A Theology
of the
Holy Spirit

A Theology of the Holy Spirit

**The Pentecostal Experience
and the New Testament Witness**

by

FREDERICK DALE BRUNER

WILLIAM B. EERDMANS/PUBLISHER
GRAND RAPIDS, MICHIGAN

Copyright © 1970 by William B. Eerdmans Publishing Company
All rights reserved
Library of Congress Catalog Card Number: 76-103445
ISBN 0-8028-1547-2

First printing, October 1970
Fifth printing, March 1976

Printed in the United States of America

To Dr. and Mrs. F. Carlton Booth

PREFACE

WHAT FOLLOWS IS AN ESSAY IN CASE-STUDY THEOLOGY. THE FOCUS of the study is the doctrine and the experience of the Holy Spirit. The particular case through and by which this doctrine is studied is the missionary movement known as Pentecostal.

The study began under missionary considerations. The late Dr. Hendrik Kraemer directed me during my course of studies at Princeton Theological Seminary to the University of Hamburg for missionary research. The late Professor D. Walter Freytag accepted me for study at the university and made available the resources of the university's well-known *Missionsakademie*. Professor D. Heinrich Meyer, Bishop of Lübeck, himself a doctor of theology in New Testament studies and a missionary for several decades in India, guided me into the study of what had for some years interested me — the Book of Acts, particularly its experience of the Holy Spirit. He encouraged me to compare the Pentecostal and apostolic understandings of the Spirit. I want to record my gratitude to these missionary gentlemen for their direction and kindness.

As the study developed I came increasingly to see that my concerns with the subject matter were principally doctrinal. The truth-question became the paramount consideration. Is the Pentecostal teaching on the experience of the Spirit in conformity with the New Testament teaching? Is Acts represented by Pentecostalism today? Should Christians seek a second, what is sometimes called a Pentecostal, experience subsequent to their Christian initiation? I found that this complex of questions was gradually forming me into what is called, in the division of theological studies, a student of systematic theology.

I was not strictly a New Testament scholar because my questions, though beginning with the first century, were too "American-pragmatic" twentieth century, too concerned with a current missionary problem, to make me a thoroughgoing biblical scholar.

But I was not principally a missionary scientist, either, because my questions were too first century, too New Testament oriented, and in these senses, perhaps, too narrow for the broad-ranging, world-oriented, and particularly nineteenth- and twentieth-century foci of mission studies.

I was in between. Which meant, I was in systematic theology. I have found that I enjoy the "middle kingdom" of systematic theology

7

between the empires of exegesis, on the one hand, and of missionary theology on the other.

I have sought to understand, first, the Pentecostal movement and its experience of the Spirit. I have attended Pentecostal and Neo-Pentecostal meetings, conferences, clinics, and prayer meetings, talked with members and leaders, read the literature. But because my concern has wanted to be more than merely academic, I have asked myself the persistent question asked by Pentecostals of any who will listen: Should I have the Pentecostal experience? As Pentecostals sometimes put it: Did I want more than a head knowledge, did I want a heart knowledge of the Pentecostal gift first known by the apostles and known now by Pentecostals themselves?

This question of "should I," and then the larger churchly question of "should we," led me as a Protestant to the New Testament. The result is this essay.

May I express a series of personal and institutional gratitudes: to the Cobb Fund of the First Presbyterian Church of Hollywood, California, my home congregation, for the larger share of the financing of my graduate studies; to the late Dr. Henrietta C. Mears of that church, my student Sunday School teacher, for initiation into Scripture and into a fellowship as close to Christian realities as I have experienced, her college department; to the evangelical theological faculty of the University of Hamburg for the privilege of association with it, and particularly, if I may say so again, to Bishop Meyer, as well as to Professor D. Georg Kretschmar, my learned co-referent; to the Rev. Dr. Darrell Guder for German mercies; to the staff of the McAlister Library of Fuller Theological Seminary for help at important periods of my research; to the Commission on Ecumenical Mission and Relations of the United Presbyterian Church in the U. S. A.; to the faculty of Union Theological Seminary, Philippines, particularly my senior colleagues, Dr. Emerito Nacpil, Dr. Gerald Anderson, and the Rev. Mr. Earl Palmer, for the high standards of their own work and for their kindness in helping me into my theological task; and, quite particularly, to those to whom this book is respectfully dedicated, for whom I and my family have special reason to feel affection.

—FREDERICK DALE BRUNER

Union Theological Seminary, Philippines
Palapala, Dasmariñas, Cavite

CONTENTS

9

ABBREVIATIONS

Apg.	Acts of the Apostles (German commentary abbreviation)
Art.	Article(s)
AV	Authorized Version of the Bible ("King James")
BC	F. J. Foakes-Jackson and Kirsopp Lake (eds.), *The Beginnings of Christianity,* Part I: Acts of the Apostles
BEvTh	Beiträge zur Evangelischen Theologie
BFChTh	Beiträge zur Förderung Christlicher Theologie
BHTh	Beiträge zur Historischen Theologie
Bl.-D.	F. Blass and A. Debrunner, *Grammatik des neutestamentlichen Griechisch.* 9th ed.
BWANT	Beiträge zur Wissenschaft vom Alten und Neuen Testament
ca.	*Circa* (about)
ch.	Chapter
col.	Column(s)
EcRev	*The Ecumenical Review*
ed(s).	Edited by, edition(s), editor(s)
EKL	*Evangelisches Kirchenlexikon. Kirchlich-theologisches Handwörterbuch*
ERE	*Encyclopedia of Religion and Ethics*
E.T.	English translation
EvTh	*Evangelische Theologie*
ExT	*Expository Times*
Fleisch I/1	P. Fleisch, *Die moderne Gemeinschaftsbewegung in Deutschland*
Fleisch I/2	P. Fleisch, *Die moderne Gemeinschaftsbewegung in Deutschland.* Erster Band
Fleisch II/1	P. Fleisch, *Die moderne Gemeinschaftsbewegung in Deutschland.* Zweiter Band, 1. Teil
Fleisch II/2	P. Fleisch, *Die moderne Gemeinschaftsbewegung in Deutschland.* Zweiter Band, 2. Teil
FRLANT	Forschungen zur Religion und Literatur des Alten und Neuen Testaments
Gr.	Greek
HNT	Handbuch zum Neuen Testament
Hollenweger	Walter J. Hollenweger, "Handbuch der Pfingstbewegung"
ICC	International Critical Commentary
IDB	*The Interpreter's Dictionary of the Bible*
idem	The same author
IRM	*International Review of Mission*
JBL	*Journal of Biblical Literature*
JEcSt	*Journal of Ecumenical Studies*
JSSR	*Journal for the Scientific Study of Religion*
JTS	*Journal of Theological Studies*

KNT	Kommentar zum Neuen Testament (Zahn)
Kol.	Colossians (German commentary abbreviation)
Kor.	Corinthians (German commentary abbreviation)
KuD	*Kerygma und Dogma: Zeitschrift für theologische Forschung und kirchliche Lehre*
lit.	Literally
LW	*Luther's Works.* American Edition
LXX	Septuagint
MD	K. Hutten (ed.), *Materialdienst: Langschnitt durch die geistigen Strömungen und Fragen der Gegenwart*
MeyerK	H. A. W. Meyer (founder), Kritisch-exegetischer Kommentar über das Neue Testament
mg.	Marginal reading
Moffatt NTC	The Moffatt New Testament Commentary
n(n).	Note(s)
n.d.	No date
NEB	The New English Bible
N.F.	Neue Folge
n.p.	No place; no publisher; no page
N.S.	New series
NTA	Neutestamentliche Abhandlungen
NTD	Das Neue Testament Deutsch (Neues Göttinger Bibelwerk)
NTSt	New Testament Studies
par.	Parallel text; paragraph(s)
RE	*Realencyklopädie für protestantische Theologie und Kirche.* 3d ed.
RGG^{2,3}	*Die Religion in Geschichte und Gegenwart.* 2d and 3d eds.
RSV	Revised Standard Version of the Bible
RV	Revised Version of the Bible
SBU	Symbolae Biblicae Upsalienses
ThEx	Theologische Existenz Heute
ThHK	Theologischer Handkommentar zum Neuen Testament
ThLZ	*Theologische Literaturzeitung*
ThR	*Theologische Rundschau*
ThZ	*Theologische Zeitschrift*
tr.	Translated by
TWNT	*Theologisches Wörterbuch zum Neuen Testament (Theological Dictionary of the New Testament)*
v., vv.	Verse, verses
WA	M. Luther, *Werke.* Kritische Gesamtausgabe ("Weimarer Ausgabe")
WChH (1957)(1962)(1968)	*World Christian Handbook.* 1957, 1962, 1968 eds.
WMANT	Wissenschaftliche Monographien zum Alten und Neuen Testament
ZKG	*Zeitschrift für Kirchengeschichte*
ZNW	*Zeitschrift für die neutestamentliche Wissenschaft und die Kunde der älteren Kirche*
ZThK	*Zeitschrift für Theologie und Kirche*

AN INTRODUCTION TO
METHOD AND PROCEDURE

PART ONE OF THE STUDY IS GIVEN PRIMARILY TO HEARING, IN ITS fulness and nuance, the intriguing and rather intricate Pentecostal doctrine of the Holy Spirit. Chapters one and two are introductory and provide the essential historical background for understanding the main theological concern of our study: the Pentecostal doctrine and experience of the Holy Spirit, especially the Pentecostal baptism in the Holy Spirit (ch. III), but then also the principal Pentecostal gifts of the Spirit (ch. IV). It seemed proper to develop the Pentecostal argument comprehensively, from all sides and with all possible means in Part One, prior to placing this argument under the critical glass of exegesis, cross-examination, and decision in Part Two.

Part Two, then, contains exegesis of the major biblical sources used by Pentecostalism and suggests appropriate theological critique. The Pentecostal use of the New Testament for the doctrine of the Holy Spirit draws most extensively from the Book of Acts and from I Corinthians chapters twelve to fourteen and we give particular attention in Part Two, therefore, to these witnesses. The first and major chapter of Part Two is devoted to the understanding of the Spirit-baptism passages in Acts (ch. V).

In the New Testament a somewhat larger literature than Acts and Corinthians reflects a doctrine of the Spirit and addresses itself to the kind of experience known in the Pentecostal movement. Therefore, in order to place the Pentecostal doctrine along a broader biblical front, in a special chapter the extra Acts-Corinthians dimensions of the New Testament are investigated and brought to bear upon the Pentecostal testimony. These dimensions taken together, we discovered, form a little systematic theology of the New Testament gospel (ch. VI).

The study comes to its conclusion and, perhaps, to its sharpest point in probing the New Testament's most serious confrontation with "spiritual things," Paul's letters to the Corinthians (ch. VII). The exegesis of I Corinthians 12-14 is important for understanding a persistent variety of spirituality in the church. The understanding of II Corinthians 10-13 provides, we believe, a final key to the inner sanctum of this spirituality.

A comparative study has special methodological problems. Neither Acts nor Corinthians nor, for that matter, any part of the New Testament was written to a specific twentieth-century problem or to Pente-

15

costalism. Each document was addressed to distinct first-century his-torical-churchly situations. (The criticism of the occasionally forced modernity of Karl Barth's *Römerbrief* has, in this connection, been kept in mind.) And yet, somehow, the New Testament witnesses need to be brought into relation to current concerns — in our case, into relation with Pentecostalism. For contemporary Pentecostalism under-stands and applies the New Testament texts in a definite way and the question must arise: Does Pentecostalism rightly understand and apply these texts?

However, the peculiar peril which the necessity of asking and an-swering this question involves is the tendency to find the New Testament texts speaking to the present situation in a direct and unrefracted way rather than mediately and derivatively. The result is liable to be a distortion of the texts' original meaning. This problem is real and cannot be either entirely overcome or taken too seriously. In spite of the peril involved the modern question must be asked and a relation between the normative New Testament witnesses and a contemporary ecumenical-evangelical problem must be discovered if the church is to be furnished with biblical direction in its current teaching and action. This necessity is at least partly implied by the properly understood (but much abused) principle of *sola scriptura*.

Yet how may the perils of distortion in this kind of study be avoided or, at least, minimized? Beyond an awareness of the problem and a compartmentalized treatment (Parts One and Two), an apparatus of notes is intended to provide a sort of sheet-anchor to the argument, to keep the correspondences in Part Two in constant contact with the realities of responsible exegesis. Hopefully, then, the study's exegesis and critique are placed on more than arbitrary or merely subjective foundations; they are to rest on — or at least critically to interact with — the best historical and biblical studies.

It is not the task of this study to write little commentaries on Acts or Corinthians. But the study must draw from the work of those whose task it was. Our work is not, properly speaking, the work of the New Testament scholar, critically to *reproduce* the New Testament witnesses in all possible purity; it is the more modest task of the mis-sionary-theologian, to *refract* these witnesses into relation to a modern missionary problem. But to refract presupposes contact with a surface, and this surface is the New Testament and its scientific representation in scholarship. From this surface, and with these understandings, Part Two enters into the delicate but we believe inescapable task of com-paring the doctrine of the Spirit in Pentecostalism with the relevant and for Christian doctrine fundamentally authoritative New Testament literature.

Part One

THE HOLY SPIRIT IN PENTECOSTAL EXPERIENCE

I

THE CONTEMPORARY PLACE
AND SIGNIFICANCE OF THE
PENTECOSTAL MOVEMENT

A. A GENERAL INTRODUCTION TO THE PENTECOSTAL MOVEMENT

THE PENTECOSTAL MOVEMENT IS ON THE GROWING EDGE OF THE Christian mission in the world today. And while some within the church might find that edge untidy and a few might even question if the movement propelling it may properly be called Christian at all, none can deny that the movement is growing. It is to be recognized that, whether approved by us or not, the Pentecostal movement is in the world with increasing numbers and significance. Pentecostalism wishes to be taken seriously as a Christian movement. Its assessment is due.

The international Pentecostal movement embraces, ecclesiastically, a sometimes inchoate, but increasingly integrated, articulate, and self-conscious body of Christians, congregations, and denominations (variations, usually, of "Assemblies" or "Church" "of God") on what is variously called the evangelical, holiness, revivalist, or conservative wing of the Christian spectrum, most of which are loosely represented in the Triennial Pentecostal World Conference and all of which were, until the 1961 New Delhi Assembly of the World Council of Churches, outside of the ecumenical movement. At the New Delhi conference the first Pentecostals — two Chilean groups — were received into the World Council. The general Pentecostal sentiment toward the application for World Council membership by these bodies may be described as unfavorable. The historical experience of Pentecostalism inclines it to a negative posture toward unitive movements, particularly with movements it understands as composed of non-conservative churches.[1]

---

[1] On intra-Pentecostal cohesion see David J. duPlessis, "The World-Wide Pente-

19

Theologically, the adherents of the Pentecostal movement unite around an emphasis upon the experience of the Holy Spirit in the life of the individual believer and in the fellowship of the church. The Pentecostal does not normally care to distinguish himself from evangelical believers in the fundamentals of the Christian faith — he is, by choice, "fundamental" in doctrine.[2] But the Pentecostal finds his distinct *raison d'être* in what for him is crucial: his faith in the supernatural, extraordinary, and visible work of the Holy Spirit in the post-conversion experience of the believer today as, he would insist, in the days of the apostles.

What is this work? The distinctive teaching of the Pentecostal move-

---

costal Movement," a paper read before the Commission on Faith and Order of the World Council of Churches, August 5, 1960, in duPlessis' pamphlet, *Pentecost Outside Pentecost* (Dallas: Privately Printed, 1960), p. 22. On World Council of Churches membership see W. A. Visser 't Hooft, ed., *The New Delhi Report: The Third Assembly of the World Council of Churches,* 1961 (New York: Association Press, 1962), pp. 9-10, 70, 219; Augusto E. Fernandez, "The Significance of the Chilean Pentecostals' Admission to the World Council of Churches," *IRM, 51* (Oct. 1962), 480-82. Notice is given of the quite recent accession to full WCC membership of a large Brazilian Pentecostal group, Brasil para Cristo (Brazil for Christ), in the *Los Angeles Times* (Aug. 24, 1969), sec. H, p. 7. Its (communicant) membership, however, is not as given, 1.1 million, but 100,000. For statistical sources see notes 7 and 8 below. See reasons for majority Pentecostal reluctance to have closer relations with the ecumenical movement in Klaude Kendrick, *The Promise Fulfilled: A History of the Modern Pentecostal Movement* (Springfield, Mo.: Gospel Publishing House, 1961), pp. 203-04; John Thomas Nichol, *Pentecostalism* (New York: Harper & Row, 1966), pp. 219, 221.

2 In only part of the fifth point of the following representative Pentecostal statement of faith would Pentecostalism conspicuously separate itself from majority conservative evangelicalism.

"(1) We believe the Bible to be the inspired, the only infallible, authoritative Word of God; (2) that there is one God, eternally existent in three persons: Father, Son, and Holy Ghost; (3) in the deity of our Lord Jesus Christ, in His virgin birth, in His sinless life, in His miracles, in His vicarious and atoning sacrifice through His shed blood, in His bodily resurrection, in His ascension to the right hand of the Father, and in His personal return in power and glory; (4) that for the salvation of lost and sinful men regeneration by the Holy Spirit is absolutely essential; (5) that the full gospel includes holiness of heart and life, healing for the body, and the baptism in the Holy Spirit with the initial evidence of speaking in other tongues as the Spirit gives utterance; (6) in the present ministry of the Holy Spirit, by whose indwelling the Christian is enabled to live a godly life; (7) in the resurrection of both the saved and the lost; they that are saved unto the resurrection of life and they that are lost unto the resurrection of damnation; (8) in the spiritual unity of believers in our Lord Jesus Christ." "The Constitution of the Pentecostal Fellowship of North America," in F. E. Mayer, *The Religious Bodies of America* (2d ed.; St. Louis, Mo.: Concordia Publishing House, 1956), p. 319. See the discussion in Nichol, *Pentecostalism,* pp. 4-5. "Pentecostalism does not distinguish itself in the principal points of Christianity from the doctrine of Protestant orthodoxy." *Les Mouvements de Pentecôte: Lettre pastorale du Synode général de l'Eglise Réformée des Pays-Bas* ("Connaissance des Sectes"; Paris: Delachaux et Niestlé, 1964), p. 21.

ment concerns the experience, evidence, and power of what Pentecostals call the baptism in the Holy Spirit. The first reception of this baptism is recorded in the New Testament account of Pentecost at Acts chapter 2, and it is from this event that Pentecostalism takes its name. Peripheral only to the understanding of the baptism in the Holy Spirit is the estimation and practice in Pentecostalism of the spiritual gifts treated, particularly, in I Corinthians twelve to fourteen.

Pentecostalism wishes, in brief, to be understood as experiential Christianity, with its experience culminating in the baptism of the believer in the Holy Spirit evidenced, as at Pentecost, by speaking in other tongues. This experience with the Spirit should continue, as in the early church, in the exercise of the spiritual gifts privately, and then publicly in the Pentecostal meetings where the gifts have their most significant sphere of operation.

There are, of course, theological differences within the Pentecostal movement but they should not be taken with more seriousness than they deserve, for the Pentcostal may always be discerned by what we may fairly call his concern for the filling of the Holy Spirit. "As great as is the fragmentation of the Pentecostal movement due to its inherent subjective element," writes Professor Meinhold, "the movement is nevertheless bound together through common views and doctrines; to these belongs first of all the concern for the direct experience of the presence of the divine Spirit."[3]

It is important to notice that it is not the *doctrine,* it is the *experience* of the Holy Spirit which Pentecostals repeatedly assert that they wish to stress. Indeed, the central attraction of the Pentecostal movement, according to one of its major leaders, consists "purely of a powerful, individual, spiritual experience."[4] The final words of this remark — "powerful, individual, spiritual experience" — contain the dominant experiential *notae* of Pentecostalism.

First, the Pentecostal feels an absence of *power* in the contemporary Christian church. He senses the opposite in reading the Acts of the Apostles in the New Testament. He feels that the difference between the church of Acts and the church of today could on the whole be characterized as the difference between a church which emphasized the Spirit and a church which has neglected the Spirit, the difference between a church in which the Spirit was an experience and a church

---

[3] Art. "Pfingstbewegung," *Weltkirchen Lexikon: Handbuch der Oekumene,* ed. Franklin H. Littell and Hans Herman Walz (Stuttgart: Kreuz, 1960), p. 1143. See also Pentecostals on the unity of the movement, in spite of its variety, in the baptism of the Holy Spirit evidenced by speaking in tongues: Guy P. Duffield, Jr., *Pentecostal Preaching* (New York: Vantage Press, 1957), pp. 15-16; Irwin Winehouse, *The Assemblies of God: A Popular Survey* (New York: Vantage Press, 1959), p. 27; Kendrick, *Promise,* p. 16.

[4] Donald Gee, *The Pentecostal Movement: Including the Story of the War Years (1940-47)* (Rev. ed.; London: Elim Publishing Co., 1949), p. 30.

in which the Spirit is a doctrine. The Pentecostal believes that he has found the source of apostolic power again in the encounter with the Spirit which he calls the baptism in the Holy Spirit. He believes that he can contribute this experience to the church.[5]

Furthermore, the baptism in the Holy Spirit is an experience, the Pentecostal believes, which every *individual* Christian — from the most gifted to the most humble — can and should experience. The experience gives to the individual Christian, it is said, a ministry, power, and spiritual sensitivity which no ecclesiastical rite, ceremony, ordination, or commission can give. The individual Christian feels himself through the Pentecostal experience to be a direct object of the *Spirit's* concern, ordained by him and by no man for service and mission in the world. And the Pentecostal *feels* this presence, this power, this spiritual imprimatur, not because it is contained in a declaration or mere promise — even in Holy Scripture — but because it is an experience: a tangible, even physical, confirmable, personal experience.

Moreover, and contrary perhaps to general expectation, highly individualistic Pentecostalism is remarkably corporate and congregational in its life. The Pentecostal church-meeting or assembly where the individual gifts are principally exercised is close to the center of the Pentecostal secret. Here the experiences of the many merge into the one and by this confluence the power of the Spirit is felt in multiplication.

There is still an additional characteristic of Pentecostal conviction which should be mentioned in any introduction to the movement: the desire for what may be called the contemporaneity of apostolic Christianity. It is important to the Pentecostal that what he reads in his New Testament be able to happen *today*. One of the most frequently quoted verses in Pentecostal literature is "Jesus Christ, the same yesterday, today, and forever" (Heb. 13:8). Fundamental to Pentecostal persuasion is the conviction that, in one Pentecostal's words, "the New Testament is not a record of what happened in one generation, but it is a blue-print of what should happen in every generation until Jesus comes."[6] This concern means, among other things, especially that the remarkable spiritual manifestations recorded in the New Testa-

---

[5] "The weighty Messages, Reports and Resolutions of the Second Assembly of the World Council of Churches," wrote Donald Gee in an editorial, "leave one with an almost oppressive sense of need, I will not say lack, of a sufficient spiritual dynamic to set them on fire and carry them forward," concluding that "there would probably be a striking unanimity among all shades of theological outlook that that dynamic must be the Holy Spirit. The Pentecostal Churches, by their special testimony to the baptism in the Holy Ghost and fire as a present experience for Christians believe they have something to offer of urgent importance and value to the whole Church." *Pentecost: A Quarterly Review of Worldwide Pentecostal Activity,* No. 30 (Dec. 1954), p. 17.

[6] DuPlessis, *Pentecost,* p. 6.

ment such as speaking in tongues, prophecy, healing, nature miracles, and visions should continue to be experienced by Christians today.

These concerns taken together — power, the individual, the Spirit, experience, the corporate, and contemporaneity — construct an introductory profile of the phenomenon of Pentecostalism.

B. THE PENTECOSTAL MOVEMENT IN SELF-PERSPECTIVE

1. THE WORLD MISSION OF THE PENTECOSTAL MOVEMENT

Pentecostals can point with justice to the world-wide sweep of their movement within a half-century. "At the turn of this century there was no Pentecostal Movement. Today, it consists of a community of more than ten million souls that can be found in almost every country under the sun."[7] Pentecostals can already claim, for example, that they are the largest non-Roman Catholic communion in France, Italy, and Portugal in Latin Europe, and in Brazil, Chile, and El Salvador, and perhaps also in Mexico in Latin America.[8]

---

[7] DuPlessis, "The World-Wide Pentecostal Movement," address to the Commission on Faith and Order, August 5, 1960, *Pentecost*, p. 22. The most reliable statistical information is contained now in Walter J. Hollenweger's prodigious study, placed in several university libraries, "Handbuch der Pfingstbewegung: Inauguraldissertation zur Erlangung der Doktorwürde der theologischen Fakultät der Universität Zürich, 1965" (9 vols.; Geneva: Privately Photocopied, 1965), hereafter cited as *Hollenweger*. For general statistical notices see *WChH* (1968); duPlessis, "Golden Jubilees of Twentieth-Century Pentecostal Movements," *IRM, 47* (April 1958), 193-201. A statistical and interpretive review is given in Kilian McDonnell, "The Ecumenical Significance of the Pentecostal Movement," *Worship, 40* (Dec. 1966), 608-29.

[8] See *Hollenweger* I, v, 14-19; II, 885-1116 (Latin America) and 1332-2340 (Europe). See also Hollenweger's article, "The Pentecostal Movement and the World Council of Churches," *EcRev, 18* (July 1966), 310. Noteworthy in Latin Europe is the strength of Pentecostalism in Italy where it is apparently twice as large as all the other Protestant groups together and more than four times as large as the well-known Waldensians. See *WChH* (1968), pp. 198-99. In Latin America, where more than half of Protestantism is Pentecostal, Brazil and Chile stand out as particularly open to the Pentecostal appeal. Over eighty percent of all Protestantism in Chile is Pentecostal, seventy percent in El Salvador, two-thirds in Brazil where there are over two million Pentecostals. See William R. Read, Victor M. Monterroso, and Harmon A. Johnson, *Latin American Church Growth* (Grand Rapids, Mich.: Eerdmans, 1969), ch. 21 "Pentecostal Growth," pp. 313-24. There seems to be some difference of opinion about the statistical strength of Mexican Pentecostalism: contrast Read-Monterroso-Johnson, *ibid.,* p. 318, and Donald McGavran, John Huegel, and Jack Taylor, *Church Growth in Mexico* (Grand Rapids, Mich.: Eerdmans, 1963), pp. 32 35 with *Hollenweger* II, 1072-89, Prudencio Damboriena, S.J., *El Protestantismo en América Latina,* 2 vols. (Bogotá: Oficina Internacional de Investigaciones Sociales de FERES, 1963), II, 116, and *WChH* (1968), pp. 115-16. However, statistical accuracy is difficult to obtain because the most rapid Pentecostal expansion has occurred in the most recent decades and, apparently, grassroots Pentecostalism does not always value statistics.

It is often reported that Pentecostalism exercises the most significant Protestant influence in warm-blooded Latin America, but it is not as well known that Pentecostalism exerts an important appeal in cooler Scandinavia as well where Pentecostals are the largest free-church community in Norway and Finland, and the second or third largest in Sweden.[9]

Pentecostal strength in the East, especially in the Communist world, is also worthy of notice. The principal historian of international Pentecostalism reports that Russia's predominantly Pentecostal "Union of Gospel Christians: Baptists and Pentecostals" is "the Christian group with the highest growth rate," and that in China Pentecostals, particularly of "The Little Flock" (or "Christian-Meeting-Place") and "The Family of Jesus" types, are the most virile and rapidly growing Protestant movements on the mainland today.[10] In Asia outside of China it is mainly in Indonesia that Pentecostalism is strong where it claims the second largest Protestant community in the archipelago.[11]

For additional literature on Pentecostalism in Latin America we may refer, generally, to Emilio Willems, *Followers of the New Faith: Culture Change and the Rise of Protestantism in Brazil and Chile* (Nashville, Tenn.: Vanderbilt University Press, 1967); more specifically, for Brazil, to William R. Read, *New Patterns of Church Growth in Brazil,* Grand Rapids, Mich.: Eerdmans, 1965; and for Chile, the founder's account, W. C. Hoover, *Historia del Avivamiento Pentecostal en Chile,* Valparaiso: Imprenta Excelsior [1909], 1948; a Roman Catholic study, Ignacio Vergara, S.J., *El Protestantismo en Chile* (Santiago de Chile: Editorial del Pacifico, S.A., 1962), esp. ch. 3, "La '3ª Reforma' "; and from the World Council of Churches, Christian Lalive d'Epinay, "La Expansion protestante en Chile," *Christianismo y Sociedad, 3-4* (1965), 19-43; *idem,* "The Pentecostal 'Conquista' in Chile," *EcRev, 20* (Jan. 1968), 16-32. For a sociological study of a conversion to Pentecostalism we may refer to Sidney W. Mintz, *Worker in the Cane; A Puerto Rican Life History;* New Haven: Yale University Press, 1960.

[9] In Norway the Pentecostals are, after the Church of Norway (Lutheran), from three to four times larger than the next two evangelical groups, *WChH* (1968), p. 201. See particular treatment of the Norwegian situation in Nils Bloch-Hoell, *The Pentecostal Movement: Its Origin, Development, and Distinctive Character* (Oslo: Universitetsforlaget, 1964), pp. 65-74; for Finland see Wolfgang Schmidt, *Die Pfingstbewegung in Finnland* (Helsingfors: Centraltryckeriet, 1935); for Sweden cf. *WChH* (1962), pp. 218-19, and *WChH* (1968), p. 205, and Bloch-Hoell, *Pentecostal Movement,* p. 91.

[10] Hollenweger, *EcRev, 18* (1966), 310 (Russia); *idem,* "Unusual Methods of Evangelism in the Pentecostal Movement in China," in "A Monthly Letter about Evangelism," Nos. 8-9 (Geneva: Division of World Mission and Evangelism of the World Council of Churches, Nov.-Dec. 1965), p. 3. For detail on Pentecostalism in Russia see *Hollenweger* I, 19-28; in China, *ibid.,* II, 1120-27.

[11] DuPlessis, "Golden Jubilees," *IRM, 47* (1958), p. 198. There is no listing for Pentecostals in the *WChH* (1957), but see *ibid.* (1962), pp. 162-64, and *ibid.* (1968), pp. 156-58 where nomenclature is ambiguous. If duPlessis' figures are correct, the Pentecostals follow only the Huria Kristen Batak Church in size among Protestants. While duPlessis, a Pentecostal, might err in the direction of enlargement, nevertheless, in some particulars the *WChH* proved unreliable. Note, finally, *Hollenweger* II, 1189-1211 where thirty-six Indonesian Pentecostal

The growth of the Pentecostal movement in the country of its origin, the United States, has also been impressive, particularly the increment in mission of the Assemblies of God, which is reported to be building one new church a day in America and to be supporting over seven hundred and fifty overseas missionaries on a missionary budget of over seven million dollars, in addition to maintaining the largest number of Bible schools in the world today.[12]

In terms of simple numbers international Pentecostalism reports the largest number of adherents in the United States (about three million), Brazil (two million), Indonesia (one million), Chile (nearly one million), and South Africa (one-half million), usually listed in that order.[13] Numerically, at the very least, the young Pentecostal movement has plowed a broad furrow into the first two-thirds of the twentieth century and reaped success.

2. THE PENTECOSTAL INTERPRETATION OF THEIR MISSION

The Pentecostal explanations of their missionary success are worth noting for the light they shed on Pentecostal conviction. Almost universal to Pentecostal inventory is the centrality of the baptism in the Holy Spirit as the source of Pentecostal power. In Pentecostalism, Acts 1:8 is believed to have found its twentieth-century exposition: "You shall receive power when the Holy Spirit has come upon you; and you shall be my witnesses . . . to the end of the earth." The "ecumenical Pentecostal," David duPlessis, explained Pentecostal conviction in addressing the Commission on Faith and Order at St. Andrews, Scotland in 1960:

> Often the question is asked, What is at the root of the success of the Pentecostal Revival? There is only one answer: Acts 1:8. . . . We have been far more interested in Apostolic Power than in Apostolic Succession. . . . We dare to believe that the blessing [of the baptism in the Holy Spirit] is as valid two thousand years after Pentecost as it was twenty years after the first outpouring of the Spirit [cf. Acts 19:1-6 with 2:1-4].[14]

groups are analyzed; and *idem*, a (to date) unpublished manuscript "Die Pfingstbewegung in Indonesien" (1966). Nichol, *Pentecostalism*, pp. 176-77, refers to three Indonesian groups which together account for almost one million Pentecostals.

[12] "During the twenty-four year period from 1936 to 1959 the number of [Pentecostal] churches increased 407 per cent, the total membership 582 per cent." Kendrick, *Promise*, p. 3. For statistical information on the world mission of the Assemblies of God see Winehouse, *Assemblies*, pp. 54-55, 197-99; cf. Carl Brumback, *Suddenly from Heaven: A History of the Assemblies of God* (Springfield, Mo.: Gospel Publishing House, 1961), pp. 64-87.

[13] *Pentecost*, No. 42 (Dec. 1957), p. 12. Cf. Eggenberger, art. "Pfingstbewegung. I. Konfessionskundlich," *RGG³*, V, 309.

[14] In duPlessis, *Pentecost*, p. 23. DuPlessis was once asked, "Are you telling us that you Pentecostals have the truth, and we other churches do not?" To which duPlessis is said to have replied with a homely illustration ending with the aphorism, "Gentlemen, . . . that is the difference between our ways of handling

And in his article "The Mission of the Pentecostal Movement" for the third edition of the prestigious *Die Religion in Geschichte und Gegenwart* duPlessis explained Pentecostalism's growth into "one of the greatest missionary movements of the twentieth century" as follows:

> The reason for this growth is not the ability or the education of the missionary or the use of new methods. The reason is simply the fact that the apostolic methods of the New Testament were followed very faithfully. Every new convert was encouraged "to receive the Holy Spirit" and then to become a witness to Jesus Christ (cf. Acts 1:8). . . . [Therefore] the missionaries of the Pentecostal movement have succeeded in establishing indigenous churches much faster than those missionaries who inevitably have had to transplant a particular doctrine or theology.[15]

The Pentecostal is persuaded that his historical success is due to his theological distinctive, the experience of the Holy Spirit in power. It is from this spiritual center that Pentecostalism understands itself and its mission. The Pentecostal groups in Brazil, for example, are reported to have affirmed that "their growth is due to the power of the Holy Spirit enabling them to witness and testify with power. This . . . is the secret of church growth."[16]

Although Pentecostals will sometimes seem aware of their shortcomings and less often apprehensive of their future, few of them doubt that hitherto God has blessed them and that they have an important historical mission to fulfill. Donald Gee thus spoke for Pentecostalism when he wrote:

> After fifty years our Lord's classic text "By their fruit ye shall know them" can safely be applied to the Pentecostal Movement. It makes no claim to perfection. . . . But, by and large, the Movement's great and solid achievements in missionary work; its fervent contribution to the cause of true Revival; and most of all its utter loyalty to the Lord Jesus Christ in His divinity and humanity, and the work of His atonement for our sins by His precious blood should still the tongues and pens of those who still publish evil of this great work of the Holy Spirit.[17]

3. THE PENTECOSTAL INTERPRETATION OF HISTORY

a. *The Fall of the Church.* It is generally taught in Pentecostal circles that after a propitious beginning the early church lost good faith

---

the same truth. You have yours on ice; we have ours on fire." In John L. Sherrill, *They Speak with Other Tongues* (Westwood, N. J.: Fleming H. Revell Co., 1964), pp. 58-59.

[15] V, 311. Cf. Melvin L. Hodges, "A Pentecostal's View of Mission Strategy," *IRM, 57* (July 1968), 304-10.

[16] Read, *New Patterns of Church Growth in Brazil*, p. 165. A major Roman Catholic student of Protestantism writes similarly and states that, in Pentecostal opinion, other factors in Pentecostal success beyond the baptism of the Spirit, are "secondary and tertiary." K. McDonnell, *art. cit., Worship, 40* (Dec. 1966), 629.

[17] *Pentecost*, No. 42 (Dec. 1957), p. 17.

and hence the extraordinary gifts and accompaniment of the Holy Spirit. "The Holy Spirit," wrote duPlessis, "continued in control until the close of the first century, when He was largely rejected and His position as leader usurped by man. The results are written in history. The missionary movement halted. The dark ages ensued."[18]

A thematic nostalgia for the power and gifts of the early church is repeatedly sounded in Pentecostal literature and language and reportedly satisfied in Pentecostal experience. There is a settled conviction that the absence in other Christian groups of the early church's experience of the Spirit is responsible for the comparative insignificance of Christianity in the world today. Behind this interpretation of history is usually the conviction that the sign of God's blessing on the church is success. "One of the main complaints of unbelievers," writes one Pentecostal, "is that if Christianity were really from God it would certainly make rapid progress on earth."[19]

While this interpretation of history is not uncommon, Pentecostalism's solution is. The way back to the early church's power and experience, it is insisted, is via Pentecost, that is, by way of the baptism in the Holy Spirit with its unusual manifestations (Acts 2:1-4). The Pentecostal experience means nothing less than "the rediscovery of Christianity!" writes Skibstedt, adding emphatically that the Pentecostal experience is *the reception of the gift of the Holy Spirit in an extraordinary, yes, in an eye-catching way.*"[20] Pentecostals are convinced that without this striking experience of the Spirit the church must only perpetuate its impotence in history.

b. *The New Reformation of the Church.* The Pentecostals frequently refer to their movement as a worthy and perhaps even superior successor to the Reformation of the sixteenth century and to the English evangelical revival of the eighteenth, and nearly always as a faithful reproduction of the apostolic movement of the first century. At the Fifth Pentecostal World Conference in the keynote address this historical conviction was given expression.

> They say Pentecost [i.e., the Pentecostal movement] is the *third* great force in Christendom. But it is really the *first* great force. . . . Who will deny that the first period of the Christian era was in every sense Pentecostal? . . . But the Church did not maintain its purity. . . . Hence, the necessity for the Reformation. . . . But this in turn . . . lacked completeness, lapsed into formality and dead ritualism which led to the need for revival. Hence the great Wesleyan revival. . . . But all of this needed a new and greater dynamic.

18 "Golden Jubilees," *IRM*, 47 (April 1958), 193-94.

19 Karl Ecke, *Der Durchbruch des Urchristentums infolge Luthers Reformation* (2d rev. ed.; Nürnberg: Süddeutscher Missionsverlag, n.d.), p. 78.

20 Werner Skibstedt, *Die Geistestaufe im Licht der Bibel,* tr. [from the Norwegian] Otto Witt (Württemberg: Karl Fix Verlag Deutsche Volksmission entscheidener Christen, 1946), p. 32, emphasis his.

Hence, the Pentecostal Revival came to ripen the grain and bring it to harvest.[21]

Pentecostals have a generally heroic view of their mission. No doubt the dual experience of success and persecution has engraved this interpretation into their consciousness. Pentecostalism feels that, accepted or not, its experience of the Spirit is the single greatest need of the traditional churches and that if these churches would accept the Pentecostal experience it could lead them to a reformation and mission comparable to its own.

c. *"The Latter Rain."* Pentecostalism not only diagnoses the past and seeks to reform the present, it also looks with special fervor to the future. Particularly close to the heart of the Pentecostal and one of the major symbols of his self-consciousness is the conviction that the movement in which he stands is, or is under, "the latter rain," as referred to by the prophets (Joel 2:23; Jer. 5:24; Deut. 11:14; cf. Joel 2:28-29; Acts 2:17-21; James 5:7). As the apostolic church represented the former rain bringing the first-fruits, Pentecostals believe that their movement is God's ordained latter rain bringing in the last-fruits of the great harvest, the immediate prophase to the second advent.

After discussing the revivals in the church through Luther and Wesley, in the fashion of the Pentecostal interpretation of history, the Pentecostal historian of the Los Angeles revival adds, significantly:

> But here we are with the restoration of the very experience of "Pentecost," with the "latter rain," a restoration of the power . . . to finish up the work begun. We shall again be lifted to the church's former level, to complete her work, begin where they left off when failure overtook them, and speedily fulfilling the last great commission, open the way for the coming of Christ.[22]

And Pentecostals believe that their movement is really the *latter* rain, i.e., the prelude to the end. "The latter-rain out-pouring of the Holy Spirit is God's final great movement of power to provide a strong witness to the church and the world before the coming of the Lord Jesus Christ."[23] The extraordinary missionary energy which new-born

---

[21] J. A. Synan, "The Purpose of God in the Pentecostal Movement for This Hour," *Pentecostal World Conference Messages: Preached at the Fifth Triennial Pentecostal World Conference, Toronto, Canada, 1958,* ed. Donald Gee (Toronto: Full Gospel Publishing House, 1958), p. 29.

[22] Frank Bartleman, *How Pentecost Came to Los Angeles: As It Was in the Beginning* (2d ed.; Los Angeles: Privately Printed, 1925), p. 88. On the "latter rain" see also Stanley H. Frodsham, *With Signs Following: The Story of the Latter Day Pentecostal Revival* (Springfield, Mo.: Gospel Publishing House, 1926), p. 249. For similar conviction, from similar roots, cf. George Huntston Williams, *The Radical Reformation* (Philadelphia: Westminster, 1962), p. 859.

[23] Synan in Gee (ed.), *Pentecostal World Conference Messages,* p. 29. In escha-

Pentecostalism has experienced, enabling it in little more than sixty years to become the evangelical majority in almost a dozen countries and to embrace the globe; the ecstasy which the movement experiences in the Holy Spirit's baptism and gifts — these lead Pentecostals to believe that the end must be near, for does not the latter rain of the Spirit immediately precede the harvest of the Son?

A very strong eschatological note has characterized the movement from the beginning, inclined to be attributed by some to the lower socio-economic level of the Pentecostals, or the crisis character of our time, or by Pentecostals themselves to their fidelity to Holy Scripture and their love for Jesus Christ.[24] None of these answers should be disregarded.

Pentecostalism looks back on church history and sees mainly failure; it looks back to its own brief history and sees mainly success; it looks to the future and sees near consummation — and in each it sees the intimate relevance of the Spirit. These features highlight the Pentecostal understanding of history.

C. THE PENTECOSTAL MOVEMENT IN REPRESENTATIVE ECUMENICAL PERSPECTIVE

Within the ecumenical movement there has been surprisingly little expressed criticism of or, until quite recently, little apparent interest in the Pentecostal movement. The most prominent ecumenical spokesmen to have given serious attention in writing to the Pentecostal movement have been Dr. Henry Pitt Van Dusen, President emeritus of Union Theological Seminary, New York, in a pair of prominently publicized articles, and Bishop Lesslie Newbigin in his Kerr Lectures on the nature of the church.

1. THE ESTIMATE OF DR. VAN DUSEN

a. *"The Third Force."* In a widely read article in *Life* magazine Van Dusen denominated the vigorous left-wing of Christianity, largely outside the ecumenical movement, "the Third Force in Christendom," ranging it alongside Roman Catholicism and historic Protestantism.[25]

---

tology the Pentecostals are "definitely adventist in doctrine and practice." Kendrick, *Promise*, pp. 13-14.

[24] The socio-economic interpretation: by most church historians, e.g., William Warren Sweet, *The Story of Religion in America* (Rev. ed.; New York: Harper and Bros., 1950), p. 422. The crisis of our times: Paul Fleisch in the conclusion to his most recent study, II/2, 386-87. For the Pentecostal interpretation see Gee, *Pentecostal Movement*, p. 2; Winehouse, *Assemblies*, p. 14.

[25] "The Third Force in Christendom," *Life, 44* (June 9, 1958), 13. Van Dusen's third force includes, in addition to the various types of Pentecostals: the Churches of Christ, the Seventh-Day Adventists, Nazarenes, Jehovah's Witnesses, and Christian and Missionary Alliance. But: "Of the third force's world membership of twenty million, the largest single group is 8.5 million Pentecostals," *ibid.*, p. 124.

He was impressed not only by the swift growth of this new force, but by the character of its worship, message, and life. He suggested that the apostles might have found themselves more at home in a Pentecostal or holiness assembly than in a more traditional Christian worship service. Pentecostal preaching, he discovered, was at once both biblical and personal; filled with scriptural reference and the practical concerns of the people. The members of this force, he observed, were evangelistic — ardently so. Their lives revolved almost *in toto* around the great Christian realities — passionately, perhaps at times feverishly — but there they revolved.

Van Dusen was also impressed with the intimate group life of the people; that they were often together in fellowship, in prayer, and in Bible study. Finally, he remarked, "they place strong emphasis upon the Holy Spirit — as the immediate, potent presence of God both in each human soul and in the Christian fellowship. Above all, they expect their followers to practice an active, untiring, seven-day-a-week Christianity."[26]

He summarized by remarking that it is only recently that Protestants have come to see the permanence and the significance of this movement. Moreover, the "tendency to dismiss its Christian message as inadequate is being replaced by a chastened readiness to investigate the secrets of its mighty sweep, especially to learn if it may not have important, neglected elements in a full and true Christian witness."[27]

b. *"The New Reformation."* In an earlier article for *The Christian Century* Van Dusen registered two major impressions left upon him by a tour of the Caribbean area: (1) "the omnipresence and relative inconsequence of the Christian Church," and (2) that Protestantism, which he saw flanked by Roman Catholicism on the one side and his "Third Force" on the other, is "the least vigorous of the three," concluding that the major discovery during his tour was this "mighty third arm of Christian outreach."[28] Then Van Dusen prophesied:

> I shall hazard a forecast: When historians of the future come to assess the most significant development in Christendom in the first half of the twentieth century, they will fasten on the ecumenical movement . . . but next to this they will decide that by all odds the most important fact in the Christian history of our times was a *New Reformation*, the emergence of a new, third major type and branch of Christendom, alongside of and not incommensurable with Roman Catholicism and historic Protestantism, in many respects startlingly analogous to the most vital and dynamic expressions of the sixteenth century Reformation. . . . To leaders of the ecumenical movement these facts appear to me to present the most confounding and commanding problems for the years just ahead.[29]

---

26 *Ibid.*, p. 122.
27 *Ibid.*, p. 124.
28 "Caribbean Holiday," *Christian Century, 72* (Aug. 17, 1955), 946-47.
29 *Ibid.*, pp. 947-48. It must be added that the Pentecostal revival is dissimilar

Should Van Dusen's predictions be prescient, we may be in touch with a formative movement.

2. THE ESTIMATE OF BISHOP NEWBIGIN: "THE THIRD ECCLESIOLOGY"

The most sustained study of the Pentecostal movement from within ecumenical circles has come from Bishop Lesslie Newbigin's lectures on the nature of the church at Trinity College, Glasgow, published under the title *The Household of God*. The question which Bishop Newbigin poses in his lectures is, "By what is the Church constituted?" or, "How are we made incorporate into Christ?" Newbigin suggests that historically there have been three major answers to these questions: (1) the hearing of the gospel with faith; (2) the participation sacramentally in the life of the historically continuous church; and (3) the reception of and abiding in the Holy Spirit.[30] Newbigin calls these answers, broadly, the Protestant, the Catholic, and the Pentecostal.

Newbigin is concerned that the Catholic and Protestant understandings of the church are, or tend to be, static. He is persuaded that there is a dynamic dimension to the understanding of the church called for by the New Testament and offered, he suggests, in Pentecostalism. He is eager to see the whole church enriched by entrance into dialogue with the Pentecostal movement. He writes,

> The Catholic-Protestant debate which has characterized the ecumenical movement needs to be criticized and supplemented from what I have called the Pentecostal angle.... The debate has to become three-cornered. The gulf which at present divides these groups from the ecumenical movement is the symptom of a real defect ... and perhaps a resolute effort to bridge it is the next condition for further advance.[31]

In an apt analogy Newbigin compares the apostle Paul's enigmatic but piercing question in Acts 19:2 — "Did you receive the Holy Spirit when you believed?" — with the questions with which a modern Protestant or Catholic might confront a prospective member of his church. The apostle's Protestant and Catholic successors, Newbigin believes, "are more inclined to ask either 'Did you believe exactly what we teach?' or 'Were the hands that were laid on you our hands?' and if

---

from the sixteenth-century Magisterial Reformation in the general absence (1) of political connections in external formation or (2) of scholarly roots or leadership theologically, and (3) in its being largely a movement within the depressed classes. In these senses it is more similar to the Anabaptist or Radical Reformation movements of the sixteenth century. For some of the evangelistic advantages and disadvantages of these features, particularly the second, see Vern Dusenberry, "Montana Indians and Pentecostals," *Christian Century*, 75 (July 23, 1958), 850-51.

30 *The Household of God: Lectures on the Nature of the Church* (New York: Friendship Press, 1954), pp. xi, 24, 82-83.

31 *Ibid.*, p. 102.

the answer is satisfactory — to assure the converts that they have received the Holy Spirit even if they don't know it."[32] Newbigin is not reluctant to suggest that the apostle's question finds its closest modern form and response in Pentecostalism. However enigmatic the "Pentecostal question" may be to us — the question, that is, of our real reception of the Holy Spirit — perhaps we need at least to hear the question and to weigh it.

Even a cursory reading of the New Testament convinces that the Holy Spirit was an important fact and a real experience in the life and in the mission of the early church. Is Pentecostalism, as Newbigin proposes, the twentieth-century restatement of this fact and experience?

D. SUMMARY AND CONCLUSION

At large and at work in the world today is a new Christian movement which by virtue of its missionary activity demands our attention and which by its claim to the description Christian demands our assessment. It is a movement of the pneumatic tradition stimulating increasing appreciation from the ecumenical movement and understanding itself as a legitimate successor to and a final heir of the great reformations of the church. The movement is at work largely outside the bounds of ecumenical Christianity but has within the last few years commenced a rapprochement and, in Neo-Pentecostalism as we shall see, even a spiritual infiltration. Its theology is distinguished by its center, the Holy Spirit, and by its insistence on a unique encounter with and a constant sensibility of this Spirit. Pentecostal experience, then, is distinguished by precisely the emphasis on experience — with the Spirit, by the individual, in power, in fellowship, and in the present. In a word, the theology of the Pentecostal movement is its experience, which is another way of saying that its theology is pneumatology.

What then is the contemporary significance of this new spiritual movement? It is the task of our study to attempt an initial answer to this question. At the very worst the Pentecostal movement poses a major ecumenical problem.[33] At the very best, in terms of numbers, growth, vitality, and influence its place is close to the heart of the international missionary movement. Pentecostalism and mission are almost synonymous. As chairman of the International Missionary Council assembly in Ghana in 1957, Dr. John A. Mackay observed in the keynote address that there are "some notable cases of organized denominations in which the Church is literally the mission. This is true

---

[32] *Ibid.*, p. 104.

[33] The influence of the Pentecostal movement is large even when negatively considered. "In every one of those twenty countries . . . the problem thrust before me as their most pressing and baffling present harassment was always the same — the presence of the 'fringe sects.'" Van Dusen, *art. cit., Christian Century*, 72 (Aug. 17, 1955), 947.

... of the Pentecostal Churches. In many parts of the world today every member of the several Churches that make up the Pentecostal World Fellowship are not only committed Christians, but ardent missionaries."[34]

In terms of the church's theology and mission Pentecostalism's significance may be that it incarnates a neglected reality of the New Testament church: the Holy Spirit in the experience of believers. What to some may seem an overemphasis of the Spirit and especially of the Spirit's more noticeable operations may, perhaps, be intended to startle the church into an awareness of its little emphasis of the same Spirit. Perhaps in the divine perspective a church that gives too much attention to the Spirit is no more culpable — perhaps less — than a church that gives him too little. Perhaps the Pentecostal movement is a voice — albeit an ecstatic and at times a harsh voice — calling the people to hear what the Spirit is capable of saying to and doing with a church that listens.

On the other hand, some might argue that Pentecostalism represents a seductive tangent from urgent modern tasks, a voice calling the church into the wilderness of spiritualism at an hour when the church needs almost anything more than it needs more "spirituality" in the popularly understood sense.

In any case, that the Pentecostal movement is significant for the church's future — whether evaluated positively or negatively — cannot be easily denied. That the Pentecostal movement must be uncritically approved or embraced because it is of growing world-wide significance need not, of course, follow. What is significant is not *eo ipso* correct. The test of anything calling itself Christian is not its significance or its success or its power, though these make the test more imperative. The test is the truth.[35] As Protestant Christians, therefore, the duty devolves

---

[34] "The Christian Mission at This Hour," *The Ghana Assembly of the International Missionary Council, 28th December 1957 to 8th January 1958: Selected Papers*, ed. Ronald K. Orchard (London: Published for the I.M.C. by Edinburgh House Press, 1958), p. 115. We may also refer to Dr. Mackay's appreciation of Pentecostalism in his article in the *Christian Century, 82* (Nov. 24, 1965), 1439. Cf. McGavran *et al., Church Growth in Mexico,* ch. 11 "The Pentecostal Contribution."

[35] Kenneth Strachan, late director of the Latin American Mission, posed the question of the growth of the "non-historical groups" on a properly broad scale. "It would be gratifying if such growth could be claimed as the inevitable result of the truth of their message and methods. . . . Unfortunately for such a thesis, some non-Christian sects are experiencing equal and even greater success. . . . Whether it be a Communist, a Jehovah's Witness, a Fundamentalist, or a blue-blooded denominationalist, the law of sowing applies equally to all: 'He which soweth sparingly shall reap also sparingly; and he which soweth bountifully shall reap also bountifully.' " *The Missionary Movement of the Non-Historical Groups in Latin America* ("Part III of the Study Conference on the Message of the Evangelical Church in Latin America, Buck Hill Falls, Pa., Nov. 10-12, 1957"; New York:

upon us to assess the Pentecostal movement, first of all, in the light of the New Testament witnesses.

There should, however, be the open acknowledgment from the first that in the New Testament at least one of the valid criteria of the presence of the Holy Spirit is power (I Thess. 1:5; Rom. 15:9; Acts 1:8). And when power is coupled with a passion to preach Jesus Christ, as it is in Pentecostalism, then without any abeyance of our critical faculties our sympathies — as Dr. Van Dusen and Bishop Newbigin have suggested — should be given new breadth and our studies fresh impetus. While ecumenical Christians have addressed themselves to the Pentecostal movement with increasing seriousness and openness it remains true that, given the place and significance of the Pentecostal movement in the modern world, Pentecostalism has not yet been addressed at its heart — in its doctrine and experience of the Spirit.

Commission on Cooperation in Latin America of the Division of Foreign Missions of the National Council of the Churches of Christ in the U. S. A. [1957]), pp. 9-10. It may be only with difficulty that the children of a business or success culture will be able to make the sometimes necessary but psychically painful distinction between volume and verity.

II

THE BACKGROUND AND
THE BEGINNINGS OF THE
PENTECOSTAL MOVEMENT

A. THE BACKGROUND OF THE
PENTECOSTAL MOVEMENT

INTRODUCTION

THE ANCESTRAL LINE OF THE PENTECOSTAL MOVEMENT COULD APPEAR
to stretch from the enthusiastic Corinthians (I Cor. 12-14) or even
the Old Testament anointed and ecstatic (e.g., Num. 11; I Sam.
10),[1] through the gnostics of all varieties, the Montanists, the medieval and
the pre-Reformation spiritualists, the so-called radical, left-wing, or
Anabaptist movements, the *Schwärmer* of the Reformation period, the
post-Reformation Quakers and, when given fresh new parentage through
the Pietist, Wesleyan, and revivalist movements of the seventeenth and
eighteenth centuries in Germany, England, and the United States, continuing in the first half of the nineteenth century briefly but very interestingly through Edward Irving in England, and lengthily and very
influentially through Charles Finney in America, issuing in the latter
half of the nineteenth century in the higher-life and holiness movements which gave birth to their twentieth-century child, the Pentecostal
movement.

If our object were primarily historical it would make a most interesting study in the history of theology and of ideas to trace the pneumatic line from its ancient roots to its modern expressions. We cannot

---

[1] See the thorough coverage of the possible glossolalic occurrences in the Old
Testament and late Judaism in Eddison Mosiman, *Das Zungenreden geschichtlich
und psychologisch untersucht* (Tübingen: J. C. B. Mohr [Paul Siebeck], 1911), pp.
37-38. Further, Paul Volz, *Der Geist Gottes und die verwandten Erscheinungen
im Alten Testament und im anschliessenden Judentum* (Tübingen: Mohr, 1910),
pp. 8-9.

do that here. We shall simply evoke in an introductory way the presence of the most compelling ancient symbol of the pneumatic movement for typological suggestion and then proceed to introduce the immediate modern ancestors of twentieth-century Pentecostalism.

Montanism (*ca.* 156 A.D.-   ) has been often referred to as the fountainhead of all the enthusiastic or pneumatic movements in Christian history. "Montanism," writes Professor Whale, "is the classic example of a sect-type destined to reappear constantly in the history of the Church from that day to this."[2] What is most interesting for our purposes to observe is the striking similarity at almost every point between the doctrinal and experiential emphases of Montanism and those of modern Pentecostalism. Professor Seeberg believes, for example, that Montanism's essential character can be summarized as follows:

> 1. The last period of revelation has opened. It is the day of spiritual gifts. The recognition (*agnitio*) of spiritual *charismata* is a distinguishing trait of Montanism. This involves primarily the acknowledgment of the Paraclete....
>
> 2. The orthodoxy of the Montanists is acknowledged — their acceptance of the rule of faith. The Monarchianism in utterances of Montanus is due to lack of theological culture....
>
> 3. The nearness of the end of the world is strongly emphasized.
>
> 4. There are strict moral requirements.[3]

The Pentecostals also believe that (1) the last period of revelation has commenced ("the latter rain") and their distinctive emphasis too is the doctrine of the Holy Spirit; (2) apart from their doctrine of the Spirit Pentecostals are usually held to be orthodox and, as with the Montanists, it is possible to argue that what doctrinal aberrations have arisen have often been due more to crudity of statement than to intentional heterodoxy; (3) the return of Christ is ardently expected; and (4) generally a strict morality prevails. Finally, as in Pentecostalism, to outsiders "the most characteristic feature of this movement," in Mosiman's estimation, "is ecstasy."[4]

Whether we attach large or minimal significance to Montanism and its emergence in the church, and whether we assign narrowness and tragedy or wisdom and necessity to the church's suppression of Mon-

---

[2] J. S. Whale, *The Protestant Tradition: An Essay in Interpretation* (Cambridge: At the University Press, 1955), p. 209.

[3] Reinhold Seeberg, *Text-Book of the History of Doctrines,* tr. Charles E. Hay (Grand Rapids, Mich.: Baker Book House, 1956), pp. 105-06.

[4] *Zungenreden,* p. 48. It is debatable, however, whether the Montanists ever spoke, or attempted to speak, in tongues. Cf. George Barton Cutten, *Speaking with Tongues: Historically and Psychologically Considered* (New Haven: Yale University Press, 1927), p. 35; S. D. Currie, " 'Speaking in Tongues': Early Evidence outside the New Testament Bearing on '*Glössais Lalein,*' " *Interpretation, 19* (July 1965), 288.

tanism, or a little of both, Montanism interests us as the prototype of almost everything Pentecostalism seeks to represent.

1. JOHN WESLEY AND METHODISM

The various pneumatic movements of the ancient, medieval, Reformation, and post-Reformation periods — interesting, indeed important, as each of these is — may be said to be germane to and fruitful for the understanding of contemporary Pentecostalism insofar as they influenced John Wesley (1703-91) and Methodism.[5] Methodism is the most important of the modern traditions for the student of Pentecostal origins to understand, for eighteenth-century Methodism is the mother of the nineteenth-century American holiness movement which, in turn, bore twentieth-century Pentecostalism. Pentecostalism is primitive Methodism's extended incarnation. "The Pentecostal movement," concluded a Jesuit student of Pentecostalism in Latin America, "is Methodism brought to its ultimate consequences."[6]

From the point of view of the history of doctrine it appears that out of the Methodist-holiness quest for an instantaneous experience of sanctification, or a "second work of grace" after justification, came Pentecostalism's centering of its aspiration in an instantaneously experienced baptism in the Holy Spirit subsequent to conversion. The Pentecostal historian Kendrick, in his genealogy of the Pentecostal experience, cites with approval Wesley's famous apology for "two":

---

[5] In his study of enthusiastic movements and their manifestations the Roman Catholic Ronald Knox understands Methodism as the most significant. "The lesser [enthusiastic] movements which might seem to foreshadow the Reformation were sporadic and unimportant, freaks of religious history. . . . [After the Reformation] the Quakers are first . . . [then] the Pietists . . . Moravianism . . . Camisards . . . Shakerism. . . . But by the middle of the eighteenth century both Quakers and French Prophets were thrown into the shade. Moravianism had produced something greater than itself . . . Methodism." *Enthusiasm: A Chapter in the History of Religion, with Special Reference to the Seventeenth and Eighteenth Centuries* (Oxford: At the Clarendon Press, 1950), pp. 4-5. On the Methodist origins of Pentecostalism see Bloch-Hoell, *Pentecostal Movement,* p. 128; Benjamin Breckinridge Warfield, *Perfectionism* (2 vols.; New York: Oxford University Press, 1931), I, 3. In future study of Protestantism I should like to give attention, in addition to several other movements of importance, to Puritanism and its theology of preparation. This was impressed upon me recently by the reading of Norman Pettit, *The Heart Prepared: Grace and Conversion in Puritan Spiritual Life,* "Yale Publications in American Studies," 11; New Haven: Yale University Press, 1966, and Robert C. Monk, *John Wesley: His Puritan Heritage* (Nashville: Abingdon, 1966), cf. p. 68.

[6] I. Vergara, *El Protestantismo en Chile,* pp. 127-28. In important parts of Latin America this pedigree is true not only theologically but also historically. In Chile, for example, it was the Methodist pastor W. C. Hoover who began the Pentecostal movement; see Vergara, *Protestantismo,* pp. 110-21 and Hoover, *Historia, passim.* The European father of Pentecostalism was the Norwegian Methodist pastor T. B. Barratt. For an interesting exchange of letters between Hoover and Barratt see Hoover, *Historia,* pp. 95-98.

" 'We do not know a single instance,' John Wesley wrote, 'in any place, of a person's receiving, in one and the same moment, remission of sins, the abiding witness of the Spirit, and a new, clean heart.' "[7] The remission of sins, in other words, and the new heart are two distinct "moments" in the life of the Christian. "A gradual work of grace constantly precedes the instantaneous work both of justification and sanctification," Wesley explained in a letter, adding "but the work itself (of sanctification as well as justification) is undoubtedly instantaneous. As after a gradual conviction of the guilt and power of sin you was [sic] justified in a moment, so after a gradually increasing conviction of inbred sin you will be sanctified in a moment."[8]

It appears that majority Pentecostalism absorbed from its Methodist parentage the convictions of the subsequent and instantaneous experience and transferred them bodily from Wesley's sanctification to their baptism in the Holy Spirit. In any case, both Methodism and Pentecostalism put their emphasis theologically someplace after justification. In Pentecostalism the theological focus is shifted almost entirely from Wesley's goal of final salvation and the sanctification which will achieve it to the baptism in the Holy Spirit and the glossolalia which will assure it. In Pentecostalism the desire for the baptism in the Holy Spirit sweeps every other doctrine into its vortex including the doctrine of sanctification.

The major influence, then, of Methodism upon Pentecostalism has been the centering of spiritual desire on experience and especially on *an* experience subsequent to conversion, to be instantaneously engaged, and hence of most consequence, requiring the meeting of certain conditions beyond conversion or justifying faith for its attainment.[9] In short, by giving special weight to the instantaneous and experienced sanctification subsequent to the new birth, Wesley preveniently shaped

[7] In Kendrick, *Promise,* pp. 40-41; from Wesley, *A Plain Account of Christian Perfection* (London: The Epworth Press, 1952 [1741; rev. 1767]), p. 24. See the dominance of the subsequent experience of sanctification in Wesley's theology established in the able study by Harald Lindström, *Wesley and Sanctification: A Study in the Doctrine of Salvation* (Stockholm: Nya Bokförlags Aktiebolaget, 1946), pp. 99, 102, 120-22, 178, 217-18.

[8] Letter of the 21st of June, 1784 in *The Letters of the Rev. John Wesley,* ed. John Telford (Standard Edition; London: The Epworth Press, 1931), pp. 221-22.

[9] Though Wesley in important places made only faith the condition for the higher experience, this must be understood in the context of his conditions for the acquiring of faith, see Documents, p. 326 below. There are not only significant theological similarities between the Methodist and Pentecostal movements, there are sociological similarities as well. Lecky's vivid description of the roots of Methodism might be applied *mutatis mutandi* to Pentecostalism. See H. Richard Niebuhr, *The Social Sources of Denominationalism* (Hamden, Conn.: The Shoestring Press, 1929 [reprinted 1954]), pp. 62-63. Niebuhr calls the Methodist revival "the last great religious revolution of the disinherited in Christendom" (p. 72). Might Pentecostalism now appropriate this description?

the Pentecostal understanding of a crisis and conscious experience of the baptism in the Holy Spirit subsequent to conversion.

Before John Wesley there may have been no such fully developed doctrine of a definite second work of grace, but since Wesley almost all those who have embraced this doctrine have been, wittingly or not, Wesley's children, and the greatest and today most prominent of these is Pentecostalism.

2. AMERICAN REVIVALISM

While theologically Methodism has exerted the major influence on the Pentecostal movement, methodologically revivalism, particularly American revivalism, has been the most formative influence. The American predecessor and contemporary of Methodism, the Great Awakening, and its unique child, frontier revivalism, radically transformed America's understanding, appropriation, and application of the Christian faith. The successive awakenings under, especially, Finney and Moody at the beginning and at the end of the nineteenth century, grooved into American Christianity and the American churches the revival methodology. Dr. Sweet could write that "revivalism . . . in a real sense may be characterized as an Americanization of Christianity, for in it Christianity was shaped to meet America's needs."[10]

Revivalism's particular contribution to American religion and hence to Pentecostalism (again a distinctly American product) was the individualizing and emotionalizing of the Christian faith, alterations which, some have argued, became increasingly necessary in an acceleratingly depersonalized civilization. Pentecostalism is revivalism gone indoors. In Pentecostalism revivalism has moved from its tents and rented halls into organized Christendom and myriad local churches. Inheriting Wesley's experiential theology and revivalism's experiential methodology, Pentecostalism went out into an experience-hungry world and found a response.

---

[10] *Revivalism in America: Its Origin, Growth, and Decline* (New York: Charles Scribner's Sons, 1945), p. 11. Elmer T. Clark, *The Small Sects in America* (Rev. ed.; New York: Abingdon-Cokesbury Press, 1949), p. 14. Dr. Sweet writes that the particularly American contributions to the churches, sects, or cults of Christendom have been Christian Science and Mormonism. Pentecostalism, which as we shall see was born in America and appears to have been exported therefrom around the world, may now perhaps be listed as the most recent American contribution to the world's religious groups. On revivalism as the *modus operandi* of Pentecostalism beyond America see, for example, the careful study of the English situation, Bryan R. Wilson, *Sects and Society: A Sociological Study of Elim Tabernacle, Christian Science, and Christadelphians* (Berkeley: University of California Press, 1961), pp. 15-118, particularly pp. 61-76, and the conclusion, p. 322; also, of Latin American experience, Willems, *Followers of the New Faith*, p. 247.

3. EDWARD IRVING

"Irvingism" appeared in the third decade of the nineteenth century in Great Britain almost as swiftly as, in its most prominent features, it disappeared. The movement was associated with Edward Irving (1792-1834), a gifted Scotch Presbyterian minister who enjoyed the friendship of Carlyle and Coleridge and an assistantship to Chalmers. Irving was increasingly drawn into millennial and "prophetic" circles to which he became the most influential convert, and he provides with his group, because of the emphasis on the gifts of the Spirit, the nearest parallel to Pentecostalism in the nineteenth century. Through Irving the Catholic Apostolic Church was founded where the primitive gifts of the Spirit were said to have been revived. Andrew L. Drummond described the principal ideas characteristic of what he called the "Tongues Movement" under Irving as follows: "The perspective is dominated by the imminent Second Coming. There must be an immediate evangelisation of the world in preparation of that event; the 'Gift of Tongues' is the means towards that end, as well as being one of the 'signs' of the Last Days."[11] But the movement associated with Irving ebbed considerably, and its existence was probably not known to the Pentecostals until in retrospect its similarities were discovered. Its influence on Pentecostalism is minimal and its interest is purely historical.

4. CHARLES FINNEY

The revivalist who first domesticated revivalism, that is, who moved it into the churches, and who has placed after Wesley the most indelible stamp upon Pentecostalism, was a man born a year after Wesley's death — Charles Finney (1792-1876). Finney's revival methodology was the shaping influence on Methodist theology in the Pentecostal churches and formed, with the holiness movement of which Finney was an influential source, the major historical bridge between primitive Wesleyanism and modern Pentecostalism. Finney's nineteenth-century writings still appear influential in Pentecostalism. A Pentecostal teacher notes that in American Pentecostalism "Charles G. Finney's one volume of Systematic Theology is used almost exclusively as a standard work of theology, particularly by the ordinary pastor and evangelist, and is the only one stocked by the average Pentecostal publishing house and book room."[12]

---

[11] *Edward Irving and His Circle: Including Some Consideration of the 'Tongues' Movement in the Light of Modern Psychology* (London: James Clarke and Co., n.d. [1934?]), pp. 146-47. For Irving's corresponding convictions on the permanence of the spiritual gifts in the church, cf. *ibid.*, pp. 114-15, 164. Cf. Nichol, *Pentecostalism*, pp. 22-24.

[12] Harold A. Fischer, "Progress of the Various Modern Pentecostal Movements towards World Fellowship," unpublished master's thesis (Fort Worth: Texas Christian University, 1952), p. 51. "Charles G. Finney," writes another Pente-

Finney's theology included an experience subsequent to conversion which he called the baptism of the Holy Ghost. In his *Memoirs* Finney discussed in this connection the inadequacies of his earliest mentor, the Rev. Mr. Gale, a Presbyterian minister:

> There was another defect in brother Gale's education, which I regarded as fundamental. If he had ever been converted to Christ, he had failed to receive that divine anointing of the Holy Ghost that would make him a power in the pulpit and in society, for the conversion of souls. He had fallen short of receiving the baptism of the Holy Ghost, which is indispensable to ministerial success. . . . I have often been surprised and pained that to this day so little stress is laid upon this qualification for preaching Christ to a sinful world.[13]

However, it was not principally Finney's doctrine of the spiritual baptism, it was his revival methods which proved of most permanent influence in American Christianity. Finney's methods in bringing men to spiritual crisis were purposely emotional and individual, that is, revivalist. Finney justified these methods by arguing that "God has found it necessary to take advantage of the excitability there is in mankind to produce powerful excitements among them before he can lead them to obey. Men are so sluggish, there are so many things to lead their minds off from religion and to oppose the influence of the gospel that it is necessary to raise an excitement among them till the tide rises so high as to sweep away the opposing obstacles."[14] Finney's influence on subsequent Pentecostalism may be said to have been, in fact, more in the realm of form and "temperature" than in the realm of content and ideas.

Significantly and symptomatically Finney's doctrine of justification has interesting correspondences. Finney rejected forensic justification and accented real sanctification as the final basis of a man's standing before God. Moreover, Finney saw justification as dependent upon a prior sanctification, thus embracing, no doubt unknowingly, the traditional Roman Catholic *ordo salutis*.[15]

costal historian, "popularized sanctification more than any other American revivalist." Kendrick, *Promise,* p. 41. Denominationally, Finney was a Presbyterian-become-Congregationalist. For Wesley's formative influence on Finney see Timothy L. Smith, *Revivalism and Social Reform* (New York: Abingdon Press, 1957), pp. 103-05.

13 (New York: Fleming H. Revell Co., 1903 [1876]), p. 55. For other treatments of the Holy Spirit and the baptism of the Holy Spirit in Finney's literature cf. *ibid.,* pp. 20-21, 65, 95, and his *Lectures on Revivals of Religion* (New York: Fleming H. Revell Co., 1868), pp. 101ff. For comment on the place of the baptism of the Spirit in Finney's theology see William G. McLoughlin, Jr., *Modern Revivalism: Charles Grandison Finney to Billy Graham* (New York: The Ronald Press, 1959), pp. 103-04; *Fleisch* II/1, pp. 144-45.

14 Cited in McLoughlin, *Modern Revivalism,* pp. 86-87.

15 It is instructive to notice in Finney's *Lectures on Systematic Theology,* ed. J. H. Fairchild (South Gate, Calif.: Colporter Kemp, 1944 [1878]) that one chap-

Finney's influence on the American scene can hardly be overemphasized. "Finney's revivalism," writes McLoughlin, ". . . transformed 'the new system' [i.e., Finney's general theology and approach] from a minority to a majority religion. By mid-century it was in fact the national religion of the United States."[16] In Finney were combined both the theology (essentially Methodism) and the methodology (essentially revivalism) which were later to find a permanent home in the movement called Pentecostal.

5. THE HOLINESS MOVEMENT

From Methodism through American revivalism and the person and work of Charles Finney (the institutionalizer of revivalism) the line is a straight one that leads through the holiness movement directly into Pentecostalism. The holiness movement seems to have arisen from a variety of causes, principal of which were the demoralizing after-effects of the American Civil War, the dissatisfaction of many within Methodist churches with the "holiness," or the adherence to Wesleyan perfectionist doctrine of The Methodist Church, and a corresponding concern for the advance of modern liberal views in theology and of wealth and worldliness in the church as a whole.[17]

The theological center of the holiness movement, true to its name and its Wesleyan heritage, was a second experience, specifically a conversion into Scripture holiness, sanctification, or as it was often called, perfect love. This center assured "the subsequent experience" an importance it was later to assume in Pentecostalism. It was directly from

---

ter is devoted to justification while six chapters are given to sanctification. For the burden of Finney's antiforensic justification argument see *ibid.*, pp. 382-403, and Documents, below, p. 332. For Wesley's related doctrine of justification cf. Documents, below, p. 331. A comparative study of the theologies of Wesley and Finney would fill a lacuna in the literature of evangelicalism.

[16] *Modern Revivalism*, p. 66. Finney was the major, and the theologically immediate, predecessor of the late nineteenth-century holiness movement, the immediate source, in turn, of the Pentecostal movement. See Mayer, *Religious Bodies*, pp. 315-16; Fleisch I/2, 14, 386, 442, and *idem*, II/1, 139, 143.

[17] Cf. Sweet, *Story of Religion in America*, pp. 352-53; John A. Hardon, S. J., *The Protestant Churches of America* (Westminster, Md.: The Newman Press, 1957), p. 295; and Kendrick, *Promise*, p. 40.

"This movement was almost exclusively a Methodist phenomenon, led by Methodists, and appealing mainly to Methodists." Clark, *Small Sects*, p. 72. Professor Warfield's discussion of the continental equivalent of the Anglo-Saxon holiness movement — the "fellowship movement" — illustrates this connection historically and theologically: "Smith's doctrine of the Higher Life is historically only a modification of the Wesleyan doctrine of 'Christian Perfection,' and the Evangelistic methods employed by him and conveyed to the Fellowship Movement were historically derived from Methodist practice. . . . They wished to apply the epithets *instantanea, perfecta, plena, certa*, which the Old Protestantism employed of the superinvention of justification on faith, to sanctification also." *Perfectionism*, I, 324 n. 42. Cf. Fleisch I/1, 153, 15-20; I/2, 11, 14, 27, and especially 287.

the holiness movement, for instance, that Pentecostalism adopted the use of the expression "the baptism in the Holy Spirit" for its second (or third) Christian experience, together with the panoply of emphases that accompany subsequent-experience theology. In the holiness movement "the scriptural phrase 'Baptism of the Holy Spirit,' which was to have an important significance in the Pentecostal movement," writes Kendrick for Pentecostalism, "was popularized as the name for the experience of sanctification, or 'second blessing.' All who came under the influence of the Holiness ministry became familiar with 'spiritual baptism.' "[18]

W. E. Boardman's *The Higher Christian Life* has usually been considered the single most influential book in the literature of the holiness movement. In Boardman's book the broad holiness principles are laid out. These principles summarize distinctive holiness theology as they later undergirded distinctive Pentecostal theology. "There is a *second experience,*" Boardman instructed his readers, "distinct from the first — sometimes years after the first — a *second conversion,* as it is called."[19] "And now to account for the two distinct experiences, each so marked and important, and so alike in character, we have only to consider two facts, viz., first, that the sinner's necessities are two-fold and distinct, although both are included in the one word salvation. We express the two in the words of that favorite hymn, Rock of Ages, when we sing, 'Be of sin the *double* cure, Save from wrath and make me pure.' "[20] It is worth noting in passing that in the nineteenth century The Methodist Church in the United States, symptomatic of its changing theological posture, shuffled off the Wesleyan phrase "double cure" and substituted for it the words "be of sin the *promised* cure."[21] It was this general "shuffling off" of the double experience which troubled some Methodists, giving them occasion to question the aspiration after holiness in Methodist ranks and so to form the holiness movement for the restoration of this second experience and the desire for it.

Boardman concluded his argument for a two-fold work in the following manner: "[Christ] has not given himself to us in half of his offices freely, then to withhold himself from us in the other half. If we are content to take him as a half-way Saviour — a deliverer from condemnation, merely, but refuse to look to him as a present Saviour

---

[18] *Promise,* p. 33.
[19] (Boston: Henry Hoyt, 1859), p. 47. Albert Outler believes that "the Methodists in America, especially in the nineteenth century, contributed to a very considerable confusion by interpreting 'perfection' in terms of 'the second blessing.' " *John Wesley* ("A Library of Protestant Thought"; New York: Oxford University Press, 1964), p. 31. Yet it is hard to see how, given Wesley's emphasis on the subsequent instantaneous experience, this interpretation could fail to follow.
[20] Boardman, *Higher Christian Life,* p. 51.
[21] Clark, *Small Sects,* p. 73.

from sin, it is our own fault."[22] Even Martin Luther is conscripted to support this two-fold scheme. "Justification in the great Reformer's sense, was *being made righteous;* that is, being *reckoned* righteous before God, and being *made* righteous in heart and life."[23] Then Boardman summarized the essential holiness persuasion: "Nevertheless the two things [being reckoned righteous and being made righteous] are distinct and different in their nature and are expressive of two great and equal wants of the sinner. He must be just in the eye of the law, justified before God. But he must also be holy in heart and life, or he cannot be saved."[24]

When brought to birth in America through the activity of Finney, Asa Mahan, the Walter Palmers, Thomas C. Upham, A. B. Earle, Boardman and others, the holiness movement spread to England where in 1875 the Keswick Convention was born, and then through R. Pearsall Smith to Germany and the continent whence was born the *Gemeinschaftsbewegung.*[25]

Out of the world-wide holiness movements the Pentecostal movement was born. The Pentecostal historian, Charles Conn, notes that "the Pentecostal movement is an extension of the holiness revival that occurred during the last half of the nineteenth century. . . . Most of those who received the Holy Ghost baptism during the earliest years were either connected with the holiness revival or held holiness views."[26]

6. ANGLO-AMERICAN EVANGELICALS AND R. A. TORREY

An unusually large number of prominent evangelical figures since Wesley and Finney and within or under the pervasive influences of the nineteenth-century holiness movements claimed to have passed through crisis, second experiences of holiness (or its equivalents: baptism of the Holy Spirit, perfect love, sanctification, the deeper experience, or victory).[27] Of particular importance, gauging from usage in Pentecostal

---

[22] *Higher Christian Life,* p. 76.

[23] *Ibid.,* p. 52.

[24] *Ibid.*

[25] For perspective on this complex see Bloch-Hoell, *Pentecostal Movement,* pp. 15-17. For a study of the American origins of the holiness movement and a championing of its influences, see Timothy L. Smith, *Revivalism and Social Reform,* pp. 103-47, and *idem, Called unto Holiness: The Story of the Nazarenes* (Kansas City, Mo.: Nazarene Publishing House, 1962), chapter one.

[26] *Pillars of Pentecost* (Cleveland, Tenn.: Pathway, 1956), p. 27. See also Kendrick's ascription of Pentecostal origins to holiness doctrinal emphases, *Promise,* p. 33. Cf. also Conn, *Like a Mighty Army Moves the Church of God: 1866-1955* (Cleveland, Tenn.: Church of God Publishing House, 1955), p. xix; Walter G. Muelder, "From Sect to Church," *Christendom, 10* (1945), 456-57; Nichol, *Pentecostalism,* pp. 5-7. See also the careful distinctions made between the holiness movement and Pentecostalism by T. Rennie Warburton, "Holiness Religion: An Anomaly of Sectarian Typologies," *JSSR, 8* (Spring 1969), 130-39.

[27] The most prominent compilation of these experiences was J. Gilchrist Law-

literature, were the late nineteenth- and early twentieth-century teachings, particularly on the Holy Spirit, of A. J. Gordon, F. B. Meyer, A. B. Simpson, Andrew Murray, and especially, R. A. Torrey — all rather prominent figures in the English-speaking evangelical world. These five formed a kind of theological fund from which the Pentecostal theology of the Spirit has drawn heavily to establish itself.[28]

R. A. Torrey is cited by Pentecostals with particular frequency and is of unusual significance to Pentecostalism in connection with the Spirit's baptism. Through a world-wide evangelistic tour with Charles Alexander in 1904 Torrey, then president of the evangelically influential Moody Bible Institute in Chicago, broadcast among evangelical Christians in many places the message of the Spirit's subsequent operations and hence served as a kind of John the Baptist figure for later international Pentecostalism.[29]

Unlike Wesley and Finney who exerted rather broad influences on Pentecostalism, Torrey's only discernible effect upon the movement was in specific connection with the spiritual baptism. But we would say without hesitation that, judging from the movement's literature, Torrey was, after Wesley and Finney, the most influential figure in the pre-history of Pentecostalism. Torrey's nearness to the Pentecostal movement's actual origins has in fact made his influence felt with more force than it might otherwise have been.

Pentecostalism found in Torrey's theology of the Spirit a special affinity. Gee writes that "it was, perhaps, Dr. Torrey who first gave the teaching of the Baptism of the Holy Ghost a new, and certainly more scriptural and doctrinally correct, emphasis on the line of 'power from on high,' especially for service and witness (Acts 1:8). His logical

---

son's *Deeper Experiences of Famous Christians: Gleaned from Their Biographies, Autobiographies and Writings* (Springfield, Mo.: Gospel Publishing House, 1911), with its thesis that "as there is a practical agreement among evangelical Christians with regard to the way of salvation, so there is a practical agreement among those who believe in a deeper Christian experience than conversion," p. ix. The two men whom Lawson understands as the most significant Christians since the apostles are Wesley and Finney. The Pentecostal leader Ralph Riggs, writing of Lawson's book, remarked that "it is good to know that the Baptism in the Spirit is more than a Scriptural doctrine; it is an experience into which many prominent Christian workers have actually entered, some in recent generations." *The Spirit Himself* (Springfield, Mo.: Gospel Publishing House, 1949), p. 100.

[28] For the relevant doctrine of these figures see below, Documents, pp. 335-41. All five of these men are cited in support of the Pentecostal baptism in the Holy Spirit in Riggs, *Spirit Himself*, pp. 47-51; Ernest Swing Williams, *Systematic Theology* (3 vols.; Springfield, Mo.: Gospel Publishing House, 1953), quotes the same five and uses substantially the same five quotations, III, 59-61.

[29] See George T. B. Davis, *Torrey and Alexander: The Story of a World-Wide Revival* (New York: Fleming H. Revell Co., 1905). Notice also the special influence of Finney's books on both Torrey and Alexander in their formative years, *ibid.*, pp. 27, 37, 56.

presentation of truth did much to establish the doctrine."[30] And both Riggs and Williams include in their standard Pentecostal treatments Torrey's claim that regeneration by the Holy Spirit and baptism with the Holy Spirit are not coterminous.

> The Baptism with the Holy Spirit is an operation of the Holy Spirit distinct from and subsequent and additional to His regenerating work. A man may be regenerated by the Holy Spirit and still not be baptized with the Holy Spirit. In regeneration there is an impartation of life, and the one who receives it is fitted for service. *Every true believer has the Holy Spirit.* But not every believer has the Baptism with the Holy Spirit, though every believer . . . may have.[31]

This statement is the most frequent quotation by a non-Pentecostal to be found in Pentecostal literature. Joined with comparable remarks by Gordon, Meyer, Simpson, and Murray, and all those influenced by them, Pentecostalism found ready at hand a large and influential body of evangelical opinion which taught and supported the later distinctively Pentecostal experience of a subsequent baptism in the Holy Spirit.

7. THE WELSH REVIVAL

The Welsh Revival of 1904-05 needs only to be mentioned before proceeding to the actual beginnings of the Pentecostal movement itself. The significance of the Welsh Revival may be found primarily in its awakening of a widespread aspiration for revival in evangelical and holiness groups in North America, Europe, and the mission world. Hardly an historical treatment of the Pentecostal movement is able to pass the Welsh Revival without a reference to the stimulus it provided for those who were very soon thereafter to join themselves to Pentecostalism. The Welsh Revival appears to have been the last "gap" across which the latest sparks of holiness enthusiasm leapt igniting the Pentecostal movement.[32]

8. SUMMARY AND CONCLUSION

Methodism was the modern soil upon which Pentecostalism flour-

---

[30] *Pentecostal Movement*, pp. 4-5.

[31] In Riggs, *Spirit Himself*, p. 47; Williams, *Systematic Theology*, III, 59; also later in Ray H. Hughes, *What Is Pentecost?* (Cleveland, Tenn.: Pathway Press, 1963), pp. 27-28; the quotation is from Torrey's *What the Bible Teaches: A Thorough and Comprehensive Study of What the Bible Has to Say concerning the Great Doctrines of Which It Treats* (London: James Nisbet and Co. [1898]), p. 271. Cf. Montanism in Adolph Harnack, *History of Dogma*, tr. Neil Buchanan (5 vols.; New York: Dover Publications, 1961), II, 101.

[32] See Mosiman, *Zungenreden*, pp. 65-67; Gee, *Pentecostal Movement*, p. 5; Bloch-Hoell, *Pentecostal Movement*, p. 17; Nichol, *Pentecostalism*, pp. 40-41, 46. For a description of pneumatic occurrences at the Welsh Revival see *Fleisch* I/2, 443-45, 448. Of special interest are the ecstatic features later to recur in Pentecostalism and the Methodist heritage of Evan Roberts, the leader of the Welsh Revival.

ished. Revivalism was in part and increasingly the American practice of Methodist theology, and Finney was the individual and the holiness movement the corporate vehicle of that theology and practice. The modern family-book of Pentecostalism has then the following main chapters: Wesley — revivalism — Finney — the holiness movement. In each chapter personal experience is given special stress. And in the Methodist and holiness movements, at the beginning and the end of this family history, the personal experience most stressed was that which was subsequent to what was called justification or conversion. It is the experience which came in the Pentecostal movement to be called the baptism in the Holy Spirit.

B. THE BEGINNINGS OF THE PENTECOSTAL MOVEMENT

1. THE EMBRYONIC BEGINNINGS

The Pentecostal movement was born in America in the midst of a period of great social change and spiritual uncertainty, the America of the late nineteenth and the early twentieth centuries. "It was during this era," writes McLoughlin, "that the country shifted from an agrarian to an industrial economy, from a rural to an urban-centered population, from an anticolonial to an imperialistic nation, from a relatively homogeneous to a polygenetic people, and from a system of relative laissez-faire to the first stages of governmental social control." And he concludes, we think a little severely, that "these profound changes and the shocks that accompanied them registered most heavily upon those country-bred, evangelically oriented, intellectually unsophisticated, and sentimentally insecure individuals who made up the bulk of the nation's churchgoers."[33]

Theologically, the first decade of the twentieth century was the period marked by the traumatic joining, at a new and crucial stage, of the bitter controversy over what was called modernism in the church: the Roman *Lamentabili* and *Pascendi* were issued in 1907, and two years later the conservative Protestant *Fundamentals* commenced publication. It is well to remember that it was from the epicenter of this period of church turmoil that the Pentecostal movement erupted.

What came to be known as Pentecostalism appears to have originated among those who were already active Christians but who, according to Pentecostals, wanted something more than they were getting from their churches. This "more" came to them in the form of the experience of speaking in tongues which, when joined to the persuasion that this speaking was the evidence of the baptism in the Holy

---

[33] *Modern Revivalism*, p. 168; cf. also Bloch-Hoell, *Pentecostal Movement*, pp. 10-11; Kendrick, *Promise*, pp. 215-16; Mosiman, *Zungenreden*, p. 70 n. 4; Kilian McDonnell, "Holy Spirit and Pentecostalism," *Commonweal*, 89 (Nov. 8, 1968), 198.

Spirit, created the embryo of Pentecostal conviction.[34] The origins of this conviction, that is to say, of the Pentecostal movement, appear to have been spontaneous, scattered, and little noticed: first, perhaps, in the late nineteenth century in the American Southeast (North Carolina, 1896), then more significantly at the very beginning of the twentieth century in the American Middle West (Topeka, Kansas, January 1, 1901), thence sporadically around the world, and finally, for the first time prominently, in the American Far West (Los Angeles, California, April 9, 1906).[35]

2. THE STANDARD BEGINNING AND SPREAD

The most striking outbreak of the Pentecostal phenomena and the one to which most Pentecostals look as the focus and fountainhead of their movement's origins occurred in Los Angeles in 1906.[36]

The catalyst and key figure in the Los Angeles events appears to have been William Seymour, whose denominational associations and contacts in Los Angeles, as recorded by a Pentecostal observer, represent a relief of the soil on which the Pentecostal movement was soon to grow.

> A colored Holiness preacher named W. J. Seymour . . . accepted the Pente-costal message . . . and he was invited to hold a meeting [at a small Naza-rene assembly in Los Angeles]. Seymour arrived there and began preach-ing on pentecostal doctrine. Severe criticism resulted and the meeting was stopped. Some Baptists invited Seymour to preach in their home at 214

---

[34] " 'It was the linking together of speaking with tongues and the baptism in the Holy Spirit that sparked off the Pentecostal Revival,' " in Gee, *Pentecost*, No. 45 (Sept. 1958), p. 17. Also Kendrick, *Promise*, p. 53; Bloch-Hoell, *Pentecostal Movement*, pp. 23-24; Morton T. Kelsey, *Tongue Speaking: An Experiment in Spiritual Experience* (Garden City, New York: Doubleday and Co., Inc., 1964), pp. 69-70.

[35] The descriptions of the beginnings of Pentecostalism are legion. The North Carolina origins are treated in Conn, *Like a Mighty Army, passim*, especially pp. 1-55. The more important Topeka beginnings are detailed in almost every study of Pentecostalism, for example more recently in Bloch-Hoell, Brumback, Kendrick, Nichol, Sherrill. For interesting early Pentecostal phenomena outside of the United States see Frederick G. Henke, "The Gift of Tongues and Related Phenomena at the Present Day," *The American Journal of Theology*, 13 (April 1909), 193-96; Mosiman, *Zungenreden*, p. 67; Sherrill, *They Speak with Other Tongues*, pp. 44-46; Nichol, *Pentecostalism*, pp. 46-48.

[36] Even Conn, who wishes to establish the primacy of his particular southeastern American Pentecostal body, the Church of God, is willing to acknowledge that the 1906 occurrences in Los Angeles have a special place in Pentecostal history. See his *Like a Mighty Army*, pp. xxii, 25. Cf. also Gee, *Pentecostal Movement*, p. 11; *Fleisch II/2*, 7. I have noted a tendency in more recent literature to move seminal Pentecostal beginnings to the Topeka incidents. I believe that Topeka is proving to be the sounder place to begin a detailed history of the Pentecostal movement. For our purposes, however, the more demonstrative and widely noticed Los Angeles events serve as an adequate descriptive base.

North Bonnie Brae Street. There, on April 9, 1906, a pentecostal revival began with the manifestations that characterized those in the middle west. The group there increased and, to take care of the crowds, a former Methodist church located at 312 Azusa Street was procured for the meetings.[37] At the Azusa Street meetings the Pentecostal movement ignited. Its fires were apparently so intense that they were felt within a short time around the world. The conflagration swept first across America itself. The reminiscences of the prominent Pentecostal leader, J. Roswell Flower, are synoptic.

> I shall never forget the day when that first messenger from Azusa Street in Los Angeles came into the community in which I lived. He testified briefly that his Pentecost had come and that he had been baptized in the Holy Ghost and spoken in tongues in accord with the pattern of Acts 2:4. His testimony was as though he had thrown a spiritual bombshell. His experience was just what those spiritually hungry people were wanting. They wanted something more [n. b.] than teaching — they wanted an experience — they wanted Pentecost. And it was not long until the "day of Pentecost" had fully come to Indianapolis and hundreds of people received a baptism in the Holy Ghost.[38]

T. B. Barratt (1862-1940), a Norwegian Methodist pastor, was in New York City on a fund-raising mission when he first heard of the events in Los Angeles. He wrote to the leaders in Los Angeles, got their counsel, received his baptism in the Holy Spirit, and returned to establish Pentecostalism in Norway, then in England, Germany, and Sweden, becoming the European father of the Pentecostal movment.[39] Many others came to Los Angeles, or were addressed by those who came from Los Angeles, and the new glad tidings spread. Within a generation Pentecostalism was a force in church history.

---

[37] Fischer, "Progress of the Various Modern Pentecostal Movements," p. 16; cf. ibid., p. 58. The only extant narrative by a participant in the April 1906 events is Frank Bartleman's How Pentecost Came to Los Angeles, especially pp. 44-58.

[38] In Gee, Pentecost, No. 36 (June 1956), inside cover. Mosiman, who was studying in Chicago during this period, notes that "on November 20th, 1906 the first [Pentecostal] adherents were baptized, and in the winter of 1908-09 there were already almost a dozen [Pentecostal] mission stations in the city." Zungenreden, p. 70. Interestingly, it was precisely during this period that the Pentecostal movement was exported from Chicago to Brazil through immigrant converts to the Pentecostal message. See Hollenweger II, 884-85, 903. See the account of the world-wide spread of Pentecostalism in Les Mouvements de Pentecôte, pp. 14-20.

[39] See chapter five of Bloch-Hoell's Pentecostal Movement, "T. B. Barratt as the European Apostle of the Movement," pp. 75-86. For a narrative of the European spread of Pentecostalism see Barratt's two books, In the Days of the Latter Rain (London: Simpkin, Marshall, Hamilton, Kent and Co., Ltd., 1909) and When the Fire Fell and An Outline of My Life (Norway: Alfons Hansen and Sønner, 1927).

3. EXPLANATIONS OF THE EMERGENCE OF THE
   PENTECOSTAL MOVEMENT

The reasons which have been suggested for the rise and attraction
of the Pentecostal movement are as varied as the movement's origins.
The Pentecostal, of course, believes his movement to be God-sent
and meeting basic human needs. Many non-Pentecostals tend to explain
the movement psychologically. Both Pentecostal and non-Pentecostal
understand the movement as arising in spiritual protest to the modernism and secularism of the church much as had the holiness movement a generation earlier.[40]

In a suggestive theological explanation, Kurt Hutten compares the
origins of Pentecostalism with the origins of other spiritual movements
at about the same period:

> Pentecostalism, whose beginnings are only a few years later than Spiritu-
> alism's, provided a very similar answer to the hunger of rationalistically
> starved souls. Rationalism, as is well known, had by then preempted the
> proclamation of the church for some time, [and] had caused the church to
> make concessions to the modern world-view bringing about a considerable
> flattening and thinning out of the church's message. . . . What was then left
> for "proclamation" were religiously warmed-over moral exhortations
> and a cultural and social program decorated with Christian vocabulary.
> This evaporation required a protest. It came through fundamentalism,
> through the holiness movement, and through the Pentecostal movement
> . . . it came also in theology through the Luther renaissance, dialectical
> theology, and the new attention to Scripture and the confessions.

Hutten concludes that the Pentecostal movement once again "made
the heavenly powers, which a rationalistic proclamation was threatening
to eclipse, into living, present realities which were visible and ex-
perienceable."[41]

Professor Liston Pope, in his careful study *Millhands and Preachers*
(New Haven: Yale University Press, 1953), provides a broad spectrum of the major sociological explanations for the rise of the Christian sect-type churches (among which, in his study, the Pentecostal
are the most prominent and numerous): (1) transiency, i.e., the fluidity
of the times, which he does not consider valid; (2) "the failure of

---

[40] For Pentecostal explanations see Winehouse, *Assemblies,* p. 14; Brumback,
Suddenly from Heaven, pp. 2-10; Riggs, "Those 'Store-Front' Churches: A Phenomenal Development in the Religious Life of America," *United Evangelical
Action, 6* (Aug. 1, 1945), 4. For recent representative non-Pentecostal explanation see James N. Lapsley and John H. Simpson, "Speaking in Tongues," *Princeton Seminary Bulletin, 58* (Feb. 1965), 3-18, especially 10-18.

[41] *Seher, Grübler, Enthusiasten: Sekten und religiöse Sondergemeinschaften der
Gegenwart* (5th rev. ed.; Stuttgart: Quell-Verlag der Evangelischen Gesellschaft,
1958), p. 515. The rise of Pentecostalism has been placed against the still broader
background of the anti-intellectualism of the period as exemplified by Bergson's
anti-Cartesian emphasis on intuition in his *L'évolution créatrice,* published, significantly, in 1907. *Les Mouvements de Pentecôte,* p. 18 n. 1.

older churches to meet the religious needs of all groups in the population," which he believes "is of unquestionable merit"; (3) the "culture shock" involved in the transition from a rural to an urban situation — i.e., urbanization — which he finds a plausible but inadequate
explanation; (4) economics, i.e., the fact of the poor being the major
group attracted, which he calls tenable; (5) psychological need, i.e.,
the craving of many for emotional outlet and expression, which he
finds credible; (6) the theological explanation, i.e., the Pentecostals'
own persuasion that genuine spiritual factors are decisive, which he
simply mentions. Then Professor Pope concludes:

> They are all gathered up in the general statement that such groups thrive
> wherever a considerable portion of the population exists on the periphery
> of culture as organized, whether the index used be that of education, eco-
> nomic status, possibilities for psychological satisfaction, or religious or-
> ganization. Members of the newer religions do not belong anywhere — and
> so they belong, and wholeheartedly, to the one type of institution which
> deigns to notice them [their churches].[42]

We do not feel it within our competence or program to assign to
any particular factor, or to any several, or even to any hierarchy of
factors the causes for the rise of the Pentecostal movement. The total
body of factors must be appreciated before there can be a finished
assessment of the Pentecostal movement.

4. PENTECOSTALISM'S APOLOGIA FOR SCHISM

The new Pentecostal movement grew swiftly, attracting both followers
and persecution, and soon many of Pentecostal conviction were splin-
tering from their former churches and forming assemblies of their own,
believing that only in separation from churches they considered apos-
tate could they be thoroughly holy and true to their new persuasion.
As Conn put it, "since reformation and holiness were resisted in the
Church, then there must be a separation if there was to be genuine
spiritual identity."[43]

---

[42] Pp. 133-35. McLoughlin's conclusions are similar, *Modern Revivalism*, pp.
466-67. For sympathetic and not unmoving discussion of the various feelings of
inferiority which appear to be in some measure satisfied by Pentecostal experiences
and fellowship see *Hollenweger* I, 184-96. Daniel O'Hanlon, S. J., believes that
"the first reason for the growth of Pentecostal churches is that when a forgotten
human being comes to one of them, he feels himself loved and understood." "The
Pentecostals and Pope John's 'New Pentecost,' " *View: A Quarterly Journal Interpreting the World-Wide Charismatic Renewal*, No. 2 (1964), p. 21. Cf. also the
studies of William W. Wood, *Culture and Personality Aspects of the Pentecostal
Holiness Religion* (The Hague: Mouton and Co., 1965), pp. 65-66, 108-09;
Wilson, *Sects and Society*, pp. 15-118; and now the valuable research project of
Luther P. Gerlach and Virginia H. Hine, "Five Factors Crucial to the Growth
of a Modern Religious Movement," *JSSR*, 7 (Spring 1968), 23-40.

[43] *Like a Mighty Army*, p. 7; cf. Conn, *Pillars*, pp. 19-22; Leonhard Steiner,
Mit folgenden Zeichen: Eine Darstellung der Pfingstbewegung (Basel: Verlag

The justifications for separation, often in the names of Jesus, Paul, Luther, Wesley, or even healthy competition, have been frequently heard and remain to this day to vex the ecumenical movement. But that the Pentecostals failed to find satisfaction in their former "non-Pentecostal" churches may not always have been due, as might too simply be adjudged, to the spirit of congenital malcontents and schismatics; perhaps Pentecostal schism was due more frequently than sometimes appreciated to men who were hungry and needy in spirit, deeply and legitimately dissatisfied with conventional Christianity, and finding no impression on or expression for their hearts except in the new Pentecostal fellowships. Their apologies for schism ought perhaps to be heard with contrition by those of us who are grateful to stand within the ecumenical and historical-denominational traditions.

5. THE RISE OF NEO-PENTECOSTALISM

At about mid-century a new constellation of Pentecostal people appeared on the horizon. These people, because they shared the Pentecostal enthusiasm for the deeper, second and specially manifested experience of the baptism in the Holy Spirit, became known as Neo-Pentecostals. Most often Neo-Pentecostals have been persons outside the standard Pentecostal denominations. Neo-Pentecostals are Protestants, and in the last several years even Catholics, who have found the Pentecostal experience to be described in the next chapter.[44]

The Neo-Pentecostal movement appears gradually and increasingly to be assuming the name "charismatic." This nomenclature may be due to the sometimes pejorative use of the term Pentecostal by outsiders. In the word charismatic the Neo-Pentecostal Christians have found a term both popular and biblical, without the associations of emotional excitement and sometimes even frenzy occasionally connected with the older Pentecostal movement. Therefore, in the future Christians from other churches will probably be hearing of the charismatic

Mission für das volle Evangelium, 1954), p. 21. The separation sometimes occurred from the other side. See the drastic action in Germany in 1909 through "the Berliner Erklärung," *Fleisch* II/2, 112. In the United States the former "Pentecostal Church of the Nazarene" in its 1919 General Assembly exscinded "Pentecostal" from its official title in order clearly to be distinguished from the rapidly rising "tongues groups" called Pentecostal; see Nichol, *Pentecostalism*, p. 72. For a Pentecostal account of the rejection of Pentecostalism by A. B. Simpson and his Christian and Missionary Alliance see Brumback, *Suddenly from Heaven*, pp. 88-97.

[44] The primary sources for the rise of Neo-Pentecostalism are John Sherrill, *They Speak with Other Tongues*, in several printings; more recently from England, Michael Harper, *As at the Beginning: The Twentieth Century Pentecostal Revival*; London: Hodder and Stoughton, 1965; and from the new movement within the Roman communion, Kevin and Dorothy Ranaghan, *Catholic Pentecostals*, "Deus Books"; Paramus, N. J.: Paulist Press, 1969.

renewal or revival as often as they hear of Neo-Pentecostalism or, in some cases, even of Pentecostalism. But behind all these names stands the same central reality: the Pentecostal or, if you will, the charismatic experience of the Holy Spirit in a life- and speech-transforming event in the career of the Christian.[45]

The origins of Neo-Pentecostalism are difficult, at this young date, to trace precisely. But it is my present opinion that the organ most efficient in the production of Neo-Pentecostalism has been the Pentecostal work among men known as the Full Gospel Business Men's Fellowship International (FGBMFI), founded in 1953 in Los Angeles, the titular birthplace of the world-wide Pentecostal movement.

Assuming early the form of breakfasts for Christian laymen, especially of Full Gospel or Pentecostal provenance, the new movement began also to draw Christian men of other churches, and not infrequently pastors, to its programs, conferences, and regional conventions, often in handsome hotel surroundings. By these means, particularly, the Pentecostal experience and its manifestations became gradually familiar to a wide range of Christians, at first across America and eventually around the world. From 1953 onward we begin to hear increasingly of denominational Protestants, sometimes even of Jews and non-Christians, and in the late sixties, finally, of Catholics obtaining the Pentecostal experience. Many of these experiences have received their most prominent documentation in the monthly *Full Gospel Business Men's Fellowship Voice,* begun the year of the organization's incorporation.[46]

At the center, presently, of the attention of charismatic Christianity is the Melodyland (formerly Anaheim) Christian Center opposite Disneyland in Anaheim, California. The Melodyland enterprise, under the leadership of Ralph Wilkerson and in periodic association with David Wilkerson (no relative) of *Cross and Switchblade* fame, conducts impressive monthly youth rallies and performs ministries to youthful dope-addicts. The Center has also sponsored annual summer charismatic clinics at which Pentecostal and Neo-Pentecostal Christians of

---

[45] Several periodicals devoted almost exclusively to describing and promoting this event have already come and gone in the short life of the charismatic movement. In the mid-sixties *Trinity* magazine edited by Mrs. Jean Stone made a swift and impressive appearance but experienced as swift and unannounced a demise. Then, shortly after, *View: A Quarterly Journal Interpreting the World-Wide Charismatic Renewal* appeared and then disappeared, replaced by the, I believe, still living *Charisma Digest,* though only an issue a year has appeared for the past two years. From outward appearances the journal with the most visible life in it at the moment is (after the now venerable *Full Gospel Business Men's Voice*) the new *Acts: Today's News of the Holy Spirit's Renewal.*

[46] In addition to the important *Voice,* a series of pamphlets compiled by Jerry Jensen on the denominational experiences of the baptism in the Holy Spirit has received wide use. See p. 118, n. 2, below.

all varieties teach and attend lectures, seminars, and electives over two one-week periods. I have discovered the programs of these clinics to offer the most contemporary ledger to the more prominent of present Neo-Pentecostals.[47]

Why has Neo-Pentecostalism arisen? Protestant churches in particular and by definition and Roman Catholic Christians since the Second Vatican Council have exercised vigorous criticism of their own churches: their irrelevance, institutionalism, and spiritual deadness. Appealing especially to harried Protestant pastors and to spiritually malnourished Protestant and Catholic laity the Neo-Pentecostal movement has promised a way out. Both Pentecostal and Neo-Pentecostal Christians claim that the power for spiritual life in the individual and in the church is found in the long-neglected but now discovered and experienced baptism in the Holy Spirit with its charismatic manifestations.[48]

Charismatic Christianity promises the church and its members the source of renewal. As long as the church feels and experiences a renewal within its own resources (which, of course, the church will properly feel are not its own resources), the appeals of Neo-Pentecostalism will probably be minimal. But wherever a church or a Christian does not feel that present resources are adequate for present problems, Neo-Pentecostalism will appear on the scene with large advantages. Thus the future of Neo-Pentecostalism would appear to be as impressive as the surrounding churches' resources are depleted. It will be interesting to watch the future.

6. SUMMARY AND CONCLUSION

If one lifts his eyes from the immediate fascination of the Pentecostal-Neo-Pentecostal movement he may see stretching before him a long line of Pentecostal predecessors — from paracletic Montanism to perfectionist Methodism, thence from Aldersgate to Azusa Street, or in the broadest view, perhaps, from Eldad and Medad (Num. 11:26) to Full Gospel breakfasts and Melodyland. The Pentecostal movement is of one piece with the preceding pneumatic tradition. But it should not be dismissed for its mere similarity. For while it has successfully assumed all of the major emphases of its forbears it has enjoyed a swift world-wide sweep denied most of them and it has developed their distinguishing doctrine to a degree unknown to any of them. It is one with its past, but in its vital present it is unique. In Christen-

---

[47] See the asterisked titles in Bibliography I for some of the better known figures.

[48] Laurence Christenson, *Speaking in Tongues and Its Significance for the Church;* Minneapolis, Minn.: Bethany Fellowship, Inc., 1968, is the primary doctrinal and apologetical explanation of Neo-Pentecostalism, by a Lutheran pastor. A number of secondary studies of the charismatic movement may be found in Bibliography II, below.

dom it is perhaps the major grassroots religious revolution of our time. Born in this century, raised largely among the poor, at mid-century entering the middle class, it is reputedly growing faster than any other modern Christian movement and is increasingly pressing its existence upon the attention of the church and the world.

III

THE BAPTISM IN THE HOLY SPIRIT IN THE PENTECOSTAL MOVEMENT[1]

INTRODUCTION: THE SETTING OF THE PENTECOSTAL DOCTRINE OF THE HOLY SPIRIT

1. THE DISTINCTIVE DOCTRINE OF PENTECOSTAL THEOLOGY

PENTECOSTALISM FINDS ITS THEOLOGICAL CENTER IN THE *tremendum* of the Spirit's coming at Pentecost as described in Acts chapter two. Yet this center needs to be defined still more precisely. For it is not the sermon in Acts chapter two which gives Pentecostalism its name or distinctive doctrine, nor even the evangelization of the hearers, nor the baptism, establishment, and life of the early church (2:41-47), though of course Pentecostalism takes each of these events at Pentecost seriously. Yet in no Pentecostal teaching that we have encountered is it these latter events on the day of Pentecost (sermon, baptism, church-founding) which are understood as uniquely Pentecostal. *Pentecost* to Pentecostals signifies, particularly, the powerful

---

[1] For the reader's convenience in this chapter — a chapter requiring considerable citation — many simple reference footnotes will be raised into the text and abbreviated. The page reference following the author's name (and, where necessary, shortened title) will form the system. In most cases the author's name indicates his only title listed in the bibliography (e.g., Buntain = his *The Holy Ghost and Fire,* Springfield, Mo.: Gospel Publishing House, 1956). Where an author has more than one title in the bibliography we shall list below the book (or in one case, article) equated in this chapter with the author's name: Brumback = *What Meaneth This? A Pentecostal Answer to a Pentecostal Question,* Springfield, Mo.: Gospel Publishing House, 1947; Eggenberger = "Die Geistestaufe in der gegenwärtigen Pfingstbewegung (Darstellung und Versuch einer Beurteilung)," *ThZ, 11* (1955), 272-95; Pearlman = *Knowing the Doctrines of the Bible,* Springfield, Mo.: Gospel Publishing House, 1937; Riggs = *The Spirit Himself,* Springfield, Mo.: Gospel Publishing House, 1949; Williams = *Systematic Theology,* 3 vols., Springfield, Mo.: Gospel Publishing House, 1953.

descent of the Spirit upon the first disciples enabling them to speak in other tongues — the Pentecostal filling with the Holy Spirit.

When the systematic theologian of the Pentecostal movement was asked, for example, "Where do we get the term 'Pentecostal'?," he answered, representatively:

> The word "Pentecostal" . . . is used to describe the events that took place on the Day of Pentecost, as recorded in Acts chapter two; or events like those which occurred on that day. To be Pentecostal is to identify oneself with the experience that came to Christ's followers on the day of Pentecost; *that is* [emphasis ours], to be filled with the Holy Spirit in the same manner as those who were filled with the Holy Spirit on that occasion.[2]

Pentecost, for Pentecostalism, means first of all and essentially Acts 2:4: "And they were all filled with the Holy Spirit and began to speak in other tongues, as the Spirit gave them utterance."

Thus Pentecost according to Pentecostals — we may even say the doctrine of the Holy Spirit according to Pentecostals — is essentially the *experience* of the Holy Spirit, and the experience of the Holy Spirit in a special way: specifically, the post-conversion *filling* of the Holy Spirit (A, pp. 61ff. below), as evidenced initially by *speaking in other tongues* (B, pp. 76ff. below), through fulfilling conditions of *absolute obedience and faith* (C, pp. 87ff. below). With this outline we have already described the center of Pentecostal experience.

The Pentecostal doctrine of the Spirit (pneumatology) is centered in the crisis experience of the full reception of the Holy Spirit. In the study of Pentecostalism it is soon discovered that Pentecostal pneumatology emphasizes not so much the doctrine of the Holy Spirit as it does the doctrine (or, as Pentecostals would prefer to say, the experience) of the *baptism* in the Holy Spirit. For it is not so much the general biblical doctrine of the Spirit or, particularly, the Pauline doctrines of the walk in or fruit of the Spirit (Rom. 8; Gal. 5), or the Johannine work of the Spirit Paraclete (John 14-16) from which Pentecostalism derives its name or its special doctrine of the Spirit, though it wishes of course to include all these emphases in its life. Pentecostal pneumatology is in fact primarily concerned with the critical experience, reception, or filling of the Spirit as described, especially, by Luke in Acts.

No other doctrine or experience — for example, sanctification, or evangelism, or healing, or the second coming, all components of what Pentecostals call the full gospel — has the unanimous voice or the cohesive power in Pentecostalism enjoyed by the experience of the special Pentecostal baptism in the Holy Spirit as recorded at Acts 2:4.

---

[2] Ernest Williams, "Your Questions," *Pentecostal Evangel*, 49 (Jan. 15, 1961), 11. Cf. Nichol, *Pentecostalism*, pp. 1-2.

Speaking at the Pentecostal World Conference in Stockholm in 1955 Donald Gee affirmed this.

> Let me remind you that it is this unique testimony that has gathered this great World Conference together. It is good that we should realize that fact. We say, quite truly, that the centre of our message is *Jesus.* But we shall gladly acknowledge that other Christians say that just as truly. That testimony would make a Christian Conference, but not a "Pentecostal" Conference, and this is a World *Pentecostal* Conference. . . . What is the unique thing that makes the Pentecostal Movement a definitely separate entity? It is the Baptism in the Holy Spirit with the initial evidence of speaking with other tongues as the Spirit gives us utterance. And on this point the Pentecostal Movement speaks with an impressive unanimity.[3]

It can be argued that apart from its doctrine of the baptism in the Holy Spirit Pentecostalism's understanding of the person and work of the Holy Spirit is not particularly unique, nor is Pentecostalism's theology generally or its soteriology specifically, sufficiently different from majority American conservative evangelicalism to justify its being made a special object of study.[4]

> It is not unusual, we may note in illustration, when the standard North European Pentecostal treatment of the baptism in the Holy Spirit announces as its purpose the treatment of the biblical doctrine of the Holy Spirit but then proceeds, in fact, to treat only that part of the biblical doctrine which is of distinct Pentecostal concern. "The intention of this brief study," the work begins, "is simply to communicate to its readers an increased knowledge of the work of the Holy Spirit as it is presented in the Bible," adding then immediately and significantly, "and in so doing we want to give particular attention to that part of the Spirit's work which we know by the designation 'the baptism of the Holy Spirit.' "[5] The book then handles entirely, as its title indicates, the single experience of the *Geistestaufe,* the Spirit-Baptism. For this *is* the doctrine of the Holy Spirit in the Pentecostal movement.

Professor Harold A. Fischer of the Pentecostal Southern California (Bible) College, in discussing pneumatology, affirms that the Pente-

---

[3] *Pentecost,* No. 34 (Dec. 1955), p. 10. Cf. Bloch-Hoell, *Pentecostal Movement,* p. 175. Note the place of the baptism in the Holy Spirit in the Assemblies of God program, "Maintaining Spiritual Priorities: Guidelines for Five Year Plan of Advance, 1969-1973," and in the important "Declaration at St. Louis," in Richard Champion (ed.), *Our Mission in Today's World: Council on Evangelism Official Papers and Reports* (Springfield, Mo.: Gospel Publishing House, 1968), pp. 70, 212-13.

[4] For the setting off of Pentecostal from other evangelical, fundamental, and holiness believers because of the distinctive Pentecostal doctrine of the spiritual baptism, see Duffield, *Pentecostal Preaching,* pp. 15-16. For discussion of Pentecostal doctrine generally see Hollenweger I, 29-183; Bloch-Hoell, *Pentecostal Movement,* ch. 7, pp. 95-171. See also note 2 above, p. 20.

[5] Skibstedt, *Geistestaufe,* p. 58. See the place of this book in the bibliography of *RGG*[3], II, 1304.

costal movement is entirely one with other conservative evangelical Christians in its understanding of the Holy Spirit's person and work, departing in one particular only:

> The only field of theology wherein Pentecostalism is distinctive is pneumatology, and that only in one particular phase of the work of the Holy Spirit. . . . Their distinctive trait is speaking with tongues as a manifestation of the Spirit. Pentecostals contend that subsequent to conversion (but can on occasion be simultaneous) there is an "enduement with power" the evidence of which is speaking with other tongues "as the Spirit gives utterance" [Acts 2:4].[6]

It can be established from the literature that the experience of the Holy Spirit in Pentecostalism is understood essentially as the experience of the *baptism* and consequent *gifts* of the Holy Spirit. Anything outside of this thematic center is peripheral, not distinctively Pentecostal, and in Pentecostal treatments for all practical purposes undeveloped.

If we wished to be unacademically schematic in making our point we would suggest that, in generally christocentric Protestantism, alongside of particularly char700iscentric Lutheranism, theocentric Calvinism, ecclesiocentric Anglicanism, kardiocentric Anabaptism, and hagiocentric Methodism may be ranged the most recent significant arrival on the stage of Protestant church history — what may somewhat awkwardly be called pneumobaptistocentric Pentecostalism.

2. THE DEFINITION OF THE PENTECOSTAL BAPTISM IN THE HOLY SPIRIT

To say "baptized" in the Spirit is, in Pentecostal opinion, to say what Scripture says in many different ways: to be filled with (Acts 2:4), to receive (Acts 2:38), to be sealed by (Eph. 1:13), or to be anointed with (II Cor. 1:21 AV) the Spirit. "It must not be considered that these different terms refer to different experiences."[7] Whenever, therefore, the New Testament records the receiving of the Holy Spirit

---

6 "Progress of the Various Modern Pentecostal Movements," pp. 58, 60. Fischer remarks that Pentecostals "agree with and do not differ from the views of the other fundamental, dispensational, biblical scholars on the distinctive person of the Holy Spirit, His deity, procession and titles, His work in eternity past . . . in creation . . . in relation to the birth of Christ, in the life of Christ. . . . Pentecostalism does not postulate anything new relative to the Spirit's work in Salvation. It recognizes efficacious grace, that one is not regenerated apart from the work of the Spirit, and that at conversion the believer is baptized by the Holy Spirit into the body of Christ effecting the union of believers in one Body." *Ibid.*, pp. 58-59. (The baptism *by* the Holy Spirit is not yet, in Pentecostal interpretation, the distinctive Pentecostal baptism *in* the Holy Spirit, see below, p. 60.)

7 Riggs, *Spirit Himself,* p. 63. Riggs adds to the already mentioned words (baptized, filled, received, sealed, anointed) the terms "fell" (Acts 10:44), and "earnest" (II Cor. 1:21-22), concluding "thus we have seven distinct terms which are used in connection with this glorious experience which is promised to believers subsequent to salvation." *Ibid.*

the word "full" or "fully" should usually be understood, for there is a difference in Pentecostal conviction, as we shall see more explicitly in a moment, between simply *receiving* the Spirit (which happens to all Christians in some measure at conversion) and *fully* receiving him (as New Testament Christians did, and as all advanced Christians do, Pentecostals believe, sooner or later after conversion). The baptism in the Holy Spirit, then, is simply the full reception of the Holy Spirit.

In describing the Christian's crisis experience with the Spirit, furthermore, the word "baptism" is congenial to Pentecostal understanding because it carries something of the traumatic signification of being overcome by an element greater than oneself. Baptism in the Holy Spirit means, in Skibstedt's formulation (p. 59), that "a person is supernaturally, experientially, and in full consciousness immersed in or submerged by the power of the Holy Spirit."

In describing the full or Pentecostal experience of the Spirit, moreover, Pentecostals usually prefer the designation "baptism *in*" (or with) rather than "baptism *of*" (or by) the Spirit. For while every Christian, on becoming a Christian, has been baptized *of* or *by* the Spirit-as-agent (I Cor. 12:13a), Pentecostals believe that not every Christian has yet been baptized by *Christ*-as-agent *in* or *with* the Spirit-as-element (Mark 1:8 par.; I Cor. 12:13b). That is, Pentecostals believe that the Spirit has baptized every believer into Christ (conversion), but that Christ has not yet baptized every believer into the Spirit (Pentecost). The Pentecostal theologian Williams has this way of explaining this somewhat complex distinction: "In the new birth the Holy Spirit is the Agent, the atoning blood the means, the new birth the result; in the Baptism with the Spirit, Christ is the Agent ('He shall baptize you with the Holy Ghost and with fire'), the Spirit the means, the enduement with power the result" (III, 47).

The Pentecostal believes, then, that since every Christian has been baptized *by* or *of* but not yet *in* or *with* the Holy Spirit, the preposition "in" is usually important for describing the special Pentecostal spiritual baptism which follows conversion.

We may gather together the Pentecostal understanding on this point by saying that the Pentecostal believes that "the promise of the Father" (Luke 24:49; Acts 1:4-5), as given its most striking definition in the announcement of the Baptist (Mark 1:8 par.), is meant to be a dramatic, critical experience — a veritable baptism *in* the Holy Spirit. Anything less experiential than the baptism in water by John, Pentecostals feel, fails to do justice to the promised character of the baptism in the Spirit by Jesus.

The baptism in the Holy Spirit in the Pentecostal understanding finds then the following formal doctrinal definition in the Assemblies of God, the largest North American Pentecostal body (as recorded in Winehouse, pp. 207-09).

> *The Promise of the Father:* All believers are entitled to and should ardently expect and earnestly seek the promise of the Father, the Baptism in the Holy Ghost and fire, according to the command of our Lord Jesus Christ. This was the normal experience of all in the early Christian Church. With it comes the enduement of power for life and service, the bestowment of the gifts and their uses in the work of ministry. Luke 24:49; Acts 1:4, 8; I Cor. 12:1-31. This wonderful experience is distinct from and subsequent to the experience of the new birth. Acts 10:44-46; 11:14-16; 15:7-9.
>
> *The Evidence of the Baptism in the Holy Ghost:* The baptism of believers in the Holy Ghost is witnessed by the initial physical sign of speaking with other tongues as the Spirit of God gives them utterance. Acts 2:4. The speaking in tongues in this instance is the same in essence as the gift of tongues (I Cor. 12:4-10, 28), but different in purpose and use.

The most important characteristics of the Pentecostal understanding of the baptism in the Holy Spirit, discernible in the definition above, are: (1) that the event is usually "distinct from and subsequent to" the new birth; (2) that it is evidenced initially by the sign of speaking in other tongues; and (3) that it must be "earnestly" sought. In the remainder of this chapter we shall study the Pentecostal distinctive in these its three salient parts: first, its *subsequence* — its difference from or its coming after initiation, baptism, or conversion; second, its *evidence* — speaking in tongues; and third, its *conditions* — the requirements for its attainment.

A. THE DOCTRINE OF THE SUBSEQUENCE OF THE BAPTISM IN THE HOLY SPIRIT

1. THE SOURCES OF THE DOCTRINE

The major source of the Pentecostal doctrine of the subsequent baptism in the Holy Spirit is the Book of Acts. The Pentecostals, in fact, will concede that their data in this connection are almost totally confined to this book. The Old Testament and the Gospels, it is pointed out, contain only prophecies of the actual experience. And while the Epistles discuss the Spirit they do not treat his subsequent baptizing in any detail. Only Acts qualifies. "There alone," Brumback explains (p. 185), "can we find a detailed description of the baptism or filling with the Spirit which was experienced by those early believers." Only in Acts do we have impressive historical demonstrations indicating an important experience of the Holy Spirit in believers' lives subsequent to initial or saving faith. "In the Book of Acts," Reed (p. 3) teaches, "are found all instances of persons receiving the baptism in the Spirit which are to be found in the Bible." The result is that the understanding of the Acts of the Apostles becomes the most important responsibility for understanding the Pentecostal experience. The truth of Pentecostalism's doctrine of the Spirit rests, then, first of all on the exegesis of the Spirit passages in Acts.

While the Pentecostal doctrine of a second work beyond converting faith appeals in special particular, exegetically, to the Book of Acts, historically, as we have seen, the way was prepared by Methodist or revival evangelicalism. The tradition of the subsequent crisis experience in the spiritual life of the Christian, we may say now summarily, was mediated into twentieth-century Pentecostalism through, primarily, Wesley and his varied heirs in the several evangelical movements of nineteenth-century Christianity. The first heir of significance was American revivalism, principally the movement connected with Charles Finney and his ideas, and then more directly the late nineteenth-century and early twentieth-century holiness movements. Then from these movements and alongside of them there were the influences emanating from persons such as the Walter Palmers, the R. Pearsall Smiths (Hannah Whitehall Smith), W. J. Boardman, and later and particularly Andrew Murray, F. B. Meyer, A. B. Simpson, A. J. Gordon, and especially R. A. Torrey, all teaching the critical importance of a second spiritual experience beyond mere initiation into the Christian life. According to these teachings, beyond the experience of Christ *for* us — conversion, salvation — there must be the experience and thus the life of Christ *in* us — the spiritual baptism, the second experience. Since the nineteenth century a significant portion of conservative evangelical Christianity, of which Keswick is only one symbol among many, has been built upon the premise of a Christian's higher (or deeper) experience.

Pentecostalism feels, therefore, that it has competent sources for its doctrine of the Holy Spirit, particularly for what is called the Spirit's subsequent work, in the theologies of Acts and of conservative or revival evangelicalism. Pentecostalism has built its doctrine of the baptism in the Holy Spirit on Scripture — particularly upon Acts — and upon tradition — particularly upon recent evangelical church history. In both these sources, biblical and historical, and, it will insist, on a third — experiential[8]— Pentecostalism finds justification for positing a decisive *subsequent* experience in the life of Christians. "Subse-

---

[8] The *exegetical* difficulties which may arise are, in the final analysis, more than balanced for Pentecostals by the *experiential* proofs of the two-fold spiritual work of conversion and of spiritual baptism in the lives of dedicated contemporary Christians. Pearlman writes, for example: "We admit that these two operations of the Holy Spirit are not differentiated in the Scriptures with mathematical precision; but there are general indications of the distinction; and that distinction has been confirmed by the experience of spiritual Christians in many churches, who teach and testify to the fact that in addition and subsequent to spiritual regeneration there is a baptism of power for Christians." *The Heavenly Gift: Studies in the Work of the Holy Spirit* (Springfield, Mo.: Gospel Publishing House, 1935), p. 26. Cf. the same argument in Williams, *Systematic Theology*, I, 39.

quence" is a Pentecostal feature but, it would argue, an inherited feature, from, it would again wish to insist, reputable sources: the acts of the apostles and of modern evangelicals.

2. THE EXEGETICAL BASIS OF THE DOCTRINE

Pentecostalism quite openly declares that unless it can support its case biblically it has no finally compelling reason to exist. Pentecostalism believes, however, that it does in fact stand on neglected biblical foundations. "The biblical grounds for the claims of the Pentecostals are solid and sound," begins a Pentecostal symposium. "We are not afraid for the doctrine to be subjected to the most exacting test in the light of theological and exegetical science. It can stand such a test without fear of embarrassment or confutation."[9] The major exegetical explanations for the subsequent Pentecostal spiritual experience of the baptism in the Holy Spirit are the following.

a. *Acts 2:1-4: Pentecost.* The principal reference instanced for the subsequent operation of the Spirit is the coming of the Spirit at Pentecost where the one hundred and twenty waiting Christians "were all filled with the Holy Spirit and began to speak in other tongues, as the Spirit gave them utterance" (Acts 2:4). Maintaining that the disciples must have been Christians prior to Pentecost and/or that in John 20:22 (" 'Receive the Holy Spirit' ") the disciples had their first, partial, and initiatory reception of the Spirit, Pentecostals find in the disciples' subsequent, full reception of the Holy Spirit at the feast of Pentecost the precedent for a similar experience and sequence among all other Christians. Williams writes:

> There is plentiful evidence that the disciples who received the Spirit at Pentecost were already in a saved state. . . . Whatever a person may think concerning this, the evidence shows that the disciples were not of the world even as Christ was not of the world (John 17:14). Their names were written in heaven (Luke 10:20). They were spiritually clean (John 15:3) and were acknowledged by Jesus as united to Him as a branch is to the vine (John 15:4, 5). Yet they had not received the Baptism with the Holy Spirit.[10]

---

[9] Anonymous introduction to *The Pentecostal Message* (Franklin Springs, Ga.: The Publishing House [of the] Pentecostal Holiness Church, 1950), p. 10.

[10] *Systematic Theology,* I, 42. William G. MacDonald writes that "the apostles . . . had several experiences chronologically of the Spirit. On Christ's resurrection He breathed out from Himself into them 'Holy Spirit' (John 20:22 . . .). Thus they became united with Christ in a new way in the experience of receiving Christ's Spirit; this may properly be called their Christian 'regeneration' or 'the renewal of the Holy Spirit' (Tit. 3:5). Fifty days later these same men were 'filled with the Holy Spirit' (Acts 2:4) and began to speak in other languages in evidence of this 'filling.' " *Glossolalia in the New Testament* (Springfield, Mo.: Gospel Publishing House, [1964]), p. 2. See this view also in Andrew Murray, *The Spirit of Christ: Thoughts on the Indwelling of the Holy Spirit in the Believer and the Church* (New York: A. D. F. Randolph and Co., 1888), p. 323.

In the absence in most Christians and churches of the Pentecostal experience recorded in Acts 2:4, Pentecostals believe they have the clue to Christianity's patent weakness. The church is not generally taught to wait, as its Lord instructed it, for a special enduement of power to equip it for its mission in the world (cf. Acts 1:8). Pentecostals believe that they are true to the event from which they take their name by waiting for this equipage. By eagerly waiting for and then receiving the specially promised Pentecostal baptism in the Holy Spirit the Pentecostal movement believes that it has fulfilled God's intention for his church, that it represents in this particular obedience the key to the church's renewal, and that it provides then in its own history the model for the divinely intended and accomplished power of world mission.

b. *Acts 2:38: The Converts at Pentecost.* The juxtaposition and the order of statements in Peter's charge to the hearers at Pentecost (Acts 2:38) lead Pentecostal exegesis to find at this pivotal passage the necessity of a sequence of spiritual experiences in the lives of all Christians after the incidence of the historical, apostolic Pentecost itself: "[1] Repent, and [2] be baptized . . . for the forgiveness of your sins and [3] you shall receive the gift of the Holy Spirit." At their repentance, comments Riggs, the Spirit "would baptize them into the Body of Christ [conversion]. Then they would take a public stand for Christ by being baptized in water in His name. Following that, they would receive the gift of the Holy Spirit."[11] First Christians are converted by the Spirit bringing them to Christ and his body, symbolized, second, by baptism in water; subsequently Christians would be spiritually filled by Christ's baptizing them in the Holy Spirit.

However, most Christians, Pentecostals feel, stop after they have received only half or two-thirds of the promise. Christians, if they wish to be the kind of Christians portrayed in the Book of Acts, should press on to claim their full inheritance as it is presented to them, in sequence, in Acts 2:38. Pentecostals have not been satisfied, they would insist, merely with being baptized into Christ; rather, they have sought their complete possession in Christ by following their conversion with the obediences requisite for receiving from the same Christ the subsequent gift of the fulness of the Spirit.

The sequence of Acts 2:38, Pentecostals believe, is a moral sequence, with its implicit imperative to follow repentance and baptism into Christ with obedience and appropriation of the Spirit. After forgiveness in Christ (Acts 2:38a), they urge from this text, comes fulness in the Spirit (Acts 2:38b).

---

[11] *Spirit Himself*, pp. 55-56. The three "baptisms" here should be noted: (1) the baptism of penitents by the Spirit into the body of Christ, at conversion; (2) the baptism in water, as confession of Christ; and (3) the baptism (of believers by Christ) into the Holy Spirit as the Pentecostal experience.

c. *Acts 8:4-25: The Converts at Samaria.* The events at Samaria provide further material for the specific Pentecostal persuasion. To all outward appearances the baptized believers in Samaria had, as have most non-Pentecostal Christians, stopped halfway. The Samaritans had not gone beyond baptism and forgiveness to the Spirit and fulness. Acts 8:14-17 records that:

> Peter and John . . . came down and prayed for them that they might receive the Holy Spirit; for it had not yet fallen on any of them, but they had only been baptized in the name of the Lord Jesus. Then they laid their hands on them and they received the Holy Spirit.

"That even after Pentecost men could come to faith and be baptized without having been baptized in the Spirit," comments Steiner representatively, "is evident from the example of the Christians at Samaria."[12]

To have been baptized merely in water, argue Pentecostals from this important Acts text, is not yet to have been baptized in the Spirit. The *spiritual* baptism is quite another experience than water baptism and should be sought by *Christians.* Acts 8, therefore, is one of Pentecostalism's major evidences for the necessity of the Christian's moving beyond conversion to the Pentecostal experience if the Christian wishes to be spiritually complete.

d. *Acts 9:1-19: Paul's Experience.* Paul's earliest Christian experiences, Pentecostals believe, indicate a subsequent encounter with the Holy Spirit. For, it is pointed out, while Paul met his Lord en route to Damascus, he received the Spirit only in Damascus (Acts 9:17). "Is the Baptism with the Spirit received at conversion?" asks a Pentecostal tract. The answer, "No, it is not." And one of the four reasons given is: "The apostle Paul was converted on his way to Damascus (Acts 9:1-6), and received his Baptism [in the Holy Spirit] three days later."[13] If in the experience of the great apostle there was a spiritual experience subsequent to conversion, it is asked, why should his less distinguished successors accept or expect anything less in their own Christian experience? Paul was not satisfied with being only a Christian; he became a Spirit-filled Christian, and Paul's whole subsequent career indicates the importance of this second fact. Paul's experience, then, should prompt all Christians to seek *two* encounters: with the Lord for conversion; with the Spirit for power in mission.

e. *Acts 10-11: Cornelius' Household.* It is with a little more difficulty that Pentecostals sustain an argument for sequence in the experience of Cornelius who was converted and baptized with the Holy Spirit, and spoke in tongues — all seemingly at once (Acts 10:43-48

---

[12] *Zeichen,* p. 175. See the declaration on the basis of this text by the Brazilian Assembléias de Deus in *Hollenweger* II, 894.

[13] A. W. Kortkamp, "What the Bible Says about the Baptism of the Spirit," Tract No. 4285 (Springfield, Mo.: Gospel Publishing House, n.d.), n. p.

par.; 11:1-18; 15:7-9). It is usually insisted, however, that Cornelius' experience and that of his household were ideal, that all believers could, even should, receive the baptism in the Holy Spirit immediately upon believing but that, unlike Cornelius and his household, the faith of most Christians is too feeble or their instruction too sketchy to enable them to receive the whole spiritual enduement at once.

But even in the ideal case, where both occur at once, a sequence will usually be introduced. "Could we not even consider that this visitation was God's ideal?" asks Riggs (p. 111), "His perfect pattern: believe Christ, receive the Holy Spirit *in immediate succession?*" (emphasis ours). It seems important to Pentecostal teaching that conversion and spiritual baptism — even when they should appear to occur together — be at least distinguished from each other and, usually, that they be placed in succession. Skibstedt explains:

> That regeneration precedes the Spirit-baptism must be seen as the general rule; nevertheless the possibility is not excluded that in certain cases both can occur at the same time ... though this seldom happens.

Then he adds, significantly:

> To be sure, though this double experience *can* occur simultaneously, nevertheless, we may not amalgamate or equate these two experiences. Regeneration is regeneration and Spirit-baptism is Spirit-baptism, even when one experiences both parts at the same time. In regeneration the divine life is communicated, and in the Spirit-baptism power is added to this life.[14]

We may summarize, then, by saying that, in the Pentecostal view, when the full experience of the Spirit is not perceptibly subsequent it must at least be separate, discrete, or distinguishable from the experience of new birth.

But it is sometimes contended, difficult as it might at first seem, that Cornelius was converted prior to the visit of Peter, that he was already a Christian, lacking only the additional spiritual baptism. This is the argument of the "three-experience" or holiness branch of the Pentecostal movement (most Scandinavian bodies and those reached by them in mission, and in North America, most prominently, the Church of God and the Pentecostal Holiness Church and their mission affiliates). DuPlessis, who comes from this branch of Pentecostalism, writes for example that Cornelius "had already experienced the grace of God, but when Peter preached to him he also received the Holy Spirit, and we speak of that incident as the Gentile Pentecost."[15] This understand-

---

[14] *Geistestaufe,* p. 73. Cf. Gee, *Pentecost* (Springfield, Mo.: Gospel Publishing House, 1932), p. 20. See the Assemblies of God definition: "This wonderful experience is distinct from and subsequent to the experience of the new birth," in Winehouse, *Assemblies,* p. 208. Somewhat puzzling, if studied, is the addendum of proofs: Acts 10:44-46; 11:14-16; 15:7-9, *ibid.*

[15] *God Has No Grandsons* (Dallas, Texas: Privately Printed, [1960]), pp. 3-4. See the extended argument of Bishop J. H. King in his sermon, "The Gentile

ing of Cornelius, however, may be described as the minority opinion of the Pentecostal movement. Nevertheless, the entire movement does seem unanimous in seeing in even Cornelius' apparently unitary experience a division of parts.

f. *Acts 19:1-7: The Disciples at Ephesus.*

> [Paul] came to Ephesus. There he found some disciples. And he said to them, "Did you receive the Holy Spirit when you believed?" And they said, "No, we have never even heard that there is a Holy Spirit." And he said, "Into what then were you baptized?" They said, "Into John's baptism." And Paul said, "John baptized with the baptism of repentance, telling the people to believe in the one who was to come after him, that is, Jesus." On hearing this, they were baptized in the name of the Lord Jesus. And when Paul had laid his hands upon them, the Holy Spirit came on them; and they spoke with tongues and prophesied. There were about twelve of them in all.

The encounter of Paul with the "disciples" in Acts 19:1-7, recorded above, is particularly important for the Pentecostal case. It would appear that the passage contemplates the possibility of faith without the accompanying reception of the Holy Spirit. Referring to Paul's query — "Did you receive the Holy Spirit when you believed?" — Riggs asks: "If all disciples receive the experience of the Holy Spirit when they believe, why did Paul ask these disciples if they had done so? His very question implies that it is possible to believe without receiving the fullness of the Holy Spirit."[16]

Pentecost" in *The Pentecostal Message,* pp. 147-50. The historian of the Pentecostal Holiness Church writes: "To suppose that Cornelius was not at the time a Christian would involve one in serious complications. He was a devout man, one who feared God, gave much alms to the poor, and prayed to God alway. . . . What Christian could boast of such? How much less should we suppose that an unconverted man could be able to measure up to such a standard?" Joseph E. Campbell, *The Pentecostal Holiness Church: 1898-1948: Its Background and History* (Franklin Springs, Ga.: The Publishing House of the Pentecostal Holiness Church, 1951), p. 181. The largest Pentecostal bodies in the United States and Brazil — the Assemblies of God — do not hold this view. Cf. the Assemblies of God commentary: "Here was a religious man who was not a Christian." D. V. Hurst and T. J. Jones, *The Church Begins: A Study Manual on the First Twelve Chapters of the Acts* (Springfield, Mo.: Gospel Publishing House, 1959), p. 111.

[16] *Spirit Himself,* p. 53. Cf. Willard Cantelon, *El Bautismo en el Espiritu Santo* (3d ed.; Springfield, Mo.: Editorial Vida, 1955), p. 28. The problem in Acts 19:2 is somewhat aggravated in the English language Authorized Version by the rendering, "Have ye received the Holy Ghost *since* ye believed?" giving the verbs a sequence which the Greek coincident aorist participle will not bear. The modern versions correct the mistranslation. The same translation error exists in the Authorized Version's Eph. 1:13: "in whom also, *after* that ye believed, ye were sealed with that Holy Spirit of promise." Some Pentecostal writers note the correct translation, though not always felicitously. Cf. Riggs, *Spirit Himself,* p. 61; Williams, *Systematic Theology,* III, 45-46. For the inspiration of the Authorized Version, however, cf. Brumback, *What Meaneth This?,* pp. 56-57. For the same treatment of these texts in the Norwegian context see Skibstedt, *Geistestaufe,* p. 72.

Furthermore, the passage teaches Pentecostals the possibility — a possibility shown to be real, they feel, in the case of many called Christians — that disciples can be not only without the experience of the Holy Spirit, but they can be quite ignorant of even the existence of the Holy Spirit. Of most importance, however, is the simple fact that these Ephesians were first disciples and only later, under special circumstances, given the full gift of the Spirit. From this passage, then, the Pentecostal believes that he has a seal to what, for him, is already a sufficiently attested fact: the crucial experience with the Spirit is not identical with the experience of becoming a believer or disciple. First men become Christians; subsequently, if they are fully obedient, they become Spirit-filled Christians.

g. *Mark 1:9-11 par.: The Baptism of Jesus.* Finally, to the preponderant evidences of Acts the biblical passage most often adduced for the doctrine of the subsequent experience of the Spirit is the baptism of Jesus recorded in the Gospels. The virgin birth of Jesus through the Holy Spirit followed years later by his Jordan baptismal experience with the Spirit provides, Pentecostals believe, the conclusive evidence of the Spirit's dual work. "If there were two operations of the Spirit in the life of Jesus," asks Williams (II, 26), "one to bring Him forth, another to endue Him for service, may it not be equally true that there is a two-fold work of the Spirit in the lives of those who 'believe on Jesus'?"

The Messiah himself, this argument shows, passed through two great experiences with the Spirit: conception, enduement with power. The Messiah's career serves then as the perfect model for all later Christians who wish to be more than Christians in name or conception only. This model should teach Christians to be dissatisfied with being merely Christians; they should strive to come to the place reached by their Lord, and by all the earliest Christians, the place where the Spirit can, a second time, intersect their lives and give them power to fulfill their specific, God-designed tasks.

Jesus' own experience, then, added to the subsequent experiences of the early church recorded in Acts, crowns the Pentecostal doctrine with a final credibility.

h. *Parry and Summary.* Do Pentecostals anticipate any serious objections to their exegesis of the "subsequence passages"? The most frequently recognized objection countered in Pentecostal literature is the argument that the doctrine of the subsequent experience with the Spirit is not widely established beyond Acts. A problem is posed by the fact, for example, that in Paul's Epistles a baptism in the Holy Spirit as an experience discrete from the one baptism is, as such, not handled. To this it will usually be replied that the nature of the Epistles — their being written to apostolically founded churches and hence, presumably, to Christians already baptized in the Holy Spirit — is sufficient explanation for the absence of the doctrine's development there. "We cannot find the answer [to the question of the nature of the baptism in the Holy Spirit] in the Epistles," writes Reed (p. 3), "because they are letters addressed to churches which were already established and in which the majority of members had already received the experience."

Apart from the record of Jesus' baptism the Gospels are placed in a category with the Epistles. "We cannot find the answer in the Gospels," Reed continues (*ibid.*), "because they contain only prophecies and promises concerning the Holy Spirit and also leave the experience itself in the future." The general conclusion is, then, as we have seen, that "we are left therefore to find the answer in the book of Acts," where alone we have the requisite historical descriptions of the chain of events leading to and issuing from the baptism in the Holy Spirit in the lives of real persons. In the Gospels and Epistles, it will be contended, we are, respectively, too early and too late; but in Acts we are "on location." The Gospels look forward to and promise the baptism in the Holy Spirit (and in one instance, Jesus' baptism, they prefigure the experience), and the Epistles build upon and assume the experience, but only Acts records it in the lives of real persons. This is the Pentecostal parry.

These seven texts then[17]— Acts 2:1-4; 2:38; 8:4-25; 9:1-19; 10-11; 19:1-7; and Mark 1:9-11 par. — constitute the *fundamenta* of the Pentecostal doctrine of a baptism in the Holy Spirit as an experience subsequent to or discrete from the new birth.

3. The Apologetical and Experiential Bases of the Doctrine

How, apart from strict exegesis, do the Pentecostals justify the need for and describe the difference between the first and subsequent works of the Spirit? Eggenberger (p. 279) complains that "a clear, generally recognized definition of the 'Spirit-baptism' as well as of 'regeneration' is lacking. Even the . . . relations between the two are not perfectly

---

[17] Some Pentecostals list only six texts omitting, significantly, the Cornelius incident. So Riggs, *Spirit Himself,* p. 61; Steiner, *Zeichen,* pp. 174-76; Glenn A. Reed, "Pentecostal Truths 322" ("Mimeographed Notes to a Course Taught at Central Bible Institute, Springfield, Missouri," 1954), pp. 17-18. Other texts used to establish the subsequent baptism in the Holy Spirit, on occasion, are: Luke 24:49; Acts 1:4, 8; 15:7-9; I Cor. 12:1-31 (according to the creedal statement of the Assemblies of God in Winehouse, *Assemblies,* pp. 207-09); John 14:17 (the Comforter "whom the world cannot receive," in Riggs, *Spirit Himself,* p. 61); Acts 3:19 (Williams, *Systematic Theology,* III, 45-46); Tit. 3:5 (Steiner, *Zeichen,* pp. 175-76). Occasionally Old Testament types are used to illustrate the two phenomena; see Riggs, *Spirit Himself,* pp. 56-57, 68; Williams, *Systematic Theology,* II, 26-28; III, 45; and Alice Evelyn Luce, *Pictures of Pentecost in the Old Testament* (Springfield, Mo.: Gospel Publishing House, n.d.), *passim.*

clear." It is, in fact, difficult to isolate a clear or a unanimous Pentecostal analysis of the Pentecostal experience from the definitions of the sometimes rather loosely related Pentecostal groups. To any given definition some Pentecostal could demur. Nevertheless, we believe that an exposure to the Pentecostal materials suggests the following irreducible outline for practically all Pentecostal groups: the Pentecostal baptism — the subsequent experience of the Spirit — is urged for Christians because it adds to initial or converting faith (1) the *indwelling* or infilling of the Spirit, and hence (2) *power* for service with the equipment, usually, of (3) the *gifts* of the Spirit. We shall take up each of these features, and the several related sub-features, in turn.

a. *The Indwelling of the Spirit.* While it is granted that all believers are somehow, or in a sense, indwelt by the Spirit, or are at the very least affected by him,[18] it is usually felt by Pentecostals that not all believers are (i) *permanently,* (ii) *personally,* or (iii) *fully* indwelt by the Holy Spirit until they have experienced the Pentecostal baptism in the Holy Spirit.

i. The Permanent Indwelling. The note of permanence finds this expression, for example (in Winehouse, pp. 87-88): "The Holy Spirit participates in and effects regeneration in the first place, which is the time when a person becomes a Christian. At a later time, the Holy Spirit takes a permanent residence within a man's being at which time he is baptized in the Holy Spirit." Until the Pentecostal baptism is experienced the Christian is felt to be deprived of the lasting residence of the Holy Spirit; prior to this experience the Spirit only operates *on,* or is *with* the Christian, he is not yet *within* him. Just as prior to the ascension the Spirit was *with* the disciples in the person of Jesus, and just as at Pentecost this Spirit came *within* the disciples, so, avers Pentecostalism in direct parallel, at conversion the Christian begins to enjoy a relationship with Christ and so *in a sense* with the Spirit; but only with the individual Christian's "Pentecost" does the Spirit come *permanently* within. "Up to that point," explains French Pentecostalism (in Eggenberger, pp. 272-73), "the Spirit 'dwells with you,' [but] from now on 'he will be in you,' John 14:17. It is through the Holy Spirit that Jesus comes to dwell in us, Eph. 3:16-17." The Pentecostal experience adds then to the Christian's indefinite relationship with the Spirit a now permanent relationship.

ii. The Personal Indwelling. Second, only through the baptism in

---

18 Pearlman writes, for example: "Indeed, the New Testament teaches that one cannot be a Christian without having the Spirit, which is the same as being indwelt with the Spirit. . . . It cannot be successfully denied that there is a real sense [*n.b.*] in which all truly regenerated persons have the Spirit." *Doctrines,* pp. 311-12. Also Harold Horton, *The Gifts of the Spirit* (2d ed.; Bedfordshire, England: Redemption Tidings Bookroom, 1946), p. 45; Williams, *Systematic Theology,* III, 44-45.

the Holy Spirit (conceived as a critical subsequent experience) does the third person of the Godhead *personally* enter the life of the believer. In a clear statement Riggs explains this Pentecostal emphasis (pp. 79-80):

> As the Spirit of Christ, He had come at conversion, imparting the Christ-life, revealing Christ, and making Him real. At the Baptism in the Spirit, He Himself in His own person comes upon and fills the waiting believer. This experience is as distinct from conversion as the Holy Spirit is distinct from Christ. His coming to the believer at the Baptism [in the Holy Spirit] is the coming of the Third Person of the Trinity, in addition to the coming of Christ, which takes place at conversion.

Before the Pentecostal baptism the Spirit is, in this interpretation, mainly the imparter or revealer of Someone else; but after the Pentecostal experience the Christian may enjoy the Spirit himself, personally and directly. Eggenberger understands the essence of Pentecostalism's baptism in the Holy Spirit to consist, in fact, in this special "God-encounter." "Views of the 'Pentecostal' Spirit-baptism," he writes (p. 282), "can be summarized in this manner: the Spirit-baptism is a meeting between the holy God and man. On this point the various Pentecostal definitions are united. The 'God-encounter' is the common core of the Spirit-baptism." Unique to Pentecostal conviction, however, is the persuasion that until the Christian receives this specific God-encounter with God-the-*Spirit,* beyond encounter with the divine Christ, the Christian's life is incomplete. All evangelical Christians would insist on the necessity of a God-encounter through Christ; but Pentecostals, arguing from the texts observed, urge the necessity of a *subsequent* encounter with the Spirit, *after* the encounter with Christ, if the Christian is to enjoy the Spirit as a person, internally, rather than as a mere instrument, externally.

iii. The Full Indwelling. Finally, the baptism in the Holy Spirit not only makes the Spirit's inner presence permanent and personal, it makes his presence full as as well. "The central fact of the Pentecostal experience," writes Donald Gee, "consists in being *filled* with the Holy Spirit," adding, "this is distinct from His previous work in regeneration as the Giver of Life in Christ."[19] The indwelling of *Christ* or the Spirit of Christ (understood apart from or before the indwelling of the Spirit himself through the spiritual baptism) is said to bring but a measure of the good things of God's salvation. "This is not to say," explains

---

[19] *God's Great Gift: Seven Talks Together about the Holy Spirit* (Springfield, Mo.: Gospel Publishing House, n.d.), p. 47. Lewi Pethrus' view may be considered extreme in adducing, apart from this Pentecostal filling, the parable of the return of the unclean spirits. *The Wind Bloweth Where It Listeth: Thoughts and Experiences concerning the Baptism of the Holy Spirit,* tr. [from the Swedish] Harry Lindblom (2d ed.; Chicago: Philadelphia Book Concern, 1945), p. 30. Similarly, Brumback, *What Meaneth This?,* p. 139.

Riggs, "that children of God in whom dwells the Spirit of Christ and who have not received the Baptism in the Spirit will not have varying measures of wisdom, knowledge, faith, etc., which come from the Lord. Being partakers of His nature and dwelling in Christ as the branch in the vine, naturally brings one a measure of the qualities which Christ has."[20] But as there is a difference between being influenced sporadically and being indwelt permanently, and a difference between experiencing an external event and experiencing a real person, so, Pentecostals explain, there is a difference between experiencing a person in a measure and experiencing a person fully. It is the baptism in the Holy Spirit which makes these important differences in the Christian's life. And not the least of these differences, and probably the one most often stressed in Pentecostal language and literature, is the fulness of the Spirit which the special Pentecostal baptism in the Holy Spirit brings the dedicated Christian.

iv. Result and Summary. The net result of these distinctions — permanent, personal, full — is almost inevitably, though not always intentionally, to place a higher valuation on the further or subsequent experience for which the first experience serves as a threshold. This tendency may be illustrated frequently in Pentecostal literature. Skibstedt, representing particularly Scandinavian Pentecostalism, writes (p. 77, with his own emphases):

> The Spirit we receive in the Spirit-baptism is indeed the same Spirit who was communicated to us at regeneration — it is only that we receive him in *so much stronger and richer measure;* and the experiencing of this blessing distinguishes itself so considerably from the experience of regeneration in that it is a so much *mightier and clearer experience.*

The English Pentecostal leader Harold Horton writes (*Gifts,* p. 45): "True it is the cross that saves and renders one a member of the family, but it is the enduement, anointing, infilling, baptism of the Holy Spirit that equips with the Gifts and renders one a miraculous member of the miracle-working body of Christ." There even appears at times a tendency in Pentecostal expression to ascribe an outward work to Jesus Christ but an inward work to the Holy Spirit, sometimes to the seeming, but of course unintentional, disparagement of the former. But, some would argue, in taking seriously the inner and equipping work of the Spirit — perhaps too seriously — the Pentecostals may have recaptured biblical ground.

In any case, Duffield's admonition (pp. 76-77) expresses the best

---

[20] *Spirit Himself,* p. 119. Cf. also in a tract: "In the New Testament men always received a 'measure' of the Spirit and were more or less filled with the Spirit at conversion. Every child of God received the 'Spirit of adoption' and is filled with the Spirit in a 'measure' when converted." Rev. J. G. Hall, "The Baptism in the Holy Spirit" (n.p., n.d.), p. 4.

sentiment if not always the express theology of the Pentecostal movement when he writes that "there is only one message for any minister of the Gospel — especially for any Full Gospel [i.e., Pentecostal] minister. We are called to preach Jesus Christ. . . . Let us be careful! Our message is not the Holy Spirit and His gifts. It is Jesus Christ and His resurrection." It cannot, in fact, be said that Pentecostal preaching and evangelism place more stress on the Holy Spirit than on Christ — though in Pentecostal literature this is very nearly the case. As a rule Pentecostal preaching appears to be fervently evangelistic in the christocentric and, in its way, even churchly sense.[21] At the same time, distinctively Pentecostal teaching, both oral and published, retains a strong emphasis upon the baptism in the Holy Spirit as a necessary subsequent experience for Christians.

This much is clear. In the Pentecostal understanding not enough happens in the new birth. The baptism with the Holy Spirit completes whatever was lacking in conversion. Apart from this further experience the Christian is able but partially to enjoy the ministry of the Holy Spirit in his indwelling permanence, person, and fulness.

b. *Power for Service.* The baptism in the Holy Spirit is necessary also if the believer is to have what is called power for service. In Pentecostalism, significantly, the baptism in the Holy Spirit is not understood soteriologically but "dynamologically"; the experience is not necessary for salvation — it is necessary, however, for spiritual power. Acts 1:8 is most often instanced in this connection: "But you shall receive power when the Holy Spirit has come upon you; and you shall be my witnesses." "The main feature of this promise is power for service," comments Williams for Pentecostalism, "and not regeneration for eternal life."[22]

21 These features may be most admirably observed in the Pentecostal booklet of essentials so influential in the Assemblies of God in Central and South America, the *Reglamento local,* ed. Rafael D. Williams (9th ed.; Santa Ana, El Salvador, C. A.: Conferencia Evangélica de las Asambleas de Dios en Centro América, 1959), where evangelism is given a prominent, yet balanced and surprisingly (local) church-centered place in the scope of the total Christian enterprise. On Christocentricity note most recently the theme of the Eighth Pentecostal World Conference in Rio de Janeiro, July 18-23, 1967: "The Holy Spirit Glorifying Christ." Impressive also is the Christian ministry represented, for example, in David Wilkerson with John and Elizabeth Sherrill, *The Cross and the Switchblade,* New York: Bernard Geis Associates, 1963.
22 *Systematic Theology,* III, 53. See Hollenweger's discussion of the non-soteriological character of the spiritual baptism where he notes that merely "a minority — mostly 'Jesus Only' groups — hold to the saving necessity of the baptism in the Holy Spirit" (I, 82). Hollenweger therefore concludes that "if one regards a sect theologically as a group which considers membership in it as necessary for salvation, then I am unacquainted — apart from insignificant exceptions — with any Pentecostal group which one must regard as sectarian" (*ibid.,* 219). For data on the marginal "Jesus Only" groups see Nichol, *Pentecostalism,*

The service for which power is provided by the baptism in the Holy Spirit is understood first of all evangelistically. "The baptism in the Holy Spirit," explains the *Reglamento local,* "imparts power for faithful witness to Christ."[23] "It is our obligation to tell all men everywhere of the salvation which He has provided," writes another Pentecostal, ". . . to give people a last chance to come into the ark of safety before the storm. The baptism of the Holy Spirit is His divine equipment to us to enable us to do that. It provides a motive, the urgency and the power with which we are qualified to carry the gospel to the ends of the earth" (in Winehouse, pp. 193-94). At the 1955 Pentecostal World Conference the German Pentecostal leader Paul Rabe expressed this conviction in the following manner: "By being born again we as individuals have been saved ourselves, but by the Baptism of the Spirit we receive power, or shall we say power to save others. . . . By being born again we have become the children of God, but by the Baptism in the Spirit we become the soldiers of Christ."[24]

The remarkable missionary activity and success in Pentecostalism are attributed by Pentecostals to their rediscovery of this apostolic experience. David duPlessis, in his article on the mission of Pentecostalism in *Die Religion in Geschichte und Gegenwart,* developed this Pentecostal conviction.

> The reason for this [missionary] growth is not the ability or the education of the missionary or the use of new methods. The reason is simply the fact that the apostolic methods of the New Testament were followed very faithfully. Every new convert was encouraged "to receive the Holy Spirit" and then to become a witness to Jesus Christ (cf. Acts 1:8). By offering their converts two distinct experiences — the meeting with the living Christ unto "regeneration" and the filling with the Holy Spirit unto "power for service" — the missionaries of the Pentecostal movement have succeeded in establishing indigenous churches much faster than those missionaries who inevitably have had to transplant a particular doctrine or theology.[25]

---

pp. 90, 116-19; *Hollenweger* I, 138-39. Though Neo-Pentecostalism, with Pentecostalism, insists that the baptism in the Holy Spirit or speaking in tongues is not a requirement for salvation, nevertheless, both assert frequently that the Pentecostal experience is, in Laurence Christenson's words, "a distinct link in the divinely wrought chain which links us to Christ." *Speaking in Tongues,* p. 53. Hence, without this experience Christians are "missing a link" in their relationship to Christ and are still somewhere outside of a full relationship with God and all that God has to give to them in the Holy Spirit. Cf. note 27, below.

[23] P. 16. Cf. Hughes, *What Is Pentecost,* pp. 19, 21. See the practiced connections between the baptism in the Holy Spirit and mission in Brazilian Pentecostalism, Read, *New Patterns of Church Growth in Brazil,* pp. 42-43.

[24] "Scriptural Principles for Receiving the Baptism in the Holy Spirit," in *Pentecost,* No. 38 (Dec. 1956), p. 8. Cf. the comparable understanding of Confirmation in other Christian traditions, below, pp. 185-88.

[25] V, 311. See also Steiner in his address at the World Conference of Pentecostal Assemblies in Stockholm, 1955 entitled, "The Pentecostal Movement and World Evangelism," in *Pentecost,* No. 33 (Sept. 1955), pp. 2-3. Cf. Aimee Semple Mc-

The promise of power, provided by the baptism in the Holy Spirit, is a central part of the Pentecostal experiential apologetic and, no doubt, of the Pentecostal appeal.

c. *The Gifts of the Spirit.* The final contribution of the baptism in the Holy Spirit to the Christian, to be discussed in more detail in the next chapter because of its development in Pentecostal theology, is the equipment with the spiritual gifts. The Christian is given the personal graces or fruit of the Holy Spirit (see, e.g., Gal. 5:22-23) as a result of his initial faith, but the ministering gifts, the charismata (e.g., those in I Cor. 12:8-10) not yet — fully. Apart from the plenary indwelling of the *gift* of the Holy Spirit it is impossible or at least difficult for Pentecostals to imagine the full exercise of the *gifts* of the Holy Spirit. We shall see that the gifts of the Holy Spirit, especially those most prized in Pentecostalism, fit quite naturally the shape of the Pentecostal gift of the Holy Spirit.

4. SUMMARY

Almost all of the major features of the subsequent baptism in the Holy Spirit according to Pentecostal interpretation — subsequence, personal ingress, indwelling, power, and gifts — may be discerned in Gee's comprehensive description.

> The New Testament appears to indicate as an unmistakable historical fact that after the first entry of the Spirit in regeneration there can be and should be also a special personal reception by believers of the Holy Spirit in his original and unique person. This experience is called the "baptism in the Holy Spirit" and its purpose is not to impart life, but to impart power. Its characteristic accompaniments are not fruits, but gifts.[26]

The Pentecostal movement believes that it has found in the Acts of the Apostles, in the witness of its evangelical forbears, and in its own personal and missionary experience, precedent and authority for its conviction that the baptism in the Holy Spirit is a critical experience subsequent to and/or distinct from conversion granting the believer the benefits of a permanent, personal, and full indwelling of the Holy Spirit and so providing power for Christian service, particularly evangelistic service, with the equipment of the spiritual gifts.

In its most essential form under this first head, the Pentecostal is persuaded that the baptism in the Holy Spirit is an experience discrete from conversion. "Sometimes it was received after tarrying; sometimes during the laying on of hands; sometimes it was completely spontane-

---

Pherson's sermon "The Baptism of the Holy Spirit: The Need of the Church Today" in her *This Is That: Personal Experiences, Sermons and Writings* (Los Angeles: Echo Park Evangelistic Association, 1923), especially p. 712.

[26] From Gee's book *Die Früchte des Geistes*, p. 6 in O. Eggenberger, "Die Geistestaufe in der gegenwärtigen Pfingstbewegung," *ThZ, 11* (1955), 278. The original English edition of Gee's book was unavailable to me.

ous; but always it came after conversion, for it is a distinct and separate experience."[27]

B. THE DOCTRINE OF THE INITIAL EVIDENCE OF THE BAPTISM IN THE HOLY SPIRIT

1. THE UNIQUENESS OF THE DOCTRINE

If it may be said that the distinctive doctrine of the Pentecostal movement is the baptism in the Holy Spirit it may also be said that what is most distinctive about this particular doctrine is the conviction that the initial evidence of this baptism is speaking in tongues.

While Pentecostalism shares with classic Methodism, the holiness movements, and with many in conservative evangelicalism, the conviction of an additional critically important spiritual experience beyond conversion, it is in the understanding of the initial *evidence* of this subsequent experience that Pentecostals are unique, and it is this evidence which marks its advocates as Pentecostal. Wesley and his holiness followers, as we have seen, made experience or feeling of a particular sort the evidence of what was called the Great Salvation. But feeling is ambiguous and has led Methodism, historically, to quite different emphases. The ambiguity of feeling was removed by Pentecostals in the discovery of the feeling *par excellence* — the transport of speaking in tongues.[28]

"The distinct doctrine of the Pentecostal churches," writes Donald Gee, "[is] that speaking with tongues is the 'initial evidence' of the baptism in the Holy Spirit. This article of belief is now incorporated in the official doctrinal schedules of practically all Pentecostal denominations."[29] "Of practically all," it must be said, for there appears to be here and there and perhaps with the advance of time a certain

---

[27] Edward J. Jarvis, "This Is That," *Pentecostal Evangel, 49* (Jan. 15, 1961), 6-7. See the ninth paragraph in the articles of faith of the Brazilian Congregação Cristã no Brasil in *Hollenweger* II, 923: "We believe in the baptism of the Holy Spirit which is received after conversion (*depois da salvação*)." From their study and experience of, particularly, the Book of Acts, Pentecostals have come to the conclusion, in the summary of a recent continental study, "that it is not sufficient for a believer to be regenerated but that he still needs a special baptism of the Holy Spirit to become in the full sense of the word an authentic Christian." *Les Mouvements de Pentecôte*, p. 35.

[28] Of spontaneous manifestations of feeling, Bloch-Hoell remarked, "the holiness movement warmly encouraged the practice of such ... and later the Pentecostal movement demanded it, emphasising one kind of motoric movement above all: glossolalia." *Pentecostal Movement*, p. 16.

[29] *Pentecost*, No. 45 (Sept. 1958), p. 17. Cf. also Gee, *Pentecostal Movement*, pp. 7-8; duPlessis, *IRM, 47* (April 1958), 193; Pearlman, *Doctrines*, p. 310; J. E. Stiles, *The Gift of the Holy Spirit* (Burbank, Calif.: Privately Printed, n.d.), p. 96; Ray H. Hughes, *Church of God Distinctives* (Cleveland, Tenn.: Pathway, 1968), pp. 32-33. Pentecostals do not normally define the baptism in the Holy Spirit apart from this initial evidence.

hesitation in allowing to tongues-speaking the spiritual baptism's only initial evidence.[30] Nevertheless, for majority Pentecostalism to date it is held to be one of the " 'verites fondamentales' " that in the baptism with the Holy Spirit " 'le signe initial est le parler in langues.' "[31] The glossolalic evidence has thus far marked Pentecostalism as Pentecostalism. It is even seriously argued that the theological act of combining the baptism in the Holy Spirit with the evidence of tongues was the catalyst creating the Pentecostal movement. Donald Gee, the most lucid Pentecostal interpreter of this "distinctive of the distinctive," remarks that "the tongues regarded simply as an isolated phenomenon, rather than as an initial evidence of the baptism [in the Spirit], had not launched a world-wide revival."[32] This doctrine is unique and for most Pentecostals it is an important explanation of the Pentecostal movement.

2. THE SOURCE OF THE DOCTRINE

Again it is on the basis of the Acts almost exclusively that Pentecostals justify their doctrine of speaking in tongues as the initial evidence of the baptism in the Holy Spirit. The Corinthian tongues-speak-

---

30 Pentecostal groups which do *not* subscribe to this particular article in its standard form: Elim Foursquare Gospel Alliance (based in Great Britain), the Schweizerischen (Swiss) Pfingstmission, and some forms of German Pentecostalism, particularly the Christlicher Gemeinschaftsverband Mülheim-Ruhr. See *Hollenweger* I, 79-97, and particularly 85, 93 for discussion. Significantly, the two Chilean Pentecostal bodies which joined the World Council of Churches in 1961 — the Iglesia Metodista Pentecostal de Chile and the Iglesia Pentecostal de Chile — differ from majority Pentecostalism in not subscribing to the tenet that speaking in tongues is the only evidence of the baptism in the Spirit. The eleventh article of the declaration of faith of the Iglesia Pentecostal de Chile affirms that "speaking in tongues, having visions, prophecies, or any other manifestation (*o cualquier manifestación*) conforming to the Word of God, is an evidence of the baptism in the Holy Spirit." *Hollenweger* II, 986. However, even majority Pentecostalism does not argue that speaking in tongues is the only evidence of the Spirit; it simply insists that it is the only *initial* evidence of the Spirit's full coming. See p. 85 below. Yet in Neo-Pentecostalism it can be written, "Scripture does not say that [speaking in tongues] is the only one. But in showing us the pattern, Scripture gives us no consistent suggestion of any other." Christenson, *Speaking in Tongues*, p. 54.

31 In Eggenberger, "Geistestaufe," *ThZ, 11* (1955), 276. Even if one may *feel* that he has received the Holy Spirit in fulness he is not to believe that he has in *fact*, unless he has this biblical evidence. See, for example, the sixteenth article of faith of the Congregação Cristã no Brasil: "When a believer receives the power of the Holy Spirit he should not say 'I have been baptized,' rather he should wait until the Holy Spirit manifests himself in accordance with the Word of God, by speaking in new tongues." *Hollenweger* II, 917. Cf. Read *et al.*, *Latin American Church Growth*, p. 315, where, with the striking exception of Chile, all of Latin American Pentecostalism is seen subscribing to the necessity of the sign of tongues.

32 In *Pentecost*, No. 45 (Sept. 1958), p. 17. Cf. also Kelsey, *Tongue Speaking*, pp. 69-70; Kendrick, *Promise*, pp. 51-53.

ing, as we shall observe more closely in the next chapter, is a particular kind of spiritual expression and Pentecostals do not wish it to be confused with the Spirit's special sign or evidence of speaking in tongues to which Acts bears witness. "For our information concerning the manifestation given to believers when baptized in the Spirit," Gee writes, "we are entirely shut up to the instances . . . in the Book of Acts."[33] It will sometimes be admitted that while Holy Scripture may nowhere explicitly say that speaking in tongues is the initial evidence of the baptism in the Holy Spirit, nevertheless the weight of the events in Acts where tongues-speaking does in fact occur upon the receipt of the Spirit compels the doctrine implicitly. The fact that tongues are not even mentioned in every instance in the Book of Acts where men are baptized or are given the gift of the Holy Spirit (e.g., Acts 2:38-41) is held to be unembarrassing to this conviction because, it is argued, when any outward evidences *are* suggested they are usually found to be glossolalic (e.g., Acts 2:4; 10:44-47; 19:6).

The Pentecostal believes that it is the divine intention to provide the baptism in the Holy Spirit with an initial evidence of the baptism's real occurrence and that the argument of the instances in Acts where an evidence *is* given is such as to be exegetically conclusive for any fair-minded reader: the evidence is speaking in tongues. "Audacious though it may sound to affirm it," Gee summarizes, "I believe that an unanswerable case can be made out, if we stand on the Scriptures alone, for the doctrine of the Pentecostal Movement that there is a manifest initial evidence Divinely ordained for the Baptism in the Holy Spirit, and a very strong case for that evidence being speaking with tongues."[34]

3. The Exegetical Basis of the Doctrine

The "classic instances" of the evidenced baptism with the Holy Spirit are usually found in Acts chapters 2, 8, 10, and 19. In Acts 8, however, no mention is made of speaking in tongues and the argument has to be sustained on grounds other than strictly textual. Therefore we shall turn first to Acts 2, 10, and 19, which are, in any event, the more frequently employed passages in Pentecostal argument, before investigating related texts.

a. *Acts 2:1-4: Pentecost.* The most celebrated effusion of the Holy

---

[33] "The Initial Evidence of the Baptism in the Holy Spirit," *Pentecostal Evangel,* 47 (July 12, 1959), 23. In another place Gee writes that "any study on this point must necessarily be confined within these limits, for the New Testament contains no plain, categorical statements anywhere as to what must be regarded as the sign." *Loc. cit.,* p. 3. See additional qualifications in Williams, *Systematic Theology,* III, 55 and Pearlman, *Doctrines,* pp. 312-13.

[34] *Pentecost,* No. 25 (Sept. 1953), p. 17.

Spirit with the manifestation of tongues occurred at the feast of Pentecost and is recorded in Acts 2:1-4 concluding, "and they were all filled with the Holy Spirit and began to speak in other tongues, as the Spirit gave them utterance." If speaking in tongues was God's evidence of his gift of the Spirit in the church's first and major experience why, it is asked, should it not also be the evidence for the church's continuing experience?

It is recognized that the Pentecost occasion was accompanied by unique and unrepeatable phenomena such as the sound of the wind, the vision of tongues as of fire, and the important ancillary fact that here only, apparently, were the tongues understood by the hearers (see Acts 2:5-13). But Pentecostals separate the unique and unrepeatable phenomena (Acts 2:1-3, 5-13) from what is called Pentecost's repeatable and pattern-making phenomenon: the filling of the Holy Spirit evidenced by the speaking in other tongues (Acts 2:4). Arguing that wind, fire, and comparable remarkable manifestations had occurred as signs under the old covenant, but that tongues never had, the conclusion is drawn that tongues-speaking is meant to be the initial sign of the Spirit's presence under the new covenant.[35]

The Pentecostal insists that the unique Pentecost event of speaking in tongues sets the only authentic pattern for every other baptism in the Holy Spirit. The apostles, it is argued, were Christians before Pentecost and yet they received the Spirit in fulness only when they were able to give evidence of this fulness by speaking in other tongues. This fact, it is felt, should establish a precedent for all later Christians. The eighth article of faith in the largest Brazilian Pentecostal body is representative, then, of the majority conviction of world Pentecostalism when it affirms that "the baptism in the Holy Spirit must [*deve*] be accompanied by the same evidence which the apostles received as their sign: 'to speak in other tongues as the Spirit [gives] utterance.' "[36]

b. *Acts 10-11: Cornelius' Household.* The Pentecostal points to the tenth chapter of Acts in further confirmation of his thesis that glossolalia is not unique to the original Pentecost itself but that the sign is intended for each full impartation of the Spirit. Peter's attendants in Acts 10 were "amazed, because the gift of the Holy Spirit had been poured out even on the Gentiles. *For* they heard them speaking

35 So Reed, "Pentecostal Truths," p. 5; Riggs, *Spirit Himself,* pp. 86-87; McPherson, *The Holy Spirit* (Los Angeles: Challpin Publishing Co., 1931), p. 168. Conn credits Jesus Christ, the initiator of the new covenant, with having spoken in tongues ("Talitha cumi," "Eloi, Eloi, lama sabachthani"), *Pillars,* pp. 45-48. Williams grants the authors of the New Testament the gift because they were Jews writing Greek, *Systematic Theology,* III, 50-51.

36 The "Fundamental Truths" of the Assembléias de Deus in *Hollenweger* II, 898. Cf. Vergara, *El Protestantismo en Chile,* p. 161.

in tongues" (Acts 10:45-46). Knowledge of the gift of the Spirit to the Gentile household was obtained specifically from the evidence of speaking in tongues ("for"). Apart from this evidence Peter's Jewish Christian companions would have been hard convinced of the full parity of the Gentile accession to the Jewish. But with this evidence the early Christians knew that only one thing could have happened: the gift of the Holy Spirit had been given in a fulness which fell short in no way of the fulness of the original Pentecost itself. Speaking in tongues signifies everywhere in the church, from Jerusalem to Caesarea, from Jews to Gentiles, the normative Pentecostal experience. Thus Acts 10 joins Acts 2 in the Pentecostal chain of witnesses to the initial evidence of the Spirit's full coming.

c. *Acts 19:1-7: The Disciples at Ephesus.* The third and final instance of speaking with tongues recorded in Acts occurs at Acts 19:1-7 where Paul, on discovering a company of Ephesian disciples who were unacquainted with the Spirit, proceeded to instruct them properly in Christian doctrine and thereafter baptized them. Then "when Paul had laid his hands upon them," the Acts account concludes, "the Holy Spirit came on them; and they spoke with tongues and prophesied" (19:6). Again the evidence of the Spirit's real coming was the recipients' unusual speech including the speaking in tongues. This passage is most frequently cited by Pentecostals when critics raise the objection that speaking in tongues occurred exclusively in apostolic times and then only for the certification of the promised gift of the Spirit to Jews (Acts 2) and to Gentiles (Acts 10). The fact that glossolalia occurred in Acts 19 some time after both the so-called Jewish and Gentile Pentecosts of Acts 2 and 10 impresses the Pentecostal and gives him added confidence that his doctrine is both biblical in content and universal in application.

The events recorded in Acts 2, 10, and 19 lay, then, what Pentecostals feel to be the surest foundations for their doctrine of initial evidence. In each instance the knowledge of the Spirit's full coming was directly and unambiguously provided through the recipients' speaking in tongues. By means of this unusual manifestation the recipients, the observers, and future readers could be assured of the real and full coming of the divine Spirit.

d. *The Other Acts Incidents (Acts 8 and 9).* The other passages adduced from Acts to illustrate the Pentecostal doctrine of the evidence of tongues are Acts 8 (the Samaritans) and, less often, Acts 9 (the conversion of Paul). Although speaking in tongues is specifically mentioned in neither Acts 8 nor 9, Pentecostals feel that there are good reasons for believing that the phenomenon occurred: in the Samaritan incident, because something striking must have happened to evoke the eager request of Simon Magus for the power of the Spirit whose coming he had just witnessed (cf. Acts 8:18-19); and in Paul's case, because of his later testimony that "I speak in tongues more than you all" (I Cor. 14:18), indicating that Paul was no stranger to the experience; and since all experiences have beginnings, presumably Paul's was no different from that of other early Christians recorded in Acts, namely, the experience of the baptism in the Holy Spirit evidenced by speaking in tongues. Both arguments for tongues in Acts 8 and 9 are admittedly presumptions but, it is felt, on the basis of the accompaniments to the gift of the Spirit in the other Acts notices, warranted presumptions.

The conclusion drawn from these five Acts texts (2; 10; 19; and 8; 9) is that since in three of the five cases the evidence is *expressly* tongues and in the remaining two cases *presumably,* there is present in Acts a doctrine which is sufficiently substantial for the church to accept as normative for its faith and life. "We submit, therefore, that the evidence is entirely sufficient for the conclusion expressed in the doctrine that 'speaking with other tongues is the initial evidence of the baptism in the Holy Spirit.' "37

e. *Mark 16:17 and Summary.* The only other passage regularly marshalled for the evidential character of the spiritual baptism outside of Acts is Mark 16:17 where it is said that believers will be accompanied by, among other signs, "new tongues." This, to Pentecostals, is the glossolalic evidence and not to have experienced this sign is to put in doubt the reality of the faith it is intended to symbolize — not so much the reality of simple Christian faith, but of the deeper Christian faith which grants the Pentecostal experience.38 The passage's authenticity is not, with Pentecostals, in question.

Does the Bible teach that the initial evidence of the gift of the Spirit is speaking in tongues? Pentecostals answer in the affirmative. They see the spiritual evidence taught in the only place where it could be taught: in the history of those who received it in the Acts of the Apostles. But they also see it promised by Jesus in the Gospels (Mark 16:17).

Had the promised spiritual sign of tongues made an appearance only at Pentecost there might have been room for doubt that it was intended as a perpetual sign. But when the first Gentiles experienced it as well, when an obscure group of Ephesian disciples had the same experience years later, and when the "Pentecostals" themselves experience it centuries later (not to mention now those who experienced

---

37 Gee, "The Initial Evidence of the Baptism in the Holy Spirit," *Pentecostal Evangel,* 47 (July 12, 1959), 3. Statistical suggestions similar to Gee's are offered by Brumback, *What Meaneth This?,* pp. 232-33, cf. p. 188.

38 So Frodsham, *With Signs Following,* p. 242; McPherson, *Holy Spirit,* p. 167; Horton, *Gifts of the Spirit*2, p. 147.

it in the years between Pentecost and Pentecostalism), it is felt that Pentecost was not only an event of the past but, in a frequently used term, that it is a *pattern* for the present and that all Christians, for these several compelling reasons, should be "Pentecostals." For speaking in tongues is not seen as an oddity; it is seen as a real necessity if a Christian is to have an unshakeable certainty that the Spirit has truly and fully come to him. This conviction is established for Pentecostals by Scripture, but it can be explained by still other means.

4. THE APOLOGETICAL AND EXPERIENTIAL BASES OF THE DOCTRINE

a. *The Argument for Experience.* Outside the specific interpretation of Acts (and Mark 16:17), the first general argument in defense of the doctrine of initial evidence is the argument from — or here, better, for — experience. To the frequent non-Pentecostal objection that the extraordinary manifestation of the Spirit in apostolic times is to be explained *heilsgeschichtlich* or dispensationally rather than imperatively or archetypically — i.e., the objection that the apostolic period was unique and not to be repeated — the Pentecostals rejoin that just as the benefits of the "once-for-all" event of the cross must still be received in order to be effective in men's lives, thus also the blessings of the "once-for-all" gift of the Spirit at Pentecost must still be received to be real in men's experience.[39]

And the Spirit must be received, Pentecostals continue, in the very *way* the apostles and early church received him — with speaking in tongues. The only experience guaranteeing that we have received the very Spirit received *by* the apostles, urge Pentecostals, is the very experience *of* the apostles. "Where else would you go for a pattern of a true baptism with the Holy Ghost?" asks Duffield (p. 18). "Shall we accept some theologian's idea? Would it be safe to trust human reasoning? I want to know that I received the fulness of the Spirit with the same accompanying signs that were manifest at the initial outpouring."

But, Pentecostals continue, while the apostles provide the divine pattern for the Spirit's reception, they can never provide a divine or even a human substitute for our own personal reception of the Spirit. Pentecost does not supplant the need for every Christian to receive the Spirit into his own experience. "The baptism in the Holy Spirit was not for the apostles only," declares the *Reglamento local* (p. 16) in its initial article on the spiritual baptism, "but is for every believer in the Lord Jesus Christ," to which it appends as proofs Acts 2:38-39 and Matthew 3:11 (the Baptist's promise of the special experience).

---

[39] Pethrus writes that to say one has received the Holy Spirit without having had any particular experience "would be about the same as saying, 'I am saved, but have never experienced salvation.' " *Wind*[2], p. 47.

There is no such thing as a dispensational Pentecost, in the Pentecostal understanding, if such an expression means that since *ca.* A.D. 30-100 the Spirit has been automatically or impersonally received. Without the experience of tongues the Christian is without the sure evidence of the Spirit — biblically and experientially. We may say that, in the Pentecostal understanding, the Pentecost-event should not be placed merely in the aorist or past tenses but it should be rendered in the perfect, for while Pentecost happened decisively in the past in the lives of the first and of all subsequently obedient Christians it should still be experienced continually in the present in the lives of committed Christians.

b. *The Argument from Reason.* Quite apart from exegesis or experience it should be considered only reasonable, Pentecostals continue, that in an event so momentous — the internal, full, and permanant reception of the Spirit himself — there should be extraordinary external effects attending the Spirit's advent. At the Fifth Pentecostal World Conference, Gee expressed this conviction as follows:

> A weak human vessel is being filled with a divine fulness. To tell us, as some wish to tell us, that such an experience can be received without any emotional manifestation is to do violence to all sense of reality. With all due respect we refuse to be satisfied that so-called 'Pentecostal' experiences without a physical manifestation are valid according to the scriptural pattern or even common logic.[40]

And what more logical announcement is there, Pentecostals ask, than the announcement *first* given: speaking in tongues?

That the Spirit employs precisely the tongue to evidence his full coming seems to Pentecostals especially reasonable. For Brandt notes that "the tongue is said to be the most unruly member of the body . . . (James 3:8). Therefore, to indicate complete domination and control of the spirit of man, we believe the tongue is the most logical member of the body for the Spirit to employ."[41] It is not strange to the Pentecostal that the Spirit releases extraordinary effects with his coming; to the Pentecostal this fact represents the height of good sense. That God's initial evidence of his Spirit in the lives of Christians is the remarkable expression of speaking in tongues is, for Pentecostals, eminently reasonable.

c. *The Argument from the Necessity of Assurance.* Finally, the Pentecostal argues not only from Scripture, experience, and reason, but from the most imperious ground of all, necessity. As the Pentecostal understands it there is an absolute necessity for *some* mani-

---

[40] *Pentecostal World Conference Messages*, p. 48. Cf. R. L. Brandt, "The Case for Speaking with Other Tongues," *Pentecostal Evangel*, 48 (June 5, 1960), 4.

[41] Brandt, *loc. cit.,* p. 30. See also Brumback, *What Meaneth This?*, p. 242; Cantelon, *El Bautismo*, pp. 16-17; William Caldwell, *Pentecostal Baptism* (Tulsa, Okla.: Miracle Moments Evangelistic Assoc., 1963), p. 35.

festation to accompany the spiritual baptism if one is ever to be assured of the Spirit's actual coming. And since no other manifestation is so clearly declared and displayed in the Acts, nor so perfectly bound to the nature of the gift of the Spirit — missionary witness — the evidence of speaking in other tongues takes on an almost compelling character.

First, it is necessary for the gift of the Spirit to be manifested by tongues-speaking if the believer is ever to have an unshakeable assurance that the Spirit is truly in his life. "When I asked Pentecostals what tongues did for them," reports John L. Sherrill, "the first answer was always, 'Assure me that I have been baptized in the Holy Ghost,'" to which Sherrill remarks sympathetically, "of course it would be a priceless asset in a believer's life: to know without question that God's own Spirit was manifested from within one."[42]

Accordingly, glossolalia heightens what is of considerable importance to the Pentecostal understanding of the baptism in the Holy Spirit: the tangibility of the experience; one may even say its physicality. "The baptism in the Holy Spirit is identified," according to the *Reglamento local* (p. 16), "by the initial physical [*física*] sign of speaking in tongues." " 'When the Holy Ghost comes in,' " the subsequent father of European Pentecostalism was advised, " 'you will know it, for He will be in your *very flesh*' " (Barratt, *Fire,* p. 109). Tongues-speaking, by being at the same time a highly spiritual *and* a highly physical experience, transforms the coming of the Holy Spirit into a knowable, clear, and datable experience, manifest in time and space.

Therefore a positive polemic takes place in Pentecostalism against what is described as "a vague 'taking by faith' " of one's baptism in the Holy Spirit.[43] Tongues make the baptism in the Holy Spirit a definite experience, removing the vagaries of faith. The Pentecostal believes that now, as in the beginning, "when we ask the Holy Spirit to come, we know that He has come by His speaking through us" (Carter, p. 110). It is quite important to the Pentecostal that he have no doubts about his actually having received his baptism in the Holy Spirit: hence the insufficiencies of the outward evidences of moral life or the inward evidences of spiritual assurance which, it is felt, take time to develop and are, even when developed, largely subjective, ambiguous, and uncertain.

It is the passion unmistakably to *know* that they have experienced

---

[42] *They Speak with Other Tongues,* p. 79; cf. *ibid.,* pp. 35-36, 115. Cf. also the contribution of James H. Hanson to a valuable symposium on tongues-speaking in *Dialog,* 2 (Spring 1963), 153.

[43] At the 1955 Pentecostal World Conference Gee remarked that tongues "made the Baptism in the Holy Spirit a definite experience. Nothing was left to a vague 'taking by faith' with a hoped for change in character and power." *Pentecost,* No. 34 (Dec. 1955), p. 10. See also p. 109 below.

the Holy Spirit — to know even physically — which distinguishes the Pentecostals' understanding of the evidence of the Spirit.

Finally, by no other means can the observing church be assured of the experience's authenticity. There must be a sign of some kind to guide the church and preserve her from deception. The scriptural sign is tongues. A baptism in the Holy Spirit without this biblical sign of tongues is, in the Pentecostal movement's general and majority understanding, an ordinary impossibility. To preserve the church from deception and to provide it with a clear criterion of inward membership, God has provided the church both biblically and experientially with an unequivocal sign. Reed (p. 12) gathers together the several persuasions under this head when he writes, "If there was to be some outward sign or evidence of the bestowment of the Spirit in His fulness, it should be (1) one easily recognized by the person himself, and by those present; (2) one that could be evident any time and always when one was filled with the Spirit; and (3) one that corresponds to the Bible pattern." For these specifications Pentecostals feel assured that only speaking in other tongues fully qualifies.

d. *The Initial Evidence.* Pentecostals will always wish to affirm, however, that although they place great stress on the initial glossolalic evidence, nevertheless, in the light of the broad witness of Scripture, there can be no argument for this sign's being the *only* evidence of the Spirit's incoming. It is the only *initial* evidence of the Spirit's baptism, but it must be accompanied by the Christian graces to be completed. "The stress," writes Gee, "must always be upon '*initial*.' It is not the final evidence of that baptism, and there is no contradiction of Paul's great saying that divorced from Love the tongues of men are both empty and offensive. But this does not invalidate the use of 'tongues' as a sign in their proper place as recorded in the book of Acts."[44] There are many evidences of the Holy Spirit, Pentecostals insist, but there must be but one *initial* evidence, and it is for this neglected initiatory sign that Pentecostals wish to contend.

e. *The Nature of Tongues.* There has been no extensive written treatment of the *nature* of tongues within the Pentecostal movement for the simple reason that the character of tongues is felt to be noncomplex. Speaking in tongues is a Spirit-inspired utterance. After this affirmation the descriptions of the experience separate and vary in detail but may be usually found to unite again, to a greater or lesser degree, around two poles, namely, that the speech is (1) ecstatic and (2) a language. Williams combines both in his remark: "In every case [of a baptism in the Holy Spirit] there is an ecstatic speaking in

---

44 *Pentecost*, No. 35 (March 1956), p. 17. Cf. also Brumback who argues in almost exactly the same manner, *What Meaneth This?*, p. 187. The fruit of the Spirit takes too long to grow to be a useful *initial* evidence. Gee, *Pentecost*, p. 27.

a language that the person has never learned."[45] One or both of these features will, at times, also be denied by Pentecostals. For example, some Pentecostals would not agree that the tongues are ecstatic and others no longer hold that tongues-speaking reproduces actual language. However, the more extensive opinion of the movement may fairly be represented as affirming both characteristics, even though the ecstasy may at times appear somewhat peculiar to observers and the language usually unknown to the hearers.

f. *The Mission of Tongues.* With all necessary qualifications, Pentecostals believe, finally, that they must remain true to their *raison d'être* and namesake — the Pentecostal glossolalic baptism in the Holy Spirit — if they are to be true to Scripture, their movement, their world mission, and not least, their mission to the whole Christian church, particularly to Protestantism towards which they feel, of course, special responsibilities. By ministering this unique doctrinal and experiential trust to other Protestant churches and individuals, Pentecostals believe that they would, in the words of French Pentecostalism (in Eggenberger, p. 280), "be opening to contemporary Protestantism the means of recovering that which it most needs: spiritual reality and conviction."

On the other hand, Pentecostals believe that whenever their glossolalic distinctive is minimized the result is the imperiling of their unique existence and their ministry as a movement. "Experience has proved," declares Gee, "that wherever there has been a weakening on this point fewer and fewer believers have in actual fact been baptized in the Holy Spirit and the [Pentecostal] Testimony has·tended to lose the Fire that gave it birth and keeps it living."[46] Pentecostals believe that it is precisely this experience — the Holy Spirit's baptism with the evidence

---

[45] *Systematic Theology,* III, 55. The books by Brumback and Christenson are the main Pentecostal and Neo-Pentecostal developments respectively. For non-Pentecostal studies of tongues-speaking see, in addition to the standard monographs by Mosiman, Rust, Léonard, and Cutten, the recent periodical literature, esp. James N. Lapsley and John H. Simpson, "Speaking in Tongues," *Princeton Seminary Bulletin, 58* (Feb. 1965), 3-18 and the literature there; also the articles in the bibliography, below, under George J. Jennings, E. Mansell Pattison, and William J. Samarin.

[46] *Pentecost,* No. 45 (Sept. 1958), p. 17. DuPlessis, reporting to Pentecostals on his meeting with the World Council of Churches Commission on Faith and Order at St. Andrews, remarked: "As usual there came the question: 'Do your people still teach that tongues is essential to the Baptism of the Holy Spirit?' And as usual I replied, 'No, unfortunately not, and where this standard is dropped, there the fervency and power of the Revival tends to diminish greatly. It seems we must either accept all the manifestations of the Spirit in Scriptural order or we lose the power that follows the Baptism in the Spirit.' " *Pentecost,* p. 19. D. W. Kerr makes the same point in "The Bible Evidence of the Baptism in the Holy Spirit," *The Phenomena of Pentecost* (Springfield, Mo.: Gospel Publishing House, 1931), p. 51.

of tongues — which is Pentecostalism's treasure to contribute to the church universal, and in Gee's words it "may well be the appointed gateway into the whole realm of an experience of the Holy Spirit as intimate and powerful as that enjoyed by the early church."[47] This experience may at least provide a gateway into an understanding of the inner meaning of the Pentecostal movement.

5. SUMMARY

Upon the doctrine of the spiritual evidence of tongues — a doctrine which to an outsider might seem to offer mainly embarrassment and little edification — the Pentecostal movement has placed much of its reputation and emphasis. One could imagine that such a doctrine would only force its adherents more and more into an impossible corner and into insignificant, unpopular sectarianism. But quite the opposite seems in fact to be the case. The movement grows rapidly and the doctrine appears to be treasured by the majority of the Pentecostal people.

Pentecostalism justifies its "fundamental verity" with the arguments of Acts, experience, reason, and the necessity of assurance, understands the phenomenon to be ecstatic languages in content, initial in evidence, and with high missionary and even ecumenical usefulness in character. Thus, far from being prepared to abandon the doctrine of the Spirit's unusual introductory manifestation, Pentecostalism finds exactly here in this unusual experience the answer to the church's and even the world's greatest needs. This conviction was given expression in the Statement of the Sixth Pentecostal World Conference in Jerusalem in 1961 where, after reviewing the powerlessness of either the conventional churches or the world's best wisdom to save men from their contemporary crises, the Pentecostal movement proclaimed in its closing words that "the only way [to save modern man] is a revival of the Pentecostal power of the Holy Spirit among all believers," concluding specifically that "a personal experience of the baptism in the Holy Spirit with its manifestations, powers, and services, according to the Scriptures, is the great need of our time."[48]

C. THE DOCTRINE OF THE CONDITIONS FOR THE BAPTISM IN THE HOLY SPIRIT

1. THE NECESSITY OF THE DOCTRINE

The baptism in the Holy Spirit is subsequent to conversion. Why

---

[47] Pentecost, No. 17 (Sept. 1951), p. 17. It should be emphasized in this connection that Pentecostalism does not wish to understand speaking in tongues as merely a goal, but as "a beginning of a new kind of Christian living." Nichol, Pentecostalism, p. 15. Cf. Hughes, What Is Pentecost?, p. 19.
[48] In Hutten, MD, 24 (Nov. 1, 1961), 247.

must this be? The baptism in the Holy Spirit is evidenced by speaking in tongues. How can this occur? The doctrine of the conditions for the baptism in the Holy Spirit is the sustained Pentecostal effort to answer both these questions; to answer why the spiritual baptism cannot usually accompany initial faith, detailing the conditions that believers usually failed to meet at that time, and to announce how the spiritual baptism can be brought to the crisis event where tongues will occur, detailing the conditions that, when fulfilled, will lead to the experience. The doctrine of conditions, then, is actually a corollary of the doctrine of subsequence and a premise for the doctrine of evidence, and as such occupies a cornerstone position in the edifice of the distinctive Pentecostal doctrine.

It is regularly suggested under the doctrine of conditions that certain fundamental steps must be taken in order for the believer to be a suitable recipient of the fulness of the Holy Spirit. The Holy Spirit "does not automatically fill men," writes Reed, "unless they meet certain definite conditions *and definitely seek to be filled*" (emphasis ours).[49] It is important to note that not only must certain conditions be met (this could happen unconsciously), but that certain conditions must be *sought* to be met (this makes the matter conscious). Unless there is a definite desire to have this experience it will not occur. The desire to have the experience expresses itself appropriately in the willingness to meet the conditions for it.

In other words, the (full) gift of the Spirit is not just a privilege received simply or perhaps unconsciously in receiving Christ; rather, it is an obligation to be sought specifically and experientially along with or as a result of receiving Christ. In a Pentecostal tract the question is asked, "Is it simply a privilege, or is it a duty, to seek this infilling . . . ?" And the answer is unequivocally, "We are commanded to seek it and are not obeying God unless we do."[50] The gift of the Spirit, we may say then in preface, is not understood as a gift which comes simply as the result of (1) receiving (2) salvation in Christ (3) by faith, but it is an obligation which comes through (1) seeking (2) the fulness of the Spirit (3) through conditions, including, of course, the condition of faith in Christ.

Pentecostals do not wish to minimize Christ in their doctrine of the spiritual baptism and the conditions leading to it. Quite the opposite. But the problem is, as Pentecostals see it, that in the lives of too few Christians do the events of baptism (or conversion) and the Pente-

---

[49] "Pentecostal Truths," p. 22. See also the *Reglamento local,* p. 16; and the even more ardent Brazilian definition in *Hollenweger* II, 898. Recently, Joseph R. Flower, "Holiness, the Spirit's Infilling, and Speaking with Tongues," *Paraclete, 2* (Summer 1968), 8.

[50] Kortkamp, "What the Bible Says," n. p. The texts cited as proofs: Eph. 5:18; Luke 24:49; Acts 1:4; Zech. 10:1.

costal baptism coincide. The solution must be, then, that beyond becoming a Christian "there are definite, stated conditions to be met; conditions that had to be met by the disciples; conditions that must be met by all who receive the Holy Ghost today" (Conn, *Pillars,* p. 96). Somehow the faith that leads to Christian baptism is not the same as or at least is not usually sufficient for the commitment which leads to the Pentecostal baptism. The Pentecostal doctrine of conditions is necessary to explain why this is the case and how it may be overcome.

2. THE SOURCES AND THE EXEGETICAL BASIS OF THE DOCTRINE

The biblical brief for the doctrine of conditions rests more widely on extra-Acts sources than is the case in either the subsequence or evidence doctrines of the Spirit in Pentecostalism. For example, the most frequently used text in support of the condition of prayer is Luke 11:13; and Galatians 3:1-5 and 3:14 are the texts most often employed for the condition of faith. And it is outside of the standard pneumobaptistic passages in Acts (viz., Acts 2; 8; 9; 10-11; 19) that Pentecostals most often establish the condition of obedience — Acts 5:32: "the Holy Spirit whom God has given to those who obey him." The Pentecostal doctrines of the subsequence and evidence of the Spirit can be found almost exclusively in Acts, but the doctrine of the obediences necessary for the full reception of the Spirit in Pentecostal development is, we may say, as wide as Scripture itself. Nevertheless, since Acts is itself so important for other features of the Pentecostal experience, it is usually in Acts that Pentecostal argument for the conditions of the Spirit will be begun.

a. *The Standard Acts Passages.* In Acts we have at least indications of the necessity of, and then more cryptically the conditions for, the spiritual baptism. Skibstedt (p. 104) writes:

> As concerns this question of the proper seeking of the Spirit-baptism we have the examples of the first Christians before us as exhortations, encouragements, and examples. Through closer examination we will find that there were very definite conditions to which they had to subject themselves, conditions which are also binding for all times. We too must subject ourselves to these conditions if we want to have these wonderful experiences of the first Christians.

If we could discover the conditions fulfilled by the earliest Christians as recorded in Acts, it is urged, we might find today the Spirit experienced in Acts. Thus the exegesis of Acts is still important for the Pentecostal conditions.

This is true even though the major Acts incidents in Pentecostal exegesis must usually be explained deductively rather than inductively in order to yield the variety of conditions found in most Pentecostal lists. Riggs, for example, understands the four conditions for the spiritual baptism to be regeneration, obedience, prayer, and faith, and he can find all these conditions even in Acts 8 and 10 where to at least some other readers these texts offer neither prayer by the recipients nor the kinds of obedience understood by Riggs, nor an additional act or type of faith (nor, in the case of Cornelius, a prior regeneration), as qualifications for the spiritual baptism. These four conditions (or so it seems to some outsiders) must be implied and supplied. At Acts 8, for instance, Riggs comments (p. 109):

> Peter had told the Sanhedrin that the Holy Ghost was given to them that obey God (Acts 5:32) and so he doubtlessly explained this to the Samaritan converts. Peter and John both had heard the Lord promise that the Father would give the Holy Spirit to them that ask Him [Luke 11:13]. So they surely told this, too, to the Samaritan converts. When these awaiting new disciples were thus prayed for and instructed, the apostles laid hands on them (as an aid to the seekers' faith) and they received the Holy Ghost.

And at Acts 19, where the account is quite brief, Riggs (p. 112) discovers his four conditions in this manner: "Who would say that [Paul] did not instruct them according to the pattern which had been followed theretofore? It is the once-for-all pattern: be saved, obey God, ask Him for His blessings, believe with all your heart, and ye shall receive the fullness of the Holy Spirit."

But a doctrine of conditions may be most easily commenced in the pre-Pentecost events of Acts 1:1 to 2:1. This passage is studied by Pentecostal interpreters and found to teach that the embryonic church (1) in obedience to its Lord (1:12) was (2) in one accord and (3) persisting in prayer (1:14; 2:1), providing subsequent generations with at least three conditions for the baptism in the Holy Spirit: obedience, spiritual unity, and prayer.[51]

But after Pentecost the difficulty in finding conditions increases with the passages, for, in most of the instances, no particular program of conditions is apparent. There could appear to be in Acts a kind of disinterest in detailing steps toward the baptism in the Holy Spirit, with the exception of the apostolic laying on of hands in two interesting passages (8:14-17; 19:6). And yet even the laying on of hands in both texts seems to be an act which is not initiated by the candidates but by the apostles. Nevertheless, to help modern seekers, Pentecostalism is able to supply the enigmatic Acts texts, usually with the help of material outside of Acts itself, with steps and conditions which will

---

[51] So, for example, Hurst and Jones, *The Church Begins*, p. 24; Riggs, *Spirit Himself*, p. 108; Pearlman, *Doctrines*, p. 317. A sample exegesis of this section might be found in the following: " 'And when the day of Pentecost had fully come, they were all with one accord!' [Acts 2:1] ... This Christian love and purity had to come before the Holy Ghost could find entrance." Conn, *Pillars*, p. 82.

lead to the translation of believers into the apostolic events recorded in Acts.

b. *A Model Interpretation of Acts 2:38.* In Donald Gee's interpretation of Acts 2:38 we have a pilot study in the Pentecostal exegesis of Acts. Gee finds in this text ("And Peter said to them, 'Repent, and be baptized every one of you in the name of Jesus Christ for the forgiveness of your sins; and you shall receive the gift of the Holy Spirit' ") three specific conditions for the baptism in the Holy Spirit: repentance, baptism, and reception. It is important for us to mark how these terms are defined in the exposition in order for us to understand the Pentecostal thought-world.

First of all, repentance is defined as the forsaking of all sin, or renouncement, and is the negative side of the conditions. Then, second, baptism in water represents the positive principle of Christian obedience and means not simply baptism but "applies to all-round obedience in everything. It means *actions*," Gee continues, "that witness before all that you have accepted the position of discipleship. Notice particularly that baptism is for 'remission of sins.' It is hopeless to expect the Holy Spirit to come in and fill you until your heart is clean" (*Gift*, p. 55). It may be observed here that baptism is given a very practical and active interpretation. Baptism means, as Gee emphasizes, "*actions*," the believer's actions — "*actions* that witness before all that you have accepted the position of discipleship." Or as Pentecostals usually express it, baptism signifies obedience. Obedience is the positive complement to and fulfillment of repentance which is primarily negative. In Pentecostal exegesis obedience as a condition for the spiritual baptism means, specifically, as Gee explained above, activity directed toward the promised removal of all remaining sin through Christ's blood, toward what is called "heart cleanness," so that the Holy Spirit may have a suitable dwelling-place in the believer.

In Gee's exposition, after the obediences of repentance and baptism follows, third, reception or faith. The place of this condition on the list is not unimportant. Gee affirms with majority Pentecostalism that "we ought not need to fight and wrestle and work to receive the Holy Spirit," for "the promises of God are all appropriated through faith, and Paul tells us especially that we 'receive the promise of the Spirit through faith.' Gal. 3:14. Ultimately there can be no other way" (*Gift*, p. 57).

It cannot be said that faith as such is omitted in Pentecostalism. It inevitably appears as a condition and is always championed. But to understand exactly what is meant by faith when Pentecostals use the term shall require much of our attention. Here it should simply be noticed that Gee above concluded his conditions with an argument for faith by remarking that "ultimately there can be no other way."

"Ultimately" means, literally, "finally; at last; in the end." We may say, in fact, as we shall see more clearly later, that faith in the Pentecostal understanding and in the Pentecostal lists of conditions is rarely, if ever, *sola* or alone, but that it is often *ultima* or ultimate. This fact is important, as we shall see, for understanding Pentecostalism.

In this representative interpretation of Acts 2:38 we hear, then, in prelude some of the thematic notes in the Pentecostal orchestration of the doctrine of conditions: (1) the attitudes or actions preceding ultimate faith, usually described as repentance and obedience (here as repentance and baptism); (2) correspondingly, the necessity of a clean heart before the Holy Spirit may fully enter the life of the believer (where it should be observed that the Holy Spirit is not yet considered as definitively or fully come: "It is hopeless," Gee emphasized above, "to expect the Holy Spirit to come in and fill you until your heart is clean"); and then joined to these preliminaries and following them (3) the insistence that human work is not necessary for the reception of the gift, for the gift is ultimately received through faith.

This exegesis of Acts 2:38 should provide an introduction to the important and sometimes difficult task of understanding how Pentecostalism finds the conditions it suggests in the passages it interprets. As we review the Pentecostal conditions themselves we shall have occasion to observe the application of the hermeneutical principles found here *in nuce*.

3. The Conditions for the Baptism in the Holy Spirit

There appear to be as many suggested conditions for the reception of the baptism in the Holy Spirit as there are, in fact, advocates of the doctrine. The following are representative lists.

Skibstedt	*Conn*	*Pearlman*
Worship	Separation from sin	Right attitude
Joyous faith	Repentance and baptism	Prayer of Christian
Earnest expectation	Hearing of faith	workers
Praise and thanksgiving	Obedience	United prayers of the
Unconditional obedience	Intense desire	church
Unity	Asking of God	Purification by faith
Endurance		Individual prayer
		Obedience

Baur	*Riggs*	*Gee*
Prayer	Regeneration	Repentance
Faith	Obedience	Baptism
Separation from sin	Prayer	Faith[52]
Separation from sinners	Faith	
Reparation and restitution		

[52] Skibstedt, *Geistestaufe*, pp. 104-13; Conn, *Pillars*, pp. 96-104; Pearlman, *Doctrines*, pp. 316-19; Baur in Dalton, *Tongues Like As of Fire*, pp. 73-74; Riggs, *Spirit Himself*, pp. 102-12; Gee, *Gift*, pp. 55, 57. The lists could be continued indefinitely.

The wide variety of suggested steps leading to the baptism in the Holy Spirit in Pentecostal lists is, we believe, patient of a three-fold division, consisting of an essential pre-condition and two subsequent conditions. These are (a) conversion, (b) obedience, and (c) faith.

a. *Conversion.* For all Pentecostals the indispensable pre-condition for receiving the gift of the Holy Spirit is conversion or regeneration. "The baptism in the Holy Spirit," declares the widely used Latin American manual of doctrine, "is for every person who has been converted to the Lord" (*Reglamento local,* p. 16). And every Pentecostal would subscribe to Conn's statement that "it is absolutely impossible for an unconverted man to receive the Holy Spirit" (*Pillars,* p. 96). What might puzzle the non-Pentecostal believer in these remarks is not so much what appears to be said — namely, that to be unconverted and to receive the Holy Spirit are irreconcilable — but what appears to be implied and is in fact later developed — namely, that to be converted and yet not to have received the Holy Spirit is at all possible. The Pentecostal doctrine of conditions teaches us, however, that conversion not only *does* (as in the doctrine of subsequence) but that it *must* precede the baptism in the Holy Spirit. The sequence — conversion, then reception of the Spirit — is not only indicative but imperative. Only after conversion, the *conditio sine qua non,* can a believer commence to fulfill the conditions that bring conversion's successor, the baptism in the Holy Spirit.

b. *Obedience.* How then can the converted man — the Christian — obtain the promised gift of the Spirit? We may gather the various answers or conditions of Pentecostal theology under the categories of obedience and faith. Eggenberger (p. 273) concurs when he writes that "the frequent statements by all Pentecostal groups concerning the way to the reception of the baptism in the Holy Spirit can be comprehended in two groups: there is a necessary trustful expectation of faith and there is a repentant obedience of faith."

We may describe the circle of conditions in the category of obedience by drawing two curves: one we may call active, the other passive. For in the first the candidate is urged to act, and in the second he is urged to cease from acting.

i. Active Obedience. (a) Separation from Sin. Obedience means first of all and actively the separation from sin. Whether understood negatively, as repentance, or positively, as obedience, under this condition the Pentecostals' implicit doctrine of sin can be discovered.

Sin is understood as something which, with Christ's help,[53] the

---

[53] It would not be fair to imply that Pentecostals teach that cleansing from sin is accomplished apart from Christ. Pentecostals all place great stress upon the blood of Christ and its cleansing power. Cf. Gee, *Gift,* pp. 55-57; Barratt, *Rain,* p. 222. Pentecostals also place great stress on the conditions of obedience and

Christian can, indeed must, remove *prior* to his being able to receive the full gift of the Holy Spirit. Obedience has as its major task the removal of sin. For "you can receive the Holy Spirit, but not with sin in your heart" (Conn, *Pillars,* p. 96).

Sin, first of all, is anything in a man's life — large or small — which may displease God. We may illustrate this conviction first from the writings of the one from whom Pentecostalism appears to have acquired its specific understanding of the conditions for the baptism in the Holy Spirit — R. A. Torrey. In his series of conditions, after discussing the first step requisite for the spiritual baptism (viz., that we accept Jesus Christ as our Savior and Lord), Torrey describes the second step.

> The second step in the path that leads into the blessing of being baptized with the Holy Spirit is *renunciation of sin.* . . . A controversy with God about the smallest thing is sufficient to shut one out of the blessing. Mr. Finney [*n.b.*] tells of a woman who was greatly exercised about the baptism with the Holy Spirit. Every night after the meetings, she would go to her rooms and pray way into the night. . . . One night as she prayed, some little matter of head adornment, a matter that would probably not trouble many Christians today, but a matter of controversy between her and God, came up (as it had often come up before) as she knelt in prayer. She put her hand to her head and took the pins out of her hair and threw them across the room and said, "There go!" and instantly the Holy Ghost fell upon her. It was not so much the matter of head adornment as the matter of controversy with God that had kept her out of the blessing.[54]

Yet not simply one's adornment or outward behavior in the world, but one's inward attitude is of major importance in the Pentecostal understanding of sin and of the conditions which will remove it. An absence, for example, of the inner attitude of humility is prejudicial to the Spirit's reception. Conn asks (*Pillars,* p. 192), "Have you obeyed God in humility? . . . Humbleness is an absolute 'must' for . . . candi-

---

faith to be fulfilled by the believer in order to appropriate Christ's blood, help, and power.

[54] *The Person and Work of the Holy Spirit: As Revealed in the Scriptures and in Personal Experience* (London: James Nisbet and Co., 1910), p. 218. See Torrey's remarks: "The Baptism with the Holy Spirit causes one to be occupied with God and Christ and spiritual things. The man who is filled with the Holy Ghost will not be singing sentimental ballads, nor comic ditties, nor operatic airs while the power of the Holy Ghost is upon him. If the Holy Ghost should come upon one while listening to the most innocent of the world's songs he would not enjoy it. He would long to hear something about Christ." *What the Bible Teaches,* p. 276. Fr. Kilian McDonnell observes that Pentecostals, "like Roman Catholics, and in contrast to the Lutheran, and orthodox Reformed, . . . are psychologically predisposed to think of sin in terms of an act, hardly ever in terms of a state." "The Ecumenical Significance of the Pentecostal Movement," *Worship, 40* (Dec. 1966), 619. For a perceptive Pentecostal view of the several doctrines of sin in the churches see William W. Menzies, "The Spirit of Holiness: A Comparative Study," *Paraclete, 2* (Summer 1968), 10-16.

dates for the baptism of the Holy Ghost." Thus the omission of right attitudes as well as the commission of wrong deeds can hinder the coming of the baptism in the Holy Spirit. John Sherrill learned from his new Pentecostal experience that "the fiercest enemies of the Spirit within are not those active sins but the passive ones: the sins of omission, indifference, inertia. I hadn't been familiar with the Holy Spirit for long before I knew that we are not made automatons by His presence. He will stay with us as long as we actively will it, work at it, yearn for His company."[55]

But however sin is understood, and it can be given wide or narrow interpretations depending upon the interpreter, it is something which must be removed or subdued if one is to receive the Pentecostal experience. For, in the frequent Pentecostal declaration, "the Holy Spirit and sin cannot abide in the same heart" (Conn, *Pillars,* p. 96).

The only conclusion possible to draw from this spiritual law might seem to be that the Holy Spirit can abide only in a heart without sin — i.e., in sinlessness. Extreme as this may at first appear, Pentecostals believe that they can and must urge this condition if two facts are understood: (1) that it is possible to speak of a "heart without sin" if by sin is understood not so much *actual* sin as *known* sin; and (2) that it must be said that the Christian's heart can be free of known sin if one realizes that the *Holy* Spirit, by definition, cannot possibly have commerce with the unholy.[56]

It is the Pentecostal conviction that when Christians remove all *known* sin the Holy Spirit can dwell in their hearts even though there may still be unconscious or unknown (and hence, apparently, unculpable) sin. In any case, as far as the candidate knows he must be without sin, for it is impossible for the Pentecostal to contemplate sin and the Holy Spirit coinhabiting the Christian's heart.

This conviction offers an additional explanation for the doctrine of the subsequence of the Holy Spirit: at conversion it is a *sinner* who is understood to receive the salvation provided in Christ. But in the majority Pentecostal view, as the converted sinner increases in sanctification he progressively qualifies for the special gift of the Spirit. The Christian is understood as quite another kind of person by the time he is ready to receive the subsequent spiritual baptism. "As sinners

---

55 *They Speak with Other Tongues,* pp. 128-29.

56 On known sin, cf. Pethrus, *Wind*[2], p. 42; Barratt, *Rain,* p. 206. The Pentecostal doctrine of sin is perhaps best understood in the light of the Wesleyan evangelicalism from which it came and on which it draws for its underlying suppositions. Cf. Wesley in the Documents, below, p. 329 and see, for example, Lawson's *Deeper Experiences* and the following representative conviction: "It is only Christians who regard faults, mistakes, temptations, lack of knowledge, and so on, as sin, who believe that the Christian cannot live without sin," p. xi.

we accept Christ," Pearlman summarizes, "as saints we accept the Holy Spirit."[57]

It does not need to be stressed that this doctrine posits a special view of sin. When it can be averred by Pentecostal leaders that (with Sweden's Pethrus, p. 51) "the only thing that can hinder you in receiving the full blessing of God is sin," it must be wondered how this blessing could ever be obtained. But Pethrus continues immediately by explaining the means to this benediction: "If we live a yielded, pure and holy life, in close fellowship with Him, the experimental side of this mighty baptism must come" (ibid.). The possibility of living a yielded, pure, and holy life in close fellowship with God, even prior to the full coming of the Spirit, is implicit in the Pentecostal conditions. How it is possible for the Christian to live this kind of a life before he enjoys the full gift of the Spirit awaits an entirely comprehensible answer. Riggs is the only Pentecostal author we have found to have specifically raised the question. He asked (pp. 102-03), "How can His children . . . be obedient, when they have not received the Holy Spirit?" Riggs' answer to this important question is not as clear as we might wish, but we reproduce it as he immediately offers it: "[Christ] had commanded them not to depart from Jerusalem until they had been filled with power from on high. Luke 24:49. This command was to be passed on to their converts, the new disciples. His command then comes also to us" (ibid.). Riggs' answer thus seems to be: it is possible for contemporary Christians to fulfill the conditions of obedience even though they have not yet fully received the Holy Spirit because it was possible for the first disciples to be sufficiently obedient before they received the fulness of the Holy Spirit at Pentecost.

But one might even raise the prior question: How is it possible to be Christians at all without having first received the Holy Spirit (Rom. 8:9)? To this particular question Skibstedt addressed himself (p. 16):

> God's Word as well as experience teach us very clearly that it is possible to become a believer and to be baptized and to experience great joy in salvation — i.e., to be a recipient of the work of the good Holy Spirit — and nevertheless not yet to have received the gift of the Holy Spirit according to the New Testament understanding.

It is possible to be a Christian and even to experience the work of the Spirit and yet not to have actually received the gift of the Spirit, Skibstedt seems here to argue, because Scripture and experience teach us that this kind of twilight existence is in fact an observable datum in Scripture and in many modern lives.

---

[57] Pearlman, Doctrines, p. 318. The pre-Pentecostal evangelical A. J. Gordon expressed this idea in a similar way, earlier, in arguing for the same distinction: "It is as sinners that we accept Christ for our justification, but it is as sons that we accept the Spirit for our sanctification." The Ministry of the Spirit (Grand Rapids, Mich.: Zondervan Publishing House, 1949 [1894]), pp. 68-69.

Or it can be argued even more frequently in Pentecostalism, as we have already had occasion to see, that every Christian *has* received the gift of the Holy Spirit, but that not every Christian has been filled with the Spirit, or received the full gift of the Spirit, or the gift of the Holy Spirit in his fulness. We are reminded again that it was Torrey's opinion, appropriated by Pentecostalism, that "every true believer has the Holy Spirit, but not every believer has the baptism with the Holy Spirit."

The obstacle keeping Christians from this full experience is simply sin. And the first step to removing this obstacle and to receiving this full experience is, simply, the obedience which sets itself to the task of removing all the sin that is known in one's life. Christ, we may say paraphrasing Pearlman, receives repentant sinners; the Holy Spirit receives or is fully received by repentant saints, i.e., by Christians who through obedience have removed all conscious sin from their lives.

(b) Heart-Purification. While viewed from one side the Pentecostal doctrine of active obedience requests a life without known sin, viewed from another side it requires "heart-purification by faith," a statement derived from the language of Acts 15:8-9: "And God who knows the heart bore witness to them, giving them the Holy Spirit just as he did to us; and he made no distinction between us and them, but cleansed their hearts by faith." Here Pentecostals find God bearing witness to the obedience he sees in the hearts of the Gentile household, rewarding them by cleansing their hearts with faith. This is the positive and resultant side of the doctrine of the separation from sin which is negative and causal. Both doctrines are conditions, but they follow this succession: removing all known sin leads to the experience or fact of heart-purification, which leads in turn to the Pentecostal baptism with the Spirit (cf. Acts 15:8-9 with Acts 10:44-46).

There is an emphasis on the purification of the heart as a condition for the baptism in the Holy Spirit which elevates this particular condition to a doctrinal status in some Pentecostal groups.[58] It receives

---

[58] See the declaration of faith of the significant Church of God in all Spanish-speaking countries in Latin America: "We believe in the sanctification which is subsequent to the new birth through faith in the blood of Jesus Christ, ... [and] in the baptism with the Spirit which is subsequent to the purification of the heart." *Hollenweger* II, 1080. Note also the interesting list of doctrinal distinctives in the Chilean Iglesia de Dios: "(5) Faith in the blood of Jesus Christ as the medium of justification; (6) Sanctification subsequent to the new birth; (7) Holiness of life; (8) Baptism of the Holy Spirit; (9) Speaking in tongues as the initial evidence of the baptism in the Holy Spirit," in Vergara, *El Protestantismo en Chile*, p. 181. For a Brazilian parallel see *Hollenweger* II, 882. For the United States see R. H. Gause, *Church of God Polity* (Cleveland, Tenn.: Pathway Press, 1958), p. 159; Campbell, *Pentecostal Holiness Church*, p. 195; Hughes, *Church of God Distinctives*, pp. 30, 34-35, 120; for personal testimonies to the three experiences, Wood, *Culture and Personality Aspects of Pentecostal Holiness Religion*, p. 24.

its fullest expression, as might be expected, in the holiness wing of the
Pentecostal movement and finds its most detailed literary development
in the writings of the two major Scandinavian Pentecostal leaders, T. B.
Barratt of Norway and Lewi Pethrus of Sweden.

The instantaneous sanctification or holiness groups teach *three* definite "works of grace" instead of two: (1) regeneration, (2) sanctification ("heart-purification by faith"), and (3) the baptism in the Holy
Spirit evidenced by speaking in tongues.[59] Pentecostals of the progres-
sive sanctification persuasion tend to make of the "purifying of the
heart" not so much a crisis experience as a preparatory condition to
arriving at *the* crisis experience of the baptism in the Holy Spirit.

From whatever side it is viewed, however, active obedience understands nothing less than the riddance by the Christian of all (known)
sin in order to provide a clean heart for the indwelling of the Holy
Spirit who is given as a witness to this obedience in the fulness of
the spiritual baptism.

(c) Prayer. One of the most frequent representations of obedience
— indeed quite often appearing as a separate condition itself — is
prayer.[60] This condition is usually built on the accounts in Luke 11:13
and Acts 1:14 where prayer precedes the impartation of the Spirit.
It is held that apart from prayer the gift cannot ordinarily be received.
The gift is "without money and without price," writes Riggs (pp.
103-04), "but He will give it only to those who *ask* for it." Skibstedt
(p. 68) affirms that "God fulfills the promises of the baptism in the
Holy Spirit as long as the candidate knows that he *needs* this power
— and *seeks* it in intensive and persevering prayer." As may be gathered
from the latter part of the last remark, it is not simply prayer that
usually obtains the gift, but a definite kind of prayer — "intensive
and persevering prayer." Riggs tells us emphatically that *"we must
ask importunately,"* and queries, "Shall we consider that He gave the
Spirit to us when asked once, even though there be no evidence then
or thereafter that He came?" (p. 104).

If the spiritual evidences of Pentecost do not follow prayer, then
either the faith or the prayer of the candidate must have been inadequate. For as there are kinds of faith — great faith and little faith —
so there are, in Pentecostal opinion, kinds of prayer — asking, seeking,
and knocking (Matt. 7:7). The latter — seeking and knocking — are
the types of prayer to which believers must extend themselves if they

---

[59] See Barratt, *Rain,* p. 221.

[60] In the largest circulating Pentecostal publication in North America, the
weekly *Pentecostal Evangel,* there appears on the inside cover of each edition a
creedal statement including, under the article on the baptism of the Spirit, only
prayer as a condition: "We believe that the Baptism of the Holy Spirit according
to Acts 2:4 is given to believers who ask for it."

are fully to meet God's requirement of importunate prayer. "This is God's elimination test," Riggs writes (p. 104), "to determine whom He considers worthy to receive this priceless gift." Intensive and extensive prayer is active obedience brought to a head. And in this kind of prayer the soul of the candidate begins to pass into the condition of passive obedience.

ii. Passive Obedience. After there has been active obedience the candidate for the promised baptism is instructed, as he now waits for the actual incidence of the gift, to become (1) as submissive as possible to the promptings of the Spirit (2) within, usually, the believing context of the Pentecostal fellowship. He is to yield himself up entirely to God and to the brotherly encouragement and prayer of other Pentecostals in the fellowship of what is usually called the "tarrying meeting." We must now turn our attention successively to the features of the individual's yielding and to the corporate tarrying meeting where this yielding usually culminates.

(a) Yielding (Emptying). The conception of yielding is frequent in Pentecostal literature. If the candidate has fulfilled all the conditions of active obedience and if he will now completely yield himself to the Spirit, he is assured of the reception of the Pentecostal baptism. Now the seeker must not attempt in any way to cooperate or to assist the process. He must become as passive as possible. Employing the analogy of water baptism Riggs (p. 66) warns that "co-operation by active participation does not assist, but rather hinders the one who is baptizing." Turning then to the actual spiritual baptism Riggs continues: "Body, soul, and spirit must be yielded. Our physical bodies must be pliable under His power. . . . Utter and complete baptism in the Holy Spirit . . . is reached only when there is a perfect yielding of the entire being to Him and one's tongue is surrendered to the control of the blessed Holy Spirit."[61] When the candidate sufficiently empties himself and becomes adequately submissive, the desired evidence finds access.

How this particular doctrinal feature is developed may be illustrated in one of the earliest recorded letters of the Pentecostal movement.

---

[61] *Spirit Himself*, p. 67. See also Pethrus, *Wind*[2], p. 61. A term used synonymously with "yielding" is "emptying." Language of this kind, familiar to students of mysticism, was probably adopted by Pentecostals from the usage of influential pre-Pentecostal evangelicals such as Andrew Murray who placed considerable emphasis upon emptying as a condition of filling. Cf. Andrew Murray, *Back to Pentecost: The Fulfillment of the Promise of the Father* (London: Oliphants, n.d.), p. 13. "It was this complete surrender of the whole heart and life [by the disciples] that made them capable of receiving the fulness of the Spirit." *Ibid.*, p. 39. The word "surrender" and the absolutes — e.g., "entire," "everything," "absolute," "complete," "full," "fulness," "whole," used throughout — were adopted by Pentecostalism from the evangelicalism noted here. See the Documents, below, p. 339.

In 1906, the important year of the world-wide spread of Pentecostalism, T. B. Barratt, the later apostle of the European Pentecostal movement, wrote from New York to Los Angeles requesting help in the reception of the baptism in the Holy Spirit as it was being newly received in the rapidly influential Los Angeles events. The letter he received in response serves as an excellent exhibition of the doctrine of yielding. We cite it in almost its entirety as it appears in Barratt's autobiography (*Fire,* p. 109, and the emphasis is Barratt's and/or the letter's):

> Los Angeles, Cal., Sept. 28, 1906
> T. B. Barratt
> Dear Brother in our Lord Jesus Christ. Greetings to you in His Name!
>   Your earnest letter touched our hearts; we are praying the full pentecostal baptism upon you! So that you may be equipped for His service as you never have been! There has to be a complete coming out, and leaving all for Jesus . . . and just *letting* God have His own precious way with us. After you have fully consecrated, and know God has cleansed your heart, then fast, and *wait upon God.* Keep yourself in a receptive attitude — and no matter what workings go on in your body, continually let and ask God to have His own way with you. You need have no fear while you keep under the blood — "Perfect love casts out all fear." Sometimes a wonderful shaking takes place, and sometimes the language comes at first, as a baby learning to talk. But let God have all — tongue, hands, feet — the whole body presented to him, as your reasonable service! When the Holy Ghost comes in, you will know it, for He will be in your *very flesh.* Be obedient on every line. Be *nothing* — that He may be all in all. We would be so glad if God should lead you to Los Angeles — many have come from afar, and have gone back with their wonderful pentecost. Hallelujah! . . . *We are very different from what we ever were before* —and we would do nothing to lose it. It fits us up for the stake, or whatever may come!
>   May God bestow this wonderful baptism upon you most speedily is our earnest prayer.
>   [signed] Mrs. I. May Throop

In this letter almost the entire gamut of the doctrine of obedience and much of the inclusive and larger doctrine of the baptism in the Holy Spirit may be seen at once. The absolutes should be observed: "the full pentecostal baptism," "complete coming out," "leaving all," "fully consecrated," "let God have all," "be obedient on every line." Passive obedience follows active obedience: "after you have fully consecrated, and know God has cleansed your heart [the two types of active obedience], then fast and wait upon God." All volitional control by the recipient must now be abandoned; the candidate must now "be *nothing* — that He may be all in all." There must be no resistance and there must be total receptivity: "Keep yourself in a receptive attitude — and no matter what workings go on in your body, continually let and ask God to have His own way with you." The receptivity must be even physical: "tongue, hands, feet — the whole body."

In this utterly receptive, self-emptying, yielded state, passive obedience on its individual side occurs.

(b) The Tarrying Meeting. The yielding of the Pentecostal candidate usually takes place in the larger context of what is called the receiving or tarrying meeting (the word "tarrying" comes from the dominical injunction in Luke 24:49 AV, "tarry ye in Jerusalem"). The tarrying meeting plays a central role in the appropriation of the baptism in the Holy Spirit. It is unfortunate that it receives so little attention in Pentecostal literature, for it would be fair to say that institutionally its importance is second to no other churchly reality except the (later to be described) Pentecostal meeting: neither formal preaching, nor the sacraments, nor any other kind of Pentecostal practice or gathering seems to occupy a place comparable in Pentecostal life.[62]

Almost all of the prior conditions of obedience are either oriented toward or are operative in this decisive place: active obedience leads to this meeting; passive obedience is exercised in the meeting; and it is for prayer that the meeting exists. A tarrying meeting may be provisionally defined as a meeting which takes place, ordinarily, after a regular assembly of the church and most frequently in the evenings, in which candidates for the Pentecostal baptism are prayed with and for by other Pentecostals with a view to the candidate's being led to the experience of the baptism in the Holy Spirit with the glossolalic evidence. It is, in short, a prayer meeting for the baptism in the Holy Spirit.

In the tarrying meeting the enquirer will be encompassed with a volume of prayer and exhortation until the spiritual *aër* becomes quite charged and warm, and as the enquirer begins to approximate ecstasy or the speaking in tongues, the intensity of the corporate prayer and exhortation will be raised and the candidate's receptivity and sensitivities heightened until the desired goal is reached, or fails to be reached. Brumback in his authoritative Pentecostal book on glossolalia justifies and explains the procedures of the tarrying meeting:

> There is a proper attitude for prayer-helpers to take toward candidates for the fullness of the Spirit, and this attitude is endorsed and practiced by the vast majority of Pentecostal believers. It is always in order to surround these candidates with an atmosphere of prayer and praise, and to offer an encouraging word. When it is evident that they are being filled with the Holy Spirit, it is perfectly proper to exhort them to continue to yield to Him. The supernatural is a strange realm to these seekers, and when the

---

[62] For interesting descriptions of the Pentecostal tarrying meeting in Brazil see Read, *New Patterns of Church Growth in Brazil*, pp. 42-43, 133, and especially 137-39. Pearlman is unusual among Pentecostal writers in donating a large place to the corporate necessities for the baptism in the Holy Spirit; see his *Doctrines*, p. 317 and above, p. 92.

praise on their lips begins to change from their own familiar tongue to a
new and unknown tongue it is reassuring to have someone near who has
already undergone that experience.[63]

Other Pentecostals are to contribute in every possible way to bringing about the evidence of the candidate's spiritual baptism, which is
the speaking in new tongues. While in the tarrying meeting volitional
activity on the part of the candidate is to be lowered to a minimum,
the responsibility and activity of the Pentecostal group is lifted to a
maximum. In yielding, the candidate should seek to be, in the words
of the letter to Barratt, "nothing"; in the tarrying meeting the candidate's circle should seek to be as spiritually active as possible in helping the yielded one reach the desired goal.

Pentecostalism has been criticized, as might be expected, for the
suggestible character of its tarrying meetings and the at times seemingly
forced nature of the ecstatic phenomena. A defense of the "forced
expectation" in the tarrying meeting is usually offered by Pentecostals
on the basis of Jesus' own command to "tarry ye ... until" (Luke
24:49 AV; cf. Acts 1:4), and his orders to his disciples, in the words
of one Pentecostal rejoinder, "to point oneself quite consciously toward
this experience in tarrying meetings. [Jesus] did exactly that which the
enemies of the Pentecostal movement accuse Pentecostals of doing.
By his command he invoked an atmosphere of eager expectation."[64]
But not all Pentecostals are as lenient. In an editorial in *Pentecost* Gee
frankly discusses some of the problems inherent in the tarrying meeting.

> The ever-present temptation that has dogged the Pentecostal Revival for
> over fifty years is to try and "make" seekers apparently speak with tongues
> so that it can be claimed that they are "through" into the promised per-
> sonal Pentecost. At the highest level this desire to help people speak with
> tongues when the power of the Spirit is manifestly upon them is entirely
> pure, for it springs from nothing but love and a longing for the seeker
> and helper to mutually rejoice in arriving at a desired spiritual objective.
> At the lowest level it can be the carnal desire of the worker conducting
> the tarrying meeting to build up a personal reputation for ability to "get
> people through." In order to make people speak with what are claimed
> to be "tongues" there have been methods adopted for which we make no
> excuse.[65]

---

[63] *What Meaneth This?*, pp. 259-60. It is interesting that Brumback can say
of Christians seeking this subsequent Pentecostal experience that "the supernatural
is a strange realm to these seekers." For a vivid description of an *ad hoc* tarrying
meeting see Sherrill, *They Speak with Other Tongues*, pp. 119-23. For details on
the spiritual and oral techniques necessary for a candidate's being brought to
speak in tongues see, e.g., Christenson, *Speaking in Tongues*, p. 130; Robert C.
Frost, *Aglow with the Spirit* (Northridge, Calif.: Voice Christian Publications,
1965), ch. 8; W. J. Samarin, "Glossolalia as Learned Behaviour," *Canadian Journal of Theology, 15* (Jan. 1969), 62-64.
[64] In Hutten, *MD, 46* (April 1, 1958), 80.
[65] No. 25 (Sept. 1953), p. 17. For a Pentecostal description of the "lower level"
aspiration see Campbell, *Pentecostal Holiness Church*, pp. 242-43.

But Gee still affirms, on the same editorial page, that in the tarrying meeting "there simply must arise a desire, indeed an eagerness, to hear seekers speak with tongues as the evidence they indubitably have received the longed-for blessing." *Abusus non tollet usum.*

Regardless of the opinions about the tarrying meeting it appears that it is in this meeting that most Pentecostal baptisms occur. No doubt the experience can and does occur in private, but we may subscribe to Hutten's judgment that "more frequently the experience occurs in the Pentecostal gathering."[66]

iii. Summary. Under the Pentecostal category of obedience practically everything in religion morally and psychologically considered may be subsumed. One must be very pure (active obedience) and very pliable (passive obedience) and very much in prayer, privately and corporately, if the divine Spirit is to descend.

The difference between the active and passive obediences, seen from the outside, is that in the active there is more of a moral and in the passive more of a psychological character. On the active side there appears to be an advocacy of the seemingly superhuman feat of sinlessness. When we are told, for example, that only sin can keep us from receiving the baptism in the Holy Spirit or that sin and the Holy Spirit cannot dwell in the same heart, we may see how seriously this condition is actually urged. On the passive side there appears to be a proposal for an almost equally superhuman self-emptying. The respective types of obedience seem to strain on the active or moral side toward the breaking point and on the passive or psychological side toward the evaporation point. We may say that the two classic poles of religious ardor express themselves in the Pentecostal conditions of active and passive obedience: an extremely optimistic self-assertion (sinlessness), and an extremely pessimistic self-negation (nothingness) — what are sometimes called the distinctively Western and Eastern varieties of religious expression.

The union of the active and passive conceptions may be found in the notion of totality. "Have you obeyed Him *fully?*" or "Have [you] yielded to God at *every point?*" are frequent Pentecostal questions. In the Pentecostal view, for there to be true obedience there must be both total repentance (so total as to exclude known sin) and total yielding (so total as to exclude one's self). It is an axiom of Pentecostal theology that only where there is full or total obedience can there be the full or total gift of the Spirit.

There is no lack of moral or religious ardor in Pentecostal obedience. We are in the presence of a distinctively religious category; whether

---

[66] *MD, 14* (Nov. 15, 1951), 110. This can be supported by most of the testimonies of Pentecostals to their spiritual baptism. See the Appendix to this chapter, below.

it is evangelical, in the classic sense, must wait for a consideration of the final condition of faith.

c. *Faith.* Pentecostalism affirms faith, but a kind of faith not usually understood as such in traditional Protestant definition. We must therefore devote a more than passing attention to the Pentecostal condition of faith in order to discover its underlying nature in its several forms: (1) in its difference in character from ordinary faith; (2) in its declared *sola fide* character; and (3) in its developed price or *analogia pecuniae* character. (4) Finally, we must study the very arresting polemic *against* faith-alone as a valid condition for the reception of the Spirit.

i. The Two Kinds of Faith. Faith is almost always included in the Pentecostal lists. Faith is usually understood as an additional act complementing obedience by which, ultimately, the gift of the Spirit is received. It is apparent from the earlier discussion of the subsequent nature of the baptism in the Holy Spirit, however, that the faith which apprehends Christ in his salvation is not usually understood as identical with the faith which apprehends the Holy Spirit in his fulness. Two types, or at least two acts of faith are usually required for the two experiences of the new birth and the baptism in the Spirit. "As there is a faith toward Christ for salvation," Pearlman expresses it, "so there is a faith toward the Spirit for power and consecration."[67] Why the first faith does not appropriate the Holy Spirit in his entire ministry is not entirely clear. However, it seems to be the general Pentecostal argument that the "further" or second faith is required (1) because the first faith was insufficiently directed and (2) insufficiently total.

(a) The Problem of Insufficiently Directed Faith. As we pointed out in the discussion of Cornelius' conversion, it will be granted that the Holy Spirit's baptism *might* be experienced on the initial act of

---

[67] *Doctrines,* p. 316. Cf. a Neo-Pentecostal formulation: "The Book of Acts teaches plainly that even after the Holy Spirit has received the believer, bringing him to a saving faith in Christ, the believer must then also receive the Holy Spirit." Christenson, *Speaking in Tongues,* p. 163. And note the pre-Pentecostal evangelicals: Gordon: "These texts [Gal. 3:2, 14] seem to imply that just as there is a 'faith toward our Lord Jesus Christ' for salvation, there is a faith toward the Holy Ghost for power and consecration." *Ministry of the Spirit,* p. 71, cf. *ibid.,* p. 68; F. B. Meyer: "As you took forgiveness from the hand of the dying Christ, take your share of the Pentecostal gift from the hand of the living Christ." *Back to Bethel: Separation from Sin and Fellowship with God* (Chicago: Fleming H. Revell Co., 1901), p. 94. See other arguments for the "two faiths" in Murray, *Spirit of Christ,* pp. 17-19 and cf. Documents, below, p. 338. See, finally, the liberal use in Pentecostal literature of the arguments for two experiences by Gordon, Meyer, Murray, Simpson, and Torrey, e.g., in Riggs, *Spirit Himself,* ch. seven, "The Baptism in the Holy Spirit Distinguished from Conversion"; Williams, *Systematic Theology,* III, 59-61.

faith, though he very seldom is. "Ideally," writes Pearlman, "one should receive the enduement of power immediately after conversion but, actually, there are certain circumstances of one kind or another which may make tarrying necessary."[68] The ideal is not usually the actual because there is a need for, at the very least, a separate and specific desire for, in the words of the title to Riggs' standard study, "the Spirit himself." There is, Pearlman (p. 236) points out, a "faith toward Christ" and a "faith toward the Spirit," and so at least in direction there are different kinds of faith.

The Spirit in his fulness is not given simply to faith in Christ, for the Spirit must, in the words of several commentators, be specifically "applied for." Riggs (p. 112) cites F. B. Meyer to the effect that (and the emphasis is his): " 'He gave [the Holy Spirit] to His Church . . . and He waits to give each *individual* member of that church his or her share in Pentecost on the one *condition* of applying for it by faith.' " This law of appropriation or application obtains, it is argued, no less for the individual's reception of the once-for-all gift of the Spirit at Pentecost than it does for the individual's reception of the once-for-all gift of salvation at the cross. "God's gift requires an appropriation" (Pearlman, p. 318). It appears, then, that at least one reason for the insufficiency of the first faith of most Christians is the fact that this faith is not specifically directed toward the appropriation of the gift of the Holy Spirit himself.

(b) The Problem of Insufficiently Total Faith. There are also reasons why the ordinary faith exercised by the ordinary Christian day by day, even when this faith is directed toward the help of the Holy Spirit, is not usually sufficient for the reception of the gift of the Holy Spirit in fulness. In the Pentecostal understanding the ordinary Christian would probably have been baptized in the Holy Spirit with the glossolalic evidence if he had had the proper amount of faith. The faith exercised by most Christians is not usually the faith meant by Pentecostals when they speak of the appropriation of the Holy Spirit by faith. It is clear that to Pentecostals there is faith and there is faith.

In a discussion of the case for faith as a condition, Barratt writes (*Rain,* pp. 214-15, emphasis his), "As you were justified and regenerated by faith, and sanctified by faith, so also you must receive the Baptism of the Holy Ghost and Fire — the Comforter, by faith," to which is immediately added the important qualification, "I am supposing that you have yielded to God at *every point.* . . . Are you willing to go *all the way with Christ?*" The "everys" and the "alls" qualify Pentecostal faith. Faith to the Pentecostal means going *all* the way with Christ; being *totally* yielded. Thus the first faith is not ordinarily

---

[68] *Doctrines,* pp. 316-17. Torrey established this idea. See below, Documents, p. 335.

sufficient for the gift of the Spirit, due not only to its insufficient object or direction (Christ and not the Spirit himself) but also, and as important, due to its insufficient content or substance.

Pentecostal faith, like Pentecostal obedience, is not normally effective until it can approach totality. Total obedience *plus* total faith should grant the total baptism in the Holy Spirit. Totality seems to hold the key to the understanding of the Pentecostal conditions. We may notice the importance of the idea of totality in a sentence of Pethrus where, after describing how he himself had finally received the baptism in the Holy Spirit, he explains why otherwise quite consecrated Christians have not yet experienced the full Pentecostal baptism in the Spirit: "They have had wonderful experiences, and surrender after surrender has been made, but because they have not come all the way and made the yieldedness complete, they have not seen the fullness of the blessing."[69] We may isolate in this sentence the Pentecostal equation: coming "all the way" (= total or active obedience) plus making the "yieldedness complete" (= total or passive obedience, or faith) issues in "the fullness of the blessing" (= the total or glossolalic baptism). The crucial terms are "all," "complete," and "fullness."

There are, therefore, two kinds of faith: a faith which appropriates and is directed toward Christ, which may or may not be total, and a faith which appropriates and is directed toward the Holy Spirit and which should or must approach totality. To this latter faith alone is given the baptism in the Holy Spirit.

ii. The Faith-Alone or Free Character of the Gift of the Spirit. There is a definite doctrine in the Pentecostal movement of the free character of the gift of the Spirit. Here it is urged that no merit of our own gains us the promise but that, appropriate to the nature of a gift, the promise is given to us freely and without cost. There is a positive disavowal of the need to struggle to be worthy in order to obtain the promised blessing. Authentically evangelical notes may be heard, for example, in the following representative Pentecostal affirmation:

> Seekers ... after the Baptism in the Spirit should always remember that this experience is also called, 'The Gift of the Holy Ghost.' Gifts are not earned or won by price or merit. Gifts cannot be forced from the giver. ... The Holy Spirit is a gracious ... God-sent Gift, and we receive Him by faith and by faith alone [Riggs, pp. 105-06].

Almost all Pentecostal representation contends for the Spirit's recep-

---

[69] *Wind*[2], p. 61. Cf. Bartleman's confession: "I had not the slightest difficulty in speaking in 'tongues.' And yet I can understand how some may have such difficulties. They are not fully yielded to God." *How Pentecost Came to Los Angeles*[2], p. 73. Cf. Wesley, Documents, below, pp. 326-27.

tion, as above, "by faith and by faith alone." This must be emphasized. But the observer cannot help but be puzzled when, for example,
immediately joined to the statement just cited is the declaration (and
the emphasis is ours) that "He will give freely, *as we meet His conditions* and ask Him for His gifts." And this is not, as we shall have
occasion to see, an isolated qualification. The freedom of the gift is
everywhere stoutly maintained. But its freedom is always predicated
on the meeting of prior conditions.[70]

We must believe that Pentecostals mean it when they say that the
gift of the Spirit is free and to be received without human effort or
merit. But it is made hard for the student of the Pentecostal movement
to know just what Pentecostals mean by this statement when, to mention just one other difficulty under this head, in very few, if any,
of the actually recorded or observed experiences of the reception
of the glossolalic baptism in the Holy Spirit does it appear that the
event occurred without considerable effort. For instance, the soberest
Pentecostal writer, Donald Gee, who wrote (*Gift,* p. 57), "we ought
not need to fight and wrestle and work to receive the Holy Spirit," on
another occasion, in reviewing Pentecostal baptisms in the Spirit in
Africa, wrote in admiration, "Oh, how they cried and groaned and
groveled in the dust, as they wrestled their way to victory [i.e., to
the Pentecostal experience]. The noise of this great visitation was heard
in a village a mile and a half away. For three hours the place was swayed
by God's Spirit."[71] Gee no doubt means, as he says, that "we ought
not need to fight and wrestle," but perhaps it is not inconsistent to
him that in many instances there appears to have been such wrestling.

But finally, that Pentecostal "by faith alone" means something different from what is usually understood by this affirmation in Protestantism, may be indicated simply by looking at the Pentecostal lists of
conditions (e.g., above, p. 92). There, faith is not alone.

Nevertheless, we wish here simply to establish and not critically to
engage the fact that there is in the Pentecostal movement a developed
doctrine of the free character of the baptism in the Holy Spirit by
faith alone.

iii. The Price or Cost Character of the Gift of the Spirit. Side by
side with the teaching just discussed exists another variation in the
intricate Pentecostal doctrine of conditions. This variation seems to
stand in almost exact contradiction to the prior doctrine, is equally
well attested, and requires therefore to be heard in this context. It
is the teaching of the high price or cost of the baptism in the Holy

---

[70] By Riggs, for example, the conditions are (1) regeneration, (2) obedience,
(3) prayer, and *then* (4) faith. *Spirit Himself,* pp. 102-12.
[71] *Upon All Flesh: A Pentecostal World Tour* (Springfield, Mo.: Gospel Publishing House, 1935), p. 65.

Spirit. Dalton gives expression to this teaching when he writes (p. 70) that "this experience is not for a select few, but for all who desire it and are willing to pay the price." Under the principle of price, furthermore, the conditions are usually made so entire as to place in deeper question the doctrine of faith alone in connection with the baptism in the Holy Spirit. A certain felt ambivalence and a definite ambiguity in the coordination of the incoordinates "free" and "cost" may be observed in the following testimony by a Pentecostal concerning her baptism in the Spirit.

> I could say then, as I can today after more than thirty-five years, "It was worth it all — worth all it cost." In fact, it cost me nothing. The joy and blessing so far outweigh the suffering of "counting the cost" and making the consecration He asked, that it was not to be compared.[72]

It appears that it can be said by Pentecostals of the baptism in the Holy Spirit that it costs absolutely nothing, not because it does not cost anything but because, in comparison with the benefit received, it is as though it costs nothing.

A like ambivalence may be found still more clearly in a pair of remarks by Skibstedt on the conditions for the spiritual baptism. First of all he stresses with all Pentecostalism the entire absence of merit in the person or work of the recipient, who "is of course conscious of the fact that this experience was not given to him because of any kind of merit but out of undeserved grace" (p. 84). But later in the same book he writes, "This experience outweighs more than sufficiently all the sacrifice which we must bring, all the seemingly allowable relations from which we must separate ourselves" (p. 112). The "musts" are noteworthy. The Pentecostal doctrine of the price of the spiritual baptism and the necessity of the candidate's paying this price is simply confusing when placed beside the following not unrepresentative Pentecostal affirmation (Riggs, pp. 64-65, emphasis his):

> All these scriptures [in Acts] emphasize the fact that this glorious experience is a gift from Heaven and is to be had by simple receiving on our part. Paul said in Gal. 3:14, "that we might *receive* the promise of the Spirit through faith" — *not* by works of righteousness which we have done; *not* by our own holiness or merit; *not* as a reward for any fasting and prayer; *not* as payment to us in any way whatsoever; but as

---

[72] Edna Garvin, "Five Words That Changed My Life," *Pentecostal Evangel, 48* (June 5, 1960), 23. In the same issue there is a religious cartoon with the caption "There's A Price to Pay," featuring the letters of "PENTE*COST*" with the last four letters ("cost") heightened and supplied with representative costs. *Ibid.,* p. 20. Cf. in Stanley H. Frodsham's biography of his wife, *Jesus Is Victor: A Story of Grace, Gladness and Glory in the Life of Alice M. Frodsham* (Springfield, Mo.: Gospel Publishing House, 1930), a sentence of Mrs. Frodsham's in a letter to her sister: " 'To get this experience costs all, and to keep it costs all — but it is worth it,' " p. 46. Cf. on the teaching of cost, Murray, *Spirit of Christ,* pp. 141, 323-24; *Back to Pentecost,* pp. 11-13, 36-44, 71.

a sheer gift of His infinite grace and love. He is offered to us freely without money and without price [n.b.]. We merely extend our hand of faith, lay hold on Him, appropriate Him, and receive Him as our own.

We can only conclude that the doctrine of faith-alone stands uncomfortable, uncoordinated, and Gemini-like beside the doctrine of cost.

iv. The Anti *Sola Fide* Polemic. Further complicating the cogency of the faith-condition is the fact that in some quarters of the Pentecostal movement a vigorous denial of the rightness of receiving the baptism in the Holy Spirit by faith alone may be encountered. In these cases the spurious "faith baptism," as it is called, is contrasted with the authentic Pentecostal baptism. The Englishman Horton, for example, writing of the spiritual baptisms enjoyed by the Acts' personalities comments, "They received because they would not be put off with a 'faith' Baptism. They would not be content with less than a Power Baptism."[73]

The most articulate voice for this particular persuasion was Mrs. Aimee Semple McPherson, the colorful Canadian-American Pentecostal evangelist of a generation ago. She once wrote, "We all know that that which we need above all else is a real genuine baptism of the Holy Ghost! *Not* just the theory, the 'take-it-by-faith-believe-you-have-it-and-go-on-experience.' We have tried this substitute too long."[74] Mrs. McPherson, with other Pentecostals, contended that in apostolic times the baptism of the Holy Spirit "was a sharp, well-defined experience. So it is today."[75]

Thus a "'faith' baptism" unaccompanied by any experience except faith itself is not sufficiently sharp and well defined to meet the standards of the biblical baptism in the Spirit. But the Pentecostal glossolalic baptism with its clear marks does meet the biblical standards. Since Pentecostals see that the spiritual baptism in the New Testament was a veritable *experience,* they fear that to make this event a matter of faith *alone* is to endanger its experiential character. But since it is impossible to have a glossolalic baptism and not feel it, Pentecostals believe that they have ensured the essentially experiential nature of

---

[73] *Gifts of the Spirit*[2], p. 223. As might be anticipated, the polemic against faith alone sometimes takes the form of a resistance to the doctrine of Christ alone, if this doctrine is understood apart from the baptism of the Holy Spirit. Cf. Barratt, *Fire*, p. 191. Ray H. Hughes believes that one of the most prominent errors of the present charismatic renewal (Neo-Pentecostalism) is the "teaching that the Holy Spirit is received by faith alone." Adding, "to be sure, everything we receive from God must be received by faith. But faith alone is not sufficient. The temple (body) must be prepared for the reception of the Spirit." "Glossolalia in Contemporary Times," in *The Glossolalia Phenomenon*, ed. Wade H. Horton (Cleveland, Tenn.: Pathway, 1966), p. 169.

[74] *This Is That*, p. 713.

[75] *The Foursquare Gospel* (Los Angeles: Echo Park Evangelistic Association, 1946), p. 195. Cf. also her *Holy Spirit*, pp. 179-80.

the baptism in the Spirit. Thus the Pentecostal polemic against faith-alone is to be interpreted in this sense: faith must be faith with an experience, indeed, with the glossolalic experience, to be adequate, New Testament, Pentecostal, and real.

The most recent prominent Pentecostal protest against *sola fide* to come to our attention occurred in the Mission Lectures at Princeton Theological Seminary in the Fall of 1959. The lecturer was David duPlessis whose concluding words in the final lecture contain both the anti *sola fide* theme and the Pentecostal appeals of more, power, and evangelization.

> In contrast to all that [in Pentecostal experience], is the vagueness that spreads over nearly all modern doctrine and experience of the Holy Spirit among Christians. It can scarcely be otherwise when the Baptism in the Holy Spirit is either denied as a spiritual crisis for the believer, or else kept as a blessing to be appropriated simply by faith, along with a warning against emotionalism. True and splendid things are being said and written by Christian leaders of our day, but when the supreme problem of the churches is the powerlessness of their members, little will be accomplished until the membership is truly revived. We need an every-member *salvation*, followed by an every-member *baptism in the Spirit*, which will produce an every-member *evangelism*, that will again *turn the world upside down*.[76]

v. The Result. The full appropriation of the baptism in the Holy Spirit according to the majority teaching of the Pentecostal movement must be accompanied by the glossolalic experience of Acts. Ordinary Christian faith does not usually qualify for this appropriation because it is (1) directed toward Christ and not the Spirit, and is (2) insufficiently total. It is in this last category — totality — that we believe we have the major clue to the Pentecostal understanding of faith as a condition for the baptism in the Holy Spirit. Faith, in the Pentecostal view, is not a mere trusting, it is absolute surrender. It is for this reason that Pentecostals can seriously speak of "faith alone," for what they understand under faith is not what has been normally understood by this word. Since faith-as-absolute-surrender, by Pentecostal definition, never takes on the character of faith until it is absolute, it can be said that faith alone (understood as this kind of faith) grants the experience of the Pentecostal baptism.

The definition of faith, then, provides the solution to the enigma of what Pentecostalism means by speaking of both the candidate's faith alone *and* his costly sacrifice as the means to the gift of the Spirit.[77] For until the glossolalic baptism occurs, the Christian's faith

---

[76] "The Holy Spirit in the Mission of the Church," printed now in duPlessis' *The Spirit Bade Me Go: The Astounding Move of God in the Denominational Churches* (Dallas: Privately Printed, 1961), p. 62, emphasis his.

[77] See the definition of faith in Finney's *Lectures on Systematic Theology*, pp. 390, 400, and Documents, below, p. 333. See also Torrey's joining of faith

must have been imperfect, and therefore, in the Pentecostal under-standing, not really faith. When faith becomes as nearly absolute as it can — that is, practically speaking, when it becomes very intense — then it experiences glossolalia and then it is really faith. In this intense sense, Pentecostals mean faith alone. And in this sense, it can be seen how faith becomes glossolalic. Intensity and ecstasy are not strangers.

The difference between ordinary Christian faith and Pentecostal faith, then, is that the former is confessed lack and the latter is attempted totality. The former is simple and all too shallow; the latter is complex and deep. The former confesses bankruptcy; the latter costs. The former is the despair of all effort; the latter is superhuman effort. And if faith can be defined in their way, then Pentecostals can say that it is by faith that one experiences the baptism in the Holy Spirit.

4. ADDITIONAL APOLOGETICAL AND EXPERIENTIAL BASES FOR THE DOCTRINE OF CONDITIONS

The case for the Pentecostal conditions, in addition to the defense of the general conditions already considered above, usually culminates in a two-fold argument for the necessity of preparation and of ap-preciation.

a. *The Necessity of Preparation.* An often suggested explanation for what to non-Pentecostals is curious — the placing of faith in a context of intense spiritual works for the securing of the promised Holy Spirit — is the Pentecostals' persuasion that these works are preparatory to faith and make the ultimate act of faith simpler. Ben-jamin Baur gives expression to this idea: "If, upon searching your heart you find that you are truly submissive to the revealed will of God and in harmony with your fellow man..., *then* it will be easy for you to exercise that simple and childlike faith in the Lord that will bring a quick response from Him" (emphasis added).[78]

Obedience facilitates faith. This is why it will be noticed that faith is not infrequently placed at the end of Pentecostal lists. For when the necessary obediences have been carried out, *then* one can believe that God will fulfill his promise. Speaking of the prior good works of Cornelius, Conn insists evangelically that it was not these good works which obtained for him the spiritual baptism: "Cornelius was

---

"apart from the works of the law" with obedience, in one of his lists of condi-tions for the baptism of the Holy Spirit in the Documents, below, p. 336.

[78] In Robert Chandler Dalton, *Tongues Like As of Fire: A Critical Study of Modern Tongue Movements...* (Springfield, Mo.: Gospel Publishing House, 1945), p. 74. Note this sequence also in Pethrus: "When all conscious sin has been taken away, then we really are in a place where it becomes easy to trust Him." *Wind*², p. 44. Also Barratt, *Rain*, pp. 214-15.

... punctilious in his works. Yet that did not bring the Holy Ghost into his heart." But then Conn adds pentecostally, "What it did bring him was an opportunity for the hearing of faith" (*Pillars,* p. 98). Cornelius' works did not bring the Holy Spirit to him, but they did bring the *opportunity* for the Holy Spirit to come to him.

So far, then, from being hindered by works, faith, in the Pentecostal interpretation, is assisted by them in its reception of the divine gift. Faith, it is believed, does not exclude works in the reception of God's gift of the Spirit; faith can and should accompany works; but faith's special place in relation to works in Pentecostal development immediately follows works as the effect follows its causes. This understanding may be observed in Riggs' significant sequence (and one should mark again the word "then"): "So we first make sure that we are right with God. Then we cease from our own works or efforts, and apply to Him for the gift which we seek. He is waiting for us to come to this point" (p. 106).

It is felt that God waits for Christians to come to this point in order to use the preparatory period for teaching Christians spiritual lessons. "God," writes Skibstedt (p. 124), "has very many lessons for us in humility and patience when he at first keeps back his gifts and blessings which we think should be always fully available." When believers must attempt again and again to receive God's gifts it is not due to any reluctance in God to give us his gifts freely; rather, Pentecostals mean, it is God's will to instruct us, through these very attempts and by his delay, in important spiritual matters. Through patient submission to the requisite conditions, the candidate for the Pentecostal baptism is initiated into spiritual attitudes conducive to the divine experience.

There is no stipulated length for this important preparatory period. The only constant is consecration — total, perfect, absolute consecration. "The act of preparation," writes Barratt, "may take place very speedily, when there is simplicity enough and perfect consecration on the part of the seeker" (*Rain,* p. 63). And those who are obliged to wait for long periods will in the end, it is confided, have no regret because of the lessons that are learned in the interim. However, the usual rule is that the more entire the consecration, the more rapid the baptism.

b. *The Necessity of Appreciation.* It is urged, secondly, that only that which is earnestly sought is deeply appreciated. "The more we inwardly seek a gift from God and the more we must therefore sacrifice in order to receive it," writes Skibstedt (p. 124), "by just that much more will we know how to value the gift when we have received it." Gee concurs and at the same time underlines the high importance of the doctrine of cost in Pentecostal theology: "The fact remains that things which are obtained cheaply are held cheaply; while that for which a great price is paid becomes a precious treasure for ever" (*Pentecostal Movement,* p. 151). This persuasion can, of course, only with difficulty (or, as we saw, with a change in definitions) be reconciled with the free or faith-alone character of the gift of the Spirit. Nevertheless, Pentecostalism believes that its conditions are justified, if they need further justification, by the common-sense laws of gratitude.

5. UNDEVELOPED INSTITUTIONS: THE LAYING ON OF HANDS AND BAPTISM

What seems to be important in the extraordinary impartation of the Holy Spirit according to the accounts in Acts, the apostolic laying on of hands, receives surprisingly little attention in most Pentecostal lists of conditions and, when interpreted, is usually understood as simply a sympathetic aid toward the more important and inward act of faith or emptying. Though the laying on of hands is rarely mentioned in Pentecostal literature we have never witnessed a Pentecostal tarrying meeting in which the laying on of hands by the leader, and usually also by as many participants as possible, has not played a very important role in the preliminary inducement or encouragement of the Pentecostal experience. The Pentecostal, of course, denies that the gift of the Spirit was an apostolic prerogative and believes that as the laying on of hands was unnecessary at Pentecost, so, on principle, it is equally unnecessary today as an *indispensable* condition for the reception of the Pentecostal gift of the Spirit.[79]

Similarly, what seems central to the ordinary impartation of the Holy Spirit in Acts and in the whole of the New Testament — baptism — is comparatively little discussed in connection with the crisis gift of the Spirit in Pentecostalism, though baptism itself seems often important in Pentecostal practice. Baptism is invariably understood as simply an outward, but a dramatic and earnest symbol of a more important inward fact or, what is much the same thing, it is understood as a confession of the Christian's sincere obedience and faith.

Perhaps the most succinct exposition of the distinction between ordinary Christian baptism and the extraordinary Pentecostal baptism in the Holy Spirit may be found in Skibstedt's analysis.

---

[79] See discussions in Riggs, *Spirit Himself,* pp. 109-10; Reed, "Pentecostal Truths," p. 18; Fischer, "Progress of the Various Modern Pentecostal Movements," pp. 60-61. It is of interest to note that the first apparently definite Pentecostal baptism in the Holy Spirit in the current Pentecostal movement — that of Miss Agnes Ozman (see below, p. 119) — occurred through the laying on of hands. Surprisingly, there is no section in the otherwise detailed *Hollenweger* on the laying on of hands. There is occasional emphasis in Neo-Pentecostalism. See, e.g., Charles Farah, "The Laying On of Hands and the Reception of the Holy Spirit," *View,* No. 1 (1966), 1-9.

The difference between the two baptisms is that commitment receives a more symbolic interpretation in water-baptism while in Spirit-baptism the consecration is felt *experientially*. In water-baptism *we* bear witness that we firmly trust *God's* promises of grace. In Spirit-baptism, however, *God* confesses himself openly to *us* as the apostle Peter explains in relation to the converts in Cornelius' house: "God who knows the heart bore witness to them, giving them the Holy Spirit just as he did to us" (Acts 15:8).[80]

Baptism, then, is understood as primarily the *believer's* deed and therefore as essentially a human event; on the other hand, the baptism in the Holy Spirit (viewed as a separate fact by Pentecostals) is understood as primarily God's doing, and as a divine event crowning the believer's prior consecration. It should be mentioned finally in this connection that most, though not all, Pentecostal bodies practice believer-baptism, by immersion, as a symbol of the believer's obedience and faith.[81]

Both the churchly laying on of hands and baptism are understood in most Pentecostal groups, then, as institutions which are primarily symbolic and external. The Pentecostal institutions of obedience and faith, on the other hand, are understood as real inner events (and not mere outward forms) which are deeply experienced by the actual recipients and not ritually superimposed by others.

6. SUMMARY AND CONCLUSION

In summary we may say that the Pentecostal conditions are necessary both to explain and to obtain the subsequent baptism in the Holy Spirit with its glossolalic evidence. The source of the doctrine of conditions is Acts and other biblical passages which teach a connection between the gift of the Spirit and conversion, obedience, prayer, and faith.

Conversion is the indispensable pre-condition for the Pentecostal

---

[80] *Geistestaufe,* p. 60. Note similar teaching outside of Pentecostalism, below, p. 185.

[81] The major reason for the rejection of infant baptism is represented in the *Reglamento local:* the infant "is unable to give a clear testimony of his faith in Jesus Christ," p. 18. The only apparent exceptions to the rule of believer-baptism are the Iglesia Metodista Pentecostal de Chile, the Iglesia Pentecostal de Chile (*Hollenweger* II, 981, 988), the Pentecostal Holiness Church in the United States (Kendrick, *Promise,* p. 185; the mode is optional), the Christlicher Gemeinschaftsverband Mülheim-Ruhr in Germany and the Kristova Duhovna Crkva 'Malkrštenih' in Yugoslavia (Hollenweger, "The Pentecostal Movement and the World Council of Churches," *EcRev, 18* [July 1966], 311). For the doctrine of baptism, generally, see Bloch-Hoell, *Pentecostal Movement,* pp. 164-67. The symbolic understanding of both the sacraments is universally Pentecostal; see, e.g., the confessions of faith in two of the largest Brazilian Pentecostal bodies in *Hollenweger* II, 898, 916. Note, however, baptism's importance for initiation — even its centrality — in some Pentecostal denominations, particularly in the Brazilian Congregação Cristã no Brasil (the "Glorias"), Read, *New Patterns of Church Growth in Brazil,* pp. 25-28.

baptism. Obedience — both active (with the goal of a sinless heart) and passive (with the goal of self-emptying) — is the Christian's essential preparation for the baptism in the Holy Spirit. When the obedience is complete the Christian should have faith. The faith which Pentecostalism prizes in this connection is not usually identical with initial Christian faith; it is a different kind or at least a different act of faith, directed primarily toward the Holy Spirit with a new quantitative intensity, and is as such neither *sola* nor *simplex*. It is a faith added to a preparatory obedience which, with this obedience, pays the price of sacrificial commitment necessary for acquiring and for appreciating the gift of the Holy Spirit. Pentecostal faith is best described as *ultima fides*.

In conversation with Pentecostalism it is usually at this point — namely, that conditions beyond "saving" faith and before and including "ultimate" faith are necessary for the reception of the Spirit — that the Christian in the Reformation tradition finds the greatest difficulty in accompaniment and where his objectivity is most tested and his sympathies most strained. For the Pentecostal may place (what may seem to us to be) an extraordinary stress upon experience and, if he wishes for himself, even upon the experience of tongues; and he may even, perhaps, locate (what may seem to us to be uncalled-for) spiritual blessings beyond baptism and, if he wishes for himself, even the fuller appropriation of the Holy Spirit — in neither case will we be pleased, but in neither case will we bristle with anathemas. But when one is asked to appropriate these or any other benefits outside of or in addition to the simple faith which apprehends Christ (or the simple grace by which Christ apprehends us) through obedience however exemplary or faith however entire, then the Protestant is compelled to enter not simply an analysis of the Pentecostal movement but a criticism as well.

And as we enter this criticism we shall, in effect, be entering into theological criticism of an evangelicalism of which Pentecostalism is simply a recent expression and a logical and theological consequence. The degree to which this evangelicalism shares with Pentecostalism the major presuppositions of the Spirit's work may be observed in reading many conservative-evangelical treatments of the doctrine of the Holy Spirit. In the following citation from the work of a major North American conservative evangelical, Dr. Harold Ockenga's *The Spirit of the Living God,* we are provided a particularly synoptic account of this doctrine of the Spirit.

> Not only are we to have the Spirit indwelling us, but filling us. This filling, however, is contingent upon several things. It is necessary for us to yield Him authority in our lives. That means supplanting self will with the will of God. ... Nothing, I think, is more difficult. This means the crucifixion of our old selves, our desires, ambitions, prejudices, love of ease, and

kindred habits. . . . The filling of the Spirit, then, is contingent upon our asking God to give us of His Spirit. . . . The disciples were filled with the Spirit after a ten-day prayer meeting, and Andrew Murray reminds us that in every case in the New Testament where the disciples were filled with the Holy Spirit it was after they had prayed to be filled. This, no doubt, was willed of God that we might show an appreciation for His highest and best gift, that we should ask to be filled with His Spirit. Do not expect that at the first simple request you will receive the choicest and most precious gift God has for any one. When ultimately, however, we have really asked, He expects us to receive that promise in faith, in order that the evidences of the fulness of the Spirit may appear. We are then to close by faith with God for His gift of the Spirit as we did close with Him in faith for the salvation purchased for us by Jesus Christ. There comes a time when we may really expect to accept and trust God for the fulness of His Spirit for the work which He has asked us to do. We are not to dishonor Him by lack of faith.[82]

---

[82] (New York: Fleming H. Revell Co., 1947), pp. 136-38. Ockenga's ideas in more recent treatments have not altered — they are, if anything, more thoroughly developed, though nowhere as succinctly stated. In *Power through Pentecost* ("Preaching for Today"; Grand Rapids, Mich.: Wm. B. Eerdmans Publishing Co., 1959) Ockenga remarks that he has "come to the conclusion that it is necessary for Christians to enter the deeper life by a critical experience if they are to enjoy all that God has for them" (p. 8). We may summarize his more recent teaching on this experience, as treated in *Power through Pentecost,* as follows.

(1) The doctrine of *subsequence.* "Every Christian has the Holy Spirit (Rom. 8:9). But it is one thing to receive the Holy Spirit and it is another thing to be filled with the Spirit and thus equipped for service" (p. 57). Cornelius, Acts 10, "shows us that in the Gentile Church it is possible for the self-conscious believer who is ethically righteous [n.b.] to receive the fullness of the Spirit at the same time that he hears about Jesus Christ. Quite generally this is not the order. Generally a person must have a conscious regeneration before he seeks to be filled with the Spirit and enters the deeper life. When his hunger and thirst for righteousness intensifies, when he prays that the Lord will meet his need, when he exercises himself unto godliness in the full evidence of his understanding, we may be sure that the Lord will lead him to someone who will tell him the full truth of the Gospel that he may be filled with the Spirit" (pp. 70-71).

(2) The doctrine of *evidence.* "We may know when we are Spirit-filled because of the resultant life of victory and of power attended by the fruits of the Spirit" (p. 81).

(3) The doctrine of *conditions.* "There is a formula in the Bible for each of the Christian's major spiritual experiences: for the assurance of regeneration, for prayer, for God's blessing upon the programme of the local church, and for the Spirit-filled life. There are five elements in this formula by which we may appropriate Pentecost. They are confession, consecration, prayer, faith and obedience" (p. 22). "As a prerequisite of being filled with the Spirit, it is necessary for a Christian to surrender everything to Christ. This may be called consecration, yieldedness, or surrender. Actually, it means that he has sold out everything for Christ's sake. . . . He is buying the spiritual life at a great cost, namely the cost of everything" (p. 23). "Men do not care enough for power to pay the price of receiving the blessing. . . . There is a price to pay for power" (p. 95). "The Spirit came historically at Pentecost and it is not necessary for us to tarry for the coming of the Spirit in our day. Nevertheless, there is much that can be said for protracted prayer meetings in order to meet the conditions which are

One may notice in this quotation the several features shared with Pentecostalism: the idea of subsequence: here "filling" beyond "indwelling," and later the "gift" after "salvation"; conditionality: "contingent," "necessary"; the several conditions of obedience: "crucifixion of our old selves" (active obedience); "supplanting self will" (passive obedience); prayer: "asking God," plus the heightened importunate prayer: "really ask[ing]"; the condition of faith: "ultimately"!; and even a modified doctrine of "evidences": speaking in tongues, however, is not meant — the victorious-life is the usual criterion; and finally, a doctrine of "appreciation."

Pentecostalism has inherited and carried to its consequences the legacy of a type of Christianity which dates at least from Wesley, perhaps from Puritanism. In our engagement with Pentecostalism, therefore, we shall indirectly be conversing with its major predecessors and its modern relatives in the circle of ideas connected with the Spirit.

---

necessary for us to be filled with the Holy Spirit or to know the Pentecostal experience" (pp. 31-32).

REPRESENTATIVE EXPERIENCES OF THE PENTECOSTAL BAPTISM IN THE HOLY SPIRIT

A. INTRODUCTION

We think that it may be helpful to append actually recorded experiences of the glossolalic baptism in the Holy Spirit by Pentecostals and by a representative Neo-Pentecostal. Here, apart from the analysis and the systematic dissection of the many-sided doctrine which have preceded, we should be able to see the parts in a larger whole and to observe in a more organic way the entering and the understanding of the Pentecostal baptism.

We have selected representative figures. Miss Ozman was the first personality understood to have experienced the Pentecostal baptism in its presently defined form.[1] Mr. Bartleman has given us the only available firsthand account of the important and standard Los Angeles beginnings of the Pentecostal movement. In doing so he includes a somewhat cryptic allusion to his own experience. The purveyor of the Pentecostal movement from America to Europe, T. B. Barratt, is not as reticent in relating his experience. The manifold feelings and impressions on his long road to the goal fill a good part of his book and of this appendix. The most celebrated Pentecostal to date was no doubt the controversial and able Mrs. Aimee Semple McPherson, evangelist and founder of the International Church of the Foursquare Gospel, an important denomination within the Pentecostal movement. She records not only her own experience but, in her large volume *This Is That* (800 pages), she relates innumerable occurrences of the baptism in the Holy Spirit in the course of her nation-wide evangelistic ministry, providing an invaluable profile of the phenomena common to the experience. Finally, as we have suggested earlier, the Pentecostal experience is, through Neo-Pentecostalism, widening its sphere of influence in the larger church. The recorded experience of the Baptist pastor John Osteen serves as an example of the appeal of the Pentecostal distinctive to Christians from other denominations.[2]

---

[1] Kendrick, *Promise*, p. 53. Cf. Bloch-Hoell, *Pentecostal Movement*, pp. 23-24; Sherrill, *They Speak with Other Tongues*, p. 38. For other records of the Pentecostal baptism in the Holy Spirit from within the Pentecostal movement we may refer to Stanley H. Frodsham's *With Signs Following*, which is almost entirely a collection of Pentecostal experiences.

[2] For other Neo-Pentecostal accounts see *Full Gospel Business Men's Voice,*

We have supplied the margin to the testimony with a key through which the reader may be directed in the text to a more systematic discussion of the material under consideration. In the margin, the key words appear as nearly opposite the material they index as possible and only the more inclusive categories are used.

Key

B. TESTIMONY

1. THE FIRST RECIPIENT: MISS AGNES OZMAN (1901)

Methodist
Holiness
Evangelicals

One of the students who was to occupy a unique place in the beginning of Modern Pentecost was Agnes N. Ozman.... Though she had been raised in the Methodist Church, Agnes had become associated ... with the Holiness movement.... She attended for one year A. B. Simpson's Bible school in New York.... She attended John Alexander Dowie's services in Zion City, Illinois. These experiences fired her with evangelical enthusiasm, so that she continued mission work in Nebraska and then in Kansas City. At this latter place she heard of the opening of Bethel Bible College and decided to join the student body.... About 7:00 p.m. [January 1, 1901] when meditating in her devotions, Agnes Ozman was reminded that believers in the New Testament church were "baptized in the Spirit" on several occasions when hands were laid on them. Acting on an impulse when [Charles] Parham re-

Acts

1953ff.; the journals mentioned in note 45, p. 53, above; Sherrill's *They Speak with Other Tongues,* and the Ranaghans' *Catholic Pentecostals.* Particular attention may be directed to the publications of the Full Gospel Business Men's Fellowship International, edited by Jerry Jensen: *Presbyterians and the Baptism of the Holy Spirit* (1963); *Methodists and the Baptism of the Holy Spirit* (1963); *Baptists and the Baptism of the Holy Spirit* (1963); *Episcopalians and the Baptism in the Holy Spirit* (1964); *Lutherans and the Baptism in the Holy Spirit* (1966); *Catholics and the Baptism in the Holy Spirit* (1968).

Laying On of Hands

Tongues
More

Seeking

Evidence

turned from the mission, she asked Parham to lay hands upon her in biblical fashion. Refusing the request at first, he finally relented and said a short prayer as he laid his hands on her. According to Miss Ozman's own testimony: "It was as his hands were laid upon my head that the Holy Spirit fell upon me and I began to speak in tongues, glorifying God. I talked several languages, and it was clearly manifest when a new dialect was spoken. I had the added joy and glory my heart longed for and a depth of the presence of the Lord within that I had never known before. It was as if rivers of living waters were proceeding from my innermost being. . . . I was the first one to speak in tongues in the Bible school. . . . I told them not to seek for tongues but to seek for the Holy Ghost." Although Agnes Ozman was not the first person in modern times to speak in "tongues," she was the first known person to have received such an experience as a result of specifically seeking a baptism in the Holy Spirit with the expectation of speaking in tongues. From this time Pentecostal believers were to teach that the "baptism in the Holy Spirit" should be sought and that it would be received with the evidence of "tongues." For this reason the experience of Agnes Ozman is designated as the beginning of the Modern Pentecostal Revival.[3]

2. A LOS ANGELES RECIPIENT: MR. FRANK BARTLEMAN (1906)

Yielding

Power for Service

Yielding

Yielding

Oh, the thrill of being fully yielded to Him! My mind had always been very active. Its natural workings had caused me most of my trouble in my Christian experience. "Casting down reasonings" (marginal reading, II Cor. 10:5). Nothing hinders faith and the operation of the Spirit so much as the self-assertiveness of the human spirit, the wisdom, strength and self-sufficiency of the human mind. This must be crucified, and here is where the fight comes in. We must become utterly undone, insufficient and helpless in our own consciousness, thoroughly humbled, before we can receive this possession of the Holy Spirit. We want the Holy Ghost, but the fact is He is wanting possession of us. In the experience of "speaking in tongues" I had reached the climax in abandonment. This opened the channel for a new ministry of the Spirit in service. From that time the Spirit began to flow through me in a new way. . . . I had not the slightest difficulty in speaking in "tongues." And yet I can understand how some may have such difficulties. They are not fully yielded to God. With me the battle had been long drawn out. I had already worn myself out, fully yielded. . . . I never sought "tongues." My natural mind resisted the idea. This phenomena [sic] necessarily violates human reason. It means abandonment of this faculty for the time. And this is generally the last point to yield. The human mind is held in abeyance fully in this exercise.

[3] Kendrick, *Promise*, **pp. 48-49, 52-53.**

And this is "foolishness," and a stone of stumbling, to the natural mind or reason. It is supernatural. We need not expect anyone who has not reached this depth of abandonment in his human spirit, this death to his own reason, to either accept or understand it. The natural reason must be yielded in this matter. There is a gulf to cross, between reason and revelation. But this principle in experience is just that which leads to the "Pentecostal"

Acts

baptism, as in Acts 2:4. It is the underlying principle of the "baptism." And this is why the simple people get in first. . . . They are like the little boys going swimming. . . . They get in first because they have the least clothes to divest themselves of. We must come "naked" into this experience. All of self is gone.[4]

3. THE RECEPTION BY THE EUROPEAN FATHER OF THE PENTECOSTAL MOVEMENT: PASTOR T. B. BARRATT (1906)

More

When praying I constantly felt the need of a *still greater blessing over my own soul!* [all emphasis is his] I stood and had from youth been standing, for holiness and the baptism of the Holy Ghost, and had no doubt often felt somewhat of the fire burning within, a touch of the unseen hand, but I knew there must be a *still deeper work and a constant victory.* All the trials I had passed through during the last year . . . brought me down — deeper down,

Seeking

before the Lord, seeking, praying, weeping in His presence, thirsting for a full baptism of the Holy Ghost — *the experience itself,* and not only the intense longing for it. . . .

Evangelicals

At a meeting where Mr. Lyal spoke at Dr. Simpson's hall, I asked them to pray for me, that my heart might be filled with the Spirit of God. However, what I first needed

Heart-purification
Preparation

was to *be cleansed in the blood of Jesus,* so that I could *believe* I was purified from all my sins. O, my dear friend, if you have been there, you know that this battle may be just as hard, possibly more so, than when you at first sought the Lord. — Sunday, eight days ago, after a long struggle on my knees, I took the Bible to the window, and my eyes fell on something there, enabling me immedi-

Heart-purification

ately to grasp *full cleansing through the blood of my precious Saviour.* — This lasted until Tuesday: then a letter came from Los Angeles. I will let you have it here. It is a remarkable letter. I read it over and over again: [We have already reproduced the letter, cf. p. 100 above.]
After having received this letter, I made up my mind that I would have the same blessing that is spoken of in

Acts

Acts 2:4 and that the friends in Los Angeles had received. I needed it both to live for God and to work for him.

Separation from Sin

Though I really had given up all before I was cleansed, still so many things came back to my memory from my past life, that I really felt sad, but I believed that Jesus

Heart-purification

had purified my heart "by *faith,*" Acts 15:9. . . . I had

---

4 Bartleman, *How Pentecost Came to Los Angeles*[2], pp. 72-75.

Acts

noticed, at times on Sunday, a remarkable warmth in my breast, but it left me. Whilst weeping Sunday afternoon, a little before five p.m., the fire came back to my breast. I had my face in a towel, so as not to disturb the inmates next door, but it did not last long ere I shouted so loudly, that they must have heard me afar off, had it not been for the noise in the street. I was bathed a while in perspiration. (They no doubt shouted aloud in the house of Cornelius — "loudly magnified God," Norwegian translation — Acts 10:46.) I could not help it; I was *seized by the Holy Power of God throughout my whole being,* and it swept through my whole body as well. Then I remembered the advice given in the letter from Los Angeles concerning the body, but I was not afraid — I was willing to die. In order to be sure that this was the work of God, I laid my hand on my pulse: The beat was as even as usual. I drank a glass of water, but the storm went on. I then got hold of Bro. Lyal, but could scarcely say a word when he came in. Then my whole body shook under the great workings of the Spirit.... I thought surely that I had received the full Pentecostal Baptism, as many do in our day, who have passed through a similar experience.... Everything seemed changed, although I had not as yet entered into the full Pentecostal glory.... I did not know, even then, that a still greater blessing was held in store for me — the *full* Baptism in the Holy Ghost and Fire!... I did not expect tongues as a definite sign of the Pentecostal blessing, but the friends at Los Angeles wrote and said I must press on to get the gift of tongues.... I want the *finished work.* In one sense *never finished* on earth, but the Pentecostal testimony or seal (gift of tongues) *to the power, and still more power!*... Former letters told of persecution, even from the Methodists, but I was told that *"the Holy Ghost only comes in when you come to an end of yourself."—* They were delighted to hear of my experience. I quote a few lines of a letter: ... "The speaking in tongues should follow the baptism. If you had remained under the power, until the Lord had finished, you undoubtedly would have spoken in tongues, not necessarily for use in a foreign field, but as a sign to you of Pentecost, the same as at the house of Cornelius and at Ephesus. Some go several days after the baptism before speaking, but unless you do speak, there is always a tendency to lead out — a leak-hole for the devil to tempt you. While we are getting a *Bible experience,* we may as well go all the way with Jesus and measure up in every particular. Many here have taken the stand, that speaking in tongues was not necessary, and after being highly anointed have claimed their Pentecost, but their power was limited and nearly all have seen their error and tarried until they spake in tongues. May the Lord bless and use you." ... I had not received any teaching concerning the tongues as a special sign of Pentecost before, in the circles where I had hitherto been.... The Lord showed me nevertheless, through this break in my

More

Evidence

More

Yielding

Evidence
Acts

Power

Evidence

experience, that it is possible to receive great anointings of the Spirit, without speaking in tongues, but that if we receive the *full* Pentecostal Baptism, as they "at the beginning," it will be a greater infilling, accompanied with tongues, prophetic language (Acts 19:6), loud praises (Acts 10:46). In the Norwegian version: "høilig prise Gud," that is: praising God loudly, but especially *tongues, which was to be the special sign of the new dispensation,* all other signs having been found among the believers before Pentecost (Mark 16:16). I wrote therefore in my account home, that "it appears to me, that when I spoke in tongues it was in connection with a power which was far beyond all that I had experienced before, that my former experience was a *glorious introduction,*" to the *Baptism in the Holy Ghost and Fire,* which I received on the 15th of November, 1906. I possibly made a mistake on the 7th of October, and disturbed the workings of the Spirit, by expecting help from others. At any rate I had to wait more than a month before the Power was turned on again, as it were, in an ever increasing degree, until I burst forth in tongues and loudly magnified God, in the Power of the Holy Spirit. This time nothing interfered with the workings of the Divine Spirit, and as a result, the same outward sign of the Spirit's presence was *seen* and *heard* as on the Day of Pentecost in Jerusalem, Hallelujah! I learnt also, that the change wrought in our lives, by the Holy Spirit, when we become the children of God (regenerated), was a different experience to the *Baptism* in the Holy Ghost, when He *fills* us, and immerses us into His own being — body, soul and spirit.... My description [in Barratt's written report to Norway] of the Baptism was as follows: "... I waited about a week after having received the mighty anointing on the 7th of October, still looking for the manifestation of tongues, but nothing happened.... Over and over again the enemy tempted me with the thought, that the *manifestation of tongues was not for me....* The reason why it took such a time was because I doubted whether I could receive the tongues, and the thought of such a strange thing taking place — that I should suddenly speak in an unknown tongue, this alone was sufficient to hinder the work of the Spirit in me. As some special manifestation in my jaws and tongue took place, my faith was strengthened, little by little, to believe that the speaking in tongues would soon be given me.... There were not many at the evening meeting, but God's power was mightily manifested. I asked the leader of the meeting, a little before 12 o'clock to lay hands on me and pray for me. Immediately the power of God began to work in my body, as well as in my spirit. I was like Daniel, powerless under the Divine touch (Dan. 10:8) and had to lean upon the table on the platform, where I was sitting, and slid down to the floor. Again my speaking organs began to move, but there was no voice to be heard. I asked a brother, a Norwegian, who had often heard me preach in

Acts

Evidence

Subsequence

Laying On of Hands

Christiania, and the doctor's wife, to pray for me once more. 'Try to speak,' the Norwegian said, but I answered, that 'if the Lord could speak through a human being, He must make me do so by His Spirit! There was to be no humbug about this!' — When they were praying, the doctor's wife saw *a crown of fire* over my head and *a cloven tongue as of fire* in front of the crown. Compare Acts 2:3-4. The brother from Norway, and others, saw this supernatural highly red light. — *The very same moment, my being was filled with light and an indescribable power, and I began to speak in a foreign language* as loudly as I could. For a long time I was lying upon my back on the floor, speaking — afterwards I was moving about on my knees with my eyes shut. For some time this went on; then at last I sat on a chair, and the whole time I spoke in 'divers kinds of tongues' (I Corinthians 12:10) with a short interval between. When speaking some of these languages, there was an aching in my vocal chords. I am sure that I spoke seven or eight different languages. They were clear and plain; and the different positions of the tongue, and the different tones of the voice, and the different accents, made me understand how different the languages were, one from the other. (Now, while I am writing this the Spirit works on my vocal chords and I have to sing.)"[5]

Acts

Tongues

4. A PROMINENT WOMAN RECIPIENT: EVANGELIST AIMEE SEMPLE MCPHERSON (1908)

Power for Service

Heart-purification Yielding

Tongues

a. *Her Experience.* I began to read my Bible afresh, with the desire of discovering the secret of a soul winner's power and success. As nearly as I could tell, the enduement of power for service was synonymous with the Baptism of the Holy Spirit. . . . I spent the week with this good lady . . . the greater part of it on my knees, praying by the hour, eating a little, sleeping a little, rising in the middle of the night, and wrapping blankets around me, dropping on my knees by the bed and praying again that my heart might be cleansed, that I might be emptied of self, sanctified wholly, and be deemed a worthy vessel, that the Lord might vouchsafe unto me His gracious induement with power for service, the Baptism of the Holy Spirit. — In a moment the blessing fell. Streams of glory from on high came pouring down, joy like the billows of the sea swept over me . . . and at last [He] took my tongue and spoke through me in a language I have never learned, the ecstatic praises of His own glorious Name, even as He filled the hundred and twenty on that memorable day of Pentecost so long ago.[6]

---

[5] Barratt, *Fire*, pp. 103, 108-09, 112-16, 120-30. (Not all of Barratt's emphases, which are abundant, have been preserved. Most paragraph or section divisions — here as hereafter in this Appendix — are marked by a dash.)

[6] McPherson, *In the Service of the King* (New York: Boni and Liveright, 1927), pp. 83, 87-89.

All at once my hands and arms began to tremble gently at first, then more and more, until my whole body was atremble with the power of the Holy Spirit. I did not consider this at all strange, as I knew how . . . batteries . . . hummed and shook and trembled under the power of electricity, and there was the Third Person of the Trinity coming into my body in all His fulness, making me His dwelling, "the temple of the Holy Ghost.". . . Almost without my notice my body slipped gently to the floor, and I was lying under the power of God, but felt as though caught up and floating upon the billowy clouds of glory. . . . My lungs began to fill and heave under the power as the Comforter came in. The cords of my throat began to twitch — my chin began to quiver, and then to shake violently, but Oh, so sweetly! My tongue began to move up and down and sideways in my mouth. Unintelligible sounds as of stammering lips and another tongue, spoken of in Isaiah 28:11, began to issue from my lips. This stammering of different syllables, then words, then connected sentences, was continued for some time as the Spirit was teaching me to yield to Him. Then suddenly, out of my innermost being flowed rivers of praise in other tongues as the Spirit gave utterance (Acts 2:4), and Oh, I knew that He was praising Jesus with glorious language, clothing Him with honor and glory which I felt but never could have put into words.[7]

b. *Her Record of Other Experiences.* Three received the baptism that night. One lady fell by the organ, another at the other side of the church. . . . One had asked the other, with tears in his eyes, to forgive him, and immediately fell back in his brother's arms under the power of the Holy Spirit. . . . The third night nineteen received the baptism of the Holy Spirit. Down they went right and left, between the seats, in the aisles, in front of the chancel rail, up on the platform. Oh, Glory! . . . This one held aloof for some time, saying: "Oh, I don't believe that all this noise and shouting and falling under the power is necessary. I believe in the Holy Spirit, but not in this enthusiastic manner." — "Well, brother, even if you don't understand it all now, do not sit back there in the seats. Come up to the altar. You feel it will be all right to seek more of Jesus, don't you?" — "Oh, yes, I will seek more of the Lord," he replied. . . . — It was only a few minutes later while praying — with the seekers, and they were going down one by one under the mighty rushing wind of the heavenly gales that were sweeping from heaven, that we heard a great shout, and something struck the floor with a thump . . . [it was] the trustee who had but shortly before declared that all of this noise and shouting was unnecessary. I doubt if there was anyone in the church who made as much noise as he. He shook from head to foot; his face was aglow with heaven's light; he

Tongues

Yielding

Acts

Tongues

More

Tarrying Meeting

Evidence

[7] McPherson, *This Is That,* pp. 44-45.

fairly shouted and roared forth as the Spirit gave him utterance, his heart was filled with joy and glory.[8]

In a few minutes the dear sister had received the baptism of the Holy Spirit and was shaking from head to foot, laughing with joy and talking in tongues. — The last Sunday the floor was covered with those prostrated under the power. Many messages were given with interpretation. — Montwait, Mass[achusetts]. Here precious saints gathered from far and near and met in blessed liberty. The first night three received the baptism of the Spirit and sinners received salvation. — On Sunday nine received their baptism, some were saved and many healed. A dear Methodist minister and his wife and daughter received their baptism. Thirty or more received the Holy Ghost in the ten days' meeting.[9]

Tarrying Meeting

At the close of each preaching service the long prayer room would quickly fill from one end to the other with earnest seekers for the baptism of the Holy Spirit. The prayers of seekers and workers went up with such unison and in such accord that their voices sounded like the rushing of many waters. Many were prostrated on the floor under the power of God while they received their baptism, others were filled with the Spirit while kneeling or standing upright on their feet, with hands and face turned up to heaven.[10]

Power for Service

"I continued to tarry for the Baptism [a Pentecostal testimony commences]. ... On Sunday ... I received the Baptism. The Holy Spirit came in like a torrent, as though He would tear my body to pieces. One of my besetting sins has been my unwillingness to speak out boldly for Christ, but when the Holy Spirit came in He made me shout the praises of Jesus until He verily split my throat. However, as one brother said to me, the Lord is able to repair any damage He does to the old temple. After being tossed about violently for quite awhile until I was panting for breath and wet with perspiration, I then lay for quite awhile in blessed quietness and poured forth praise to God in tongues for over half an hour."[11]

Obedience

Power

Evidence

"Mrs. McPherson, [another testimony reports], was particularly strong in her preaching concerning the baptism of the Holy Ghost. ... She placed much emphasis on the fact that a blood-washed soul and a clean body were necessary to prepare the individual to become the temple of the Holy Ghost. In other words, she believes that the doctrines of perfect love and entire sanctification must precede the baptism of the Spirit which bestows power through the gifts of the Spirit and bears the fruit of the Spirit. She was inducted after much prayer and long waiting. She believes that there must be some special evidence,

8 *Ibid.,* p. 96.
9 *Ibid.,* p. 110.
10 *Ibid.,* p. 166.
11 In *ibid.,* p. 217.

as on the day of Pentecost and other subsequent similar
occasions, given to every individual who has thus been
baptized."[12]

More

Do you feel your need of strength and power [Mrs.
McPherson asks]? Does your soul cry out for a greater
revelation of Jesus and His Word, for a greater vision and
a broader horizon? Then *tarry until* you are endued with
power from on high.[13]

5. A CONTEMPORARY NEO-PENTECOSTAL RECIPIENT: THE REV. MR.
   JOHN OSTEEN (1960)

More

I stand as one of the group of pastors who are desper-
ately concerned and deeply disturbed and confused over
the lack of power ... there has been a growing concern
in my heart, for I knew that something ought to be there
which was not there, and could not be found.... I read

Acts

in the Bible about the early church and its supernatural
power and I so longed for such as that.... Men and
women are tired of deadness and failure. — My subject
was in the form of a question. "When did Jesus baptize
you in the Holy Ghost and Fire?" If we know when we
are baptized in water, we would certainly know when and

Subsequence

if we had been baptized in *fire*. I confessed to them that
I had not had this experience, but was setting my heart
and soul toward God to have it! — I discovered that even
though Jesus was the Son of God, nothing was ever heard
of His supernatural ministry on earth until the Holy
Ghost came upon Him.... Directly, there came into my
hands a strange feeling, and it came on down to the
middle of my arms and began to surge! It was like a
thousand — like ten thousand — then a million volts of
electricity. It began to shake my hands and to pull my
hands. I could hear, as it were, a zooming sound of the
power. It pulled my hands higher and held them there as
though God took them in His. There came a voice in
my soul that said, "Lay these hands on the sick and
I will heal them!" ... [he then performed some healings]
but I didn't have the baptism.... In an air-conditioned
room, with my hands lifted ... and my heart reaching up
for my God, there came the hot, molten lava of His
love. It poured in like a stream from Heaven and I was
lifted up out of myself. I spoke in a language I could
not understand for about two hours. My body perspired
as though I was in a steambath: the Baptism of Fire! —
This was about two years ago. Between seventy and eighty
of our people have received this glorious experience. Men

Power

and women who wearily trudged to prayer meeting and
drove themselves to be faithful have become flaming
evangels for Jesus![14]

---

12 In *ibid.*, pp. 369-70.
13 *Ibid.*, p. 659.
14 John H. Osteen, "Pentecost Is Not A Denomination: It Is An Experience,"
Full Gospel Business Men's Voice, 8 (June 1960), 4-9.

C. SUMMA SUMMARUM: THE CATEGORY OF "MORE"

The Pentecostal passion for "more" is, for us, the most pervasively interesting feature in the Pentecostal *testimonia* reviewed above. Miss Ozman found, through her glossolalic experience, "the added joy and glory my heart longed for." Pastor Barratt, though a Christian minister, "felt the need of a *still greater blessing over my own soul!* ... I knew there must be a *still deeper work*" (his emphasis). And the Rev. Mr. Osteen had a troubling sense of need, of a "lack of power. ... I knew that something ought to be there which was not there, and could not be found." He longed for the supernatural power which he saw at work in Acts but absent from his life and from the life of the church around him. Speaking for the church he felt he could say, "Men and women are tired of deadness and failure." For all of these seekers, release, joy, and power came in the experience subsequent to their conversions, evidenced by tongues, and obtained by consecrated seeking. Acts had now not only been read, it had been experienced. The seekers had become possessors. In the words of Barratt's correspondent, "When we have this Baptism, we are very different from what we ever were before."

We do not think that one errs in believing that in the desire for more there is a satisfying and almost comprehensive explanation for the need of the Pentecostal experience of the baptism in the Holy Spirit. We believe that we can trace the genesis of this desire for more.

1. The desire begins in the innermost parts of the Christian. He senses deep insufficiency, impotence, sin. This is so precisely as a Christian.[15] This nagging, troubling inner need is the absolute beginning of the desire for more.

2. The desire is nourished by the reading, in particular, of the Acts of the Apostles and so the exposure to the miracle-world of the early church.[16] In Osteen's words, cited earlier, "I read in the Bible about the church and its supernatural power and I so longed for such as that." The inner dissatisfaction deepens. For the contrast with the white-hot ardor of the church in Acts serves only to heighten the black night of the heart. Above all, the *power* of the early church serves to intensify the seeker's sense of spiritual impotence.

3. Fellowship with Christians who know of a higher spiritual experience plays, then, an important part. Indeed, chronologically it is perhaps as often true that this fellowship is itself the first-cause of the sense of Christian frustration and later of Christian victory. The holiness (in our time

---

[15] "I not only understand that there *was* more for me, but felt there *must* be more for *me,* or otherwise my Christian life would be a failure. My Christian life was not satisfying to God nor to myself. Of this I was fully convinced ... there was more to be had." Pethrus, *Wind²,* p. 20. Gee remarked that the Pentecostal movement "attracted hungry hearts among the most spiritual ranks of Christians. They longed for more of God. They longed to enjoy greater manifestations of the Holy Spirit." *Pentecost,* No. 28 (June 1954), p. 17.

[16] Brumback's observation is representative of many: "Long, prayerful hours spent in searching the Book of Acts and the Epistles convinced these believers that the early Christians enjoyed a much richer and fuller experience than they themselves had yet received." *What Meaneth This?,* p. 279.

more frequently, the victorious-life) theology of the new Christian fellowship waters what inner need had planted and Acts had cultivated. In this theology is advocated and experienced a distinct subsequent blessing for the Christian beyond conversion, granting beyond the forgiveness of sins the conquest of sin, beyond grace power, beyond the Christ-for-us the Christ-in-us, and beyond salvation in Christ the baptism in the Holy Spirit. The holiness-victory promise is tremendous. It offers precisely what the inner man lacks and what Acts seems to teach. The desire is now full-grown. Only its satisfaction remains.

4. On enquiry one discovers, as we have developed throughout, that there are definite conditions to be met in order to obtain this benediction and (if one is in a Pentecostal community) that the initial evidence of its reception is, as in Acts, the Pentecostal speaking in tongues (in non-Pentecostal contexts, the victorious life). The desire for more than usual is conditioned on more than usual obedience and faith and is evidenced by a more than usual experience. The air is absolutes: the full Pentecostal blessing comes when there is entire consecration, absolute surrender, and entire yielding, issuing in the full indwelling of the Holy Spirit and supernatural power for service. The desire for more is now not only planted, cultivated, and watered, but it is (to alter the analogy) instructed. It now knows what to look for and how to get there.

5. Either in prayer with others who have experienced the Pentecostal baptism, or in prayer alone, the more comes. The desire now becomes a satisfaction. The satisfactions are not difficult to imagine: one has now more than ordinary assurance that he is an object of God's love and action; there is a sense of being one with the early church in its very experience; there is a sense, too, of being one now with a contemporary Spirit-filled movement which has also experienced this more — a fellowship of the more arises; and now, in this fellowship, having already learned by experience the absolutes that make up the deeper Christian life, one finds it easier to give oneself absolutely to the whole of the church's life and to bringing others to this fuller experience. One senses, therefore, a veritable increment in power, in faith, and in the Christian life. The desire for more envelops itself more and more into more and we have the Pentecostal Christian. His activity, his mission, and his characteristic style of life are not as difficult to explain, we believe, when they are viewed in the comprehensive perspective of the idea of more.

IV

THE GIFTS OF THE HOLY SPIRIT
IN THE PENTECOSTAL MOVEMENT

INTRODUCTION

1. THE GIFT AND THE GIFTS OF THE HOLY SPIRIT

When the believer is baptized in the Holy Spirit he qualifies for the gifts of the Holy Spirit. The believer may receive his particular gift of the Spirit either with his baptism in the Spirit or at some time afterwards — Pentecostal opinion differs here slightly and insignificantly. In any case, the gift of the Spirit grants the gifts of the Spirit.

Pentecostals wish, however, to distinguish carefully between the two phenomena — the gift and the gifts — as the experiences, respectively, of Acts and Corinthians. For the gift occurs only once, while the gifts should be experienced continually. But the gifts cannot occur at all — or they cannot occur fully — until one has the gift of the Holy Spirit, i.e., until one is baptized in the Holy Spirit with the initial glossolalic evidence. Only when the Holy Spirit permanently, personally, and fully enters the believer's life does the believer become eligible for the full equipment of the spiritual gifts. Finally, the gifts of the Spirit have their special purpose, as the gift of the Spirit has its general purpose, in "power for service," in providing "a spiritual capability far mightier than the finest natural abilities could ever supply."[1] Baptized with the gift, and endowed with one or more of the gifts, the Christian is finally equal to his task in history.

2. THE NON-SUSPENSION OF THE GIFTS

The Pentecostal places unusual stress upon the gifts of the Spirit

---

[1] Gee, *Concerning Spiritual Gifts: A Series of Bible Studies* (Rev. ed.; Springfield, Mo.: Gospel Publishing House, 1947), p. 15. For discussion of the relations between the gift and the gifts of the Spirit see Melvin L. Hodges, *Spiritual Gifts* (Springfield, Mo.: Gospel Publishing House, 1964), pp. 4, 15-16.

and particularly upon the gifts discussed in I Corinthians 12 to 14.[2] He believes that the spiritual gifts should be taken with their deserved seriousness and, like Blumhardt, he finds in their full restoration the return of the church to its early power. But he holds that the gifts were never really suspended; only the infidelity of the church occasioned the gifts' eclipse and made them appear to have been suspended or superseded. Gee writes, for example, that there is no "sound and convincing argument against the continuance of the early Pentecostal phenomena of the Church ... the Church ceases to enjoy His gifts through her own lukewarmness and unbelief, and not because God arbitrarily withdraws them as unnecessary today."[3] In the Pentecostal movement, it is averred, God is showing what he can do with a church that recognizes and exercises the gifts of his Spirit.

According to most Pentecostal discussions, the spiritual gifts find their legitimacy in the testimony of Scripture, and their urgency in the needs of men.

a. *The Witness of Scripture.* The major texts marshalled from Scripture to support the Pentecostal argument for the non-suspension of the spiritual gifts, in addition to I Corinthians 12-14, are, "the gifts and calling of God are without repentance" (Rom. 11:29 AV), "Jesus Christ is the same yesterday and today and forever" (Heb. 13:8), and the promise of Jesus to accompany those who believe with miraculous signs (Mark 16:17-18, cf. v. 20). To the Pentecostal these texts mean that the spiritual gifts which God once instituted and to which the apostles gave testimony are irrevocable and constant, the changeless Christ himself being the chief guarantee.

---

[2] The gifts listed, for example, in Eph. 4:7-11 and Rom. 12:3-8 receive, it would be fair to say, little attention in Pentecostal literature. However, see Gee's *The Ministry-Gifts of Christ* (Springfield, Mo.: Gospel Publishing House, 1930) for a treatment *extra-Corinthios*. But even here Gee subordinates the Romans-Ephesians "offices" to the actual "Spiritual Gifts" of I Cor. 12-14. For reasons cf. Horton, *Gifts of the Spirit,*[2] p. 35. For a perceptible change in temper and emphasis see Gee's *Fruitful or Barren? Studies in the Fruit of the Spirit* (Springfield, Mo.: Gospel Publishing House, 1961) and especially Gee's 1963 lectures, *Spiritual Gifts in the Work of the Ministry Today* ("The L.I.F.E. Bible College Alumni Association Lectureship on Spiritual Gifts, 1963"; Los Angeles: n.p., 1963), pp. 14, 66.

[3] *Pentecostal Movement,* p. 10. In another place he writes: "It is surely a serious thing to accuse God of *withdrawing* these gifts if the real fact is that the church *lost* them through lukewarmness!" *Concerning Spiritual Gifts,* p. 10. Similarly, Brumback, *What Meaneth This?,* p. 61; Duffield, *Pentecostal Preaching,* p. 53. So also Edward Irving, see the references in note 11, p. 40 above; and recently Hans Küng, S. J.: "Where a Church or community thrives only on office-holders and not on all the members, one may well wonder in all seriousness whether the Spirit has not been thrown out with the charismata." "The Charismatic Structure of the Church," *The Church and Ecumenism,* ed. Hans Küng ("Concilium: Theology in the Age of Renewal," 4; New York: Paulist Press, 1965), p. 58.

Furthermore, the absence of any texts to the contrary, the fact, that is, that no divine intention is ever biblically suggested for the termination of the gifts with a particular period argues, the Pentecostal believes, for the non-suspension of the gifts. Hence the Pentecostal ardently disagrees with the church's frequent relegation of the gifts of the Spirit to the apostolic or post-apostolic age. Scripture positively promises the church spiritual equipment with gifts; Scripture never negatively argues for their removal — these form the principal biblical *apologia* for Pentecostalism's affirmation of the gifts of the Spirit.

b. *The Needs of Men.* Shaping the Pentecostal persuasion beyond the clear witness of Scripture are the clamant needs of men. These needs, it is insisted, are as desperate in the twentieth century as they were in the first. If the church's gifts were to expedite her mission to the world in the first century, why, it is asked, should they be any less necessary for the church's mission in the twentieth? "Has [God] happened upon a period of temporary helplessness in this age of desperate human need?" asks Horton.[4] Scripture makes the gifts right; but men make the gifts necessary. Pentecostalism believes that it has always been God's intention to clothe his church, as he did his Messiah, with power adequate for mission. The source of this power is the baptism in the Holy Spirit; the medium of this power is the gifts of the Holy Spirit.

Armed with the arguments of Scripture's witness to the gifts and its silence on their suspension, and with the surety of the changeless character of Christ and the unchanging needs of men, the Pentecostal feels certain that the only honest explanation for the paucity of the gifts' manifestations in our time is the church's unwillingness to take God's provisions seriously.

A. THE PENTECOSTAL MEETING: THE LOCUS OF THE GIFTS

1. The Elements of the Meeting

In the Pentecostal assembly the gifts are believed to have been restored. Here I Corinthians chapters twelve to fourteen suddenly come alive. Here the varied gifts of the Spirit are offered expression. The Pentecostal church meeting has been described as pew-centered, and the description is apt. In contrast to generally pulpit-centered Protestantism and altar-centered Catholicism, Pentecostalism finds its center in the believing community. The Pentecostals are concerned, as one put it, that "we never reach the point where our congregations are composed of on-looking spectators rather than participating worshippers."[5] To avoid this deflection Pentecostals attempt to offer every

---

[4] *Gifts of the Spirit*[2], p. 39.
[5] David A. Womack, "Are We Becoming Too Formal?," *Pentecostal Evangel,*

believer an opportunity actively and personally to participate in the church's life. The paramount locus for this participation is the church meeting. Here the gifts are to find their most proper and prominent sphere of operation. The major elements of the meeting can be described briefly under the heads of music, prayer, and ministry.

a. *The Music and the Mood.* The Pentecostal meeting is marked by wide participation, first of all, in music. A sociological observer remarked of the Pentecostal meeting, accurately, that "there is action from beginning to end and it is in large part a musical service. . . . Throughout there is much singing and when these people sing, they sing not only with their voices but with their hands, and their feet and their bodies."[6] As a student of Brazilian Pentecostalism has noted, songs and choruses usually constitute in fact (though never in theory) the liturgical element of the Pentecostal meeting.[7]

In attending Pentecostal meetings it has been our observation that frequently an amateur church orchestra appears on the platform in front, composed often of small children who must just be learning music, elderly men who must have learned their music years ago, and all the ages and types in between — and all, presumably, members of the church. The music is animated and loud with decisive rhythm; it is often accompanied with congregational clapping of hands (a Pentecostal feature), and it is not infrequently led from the front by a vigorous song-leader. The music, even in Europe, has a distinct "American" folk beat, lending itself to full bodily participation.

The mood of the meeting, formed largely by the music, is usually far from joyless and morose as might be expected in the generally poor Pentecostal communities. We have been interested also to observe the unusually large number of whole families in the Pentecostal assembly — father, mother, and children — sitting together singing heartily, and those who are too young to sing, clapping heartily. The mood of the singing is often communal and joyous in contrast to what, in some Protestant churches, we may fairly describe as perfunctory and sad.

Joy is, in fact, a mark of the usual Pentecostal assembly. Most of those in attendance at the meeting seem glad to be there. The Pentecostal often asks why joy and its expression should be permitted to almost every kind of human convocation except the church. Pentecostals argue that it is an elementary human desire to wish to be

---

48 (Dec. 4, 1960), 3. On the impressive "participation" feature of Pentecostalism see Read, *New Patterns of Church Growth in Brazil*, pp. 136-37, 225-26; Christian Lalive d'Epinay, "The Pentecostal 'Conquista' in Chile," *EcRev*, 20 (Jan. 1968), 16-32; from the Scandinavian perspective, Bloch-Hoell, *Pentecostal Movement*, pp. 162-63; and a recent Catholic appreciation, K. McDonnell, "The Ideology of Pentecostal Conversion," *JEcSt*, 5 (Winter 1968), 112-15.

6 A. T. Boisen, "Religion and Hard Times: A Study of the Holy Rollers," *Social Action*, 5 (Mar. 15, 1939), 23. Cf. also Mosiman, *Zungenreden*, p. 71.

7 Emile Léonard in *Hollenweger* II, 908.

happy and a fundamental responsibility of the church to provide opportunity and expression for this happiness. It is in the church, indeed, that authentically happy news is present, proclaimed, and believed to a degree unknown in the world outside of the church. Pentecostals, then, believe that the best and most appropriate place for happiness and for its expression is the church of the gospel.[8]

The Pentecostal assembly is a place of great emotional expression. Gee describes the special attraction of a Pentecostal meeting to him in these descriptive words, "There was some indefinable difference; an individual liberty; a simple spirituality; a lack of ministerial formality; an emphasis upon the distinctive testimony of the Pentecostal Movement [i.e., the spiritual baptism]; a place for spiritual gifts; an utter abandon that can only be summed up as peculiarly and uncompromisingly 'Pentecostal.' "[9] It must be admitted by observers that these features or moods are frequently in evidence in Pentecostal assemblies, with ecstasy, and sometimes with agony, and the opportunity for their expression seems to be a major factor in the attractiveness to many of the Pentecostal meeting.

b. *Prayer.* The meeting is also characterized by prayer and this too is communal. It is a truism of Pentecostal worship that the entire congregation prays. And the congregation prays not only in silence but as often in vocal concert or cacophony. The church is filled with sound at prayer (indeed, most always). There is no lack of vital congregational participation in this important activity. The prayer, too, borders constantly on ecstasy; one or both hands are often raised in petition or praise, reminiscent of the old Jewish habit; very often the entire congregation descends to its knees, turns its back to the platform (this being a more accurate description than the chancel), and uses the pews (or, as often, the chairs) as a place of prayer. The Pentecostal church is a house of prayer for all members. "No church," one Pentecostal leader has written, "can call herself a church which depends upon trained leaders to do the praying."[10] It is hard to say whether more of the average Pentecostal meeting is consumed in music or in prayer — but consumed it is in large part by both, and in both by everyone, and in both with considerable feeling. The particular gift of prayer which seems so resident in Pentecostal assemblies is attributed ultimately, as are almost all other Pentecostal dis-

---

[8] Cf. Riggs on the uninhibited joy of Pentecostal "store-front" churches. "Those 'Store-Front' Churches," *United Evangelical Action,* 6 (Aug. 1, 1945), 4. Cf. Fr. O'Hanlon's respect, "The Pentecostals and Pope John's 'New Pentecost,' " *View,* No. 2 (1964), p. 23; and Malcolm J. C. Calley, *God's People: West-Indian Pentecostal Sects in England* (London: Oxford University Press, 1965), pp. 143-44.

[9] *Pentecostal Movement,* pp. 209-10. See also the section "The Distinctive of Worship," in Hughes, *Church of God Distinctives,* pp. 73-93.

[10] Buntain, *Holy Ghost and Fire,* p. 59. Cf. Mosiman, *Zungenreden,* pp. 71-72; Read, *New Patterns of Church Growth in Brazil,* p. 21.

tinctions, to the baptism in the Holy Spirit enjoyed by most Pentecostal members.

c. *The Ministry of the Congregation.* In many Pentecostal assemblies the congregation takes a vital part in not only the music and the prayer of the meeting, but in the ministry of the spoken word as well. Most Pentecostals seem not to deprecate an ordained or preaching ministry of some sort, though many Pentecostal groups began with some suspicions of a professional ministry. But Pentecostals almost unanimously insist that the ministry be based on a recognition of the spiritual gifts necessary for the pastoral task and be supplemented with the wide variety of spiritual gifts exercised by the rest of the Christian community. Pentecostalism may, in fact, be described as an institutional expression of the revolt against the "one-man ministry."

The individual member of most Pentecostal churches must feel as he comes to the meeting that *he* may have something worthwhile to share with the whole assembly if the Spirit should prompt him; and if not, another brother or sister should have something inspiring to share with him. Most Pentecostal meetings include what is called a time of testimony in their schedule. Individuals are encouraged to share from their Christian experience for the benefit of all and for the praise of God. The testimony is often of personal spiritual experience during the preceding week; of answers to prayer; not infrequently the testimony concerns some kind of healing; occasionally the subject is an evangelistic experience; sometimes a Bible passage is shared; but always, what is at the heart of the particular Pentecostal Christian is brought to the heart of the Pentecostal assembly, and the result is, as far as we have been able to observe, real edification.

There has been criticism of testimony meetings of this kind. For instance, Professor Baëta of Ghana writes (of the separatist churches in his country):

> Church services of "witness" are regularly held in which members give testimonies about the granting of such requests. The nature of the hopes held out must provide an answer to those who wonder why historical church workers do not appear to be able to attract such large crowds as the separatists can draw. But the far more important questions are, of course: Is this the true essence of Christianity? Is it legitimate to present what are merely some of the beneficial by-products, as the whole thing?[11]

Without entering into serious debate at this point, and while appreciating Professor Baëta's concern, one might simply ask in a preliminary way, do historic churches often enough offer services of testimony for the laity at all; hold out any kind of hope for Christians

---

11 Christian G. Baëta, "Conflict in Mission: Historical and Separatist Churches," in *The Theology of the Christian Mission,* ed. Gerald H. Anderson (London: SCM Press, 1961), p. 294.

in mundane life — e.g., in answers to prayer in quite material, physical, or economic matters; or is there occasionally a tendency to spiritualize some of the biblical promises quite away? Finally, one may question whether separatist churches, at least of the Pentecostal type, actually do hold out the answering of prayer requests as, in Professor Baëta's words, "the whole thing." We grant that often the answers and requests in prayer appear to be primitive, unrefined, and narrow in their conception. But for those who offer these prayers or receive what they believe are answers to them, their prayers are as concrete, real, and "primitive" to them as the needs of their difficult lives.

As was suggested earlier, many Pentecostals grant a dignity to the preached Word and they may be seen waiting in great expectancy as the Bible is preached (and in its way it is), but they are convinced, biblically and experientially, that they need to hear the Word from more than a solitary professional, that "they need the inspiration that comes from actual persons who, by song and testimony, tell of what God is doing for them."[12] Pentecostals feel that free and full lay participation in the church meetings offers a *practical* dimension to the church service which would otherwise be lacking. As Buntain explains, the laity, "if encouraged, will by their testimonies and life preach greater practical sermons than [the minister's] messages from the pulpit."[13]

Most Pentecostals believe, with Dr. Van Dusen, that because of the vital congregational participation the apostle Paul would probably be more at home in a Pentecostal assembly than in a Protestant cathedral. Speaking in this manner of the apostle Paul, the Pentecostal pastor Karl Ecke conceded to the Protestant churches in Germany, for example, "that Paul would have quickly recognized that justification by faith rings with great clarity from the evangelical pulpit. And yet, so much would offend him, and first of all, the silence of the church in prayer and worship."[14] This "silence in the church" is attributed by Pentecostals again, as are most of the church's failings, to the absence of the church's promised Holy Spirit.

One of the most salutary results of the church's rediscovery of the

---

[12] Buntain, *Holy Ghost and Fire*, p. 62.

[13] *Ibid.* "Prepared addresses must continue to be the prime source of teaching," Buntain notes soberly, "but those who reject the practical or home teaching of free-hearted 'fellowship' are standing in the way of men and women who need something beyond the solemn pulpit utterances to keep them in victory." *Ibid.* McDonnell believes that in Pentecostal meetings "the subjective testimonies of participants [have] precedence over an objective message." "The Ecumenical Significance of the Pentecostal Movement," *Worship, 40* (Dec. 1966), 619. We have not noticed that this is so.

[14] *Durchbruch*, p. 1. "It would also offend Paul that one person alone out of the congregation appeared to be the active agent in the worship service," Ecke believes, "instead of the variety of gifts which resides in the congregation being granted the opportunity of unfolding." *Ibid.*

Pentecostal distinctive, it seems to be believed, would be the restoration, with the *gift,* of the *gifts* of the Holy Spirit and the correspondingly vital participation of the entire congregation in the life of the church, and especially in the life of the church meeting.

2. THE EFFECTS OF THE MEETING

The aggregate effect of the exercise of the various elements of the meeting discussed above, with the operation of the particular individual gifts of the Spirit to be discussed below, is to make the Pentecostal meeting not only expectant but explosive. One cannot help having at least one of two very specific feelings during a typical Pentecostal meeting: the openness of heaven and/or the inflammability of the congregation.

a. *The Openness of Heaven.* First, one senses that the congregation feels itself in constant readiness for divine invasion. The supernatural is ever latent and sometimes patent in the Pentecostal meeting. It can at any time sweep into the meeting, through a prophecy, or a speaking in tongues, or a testimony, and it is always somewhat perceptible in the several elements of the meeting itself. The natural is in constant intersection with the supernatural and in constant susceptibility of being swallowed up by it. The result is sometimes awesome — not greatly unlike that described in Acts (2:43), "and fear came upon every soul; and many wonders and signs were done."

There is a sense in the Pentecostal meeting that the divine is not only (as in our churches) an object of worship but that he is also, and especially, a subject of action. To be sure, the non-Pentecostal feels that the divine acts and speaks in a special way through the preached Word of the ordained minister, and perhaps even in a general way in the hearing, confession, prayer, and sung praise of the congregation. The Pentecostal, however, feels that the divine speaks throughout the entire service in a special way through, at different times, in different manners, and by different persons, the entire congregation. The result is the Pentecostal congregation's feeling that heaven is open not only in the preacher's proclamation but in the assembly's participation.

b. *The Explosiveness of the Assembly.* The second impression obtained from a Pentecostal meeting is that, were the leader of the assembly not skilled in directing the corporate emotion, the meeting could explode into chaos — in the vernacular, "the roof could blow off." There is such freedom in expression in many Pentecostal meetings — for example, in many Pentecostal groups one may begin to speak in tongues at almost any point in the service — and there is such high emotion everywhere in evidence or in suppression, that the meeting sometimes seems not only sensitive of being in direct contact with the divine but in danger of rank confusion. Yet as Gee remarks of the Pentecostal meeting, "it may arouse antipathies, but it will never be insipid."[15] It may be inevitable that perfect freedom yields a predictable confusion. The perennial problem is raised again, in Dr. Mackay's phrase, of ardor or order — which should be sacrificed? Is it best to have perfect freedom and the perhaps inevitable disorder which will accompany it, or perfect order and the perhaps inevitable limitations which will accompany it? Is the openness of heaven worth the explosiveness of the assembly? Must there be disorder for there to be the divine? How can there be a responsible ministry of gifts and right participation by the entire congregation and yet the decency and order which Paul requires? These are just some of the more serious questions raised by the remarkably engaging Pentecostal meeting.[16]

B. THE INDIVIDUAL GIFTS

1. INTRODUCTION

a. *The Non-Remarkable Gifts.* For several of the individual gifts of the Spirit listed in the New Testament and therefore appropriated by the Pentecostals it can be definitely affirmed that there is no unique or special interpretation. It can only be said that Pentecostalism *emphasizes* the gifts in general and that it emphasizes those gifts in particular which are traditionally least emphasized: especially healing, prophecy, and tongues. The less remarkable and less manifest gifts are very little discussed and consciously little practiced.

However, Pentecostalism often sees much more than the Protestant Christian is accustomed to seeing in even the least spectacular gifts. The gifts of the word of knowledge and the word of wisdom (I Cor. 12:8), for example, in addition to being understood as spiritual help in knowing and teaching, can be taken to mean the supernatural revelation of unknown, esoteric, and future things.

Furthermore, in the life of the Pentecostal movement, as far as we have been able to observe, there appears to be no deliberate or widespread practice of the non-remarkable gifts *per se.* Therefore, if it can be said that Pentecostalism stresses the spiritual gifts, then it would

---

[15] *Concerning Spiritual Gifts,* p. 107.

[16] Dr. John Mackay reasoned: "If it is a choice ... between the uncouth life of the Pentecostals and the aesthetic death of the older churches, I for one choose uncouth life." In Sherrill, *They Speak with Other Tongues,* p. 140. Hollenweger, in a prospectus announcing the appearance of his handbook, wrote that his studies brought him to the conclusion that the strength of the Pentecostal movement "does not lie in theology nor in doctrine but in the attempt to create congregations which are open to spontaneous contributions and who take seriously in worship the non-literary, 'oral' man, i.e., the majority of our population. This is a serious challenge to the traditional churches." "Handbuch der Pfingstbewegung (Handbook of Pentecostalism)," [Prospectus, 1966], p. 3.

THE GIFTS OF THE HOLY SPIRIT

be more accurate to say that it stresses the extraordinary spiritual gifts. For there is no serious emphasis in the Pentecostal movement on the gifts associated with (to take but one New Testament list) wisdom, knowledge, or faith, all somewhat intangible endowments. It is the more striking gifts which are the special Pentecostal concern.

b. *The Remarkable Gifts.* The more remarkable gifts of the Spirit have pride of place in the Pentecostal movement. It is not untypical, for example, when Ecke feels that he can define the spiritual gifts in their entirety under only two of the more extraordinary types: "It is well known that the apostle Paul described the spiritual gifts — i.e., the utterances and songs especially effected through the Holy Spirit and beyond the power of men which are delivered in the mother tongue (prophecy) and in other tongues (tongues-speaking)— as the permanent normal possession of the church (e.g., I Cor. 12:4-7)."[17] The more visible or distinguishable gifts are felt to be especially suited to the special character which Pentecostalism assigns to spiritual gifts as a whole: the character of signs, giving the church's witness attraction and attestation.

c. *The Sign Character of the Remarkable Gifts.* The Pentecostal understands all of the gifts of the Spirit as partaking of the nature of signs, but of course the more apparent of the gifts provide the more apparent of the signs and so justify their special importance. The sign character of the gifts of the Spirit as a whole, particularly of the more spectacular gifts, is derived primarily from the following sources.

(1) *Mark 16:17-18, 20:* " 'And these signs will accompany those who believe: in my name they will cast out demons; they will speak in new tongues; they will pick up serpents, and if they drink any deadly thing, it will not hurt them; they will lay their hands on the sick; and they will recover.' ...And...the Lord worked with them and confirmed the message by the signs that attended it."
(2) *I Cor. 14:22:* "Thus, tongues are a sign not for believers but for unbelievers."
(3) *The entire development of Acts:* Cf., especially, Acts 2:43; 4:30; 5:12; 6:8; 8:13; 14:3; 15:12; 16:22.

It is felt by Pentecostals that the church has failed to seek these biblically promised accompaniments and has therefore given a generally impotent and enervated witness in the world.

Pentecostalism cherishes the striking gifts of the Spirit particularly for their ability to arrest the world's attention and to certify the church's

---

17 "Die Pfingstbewegung: Ein Gutachten von kirchlicher Seite" (Privately Printed, 1950), p. 3. See Fleisch's theory for the unusual emphasis which tongues and prophecy receive in Pentecostalism, *Fleisch* II/1, 122; II/2, 149-50. Cf. Gee, *Pentecostal Movement,* p. 8. See, however, Gee's more recent complaint: "On the whole, when we are told that 'The Gifts' are being exercised within our churches we find far too often that the reference is only to messages in tongues and their interpretation." *Spiritual Gifts in the Work of the Ministry Today,* p. 13.

work.[18] It was speaking in tongues, it is pointed out, which attracted the curious crowd on the day of Pentecost (Acts 2:5-13); it was the healing of a lame man which provided the second major apostolic opportunity to preach (Acts 3:11); and subsequent opportunities were comparably prepared and accompanied by signs. The early church lived and evangelized by magnetic and confirmatory signs; so, it is urged, should we. "For the very same reason that the signs followed the message in the first century (viz., the providing of a miraculous background for the message and the investing of the disciples with divine authority)," writes Brumback, "they should follow the same message today."[19] The special character of the remarkable gifts as signs, attractions, and certifications is a major Pentecostal argument for the utility and necessity of these gifts today.

2. THE GIFT OF HEALING

The arguments of sign, attraction, and attestation are used with special force, as might be expected, with the gift of healing. Nothing attracts men and attests the gospel, it is felt, quite like the healing of infirmities. Indeed, healing fills out the full gospel of a *full* salvation, argue Pentecostals. Not only sin but sickness finds an answer in the Pentecostal full gospel. One of the earliest German Pentecostal documents, "What Is the Pentecostal Movement?," expresses this conviction in these words:

> We are convinced that for millions of modern men in the higher and lower classes of our people there is no other return to Scripture-faith than through new miracles combined with an apostolically empowered and clear proclamation of the gospel of a full salvation, of deliverance for spirit, soul, and body.[20]

The case for healing is built paradigmatically upon the ministry of

---

[18] Cf. Brumback, *What Meaneth This?*, pp. 81, 323; L. Thomas Holdcroft, "The Gift of the Gifts of Healings," *Paraclete*, 2 (Spring 1968), 11. Gee believes that the gifts "may reverently be called God's method of divine advertising for the preaching of the Gospel." *Spiritual Gifts in the Work of the Ministry Today*, p. 84.

[19] *What Meaneth This?*, p. 81. Also Horton, *Gifts of the Spirit*[2], pp. 14-15, 216.

[20] In Hutten, *MD, 14* (Dec. 1, 1951), 124. Pentecostal expansion in Latin America in the fifties is attributed in significant measure to healing campaigns. See Read *et al., Latin American Church Growth*, p. 323. Cf. Steiner, *Zeichen*, pp. 121-22; Gee, *Concerning Spiritual Gifts*, p. 12; Horton, *Gifts of the Spirit*[2], p. 114. "Full Gospel" is an alternate name for Pentecostalism and usually means the message or movement which emphasizes (1) salvation, (2) the baptism in the Holy Spirit, (3) healing, and (4) the second coming. Cf. McPherson, *Four-square Gospel*, pp. 13-14. The holiness wing of the Pentecostal movement includes an experience of sanctification in the definition of the full gospel. Cf. Conn, *Like a Mighty Army*, p. 104.

Jesus, and theologically is rooted not in the doctrine of the Holy Spirit but in the doctrine of the atonement.[21]

The healing meetings of Pentecostalism have, with speaking in tongues, contributed most to the movement's notoriety in the eyes of the general public. There is an emphasis on healing in many Pentecostal circles which makes it almost a second Pentecostal distinctive. In his history of the Pentecostal movement Gee puts the gift in the majority Pentecostal perspective.

> Although not directly and essentially a part of the distinctive Pentecostal witness to the Baptism of the Holy Ghost with signs following, yet from the beginning of the Pentecostal Movement there has been a recognized place for the intimate relationship of faith for physical healing arising from the same grace of the risen and glorified Christ who bestows the Holy Spirit.[22]

With their emphasis on healing, the Pentecostals have not always been able to avoid a certain anti-medical bias, although this appears to be sporadic and perhaps not typical, and there has generally been a voice of moderation within the movement. An influential manual of doctrine, for example, adds to its locus on healing this cautious though revealing note: "The believer who seeks medical aid or advice when the extent of his own faith is not sufficient for the miracle of healing, should not be censured," adding perhaps a bit defensively, "he should be encouraged to maintain his faith in God no matter what medical help he has received."[23]

[21] The major texts are Isa. 53:3-6, 10 and the parallel in I Pet. 2:24. Cf. *Reglamento local*, p. 16; Bloch-Hoell, *Pentecostal Movement*, pp. 148-49; and the title of the section on healing in the Chilean Iglesia de Dios: "Sanidad divine proveída para todos en la expiación," Vergara, *El Protestantismo en Chile*, p. 180. Pentecostals occasionally wish to make a distinction between faith healing, as for instance in Christian Science, and divine healing as practiced in Pentecostalism. Cf. Conn, *Like a Mighty Army*, p. 77 note. John 14:12 is often added to Isa. 53 and I Pet. 2:24 in biblical evidence. So, for example, Duffield, *Pentecostal Preaching*, p. 53. Neo-Pentecostalism may emphasize the Holy Spirit in relation to healing if Kathryn Kuhlman is representative. See her *I Believe in Miracles* (Englewood Cliffs, N. J.: Prentice-Hall, 1962), pp. 198-99.

[22] *Pentecostal Movement*, pp. 40-41. "Divine healing is a related, yet separate subject and has never been the peculiar testimony of the Pentecostal Revival alone." Gee, *Spiritual Gifts in the Work of the Ministry Today*, p. 13. Also Conn, *Pillars*, p. 30; *idem, Like a Mighty Army*, p. 77.

[23] *Reglamento local*, p. 17. For examples of what might be considered the extreme anti-medical view in Pentecostalism see Howard Carter, *The Gifts of the Spirit* (Minneapolis, Minn.: Northern Gospel Publishing House, 1946), pp. 72-73; Horton, *Gifts of the Spirit*[2], p. 108; Conn, *Like a Mighty Army*, pp. 76, 204 n. 30. See extensive discussion in *Hollenweger* I, 100-22 and his observation that "the majority of the Pentecostal groups believe in healing through prayer, but now they do *not* any longer reject medical help." *Ibid.*, I, 106. For information on the major Pentecostal healers — William Branham, Gordon Lindsay, Hermann Zaiss, Oral Roberts, A. A. Allen, Tommy Hicks, T. L. Osborn, Harold Herman,

The practice of some of the most noted Pentecostal evangelists and healers (e.g., Oral Roberts, T. L. Osborn) has at times, however, been the occasion of embarrassment and even of criticism within the Pentecostal movement itself. However, this should not be taken to indicate a diminished interest within Pentecostalism in healing as such: this does not appear to be the case, and it is reported that in the newer Pentecostal groups the interest in healing seems especially strong, particularly in Africa. Meanwhile, the view seems still generally held, even by the somewhat moderate, for example the Swiss Steiner, that "over every sickness there stands, however, in the last analysis, the will of God to heal."[24]

3. THE GIFT OF PROPHECY

What is believed to be the gift of prophecy is exercised in most Pentecostal assemblies. One seemingly possessed by the Spirit will speak biblically reminiscent sentences or phrases in the vernacular, usually of exhortation and most often with an eschatological and sometimes visional context and content. Prophecy is similar to tongues in occurring most often in an ecstatic or para-ecstatic condition and in understanding itself as a medium of the Spirit. Mosiman can even say of prophecy that "it differs from tongues-speaking only in that it is spoken in understandable speech."[25]

Prophecy is usually defined, even by the more careful in the Pentecostal movement, as something more than simply Spirit-inspired utterance, but as in fact the voice of the Spirit himself: in prophecy, we are told, we have "the *speaking* Spirit."[26] In the normal Pentecostal assembly prophecy as well as tongues will occur. The ratio of prophecy to tongues in an ordinary assembly seems to vary depending upon the amount of excitement present: in the more subdued atmospheres, prophecy predominates; in the more surcharged, tongues.

Finally, since prophecy is felt to be spontaneous and direct spiritual

---

Jack Coe, O. L. Jaggers, and others — see both *Hollenweger* I, 101-13 and Nichol, *Pentecostalism*, 221-26.

[24] *Zeichen*, p. 173. For recent views see the new Pentecostal journal *Paraclete*, 2 (Spring 1968). Note the general caution in Gee's editorials in *Pentecost*, No. 47 (Mar. 1959), p. 17, and No. 48 (June 1959), p. 17, and his most recent comment that the Pentecostal ministry of healing "has won some notable victories for the glory of God, but also it has suffered shameful defeats. Its right use has attracted multitudes, but its abuse has turned multitudes away." *Spiritual Gifts in the Work of the Ministry Today*, p. 85. For criticism from within Pentecostal circles see *Hollenweger* I, 103-04; Carl F. H. Henry, "Pentecostal Meeting Makes Holy Land History," *Christianity Today*, 5 (May 22, 1961), 30; Hutten, *MD*, 24 (May 1, 1961), 106, and (Oct. 15, 1961), 236.

[25] *Zungenreden*, p. 115.

[26] Gee, "Speaking with Tongues and Prophesying," Address at the 1955 Pentecostal World Conference, *Pentecost*, No. 34 (Dec. 1955), p. 11. Cf. Riggs, *Spirit Himself*, pp. 153-56.

communication, it is not to be confused with preaching or prepared remarks where the substance is obtained by more conventional or indirect means than immediate inspiration. The Spirit delivers his mind and heart spontaneously and directly to the assembly through his prophets. However, there does appear to be some recognition of the dangers inherent in a gift purporting to supply the direct voice of the Spirit. Yet even in the most restrained voices of the Pentecostal movement there seems to be a willingness to risk the dangers in order to have the gift — so highly prized is the gift itself.[27]

4. THE GIFT OF TONGUES

a. *The Centrality of the Gift and Its Relation to the Evidence of Tongues.* To the gift of tongues special honor is assigned in the Pentecostal movement. This might be expected since the Pentecostal baptism in the Holy Spirit — the major Pentecostal phenomenon — is evidenced, as we have seen, by speaking in tongues. Speaking in tongues, whether understood as the crisis evidence or as a continuing gift of the Spirit, occupies such a central place in the Pentecostal assembly that Pentecostalism is sometimes known as "the tongues movement."

As we had occasion to see in another context (above, p. 79), speaking in tongues in Pentecostalism is sometimes explained dispensationally as God's unique sign to his church in the present age. Other signs were given in the Old Testament period but never tongues. Indeed, it is said, all the other gifts listed in I Corinthians twelve were manifested at some time earlier in the divine economy; but only tongues and the interpretation of tongues were reserved for the church period as the signs of the Spirit's special presence.[28] As a result, Pentecostals cherish tongues and the gift of their interpretation as God's special gift for the present time.

Although in Pentecostal definitions the speaking in tongues which evidences the baptism in the Holy Spirit is said to be the same "in essence" as the continuing gift of tongues exercised in the church, nevertheless, there is an insistence that the two are different "in purpose and use." They are the same in essence in that in both the source of inspiration is the Spirit and the form which the inspiration

---

[27] The dangers are most apparent when prophecy is contrasted with Scripture. Cf. Carter, *Gifts of the Spirit*, p. 77. However, most Pentecostals seem to insist on the conformity of prophetic utterance to Scripture; see Steiner, *Zeichen*, p. 177; Riggs, *Spirit Himself*, p. 161; and the emphatic caution of Hodges, *Spiritual Gifts*, pp. 18-21. Some Latin American and African Pentecostal groups appear to form an exception due, perhaps, to the pervasive spiritualistic influences of the environments. See Read, *New Patterns of Church Growth in Brazil*, pp. 39-40, 209-11 and *Hollenweger* I, 97-99, 126-28.

[28] So McPherson, *Holy Spirit*, pp. 167-69; Barratt, *Fire*, pp. 222-23; Carter, *Gifts of the Spirit*, p. 8; Gee, *Concerning Spiritual Gifts*, pp. 62-63; Christenson, *Speaking in Tongues*, p. 30.

A THEOLOGY OF THE HOLY SPIRIT

takes in both cases is said to be some kind of language. They are different in purpose and use in that the *evidence* of tongues is to confirm the baptism in the Holy Spirit while the *gift* of tongues, following I Corinthians fourteen, is to edify believers and to convict unbelievers.[29]

Although these two uses are to be kept distinct, it is usually insisted that the gift of tongues should continue to be enjoyed by every Pentecostal who has experienced the evidence of tongues. This reasoning is not difficult to follow, for given the necessity of the evidence of tongues in the spiritual baptism, not to continue speaking in tongues after having begun seems to most Pentecostals to be not only unspiritual but unnatural, indicating, it is sometimes argued, a lack of faith (Mark 16:17) and of obedience (I Cor. 14:5).

Thus while the evidence and the gift must be distinguished one from another (usually as the experiences of Acts and Corinthians, respectively), nevertheless, in normal circumstances the one should lead inevitably to the practice of the other. This is another indication of the value placed in Pentecostalism on speaking in tongues.

b. *The Nature and Content of the Gift.* The nature of the glossolalia in Pentecostal interpretation has already been discussed (above, pp. 85-86), but the nature of the *gift* of tongues differs from the nature of the evidence of tongues in the further sense that while the evidence occurs impulsively, outside the believer's control, the gift should be at least increasingly under the believer's control. The process at work in the gift of tongues is explained in the same uncomplex manner as it is in the evidence of tongues: as an inspiration of the Spirit expressing itself in a language. Therefore, the gift of tongues obtains in usual Pentecostal interpretation the following kind of definition: it is "the power to speak supernaturally by the Holy Spirit, in a language not known to the one possessing the gift."[30]

The content of the public gift of tongues when interpreted has been analyzed as falling into three major types which we may call: (1) prophetic, concerning the church's future; (2) promissory, concerning the church's present; and (3) exhortative and admonitory, concerning sin

---

[29] Cf. Winehouse, *Assemblies,* p. 209; Brumback, *What Meaneth This?,* pp. 249-50, 296; MacDonald, *Glossolalia in the New Testament,* p. 14.

[30] Carter, *Gifts of the Spirit,* p. 103. Real languages: Horton, *Gifts of the Spirit²,* p. 159; Reed, "Pentecostal Truths," p. 26; Carter, *Gifts of the Spirit,* who writes, "It is no exaggeration to say that the gifts of other tongues have been proved thousands of times by people who have known the language spoken, and who have confirmed the interpretation as being perfectly accurate," p. 115. So also Brumback, *What Meaneth This?,* p. 113; Christenson, *Speaking in Tongues,* pp. 22, 25; Jon Rutheven, "Is Glossolalia Languages?," *Paraclete,* 2 (Spring 1968), 27-30. See, however, Gee, *Pentecostal World Conference Messages,* p. 47 and Sherrill, *They Speak with Other Tongues,* pp. 89-103. I have noted a recent resistance to tongues understood as (in the NEB) "ecstatic utterances." Christenson, *Speaking in Tongues,* pp. 24, 83-84, 93. For non-Pentecostal studies see note 45, p. 86 above.

and righteousness in the local assembly.[31] The public gift of tongues has as its purpose nothing less than preaching or prophecy: the inspired direction of the people of God; and it differs from prophecy only in its coming in a more numinous and, as it were, other-worldly form. Finally, it has been observed that in many if not most modern instances of the exercise of the gift the speaking subject is either Jesus or the Holy Spirit, thus offering, like prophecy, the divine directly and "speaking."[32]

c. *The Private, Public, and Feminine Uses of the Gift.* The use of the gift of tongues is essentially two-fold; it is, explains Skibstedt, "of great value both for the personal edification of the individual and, when mediated through the gift of interpretation, for the common edification of the entire assembly."[33]

The first use of tongues is private and its purpose is personal edification in prayer. This understanding is found in the apostle Paul: "One who speaks in a tongue speaks . . . to God" and "edifies himself" (I Cor. 14:2, 4). Here God is praised and petitioned in spiritual speech "too deep for words" in one's own language (cf. Rom. 8:26) and the result is the enrichment of the petitioner. Pentecostals speak often of the benediction which this kind of prayer brings. "Those who have spoken in tongues in private worship and devotion," writes Williams, "can testify to the enriching, spiritual rest, and refreshing to the soul that results from such communion with God."[34] This intimate experience in prayer is valued by Pentecostals and their esteem is not

---

[31] The division suggested by Hutten, *MD, 14* (Nov. 15, 1951), 112-13. See examples in *Fleisch* II/2, 22.

[32] Hutten, *MD, 14* (Nov. 15, 1951), 112. Cf. Mosiman, *Zungenreden*, p. 77.

[33] *Geistestaufe*, p. 86. By 1963 Gee had apparently come to see the private use as the almost exclusive one: "We are left with the plain inference that the proper sphere of the Gift of Tongues is in private devotion, and for that reason it need not occupy us unduly as a Gift for ministry." *Spiritual Gifts in the Work of the Ministry Today*, p. 68.

[34] *Systematic Theology*, III, 49-50. Frodsham writes that "in these last days there is everything to break down the faith of the believer, but here we are shown God's mysterious means (the speaking in tongues) of building him up in the faith. Hundreds can testify that when they have been alone, praying in tongues for an hour or so, in sweet communion with God, they have been built up, strengthened and encouraged in their spiritual lives." *Rivers of Living Water and the Secret of a Perpetual Pentecost* (Springfield, Mo.: Gospel Publishing House, n.d.), p. 66. Neo-Pentecostalism, too, finding Paul saying that the tongues-speaker "edifies himself," believes, therefore, that *all* Christians should speak with tongues in private devotions and prayer. Christenson, *Speaking in Tongues*, pp. 28, 126, 129; Harper, *As at the Beginning*, p. 104. Indeed, before Christians can even edify the church through prophecy (I Cor. 14:4[b]), it is argued, they should be able to edify *themselves* through speaking in tongues (I Cor. 14:4[a]). Joseph R. Flower, "Holiness, the Spirit's Infilling, and Speaking with Tongues," *Paraclete, 2* (Summer 1968), 9. See the sympathetic views of Van Dusen in Sherrill, *They Speak with Other Tongues*, p. 30; Hollenweger, "Evangelism and Brazilian Pentecostalism," *EcRev, 20* (April 1968), 165.

decreased by the knowledge that Paul himself enjoyed the same experience (I Cor. 14:18). Pentecostals wish this experience for all Christians. Paul's difficult question, "Do all speak in tongues?" (I Cor. 12:30), implying that all do not, is referred in Pentecostal argument to the *public* use of tongues and not to the private which, it is contended, all Christians should enjoy. In the private use of tongues, finally, the gift of interpretation is unnecessary since others are not ordinarily present.

The second use of tongues is public or congregational and when accompanied by its complement, the gift of interpretation, has as its purpose the edification of believers (I Cor. 14:5) and the conviction of unbelievers (14:22). Here the gift of tongues reaches its full power, and when heightened miraculously by the gift of interpretation, the effect appears to be, in fact, inspirational to the faithful and confounding to the unbelieving. The distinctive mark of the Pentecostal church service is the exercise of this gift and its interpretation.

Paul's prohibiting women to speak in church, in the context of his discussion of speaking in tongues (I Cor. 14:34-35), is felt to be not "absolute" or admitting of no exceptions. For, it is usually contended, in earlier forbidding women to pray or prophesy in church with unveiled head (I Cor. 11:4, 5) Paul implies that *with* proper veiling a woman may pray or prophesy in church, thus over-ruling or supplementing Paul's later and seemingly absolute remarks in I Corinthians fourteen.[35]

In summary, it is in the private use of tongues that the individual Pentecostal finds a new means of praise and personal blessing, and it is in the public exercise of the gift that corporate Pentecostalism is provided externally with its most recognizable feature and internally with edification, conviction, and sometimes, of course, problems.

d. *The Alleged Apostolic Devaluation of the Gift.* The high assessment of the gift of tongues must face the overall argument of I Corinthians 12-14. It appears to a simple reading of this passage that the gift of tongues is prudently demoted by the apostle. But Pentecostalism has another exegesis. It will be pointed out that (1) the mere location of the gifts of tongues and their interpretation at the bottom of Paul's lists (I Cor. 12:8-10, 28-29) is no sufficient criterion of the apostle's devaluation since in other biblical lists the most valued commodity can be placed at the end also (e.g., II Pet. 1:5-7; I Cor. 13: 13); (2) a careful perusal of I Corinthians 14 will uncover the fact

---

[35] Brumback, *What Meaneth This?*, pp. 312-13; Horton, *Gifts of the Spirit*[2], p. 207; Elmer C. Miller, *Pentecost Examined by a Baptist Lawyer* (Springfield, Mo.: Gospel Publishing House, 1936), p. 117. Arnold Bittlinger prefers to omit the verses on women altogether, for somewhat tenuous reasons; *Gifts and Graces: A Commentary on I Corinthians 12-14*, tr. Herbert Klassen and Michael Harper (London: Hodder and Stoughton, 1967), p. 110 note.

that Paul, in the words of one interpreter, had "infinitely high esteem" for the gift of tongues, and Paul's citations to this effect can be listed. Indeed, it will be shown that because of Paul's special chapter-long treatment of the gift the conclusion must be drawn that he saw unusual worth in its manifestation. Steiner can in fact write that "according to I Corinthians, prophecy and speaking in tongues are treated as especially significant."[36]

But even should it be granted that tongues-speaking appears in Paul's estimates among the least of the gifts, Pentecostals propose that by virtue of its being least then, on Paul's analogy, it should be invested with the greater honor ("those parts of the body which we think less honorable we invest with greater honor," I Cor. 12:23) and should be, therefore, in greater prominence, for "if we do not possess the greater gifts we ought to have the least."[37] Finally, should Paul's express preference of prophecy to tongues be raised, Pentecostalism will insist that this also is relative, for the apostle places the gift of tongues, when accompanied by interpretation, on an exact level with prophecy when he writes that "he who prophesies is greater than he who speaks in tongues, *unless* someone interpret" (I Cor. 14:5), forming the equation: tongues plus interpretation equals prophecy.[38]

Thus, argue Pentecostals, the gift of tongues is by no means to be despised. Pentecostalism, far from seeing the demotion of the gift of tongues in I Corinthians 12-14, wishes to underline the apostle's remark in the critical fourteenth chapter: "I want you all to speak in tongues" (I Cor. 14:5).

e. *Summary.* When Pentecostalism's interpretation of I Corinthians twelve and fourteen is reviewed one sees the tenacity with which the gift of tongues is held and the ingenuity with which it can be de-

---

[36] *Zeichen*, p. 177. Cf. Horton, *Gifts of the Spirit*[2], p. 145. Brumback believes that Paul's criticism in I Cor. 14 concerns only the Corinthians' failure to provide tongues with interpretation and a limited number of utterances; see his list of fifteen texts from I Cor. 14 proving the apostle's high esteem for speaking in tongues, *What Meaneth This?*, pp. 167-69.

[37] Carter, *Gifts of the Spirit*, p. 106. He adds: "It should, therefore, be the possession of all God's people." *Ibid.* "For," writes Horton, "Tongues and Interpretation, like fingers and toes, being among the feebler members, are the most generously distributed, and, like veins and nerves, more jealously and carefully safeguarded." *Gifts of the Spirit*[2], p. 44. The gift of tongues "is among the least of the Gifts, and for that further reason it is by far the most frequently distributed and used." *Ibid.*, p. 145; similarly, Christenson, *Speaking in Tongues*, pp. 134-35; also, unexpectedly, the Catholic observer McDonnell, "Holy Spirit and Pentecostalism," *Commonweal*, 89 (Nov. 8, 1968), 200 and his "The Ecumenical Significance of the Pentecostal Movement," *Worship*, 40 (Dec. 1966), 614.

[38] Barratt, *Rain*, p. 45; Carter, *Gifts of the Spirit*, p. 78; MacDonald, *Glossolalia in the New Testament*, p. 15. The Anglican pastor Kelsey, who is sympathetic to Pentecostal manifestation, even sees speaking in tongues as a more dependable spiritual sign than prophecy which, he believes, can be ego-serving. *Tongue Speaking*, p. 17.

fended. Donald Gee believes that its defense is not only warranted but necessary. He finds in the revival of the gift of tongues within the Pentecostal movement a divine impetus for the reevaluation by the historic churches of the whole subject of spiritual gifts.[39] Therefore Pentecostalism does not wish to apologize for its estimation of the gift of tongues and it insists that any apparent over-emphasis which tongues-speaking receives to the seeming neglect of other gifts is due more to its underestimation in the eyes of the rest of the church than to its arbitrary exaltation in Pentecostalism.

5. THE GIFT OF THE INTERPRETATION OF TONGUES

The gift of the interpretation of tongues is explained in the same simple manner as the gift of tongues. The gift is believed to provide a *real* interpretation, hence agreeing in content with the message in tongues, but at the same time it is believed to be a *spiritual* gift, hence offering more than simply a literal translation of the message.[40] Mosiman explains:

> The activity of tongues-interpretation is not dependent upon a conscious understanding of the speech of the "inspired" speaker. The interpretation is not a translation ... of one language into another.... The interpretation ... is the reproduction into conventional speech of the thoughts and feelings which have been expressed in tongues-speaking.[41]

In actual practice, to our observation, the exercise of the gift of the interpretation of tongues differs imperceptibly from the exercise of the gift of prophecy: the interpreter, like the prophet, stands, addresses the assembly in an earnest, ecstatic, exhortatory, and usually eschatological manner, as an instrument of the Spirit and for the edification of the assembly. The interpreter, in other words, is semi-glossolalic and semi-prophetic, and his work completes the gift of tongues as it resembles the gift of prophecy.

SUMMARY AND CONCLUSION

We may say of the gifts of the Holy Spirit in the Pentecostal movement that the more subtle or mental of these gifts — e.g., the gifts of the word of knowledge, or wisdom, teaching, administration, aids — receive little more emphasis, indeed, probably less, than in the non-Pentecostal churches. But in two important respects the gifts of the

---

[39] *Concerning Spiritual Gifts*, p. 115. See also his 1963 lectures: "We suggest a contribution by the Pentecostal movement to the whole Church of the greatest value when we testify to the desirability of having His presence made manifest by means of spiritual gifts. We dare to believe that this is one of the supreme purposes of God in sending the Pentecostal Revival in the twentieth century." *Spiritual Gifts in the Work of the Ministry Today*, p. 24. Also Finsaas in Christenson, *Speaking in Tongues*, p. 98.

[40] Steiner, *Zeichen*, p. 177. Gee, *Concerning Spiritual Gifts*, p. 96.

[41] *Zungenreden*, pp. 114-15.

Spirit are highlighted: in their corporate expression in the Pentecostal meeting and in their striking expression in individual Pentecostals.

In the Pentecostal meeting the outsider may be obliged to recognize that the Pentecostal movement has discovered a cardinal biblical truth: the truth that, in the words of one Pentecostal leader, "religion is a life to be lived in fellowship; a conflict which can be carried on only in groups. . . . This religion finds expression through a Church wherein every person from the minister down to the lowliest member 'according to the grace that is given to us' is called to exercise his gift, effectually working for the general good of the whole."[42] The discovery and the application of this truth no doubt explain in large measure the world-wide appeal of the Pentecostal movement. And its relative neglect may explain in part some of the problems of the historic churches.

Pentecostalism takes the congregational exercise of the individual gifts with a final seriousness. In the Pentecostal meeting the priesthood of believers *within the congregation* is believed and attempted on a scale unparalleled, to our knowledge, in any other branch of the church. As in the New Testament, the congregational fellowship of believers is experienced as nothing less significant than the center of the Christian life. "I think we must say that a real congregational life," writes Bishop Newbigin in his appreciation of Pentecostalism, "wherein each member has his opportunity to contribute to the life of the whole body those gifts with which the Spirit endows him, is as much of the *esse* of the Church as are ministry and sacraments."[43] If Pentecostalism has raised this *esse* in its acute form it may deserve our appreciation.

At least since Montanus, perhaps since Corinth, the gifts of the Spirit have appeared to be more a source of embarrassment than of encouragement to the Christian church. Pentecostalism, by raising the doctrine of the gifts of the Spirit in even its most embarrassing forms, may be performing a needed, perhaps even a very important ministry.

---

[42] Buntain, *Holy Ghost and Fire,* p. 62.

[43] *Household of God,* pp. 117-18. And from the Roman Catholic perspective Hans Küng writes that in his opinion "there is probably no section of the Constitution on the Church [of Vatican II] that will prove more fruitful for ecumenical discussion than that on the charismata" and that "to rediscover the charismata is to rediscover the real ecclesiology of St. Paul." "The Charismatic Structure of the Church," *The Church and Ecumenism* ("Concilium," Vol. 4), pp. 41, 49.

Part Two

THE HOLY SPIRIT IN
NEW TESTAMENT WITNESS

PRELIMINARY REMARKS

Having analyzed the Pentecostal doctrine and experience of the Holy Spirit at its center and in its parts, it is now in order to place the Pentecostal understanding under the light of the New Testament witness. We shall seek throughout this second part, at appropriate places, to compare the Pentecostal doctrine with the New Testament's.

Exegesis has as its first responsibility the discovery of the proper text and of the meaning of the text in the setting in which it was written. The responsible historical-critical commentary makes this discovery its primary task. All other exegesis must be based upon this carefully laid foundation. That we have attempted to base our "comparative exegesis" upon this foundation is indicated in the conversation carried on in the notes.

We should say that in Acts, to which special attention is necessarily devoted, we cannot presume a competence to assign the text's main features *primarily* to Luke's literary work, or as is now more clear, to his theological work, rather than to events in history which the author of Acts seeks to reflect and, of course, to interpret, *if* such an assignment should in practice involve making the text as it stands mean less, or bear less weight in the church, than it intends to mean and bear. To do this — to say, for example, that Luke is principally an artist, of either aesthetic or theological provenance, and therefore in doctrine often simply mistaken, distorting, or the victim of his sources, or of his de-eschatologized or *frühkatholische* theology, even if any one of these or more should be true — would mean not only to go beyond our competence, but in our task to appear to concede to Pentecostalism that while it works with Acts we work with something better — for example, with *Paul's* doctrine of the Spirit — or with something worse, namely with Luke's pretensions. This must mean in our case to concede Acts as it stands to Pentecostalism.

It has become our conviction that such a concession is not only not necessary, but in many cases not right, as the following pages will seek to make clear. The final question at stake in our confrontation with Pentecostalism is not: was Luke right or wrong, astute or aberrant, accurate or fanciful, but: does Pentecostalism rightly or wrongly understand Luke, accurately or mistakenly interpret him, properly or improperly apply him? Hence we feel obliged in most cases to take the text as it stands and to take it with a full seriousness and as authority. This will involve, of course, critical work. But when the text is discovered and rendered it is not the text, or Luke, whom we wish to put on trial, but ourselves, Pentecostalism, and the church. Ours is the task of hearing the text — what it said then and what it means now.

Thus our particular responsibility in this section is to bring what the first-century witnesses report into a very concrete, contemporary missionary situation — into relation with twentieth-century Pentecostalism. Essentially, then, our task is not *religionswissenschaftlich* but *missionswissenschaftlich*. Our major questions throughout this second part will be two-fold: (1) *theologia Scripturae:* What is the doctrine and experience of the Holy Spirit taught in this particular text of the New Testament? and (2) *theologia missionis:* How does this biblical datum correspond to the doctrine and experience of the Holy Spirit borne witness to in Pentecostalism? It is the establishment of this relationship which we see as our final responsibility.

The plan of this second part of the study then is first to study Acts, particularly its Spirit-baptism texts and, where profitable, to show comparison with Pentecostal doctrine (ch. V). This study in Acts is to be followed by a systematically arranged investigation of the condition, means, and evidence of the Holy Spirit — what we shall call *the Way of the Spirit* — in the light of the New Testament witnesses outside of Acts, in correspondence with and in consequence for the witness of Pentecostalism (ch. VI). A study of the relevant spiritual problems in the church in Corinth and the apostle's approach to their solution concludes the second part (ch. VII).

The church in the twentieth century wishes to learn what the definitive first-century apostolic witness said about the gift then received and which the church in our time has also received and wants much better to understand and fully to experience — the gift of the Holy Spirit. Pentecostalism has given us the opportunity of going to the very heart — to the Spirit — of the New Testament.

V

THE BAPTISM OF THE HOLY SPIRIT
IN THE ACTS OF THE APOSTLES:
A COMPARATIVE STUDY

A. ACTS 1:1 — 2:13. THE BAPTISM OF THE HOLY SPIRIT AT PENTECOST: ITS PROMISE AND ITS OCCURRENCE

1. ACTS 1:1-2: THE FUNCTION OF THE HOLY SPIRIT IN ACTS

Luke begins the second volume of his work by employing two important expressions through which he apparently intended to have his present volume understood and interpreted:

> In the first book, O Theophilus, I have dealt with all that Jesus *began* to do and teach, until the day when he was taken up, after he had given commandment *through the Holy Spirit* to the apostles whom he had chosen (1:1-2).

First, what Jesus *began* to do and teach he now continues. "This second volume," comments Stählin, "clearly intends to present the second period of Jesus' work."[1] What Jesus commenced in the flesh as

---

[1] *Die Apostelgeschichte* ("NTD"; 10th ed.; Göttingen: Vandenhoeck und Ruprecht, 1962), p. 11. Also Bo Reicke, *Glauben und Leben der Urgemeinde: Bemerkungen zu Apostelgeschichte 1-7* (Zürich: Zwingli, 1957), p. 10. Cf. Schweizer, art. *pneuma, TWNT,* VI, 402, 15-16; 403, 23-25; and the discussion in J. H. E. Hull, *The Holy Spirit in the Acts of the Apostles* (London: Lutterworth, 1967), pp. 179-80. See, however, H. A. W. Meyer, *Kritisch-Exegetisches Handbuch über die Apostelgeschichte* ("MeyerK"; 3d ed.; Göttingen: Vandenhoeck und Ruprecht, 1861), pp. 25-26, and Hans Conzelmann, *Die Apostelgeschichte* ("HNT," 7; Tübingen: Mohr, 1963), p. 20. Our use of the name "Luke" is merely traditional and convenient; the relation of the author of Luke-Acts to Paul's physician companion is not considered. Our use of the phrase "baptism of the Holy Spirit" is mainly euphonic and is not intended to differ in any way from Pentecostalism's more usual expression, "baptism in the Holy Spirit." Finally, references to sayings of Jesus, Peter, Paul, and others in Acts do not intend to deny Luke's creative work: again, the device of traditional reference is in the interest of simplicity.

recorded in the Gospel, he now continues in his new humanity, the church, as recorded in Acts.

Second, Jesus' post-resurrection ministry, epitomized in the missionary commandment (Luke 24:46-49; Acts 1:8), is to be understood as a ministry performed "through the Holy Spirit." The meaning of this initial reference to the Spirit in the Book of Acts is first of all this: Jesus himself is the subject of the Spirit's work in history.

Luke wishes here in an impressive introductory manner to connect the work of Jesus with the ministry of the Spirit. What Jesus did or continues to do was and is "through the Holy Spirit." Luke does not wish for the Holy Spirit, who is to play such an important role in Acts, to be separated from the work of Jesus Christ as though the Holy Spirit could be understood to have a separate, independent, or even analogous work of his own. Luke's first sentence makes clear an intention of his entire book: the Spirit is not to be dissociated from Jesus. The Spirit *is* Jesus at work in continuation of his ministry.

The work of the Holy Spirit in the history of the apostles about to be recorded by Luke, then, is to be understood in the light of its initial sentence (1:1-2). The work of the Holy Spirit is the extension of the ministry begun and now continued by Jesus Christ himself, and the deeds of the church — the acts of the apostles — are the fruit and expression of that ministry.

The doctrine of a distinctive work of the Holy Spirit *beyond* Jesus' work, a doctrine taken often from the Book of Acts, must be assessed in the context of Acts' programmatic first sentence.

2. Acts 1:4-5: The Promise of the Baptism of the Holy Spirit

And while staying with them he charged them not to depart from Jerusalem, but to wait for the promise of the Father, which, he said, "you heard from me, for John baptized with water, but before many days you shall be baptized with the Holy Spirit" (1:4-5).

To receive the promised baptism with the Holy Spirit the apostles are commanded not to leave Jerusalem. Jerusalem, in Luke's conception, is to be the site of the penultimate event of salvation history prior to the ultimate of the return of Christ (v. 11b). Here in Jerusalem, holy-history is to find again its vital center and its new beginning. The importance of Jerusalem to Luke-Acts cannot easily be overestimated.

Of most significance to us, the condition for the baptism of the Holy Spirit — remaining in Jerusalem — is not psychological, it is geographical; it is not so much "spiritual" as it is spatial. That is, it is not the *waiting,* it is the waiting in *Jerusalem* which is stressed. Whether Jesus' utterance can even properly be called a "condition" at all, in the frequently used sense of spiritual qualification, is debatable. In concluding his Gospel, for example, Luke used the verb "stay" or literally "sit" (*kathisate*) to describe Jesus' command to the apostles: *"Kathisate* in the city until you are clothed with power from on high" (Luke 24:49). Whether the verb is "wait" (*perimenein*, 1:4) as in Acts, or "sit" as in the Gospel, it is as unstrenuous and as non-subjective a condition as it seems possible to suggest. It does not really appear that Jesus contemplated giving the apostles what are usually understood as conditions when he announced the Spirit's coming. For Jesus did not preface his charge with a conditional "if" — "if you remain in Jerusalem you shall be baptized in the Holy Spirit"; rather, upon charging the disciples to remain in Jerusalem he simply promises the Holy Spirit (vv. 4b-5).

A careful study of the words used in this paradigmatic announcement of the baptism of the Holy Spirit heightens the character of the Spirit as gift. First, the baptism of the Holy Spirit in Acts is called not "the opportunity," "responsibility," or even "privilege" of the believer, but "the *promise* of the Father" (v. 4). The baptism of the Holy Spirit thus comes in the name of promise not law, hence as gift not challenge. The name of the Spirit here also teaches us that the source of the baptism in the Spirit is not human, it is divine: the Spirit is "the promise of the *Father.*"

The word "promise" (*epaggelia*) has a pedigree in the New Testament (cf. outside Luke 24:49 and Acts 1:4; 2:33, 39; and notably Rom. 4:13, 14, 20; Gal. 3 *passim*, especially v. 14; Heb. *passim*). It is usually involved in its major New Testament contexts with grace and contrasted with effort (cf. particularly Rom. 4 and Gal. 3). It is braced in Acts, e.g., with the equally rich sister word *dörea*, "free gift," in Peter's first offer of the "baptism of the Holy Spirit" after Pentecost (Acts 2:38-39). In Acts implicitly as elsewhere in the New Testament explicitly, the divine promise has as its classic opposite the law, i.e., demand, specifically the demand for spiritual effort.[2]

The promise of the Spirit is a present, with all the happy associations of a present, particularly from a father, with a present's significance as free, without price, cost, or condition. "The divine promise in the New Testament is always *epaggelia* not *huposchesis*, 'pollicitum' not 'promissum,' a gift graciously bestowed and not a pledge obtained by negotiation."[3]

It is instructive to notice in preface that in each of the major Spirit-baptism passages in Acts — 1:4 (pre-Pentecost); 2:33 (Pentecost); 2:38-39 (post-Pentecost); 8:20 (Samaria); 10:45 (Caesarea; also 11:17); and perhaps implicitly 19:2 (Ephesus: *elabete;* cf. also 15:8 *dous*) — the Holy Spirit finds either the name "promise" or "gift." The

[2] Conzelmann points out that Luke's use of *epaggelia* is not unique and belongs to the early church's regular vocabulary. *The Theology of St. Luke,* tr. Geoffrey Buswell (London: Faber and Faber, 1960), p. 220.

[3] J. B. Lightfoot to the relevant passage Gal. 3:14b: "that we might receive the promise of the Spirit through faith." *Saint Paul's Epistle to the Galatians: A Revised Text with Introduction, Notes, and Dissertations* (9th ed.; London: Macmillan, 1887), p. 140.

Spirit in Acts is never achieved or "obtained" (cf. Acts 8:19-20 *ktasthai!*),
he is always a present, i.e., he is the Spirit *of God*. Therefore, here at
the opening of Acts Luke gives the Spirit the name by which he is
rightly to be understood in the remainder of the book: he is "the
promise of the *Father.*"

Jesus continued by reminding the apostles that they had heard of
this promise from him and that "John baptized with water, but before
many days you shall be baptized with the Holy Spirit" (v. 5). Grammatically, the voice of the promised baptism is important: it is passive
(*baptisthēsesthe*). The passive means that the baptism of the Spirit shall
not be the result of the recipients' activity; the subject of the spiritual
baptism is not to be the recipient and his effort but the promiser
and his will.

Comparable to the promise used in Acts is the earlier promise in
Luke's Gospel, also passive: "until you are clothed (*endusēsthe*) with
power from on high" (24:49). In Luke's Gospel the promise of the
Spirit is not understood as a human or even spiritual achievement but
as a divine gift: it descends significantly, "from on high," out of men's
reach.

Finally, even the last words of the Acts' promise (in the Greek
text), seemingly insignificant, breathe grace: the promise will not be
long in coming, and evidently without any necessary connection to the
disciples' readiness: it shall be "before many days," i.e., soon.

This is the first announcement of the baptism of the Holy Spirit in
Acts. Had there been a wish to generate a fuller participation by the
apostles (or future readers) in the procuring of the coming gift we may
have expected a teaching with more challenge, or an invitation with
several conditions. Sitting is not the posture of heroes. The command
to remain in Jerusalem could have been supplemented in Luke's record
with instructions on how to wait, how best to fill the time while waiting,
or with requisite obedience in prayer and devotional exercise. But we
have no account of these; only the quiet "wait," "remain," "sit."

Still another possibility would have been to put the promise in the
subjunctive: "You may (or might) be baptized with the Holy Spirit,"
or even "You can be baptized with the Holy Spirit," rather than in the
simple future indicative, "you shall be baptized," which places no
demands on the apostles and which suggests no uncertainty of the
promise's implementation. The subjunctive, however, would have caused
soul-searching in the little company.

A further possibility would have been to record Jesus as promising
the Spirit to *some,* to those, namely, who fulfilled certain conditions:
"Some of you shall (or may) receive the Spirit." This would have suggested that only those who were spiritually prepared for the gift would
be the recipients of it. This could have meant that only those who
were sufficiently emptied, as it is said, would be appropriately filled.

The word "some" would have made the promise conditional, for no one would wish to miss being one of the some.

It is as surprising as it is significant, therefore, to notice the absence of either grammatical or inner conditions for the baptism of the Holy Spirit, apart from the injunction to wait in Jerusalem, in this its standard announcement. In remarkable simplicity Jesus is recorded as promising the baptism of the Holy Spirit inclusively to all (*baptisthēsesthe*, 1:5), and it is later given to all (2:4). One of the most noteworthy features of the baptism or gift of the Holy Spirit in Acts is in fact that it is given to *every* believer present, without exception or qualification — from the one hundred and twenty at Pentecost to the twelve at Ephesus (19:1-7). There is no record in Acts of any believer in a group of believers failing to receive (or partly receiving) the promised Holy Spirit when he descended. The Holy Spirit comes as inclusively as he does unconditionally. Both belong to his character as gift.

Moreover, there is no recorded reference in any filling or giving of the Holy Spirit in Acts to the subjective measure or depth of faith or obedience in the many different recipients. Not every one on every occasion had exactly the same subjective inner states and conditions. Yet this did not seem to matter. Perhaps God's gift has the finest opportunity of showing itself as a gift when it overlooks conditions. In any case, Jesus' promise of the baptism with the Holy Spirit *is* inclusive, passive, indicative, and simple future.

In every way possible the opening page of Acts seems seeking to avoid the slightest tendency in its readers to think of the Spirit, who will be so central to the book, as a reward for effort or as decisively or conditionally dependent upon the recipients' subjectivity beyond faith in Jesus' promise. The opening paragraph of Acts has set the standard terms by which the Holy Spirit in the remainder of the book is to be understood. This paragraph is the lexicon of the Spirit in Acts. As the opening sentence united the Holy Spirit with the work of Jesus, so the opening paragraph clothes the Spirit in his proper name: the promise. The Holy Spirit is, even at the very beginning, Jesus' way of working in his church (vv. 1-2), and the church will receive him freely, inclusively, and indicatively — as a promise (vv. 4-5).

3. ACTS 1:8: THE PROMISE OF THE POWER OF THE HOLY SPIRIT

The final relevant reference to the Holy Spirit prior to Pentecost[4] is incorporated appropriately enough in the "table of contents" to the Book of Acts — 1:8 — a text very important to Pentecostalism as we have observed. As Luke had recorded the theme to his Gospel in a dominical word concerning the Holy Spirit's relation to Jesus (Luke 4:18), so similarly the Spirit's relation to Jesus is stressed

---

[4] In v. 16 Luke understands the Spirit in the traditional Jewish prophetic way.

in Acts' thematic statement. Jesus turns the apostles' curiosity about the future kingdom away from speculation and to the sphere and plan of mission which is the means of the kingdom and the theme of the Book of Acts.

> But you shall receive power when the Holy Spirit has come upon you; and you shall be my witnesses in Jerusalem and in all Judea and Samaria and to the end of the earth (1:8).

If we observe this verse carefully we shall notice features that are already beginning to recur in the Acts' doctrine of the Spirit. The promise (it *is* a promise!) is again a simple future rather than a complex possibility in the subjunctive or imperative.

Further, perhaps even the preposition used here — *epi* ("upon") — prominent also in Peter's Pentecost address (cf. 2:17, 18, 19) is meant to point to the sovereign, gracious giver, and away from the recipients: the Holy Spirit comes "upon" (*ep*elthontos . . . *eph*, 1:8). The Spirit (in Volz's observations on the Hebrew *'al* which the Greek *epi* translates) "comes from above (*'al*), that is in contemporary idiom, the Spirit is a divine gift."[5] Prepositionally, we may say that the Spirit's direction of origin in Acts is not *ek* but *eph*, he comes not from within but from "on high" (Luke 24:49). That is, the Spirit does not arise from within the emotional or spiritual life of the recipient, he is not dependent upon or subject to one's inner states. The Spirit comes from above and upon, i.e., from God.

When the Spirit has come upon his people there shall be power; but, according to the text, not power *per se* or for us, but for a higher task: "you shall be *my* witnesses." The "my" is accentuated by its position in the original. Significantly, the object of the spiritual witness shall not be the gift, power, or baptism of the Holy Spirit. Jesus is the object, but more than object, he is first of all the subject of the witness of the Spirit. The apostles are *his* (genitive possessive) witnesses, belonging to him and in his possession. The power of the baptism of the Holy Spirit is first and foremost a power which joins to Christ. Our seeing this clearly depends upon the observation of the verb used here to describe the result of the power of the Holy Spirit: *esesthe,* "you shall *be.*" It is a copula, a joining verb. The result of the power of the baptism of the Holy Spirit according to Acts 1:8 is first of all not what men do but what they become. The greatness of the baptism of the Holy Spirit is not that it is an event *beyond* the joining of a man to the ascended Christ but that it is precisely this event itself. To be baptized in the Spirit is to become Christ's. The baptism of the Holy Spirit joins men to Christ in such a way that the recipients become *his,* i.e., Christians. The power of the Holy Spirit is his ability to join men to

---

[5] *Der Geist Gottes und die verwandten Erscheinungen im Alten Testament und in anschliessenden Judentum* (Tübingen: Mohr, 1910), p. 98.

the risen Christ so that they are able to represent him. There is no higher blessing.

And this promise and its power, like its predecessor's (1:4-5), is inclusive and not selective (*esesthe*), which is another way of saying that it is gracious and not conditional. There are no conditions in Acts 1:8. This promise is recorded, of course, with particular reference to the apostles. But as in the Gospels, what is said here is meant to apply derivatively to future generations. We can never be witnesses (*martures*) in one sense of the word: eye-witnesses of the historical and risen Lord. However, the power received by the descent of the Holy Spirit upon the lives of the apostles was not an apostolic prerogative, for if it were, none but the apostles would be joined to Christ.

Jesus joins men to himself through his Spirit: this is the power, the glory, and the ministry of the baptism with the Holy Spirit. Only when the Spirit came upon the apostles were they joined with the newly ascended Lord, and only then did they have the commensurate authority and ability to bear witness to him. And throughout Acts it is to Christ, to his work and salvation, and not to an independent, second work of the Holy Spirit that the apostolic preaching in fact bears witness. The power of the baptism of the Holy Spirit is the power of Christocentricity.[6]

Finally, Acts 1:8 contains the chapter-titles of Acts: "in Jerusalem and in all Judea and Samaria and to the end of the earth." As Acts unfolds the reader discovers that at each critical chapter the Lord "through the Spirit" employs extraordinary means to instruct the church in the universality and unconditionality of the gospel: even for the racially and religiously suspect Samaritan (ch. 8), even for the spiritually unclean Gentile (chs. 10-11). The first half of Acts is largely a story of how the church learns the nature of the gospel (and this includes the nature of the Holy Spirit) as promissory, free, universal, and received apart from obedience to the law or special conditions of holiness — i.e., that salvation is received simply by faith. This fact is sealed in the Jerusalem council (ch. 15). Thus Acts becomes an object lesson in the nature of the church and its mission.

A Galatian text serves as a fitting theological conclusion to Pentecost's introduction:

> Christ redeemed us from the curse of the law ... that in Christ Jesus ... we might receive the promise of the Spirit through faith (3:14).

Between Christ's promise and Pentecost, Acts records in successive scenes: Christ's ascension (1:9-11), the return to Jerusalem and the up-

---

6 Perhaps significantly, after Pentecost and the christological reference in the sermon at the Caesarean "Pentecost" (Acts 10:38), allusion to the Holy Spirit *per se* does not occur in the record of an apostolic missionary sermon. (Stephen's remark at Acts 7:51 is neither an apostle's nor, in the usual sense, missionary.)

per room (1:12-14), followed by a longer account of the enlarging of the apostolic circle (1:15-26). In this eighteen-verse interlude Pentecostalism often finds a verse by which to establish a condition for the coming of the Holy Spirit in his Pentecostal power: "All these with one accord devoted themselves to prayer, together with the women and Mary the mother of Jesus, and with his brothers" (1:14). However, Luke is not recording a condition (or conditions). The company is not praying because Jesus conditioned the Spirit's coming upon prayer either sufficient, unified, or ardent. The introduction to Acts was conspicuous for the absence of conditions of this nature. The *fact.* therefore that the believers prayed is the more understandable: it is in the atmosphere of grace that prayer flourishes.

Of most significance, the record does not say that there was prayer for the Holy Spirit. The Spirit is not mentioned. Luke, in fact, mentions no object of prayer at all. The absence in this text of the condition of prayer or the object of the Holy Spirit makes it difficult for the argument to be convincing which finds here the condition of prayer for the baptism of the Holy Spirit. The united and devoted prayer of the Christians in the upper room is notable when it is allowed to be a fact, it is troubling when it is required as a condition. The fact of prayer is placed in a phrase enough verses removed from the actual Pentecost event to keep it from appearing to be the cause of Pentecost. Pentecost was not occasioned by the disciples' marvelous prayer-life or their fulfilling of conditions. Pentecost, according to Peter's sermon, came by one means: by the exaltation of Jesus Christ to the right hand of the Father where *he* received and gave the Spirit in the same name by which he had been announced — as "the promise" (2:33; 1:4).

4. ACTS 2:1-13: PENTECOST

Pentecost is ushered in with an historical notice: "When the day of Pentecost had come" (lit., was fulfilled). Rather than pointing to the fulfillment of any or several spiritual requirements — for instance, "when the disciples had fully met the price of Pentecost," Luke points to history and to the sovereign timing of God.

When the day came "they were all together in one place" (v. 1b). If one wishes to find in their being together in one place a moral accomplishment he may, but the text offers no special encouragement.

Then the Pentecost event occurs.

> And suddenly a sound came from heaven like the rush of a mighty wind, and it filled all the house where they were sitting. And there appeared to them tongues as of fire, distributed and resting on each one of them. And they were all filled with the Holy Spirit and began to speak in other tongues, as the Spirit gave them utterance (2:2-4).

"From heaven," and "suddenly," the gift appears. The suddenness removes any graduated nuance and the "from heaven" gives the Spirit his proper direction of origin and takes the source of the gift from men's hands and hearts.

The final word in v. 2 gives us a glimpse — one of the very few — into the subjective condition of the disciples: "where they were *sitting* (*ësan kathëmenoi*)." Luke might have said, "where they were praying," or "kneeling," or perhaps even "seeking," or "yielding." But Luke, who otherwise reserves a large and prominent place for prayer, particularly in relation to the Holy Spirit (cf., e.g., Luke 3:21; 11:3 D; 11:13), must appear to have missed an opportunity here. Or perhaps an intention was expressed in the omission: the gift, especially this first and, as Pentecostals say, this pattern-making gift at Pentecost, must be seen as a gift. Not even the church's prayer must be brought into a too close proximity or prominence when the promise "suddenly," "from heaven," appears in history.

The tongues as of fire sat on "*each* one of them," "and they were *all* filled with the Holy Spirit." As we have observed earlier, there is no record in Acts of one or several persons being passed over with the full gift of the Spirit due to the insufficient meeting of conditions. It is another relevant feature of the doctrine of the Holy Spirit in Acts that when the Spirit comes he is not recorded as coming partially, as only participating in the life of the recipient, applying justification, and then leaving to return in fulness, sanctification, or power at a later time when the justified person is more worthy, empty, or clean. There is no partial filling of the Holy Spirit in the Book of Acts. The Holy Spirit, in relation to believers, is evidently not only not selective (coming on only a few) and not conditional (coming on only the worthy), he is not partial (coming only part-way). The gift of the Spirit is the filling of the Spirit. This is the testimony of the Book of Acts from its beginning. Wherever the Holy Spirit comes to a man he comes, to use the familiar language, to fill, not only to effect; to dwell, not simply to visit. Finally, the Holy Spirit is a person, and therefore where he is, he is fully, and not two-thirds or three-quarters.[7]

"And [they] began to speak in other tongues, as the Spirit gave them utterance" (v. 4b). There had been no indication in Luke's Gospel or in Acts heretofore that speaking in tongues would be in the church's experience. Nor were the disciples at Pentecost recorded as seeking this particular experience. Yet nothing more aptly expressed the will of God for the world mission of the church than proclaiming the great deeds of God in the world's languages. This is what gives the Pentecost story its beauty and meaning. To be filled with the Holy

---

[7] Herman Gunkel writes that "expressions such as 'be filled with the Holy Spirit'... appear... to flow from the view... that as much of the Holy Spirit will be given a person as he can contain." *Die Wirkungen des heiligen Geistes nach der populären Anschauung der apostolischen Zeit und der Lehre des Apostels Paulus: Eine biblisch-theologische Studie* (2d ed.; Göttingen: Vandenhoeck und Ruprecht, 1899), p. 29. But *every* reception of the Spirit is, in Luke's teaching, a filling of the Spirit.

Spirit is to want others to know God's deeds in Christ. The Holy Spirit moves men to praise the "mighty works of God" (v. 11).[8]

It appears to be Luke's opinion, expressed at least in his choice of words, that the event at Pentecost was unique in being a "speaking in *other* (*heterais*) tongues," i.e., in other languages (cf. the synonym in vv. 6 and 8: *dialektō*). In neither of the other two (and only) records of glossolalia in Acts does Luke add the word "other" to tongues (cf. 10:46; 19:6). Furthermore, there was no one recorded as present at either Caesarea (Acts 10) or Ephesus (Acts 19) who needed a speaking in other languages; only at Pentecost do we have a record, as Luke intends it, of several diverse linguistic groups to whom the gospel is preached by means of miraculously given tongues.

Not only the sounds and visions as of wind and fire disappear with Pentecost, but the speaking in *other* tongues, i.e., in other languages as well. Most of the phenomena attending Pentecost were swept away after Pentecost; in Acts the one constant — stressed especially in the major Spirit passages — is the essence of the matter: the Spirit of God is the Spirit of *God*, i.e., a gift.

The absence of the *seeking* of the speaking in tongues is significant. It, with the intelligibility of the tongues, places seriously in question the adequacy of Pentecost as a "pattern" for the Pentecostal baptism in the Holy Spirit. The Pentecostal historian Kendrick, writing of Pentecostal origins, remarks that Agnes Ozman "was the first known person to have received such an experience as a result of specifically seeking a baptism in the Holy Spirit with the expectation of speaking in tongues" (p. 53). However, neither in Acts 2 nor in Acts 8, 10, or 19 — the primary Pentecostal texts for tongues as evidence — are tongues recorded as *sought*. Thus there is an internal contradiction in the creedal use of Acts 2:4 in each *Pentecostal Evangel,* the major American Pentecostal journal: "We believe that the Baptism of the Holy Spirit according to Acts 2:4 is given to believers who ask for it." For the tongues-baptism in the Holy Spirit, according to Acts 2:4, is not asked for. In fact, in neither Acts 2, Acts 8 (where no tongues are recorded at all), Acts 10, nor Acts 19 is either a baptism in the Holy

---

[8] While the glossolalia may be in part described as worship we do not believe that worship, in the narrower sense, is the most accurate way to describe the purpose of the tongues of Pentecost. The purpose of Pentecost's glossolalia appears to be mission, as indicated mainly by the expression "other tongues" (*heterais glōssais*) — both by the fact that the tongues *are* "other" and plural and by their reference to the catalogue of nations (Acts 2:9-11). It appears that according to Luke's account the Pentecost glossolalia were intended to attract outsiders and thus to expedite Peter's sermon. Acts 2:14-47 interprets the meaning of Acts 2:1-13. For literature on glossolalia see now particularly A. J. Mattill, Jr., and Mary Bedford Mattill, *A Classified Bibliography of Literature on the Acts of the Apostles* ("New Testament Tools and Studies," 7; ed. Bruce M. Metzger; Leiden: E. J. Brill, 1966), pp. 343-51.

Spirit *or* speaking in tongues asked for by the recipients. Must this not affect the Pentecostal doctrine of a specifically sought baptism in the Holy Spirit with its evidence of tongues?

B. ACTS 2:14-39: THE MEANS OF THE BAPTISM OF THE HOLY SPIRIT ESTABLISHED AT PENTECOST: CHRISTIAN PREACHING AND BAPTISM

1. Acts 2:14-36: Christian Preaching

It is in Luke's interest as he develops the Pentecost events in Acts 2 that the meaning of Pentecost be found not in the interior spiritual life of the disciples nor even in the gift of the Holy Spirit, but in the preaching of Jesus Christ. In the center of Luke's attention at Pentecost — even quantitatively — is not what we usually think when we say "Pentecost," i.e., the Spirit, it is Jesus Christ; not spiritual ecstasy, but a Christian sermon.

Peter takes up the mocking of some, points out that what they have just seen and heard is the fulfillment of God's promise in the prophet Joel to pour out his Spirit upon (*epi!*) all flesh, stressing "And it shall be that whoever calls on the name of the Lord shall be saved" (v. 21). Joel, like Luke (like Peter), finds the *point* of the great eschatological Spirit-event not so much in the pouring out of the Spirit as such as in the universal promise of salvation *for which* the Spirit is poured out.

And "beginning from this scripture" Peter proceeds to preach Jesus of Nazareth, what he did and means and what he has just now accomplished (v. 33), concluding with the piercing accusation that this very Jesus, whom God made Lord and Christ, had been the victim of their crucifixion. Peter's movement in his sermon, comparable to Joel's movement in his prophecy, is the *one* movement of the Holy Spirit: away from the Spirit to the Christ. *This* is the Holy Spirit's power; this is his office (1:8). The ministry of the Spirit is Christo-centricity. The means of the Spirit is Christian preaching.

2. Acts 2:37-39: Christian Baptism

The Spirit-moved sermon awoke conviction in the heart of the hearers. Luke teaches here historically what Paul elsewhere teaches more systematically: that the move to faith is the work of the Holy Spirit.[9]

---

[9] This is our objection to the widely held opinion that Luke with the "popular view" (Gunkel) of his time fell far behind Paul by failing to attribute faith to the work of the Holy Spirit. The sermon in Acts 2 is the result of the Pentecost outpouring of the Spirit and can only be understood in this sequence. Therefore Gunkel's tracing faith here to the *sermon* but not, consequently, to the Holy Spirit who caused the sermon, seems to us short-sighted. *Wirkungen*², p. 7. *Contra* also the most modern representative of Gunkel's theory of the Holy Spirit in Acts, Schweizer, art. *pneuma, TWNT,* VI, 430-31 (cf. *idem, Gemeinde und Gemeindeordnung im Neuen Testament* [Zürich: Zwingli Verlag, 1959], p. 86).

Faith, including the spiritual gift which comes with faith (cf. 15:8-9), is not a work of the hearers, it is first of all the work of the Holy Spirit in the sermon (13:48; 16:14; 18:27).

The hearers' response to the sermon, "What shall we do?" is answered by Peter's important words, "Repent, and be baptized every one of you in the name of Jesus Christ for the forgiveness of your sins; and you shall receive the gift of the Holy Spirit" (2:38). In this reply Luke records his comprehensive summary of the reception of Christian salvation. We must investigate it, therefore, very carefully.[10]

We begin with repentance. Repentance is not adequately defined as regret; this the hearers already had (v. 37). Repentance here is the Spirit-enabled decision to be baptized. This repentance-decision, or the step to baptism, is *preceded* and *prompted* by God's stepping toward men in the saving events of passion, Pentecost, and preaching. Therefore repentance is not a long inner work (as would be expressed by an imperative verb in the present tense) but the once-for-all accepting of God's offer through preaching of forgiveness by baptism (this is expressed perfectly here by the aorist imperative). Repentance is being baptized.

Of most importance, the response which is men's in repentance is not merely required in preaching or offered and symbolized in baptism, it is *enabled* through both preaching and baptism. In this sense, too, repentance is accepting baptism. Repentance is not something to be done at home or worked on; it is *received* "in the church," as a response to God's offer and work tendered in human words and human acts (the acts of *others!*) in preaching and baptism. God *gives* repentance (Acts 11:18: "God has granted repentance unto life") and men should accept it where here it is placed: in the invitation to Christian baptism.

The baptism offered by Peter is "in the name of Jesus Christ," that is, it is to bring men into his fellowship and possession. As in the proclamation of the gospel, so in baptism, the only name that *needs* to be heard is the name of Jesus Christ. This observation involves,

---

Schweizer's opinion that Luke does not trace faith to the work of the Spirit is the more surprising since he can write in another connection of Acts that "before all, however, the preaching of the disciples is attributed [by Luke] to the Spirit," art. *pneuma*, *TWNT*, VI, 406, 5-6.

[10] Ulrich Wilckens writes that "while in the other sermons [in Acts] only one or two of the motifs [of saving preaching in Luke's view] appears at a given time, here in Acts 2:38-40 we have a combination and coordination of all of the motifs." *Die Missionsreden der Apostelgeschichte: Form- und traditionsgeschichtliche Untersuchungen* ("WMANT," 5; Neukirchen Kreis Moers; Neukirchener Verlag, 1961), p. 178. Thus the absence of a specific reference here to the laying on of hands, *pace* Dupont, is significant. L. Cerfaux and J. Dupont, *Les Actes des Apôtres* ("La Sainte Bible"; Paris: Les Éditions du Cerf, 1964), p. 49.

of course, no slighting of the possibly later trinitarian baptismal formula. For even in trinitarian language there *is* only one divine name (*to* onoma; cf. 4:12 and the *singular* name in Matt. 28:19). There is not a baptism in Jesus Christ followed or preceded by discrete baptisms in the Father, and then again in the Spirit. God is one, his name is one, and there is therefore only one baptism (Eph. 4:5). To be baptized in, into, or as here, literally, "upon" the name of Jesus Christ means to become his, and to become *his* means, by definition, to receive his Spirit (1:8; cf. I Cor. 6:17; Rom. 8:9). To argue otherwise is to posit a Spirit-less Christ.[11]

The baptism in the name of Jesus Christ, according to Luke's account, includes both the forgiveness of sins *and* the reception of the gift of the Holy Spirit (2:38b) — together. This single two-fold benefit corresponds exactly to the Old Testament promise of the coordinate forgiveness of sins and gift of the Spirit (Jer. 31:31-34; Ezek. 36:24-27). The baptism is, in the careful formulation, "for the forgiveness of your sins; *and* you shall receive the gift of the Holy Spirit."

It is particularly important to emphasize that sins, according to this important Acts text, are not cleansed away by devout effort so that the Spirit may be received after the candidate's cleansing of his heart. Instead, God promises to remove sins in the water of baptism and therewith to grant the sanctifying gift of the Spirit (cf. Acts 22:16). The cleansing from sin, like the gift of the Spirit, is God's work and therefore God's present. There is no cleansing initiation mentioned in the New Testament except that which is recorded here (cf. Acts 15:8-9; I Cor. 6:11).[12]

---

[11] In his desire to avoid sacramentalism with its apparent binding of God to baptism, Markus Barth seems to have missed the meaning of the biblical one-baptism and his entire book on baptism becomes inevitably a *de facto* apologetic for two baptisms: "water baptism" and a separate, sovereignly given "Spirit-baptism." See for example on the text at hand, Barth's *Die Taufe—ein Sakrament? Ein exegetischer Beitrag zum Gespräch über die kirchliche Taufe* (Zollikon-Zürich: Evangelischer Verlag AG, 1951), p. 143 and pp. 184-85 below. However, Luke is not purely spiritual in the usually understood sense, even though he, like Barth, places the highest worth upon the Holy Spirit. Nor is Luke what Barth fears others find him to be — a sacramentalist. Luke is both — simultaneously — and therefore neither in their usually understood senses. That is, Luke is an incarnationalist and he understands the gift of the Holy Spirit as given through the earthly, human means of the one baptism. This fact — the incarnational joining of the divine and the human, of the Spirit and baptism in one great event — finds one of its clearest expressions in the New Testament at Acts 2:38. Christ's baptism, like Christ, is not divided. Cf. W. F. Flemington, *The New Testament Doctrine of Baptism* (London: S.P.C.K., 1953), p. 81, and especially the Baptist scholar G. R. Beasley-Murray, *Baptism in the New Testament* (London: Macmillan, 1962), pp. 102-03, 107, in remarks addressed critically to Barth's separation of a water baptism and a Spirit-baptism.

[12] Calvin's understanding of the sacraments requires him to alter Luke's order: "True, baptism is placed before the forgiveness of sins in the order of words;

We must stress that the forgiveness of sins is *coupled with* (*kai consecutive*) the gift of the Holy Spirit: "*and* you shall receive the gift of the Holy Spirit." The future tense of the reception of the spiritual gift is as future as the baptism with which it is connected. The gift of the Spirit is here directly joined with and promised to the forgiveness which comes with baptism: "be baptized every one of you in the name of Jesus Christ for the forgiveness of your sins; and you shall receive the gift of the Holy Spirit." And the gift is promised "to your children and to all that are far off, every one whom the Lord our God calls to him" (v. 39). Significantly in this phrase, to be observed more particularly in a moment, the condition for the spiritual blessing is God's call and not men's preparations, and to whomever he calls he gives his Spirit as *gift* ("and you shall receive the *gift* [*dörean*] of the Holy Spirit").

> *Dörea(n)*, like *epaggelia* ("promise"), is used in the most gracious associations in the New Testament. For instance, in describing the gospel in his *locus classicus* Paul writes that we are "justified freely (*dörean*) by his grace" (Rom. 3:24). *Dörean* is a word meaning literally "for nothing," "unmerited," "given as a gift," "without a cause." We may translate it in our context, "without a condition."

It is not insignificant, therefore, that Luke (Peter) selects the word *dörea* in describing the standard impartation of the Holy Spirit. Rather than telling his inquirers to await the Holy Spirit in a second Pentecost event with wind, fire, and tongues, Peter offers Christian baptism. Rather than telling the candidates to "wait," as the Lord had instructed him, Peter offers baptism. After Pentecost the command to "wait" in connection with the Holy Spirit is not repeated in the New Testament. And the apostolic wait in Jerusalem applied only to that unusual period in the apostles' career between the ascension of Jesus and his gift of the Spirit to the church at Pentecost. Subsequent Christians do *not* need to wait in Jerusalem for the promise of the Father.

Our text teaches us that since the occurrence of Pentecost Christian baptism becomes the locus of the Spirit's reception in response to the Spirit's pressure in preaching. Henceforth, baptism is Pentecost. Peter invites no one to the upper room. He teaches no one how to speak in tongues. The exterior forms of Pentecost (wind, fire, visions, tongues) leave; the essential content remains. The content is God's free gift of the Holy Spirit. And after Pentecost this gift is offered, as here, with forgiveness, in the humble rite of baptism. Baptism becomes the bap-

---

but in the order of reality baptism follows forgiveness; for baptism is nothing else than the sealing of the goods which we receive through Christ in order that these might now be in effect for our conscience." *Die Apostelgeschichte: Auslegung der heiligen Schrift in deutscher Übersetzung*, Bd. 2 (Neukirchen Kreis Moers: Verlag der Buchhandlung des Erziehungsvereins, n.d.), p. 54 *ad loc*. Cf. however Wilckens, *Missionsreden*, p. 178.

tism of the Holy Spirit. Peter in Acts 2:38 offers no other definition. He does not contrast baptism and the gift of the Spirit, he joins them. As we shall presently see, it is one of the major purposes of Acts to show that baptism and the gift of the Holy Spirit belong indissolubly together. This is the special lesson at Acts 8 and 19.

According to this important text, Acts 2:38, we must stress in summary that incorporation into Christ grants the Spirit; in the name of Christ the forgiveness of sins always includes, positively, the gift of the Spirit. The forgiveness covers our major problem; the gift brings our major provision.

Peter concludes this classic and definitive description of salvation's one reception by repeating the nature of the whole saving and baptismal event: "For the *promise* is to you and to your children and to all that are far off, every one whom the Lord our God calls to him" (v. 39). All the features attending the baptism of the Holy Spirit since its introduction in chapter one are present here in the comprehensive review of its first transmission after Pentecost: the inclusive promise whose sole condition is the call of the sovereign donor, the Lord God. "Those whom the Lord God calls [v. 39]," Stählin comments, "and those who call on the Lord [v. 21] are the same; . . . in the decision for Christ . . . a preceding election of grace is fulfilled."[13]

The means used by Luke to this point to define the gift of the Spirit — whether in verbs (indicative, passive, inclusive second person plural), nouns ("promise," "gift"), or even prepositions ("upon") — all point to the pure grace and divinity of the Spirit — to the *Holy* Spirit.

And this Holy Spirit, consonant with the names given him in Acts, is given through the "means of grace." These means, established as the first-fruits of Pentecost, are Christian preaching (2:5-37) and its seal, Christian baptism (2:38-41).

C. ACTS 2:40-47. THE EVIDENCES OF THE BAPTISM OF THE HOLY SPIRIT ESTABLISHED AT PENTECOST: CHRISTIAN BAPTISM AND LIFE

The hearers respond to Peter's offer and to his subsequent exhortation to "save yourselves from this crooked generation" (v. 40) in the following simple manner according to Luke's record: "So those who received his word were *baptized*" (v. 41). Luke does not yet present any other initial evidence of the baptism of the Holy Spirit. It is not the signs of Pentecost which are recorded, it is the sign of baptism. Baptism in water becomes the *medium exhibitivum* of the baptism in the Spirit. The initial Pentecost event did not institute replicas, it instituted Christian preaching and baptism. It is not little Pentecosts that are either here recorded or are in Acts intended to follow the one

---

[13] *Apg.*[10], p. 54.

Pentecost. Pentecost endows the church with Word and sacrament. In our text (v. 41) it is in the single term "baptized" that the whole of the salvation definitively released at Pentecost and announced in preaching is sealed. Salvation is offered in baptism in Christ's name (vv. 38-39) and is evidenced by the same means (v. 41). Baptism is the sure visible evidence taught in Acts of the reception of the forgiveness of sins with the coordinate gift of the Holy Spirit.

Other evidences may attend the baptism, but they are not decisive; they are left to a happy and free irregularity throughout Acts. Here (vv. 42-47), for example, in addition to baptism we have a record of Christian fellowship, the desire for the apostolic Word, the Supper, prayer, and almost the whole spectrum of normal, healthy church life. In other places in Acts the gift of joy is accentuated (8:39; 16:34); in others, openness (*parrēsia*) (cf. 4:8 with 4:13 and 4:29 with 4:31). But normally and usually, since Luke is writing not so much an interior history of believers as an exterior history of the church of the apostles, only the fundamental event is recorded, the rite of church initiation (for the church is Luke's concern): baptism.[14]

Here we have the first recorded "baptism of the Holy Spirit" since the coming of the Spirit at Pentecost. In the baptism of the Holy Spirit according to the doctrine of Acts prefigured and classically presented here and developed over and again hereafter, baptism is the Spirit's own sufficient evidence. For Christian baptism — and here we summarize and look out in prospect over the whole teaching of Acts — is spiritual baptism. There is only *one* baptism (Eph. 4:5).[15]

D. ACTS 4:31; 5:32: PRAYER, OBEDIENCE, AND THE HOLY SPIRIT

Two brief passages frequently used to introduce special conditions for the filling or gift of the Holy Spirit are now to be investigated: the first for the condition of prayer (4:31); the second for the condition of obedience (5:32).

1. PRAYER AND THE HOLY SPIRIT (ACTS 4:31; cf. LUKE 11:13; EPH. 5:18)

Acts 4:23-31 contains the account of the church's first recorded prayer meeting after Pentecost, the result of which Luke records as follows: "And when they had prayed, the place in which they were

---

[14] To have stressed Luke's "exterior" concentration is the special merit of Heinrich von Baer's study of the Holy Spirit in Luke: "The inner experiences are characterized only through their outward and manifest effects." *Der heilige Geist in den Lukasschriften* ("BWANT," 3/3; Stuttgart: W. Kohlhammer, 1926), p. 204.

[15] Cf. Wilckens, *Missionsreden*, p. 183.

gathered together was shaken; and they were all filled with the Holy Spirit and spoke the word of God with boldness" (v. 31).

In the first place it is important to observe that the Holy Spirit, according to the text, was *not* given because he was asked for. This is sometimes overlooked. The disciples asked for boldness in speaking the Word. Nevertheless — or therefore! — the result *is* the filling of the Spirit. Interestingly, there is no record in Acts of men praying that they might receive the Holy Spirit.[16] We may be sure that it is proper, indeed desirable, for believers to ask for the Spirit continually (so Luke 11:13), but it is not necessary to do so in so many words in order to have the Spirit's presence or assistance, as the present Acts text among others teaches. We may be led, in fact, to believe from this text that wherever there is the prayerful desire among Christians for the service of Christ there is the full gift of the Spirit. The Luke 11 and Acts 4 texts are, respectively, addressed to and expressed of *Christians* and, taken together, they do not teach the necessity of prayer for the first full reception of the gift of the Holy Spirit. They do teach that simple Christian prayer receives the Father's continuing provision of his Holy Spirit whether the Spirit himself is specifically requested (Luke 11) or not (Acts 4).

It is in this context that we may best investigate still another text often used to teach Christians that they have less of the Holy Spirit than the fulness offered in the Pentecostal baptism in the Holy Spirit, Ephesians 5:18: "And do not get drunk with wine, for that is debauchery; but *be filled* (*plērousthe*) with the Spirit." It needs only to be pointed out that this verb contemplates not the once-for-all reception of the Holy Spirit (in that case the aorist imperative would have been used), but the Christian's present and continuing responsibility and privilege of *being* (passive) filled with the Spirit.[17] The scope of the passage is little

---

16 Contrast Andrew Murray's claim that whenever the disciples were filled with the Spirit it was when they prayed to be filled, cited and followed by Ockenga, *Spirit of the Living God*, pp. 136-38, and p. 116 above. In Acts 1:14 we are not given any object of prayer and in Acts 8:15 it is not the recipients who are recorded as praying. Is prayer "far more important" to Luke than baptism as a means of receiving the Holy Spirit (Schweizer, art. *pneuma*, TWNT, VI, 411)? Affirmation is unnecessary since Christian baptism is neither normally without prayer (cf. Luke 3:21-22; Acts 22:16) nor in these places is it simply prayer *per se* which is recorded as the means of the Spirit's fundamental reception — it is baptism. According to even Luke, who heightens the fact of prayer at Jesus' baptism, it is not just prayer anywhere, it is prayer at baptism where Jesus' classic encounter occurs. After this encounter, in all believers' lives, prayer is a continuing means of the reception of the Spirit. But prayer and baptism should not be played off at each other's expense — least of all in Luke's name. See now the monograph of Wilhelm Ott, *Gebet und Heil: Die Bedeutung der Gebetsparänese in der lukanischen Theologie*. "Studien zum A. und N.T.," 12; München: Kösel, 1965.

17 The clearest illustration of the difference between the fundamental initiation gift of the Spirit and the continual giving of the Spirit for Christian living, may

different from Luke 11:13: both consider the believer's continuing (and not introductory) relation to the Holy Spirit. Neither bothers either adjectivally or adverbially to define, deepen, or absolutize the simple "ask" or "be filled" because both see the Holy Spirit in the context of the person and work of Jesus Christ, which means that they see the Spirit not as the believer's monumental accomplishment but as God's graciously offered provision for living the Christian life.

2. Obedience and the Holy Spirit (Acts 5:32)

The text most frequently marshalled for the condition of obedience in Pentecostal discussions is Acts 5:32: "And we are witnesses to these things, and so is *the Holy Spirit whom God has given to those who obey him.*" The text is interpreted, as we have seen, in this manner: Not all Christians have the full Pentecostal gift of the Holy Spirit because, as the text is said to indicate, not all Christians have been fully *obedient* to the conditions necessary for the full reception of the Holy Spirit.

However, the obedience spoken of in Acts 5:32 rather than being a condition is the result of the gift of the Holy Spirit. The text does *not* say either that the Holy Spirit *will* be given to those who shall obey him, or that the Holy Spirit *was* given to those who previously obeyed him, but, interestingly and suggestively, that the Holy Spirit was given in the past to those who are *now* obeying him. The text reads literally: "and so is the Holy Spirit whom God gave [past] to those who are [present] obeying him." One meaning of the text is at least this: obedience is the present *result* of the *prior* gift of the Spirit.[18]

Second, not only the text but the context must be carefully observed. Peter and the apostles were speaking to the high priest and Sanhedrin (vv. 27-29). The obediences lacking in this audience were not the obediences of sufficient religious observance, prayer, sacrifice, or zeal. They had, if it is possible, too many of these "obediences." The one obedience needful they lacked: the obedience *of faith.* Contained in Peter's remark therefore is a rebuke: "God gave his Holy Spirit not to you who think that you are obeying him through your spirituality but who continue to disbelieve his Son; he gave him to us who believe in Jesus and are thus obeying him in the ministry of his Word."

---

be observed in comparing Gal. 3:2 and its aorist with Gal. 3:5 and its present participle. See below, pp. 236-39. There should be only encouragement of the Christian's seeking successive fillings of the Spirit as often as desired. There should be objection only to the insistence that, after one becomes a Christian, there is *one other* filling still outstanding before the Christian is complete before God. The latter is heresy; the former, normalcy.

[18] Schweizer misses this when he writes that "according to Acts 5:32 obedience must precede the reception of the Spirit." Art. *pneuma, TWNT,* VI, 410, 14. See to the grammar of Acts 5:32 Ernst Haenchen, *Die Apostelgeschichte* ("MeyerK"; 12th rev. ed.; Vandenhoeck und Ruprecht, 1959), p. 206 n. 5.

This text does not offer aid and comfort to the multiplication of devout conditions in the name of obedience. For it was precisely rigorous obediences which, in fact, kept the Sanhedrin from faith in Christ and therefore from receiving the Holy Spirit. There *are* "obediences" which block the way to God's gift (cf. Rom. 9:30 — 10:4; Col. 2:20-22).

But first of all, the obedience spoken of in Acts 5:32 is an obedience which *flows from* the prior gift of the Holy Spirit. This is the lesson of Pentecost as well, observed most strikingly in the career and obedience of Peter himself. The obedience lacking in the Sanhedrin and present in the apostles was simply faith in Christ. To draw from Acts 5:32 the multifarious Pentecostal conditions of obedience must be calculated to create more quickly a Sanhedrin than a church.

> Cf. Sjöberg, article *pneuma, TWNT,* VI, 381, 15ff. with the Pentecostal conception outlined in Part I:
>
> > In Rabbinical teaching ... there was an acknowledged connection between the Holy Spirit and a life of obedience to God. The gift of the Spirit is there understood primarily as a reward to an obedient life. The possession of the Spirit is presented first of all as the result of a righteous life, not as the ground of such ... where there are righteous men, there the Holy Spirit will be given.[19]

E. ACTS 8:4-24: THE BAPTISM OF THE HOLY SPIRIT AT SAMARIA

1. ACTS 8:4-17 ESPECIALLY 14-17: THE ILLUSTRATED UNION OF BAPTISM AND THE GIFT OF THE HOLY SPIRIT

In the account of the Samaritan conversions we have the only record in the New Testament of persons who believed, accepted Christian

---

[19] See Sjöberg's other examples in the same article of the doctrine of the Spirit in Rabbinic teaching; they may all be compared fruitfully with the Pentecostal doctrine outlined in Part I.

The valuable detailing of the use of Acts 5:32 in Pentecostal practice and of the roots of the Pentecostal understanding of obedience in Hollenweger's "Geist- und Bibelverständnis bei Spiritualisten der Gegenwart: Eine frömmigkeits- und dogmengeschichtliche Untersuchung unter besonderer Berücksichtigung der Schweizerisches Pfingstmission und ihrer historischen Wurzeln" ("Akzessarbeit bei Herrn Prof. Dr. Fritz Blanke"; Zürich: Mimeographed copy of the typewritten manuscript, 1960), p. 91 is directed, in our opinion, somewhere this side of the heart of the matter. As we shall detail in the next chapter on a broader scale, the problem in Pentecostalism is not that Pentecostals take the Bible too seriously or too literally but that Pentecostalism as a rule does not take that which the Bible exists to teach seriously enough — the Bible's message and *raison d'être*, the gospel. The Pentecostal conviction, in Hollenweger's words, that "we must fulfill the whole Scripture" (*ibid.*) is precisely the message of *the law* (cf. Gal. 3:10-13 and the development below, pp. 226-32) with which Paul *contrasts* the message of the gospel. The false Pentecostal Bible understanding, in our opinion, flows at its deepest level from a false understanding of the gospel, not from a failure to understand Scripture less literally.

baptism, and had nevertheless not yet received the Holy Spirit. The reason for this hiatus is as important for us to grasp as it was for the nascent church in Jerusalem.

> Now when the apostles at Jerusalem heard that Samaria had received the word of God, they sent to them Peter and John, who came down and prayed for them that they might receive the Holy Spirit; for it had not yet fallen on any of them, but they had only been baptized in the name of the Lord Jesus. Then they laid their hands on them and they received the Holy Spirit (8:14-17).

It should be noticed first that the remedy for the absence of the Holy Spirit was not sought or found, according to this text, in any disposition or action of the Samaritans.[20] Nor according to our text are any steps for receiving the Holy Spirit proposed to the Samaritans. The Samaritans are asked no questions and they are placed under no commands. The problem lies not with the Samaritans. We have no record that it lay with Philip,[21] who in fact in the next scene (8:26-40) is instrumental in the conversion of the Ethiopian eunuch without any supplementation by the apostles. Indeed, we have no record of subjective lack on the part of any party in this account. The discovery in Acts 8:14-17 of insufficient commitment on the part of any parties or a finding of the imperfect fulfilling of any conditions must be imported into the text, they cannot be exported from it.

Observe the importations of the Pentecostal Riggs (p. 109):

> Peter had told the Sanhedrin that the Holy Ghost was given to them that obey God (Acts 5:32) and so he doubtlessly explained this to the Samaritan converts. Peter and John both had heard the Lord promise that the Father would give the Holy Spirit to them that ask Him. So they surely told this, too, to the Samaritan converts. When these awaiting

---

[20] *Contra* Schlatter who concludes here and to Acts 18:24-28 and 19:1-6 that "the different approaches may have well been in response to the different situations of faith and conscience." *Die Apostelgeschichte* ("Erläuterungen zum Neuen Testament," 4; Stuttgart: Calwer Vereinsbuchhandlung, 1928), p. 233. More recently, Donald G. Bloesch: "The Samaritans had been baptized, but their new birth was aborted because they had not forsaken their old way of thinking and living. They had believed with their minds (*credentia*) but not with their hearts (*fiducia*)." "The Charismatic Revival: A Theological Critique," *Religion in Life, 35* (Summer 1966), 370. But see already correctly Meyer: "To explain the matter by the subjectivity of the Samaritans whose faith, as it is supposed, had not yet penetrated to sufficient depth, has no justification in the text, least of all since we do not hear of the apostles giving further instruction but instead read only of their prayer and laying on of hands." *Apg.,*[3] p. 167.

[21] *Contra,* in different ways, the Pentecostal Gee, *Ministry-Gifts,* p. 51; the Anglican Arthur James Mason, *The Relation of Confirmation to Baptism: As Taught in Holy Scripture and the Fathers* (London: Longmans, Green, and Co., 1891), p. 23; the Roman Catholics Nikolaus Adler, *Taufe und Handauflegung: Eine exegetisch-theologische Untersuchung von Apg. 8:14-17* ("NTA," 19, Bd., 3. Heft; Münster Westf.: Aschendorffsche Verlagsbuchhandlung, 1951), pp. 116-17; Dupont in Cerfaux and Dupont, *Actes,* p. 88.

new disciples were thus prayed for and instructed, the apostles laid hands on them (as an aid to the seekers' faith) and they received the Holy Ghost. However, the imposition of the apostles' hands was not simply an aid to the seekers' faith, it was the normal accompaniment of baptism (9:17-19; 19:5-6; Heb. 6:2), i.e., of initiation, and *as such,* not as either an independent initiation rite or as an intensifier of the initiates' faith, it has its significance.

What the Samaritans lacked, as far as we are told, was not the laying on of hands, it was the *Holy Spirit* (vv. 15-16).[22] In no other place in Acts, except at Acts 19:6, are the hands of apostles recorded in connection with the gift of the Holy Spirit — neither at Pentecost, nor in the post-Pentecost accessions, nor even in Paul's conversion itself where Ananias, who was not an apostle, was, according to Luke's account, the agent (or audience) of Paul's initiation. Even in Acts 19:1-7 it was not the apostolic laying on of hands which was either missing or taught but, as a careful reading of the text will reveal, the desideratum was Christian baptism of which the laying on of hands was simply, as always, a part.

We must look for the solution to the Samaritan puzzle in another direction. Samaria was the church's first decisive step out of and beyond Judaism. This was no casual event. Only the accession of the Gentiles (ch. 10) can be compared with it. Samaria was both a bridge to be crossed and a base to be occupied. A bridge to be crossed because Samaria represented the deepest of clefts: the racial-religious. A base to be occupied because the church no longer resides in Jerusalem or among Jews alone, but becomes a mission.

We know from other accounts in the New Testament of the feeling of the Jew for the Samaritan, and we know from the important records in Acts 10-11 and 15 of the painful and critical decision which the reception of Gentiles posed for the Jewish church. The reason behind the absolutely unique division of what everywhere else since Pentecost is one — Christian baptism and the gift of the Spirit — may most satisfactorily be found in the divine will to establish unequivocally for the apostles, for the despised Samaritans, and for the whole church present and future that for *God* no barriers existed for his *gift* of the Spirit; that wherever faith in the gospel occurred, there was the *work* of God's Spirit and there accordingly God purposed to give the *gift* of his Spirit; that baptism in the name of Christ as everywhere else now even in Samaria must include the gift of the Spirit; in a word, that the gift of God's Holy Spirit was free and for all. To teach this basic and important fact — it was the fact of the gospel — God with-

---

22 Because of this term in the text ("Holy Spirit," *pneuma hagion*) I am unable to find convincing, though it is plausible, the argument which sees reference here only to charismatic gifts or manifestations of the Spirit and not to the Holy Spirit *simpliciter.*

held his gift until the apostles should see with their own eyes and —
let it not be overlooked — be instrumental with their own hands in
the impartation of the gift *of God* (v. 20), merited by nothing, least of
all by race or prior religion.

The role of the apostles should not be minimized. As the sole witnesses of the ministry, death, and above all of the resurrection of
Jesus Christ, and as the specially appointed bearers of this saving
tradition to the world, they were dominically invested with authority
and it is no accident therefore that it was they and not simply any
disciples in Jerusalem who were sent to Samaria. Later, less august
officers than Peter and John can be dispatched to important new situations — e.g., Barnabas to Antioch (11:22). But in the crossing of the
first threshold into the non-Jewish world, as Luke wishes dramatically
and stylistically to present it, the leading apostles themselves came.[23]

The fact that God willed to connect with the apostles' coming, prayer,
and laying on of hands his gift of the Holy Spirit heightens not only
the significance in the divine economy of the apostles but of the
church and of its apostolic foundations. It was evidently not the divine
plan, according to Luke's understanding, that the first church outside
Jerusalem should arise entirely without apostolic contact. For this to
have occurred could have indicated the indifference of the apostolic
tradition — viz., of the history of Jesus Christ — and of the unity
of the church. Both the tradition and the union were preserved through
the apostolic visitation. The Samaritans were not left to become an
isolated sect with no bonds of union with the apostolic church in
Jerusalem. If a Samaritan church and a Jewish church had arisen
independently, side by side, without the dramatic removal of the
ancient and bitter barriers of prejudice between the two, particularly
at the level of ultimate authority, the young church of God would
have been in schism from the inception of its mission. The drama of
the Samaritan affair in Acts 8 included among its purposes the vivid
and visual dismantling of the wall of enmity between Jew and Samaritan and the preservation of the precious unity of the church of God
through the unique divine "interception" and then prompt presentation of the Spirit in the presence of the apostles.

---

[23] The importance, indeed the absolute importance, of the apostles as the eye-
witness *martures* of the resurrection appearances, and of the early church to
which they belonged as the sole custodian of the saving tradition of God's act in
Christ, and with which, therefore, one must be in union, cannot be minimized.
See, particularly, Werner Georg Kümmel, *Kirchenbegriff und Geschichtsbewusstsein in der Urgemeinde und bei Jesus* (Uppsala: SBU, 1943), p. 7; Leonhard
Goppelt, *Christentum und Judentum im ersten und zweiten Jahrhundert: Ein Aufriss
der Urgeschichte der Kirche* ("BFChTh," 2. Reihe, 55 Bd.; Gütersloh: C. Bertels-
mann Verlag, 1954), p. 83; Birger Gerhardsson, *Memory and Manuscript: Oral
Tradition and Written Transmission in Rabbinic Judaism and Early Christianity*
(Uppsala: Almqvist and Wiksells, 1961), pp. 220-25.

The centrality of the apostles and the unity of the church — these are among the important lessons of Acts 8 — but they are overarched by that for which both the apostles and the one apostolic church existed. The gospel, in its grace, freedom, and universality, constitutes the major *scopus* of the Samaritan incident. The illumination before the eyes of the whole church — Jewish, Samaritan, and thereafter ecumenical — of the free gospel of Jesus Christ which is sealed to all those who receive it by the free gift of the Holy Spirit: this is the dominant purpose not only for the writing of the Samaritan record, but for the writing of Acts 1-15 as a whole.

The uniqueness of the Samaritan event is affirmed even by those who use it to teach special doctrine.[24] The account is accentuated by two important words in verse 16.

> [The Spirit] had *not yet* fallen on any of them, but they had *only* been baptized.

Luke reports that the Samaritan believers had *only (monon)* been baptized, indicating that enough had not yet occurred, as indeed it had not. To be baptized and not to have received the Spirit was an abnormality, in fact, as the passage goes on to teach, an impossible contradiction in Christian realities.

This impossibility is heightened by a still more important word in verse 16. The word introduces the verse and is accentuated by its position at the head of the Greek sentence: "Not yet [*oudepö*] had the Holy Spirit fallen on any of them." The meaning is this: The Spirit *is* to come with baptism, but this coming had "not *yet*" occurred. The relation of baptism to the Spirit, the "not yet" indicates, is the relation of cohesion.

There is an important distinction between the Greek words *oudepö* and *ou,* just as there is in most languages some symbolic distinction

---

[24] Cf., e.g., Mason who reserves the gift of the Holy Spirit for confirmation and who remarks to Acts 8:16 in the process of his development: "And yet the language employed appears to indicate that there was something unsatisfactory in such a position. 'They had *only* been baptized.' It was an unusual situation for Christian men to be found in, baptized, and yet not possessed of the specific gift of 'Holy Spirit.' Christian initiation — so it is implied — ought normally to have included this gift. It was as if they had been stopped in the middle of their Baptism — one part of it validly conferred and not needing to be repeated, but another kept in reserve. Their Baptism was not as yet consummated by that great blessing to which it was an introduction. . . . This natural and destined completion it only received through the prayers and the imposed hands of the Apostles who came down from Jerusalem for the purpose." *Relation of Confirmation to Baptism,* p. 20. The last phrase needs correction. Cf. Johannes Behm: "the assertion that the apostles went to Samaria for the purpose of communicating the Holy Spirit . . . is not textual. The *purpose* of the trip is not given us at all in Acts 8:14, only the *occasion:* the conversion of the Samaritans." *Die Handauflegung im Urchristentum nach Verwendung, Herkunft, und Bedeutung in religionsgeschichtlichem Zusammenhang untersucht* (Leipzig: A. Deichert, 1911), p. 30 n. 1.

between an event not yet happening and not happening. When it is said that "x happened but y did *not* happen," a definite set of meanings is conveyed: not only are the two events not connected, they are to a certain degree contrasted. However, when the word "yet" is added to "not" we are given a picture of the components of one entire event. Thus when Luke wrote that the Samaritan believers had only been baptized but that the Holy Spirit had not *yet* fallen he meant that it is exactly the coming of the Spirit which completed Christian baptism and that the gift of the Spirit *will* therefore be given to that with which it properly belongs — as indeed it very promptly was. With the formal "not yet" and "only" of Acts 8:16 we are led not only into the heart of the meaning of this passage but into the inner world of the writer's and the early church's conviction *vis-à-vis* baptism and the gift of the Spirit.[25]

The qualifications of Acts 8:16 indicating temporary suspension of the normal — the "only baptized" and the "not yet" given Spirit — are, we should note, singular in the Book of Acts and they *presuppose* the union of baptism and the Spirit. In no other place in the New Testament is Christian baptism given the qualifications of Acts 8:16. And promptly in Acts 8:17 we are informed that the singular disconnection was immediately bridged.

The vacuum is filled apart from any new regimen of conditions being imposed upon the Samaritans. This is, for our study's considerations, the most important fact. What is taught in Acts 8:14-17 is significant: *the divinely purposed and accomplished union of baptism in the name of Jesus Christ with the gift of the Holy Spirit apart from all subjective conditions.* The Spirit is temporarily suspended from baptism here "only" and precisely to teach the church at its most prejudiced juncture, and in its strategic initial missionary move beyond Jerusalem, that *suspension cannot occur.* This the New Testament's only record of Christian baptism without the immediately present gift of the Christian Spirit, and the immediate resolution of this enormity, teaches in a most impressive but not unconfusing manner the New Testament's normative and important doctrine of the "one baptism" of the church. Baptism in the name of Christ *cannot* but be baptism in the Holy Spirit; Christian baptism cannot but be accompanied with the gift of the Holy Spirit (2:38-39; 19:1-7). This unitive fact is also and especially the doctrine of the Samaritan incident.[26]

---

[25] The construction of Acts 8:16 "assumes precisely the solidarity [*Zusammengehörigkeit*] of baptism and the Spirit." Conzelmann, *Apg.*, p. 55.

[26] "In reality, the intent of both passages [Acts 8:14-17; 10:44-48] is to teach precisely the inseparability [*die unlösbare Zusammengehörigkeit*] of baptism and the receipt of the Spirit." Rudolf Bultmann, *Theology of the New Testament,* tr. Kendrick Grobel (2 vols.; New York: Charles Scribner's Sons, 1951), I, 139; *idem, The History of the Synoptic Tradition,* tr. John Marsh (Oxford: Basil Blackwell, 1963), p. 247 n. 1. Cf. Haenchen, *Apg.*[12], p. 147 to Acts 2:38.

The possibility that the Samaritans spoke in tongues when they received the Spirit is not unreal. However the haste with which this conclusion is sometimes drawn seems to us precipitous. Simon "saw" (v. 18) that the Samaritans had received the Holy Spirit. But may he not have seen, for example, the joy mentioned of the eunuch in the following incident (v. 39), or the fellowship and love of the converts at Pentecost (2:41-47), or any other of the fruits of the Spirit mentioned throughout Acts? These moral attributes can be as miraculous, as sudden, and as visible as the striking manifestation of tongues.

Furthermore, speaking in tongues is not mentioned in the text. If it were Luke's or the early church's conviction that no one should suppose he had received the Holy Spirit until he had spoken in tongues — if this were so important that the absence of the form was prejudicial to the fact — why does Luke so consistently fail to mention this *sine qua non*? Why does he not mention it at all places and, *of* all places, here, where for a period there was knowledge that the Holy Spirit had not yet been received? Here, certainly, on the one occasion in the New Testament where momentarily Christian baptism appears to be without the spiritual gift, the doctrine of tongues as the Spirit's only initial evidence should have been taught with prominence. Our only conclusion can be that Luke had no such doctrine. Paul does not teach it, nor do the Gospel accounts;[27] it cannot be found elsewhere in the New Testament, and it is not even taught as normative in Acts. The doctrine lacks sufficient support. Tongues-speaking may indeed have occurred in Samaria and we have nothing against it; but neither have we any record of it, and where a text is silent, especially about a matter as important as the evidence of the Holy Spirit, perhaps it is best for the interpreter to remain silent too.

> The incarnation, life, death, resurrection, ascension, and heavenly session of Jesus Christ must be seen as one indivisible saving deed, all the benefits of which the believer receives *together* in one Christian baptism and not gradually or in parts, one before the other, in separate baptisms. The believer must not have separate crisis experiences of first Christmas, then Good Friday, then Easter, then Ascension, and finally Pentecost before he is a full Christian.

These facts taken together should inhibit recurring efforts to build a convincing doctrine of a second Spirit baptism, or of a special gift

---

27 To Mark 16:17 see the various commentaries. Though Mark 16:17 may mirror the early life of the church, decisive for our considerations is the fact that it is not a part of Mark's Gospel. See, e.g., Vincent Taylor, *The Gospel according to St. Mark: The Greek Text with Introduction, Notes, and Indexes* (London: Macmillan, 1959), pp. 610, 613. If it is insisted that Mark 16:17 be used for the doctrine of the initial evidence of the Spirit by tongues then, consistently, Mark 16:18 must also be employed for the initial evidence of the Spirit by one or two poison immunities.

of the Holy Spirit, or of the imperative (not, necessarily, the practice) of the episcopal imposition of hands in confirmation, upon this unique text. If a biblical doctrine must be taught in more than one book and often and systematically in order to be binding for the church, then it needs to be taught in more than one place in one book (and in that one place, certainly, it must be *taught*).

In this text, as we have seen, Christian baptism and the gift of the Holy Spirit are taught not as contrasted or separated realities but as the correlates of the one reception of Christian salvation. The doctrinal constructions which have been raised on the frail and isolated foundation of Acts 8:14-17 (with the illegitimate help, often, of the John-baptized of Acts 19:1-7; see the exposition below) — from positions as seemingly disparate as the spiritual baptisms of Pentecostalism and Markus Barth to the sacrament of confirmation episcopally administered in some Anglo and Roman Catholicism — are enough to make one ask with the Psalmist, "Lord, if [this] foundation be removed, what will the righteous do?"[28]

This is not the place to go into the fact that a doctrine of a separate gift or fulness of the Holy Spirit, through either a later spiritual baptism or a subsequent sacrament of confirmation, suffers under the handicap of being neither taught nor instituted by Jesus in the Gospels, nor discussed in the Pauline epistles, nor even mentioned in the literature of the post-apostolic church.[29] The initiation laying on of hands is mentioned twice in Acts — here and at Acts 19:6 — and in Hebrews 6:2, and in all three incidents, significantly, in close connection with that over-arching reality of which it is a part — baptism.

---

[28] For these several church types in this connection see the extended note below, pp. 184-88. I must confess that Acts 8:14-17 taken alone (or with Acts 19:1-7) might lead one to a textually supportable conviction of some kind of church confirmation. But I do not presently believe that it should, unless this church confirmation is baptism.

[29] Mason argues from both apostolic and post-apostolic literature for confirmation as the sacrament for the (full) gift of the Holy Spirit but must write that "it may clear the mind of the reader to be told that the name of Confirmation is only a Western name, and is not found until the fifth century, and that in the Eastern authors, and the earlier Western ones, that which we understand by Confirmation is only described by its constituent acts or elements as parts of the order of Holy Baptism." *Relation of Confirmation to Baptism,* pp. xii-xiii. Mason, however, is able to avoid embarrassment as follows: "To us it is no incorrect description of the relation of Confirmation to Baptism when the Fathers say that in Baptism the Holy Ghost is given, meaning thereby that He is given in that part of the baptismal sacrament which we know by the name of Confirmation." *Ibid.,* p. xv. See, however, Behm: "The writings of the apostolic Fathers and the apologists are completely silent on the subject of the laying on of hands. . . . All the more surprising is the fact that these ancient writers speak of the two-fold gift of baptism in a way very similar to the New Testament, [namely] of the forgiveness of sins and new life in the Holy Spirit." *Handauflegung,* p. 177. For studies of Acts 8:9-24 see Mattill, *Classified Bibliography,* pp. 378-80.

Acts 8 does not exist to teach the *separation,* it exists to teach the *union* of baptism and the gift of the Spirit. We may say then that the various interpretations which have been placed upon Acts 8 in order to develop a biblical doctrine of a second and for the first time full irıpartation of the Holy Spirit, either experientially or episcopally, are without foundation in either this text or the larger biblical context.

2. ACTS 8:18-24: HOW NOT TO SEEK THE HOLY SPIRIT (THE SIMON MAGUS EPILOGUE)

Luke had not said in his record of the Samaritan conversion that the Holy Spirit was given *through (dia)* the hands of the apostles; he had simply paralleled imposition of hands and the gift of the Spirit: "Then they laid their hands on them and they received the Holy Spirit" (v. 17). God may indeed have given his Spirit "through" the hands of the apostles, whatever this might mean. This is at least very nearly the case and one need perhaps have no objection to this expression as such. God did give the Holy Spirit in some connection *with* the laying on of the apostles' hands. Yet there might have been undesirable implications had the Holy Spirit been recorded as channeled exactly "through" the hands of the apostles. The reference to prayer (v. 15) helps to avert some of these implications. However, to make the record clear at once it is not yet said in Acts 8:14-17 that the Holy Spirit was given through the hands of the apostles.

Simon, however, makes the fine and perhaps fatal equation. Luke tells us that "*Simon* saw that the Spirit was given through the laying on of the apostles' hands" (v. 18) and Simon therefore offers the apostles means to secure what he understands to be an apostolic power: " 'Give me also this power, that any one on whom I lay my hands may receive the Holy Spirit' " (v. 19). What Simon thought he saw is, in any case, not as serious as the way (or even the fact) that he sought it. Peter's answer rings down to our century:

> But Peter said to him, "Your silver perish with you, because you thought you could obtain the gift [*tēn dōrean*] of God with money! You have neither part nor lot in this matter, for your heart is not right before God. Repent therefore of this wickedness of yours, and pray to the Lord that, if possible, the intent of your heart may be forgiven you. For I see that you are in the gall of bitterness and in the bond of iniquity" (vv. 20-23).

The entire Simon passage is important for the understanding of the gift of the Holy Spirit and is in fact the only independent negative instruction of any length which we have on the subject of the Holy Spirit in Acts.

Simon desired the Spirit that he might (1) have greater spiritual power; (2) he was willing to make a costly sacrifice to obtain this power; and (3) he was obliged, however, to face the consequences of this spurious spiritual quest.

First, Simon was impressed by what the gift of the Holy Spirit does — it gives power. Consequently he desired to have and to confer this power himself: " 'Give me also this power, that any one on whom I lay my hands may receive the Holy Spirit.' " This motive and its subsequent judgment should constitute a warning: the desire to have, get, or give the gift of the Holy Spirit due primarily to the *power* it grants is a dangerous desire. The fact that in our subject it is by the appeal of power that a special baptism of the Holy Spirit is most often urged is not a propitious sign.

Second, Simon was willing to make a considerable sacrifice to obtain the gift of the Spirit. It was not the crass offer of money alone which repelled Peter, it was the offensive "notion" (*epinoia,* v. 22; cf. *eno-misas,* v. 20) that the *gift* of God can *by human means (dia chrëmatön)* be *obtained (ktasthai).*

We may take up each of these important terms in turn. 1. The *object* of Simon's sacrifice was *tën dörean tou theou,* "the [free] gift of God" (v. 20). Simon thought he was asking for a separate, distinct, and further gift when he sought the power of the Holy Spirit for himself. He must not have known that there is no such further or higher gift if it is conceived as such — there is only "the" gift of being a Christian — the gift of the Holy Spirit. And this gift is the gift *of God (tou theou).*

2. The *means* of Simon's sacrifice is *dia chrëmatön. Chrëma* means "property, wealth, means" (so Mark 10:23 par.; Luke 18:24), or "money" as here (Bauer, *Woerterbuch*5, p. 750). It is something valuable which men possess; it is brought by the active party (e.g., Barnabas, 4:37), and it is something usually wanted by the passive or receiving party (e.g., Felix, 24:26). It can very honorably be offered (e.g., Barnabas), and is honored thus highly among men (cf. Acts 4:34-37). Its offering can be a noble fruit of grace. But — and with this we return to our text — it can never be offered to *obtain* grace, or else grace ceases to be grace. God's gift comes *dia charitos,* not *dia chrëmatön.*

3. The *verb* of Simon's sacrifice is *ktasthai.* Two verbs are used in Acts for the reception of the Spirit: *ktasthai* (obtain) here alone (8:20), and everywhere else *lambanein* (receive) (cf. 1:8; 2:33; 8:17; 10:47; 19:2). *Ktasthai* like *chrëma* has an interesting and instructive usage in Acts. It occurs in three places: in 1:18 of Judas, in 8:20 of Simon, and in 22:28 of a Roman tribune. In all three cases the procuring is connected with a price paid. In each usage there is what may be called a commercial element present. In the light of these Acts passages we may direct three typological questions to our theme: Is there what we may call a "Judas" or "field of blood" interpretation of the Spirit wherever God's gift is said to be procured as a "reward"? Is there an interpretation which we may call "Simonic" wherever the power of the Spirit is thought to be procured through our resources? Finally, is there a "tribunal" understanding of the Spirit wherever one may say, "I secured this gift through a large sacrifice"? (See for the relevance of these questions "The Price or Cost Character of the Gift [of the Spirit]," pp. 107-09

above). In the New Testament no sacrifice paves the way for the Spirit except one, see below, "The Condition of the Spirit," pp. 225-32. The relevance of the Simon Magus passage to our theme is this: The Spirit is, in the language of Acts 8:20, *the (tën)* gift — the *gift (dörean)* — of God *(tou theou)*.

If God's *gift* can be actively obtained by special people after initiation rather than freely received by all in initiation, by sacrifice rather than by faith, then what is called a promise is in reality a reward and therefore no longer exclusively either a gift or God's.[30]

Peter's rebuke is one of the harshest in Acts (8:20-23). The spirit that seeks to obtain God's free gift through costly means is not a good spirit. It is a spirit "in the gall of bitterness and in the bond of iniquity" (v. 23). It needs to pray: not for the Holy Spirit, but for forgiveness for having attempted to obtain him (8:22b). It needs to repent: not in order to receive the Holy Spirit, but in order to cease being the spirit it is. It is no surprise therefore that Simon was regarded by the apostolic and post-apostolic church as "the father of all heresy" and that he bore, appropriately, the name "Magus" (magician, cf. v. 9).[31]

There is, in fact, no great distance between magic and conditions. Both seek beyond faith to get ahold of supernatural powers. Both are out of place in the church. However, in one form or another both have always remained to vex the church. Gnosticism, which has no merely accidental connection with Simon Magus, posed the first and probably the most formidable of the early church's struggles for life. Paul's letters to Corinth are the classic memorials to this warfare. We shall discover that Simon's "notion" develops into the "Corinthian theology" of Paul's opponents, and that both find perhaps their most recent correspondence in the theology of Pentecostalism.

The Simon Magus passage serves as a lasting warning to the making of conditions for God's free gift. Only once before had Peter to speak as severely: with Ananias and Sapphira for "lying to" and "tempting" the Holy Spirit (5:3, 9). How had they lied to the Spirit? By claiming

---

30 The general Pentecostal understanding of the biblically important word "gift" may be illustrated again briefly here as follows: "The more earnestly we covet a gift from God and the more we sacrifice to obtain it, the more we will prize it when it is obtained." In Barratt, *Fire*, p. 115. (Cf. Ockenga: "Do not expect that at the first simple request you will receive the choicest and most precious gift God has for any one." *Spirit of the Living God*, p. 137.) Prayer "is God's elimination test to determine whom He considers worthy to receive this priceless gift." Riggs, *Spirit Himself*, p. 104.

31 See Hans Jonas, *The Gnostic Religion: The Message of the Alien God and the Beginnings of Christianity* (Boston: Beacon Press, 1957), p. 103; Leonhard Goppelt, *Die apostolische und nachapostolische Zeit* ("Die Kirche in ihrer Geschichte. Ein Handbuch"; Bd. 1, Lieferung A; Göttingen: Vandenhoeck und Ruprecht [1962]), pp. 63-64. See especially the exposition of the Corinthian letters, below, pp. 285-319.

to have given him everything when they had not. How had Simon
sinned against God? By presuming to give God something for his gift
when God alone is its giver; by supposing that one must "pay a price"
for what God makes free. The important matter in the Christian faith
is that God gives everything (cf. I Cor. 4:7). Therefore, the gift of
God can only be — received.

> Who has ever made a gift to him,
> To receive a gift in return?
> Source, Guide, and Goal of all that is —
> To him be glory for ever! Amen.
> (Rom. 11:35-36 NEB)

Four strong words are used in Acts to teach and to guard the doctrine
of the Holy Spirit: *epaggelia* ("promise," 1:4; 2:33, 39; cf. Luke 24:49);
dōrea ("gift," 2:38; 8:20; 10:45; 11:17); *didonai* ("to give," cf. *edōken*,
"he gave," 5:32; 11:17-18); and *lambanein* ("to receive," 1:8; 2:38;
8:17; 10:47; 19:2), and all four combat the error of the conditional
understanding of the Holy Spirit. The Holy Spirit is the promise-present
of the Father and, as such, a perfect free-gift given — not merely offered
— to believers who simply receive (never obtain) him. As we have
already noted, at least one of the four cardinal words is present in every
context in Acts where the decisive giving of the Holy Spirit is described.
These four words act as lights to illumine the meaning of the Holy Spirit
wherever he descends. They keep the church's mind within the boundaries
of grace. In their light the Holy Spirit is kept Holy. Together they spell
the freedom of grace. In their presence there can be no notion that the
gift of the Holy Spirit is an acquisition procured as a reward through
conditions beyond faith in Christ.

The important doctrine of the reception of the Holy Spirit in the
Book of Acts, as observed already in the important opening chapters,
as preserved in the especially important eighth chapter, and as developed throughout the subsequent chapters in Acts, may be formulated provisionally in a proposition: The Holy Spirit is given by God
alone through the *vox humanum* of the gospel as the Father's promise
and is simply received by men in Christ's name as a free gift through
faith sealed in baptism.

EXTENDED NOTE: THE "SECOND WORK" OF MARKUS BARTH,
OF SOME ANGLO-CATHOLICS, AND OF TRADITIONAL ROMAN
CATHOLICISM

1. MARKUS BARTH

Markus Barth's *Die Taufe — ein Sakrament? Ein exegetischer Beitrag
zum Gespraech ueber die kirchliche Taufe* (Zürich, 1951) is an extended
effort to establish in Scripture two baptisms. See above, p. 167, n. 11.
Acts 8 provides his major source. In order to develop the two baptisms
("Water-baptism," "Spirit-baptism" — interestingly, the two substantives
do not occur in the New Testament) Barth does the following: (1) sees

Christian baptism ("Water-baptism") as synonymous, and no more, with Johannine baptism: "One cannot, simply because of a basically different message and of a different faith, distinguish John's baptism from Christian baptism" (p. 172; cf. p. 184). We should think that for reasons as important as these — different message and different faith — Johannine and Christian baptisms *must* be distinguished, as indeed they are, cf. Acts 19:1-6. For Barth's unprecedented translation of Acts 19:4-5, however, see pp. 165-66 of his work. Barth (2) understands the submission to "water-" baptism in the name of Christ to be the work of men — moral, juridic, and sociological, *ibid.,* pp. 52-55. And since human and spiritual baptism are to be kept separate, according to Barth's insistence, the candidate can perform the necessary moral and other acts prior to and without the benefit of the baptism in the Holy Spirit. Barth therefore (3) discovers in the New Testament, in spite of protestations to the contrary, *two* Christian baptisms (Barth's substantives "Water-baptism" and "Spirit-baptism," and their separate occurrences, sufficiently indicate this fact; see pp. 158-59 of his book).

Markus Barth's doctrine of the two baptisms, in the name of God's freedom and in the legitimate desire to avoid sacramentalism, is a doctrine in danger of docetism, where God's uniting himself with the human is interpreted as more a shame than a salvation. However, *pace* Barth, the divine freedom is not endangered when the assurance of salvation is mediated through baptism rather than transient spiritual feeling. Barth warns that we must dispense with the tendency "to identify or to comingle man and God, the earthly congregation and the divine breath" (p. 145). But this comes close to being a denial of the incarnation (cf. I John 4:2-3). Unfortunately, in his last work, Barth *pater* followed his son in the doctrine of baptism. Karl Barth, *Church Dogmatics,* IV/4 (1969), pp. x, 62, 75.

2. SOME ANGLO-CATHOLICS

Some representatives, particularly, of "High" or Anglo-Catholic Anglicanism argue for the first full, permanent, and indwelling gift of the Holy Spirit in a second, subsequent, supplementary event or sacrament (not necessarily, as in Pentecostalism, in a second "experience"). The major line of representatives in this school includes: Fr. F. W. Puller, *What Is the Distinctive Grace of Confirmation?* 1880; Arthur James Mason, *The Relation of Confirmation to Baptism,* 1891; Dom Gregory Dix, *The Theology of Confirmation in Relation to Baptism,* 1946; L. S. Thornton, *Confirmation: Its Place in the Baptismal Mystery,* 1954.

For the parallels to Pentecostalism note, e.g., Mason's *(op. cit.)* remarks:

(1) to the doctrine of subsequence:

It is natural to suppose that the Paschal gift stands related to the Pentecostal as Baptism is related to Confirmation . . . ; but whether this be an exact statement of the case or not, the successive bestowals, at definite moments, of gifts akin to each other but not identical, prepares us for those words of Holy Scripture which teach us directly concerning the double sacrament of our initiation into Christ (pp. 17-18; cf. p. 455).

(2) to the doctrine of conditions:

My object is only to ascertain what it is that we receive by Confirmation in addition to the purely Baptismal grace, when all the right conditions are fulfilled (p. 5).

(3) the conclusion:

Unless I have signally failed in the setting forth of the Scriptural and Patristic texts, two points will by this time be, I believe, abundantly clear; first, that if we are to be guided by primitive antiquity, Confirmation is an integral part of Holy Baptism, in such a sense that what we usually call Baptism is, without it, an unfinished fragment, although conveying priceless blessings; and secondly, that the *res sacramenti,* the objective bounty extended by God for our acceptance, in this crowning part of Baptism, is that which bears the title of the gift of the Holy Ghost. In so special and unique a sense does this gift belong to Confirmation, that, notwithstanding all previous operations of the Holy Ghost upon the soul, the baptized but unconfirmed believer may, unless the Divine action departs from its ordinary course, be truly said not to have received the Holy Ghost (p. 414).

For the most modern representation of this school see Thornton *(op. cit.)* and his thesis:

As the Persons of the Godhead are complementary to one another, so the dispensation of the Spirit is complementary to the work of the Redeemer. So also our identification with the Christ in his life-story through baptism is crowned by *His* bestowal of the Spirit in confirmation. The notion which isolates the laver of baptism in a self-completing circle of its own runs counter not only to the evidence for two stages of initiation, but also to every other aspect of "unity in plurality" surveyed in the present work. The whole plan of St. Luke's two volumes is a case in point (p. 183; cf. also pp. 11, 18-19, 180).

For a recent symposium on the confirmation question, mostly Anglican, see Kendig Brubaker Cully (ed.), *Confirmation: History, Doctrine, and Practice.* Greenwich, Conn.: Seabury, 1962; cf. also "Neuere englische Literatur zum Taufproblem," *ThLZ* (1951), coll. 709-16, especially 715-16. For scholarly debate with the school's argument see G. W. H. Lampe, *The Seal of the Spirit: A Study in the Doctrine of Baptism and Confirmation in the New Testament and the Fathers* (London: Longmans, Green, 1951), who provides in his introduction a helpful survey of the line from Puller through Mason and Dix to Thornton. To Thornton's argument, represented for example in the following remark, "First comes Baptism for the remission of sins; then the promised circumcision of the heart in the seal of Confirmation. When these two stages are completed, then and not till then the indwelling of the Spirit takes place" *(op. cit.,* p. 9), Lampe replies *(The Seal,* pp. xiii-xiv):

It would require the plainest and most direct authority of Scripture, recognized and upheld by the constant and uniform testimony of the Church's tradition, to compel us to accept a doctrine apparently so much at variance, not only with the facts of experience, but also with the essential character of the Gospel. . . . On Thornton's view no non-episcopal body, and no church whose bishops cannot claim to represent the "apostolic ministry," possesses the Holy Spirit. Their members have never been "brought into full relationship" with Christ, for they "have not yet entered into the full mercies of the Covenant."

Lampe concludes:

It is difficult, if not impossible, to understand how there can be remission of sins, adoption, or regeneration, without His indwelling presence. As Dr. Bright remarked in reply to the views of Puller and Mason: "A theory which admits that baptism involves regeneration and the 'quickening touch' of the Spirit, and 'in a sense' a reception of Him by reason of 'incorporation into Christ' yet denies to the baptized, as such, that personal indwelling of the Spirit which is the 'great prerogative of the Gospel dispensation', forbids them to consider themselves as 'temples of the Holy Ghost', confines the 'baptism of the Holy Ghost' to confirmation ... can hardly be said to commend itself by consistency, and would seem to require a serious alteration in the pastoral teaching of the clergy" (p. 317).

For our purposes the most interesting matter to observe is the exact parallel between the high-liturgical and the popular-experiential doctrines of the Holy Spirit as represented respectively in a type of Anglo-Catholicism and in Pentecostalism. Mason cites approvingly "a most devout living writer of the English Church" who remarked that confirmation " 'may be viewed, *inter alia,* as the quasi-sacrament of what some Christians call the "second blessing"; the realisation of the highest life of the new-born soul in the more fully received power of the Spirit' " (*op. cit.,* p. 451).

3. Traditional Roman Catholicism

It is instructive to notice, finally, in poles as seemingly disparate as Pentecostalism and Roman Catholicism, the development from Acts 8 of a second experiential (Pentecostal) or sacramental (Catholic) blessing. (Cf. Behm, *Handauflegung,* p. 25: "Our text [Acts 8:14-17] is the *locus classicus* for the Roman church doctrine of Confirmation as the reserved right of bishops and of the laying on of hands at Confirmation.")

The Roman Catholic commentator A. Steinmann (*Apg.*[4], 1934, p. 82) writes to Acts 8:14-17:

The significance of this text lies essentially in its presentation of the relationship between Baptism and Confirmation. As here, so also in the remainder of Acts, both sacraments are not thought of as being so closely bound that they cannot be considered independently of each other.

Steinmann finds the separation of baptism and confirmation even in Acts 2:38-39, seeing the promise of the Spirit first fulfilled in Acts 4:31; he also prefers to understand Cornelius as a Christian prior to Peter's sermon (*ad loc.*). To Acts 8:14-17 see also Adler's conclusion, *Taufe und Handauflegung: Eine exegetisch-theologische Untersuchung von Apg. 8:14-17,* 1951, pp. 116-17. Note, however, the remarks of the Roman Catholic exegete R. Schnackenburg (*Das Heilsgeschehen bei der Taufe nach dem Apostel Paulus,* 1950, p. 78) to the absence of a doctrine of confirmation at least in the Pauline literature.

Finally, for a parallel of semi-official Roman Catholic confirmation doctrine to the Pentecostal Spirit-baptism doctrine see the formulations of St. Thomas Aquinas:

> So therefore does man receive spiritual life in Baptism, which is a spiritual regeneration: while in Confirmation man arrives at the perfect age, as it were, of the spiritual life. Hence Pope Melchiades says: "The Holy Ghost, Who comes down on the waters of Baptism bearing salvation in His flight, bestows at the font, the fulness of innocence; but in Confirmation He confers an increase of grace. In Baptism we are born again unto life; after Baptism we are strengthened" (*Sum. theol.* III, q. 72, art. 1).

> And therefore by the sacrament of Confirmation man is given a spiritual power in respect of sacred actions other than those in respect of which he receives power in Baptism. For in Baptism he receives power to do those things which pertain to his own salvation, forasmuch as he lives to himself: whereas in Confirmation he receives power to do those things which pertain to the spiritual combat with the enemies of the Faith (*ibid.,* art. 5).

For the Pentecostal parallels almost the whole of Part I above could be cited, but one citation will suffice here from the Hamburg-Germany Pentecostal pastor Paul Rabe in an address to the Pentecostal World Conference in 1955:

> By being born again we as individuals have been saved ourselves, but by the Baptism of the Spirit we receive power, or shall we say power to save others. . . . By being born again we have become the children of God, but by the Baptism in the Spirit we become the soldiers of Christ. "Scriptural Principles for Receiving the Baptism in the Holy Spirit," An Address . . . given at the World Conference [of Pentecostal Assemblies], in *Pentecost* (December, 1956), p. 8.

Valuable now for introduction to the current baptism debate as a whole and for the several traditions in particular is Dale Moody, *Baptism: Foundation for Christian Unity;* Philadelphia: Westminster, 1967: on Markus Barth see *ibid.,* pp. 64-71, esp. p. 68; on the Anglican discussion, pp. 162-216; and on the Roman tradition, pp. 14-44.

F. ACTS 8:26-40: THE ETHIOPIAN EUNUCH'S BAPTISM OF THE HOLY SPIRIT

Luke may have introduced this account to avoid the supposition that only apostles could participate in a genuine or full conversion. Immediately following the Samaritan episode, Philip, prompted by the Spirit (v. 29), joins himself to the Ethiopian eunuch and proceeding from a conversation over an Old Testament text bears witness to Jesus. Philip's witness evidently involved reference to baptism, for the eunuch asks, "Here is water, what is to keep me from being baptized?" (v. 36). They both entered into *(eis)* the water and Philip baptized him (v. 38).

How do we know that the Holy Spirit was present, active, and given here? The Holy Spirit arranged the meeting (v. 29), concluded it (v. 39a), and was probably the source of the homebound eunuch's joy *(chairön),* for in several places in the New Testament joy is regarded as the special fruit of the Spirit (cf. 11:23-24; 13:52; the context of 2:46; Gal. 5:22 *et al.*). Furthermore and conclusively, we may know that we are in the presence of an authentic and whole spiritual initiation because Jesus had been preached and in response the eunuch had been baptized.

In a few older texts (among them the important A from the fifth century) there is a record of the Holy Spirit's coming: literally, "The Holy Spirit fell upon the eunuch." In other important texts, however, there is no explicit reference to the coming of the Holy Spirit. But in Acts baptism in Christ, as we learned at the beginning (2:38-39 and 41) and as may be gathered from the evidences of this text, is baptism in the Spirit. Forgiveness of sins is not mentioned in this text either, or that the eunuch believed. But baptism says all these things. In Acts, baptism says "faith" and "forgiveness," no less surely than it says "the gift of the Holy Spirit" (2:38-41). Baptism in Acts is the inclusive term for all the facts of personal salvation: the message of the gospel, repentance, forgiveness, the gift of the Holy Spirit, and reception into the church.[32] The eunuch was baptized — that tells us all that we need to know. Acts 8:26-40 leaves us with no sense of incompletion, no sense of an imperfect initiation as did, purposely, Acts 8:4-16. We have in the present text, by all of Luke's normal indications, a whole initiation.

What was the condition of the baptism of the Holy Spirit? We might say preaching and baptism and not err grievously, but precision of language leads us to prefer to "condition" the church's traditional designation: means of grace. Later (eighth century [E *et al.*]) editors attempted to introduce a genuine condition into the text — verse 37 — by adding the very significant words (among others): " 'If you believe with *all* your heart, you may' " (RSV margin). Beyond strong textual grounds, I find important theological reason for suspecting this reading. Nowhere else in the New Testament is believing with *all* one's heart made a condition of salvation. If it were who could be saved? Even to imperfect, incomplete — i.e., simple — faith God gives himself completely. "Lord, I believe, help my unbelief." But happily, the editors' absolute condition is not in our gospel, nor in our text.

---

[32] See Miss Silva New's (Dr. Silva Lake's) conclusion: "Belief in Jesus (or in His Name), baptism, the remission of sins, the laying on of Apostolic hands, and the reception of the Spirit seem to have formed a single complex of associated ideas, any one of which might in any single narrative be either omitted or emphasized." "The Name, Baptism, and the Laying on of Hands," *The Beginnings of Christianity,* ed. F. J. Foakes-Jackson and Kirsopp Lake (Part I: The Acts of the Apostles; London: Macmillan, 1933), V, 134. Only one correction to Dr. Lake's conclusion seems necessary, as the present Acts text indicates: the *apostles* did not administer every baptism in the primitive church. Therefore, "the laying on of Apostolic hands," in the narrow sense, is not textual. See also Beasley-Murray's critique, *Baptism in the New Testament,* pp. 113-14.

G. ACTS 9:17-19: PAUL'S BAPTISM OF THE HOLY SPIRIT

In the prefatory announcement to Ananias of the divine intention for Paul it is relevant to notice that power is not mentioned, rather: " 'I will show him how much he must suffer' " (pathein, "suffer," placed at the end for emphasis, v. 16). In a preoccupation with power the importance, indeed the divine necessity (dei: "must") of suffering can be overlooked. There is much suffering in Acts. The Book of Acts is not theologia gloriae nor is its power merely triumphalist, though a superficial reading might give this impression. The power in Acts may be called power in prison.[33]

Ananias, who is neither apostle nor bishop, grants Paul the laying on of hands. The laying on of hands is not an apostolic or episcopal prerogative.

Paul is given no conditions for the baptism of the Holy Spirit; he is simply informed that Jesus has sent Ananias so that he might see and "be filled with the Holy Spirit" (v. 17b). "And immediately something like scales fell from his eyes and he regained his sight. Then he rose and was baptized, and took food and was strengthened" (vv. 18-19).

No mention is made in the text of the occurrence of the promised filling of the Holy Spirit. Is this because the promised filling did not occur? Such an assumption is foreign to the intention of the text. In Ananias' promise (! without any conditions) the filling of the Spirit is coupled with the restoration of sight (v. 17b). As we have discovered, it is Luke's fashion to summarize in one predicate the whole of a promise to avoid repetition (cf. 2:38-40 with 2:41). We are told in the following order that (1) hands having been applied during the promise, (2) the scales fell and Paul sees again (3) and is baptized. These facts taken together and in the light of the promise say that the Spirit was given with this event or, summarily, that to "be baptized" = to "be filled with the Spirit." Baptism and the reception of the Spirit are so synonymous as to be identical. Christian baptism is spiritual baptism.[34]

---

[33] There is insufficient attention to the suffering dimension of Acts in some modern analysis. For example, while an undeniable "triumphalism" breathes through Acts it must not be forgotten that not only Peter in the first half of Acts but Paul in the last half, as representative and model figures of the church, are as often in prison as in public. And significantly, while Acts ends with its famous and triumphant "unhindered" (28:31), it should be remembered that it is said of a man, typically, "in chains" (28:20; cf. 21:33; 12:6, 7).

[34] "Ananias speaks to the blinded Paul: 'that you may regain your sight and be filled with the Holy Spirit.' The last words are a paraphrase of the baptism which is then recorded." Wilhelm Heitmüller, Im Namen Jesu: Eine sprach- und religionsgeschichtliche Untersuchung zum Neuen Testament, speziell zur altchristlichen Taufe" ("FRLANT," 1/2; Göttingen: Vandenhoeck und Ruprecht, 1903), p.

H. ACTS 10:44-48; 11:13-18: THE BAPTISM OF THE HOLY SPIRIT OF CORNELIUS AND HIS HOUSEHOLD IN CAESAREA

1. ACTS 10:44-48: THE EVENT

Three times in a vision a voice announced to Peter that "what God has cleansed, you must not call common" (10:15-16; cf. 11:9-10). This announcement indicates that the cleansing of the future recipients of the Holy Spirit is in God's eyes an already accomplished fact and is neither to be doubted by Peter *nor* (for our purposes an important consideration) demanded of Cornelius. The major point of the Cornelius account is to be the breaking of Peter's (and the circumcision party's, cf. 10:45) insufficiently Christian notions of holiness.

As Philip had been led by the Spirit to the eunuch, so now Peter is led by the Spirit to Cornelius (10:19-20; 11:12-14). He proclaims the gospel and the Spirit descends (10:44-48). The purpose of the Cornelius episode is to teach the church, as dramatically as had the Samaritan initiation, that God accepts *all* men apart from the keeping of any legal prescriptions by freely giving the gift of the Holy Spirit to faith.[35]

In this account the unique similarity of the Spirit's coming to his coming at Pentecost is of special interest. Through a striking divine intervention by which the Gentiles were inaugurated into the church just as the Jews had been ("just as we have," 10:47; cf. 11:15) a certainty was provided that Gentiles stood on no less equal footing, no slightly lower level in the church than did the Jews.

What sign would have been conclusive in demonstrating to the sceptical circumcision party perhaps in particular (10:45; cf. 11:2-3) that the occasion of Gentile initiation was no less auspicious than that of Jewish initiation? The tongues of Pentecost.[36] Therefore this sign is specifically mentioned (10:46). Tongues were a sign not because they were expected, required, or usual, but precisely because they

---

302 n. 3. Stählin sees in the parallel "that" construction of vv. 17 and 18 a clear indication that "the reception of the Spirit is connected with the visible sign of baptism." *Apg.*[10], pp. 137-38.

Laying on of hands appears normally to have accompanied baptism (Acts 19: 5-6; Heb. 6:2) and to have been an integral part of it in much the same way that the forgiveness of sins and the gift of the Holy Spirit were interconnected and integrated (Acts 2:38). Accordingly, Acts 9:17-18 = Acts 22:16.

[35] See Martin Dibelius, *Aufsätze zur Apostelgeschichte,* ed. Heinrich Greeven (Göttingen: Vandenhoeck und Ruprecht, 1951), p. 103.

[36] However, there remains some doubt as to whether Luke intended to record *precisely* the same phenomena: at Pentecost alone are the tongues described as "other" (*heterais*) (2:4; cf. 2:8, 11), i.e., as other languages. Cf. Nikolaus Adler, *Das erste christliche Pfingstfest: Sinn und Bedeutung des Pfingstberichtes Apg. 2:1-13* ("NTA," 18/1; Münster i.W.: Aschendorffsche Verlagsbuchhandlung, 1938), p. 108.

were unexpected, unrequired, and unusual — resembled only by Pentecost — convincing even the most hard-necked that God wanted the Gentiles as well as the Jews among his people. Had there been faith to believe that Jesus Christ is "Lord of all" (10:36) there may have been no need for this drama. The clear teaching of the New Testament is that the need for the spectacular is more often a feature of unbelief than of belief, for in the words which our Lord often repeated: "an evil and adulterous generation seeks for a sign" (Matt. 12:39; 16:4 par.; cf. John 4:48b; 7:3-6).

It should also be noted as significant, then, that here as at Pentecost tongues came not as a sought evidence of the baptism of the Holy Spirit but as a complete surprise ("amazed," 10:45). Speaking in tongues occurs in Acts 2 and 10 but in both instances the occurrence is *unsought, unexpected,* and *undemanded.* This fact is very detrimental to the Pentecostal doctrine of the required and sought initial evidence of the baptism in the Holy Spirit.

Furthermore, the Caesarean event cannot be interpreted by means of Pentecostalism's doctrines of either the *subsequent* or the *conditional* baptism in the Holy Spirit. The tongues came neither subsequent to conversion nor through conditions fulfilled prior to their incidence. They occurred here *at conversion.* Nor here, or elsewhere in the New Testament, is tongues-speaking recorded as occurring in a single seeking *individual,* as it is, however, in most Pentecostal instances. In Acts, on the three occasions where tongues occur, they come to an entire group at once, with prophecy, bringing complete Christian initiation, and occur, in all three cases, apart from recorded effort on the part of the recipients. Speaking in tongues in Acts is on all three occasions a corporate, church-founding, group-conversion phenomenon, and never the subsequent Spirit-experience of an individual.[37]

Of most importance, the gift of the Holy Spirit here is conversion, not a later experience. The argument that Cornelius was converted prior to his hearing, so that what happened here was a second (or even third) experience is insubstantial. Peter was to be summoned, Cornelius was told, " 'to declare to you a message by which you will *be saved,* you and all your household' " (11:14). The gift of the Spirit, as always, was no further experience, it was *the* experience of salvation. And this salvation was without conditions and "without price" — it was simply given through the gospel (cf. Gal. 3:2).

The unity in Acts 10 of the baptism of the Holy Spirit and conversion establishes the fragility here (and in Acts 8) of the Pentecostal thesis: "Sometimes [the baptism of the Holy Spirit with tongues] was received after tarrying; sometimes during the laying on of hands; some-

---

[37] I owe this insight to Otto Dibelius, *Die werdende Kirche: Eine Einführung in die Apostelgeschichte* ("Die urchristliche Botschaft," 5. Abt.; 5th rev. ed.; Hamburg: Im Furche-Verlag, 1951), p. 103.

times it was completely spontaneous; but always it came after conversion, for it is a distinct and separate experience."[38] This thesis is also corrected by Acts 2 (see Peter's view of Pentecost, Acts 11:17, and the development below, p. 196) and even more clearly in Acts 19 — Pentecostalism's final courts of appeal. That conversion and the coming of the Spirit are one and identical and not two and separate is most clearly attested here in the Cornelius account. Pentecostalism's thematic texts form then, paradoxically, specific antitheses to a doctrine of a subsequent, sought, or conditional baptism in the Holy Spirit.

But may not the Cornelius account be an instance where we see the gift or baptism of the Holy Spirit coming quite apart from baptism itself? At first this could appear to be the case, and the divine parallel with Pentecost — the immediacy of the gift — could suggest it. However, the parallel ceases before this conclusion can be drawn: Cornelius and his household are promptly baptized. The Holy Spirit may come immediately prior to baptism (at least in this single instance), immediately after baptism (cf. 19:5-6), or with baptism (Acts 2:38), but never, anywhere in the New Testament after Pentecost, apart from baptism. The intimate connection between baptism and the Spirit, established at Pentecost (2:38-39), dramatically confirmed at Samaria (8:14-17), finds expression again here in Caesarea. Since it was evidently impossible for the apostles to associate the gift of the Holy Spirit with anything but baptism, the new converts were immediately baptized (10:48).[39]

Baptism, it should be noted therefore, was not considered a superfluous rite, dispensable now because the "real thing" had already occurred. The gift of the Holy Spirit without baptism was as unthinkable to the church as baptism without the gift of the Holy Spirit (8:14-17; 19:2-7). The apostles' unique immediate experience at Pentecost did not lead them to think that the Holy Spirit would always (or ever) come as he had with them, separated in time from baptism. Their instructions at Pentecost and here at the "Gentile Pentecost" confirm this.

Constantly, from their Lord's vicarious experience (Mark 1:9-11 par.) to the church's daily experience — and this cannot be stressed too strongly — the apostles saw the descent of the Spirit as intimately connected with baptism. The baptism with the Holy Spirit and baptism, they knew, belonged together in such a way as to form the "one bap-

---

38 Edward J. Jarvis, "This Is That," *Pentecostal Evangel, 49* (Jan. 15, 1961), 7.
39 Cf. Flemington, *New Testament Doctrine of Baptism*, p. 151; Ragnar Asting, *Die Heiligkeit in Urchristentum* ("FRLANT," N.F., 29; Göttingen: Vandenhoeck und Ruprecht, 1930), p. 123; R. E. O. White, *The Biblical Doctrine of Initiation* (London: Hodder & Stoughton, 1960), p. 196. The fact that Peter "commands" and apparently does not himself administer baptism (cf. Cerfaux-Dupont, *Actes*, p. 109) can indicate again the relative indifference of an *apostolic* laying on of hands at baptism (cf. I Cor. 1:14-16).

tism" of the church (Eph. 4:5; cf. I Cor. 12:13; John 3:5; Tit. 3:5). This
is the doctrine, both here and in Acts as a whole, of baptism and the
Spirit. Christian *baptism* and the gift of the *Spirit* come together forming both actually and figuratively the baptism in the Spirit.[40]

2. ACTS 11:13-18: THE REVIEW

In chapter eleven Peter rehearses to the church in Jerusalem what
had happened in Caesarea. He stresses that the Holy Spirit had come
upon the Cornelius household "just as on us at the beginning" (v. 15).
This remark is important. Peter does not say that the Holy Spirit came
upon Cornelius' household "just as he always does with everyone."
Had Peter said this we would have to suppose that in the earliest church
the Holy Spirit was always, or at least normally, given with speaking
in tongues. But that the only parallel Peter knows to draw to Caesarea
is what had happened "at the beginning" reinforces the probability that
after Pentecost the Pentecost manifestations were not only not normative but probably not known.

Then Peter recalls, as a result of the Caesarean experience, the
words of the Lord, "how he said, 'John baptized with water, but you
shall be baptized with the Holy Spirit'" (v. 16).[41] This is the first time
that the expression "be baptized with the Holy Spirit" is used since
Acts 1:5 and it is the last time it is used in the New Testament. The
phrase occurs on only two occasions in Acts: in promising the first
Pentecost (1:5) and in reviewing the last (11:16). The usual expression becomes very early "receive the Holy Spirit" (2:38; 8:17; 10:47;
19:2) and the Spirit's name is predominantly "the gift" (2:38; 8:20;
10:45; 11:17) or "the promise" (1:4; 2:33, 39; cf. Luke 24:49) and
never in the New Testament "the baptism."[42]

---

[40] See Alfred Seeberg, *Der Katechismus der Urchristenheit* (Leipzig: A. Deichert'sche Verlagsbuchhandlung Nachf. [Georg Böhme], 1903), p. 218 to Acts
10:47-48; also Behm, *Handauflegung,* p. 169. It is one of the most interesting
features of Acts that it is in precisely the two passages where an historical separation of Christian baptism and the gift of the Spirit is described (Acts 8 and 10)
that the theologically purposed and historically accomplished *union* of the two is
most forcefully taught. In these two places Luke records separation only to teach
union. To confuse what Luke records with what he teaches is as erroneous as it
is frequent.
[41] Schweizer understands Acts 11:16, with Acts 1:5, as a Lukan "insertion" and
says therefore that 11:16 "proves that for Luke baptism was considered as at
most in an accidental connection with the all-important [*allein wichtigen*] out-
pouring of the Spirit." Art. *pneuma, TWNT,* VI, 411. Conzelmann rebuts by
saying simply, "On the contrary!" *Apg.,* p. 67. It is, of course, true that Luke
places the highest valuation possible upon the reception of the Spirit — all Acts
testifies to this. But Christian baptism's normal relation to this decisive gift is,
in Luke's doctrine, not accidental but instrumental.
[42] The noun term "baptism of (in, or with) the Holy Spirit" does not occur
in the New Testament. Our use of the expression in the titles to the several

To be literal, being "baptized with the Holy Spirit" is not a doctrine which Acts teaches for the on-going church since the phrase occurs only at the crisis initiations of the Jews and of the Gentiles into the church. After Caesarea the phrase disappears from the vocabulary of Acts (see the closest New Testament parallel, I Cor. 12:13). The shift in expression from "be baptized with the Holy Spirit" to "receive the gift of the Holy Spirit" occurs at the very beginning of Acts: the promised baptism (1:5) becomes at its first transmission the promised gift (2:38). But because in Acts the gift of the Spirit is so integrally connected with baptism, baptism and the gift of the Spirit may be said, with a certain picturesqueness of speech, to form the "baptism with the Holy Spirit" (cf. outside Acts, I Cor. 6:11; 12:13; John 3:5; Tit. 3:5-6). Ever since the Jewish-Gentile initiations the expression "baptism of the Holy Spirit" is only appropriate in the church, however, when it is used in the fullest sense of its main words, namely, when it applies to a real *baptism* and to the equally real reception of the *Spirit*.[43]

In the account before us Peter moves from the expression "be baptized with the Holy Spirit," an expression (we repeat) which he recalls not from the constant experience or vocabulary of the church but from the pre-Pentecost promise of Jesus (11:16), to the more usual designation, " 'If then God gave the same gift (*dörean*) to them as he gave to us when we believed in the Lord Jesus Christ, who was I that I could withstand God?' " (v. 17).

Thus for the third time in three verses (vv. 15, 16, 17) Peter overarches the entire history of the church theretofore and reaches back to the circle of events at and before Pentecost to find a connection with what had just transpired in Caesarea: (1) v. 15: " 'as on us *at the beginning*' "; (2) v. 16: " 'I remembered the *word of the Lord*' "; (3) v. 17: " 'God gave the same gift to them as he gave to *us.*' " We may safely conclude then that the Caesarean occurrence of tongues was not the normal initiatory experience of the church and that its only correspondence was Pentecost.

According to Peter's review the object of faith for the gift of the Spirit, *both* for the apostles in Jerusalem and for the household in Caesarea, was Jesus Christ and not (separately) the Spirit: " 'If then God gave the same gift to them as he gave to us *when we believed in*

---

sections is simply a concession to Pentecostalism. "Gift of the Holy Spirit" would be the more appropriate designation in an Acts study.

[43] Kümmel points out that no *antithesis* between water and Spirit baptism and hence no problem need be seen in the Baptist's prediction, "I have baptized you with water; but he will baptize you with the Holy Spirit" (Mark 1:8 par.), since both phrases refer to a *baptizing* and this term must be taken realistically. "Das Urchristentum: Nachträge zu Teil I-III," *ThR*, N.F. *18* (1950), 45. So also Asting, *Heiligkeit,* p. 123; von Baer, *Heilige Geist,* p. 170. See also the discussion below, p. 219.

the Lord Jesus Christ...' " (11:17).[44] But of equal moment, if, as is
likely, Peter here compares the faith of the Caesareans with the faith
of the apostles at Pentecost — "when *we* believed" — then we have
the significant information that the apostles considered *Pentecost* to be
the *terminus a quo* of their faith, hence the date of their conversion.
It was only when they received the Spirit that they felt able to say that
they believed.[45] For Peter, then, the filling of the Holy Spirit was equivalent to believing (2:4: "they were ... filled with the Holy Spirit" =
11:17 "we believed"). The apostles became Christians in the same way
that Cornelius' household had become Christians: by receiving the
gift of the Holy Spirit through faith in Jesus Christ. For neither group
was the reception of the Holy Spirit a second or higher experience
accomplished along a route of arduous conditions: the gift was *the*
(*hē* dörea, 10:45; 11:17) full and faith-giving gift of the Spirit. There
may be few more suitable ways to define the filling of the Holy Spirit
than as the gift of faith.

When Peter concludes his report by asking, " 'Who was I that I could
withstand God?' " (v. 17), does he mean withstand God by not granting baptism which is the act of Christian initiation? Probably (10:47).
If *kōluein* ("withstand," "hinder") in the New Testament has a baptismal reference, as Cullmann and others have argued, then this possibility becomes still more real. This would mean that not simply human
afterthought led Peter to baptize the converts, but the very *Drang* of
God himself. Then baptism is God's pressure on the church, as it is
on the believer, to seal what has happened through the gospel. Then the
work of God commencing with the preparation of the recipient (10:3-6;
11:13-14), continuing in the sending of the gospel messenger (10:19-
20; 11:12), reaching its high point in the conversion work of the Spirit
through the message (10:43-44; 11:15-17), is completed in the water
of baptism (10:47-48). The whole is the work of God, baptism not
excluded. And the whole *is* a whole, not to be severed at any part.

The Spirit can be said to be given with the message of faith (Acts
10; cf. Gal. 3:2, 5) as he is, and with baptism (Acts 2:38-39) as he is;
but these are not two disparate parts, they are one organic whole and
should occur together (cf. 2:41: "that day"; 16:33: "at once"). Baptism is the conclusion of the missionary sermon and the concretion of

---

[44] The subject of the Greek *pisteusāsin* ("they believed"? So Züricher Bibel;
"we believed"? So RSV) is difficult to ascertain but is probably meant to refer
both to the apostolic circle and to the Caesarean converts.

[45] "If we let Peter's speech work on us its complete force we will see that
according to Luke's viewpoint the time of Peter's conversion was Pentecost."
Von Baer, *Heilige Geist*, p. 96. Also Friedrich Büchsel, *Der Geist Gottes im
Neuen Testament* (Gütersloh: C. Bertelsmann, 1926), p. 249. The Spirit-events of
Acts 2, of Acts 10-11, and their theological formulation in Acts 15:7-11, are the
decisive refutations of Schweizer's thesis that in Luke "the faith [of men] is
never traced to the Spirit." Art. *pneuma, TWNT*, VI, 410, 8-9.

its promises. The God who brings the gospel to bear on the heart through his Spirit working in the message presses church and believer to immediate baptism where his work will be sealed (cf. 8:36; 9:18; 10:47). Peter felt this pressure and did not feel worthy to withstand it. Baptism and the gift of the Spirit belong together.[46]

The whole Caesarean account ends on a sovereign and lofty note indicating once again, as Acts never tires of doing, the source behind the whole good work:

> And they glorified God, saying, "Then to the Gentiles also God has granted repentance unto life" (11:18).

Repentance, which men are called upon to effect (2:38; 3:19), is the gift of God (11:18). God gives repentance through the message of the gospel which sets repentance in motion, and he seals it in baptism (cf. 2:37 with 2:41; 10:44 with 10:48). Repentant faith, no less than forgiveness and the Spirit, is at its source the one gift of God made available, or better made active, in the serving of the gospel Word, and made actual in baptism.

The ascription of Acts 11:18 to tradition rather than to Luke's own conviction in the studies of Conzelmann and Wilckens seems to us not entirely fair to Luke.[47] Does Luke introduce testimony which he finds out of harmony with his own conviction? Does Acts 11:18 fail accurately to represent what did in fact here happen to Cornelius? Do the conversions which Luke describes in Acts (e.g., Paul's) diverge from the theological sense of Acts 11:18? We may compare with 11:18 comparable formulations in Acts which teach the sovereignty of God:

> For the promise [of the gift of the Holy Spirit] is to you and to your children and to all that are far off, *every one whom the Lord our God calls to him* (2:39).

> And his name, by faith in his name, has made this man strong whom you see and know; and *the faith which is through Jesus* has given the man this perfect health in the presence of you all (3:16).

> *God,* having raised up his servant, sent him to you first, to bless you *in turning every one of you from your wickedness* (3:26).

> *God* exalted him at his right hand as Leader and Savior, *to give repentance to Israel and forgiveness of sins* (5:31).

> And when the Gentiles heard this, they were glad and glorified the word of God; and *as many as were ordained to eternal life believed* (13:48).

> And *God* who knows the heart bore witness to them *giving them the Holy Spirit* just as he did to us; and *he* made no distinction between us and them, but *cleansed their hearts by faith* (15:8-9).

> *The Lord opened her heart to give heed to what was said by Paul* (16:14b).

> He greatly helped those *who through grace had believed* (18:27c).

---

[46] Cf. Conzelmann to Acts 11:17. *Apg.,* p. 67.

[47] Conzelmann, *Theology of Luke,* p. 100 n. 1; p. 228 n. 2; Wilckens, *Missionsreden,* p. 181.

I. ACTS 14:19-28: PAUL'S FIRST STRENGTHENING MESSAGE

When Paul and Barnabas had made many disciples in Derbe they recirculated through the cities where they had preached the gospel earlier, "strengthening the souls of the disciples" (v. 22). This little paragraph is important because it delivers to us *in nuce* the essential content of Paul's message to Christians. Since in Pentecostalism the baptism of the Holy Spirit is usually taught to those who are already Christians and in connection with what is called the higher, deeper, or victorious life, this passage is instructive.

What was essential to Paul's "strengthening" (*epistërizontes*, 14:22) message according to Luke's record?

> When they had preached the gospel to that city and had made many disciples, they returned to Lystra and to Iconium and to Antioch, strengthening the souls of the disciples, exhorting them to *continue in the faith*, and saying that *through many tribulations we must enter the kingdom of God* (14:21-22).

First and foremost, Paul encouraged Christians to remain in the faith once given (the article indicates the *fides quae creditur*). Paul's higher-life message was not so much an exhortation to "go on" to higher things as it was to remain in lofty faith (cf. Barnabas in Antioch, 11:23). The Christian goes on by starting over again (Luther), he "lives by faith" (Paul, Rom. 1:17). Paul did not evidently teach an experience or responsibility higher than faith — for example, emptying, absolute surrender, total obedience — as though anything could be higher than faith or as though faith were only a beginning (cf. Rom. 1:17a: *ek . . . eis*).

And the faith of which Paul speaks, we learn from the context, is faith in Christ. As faith does not need a new definition or addition (e.g., absolute surrender) to be complete, so it does not need a new object — for example, Pentecostalism's Holy Spirit — to go deep. The new name in Antioch was "Christians" not "Spiritists," 11:26; the reasons: 11:20, 21, 23, 24. In Paul's messages in Acts the Lord Jesus Christ is the central and sufficient object of faith. According to Luke's record the Holy Spirit is not mentioned in any message during this missionary journey.[48]

Second, Paul apparently did not strengthen the disciples by offering them more power than they already had in faith by teaching a "life of rest" or victory above difficulties. He tells them simply and realistically that *"through* many difficulties we must enter the kingdom of God"

---

[48] The Holy Spirit is never spoken of as a separate object of faith in the New Testament (there is no command to "believe in the Holy Spirit," *pisteuein en* or *eis to pneuma hagion*) because the Holy Spirit is "in Christ Jesus" (cf. Gal. 3:14; Rom. 8:2, 9-10; John 14:26: "in my name"). See the systematic development below, ch. VI.

(v. 22). The way of the Christian life is not the higher way *over* (*huper*: a key word in II Cor.) difficulties but the "lower," earthy way *through* them.

And this hard way is not overcome by a divine experience granting so much power that difficulties are no longer really difficulties.[49] Rather it is a divine *necessity* (*dei*) that these difficulties be. The "second experience," if it may be called that, of which Paul here speaks is not the baptism in the Holy Spirit but "the kingdom of God" (v. 22b). Between baptism and the coming of the kingdom there is no necessary second experience. But there are many difficulties!

That toward which Paul directs the eyes of the new Christians, then, is their faith in the beginning — in that they should remain — and the kingdom at the end — toward that they should press. And the medium between the two which Paul here chooses to stress is difficulty not power. There were no interim blessings to divert the eyes. In Paul's teaching as recorded by Luke, then, there is in effect no deeper-life message as distinguished from the gospel, with an added second experience; there is only the gospel of faith with its honesty.

Paul then ordained elders for the churches (v. 23); the churches needed these more than a second blessing. Paul concluded his strengthening mission by "commending them to the *Lord* in whom they *believed*" (v. 23). Thus again Paul's message to Christians, like his message to non-Christians, is (cf. 11:23) *solus Christus, sola fide*. Paul's first missionary journey can terminate in Antioch where it had begun with the report that God had been with them and that *he* had opened to the Gentiles a "door of faith" (v. 27). "It is enough."[50]

J. ACTS 15:1-29: THE FURTHER WORK OF THE CIRCUM-CISION PARTY AND THE JERUSALEM CONFERENCE

> But some men came down from Judea and were teaching the brethren, "Unless you are circumcised according to the custom of Moses, you cannot be saved" (v. 1).

The doctrine of the men who came down from Judea was, simply put, that faith in Christ was not enough. Faith must be supplemented by a fuller obedience to the teaching of Scripture, and in this case particularly, by circumcision. The essence of the circumcision party's teaching was not that faith in Christ was unnecessary for Gentiles but that faith

---

[49] An opinion influential in Pentecostalism and beyond (e.g., in evangelical victorious-life teaching), especially since Wesley: see his *Plain Account, passim,* but especially pp. 9-10, 23. See excerpts in the Documents, below, p. 330.

[50] In the picture of God's opening the door of faith Luke emphasizes in a conclusive way both "that it is faith . . . which is for all the one means of access to God and to salvation . . . , and that it is God himself who provides this faith." Stählin, *Apg.*[10], p. 197. Linguistically and theologically the Thessalonian correspondence of Paul is a fascinating commentary on Acts 14:22. See my dissertation, II, pp. 127-28 for exegesis.

alone was insufficient for full standing before God: obedience must be added to make faith and salvation complete.

Paul and Barnabas could not allow even the seemingly most harmless of religious rites — even if taught with great authority in Scripture (cf. e.g. Gen. 17:14) — to be admitted as a "further work": "Paul and Barnabas had no small dissension and debate with them" (v. 2). For they knew that hidden under even the smallest of conditions is the larva of law. Though this does not appear in the men's opening appeal for fuller obedience (v. 1) it comes to light in the convened theological conference in Jerusalem when the believers who belonged to the party of the Pharisees declared: " 'It is *necessary* to circumcise them, *and to charge them to keep the law of Moses'* " (v. 5). Here becomes patent what is latent in every condition: the crushing weight of the whole law.

Peter responds with a summary of the sufficiency of the message of faith (vv. 7-11). God's full will for the Gentiles could be compressed into a single phrase: that they "should hear the word of the gospel and believe" (v. 7). Then Peter described how this occurred in a fine theological sentence:

> And God who knows the heart bore witness to them, giving them the Holy Spirit just as he did to us; and he made no distinction between us and them, but cleansed their hearts by faith (vv. 8-9).

The fact that God gives his Spirit not after but through the cleansing of hearts by faith is established splendidly in this text through the parallel simultaneous or coincident aorist participles (*dous . . . të pistei katharisas*). The gift of the Spirit and faith are not only contemporaneous, they are *God's* acts (or act!) as well. The aorist tenses tell us that the gift of the Holy Spirit was not given in portions (e.g., partially in a first experience, fully in a second), nor was the cleansing a gradual process leading up to the gift. The Holy Spirit and the cleansing were given in the same moment: indeed, in the moment of faith (*të pistei,* v. 9). We are saying then a good deal more than we may at first appreciate when we say with Luke (and Peter) that the gift of the Holy Spirit is aorist. The cleansing of the heart, faith, the gift of the Holy Spirit are then essentially all *one act of God* and not three moral conditions, or two moral conditions and a result.

The strict Judaistic concern was the concern of holiness (cf. e.g. Mark 7:1-15 par.; Gal. 2:12). Surely, they reasoned, God would not give his Spirit to men who had not fully obeyed his clear commands in Scripture; and not fully to obey God's commands must certainly involve heart uncleanness. Out of what was thought to be obedience to the clear teaching of their Bible the circumcision party evidently contended for an absolute and full obedience to the expressed will of God before a man could have full salvation, and this obedience found for them its most essential initial evidence in circumcision.

We know of few theological sentences more significant to twentieth-century Pentecostal or holiness concern, therefore, than Acts 15:8-9. As we observed in Part I of this study, conditions are there prescribed with a view, essentially, to achieving "heart-cleansing" or a "deeper faith" in order to obtain at last the full and permanent gift of the Holy Spirit. However, according to our text *each* of these "moments" — cleansing, faith, and Spirit — is a *single* moment and a gift of God, better *the* gift of God, or antithetically, God's work and not men's.

According to Acts 15:7-9, God's cleansing is not one step, his gift of faith another, his gift of the Spirit the last. Rather God cleanses men's hearts through faith by giving them the Holy Spirit through the gospel.[51] Faith is the work of God in cleansing men's hearts (*"God . . . cleansed their hearts by faith,"* vv. 8-9).[52]

Thus we may say to the Pentecostal conditions from this important text: the "heart-cleansing" which is so painfully pursued God achieves; the faith which is so assiduously cultivated God grants; the Holy Spirit who is so scrupulously sought God gives — and the means is simply the divine gospel which is the power of *God* unto salvation (cf. Rom. 1:16).

It must have been overlooked by the adherents of the doctrine of heart-cleansing, as it is called (and it is taken from this text, Acts 15: 8-9), that the subject of the sentence is God (v. 8). The giving, the cleansing, the faith are all described as his work. This must come as a relief to those who discover it and who learn that God does not demand *their* accomplishment of these momentous realities before he will give himself, but that, typical of grace, God gives himself by giving these realities. The conversion of Cornelius is the clearest exposition of this fact.

Nevertheless, the fact that response-ability is not overlooked in this important text may be observed in the opening phrase: " 'And God who knows the heart bore witness to them' " (v. 8). We are given neither a psychological nor a moral description of what God saw in the heart; it was not a clean heart for he cleansed the heart thereafter

---

[51] Acts 15:8-9 forms Luke's final theological rebuttal of the Gunkel to Schweizer thesis that the Spirit in Acts is unconnected to faith and only loosely related to baptism. Schweizer notices that "faith, not baptism, cleanses one for the reception of the Spirit according to Acts 15:8-9." Art. *pneuma, TWNT,* VI, 411, 34-35. But Luke can also describe baptism as a cleansing means (cf. Acts 22:16: "Rise and be baptized, and wash away your sins, calling on his name"). And in Acts 2:38, Luke's model understanding of the church's reception of the Spirit, Christian baptism is presented as the means of the forgiveness of sins and hence as in a cleansing relationship to the co-ordinated reception of the gift of the Holy Spirit.

[52] See Haenchen, *Apg.*[12], p. 386 to v. 9. Also Stählin: "God bore witness to his election of love by accomplishing through the threefold gift of the gospel, faith, and the Holy Spirit that which according to the Judaizers could be accomplished only through the observance of the Holiness code: the cleansing of hearts." *Apg.*[10], p. 202.

(v. 9). It may have been faith ("believe" is the word immediately preceding this phrase, v. 7), but then God was but looking on his own work (v. 9b; cf. 13:48; 18:27; 2:39b). If as Paul says, "faith comes from what is heard, and what is heard comes by the preaching of Christ" (Rom. 10:17), then Peter (Luke) is expressing the same conviction here for it was God who sent the preacher (Acts 10:5, 19-20, 30-33; 11:12-13) and it was God who gave the hearers repentance (11:18) or faith (15:9). We are not *told* what God saw; Peter is not so much interested in what God saw as in what God did: He gave the Holy Spirit just as he had to the disciples in the beginning, making no distinction between Jews and Gentiles, but cleansing their hearts by faith (vv. 8-9).

In any event, Cornelius and his household responded in faith, they believed, and no interpretation should be allowed to do violence to the human response, nor to this text, nor to its larger context which gives responsible faith an importance we dare not overlook or make fatalistic. The famous warnings with which the apostles often concluded their sermons would not be understandable if faith were not a responsibility (cf. 2:40; 3:23; 13:40-41).[53] Believing is God's gift; at the same time — or rather, as a direct *result* — it is the hearers' solemn responsibility to receive it. As long as it is kept in mind that what God does is infinitely the greater and that what the hearer receives is on all sides enabled by what God does and gives — the gospel, the preacher, baptism, the church — then men will not fall into the sin of presumption and take credit for their faith or, what is worse, for their absolute faith. God alone can do the absolute, and for men either to claim it or demand it seems very like the primal sin.

Furthermore, faith is without adjectives in Acts; faith is, as everywhere in the gospel, *sola fides* — without adornments or supplements — but with innumerable fruits. But faith for the reception of God's gift must be alone or it will not be; faith must be without adjectives or the gospel becomes law. The greatness of Acts 15:7-9 is this: it combines so wholly and theologically, so satisfactorily, the simple divine and human event of salvation. Its significance in relation to the problem in this study is that it clearly announces the (exclusive) cleansing, working, and giving Subject of the gift of the Holy Spirit.

Peter concludes his theological clarification by asking those who wished a fuller gospel — i.e., a gospel where a specific obedience to a law of the Bible was added to faith in Christ before a man had full standing before God — " 'Why do you make a trial of God by putting a yoke upon the neck of the disciples which neither our fathers nor

---

[53] See also the preaching of Jesus mirrored by Matthew in the conclusion to the Sermon on the Mount with its four warnings; or the point of many parables. I discuss the thorny question of infant baptism below, p. 218, n. 76.

we have been able to bear?' " (v. 10).[54] Ananias and Sapphira had tempted God by claiming an absolute surrender when they had not made it; Simon had tempted God by offering a kind of absolute surrender when God himself had made it; the circumcision-holiness party were now tempting God by *demanding* of others, of even believers, an absolute surrender, or an obedience, which God alone gives and had given. The experience of the fathers and of the church was that neither was able to bear the oppressive yoke of absolutes.

Peter's final words are: " 'But we believe that we shall be saved through the grace of the Lord Jesus, just as they will' " (v. 11). Grace is everything, and only where grace *is* everything is there a gospel at all. Furthermore, it is *through* (*dia*) the grace of the Lord Jesus that we *believe;* literally v. 11 reads, "but through the grace of our Lord Jesus Christ we believe to be saved." It is through grace that we believe, as every Christian knows (cf. 18:27: "those who through grace had believed").[55] And salvation — not just "partial salvation," as if there ever were such a creature; but the one salvation, the only salvation there is — is the result of the faith which comes through grace. So rich and so complete, and so now completed, is Peter's exposition of the gospel. Peter slips away now from the history of Acts entirely, but these his final words are among the clearest in the whole of the New Testament in their illumination of the gift of God.

The decision of the Jerusalem council is that the holiness concerns of the circumcision party and their unevangelical biblicism are not to be allowed to cloud the gospel of *sola gratia, sola fide*. The circumcision party's troubling teaching (cf. Gal. 1:7; 5:10) of a further work, unsettling the believers, is to be disregarded (15:24). The ethical instructions contained in the apostolic letter (vv. 22-29) are not new conditions for a fuller salvation, but good advice for Christians already enjoying a full salvation through faith. The letter concludes thus

---

[54] Haenchen's attempt (*Apg.*[12], pp. 99-100; p. 387 nn. 1 and 2; cf. among others also Philip Vielhauer, "Zum 'Paulinismus' der Apostelgeschichte," *EvTh, 10* [1950-51], 5-10; Conzelmann, *Theology of St. Luke*, pp. 160-61, 146-48) to make Luke's formulation of the law-problem *greatly* different from Paul's is, for us, unconvincing. The fact that Luke places Acts 15 at the crown of his entire development (cf. Conzelmann, *ibid.*, pp. 211-12) indicates as can nothing else that he understood freedom from the law as of the very highest importance for his composition and for the church. To be sure, Luke does not evidence Paul's sublime grasp of the law-gospel problem — but, then, who can?

[55] Acts 15:11 is rendered differently in all of the standard versions. We think that the absence of a *hoti* indicates, or can indicate, the formula of faith through grace as well as it indicates the doctrine of salvation through grace: *alla dia tēs charitos tou kuriou Iēsou pisteuomen sōthēnai* (but through the grace of the Lord Jesus we believe [have faith] to be saved). If this hypothesis is correct, then Peter's theological formulation in Acts 15:7-11 is almost peerless. We were pleased to discover· Stählin's recent voucher of this possible translation. *Apg.*[10], p. 203.

not with a warning but with the evangelical words: " 'If you keep yourselves from these [pagan practices] you do well' " (v. 29).
The result of the Jerusalem conference? There are to be no further
works for the reception of God's one salvation. Indeed, there are to be
no works for this reception at all, but faith only, which is exactly the
despair of all works as means for having God. Making holiness of
heart a condition of salvation, which was the circumcision party's contention, was recognized. But the author of the work of holiness is made
God alone. It may be impossible for a man's heart to be unclean if
the Holy Spirit is to enter it — the constant theme of holiness and
Pentecostal teaching, a theme we shall later investigate theologically
— but, in any case, the cleanliness is not the work of men, it is the
simple gift of faith (*të pistei*) in the God who receives and cleanses
precisely the unclean, the unworthy, and the sinful. Fundamentally,
holiness is the gift of faith — a gift given by God and empirical to
him alone. The failure to see this paramount truth here and throughout the New Testament is a major failure in holiness-Pentecostal
teaching.[56]

The result of the Jerusalem conference is that the church is liberated
from a "fuller" gospel of a "fuller" faith than that with which it had
been once and for all entrusted and which God once-for-all gives,
thus freeing the church of the first and subsequent centuries from the
necessity of a troubled and unsettled conscience before God, and from
the law (v. 5; cf. Rom. 7:1-6; 10:4) and its unbearable yoke. If we
reserve the message and fruit of faith, and if we recognize faith's giver,
we may say that the result of the Jerusalem conference for Christian
theology is the abolition of conditions.

K. ACTS 16:11 — 18:11: SIX GREEK CONVERSIONS

Between the Jerusalem conference where the relation of faith to
salvation and the Holy Spirit is clarified, and the events in Ephesus
circling around baptism and the Holy Spirit (18:24-28; 19:1-7) there

---

[56] Circumcision implies, among other less important things, that faith is not
sufficient before God and that at least *one thing more* must be done in order
to be fully pleasing to him. If one starts with only *one* other act beyond the faith
given him in the beginning, how may he ever be certain that this act is at last
sufficient before God? Indeed, to step out of the sphere of *sola fide* in *solum
Christum* into the sphere of absolute surrender for a fuller salvation through a
second experience is to step out from under the yoke that is easy and the burden
that is light into and under the yoke that is unbearable: the yoke of the law with
its burden of never knowing when one has done *enough*. Luther asserted that
with supplements "faith and the whole Christ crash to the ground. . . . For
the two — Christ and supplements — do not suffer each other together in the
heart so that I rest my trust on both; rather, one must get out of there: either
Christ or my own doing." *WA* 37, 46, 21 cited in Paul Althaus, *Die Theologie
Martin Luthers* (Gütersloh: Gütersloher Verlagshaus, Gerd Mohn, 1962), p.
196 n. 6.

are six occasions in which men and women become Christians and so, by definition, six different occasions in which the Spirit is given:

(1) The Philippian Lydia (16:11-15)
(2) The Philippian Jailer (16:25-34)
(3) The Thessalonians (17:1-10a)
(4) The Beroeans (17:10b-15)
(5) The Atheneans (17:16-33)
(6) The Corinthians (18:1-11).

By way of these six quick portraits we may catch a profile of Luke's doctrine of Christian initiation in Acts. The Greek circuit (16:11 — 18:11) teaches us historically as the Jerusalem council is to have taught us theologically the constant, normal, yet supernatural means by which men become Christians.

Leading the way to the Spirit's reception in each case is not a string of conditions but the oral transmission of the gospel (16:13-14, 25, 31, 33-34; 17:2-3, 13, 17-18, 22-31; 18:4-5, 11).[57] The heart of the hearer is prepared not by any activity of his own but by the electing and sovereign Lord (16:14; 18:9-10). Diverse persons (*tines,* 16:14; 17: 4, 34) are transformed into "brothers" (16:40; 17:6, 10, 14; 18:18), our accounts tell us, by believing (16:31; 17:12, 33; 18:8; cf. 16:34, 15), or being persuaded (17:4; 18:4), or being baptized (16:15, 33; 18:8), the normative aorists in all cases instructing us that the persuasion of faith was sealed and evidenced in the moment of baptism. The grammar also indicates that in Luke's opinion faith, persuasion, and baptism were not so much three discrete entities as they were synonyms for the one commitment which, by God's power, makes the Christian and grants the Spirit.

We know that the Spirit was given not because he is ever mentioned — he is not — but because Jesus Christ was proclaimed and believed, and this is the great work of the Spirit (1:8; 4:31; 15:8; cf. I Cor. 12:3; Rom. 8:9). We can believe that the Spirit was received when we are told simply that the hearers were baptized, for this momentous event in Acts presupposes the foregoing work of the gospel and the consequent faith of the hearer. Baptism really is the evidence of the Holy Spirit for it evidences the effective work of the gospel and the effected faith of the hearer, and both are due, as we have seen, to the Spirit (1:8; 15:8-9; cf. 16:15, 33; 18:8).

But the Greek histories of Acts 16-18 do not fail to give us a sampling of other of the most important evidences of the Spirit: love, as testified to most concretely in the opening of the home (see the interesting use of *oikos* in the texts), the "lust for fellowship" (16:15, 33-34; 17:5) with the new Christian brothers, and joy in believing

---

57 See Büchsel's summary: "A reception of the Spirit without a preceding proclamation of the gospel does not occur in Luke. The connection between Word and Spirit is inseparable." *Geist Gottes,* pp. 256-57.

(16:34; cf. I Thess. 1:6). For the fruit of the Spirit is, first of all, love and joy (cf. Gal. 5:22). Luke, like Paul, is interested in no other evidences of the Holy Spirit for the on-going church than the baptism which joins the believer to the new humanity (17:4 *proseklëröthësan!;* cf. Gal. 3:27-28) and the character which flows from it by the same Spirit into the life of the church and the world (16:14-15, 33-34; cf. 2:38-47; Gal. 5:22-23).

L. ACTS 18:24-28: APOLLOS AND THE BAPTISM OF THE HOLY SPIRIT

> [Apollos] was an eloquent man, well versed in the scriptures. He had been instructed in the way of the Lord; and being fervent in spirit, he spoke and taught accurately the things concerning Jesus, though he knew only the baptism of John. He began to speak boldly in the synagogue; but when Priscilla and Aquila heard him, they took him and expounded to him the way of God more accurately (vv. 25-26).

It is not easy to determine whether Luke hesitates to apply to the Jewish Apollos the encomiums "disciple," "brother," or "believer" from doubt of Apollos' Christian standing or whether Luke is attempting to describe a Christian by using the descriptions "he had been instructed in the way of the Lord," "[he] taught accurately the things concerning Jesus," "being fervent in the spirit." In any case, what is important to Luke is that Apollos "knew only the baptism of John." Apollos taught the things of Jesus accurately but he did not yet know how to apply or end his teaching by offering baptism into the name of Jesus Christ (cf. 19:5-6; 2:38).

John's baptism was *only* with water; the baptism into Jesus Christ is nothing less but it is much more; it is baptism with the Spirit (cf. 1:5; 2:38; 19:5-6). This Apollos did not yet know. Consequently, Apollos' hearers might be persuaded, might even believe, but without baptism, the divinely instituted locus of the Spirit, and without an opportunity for the believers' persuasion and faith to come to expression, to become public in the openness of baptism, Apollos' converts were inadequately initiated. The classic example of this is probably the strange "disciples" in the account immediately following (19:1-6).

Apollos' preaching was no doubt the work of the Spirit, and concerning Jesus it was accurate to a point, but until the work of the Spirit in preaching found its intended point, goal, and application in his work in baptism, Apollos and his hearers were in need of more accurate instruction (v. 26 = 19:4-6).

The Apollos at Ephesus passage teaches the importance of baptism to preaching; without baptism in the name of Christ following preaching in the name of Christ the preacher's work and the believers' lives are incomplete. It does not seem important to Luke to tell us what happened in Apollos' inner life as a result of Priscilla and Aquila's more accurate instruction; important for us to see is apparently only that Apollos learned to include in his proclamation what he had previously left out — Christian baptism.

We think that Luke's concern in this pericope, therefore, is not so much the preservation of the *Una sancta* (Käsemann) or *heilsgeschichtlich* (Schweizer), but evangelistic, i.e., the sealing of preaching with baptism.

M. ACTS 19:1-7: THE EPHESIAN DISCIPLES AND THE BAPTISM OF THE HOLY SPIRIT

> While Apollos was at Corinth, Paul passed through the upper country and came to Ephesus. There he found some disciples. And he said to them, "Did you receive the Holy Spirit when you believed?" And they said, "No, we have never even heard that there is a Holy Spirit." And he said, "Into what then were you baptized?" They said, "Into John's baptism." And Paul said, "John baptized with the baptism of repentance, telling the people to believe in the one who was to come after him, that is, Jesus." On hearing this, they were baptized in the name of the Lord Jesus. And when Paul had laid his hands upon them, the Holy Spirit came on them; and they spoke with tongues and prophesied. There were about twelve of them in all (19:1-7).

This paragraph is connected with the preceding one for we are still in Apollos' former field of service, Ephesus (18:24), and the problem is the same (and its result?): John's baptism. Here as with Apollos we have the curious mixture of Christian and non-Christian nomenclature: the Ephesian men were "disciples," the normal description in Acts for Christians (over a dozen times through Acts 15; cf. thereafter 16:1; 18:23, 27; 19:9, 30; 20:1, 30; 21:4, 16); nevertheless they had not yet received the Holy Spirit (v. 2)! They too had believed but they had not yet been baptized in "the name of the Lord Jesus." They too had everything and yet nothing; they believed and yet had not received the Holy Spirit, for they had not yet had Christian baptism.[58]

Consequently this passage (with Acts 8) is a major source for the Pentecostal brief. For here we have believers who have not yet re-

---

[58] Goppelt believes that " 'the disciples' in Ephesus ... were in reality not disciples, i.e., Christians, but adherents of John the Baptist." *Apostolische und nachapostolische Zeit*, p. 61 n. 36. So also Conzelmann, *Apg.*, p. 110. Dupont calls them Christians but "d'un genre un peu particulier." Cerfaux-Dupont, *Actes*, p. 166. But contrast Stählin, *Apg.*[10], pp. 252-53. See Rudolf Knopf for, in our opinion, the clearest description of these disciples: "The disciples of John the Baptist should obviously be understood as a kind of Christians. They were believers, but believers in a quite imprecise way, in the Messiah preached by John the Baptist, and it was for this Messiah that they were waiting; they were baptized, but not in the name of Jesus; and the Holy Spirit, the common equipage of all Christians, they had not received." *Die Apostelgeschichte* (Göttingen: Vandenhoeck und Ruprecht, 1906), p. 618.

ceived the Holy Spirit. Finding this discrepancy Pentecostalism then suggests its conditions for the filling of the void.

See Riggs' (p. 112) interesting manner of finding all four of his Pentecostal conditions — conversion, obedience, prayer, and faith — in this passage:

> Who would say that [Paul] did not instruct them according to the pattern which had been followed heretofore? It is the once-for-all pattern: be saved, obey God, ask Him for His blessings, believe with all [n.b.] your heart, and ye shall receive the fullness of the Holy Spirit.

Note also Gee:

> But the little group of disciples swiftly moved in a matter of fuller obedience; and then the apostle prayerfully laid his hands upon them and they received (Gee, *Gift*, p. 7).

First of all it may be pointed out that Paul's basic assumption is that the reception of the Spirit occurs simply with faith, for Paul's initial question was, "Did you receive the Holy Spirit when you *believed*," not "when you prayed," or "when you emptied yourself," or even, as erroneously in the AV, "*after* you believed," or "when you had sufficiently obeyed" or "yielded."[59] Faith, according to Paul, is the receptacle of the Spirit. Again the aorist of faith rather than the present participle signifies the faith present at baptism. That this is the case is underlined in the following question when, on learning of the group's ignorance of the Holy Spirit, Paul senses that the problem can lie only with baptism where faith is expressed and the Spirit received for he asked, "Into what then were you baptized?" And as he evidently had suspected it *was* here that the abnormality had its roots for the Ephesians had been baptized "into *John's* baptism."[60]

After explaining to the Ephesian disciples that Christian faith is "in *Jesus*" and that therefore Christian baptism is into Jesus, not into John, Paul for the first time baptized the twelve into (*eis*) "the

---

[59] The question could imply that it would be possible to believe in Jesus Christ and yet *not* receive the Holy Spirit. So Cerfaux-Dupont, *Actes*, p. 166, referring to Acts 8. However, this implication is circumvented by the rest of the narrative.

[60] Cf. Hans Heinrich Wendt: "The presupposition of this 'into what then [were you baptized]' is this: had they been baptized in the name of Jesus as the Christ who had come then they must have had the realization, through him, of the Holy Spirit and have received the Spirit in baptism." *Kritisch-exegetisches Handbuch über die Apostelgeschichte* ("MeyerK"; 6.-7. rev. ed.; Göttingen: Vandenhoeck und Ruprecht, 1888), p. 143. So also Heitmüller, *Im Namen Jesu*, p. 302; Flemington, *New Testament Doctrine of Baptism*, p. 47; Stählin, *Apg.*[10], p. 253; Conzelmann, *Apg.*, p. 110. Behm writes, representatively, that Paul's question "is only intelligible when underlying it is the opinion that baptism and the communication of the Spirit belong together." *Handauflegung*, p. 20 n. 1.

name of the Lord Jesus," with the laying on of hands, and the Ephesians received the Holy Spirit.

The significance of Paul's important question on baptism (v. 3a) can be appreciated by observing what Paul did not ask. (1) When Paul discovered by his first question that the men did not know the Holy Spirit Paul did not then ask, "What kind of (faulty) instruction did you receive then?" and proceed to teach them the (right) doctrine of the Holy Spirit. Instead, Paul asked, "Into what then were you baptized?" and on learning of their Johannine baptism he proceeded to teach them *Jesus Christ* (v. 4). In other words, on learning of their ignorance of the Holy Spirit Paul's subject, surprisingly, was *not* the Holy Spirit, it was Jesus Christ. This is significant. The remedy for those who know little or nothing of the Holy Spirit is not special instruction or knowledge on access to the Spirit, or a new set of conditions, a new regimen of emptying, added obediences, deeper commitment, or ardent prayer, but instead simply the great fact: the gospel of faith in the Lord Jesus Christ and baptism in his name.

(2) Paul did not ask, "Did you not know that after mere faith you are to press on to a second experience where you will receive an enduement of power through the baptism in the Holy Spirit?" Instead Paul wondered if these Ephesians had ever had faith in *Jesus* at all or, what is the same thing, if they had ever been baptized into him, for if they had they would certainly have received his Spirit. Paul learned, indeed, that their faith was not in Jesus who had come but in a Messianic figure who was yet to come — the character of the message of John the Baptist (vv. 3-4). Paul therefore did not teach a second blessing here or a discrete spiritual baptism which goes beyond a "mere" baptism in water. He taught the one great blessing — faith in Jesus — and proceeded precisely to baptize in Jesus' name (which included, as always, a laying on of hands). Whereupon they received the Spirit.[61]

(3) Paul did not ask, "Who then laid hands on you?" or "Did you fail to visit (or call) the apostles?" Paul's subject is not the apostolate, episcopate, or the laying on of hands, but faith and baptism into Jesus Christ. Paul's subject is not at all the necessity of tongues as the initial evidence of the Spirit. No moral or ecclesiastical conditions and no ecstatic evidences are laid upon or required of the Ephesians before they can have the Holy Spirit whom they do not know. Faith and its initiatory expression in baptism — baptism into Jesus Christ (and not, discretely, into the Holy Spirit) — is Paul's whole message according to Luke's record. Furthermore, the active party in this passage is not the Ephesian disciples who set about to fulfill the neces-

---

61 "The Messiah whom the Baptist described as coming, Paul described as, in Jesus, having come. The hearing of this — for them — new message of Paul led them to the decision to be baptized into this *Jesus*." Wendt, *Apg.*[7], p. 413.

sary obediences, it is Paul who, without uttering a single recorded command, teaches Jesus as the Christ.

(4) Paul did not ask, for example, "Did you fail to believe *enough?* Was your surrender full? Did you empty yourself entirely? Did you obey in every particular?" In comparison with the ardor of these questions Paul's actual question seems pale, "Into what then were you baptized?" On discovering their Johannine rather than Christian baptism Paul did not, according to the text, attempt to probe into the subjective, spiritual condition of the recipients. His procedure may in fact seem strangely objective to us. He is not recorded as looking for the fault through a spiritual or inner examination of the real state of the Ephesians' hearts or commitment. He leaves this, perhaps, to the only one who knows hearts (1:24; 15:8). Paul simply taught faith in the Lord Jesus Christ, and when he was assured of this he baptized. It was, and is, that elementary.

Spiritual baptism as it is taught by Pentecostals, distinguished from Christian baptism, is quite beyond the purview of this passage. Paul is not "going on" to higher things, he is going back to the fundamental thing — to the very beginning where every believer receives the Holy Spirit according to the apostolic understanding — in believing in Jesus and consequent Christian baptism. The Holy Spirit — and we may say it with all reverence for this is the teaching of Acts — comes as the result and the "gift" and not as the center or the theme of the Christian message. For it is the Spirit's ministry that the gospel be the gospel of Jesus Christ and not the gospel of the Holy Spirit (cf., e.g., Pentecost) and that the Spirit be received not because *he* is specifically sought but because Jesus Christ is proclaimed. The only occasion for a spiritual baptism according to Paul's (or Luke's) understanding is Christian baptism. For the Spirit never comes apart from Jesus Christ.

Luke's Acts is an independent exposition of the truth of the Matthean formula that to be baptized into the divine (or triune) name is, by definition, to be baptized at the same time into the Holy Spirit (Matt. 28:19). There is no necessity for separate baptisms into each "person" of the trinity, for it is the good pleasure of the Father, in Paul's words elsewhere, that in the Son the fulness of the Godhead dwell bodily (cf. Col. 1:19; 2:3, 9). This theological formulation of Paul's in Colossians is taught historically (and theologically) by Luke in Acts, particularly in this paragraph where "the missing Holy Spirit" is supplied not through new information about the Holy Spirit but through "the missing Lord," i.e., through the proclamation of the Lord Jesus Christ and baptism into his name.[62]

Ever since Jesus, for Christians to believe in the Messiah and yet to

---

[62] Contrast Ockenga, *Power through Pentecost,* pp. 95-97. Haenchen points out properly that this is in Luke's sense no re-baptism; it is the hearers' first and only *Christian* baptism. *Apg.*[12], p. 489.

be baptized "into John's baptism" is of course an anomaly. And that is the problem behind this passage. Only when faith in the Lord Jesus Christ is joined with baptism in him has the Christian, of course, received authentic Christian initiation. The missing link in the Ephesians' spiritual formation, therefore, was not teaching on how to be baptized in the Holy Spirit, it was faith and baptism in Jesus. And when this faith and baptism were given, so also, gratuitously, was the Spirit.[63]

It remains for us to investigate the concluding moments of the episode. Interesting is the fact that in Paul's discussion of the Johannine baptism, which he found to be the root of their Spiritlessness, Paul centers his and the Ephesians' attention not on any liturgical features of the rite of baptism (cf. I Cor. 1:14, 17) but again, evangelistically, upon faith in the present Jesus.[64]

Though Paul is recorded as *teaching* only Christian faith and baptism in Acts 19:2-5, yet Luke specifically mentions Paul's laying on of hands as the immediate precursor of the gift of the Spirit (v. 6). This must not be overlooked. The laying on of hands was no doubt an integral part of the baptismal service, with prayer, and should not be separated from baptism as an independent rite granting the Spirit.

For it is clear from what had preceded that the Ephesians' failure to know the Spirit was not due to their failure to call upon or seek an apostolic laying on of hands. Paul did not ask in either of his questions, as we observed, "Did you receive the Holy Spirit through apostles or their emissaries?" or "Who, then, laid hands upon you?" Nor did his ensuing discussion concern hands or apostles. The laying on of hands is brought into closest connection with baptism (cf. the "and" of v. 6) and was a part of baptism (for the emphatic *te* of Heb. 6:2 cf. *Bl.-D.* paragraph 443, 3).

The parallel in Acts 19:6 of Paul's action in Ephesus and Peter's earlier laying on of hands in Samaria (8:17) is striking and perhaps intended, for the paralleling of Peter's and Paul's activities makes one of the most interesting features of Luke's composition.

This much we may say: then as now there was probably never a baptism unattended, and rarely one in which the administrant did not prayerfully lay his hands on the baptized person. The laying on of hands probably constituted the conclusion of the baptismal act just

---

[63] Cf. Behm, *Handauflegung*, pp. 20-21.

[64] It should be noted that while the liturgical features are not of the essence to Paul, I Cor. 1:14, 17 does not teach that baptism was a matter of indifference to him. "It is not baptism which is marginal, but who *administers* baptism, since it is God's deed in baptism which matters, not the person of the baptizer." Hans Lietzmann and Werner Georg Kümmel, *An die Korinther I, II* ("HNT," 9; 4th rev. ed.; Tübingen: Mohr, 1949), p. 168. See also the commentaries on Corinthians by Weiss, Bachmann, Schlatter *ad loc.*

as the whole rite of baptism constituted the conclusion of the missionary sermon. It was at this solemn terminus that the Holy Spirit came upon the Ephesians.[65]

We would be willing to believe in an apostolic prerogative for the gift of the Spirit, for it is an apostle who here lays on his hands, if there were a developed doctrine of the same in Acts or in the New Testament elsewhere. But the laying on of a non-apostle's hands is all that is mentioned in Paul's conversion itself (9:17-19, and Ananias' laying on of hands *preceded* Paul's baptism as an act of healing and prayer, indicating no necessary legal, temporal, or ecclesiastical order in the rite). The eunuch received baptism, as we saw, without an apostle present (8:26-40). And Paul in another place registers his gratitude for not having participated in many Corinthian baptisms (I Cor. 1:14, 17). The obstacles to a doctrine of the apostolic laying on of hands for the full gift of the Spirit are, we believe, as insuperable as those to the doctrine of tongues as the initial evidence of the Spirit (and the two go together in precisely the two most unusual situations: Acts 8 and 19). The laying on of hands by apostles (and others) is mentioned in Acts but it is never taught in Acts, Paul, the Gospels, or elsewhere as a necessity for the Spirit's reception.

Apostolic laying on of hands, tongues, and prophecy, all occurred with the coming of the Spirit here. All accompanied the gift tangentially; none is taught as the Spirit's pre-condition either essentially or peripherally and none is sought by or required of the Ephesian disciples. The teaching of Acts 19:1-7 is that the Ephesians lacked the Holy Spirit due to no failure to summon, intentionally, either apostles, full surrender, or tongues, but unintentionally in having been baptized into John's baptism rather than into Jesus Christ's.

As in Acts 8 and 10, so here in Acts 19 eloquently, the reverse of either a conditional, second, spiritual baptism or a sought and required initial spiritual evidence is taught. Christian baptism with its coefficients of faith in Christ and the gift of the Spirit is the burden and the light of this passage. That the Ephesian converts here spoke in tongues is merely interesting — nothing more.

Few passages teach the essential union of faith, baptism, and the Holy Spirit as clearly as Acts 19:1-7. With its clear-cut questions,

---

[65] Bultmann, *Theology of the New Testament,* I, 134-35; G. B. Caird, *The Apostolic Age* (London: Gerald Duckworth, 1955), p. 70 n. 4: "If we insist on finding a rationale for this practice, the only one which covers all cases is that of Augustine: 'What else is the laying on of hands but prayer over a man?' [*de bapt.* 3, 16]." Cf. also Büchsel, *Geist Gottes,* pp. 262-63; Haenchen, *Apg.*[12], p. 489; Rudolf Schnackenburg, *Das Heilsgeschehen bei der Taufe nach dem Apostel Paulus: Eine Studie zur paulinische Theologie* ("Münchener Theologische Studien"; München: Karl Zink Verlag, 1950), p. 78; and see the other Roman Catholic exegete Alfred Wikenhauser, *Die Apostelgeschichte übersetzt und erklärt* ("Regensburger Neues Testament," 5; 3d rev. ed.; Regensburg: Verlag Friedrich Pustel, 1956), p. 98.

"Did you receive the Holy Spirit when you *believed?*"; "Into what then were you *baptized?*" we have almost a classic definition of how the Holy Spirit comes and of the union in the apostolic consciousness of faith, baptism, and the gift of the Holy Spirit. The unambiguous result of faith-baptism into *Christ* is that the Holy Spirit is given — or to use the more charged expression, that "the baptism in the Holy Spirit" is simply Christian baptism.[66]

We have now surveyed all the major texts for the Pentecostals' doctrine of the baptism in the Holy Spirit. On Pentecostalism's own admission it is in Acts and "there alone [that] we find a detailed description of the baptism or filling with the Spirit which was experienced by those early believers."[67] Pentecostalism's doctrine from these Acts texts (and therefore claimed for the New Testament) can be summarized as follows:

> The New Testament appears to indicate as an unmistakable historical fact that after the first entry of the Spirit in regeneration there can be and should be also a special personal reception by believers of the Holy Spirit in his original and unique person. This experience is called the "baptism in the Holy Spirit" and its purpose is not to impart life but to impart power. Its characteristic accompaniments are not fruits but gifts.[68]

We have just seen the basis this thesis has in Acts 19, one of Pentecostalism's major texts. The Holy Spirit in Acts 19 had not made a "first entry," he had not yet come at all (v. 2). There is no second experience of the Holy Spirit in Acts 19. What makes this record so impressive is that for the first time the Ephesians received the Holy Spirit and this not through unique conditions but through the standard and normative Christian message and its baptism.

There was also only one reception of the Holy Spirit by Cornelius' house (10-11). No "two experiences" are recorded there — first regeneration, then the later personal reception of the Spirit — there as here and throughout the New Testament (cf., e.g., Tit. 3:5-6; John 3:5; I Cor. 6:11) new birth *is* spiritual baptism. Cornelius did not have a later experience, he had *the* Christian experience.

Acts 8 is the other major source for the Pentecostal "two," but

---

[66] Note Bultmann's conclusion: "It has to be emphasized that Acts, like Paul, conceived of Baptism, as did Hellenistic Christianity, as the sacrament of the gift of the Spirit. The apparent exceptions actually go to prove that for Acts Baptism and the reception of the Spirit belong together [Acts 8:14ff.; 10:44ff.]. ... Most of all the contrast of John's baptism with the Christian rite in [Acts] 19:1-7 shows that for the latter the gift of the Spirit is characteristic." *History of the Synoptic Tradition*, p. 247 n. 1. Similarly, *idem, Theology of the New Testament*, I, 139; Wilckens, *Missionsreden*, p. 183; Heitmüller, *Im Namen Jesu*, p. 302: "In the same way [Acts] chapters 8 and 19 presuppose, in the final analysis, that the Christian receives the Spirit in baptism."

[67] Brumback, *What Meaneth This?*, p. 185.

[68] Gee, *Die Früchte des Geistes*, p. 6 cited in Eggenberger, "Geistestaufe," *ThZ, 11* (1955), 278.

with as little ground as in Acts 19 and 10-11. In Acts 8 there is no recorded first entry of the Spirit into the Samaritans followed by a special, personal reception of the Spirit later. The Samaritans had "not yet" received the Spirit at all for reasons we believe we have made clear from the text. When the Samaritans received the Holy Spirit they simply received him for the first time.

The same is the case in Acts 2. Here Jesus' promise of the Holy Spirit in Acts 1 comes to its fulfillment as the result of his ascension (2:33). The disciples had this *one* and absolutely decisive filling of the Holy Spirit — and it *was* full (2:4) needing no later completion.[69]

Wherever the Holy Spirit comes — and this is unequivocally the witness of Acts — he comes as befits his person and grace, his name as promise and his nature as gift — fully. There is, as we have stressed earlier, no record in Acts or in the rest of the New Testament of a first, partial infilling of the Holy Spirit completed, perfected, or filled later by a second personal reception of the Spirit.

There will of course be any number of future ministrations of the Spirit, future fillings (cf. e.g. Acts 4:31 with 2:4 and Gal. 3:5 with Gal. 3:2; and see Eph. 5:18), for the Spirit is alive. But these fillings are not to fill out what was lacking in the Spirit's first coming. They are the great privileges of the Christian life, not a burden to be obtained through a program of conditions. The fundamental, basic gift of the Spirit in Acts comes but once, in Jesus Christ, and does not need filling or improvement or "more." In neither Acts 2, 8, 10, or 19 — the standard Pentecostal texts for the doctrine of the believer's subsequent baptism in the Holy Spirit — is there a record of the Spirit's first and partial entry followed then by his second and finally personal reception. It is worth noting, then, that Pentecostalism builds its doctrine of a necessary second entry of the Holy Spirit on texts that teach his one entry.

N. ACTS 20:17-38: PAUL'S FINAL STRENGTHENING MESSAGE

In the address to the Ephesian elders we have Paul's longest message to Christians recorded in Acts. In it he reviews his three-year ministry in Ephesus and can confidently assert that "I did not shrink from declaring to you *anything* that was profitable" (v. 20), immediately summing up the content of this comprehensive teaching as "repentance to God and of faith in our Lord Jesus Christ" (v. 21).

Interesting once more — as we have been discovering throughout

---

[69] It is sometimes asserted that Jesus' first gift of the Spirit was recorded in John 20:22, his second, fuller gift — the Pentecostal baptism in the Holy Spirit — in Acts 2:4, p. 63, above. However, this is to take two traditions of the same event — the Johannine and the Lukan — and to place them in chronological sequence.

Acts — is the absence in Acts 20:21's summary of reference to the Holy Spirit or to the baptism in the Holy Spirit. But this is due not to a lack of spirituality or to a failure to appreciate the Holy Spirit as "profitable" by either Paul or Luke. In Acts the attention of the apostolic messages is lifted almost exclusively to God's great deeds in Christ — this is the only authentic spirituality which Acts seems to recognize.

However, the Holy Spirit is mentioned more in this message to the Ephesian elders than in any other message since Pentecost. Indeed, outside of Pentecost (and one *christological* reference at the Caesarean Pentecost, 10:38), the Holy Spirit is not recorded as a subject of missionary preaching. Yet as we shall see even in this message in Acts 20 where the Holy Spirit is mentioned, he is not taught as a challenge or opportunity to be acquired by truly dedicated elders or as a possible or as a past deeper experience. Rather, the Spirit is pictured here as the companion of the church's and the Christian's way (vv. 22-23, 28). Paul can summarize his missionary message as a message of repentance toward God and faith in Christ and thereby not neglect the Holy Spirit because this one great act embraces the work of the Spirit (cf. 1:8; 2:11). The Spirit does not have to be mentioned to be present, or taught to be received, he is "in Christ" and "through Christ" (cf. 1:2; 2:38-39; 4:29-31; 10:43-44; 11:17; 15:8-11; 19:4-6) — this is the message of Acts as it is of the epistles.[70]

Finally, in warning of impending heresy and apostasy (vv. 29-30) Paul commends the elders "to God [or *kuriö*, B pc] and to the word of his grace, which is able *(dunamenö)* to build you up and to give you the inheritance among all those who are sanctified" (v. 32). Paul need not commend his elders to a unique or subsequent message of power or deepening in order to strengthen the elders for the coming onslaughts of heresy and the world; he can commend them to the same message by which they became Christians, which never grows old, is never exhausted, imperfect, needy of supplementation, additional power, height, or depth — he can commend them to "God and to the word of his *grace,*" which is itself *dunamenö* — powerful — to build men up. God's word through Paul to the elders is in effect also God's

----

70 Neill Q. Hamilton writes that in Paul's understanding "the Spirit is pre-eminently the One Who throws light upon Christ. Therefore in all His action He seeks to fill the consciousness of men with the picture of Christ — and to do this He must avoid making *Himself* the object of consciousness." *The Holy Spirit and Eschatology in Paul* ("Scottish Journal of Theology Occasional Papers," 6; Edinburgh: Oliver and Boyd, 1957), p. 6 n. 4. This tallies with Luke's doctrine as we have discovered it in Acts. It is questionable if Acts should be called, as is sometimes suggested, "The Acts of the Holy Spirit." If we have understood the intention of the Spirit's doctrine in Acts a title such as "The Book of the Apostolic Proclamation of Jesus Christ" might be preferred — or, simply, as it now stands, "The Acts of the Apostles."

word in another place to Paul himself, " 'My grace is all you need' "
(see II Cor. 12:9 NEB).

O. ACTS 22:16: PAUL'S TESTIMONY TO HIS BAPTISM

In the final reference to baptism in Acts, Paul's defense before the
Jerusalem public, we have a fine summary of Acts' teaching vis-à-vis
Pentecostalism.

Paul recalls Ananias' instructions, " 'And now why do you wait?
Rise and be baptized, and wash away your sins, calling on his name' "
(22:16). The removal of Paul's sin is to be accomplished in baptism.
The first reference to baptism after Pentecost in Acts also makes this
connection, " 'Be baptized . . . for the forgiveness of your sins' " (2:38).

Sin, according to Acts, is not removed by the ardent inner or outer
activity of the candidate; it is removed by God's gracious and cleansing
gift of baptism. The separation from sin which Pentecostalism (following R. A. Torrey and others) insists upon as a condition for God's
gift is not accomplished by dedicated rigor but by God's forgiveness
applied in baptism. The demanded "heart-cleansing" is accomplished
by God's cleansing work of faith (15:9), i.e., in baptism (2:38; 22:16).

It may be asked, Why does this passage not say, " 'Rise and be
baptized and wash away your sins and receive the Holy Spirit' "? Is it
because the Holy Spirit is not received when sins are washed away?
Is it because the Holy Spirit is received later on when Paul is more
worthy? No! The Holy Spirit is received with the forgiveness of sins
(2:38; I Cor. 6:11; Tit. 3:5).[71] Neither Paul nor anyone else will
ever be more worthy of the Holy Spirit than when God has washed
away his sin. Significantly, in the earlier account of Paul's same encounter with Ananias the filling of the Holy Spirit is promised (9:17).
But the absence of reference to the Spirit in this parallel text informs
us again that specific mention of the Holy Spirit is not necessary for
the Holy Spirit to be in fact present.

The gift of the Holy Spirit is not mentioned in Acts 22:16 not
because Paul did not receive the Spirit then, but because when the
forgiveness of sins is received so is the Holy Spirit (see 2:38-39).
It is as unnecessary to mention the Holy Spirit in this text as it is
faith or repentance, which of course also belong to baptism. Where
Christian baptism is present there are present also all the other elements of the one gift of salvation, just as where only faith is mentioned
at an initiation (17:12, 34) there are also present baptism, forgiveness,
the Spirit, and any other benefits in Christ we may wish to name.[72]

Cleansing, justification, sanctification, all occur under the name of
Christ and through the work of the Spirit in baptism; indeed, a text

---

[71] Cf. Schnackenburg, Heilsgeschehen, p. 103.
[72] Cf. Silva New's formulation in n. 35 above.

from Paul himself provides the best commentary to Luke's doctrine of baptism:

> You were washed, you were sanctified, you were justified in the name of the Lord Jesus Christ and in the Spirit of our God (I Cor. 6:11).

But where baptism is interpreted in a non-responsible or non-responsive manner the present Acts text serves as a useful corrective. *Paul is to arise and be baptized.* If anyone wishes to call this a work or condition — and he is advised not to use this terminology — then the walk to baptism is the only "condition" present. Nevertheless let it be stressed, as Luke has himself stressed, that this walk is enabled by the faith worked through the sovereign Lord (cf. e.g. Acts 3:16).

It *is,* however, man's *responsibility* and we can err in the other direction when we fail to take *this* responsibility (i.e., no spiritualistic, rigoristic responsibility, but that of simple baptism) with the seriousness with which it is taken in Acts.

As if to heighten this responsible dimension the two major verbs after "rise," namely "be baptized" and "wash" are placed in the aorist imperative *middle*. The middle voice need not mean "baptize yourself" and cannot mean "cleanse yourself," but rather should and grammatically can be understood to mean "let yourself be baptized and thus cleansed" (*Bl.-D.* par. 317). Nevertheless, it is *Paul* who is to *let* this happen — and in these two terms, "Paul" and "let," we have the responsible and yet the divine dimensions of Christian baptism, and to lose either side is to lose much.[73]

Paul is commended to no lists of conditions but he *is* to *let* himself be baptized. And in baptism *God* applies all the conditions accomplished already, if we may use a Pauline expression, by the "one man's obedience" (Rom. 5:19).

Responsibility is further stressed by the last verb in the sentence, also in the middle voice, "calling on his name." *Paul* was to call on the name (cf. 4:12; 2:38). Evidently prayer was a feature of the baptismal ceremony and prayer by the one to be baptized as well, no doubt, as by those who baptized.[74] This custom confirms as solidly as

---

73 On a parallel passive construction at Acts 2:40, " 'Save yourselves from this crooked generation,' " Stählin comments that the literal meaning is " 'Let yourselves be saved!' " and adds: "The imperative passive of the Greek here is an especially characteristic form of New Testament preaching (cf., e.g., also II Cor. 5:20; I Pet. 2:5; 5:6; further Rom. 12:2; 13:4; Eph. 4:23-24; Gal 6:7); it means challenge and provision at the same time: God wants to act on you ... let him act on you! ... The acting by which this let-happen-on-you becomes completely perceptible is the baptism in Christ." *Apg.*[10], p. 55.

74 Note Schnackenburg's reflection on Paul's usage: "Baptism is the act by which a person gives his confession of Christ as Lord (Rom. 10:9-10) and by which, conversely, in all probability the name of Jesus was pronounced over the one being baptized (Jas. 2:7; I Cor. 6:11)." *Heilsgeschehen,* p. 120. Cf. Heitmüller, *Im Namen Jesu,* especially pp. 92-93, 127.

one could wish the responsible character of Christian baptism, without in the slightest jeopardizing, but in fact magnifying the work of divine grace in baptism for it is received gratefully. "As certainly as repentance is the divine gift of baptism, so certainly must it also remain the historical deed [*Tat*] of men" (Lohmeyer).[75] Grace does not have to be unconscious to be grace.

Acts 22:16 will teach us, then, that it is the will of God that sin be washed away at baptism by God and that it is the hearer's responsibility to betake himself in faith to this place and to let himself be baptized. This text summarizes well the entire teaching of Acts concerning spiritual baptism. In this text Paul explains in a sentence the sin-removing event of his life and it meshes smoothly with the now massive doctrine which we have behind us in the multicolored texts of Acts. Sin is removed not before or after baptism by the intense spiritual labor of one who is already a Christian, it is removed in the baptism which makes a man a Christian. This is the grace of God.[76]

---

[75] *Das Urchristentum: 1. Buch, Johannes der Täufer* (Göttingen: Vandenhoeck und Ruprecht, 1932), p. 78; cf. *ibid.*, pp. 72, 76, 103.

[76] The infant baptism question immediately rises for every serious reader. Are responsible baptism and infant baptism compatible? At first appearance one must feel obliged to reply, no. And there is, correspondingly, the rise of a critical discussion of infant baptism in the church, punctuated most impressively recently by Karl Barth's final fragment (*Kirchliche Dogmatik,* IV/4). The seventies may well be the decade of a baptism debate in the church.

The practice of circumcision, certainly, was abolished by the work of Christ; but the principle of infant, family, or group initiation I find nowhere annulled. Indeed in Acts, in the house-formulas, I find such initiations actually suggested. Luther's argument, that there must be both strong positive *and* negative teaching in Scripture on matters as important as salvation and initiation, carries weight with me. I presently believe that the burden of proof lies with those who would abrogate the infant initiation of the church under Israel. I do not find this abrogation in the New Testament, though perhaps I am blind. And of at least equal importance I do not see any warning against the continuation of the bringing of children into the church among the Gentiles.

May I refer for fruitful cross-reference to I Cor. 10 (*pace* Beasley-Murray, *Baptism in the New Testament,* pp. 181-85) and the paralleled "sacramental" experience of the old and new church: infants, also, before they "knew" the meaning of the crossing of the Red Sea "knew" the salvation of crossing it. This, I believe, is also the sequence of knowing, cognitive or not, of infants baptized in the Christian church. A whole host of questions and problems then arises concerning all those baptized in the "Christianized West" (and *not* baptized elsewhere). But I presently find the continuation of I Cor. 10 itself a sufficient answer to some of these questions. Moreover, at the moment, I prefer these questions and problems, serious as they are, to those still more serious ones I must answer if I reject infant baptism. But there are still questions and problems.

ADDITIONAL NOTE: THE SYNOPTIC ACCOUNTS OF JESUS' BAPTISM AND THE SUBSEQUENT TEMPTATIONS IN THEIR RELEVANCE TO PENTECOSTAL DOCTRINE

1. THE BAPTIST'S PROMISE

If the early church *connected* and did not *contrast* or separate baptism in water and the gift of (or baptism in) the Holy Spirit as all the major and especially the problematic texts in Acts teach, then how is this to be explained in the face of the apparent contrast in John the Baptist's announcement, " 'I have baptized you with water; but he will baptize you with the Holy Spirit' "? (Mark 1:8 par.; cf. Acts 1:5; 11:16).[1]

First, it is important to observe that John the Baptist's apparent contrast is only apparent. It is noteworthy that in his announcement the mediums of water and Spirit are contrasted but not the act of *baptism* (" 'I have *baptized* you with water; but he will *baptize* you with the Holy Spirit' "). The Baptist announced that "the mightier one" would make baptism much more than simply baptism but, significantly, nothing less. In the first-century milieu the term "baptize" was not primarily pictorial; it had its firm place in the cultic life of Palestine and meant, first of all, simply "baptize." Baptism in the Spirit meant what the words say, *baptism,* and that, namely, *in the Spirit.*[2]

It was the special contribution of John the Baptist to the church, moreover, that the coming of the Spirit was connected not only with baptism but with the Christ: " 'He *(autos)* will baptize you with the Holy Spirit.' " The promised spiritual baptism was thus ensured of thorough

---

[1] For debate on the origin and original of this phrase cf., for example, Wilhelm Michaelis, *Täufer, Jesus, Urgemeinde: Die Predigt vom Reiche Gottes vor und nach Pfingsten* ("Neutestamentliche Forschungen," 2. Reihe, 3. Heft; Gütersloh: C. Bertelsmann, 1928), pp. 22-23 and Bultmann, *History of the Synoptic Tradition,* p. 247 n. 1; cf. Taylor, *Mark,* p. 157. To the *kai puri* addition in Matthew and Luke cf. Schweizer, art. *pneuma, TWNT,* VI, 396-97.

[2] See Walter Wink, *John the Baptist in the Gospel Tradition* (London: Cambridge University Press, 1968), pp. 36-37. Cf. Lohmeyer: "One thing, however, combines the contrast: here as there it is a 'baptism.' " *Das Evangelium des Markus* ("MeyerK"; 15th ed.; Göttingen: Vandenhoeck und Ruprecht, 1959), p. 19; cf. *idem, Das Evangelium des Matthäus: Nachgelassene Ausarbeitung und Entwürfe zur Ubersetzung und Erklärung,* ed. Werner Schmauch ("MeyerK"; Sonderband, 3d ed.; Göttingen: Vandenhoeck und Ruprecht, 1962), p. 43; also Kümmel, "Urchristentum," *ThR,* N.F. *18* (1950), 45; Asting, *Heiligkeit,* p. 123; von Baer, *Heilige Geist,* p. 170. See the suggestive hypothesis of J. E. Yates, *The Spirit and the Kingdom* (London: S.P.C.K., 1963), pp. 177-78, 212-13, 220.

Christocentricity. In the history of the church John's baptism was superseded because through the power of Christ's name baptism was no longer able to be *merely* baptism in water. For as we saw in Acts, Christian baptism was furnished with the gift of the Spirit (Acts 2:38-39; 19:2-6; and not least 8:14-17; 9:17-19 [with 22:16]; 10:44-48).

The deepening of baptism's earliest meaning had, however, an even profounder source than the Baptist's promise or the church's experience. This source was Jesus' own baptism. "In the preaching of John the Baptist water and the Spirit were still separated; but they will not stay separated. That they come together, that is the work of Jesus" (Schlatter).[3]

2. JESUS' BAPTISM

As the prototype of Christian baptism's occasion and as its royal institution, at Jesus' baptism (*n.b.* in *water*) the Spirit descends.[4] The connection between baptism and the coming of the Spirit is made particularly vivid in Mark's account: "immediately" (1:10). The connection is immediate and so direct as to make of what could be two — baptism in water and the descent of the Spirit — one. If Acts were not enough, Jesus' own experience solders the former two — baptism and the gift of the Spirit — into the divine one baptism. Spiritual baptism is formed and inaugurated in no less than the person of its elect dispenser: Jesus Christ.

The meaning of the descent of the Spirit is the assurance of sonship and vocation: " 'Thou art my beloved Son' " (Mark 1:11 par.). The power which is connected with the Spirit's descent is not so much an infusion of new energy as it is the announcement (in Jesus' case perhaps preferably, the assurance) of a relationship, the relation of sonship.

Certainly the presence of the Holy Spirit means power. But here the heavenly voice interprets the Spirit. And the meaning of the Spirit according to the voice from heaven is found primarily in God's relation of love to Jesus and only derivatively in Jesus' relation of power to the world: " 'Thou art my beloved Son; with thee I am well pleased.' " It appears therefore to be the almost united message of the New Testament that spiritual power flows from the message of God's love and from nothing else (cf.

---

[3] *Der Evangelist Johannes: Wie er spricht, denkt und glaubt: Ein Kommentar zum vierten Evangelium* (3d ed.; Stuttgart: Calwer Verlag, 1960), p. 89 to John 3:5. Schlatter's remark applies to the Synoptics as well, not least to Luke who is sometimes accused of separating baptism and the gift of the Spirit. Conzelmann, however, notes that while "John [the Baptist's] preaching and baptism are without the Spirit; the Spirit, baptism, and forgiveness [in Luke's teaching]... are indissolubly linked." *Theology of St. Luke*, p. 228 n. 1. See finally to the situation Lampe's conclusion: "The great event which changed Johannine into Christian Baptism was... the Baptism of Jesus." *Seal*, p. 33.

[4] "The early church did not find the 'institution' of baptism in Matt. 28:19 but in the baptism of Jesus by John in the Jordan." Georg Kretschmar, "Himmelfahrt und Pfingsten," *ZKG*, 66 (1954-55), 250 n. 187. Luke does move the emphasis toward the *prayer* at Jesus' baptism (Wink, *John the Baptist*, p. 83), but it is prayer at Jesus' *baptism*. To the dove see Greeven, art. *peristera, TWNT*, VI, especially 67-68. It is important to observe that Jesus is never said to have been "baptized" by the Holy Spirit "perhaps to avoid the suggestion of initiation." White, *Biblical Doctrine of Initiation*, pp. 96-97.

again Acts 20:32; II Cor. 12:9). Therefore it is not surprising that the first meaning of the descent of the Spirit as exposited by the heavenly message is sonship.[5]

It should be further noted that the Holy Spirit, with the accompanying voice of assurance, comes *from heaven* (stressed in all three Synoptic accounts), not from the baptizer or from the water or, we may even say, from baptism, though God deigns to use these. Moreover, we are not told that Jesus asked for this endowment,[6] or that he was obliged to fulfill any conditions to obtain it, or even that he expected it.[7] Nor, according to our accounts, was the evidence of the Spirit glossolalic or even ecstatic.

The occasion, evidence, and conditions (or lack of them) in the baptism of Jesus are seen to synchronize with the same in Acts: the Spirit descends from heaven in simple baptism. When we have studied the remainder of the New Testament, we shall discover that a fundamental part[8] of the New Testament's doctrine of the baptism of the Holy Spirit — at the very least in the formal connection of the water of baptism and the descent of the Spirit, and in the theological connection of both with the assurance of sonship — is contained proleptically and typically in this its first and certainly most sublime occurrence.

One must, however, be cautious in drawing the correspondence between Jesus' baptism and the church's — and certainly, in drawing it too far. One may wonder if there is not a certain lack of sensitivity in Pentecostals' paralleling their own conversion with Jesus' virgin birth, and of their subsequent spiritual experience in tongues with Jesus' baptism.[9] Can it properly be said that Jesus underwent "two experiences"? And can it be said that Jesus "needed" to have a "second" experience?[10] As surely as

---

[5] This meaning is developed for the church by Paul: especially Gal. 4:4-6; cf. 3:7 with 3:14; Rom. 8:15-17. See below, "The Evidence of the Spirit: Christian Faith," pp. 267-73.

[6] Luke tells us only *that* he was praying (3:21).

[7] Schlatter manages to capture an appreciation of the wider significance of Jesus' baptism: "To him who sensed his life to be God's work and gift it was impossible to begin his career on his own initiative; he had to wait until God called him." *Die Geschichte des Christus* (2d ed.; Stuttgart: Calwer Vereinsbuchhandlung, 1923), p. 91. We would only caution that we have no record that "Jesus had to *wait*" for this gift, and of most significance, none that "Jesus *had* to wait." Jesus may indeed have expected the Spirit's enduement. The Old Testament spoke of the Spirit coming upon those whom God used. Nevertheless, what is important for our purposes — and quite objectively too — is the fact that there is no *record* of this expectation in Jesus' career.

[8] But no more. There is in Jesus' baptism, of course, no recorded preceding gospel proclamation, forgiveness of sins, or cleansing.

[9] Cf. above, p. 68. Note duPlessis' more recent comparisons in *The Spirit Bade Me Go*, p. 65 and "Jesus Christ the Baptizer," *Acts, 1* (Sept.-Oct. 1967), 15.

[10] Cf. the Pentecostal predecessor F. B. Meyer: "Jesus Christ was conceived of the Holy Ghost.... Why then must He be anointed? Because His human nature needed to be empowered by the Spirit, before even He could do successful service in this world. Jesus waited for thirty years until He was anointed ... never forget that our Lord's ministry was not in the power of the second person of the blessed Trinity ... but ... the third." *A Castaway and Other Addresses* (Chicago: Fleming H. Revell Co., 1897), p. 86.

Jesus' baptism was a vital and unquestionably real and empowering experience, can it be said that his "first" experience, like that of the Pentecostals', was only a "participation" in the divine, a partial filling, imperfect and needing power and supplementation? Did Jesus need to "press on" or "wrestle through," as it is said, to this "higher" experience? Did Jesus' spiritual baptism occur in a waiting-meeting, was it obtained through entire emptying and evidenced by the speaking in tongues?[11] Or did his encounter with the Spirit occur at baptism — apart from any mentioned conditions, evidenced simply by the Father's assurance of good pleasure at baptism?

Jesus' baptism corresponds with the church's in being in water, in being accompanied (immediately) with the Spirit, and in meaning sonship. But how does Jesus' spiritual baptism correspond to Pentecostalism's subsequent (after-conversion), conditional (beyond-faith), and evidential (tongues-speaking) baptism in the Holy Spirit? We must interpret the Pentecostals' comparison of their regeneration with Jesus' virgin birth, and of their speaking in tongues with Jesus' baptism as unfounded, and then as unfortunate and christologically inappropriate.

Both John's promise and Jesus' baptism teach, with Acts, that baptism and the descent of the Spirit belong together. The significance of Jesus' baptism for the church's baptism therefore is large:

> The fact that Christian Baptism is a re-presentation of the Baptism of Jesus implies that it is through Baptism in water, and not through any other ceremony ... that the believer enters into the possession of the Spirit which is imparted through his membership in Christ.[12]

3. THE TEMPTATIONS

The temptations are probably intended to be viewed in an organic connection with the preceding baptism. May they be extended in their reference beyond Jesus to the church? When done cautiously — that is, in realizing that the first reference of the temptations is probably to Jesus' execution of his call — they not only may but are most likely intended to be referred to the church for her warning and edification.[13] The sons, like the Son, are tempted to misuse their new relationship and vocation, and the evangelists' records are outlines of the form and content these temptations may assume. They are not a little relevant to our subject.

The Son's first temptation involves at least the temptation to seek a

---

[11] Cf. above, pp. 87-117, for the terminology used in describing the Pentecostal conditions. Büchsel believes that "it deserves special attention that the reception of the Spirit [at Jesus' baptism] is not presented as the result of aescetic actions." *Geist Gottes*, pp. 156-57. Volz's discussion of the *Ebed Yahweh* (Servant of the Lord) in Isaiah 61:1 and context is most instructive in connection with ecstasy: "In the work of the *Ruah* (Spirit) there is no mention whatsoever of the ecstatic element; nowhere is the ecstatic element so removed as in the *Ebed*. He is the exact opposite of an ecstatic personality. He does not cry out and one does not hear his voice in the streets. The *Ruah* does not even express himself in striking miracles, but in a special ethical and thoughtful task." *Geist Gottes*, p. 98.

[12] Lampe, *Seal*, p. 45.

[13] "The Temptation story shows how obedient submission of the will to God characterizes Church and Messiah alike — particularly in regard to the problem of miracle." Bultmann, *History of the Synoptic Tradition*, p. 256.

spiritual evidence beyond baptism, i.e., further proof of being, as there confirmed, the "Son of God": " 'This is my beloved Son,' " ... " 'If you *are* the Son of God, command these stones to become loaves of bread' " (Matt. 3:17 and 4:3 par.).[14] This is the temptation to go beyond the "voice of baptism." It is the temptation to seek a more concrete evidence, an evidence of observable and powerful transformation (here: of stones to bread; in Pentecostalism: of a tongue to "tongues"), rather than to remember the assuring evidence of sonship in baptism. The Ur-temptation may be the quest for evidences.[15]

While in the first temptation the particularly tempting was the transformed, in the second temptation (in Matthew) the particular appeal is to the spectacular (here: "throw yourself down"; in Pentecostalism's ecstatic baptism almost literally the same). The adversary's attractive and striking doctrine of evidence could be found in Scripture (Matt. 4:6; Luke 4:10 = Psalm 91:11-12). It is tempting to believe that if one can have a spectacular experience it must be a divine experience. But Jesus calls this expectation tempting God or, in modern English, "using God," for it is the attempt (perhaps even through "absolute surrender," since hurling oneself from a precipice is not lightly undertaken), by a remarkable means, to *require* God to reveal himself. Can the agonies of the Pentecostal tarrying-meeting involve a similar temptation?

While Jesus was tempted in the earlier encounters to seek concrete and spectacular evidences, in the final temptation (in Matthew) the appeal is to power and glory (here: "the kingdoms of the world"; in Pentecostalism: "power for service"). This is an especially appealing temptation, since it is for a good end. Did not Jesus wish to see the world his? (Do we not wish to have power toward the same end?) But it is just this fact — just the goodness of the end offered — which makes this temptation into a temptation in the fullest sense of the word. The desire for spiritual power is perhaps the most refined of temptations and if it ever becomes paramount it can lead perhaps to power but not to the service of *God* (Matt. 4:10; Luke 4:8; cf. Matt. 7:22-23!).

The temptations which follow Jesus' baptism have particular relevance to the problem of this study. Though, or even because it is spiritual, baptism is a simple, and in some senses an unsensational and an outwardly unpowerful event. (This is especially true in the case of an infant's baptism.) In the quietness of its assurance it may seem to give no special promise of a (i) transforming, (ii) spectacular, or (iii) powerful endue-

---

14 Schlatter believes that "the goal of [this] temptation is not the stimulation of doubt. What is required of Jesus is decisions, options through which he would misuse his relationship to God." *Der Evangelist Matthäus: Seine Sprache, sein Ziel, seine Selbständigkeit: Ein Kommentar zum ersten Evangelium* (5th ed.; Stuttgart: Calwer Verlag, 1959), p. 102. It is true that the stimulation of doubt is not the *goal* of the temptation, but it is the *means*. Doubt is often the first step toward misusing one's relationship with God. See the remarkable psychology of Genesis 3.

15 "It is precisely to Jesus' possession of the Spirit that the temptation is addressed." Büchsel, *Geist Gottes*, p. 174. It was to the quest for evidences that Zechariah in the nativity narratives succumbed (Luke 1:18: " 'How can I be *sure* of this?' ").

ment. Yet when Jesus had refused these impressive evidences and had remained instead in the quiet assurance of sonship which is baptism, we read in Luke that Jesus returned from these temptations "in the power of the Spirit" (4:14).[16]

___

[16] C. K. Barrett believes that one reason for the relatively infrequent reference to the Holy Spirit in Jesus' subsequent teaching in the Synoptic tradition is Jesus' will, deepened through the temptations, to go the unspectacular way of lowliness and of outward weakness in his mission. *The Holy Spirit and the Gospel Tradition* (New York: The Macmillan Co., 1947), p. 159. Cf. on this theme the exposition of II Corinthians below, pp. 303-19.

VI

THE WAY OF THE HOLY SPIRIT ACCORDING TO THE NEW TESTAMENT AND THE CONSEQUENCES FOR PENTECOSTAL DOCTRINE: A SYSTEMATIC SURVEY

A. THE CONDITION OF THE SPIRIT: THE WORK OF CHRIST — RELEASE FROM LAW

1. THE NEW TESTAMENT DOCTRINE (JOHN 7:37-39; GAL. 3:10-14; 4:4-7; ROM. 8:1-4)

a. The New Testament writers realized that something must be altered, that some condition must be met if men were to receive God's Holy Spirit. A citation from John's Gospel will serve to introduce the principal New Testament condition:

> On the last day of the feast, the great day, Jesus stood up and proclaimed, "If any one thirst, let him come to me and drink. He who believes in me, as the scripture has said, 'Out of his heart shall flow rivers of living water.'" Now this he said about the Spirit, which those who had believed in him were to receive; *for as yet the Spirit had not been given, because Jesus was not yet glorified* (John 7:37-39).

The Spirit is received, according to this text, by simple faith in Jesus (it should be noticed that nothing is added to this faith in either of its two references in the text: it is *sola*), but prior even to this *fide* reception there is a more basic condition to be fulfilled. The giving of the Spirit is dependent, first of all, upon the "glorification" of Jesus, which in John's Gospel means the death, resurrection, and ascension of Jesus Christ (John 12:16, 23-24; 13:31-32; 17:1). The indispensable pre-condition for the giving of the Spirit is the work of Christ.

b. It was left for Paul to develop what he saw as the deeper the-

225

ological reasons behind the necessity of the precedence of Christ's work to the gift of God's Spirit.

Paul saw a profound incompatibility between the condition of man and the righteousness of God (cf. Rom. 1:19—3:20). How could this incompatibility be overcome? What must be done in order for man to obtain the righteousness requisite for entering a relationship with the righteous God?

On the answer to this question hangs the distinctiveness of the Christian message.

In Galatians 3:10-14, a text of the greatest importance, Paul considered an answer suggested by the law: life with God may be acquired through men's spiritual *doing (poiein)* — deeds — in obedience to the law: "he who *does* them [the works of the law] shall live by [means of] them" (Gal. 3:12). Doing the law gives life with God: this, in Paul's judgment, is the essential message of the law. Yet Paul saw in the same law a curse upon those who did not *totally* obey (Gal. 3:10= Deut. 27:26). Indeed, and more profoundly, Paul saw a curse upon all those who even sought to make their obedience to the law the basis of their life before God (this is the force of the crucial preposition *ek* rendered "rely on" by the RSV, Gal. 3:10; see also Gal. 2:16). To think that one has God *because* one has deeds is, in Paul's thinking, the real curse of the law. Therefore, in order to see believers (*sic*, for such was the condition of those to whom Paul wrote) in a *full* relationship with God Paul, in contrast to his opponents in Galatia, did not urge a still greater obedience to the law; rather, in the perspective of Christ's perfect accomplishment on the cross, *Paul saw the law with its condition of deeds set aside* as the way of men to righteousness or right relations with God, and that means, in Paul's thought, as the way of men to the Holy Spirit (Gal. 3:14 in context).

Paul came to see the righteousness requisite for the Spirit fulfilled not by those who through their deeds sought their way to the Holy Spirit, but by Christ who through his deeds made his way to us, fulfilling the law himself, and so bringing to us *with himself* the fulness of the Holy Spirit as a free gift. Paul teaches, then, that through the absolute obedience of Jesus Christ the Holy Spirit comes to men and that it is not men who through their absolute obedience must come to the Spirit. Paul explains (and the absolutes should be noted):

> For all *(hosoi)* who rely on works of the law are under a curse; for it is written, "Cursed be every one *(pas)* who does not abide by all *(pasin)* things written in the book of the law, and *do* them." Now it is evident that no man *(oudeis)* is justified before God by the law; for "He who through faith is righteous shall live"; but the law does not rest on faith, for "He who *does* them shall live by them." *Christ redeemed us from the curse of the law,* having become a curse for us — for it is written, "Cursed be every one *(pas)* who hangs on a tree" — that *in Christ Jesus* the blessing

of Abraham might come upon the Gentiles, that we might *receive the promise of the Spirit through faith* (Gal. 3:10-14).[1]

The Holy Spirit comes — and this in relation to our subject is of considerable importance — "in Christ Jesus" (v. 14a) and not as a second experience independent of or in addition to Jesus Christ.

Of first importance in the present text, however, is the relation of Christ's *work* to the coming of the Spirit. Jesus Christ's redeeming work according to Paul is redemption from the curse (v. 13) and sovereignty (cf. Gal. 4:5 "under the law") of the law. *The* condition to be fulfilled in order for the Spirit to come to men is the redemption of men from the law (see the theologically important precedence of Gal. 3:13 to 3:14 and of Gal. 4:5 to 4:6; cf. also the movement in Rom. 8:1-4).

What then is the law from which men must be redeemed and what are "the works of the law" which superintend a curse upon "all" who live before God by them or who in seeking to live by them fail in total obedience (Gal. 3:10)?

First of all, the law itself is holy and spiritual and its command is holy, righteous, and good (Rom. 7:12, 14). The *works* of the law *(erga nomou)* are the deeds done in obedience to the righteous command of the law in contrast to deeds done in obedience to one's own whims. Originally the phrase had a good sense: the works of the law were understood as the deeds of obedience toward the divinely revealed will.

Moreover, two features characterize the law in Paul's citations in Galatians 3:10-12 and it is these features which are most relevant to our subject. The law's conditions are (1) absolute ("abide by *all* things," v. 10) and (2) to be done ("abide by all things . . . , and *do* them," v. 10c; cf. v. 12, "He who *does* them shall live"). Only when a man (1) *fully* (2) *does* what is conditioned does the law provide what is needed: this is the character and the way of the law and its problem. The call of the law is the call to total obedience in order to receive righteousness before or life with God (v. 11). And the law is — and this is its third characteristic in Galatians 3:10-12 — a call to live before God *on the basis* of this total obedience: " 'He who does [the works of the law] shall live *by* them' " (v. 12; cf. again the *ek* of v. 10). It is primarily because of this basis *(ek),* because of this means or way of life, and not because of the impossibility of full obedience, that Paul

---

[1] For the entire paragraph, Gal. 3:10-14, see especially the development by (Schniewind and) Friedrich of *epaggelia* in *TWNT*, II, 578-79; cf. also the still valuable Johannes Glöel, *Der Heilige Geist in der Heilsverkündigung des Paulus: Eine biblisch-theologische Untersuchung* (Halle a. S.: Verlag von Max Niemeyer, 1888), p. 95. It is not unimportant that in Gal. 3:14 the Holy Spirit comes "in Christ Jesus" and, specifically, as "the promise." This is the teaching also of Acts (1:4; 2:33, 38-39; cf. Luke 24:49). Galatians 3:14 serves as a kind of theological summary of Acts' more extended historical argument.

in the present argument repudiates the way of the law to the Spirit.[2]

Seeking to live before God on the basis of one's own obediences to the law is repugnant to Paul in the light of the perfect redemption from the law and the perfect assimilation of the curse of the law by Christ's death on the tree. For Paul, Christ's death signed the termination papers for the reign of the law in the lives of men. "For Christ is the end of the law, that every one who has faith may be justified" (Rom. 10:4). Henceforth to seek to have life from God on the basis of one's own devout obediences to the law, in the knowledge of Jesus Christ's obedience, could appear to Paul as only a contempt for the sufficiency of the work of Christ. Life before God must now be lived on the basis — on the exclusive basis — of Jesus Christ's finished work, i.e., by faith. The law, however, ultimately involves the invitation to life before God on the basis of one's own deeds and this to Paul is the reprehensibility of life-by-law.

The way of the works of the law, then, is a way built upon a road of absolute spiritual requirements and traversed by the appropriate deeds leading *to* the Spirit. Paul contrasts this way with another: the redeeming death of Jesus Christ removing men "out from under" the curse accruing to those whose life with God is based upon their doing. For Paul it is the *Spirit* who "come(s)" and therefore he can only be "receive(d)" (Gal. 3:14). According to the way of the law, however, the *seeker* must come, by way of deeds absolutely and perhaps even *biblically* done (Gal. 3:10b: "abide by all things written in the *bibliö* of the law" = Scripture) and *then* the Spirit who is life will be given (Gal. 3:10b-12b).

The ways of law and gospel then are two different ways: the one is the way of men to the Spirit; the other is the way of the Spirit to men. The condition to be fulfilled for the way *to* the Spirit is the devout or biblical works of men; the condition already fulfilled for the way *of* the Spirit is the work of Christ now recorded for us in Scripture. The nomistic direction for acquiring God's gift is "upward," from man to God; the evangelical direction is "downward," from God to man. The nomistic means to the end is devout biblical *deeds;* the evangelical is the deed of the *solus Christus* witnessed in the apostolic testimony of Scripture.

---

[2] Heinrich Schlier, *Der Brief an die Galater* ("MeyerK"; 11th ed.; Göttingen: Vandenhoeck & Ruprecht, 1951), pp. 89-92. On works-of-law as way-of-life Lohmeyer points out that in Hebrew thought "works" are "the religious *existence* which the righteous should have before God," and therefore they mean "first of all the total historical existence of man." "Probleme paulinischer Theologie, II: 'Gesetzeswerke,' " *ZNW*, 38 (1929), 188, 195 (emphasis ours). To be justified before God "apart from works" means then, in the deepest sense, to be acceptable to him "apart from the way we *are*" or, in modern terms, "*as* we are." This is good news.

c. The Galatian interlopers wished to introduce special laws or conditions of obedience in order to bring about the greater removal of sin in order, finally, to procure the full gift of salvation. However, it is one of Paul's central messages that laws and conditions are not curbs but are *incentives* to sin due to the impotence and impudence of the flesh; consequently, if men are to be freed from sin they must not be saddled with laws, they must first and radically be freed from them (Rom. 7 *passim;* Gal. 2:18-19; 3:19; Col. 2:13-14). This freeing, this liberation from law is the redeeming work of Christ, classically formulated in Paul's summary:

> There is therefore now no [*ouden*, stressed] condemnation for those who are in Christ Jesus. For the law of the Spirit of life in Christ Jesus [*n.b.* the Spirit's location] has set me *free from the law of sin and death*. For God has done what the law, weakened by the flesh, could not [*adunaton*] do: sending his own Son in the likeness of sinful flesh and for sin, he condemned sin in the flesh, in order that the just requirement of the law might be fulfilled in us, who walk not according to the flesh but according to the Spirit (Rom. 8:1-4).

Adherence to the law does not procure the Spirit — this is an *adunaton* — rather, and most significantly, *the Spirit of life in Christ Jesus procures us and in so doing sets us free from the law.* And thus, freed from law, walking according to the freely given Spirit, the second miracle of the Christian life occurs: the fulfillment of the just requirement of the law. This sequence in the believer's history — release-fulfillment — is the reverse of most mystic or spiritualistic expectation and formulation which is usually: fulfillment-release.

That the spiritualistic and the legalistic are not polar opposites but in fact correlatives has been one of the discoveries of this study and may be observed in many places in Part I. If the Spirit does not *come* to us freely in Christ then we must *go* to him through some kind of spiritual achievement and this means, ultimately, via law. The combination of legalism and spiritualism is not new, however. W. D. Davies, "Paul and the Dead Sea Scrolls: Flesh and Spirit," in *The Scrolls and the New Testament,* ed. Krister Stendahl (New York: Harper, 1957), p. 180, points out that "one of the most striking aspects of the Scrolls is the coincidence in them of a 'legalistic' and a 'charismatic' piety. The obedience to the Law demanded in the sectarian sources is even sharper than in Rabbinic Judaism."

Compare the "lust for law" in the spiritualist Montanists as discovered by G. N. Bonwetsch, *Die Geschichte des Montanismus* (Erlangen: Deichert, 1881): "Through the intensification of spiritual discipline the *nova prophetia* intends to make perfect the *nova lex*" (p. 81); "Whoever does not fulfill the conditions of the Paraclete but satisfies himself with only the general Christian revelation is no perfect Christian, he is only a psychic [i.e., a carnal person, contrasted with a pneumatic, a Spirit-filled person]" (p. 124; cf. *ibid.,* pp. 126, 136). See Bonwetsch's conclusion that Montanism represented in fact a seriously erroneous conception of the Christian faith which, in the last analysis, derived "from the understanding of the gospel as a new law" (pp. 149-50). "Therefore when the church opposed [Tertullian's Montanist legalism] it evidenced how much it still possessed a sense for evangelical freedom, although there may have been some worldly considerations which contributed to the church's opposition" (p. 98).

Note further the conditions and *"Entgrobungen"* of the sixteenth-century radical Protestants as reflected classically in Luther's "Against the Heavenly Prophets" (1525), especially *WA* 18, 137-39=*LW* 40, 146-49. At one place Luther writes, "With all [Karlstadt's] mouthing of the words, 'Spirit, Spirit, Spirit,' he tears down the bridge, the path, the way, the ladder, and all the means by which the Spirit might come to you. Instead of the outward order of God in the material sign of baptism and the oral proclamation of the Word of God he wants to teach you not how the Spirit comes to you but how you come to the Spirit" (*LW* 40, 147).[3]

It is the apostolic conviction that spiritual law cannot curb sin and that it in practice proves to be in fact the *aphormë* (Rom. 7:8, 11), the "supply base" for sin's warfare against God's will in men.[4] Law is a power, but not against sin: "the power *of* sin," Paul writes, "is the law" (I Cor. 15:56b).

d. The demand of the law for absolute obedience to God is not lightly dismissed by the New Testament gospel. It is confirmed especially in the life and death of Jesus Christ. The full obedience, the absolute surrender, the total separation from sin required by holiness teachers of all time for the full reception of the Spirit or of a right relationship with God are recognized and affirmed by the apostolic gospel.

But a difference separates the two classic religious ways — the ways, respectively, of law and gospel, to and of the Spirit — and this difference may be discovered by observing the location of absolutes.[5] The way of the law places the absolutes on men; the way of the gospel places the absolutes on the Messiah. The necessity of the law's righteous

---

[3] For this theme see besides the excellent introduction in *Luther: Ausgewählte Werke,* ed. H. H. Borcherdt and Georg Merz ("Münchener Ausgabe"; 3d ed.; München: Kaiser, 1950), IV, 361-63; also Karl Holl's "Luther und die Schwärmer," in *Gesammelte Aufsätze zur Kirchengeschichte: I. Luther* (7th ed.; Tübingen: Mohr, 1948), pp. 420-67. The best modern study of Luther's doctrine of the Holy Spirit is: Regin Prenter, *Spiritus Creator,* tr. John M. Jensen (Philadelphia: Muhlenberg Press, 1953), especially pp. 247-302. For a later evangelicalism's teachings see the Documents, below, pp. 323-41.

[4] Cf. Walter Gutbrod, art. *nomos, TWNT,* IV, 1066,34-35. Gutbrod's article is very helpful for the understanding of the law in the New Testament.

[5] To the absolutes, cf. besides the Pentecostal conditions in Part I, above, Paul's *pas* in Gal. 3:10, 13, and the Qumran parallel noted by W. D. Davies, "Paul and the Dead Sea Scrolls: Flesh & Spirit," *The Scrolls and the New Testament,* p. 281 n. 81.

demands being fulfilled is of central concern to the gospel. But the gospel removes the burden of absolute fulfillment from the back of the believer to the cross of Christ and we may say that this is what makes it *gospel.* Then by God's freely granting acquittal, acceptance, righteousness, peace, and the Spirit to the liberated believer in Christ, the intention — the just requirement (RSV) or commandment (NEB) — of the law, far from being flaunted, is fulfilled in those who walk according to the Spirit and we may say that this is what makes the gospel *the gospel of righteousness* in the fullest sense.

And this life in the Spirit, lived by faith, actually fulfills the commandment of the law in the law's two main senses: (1) faith gives God the honor for the whole work of salvation from beginning to end, thus essentially fulfilling the law of love toward God: faith lets God be God; and (2) faith in God's sufficient salvation in Christ has within it, by the Spirit, the power to remove the believer's eyes at last from himself and from his own attempted religious sufficiency and to turn him outward toward the neighbor whom he now has strong reasons, motives and, in the Spirit, power for loving as freely and unconditionally as he himself has been loved, thus essentially fulfilling the law of love toward men: faith lets men be human.

Thus what one way makes the condition for the receiving of the full gift of God — namely, the believer's sufficient obediences — the gospel answers in double reversal: (1) God's gift of Christ's sufficient obedience is the already fulfilled condition for the Spirit, and as a result (2) "in him" believers are freely given the full gift of the Holy Spirit as the power of real obedience and righteousness. But this obedience, it must be stressed, is not *for* the Spirit — he is always the pure gift — the obedience is *from* the Spirit. The Spirit is the *source,* not the *goal* of the moral life. It is Christ's redemption from and not men's pursuance of the law which is *the* condition and the way of God's gift of his Holy Spirit to men in Christ Jesus.[6]

The absolute conditions required for the full reception of God's presence by advocates of any "way" of religious law may at times include commendable obediences; but in location — on men rather than Christ — they are false.

> And you, who were dead in trespasses and the uncircumcision of your flesh, God made alive together with him, having forgiven us all our trespasses, having *canceled* the bond which stood against us with its legal demands; this he *set aside,* nailing it to the cross (Col. 2:13-14).[7]

---

6 To the entire subject of freedom from the law see Schlier, art. *eleutheros,* *TWNT,* II, 492-500.

7 To the "legal demands" *(dogmata)* in Colossae note Lohmeyer's comment (and the relevance): "The 'demands' are those requirements which, according to the Colossian [false] teaching, should lead individuals to being 'filled' with all the divine fulness; 'demands' are those things which, according to Paul [however], work the very opposite: the compulsion to sin and death. When God

For Christ *ends* the law and brings righteousness for everyone who has faith (Rom. 10:4 NEB).

2. THE CONSEQUENCES FOR THE PENTECOSTAL DOCTRINE OF SIN

a. Pentecostalism and the New Testament are one in the conviction that the removal of sin poses the major problem for the reception of the Holy Spirit. The difference commences when the solution for sin — righteousness — is described. Pentecostalism calls on the believer to do all in his power to remove what is understood as sin in order to appropriate what is called the cleansing power of Christ's blood in order in turn to be finally ready, clean, worthy, or yielded for the indwelling of the Spirit.

Therefore, from a certain perspective it must be conceded that the Pentecostal deserves the Spirit. However, the apostolic gospel declares that it is the undeserving who are considered righteous and are hence the Spirit's recipients.

> Now to one who works his wages are not reckoned as a gift but as his due. And to one who does not work but trusts him who justifies the *ungodly,* his faith is reckoned as righteousness (Rom. 4:4-5).[8]

According to the witness of Paul it is not the sinless, clean, or worthy who receive God's gift as their due through their fulfilling of even the most righteous conditions; it is the ungodly, the unclean, the unworthy who receive the gift through their trust in another's righteousness. The consequences of the New Testament's solution for sin must be the untenability of the Pentecostal doctrine of sin as it finds summary expression in the following formulas, studied in Part One.

i. "You can receive the Holy Spirit, but not with sin in your heart!" However, if it is to sinners and not to the righteous that Jesus comes, and if the Holy Spirit comes "in Christ Jesus," then the Holy Spirit comes to sinners — indeed, if he did not there could be no freedom from sin (Rom. 8:2, 4). *Only* sinners receive the Holy Spirit.

ii. "The Holy Spirit and sin cannot abide in the same heart." However, the Holy Spirit and sin do abide in the same heart unless the Pentecostal is willing to affirm his sinlessness. But sin is freely forgiven by grace, cleansed by faith (Acts 15:8-9), washed away by baptism (I Cor. 6:11; Acts 22:16); and in the power of these initiation acts, in the Spirit, sin is constantly fought away by obedience (Rom. 8:13; cf. 6:12-23). Sin remains (Rom. 6:12); but by recognizing what Christ has done *for* us in his death and *with* us in baptism men are not only called on but are enabled to reign over sin (Rom. 5-8).

---

canceled this bond, he also set aside all 'demands.' " *Die Briefe an die Philipper, an die Kolosser und an Philemon* ("MeyerK"; 11th ed.; Göttingen: Vandenhoeck & Ruprecht, 1956), p. 117.

[8] See Hans Wolfgang Heidland, art. *logizomai, TWNT,* IV, 293,30—295,10 for an excellent discussion of this important passage.

This reign is not without struggle, as the important present tense verbs in Paul's discussion of the Christian life indicate (cf., e.g., Rom. 6:12-13; 8:13; I Cor. 9:27).

The remarkable and evangelical reason for the Christian's struggled sovereignty over sin is not the fulfilling of conditions giving the *banishment* of sins but, first of all and basically, the *forgiveness* of sins: "sin will have no dominion over you, *since you are not under law but under grace*"! (Rom. 6:14). The Christian life of mastery rests upon and is enabled by the gift of life under grace. Grace, according to Paul, is the condition of the believer's mastery of sin. It is the tragedy of Pentecostalism, on the other hand, that it makes the mastery of what it considers sin to be the condition for the grace of the Holy Spirit. Grace itself, or the forgiveness of sins, appears in Pentecostalism to play a role only in the Christian's conversion, rarely appears in other discussions, and thus ceases for all practical purposes to be the center, accompaniment, and determinant of the whole Christian life. The reversal of the apostolic sequence of grace-then-obedience lies at the bottom of the Pentecostal error.

The means by which this reversal is sometimes accomplished is the contrast, adopted from what is frequently known as victorious-life Christianity, of "Christ for us" with what is said to be the far deeper and better "Christ in us." Cf., e.g., the Pentecostal Mülheimer New Testament note to Colossians 1:27: "Many believers count on the 'Christ *for* us' but not on the 'Christ *in* us'; and yet it is the 'Christ in us' who is the hope of glory. That means: the heavenly resurrection-life can only be imparted to us when we let Christ live in us. The forgiveness of sins, as important and necessary as it is, does not suffice for this" *(ad loc.)*. Of course, if it were true that the forgiveness of sins did not suffice to bring Christ into our lives then the believer would be obliged to go on to a higher, better experience, faith, or obedience in order finally to obtain that which *would* suffice to bring Christ into our very beings. However, apart from the fact that in Colossians 1:27 the "you" of the "Christ in you" is *plural* (*en humin*), not singular, meaning that the expression is not primarily individual or internal but communal and congregational, the most important fact is that Christ *is* in believers, individually, in faith. Faith is the receptacle of Christ. Where there is faith in Christ, there Christ is in faith. That is simply the gospel. Furthermore, "Christ in us" is not a higher, better form of "Christ for us." "Is Christ divided?" Where Christ is for us he is in us, else he would not be truly for us. Nor is the simple faith which receives Christ and forgiveness to be demoted by letting it do only an external work while some other disposition (such as "letting go") will finally suffice to get Christ into us. The sufficiency of Christ's once-for-all work and of faith alone which receives him — *fully*, i.e., for us and in us — is frequently but subtly demeaned in victorious-life teaching. Not only is Christ's person divided but his people are robbed. The believer is thrown from a gratitude for God's work outside himself into a grovelling within himself. The gracious fact of the inner Christ is made to depend upon tricky inner doings or undoings of the believer (for example, "yieldings," "appropriating," "full surrender," *et al.*). Thus the way of law enters via the teaching of "Christ in us" — a strange irony. The only corrective is emphasis where the New Testament overwhelmingly places it: on the whole Christ, received once and for all by simple faith; on the Christ who is so much for us that he is in us.

b. The Pentecostal doctrine of sin is directly traceable to the inadequate doctrine of the forgiveness of sins and this in turn is the cause of the doctrine of a higher, second, or subsequent experience. The Swedish Pentecostal leader Lewi Pethrus wrote, we recall:

> During the year 1905 God met me again, and made it very clear that there was more than forgiveness and sonship to be received from Him. I not only understood that there *was* more for me, but I felt there *must* be more for me, or otherwise my Christian life would be a failure.

In this summary the leader of what is reputed to be the largest North European Protestant congregation places his finger on the heart of the Pentecostal problem — the under-evaluation of the forgiveness of sins — and thus on the heart of the Pentecostal passion — for "more," particularly more of spiritual experience.

Forgiveness must inevitably appear insufficient and preliminary if beyond it a still higher benefit is posited. Wherever forgiveness is mere there will be passion for more. Where forgiveness and the sonship it includes are understood as only a part of what God has to give men and not as the very content of God's gift, then there must be the discovery of means other than forgiveness to attain privileges higher than sonship.

There is however no privilege comparable to the forgiveness of sins with which adoption into divine sonship is granted, and when a man can stand before God he stands beneath no other benefit. "If God is for us," we may ask, "what can still stand above us?" The New Testament speaks in awe of the forgiving wonder accomplished in God's sending of Jesus Christ for the sins of the world and it focuses all its powers of attention on this living center. The Holy Spirit's power exists in nothing less *or more* than in the illumining and implementing of this universal wonder. God's justification of the sinner is the meaning of the New Testament. (And sanctification, from the believer's side, is simply taking justification seriously.) The deep realization of the meaning of the forgiveness of sins is the essential meaning of the gift of the Holy Spirit.

c. That this realization largely still awaits Pentecostalism may be illustrated in the following thematic remark, noticed more than once in Part One: "As sinners we accept Christ; as saints we accept the Holy Spirit." Not only is the separation of the Spirit from Christ serious (is Christ without the Spirit?) but it is suggested that while sinners can accept Christ, the Holy Spirit must be obtained by men more highly qualified. The Pentecostal conditions define the meaning of "saints." The Holy Spirit is more difficult to obtain because while Christ comes to the sinner apart from special conditions of righteousness, the Holy Spirit, for his part, does not come in his fulness until men fulfill specifically required conditions of righteousness, i.e., until the initiated believer approximates what is called a heart without sin. While no burden is placed on the unbeliever, the believer is required nothing less than the supreme accomplishment — the removal of sin — and this *prior* to the supreme divine bestowment, the full gift of the Holy Spirit. (Without the filling of the Holy Spirit men are given the Herculean task of removing all known sin — in order, finally, to obtain this full Spirit. But if men can do all this *without* the full Spirit why is he necessary?)

The New Testament is not at war with the repudiation of sin — this repudiation is the believer's task in the Spirit. But the New Testament *is* at war with the notion that it is first man's war with and overcoming of sin that secures God's gift (cf. Rom. 10:3).

d. The Pentecostal interpretation of sin reaches its limits in the doctrine of "known sin." The teaching at this point was able to be comprehended in the following manner: "In seeking the baptism with the Spirit we should always remember that the first requisite is to be cleansed from all known and conscious sin."[9]

One can only ask: What of the person convinced of his own intrinsic righteousness — perhaps the profoundest of sins — must he not in special particular be blinded, by his very supposed righteousness, into a conviction that he has no known sin? What of the person with the obtuse conscience whose sin is arrant but whose consciousness of it by this very fact is hardened into unconsciousness? And what of the person, most importantly, *with* a conscience — seeing himself as he is, must he not by this fact be driven to despair? But what is forgiveness for? How long does it last? As long as one is himself righteous? Then why God's forgiveness at all?

Furthermore, on Pentecostal premises as well as in reality, is sin less culpable for being unknown? Finally, who was it in our Lord's parable who returned to his house with God's righteousness, the man conscious of no known sin (Luke 18:9-12) or the man whose prayer must be understood as the confession of the failure to have met any conditions at all: "God, be merciful to me a sinner"?[10]

---

9 Pethrus, *Wind*², p. 42. The Pentecostal order is "cleansing," *then* the coming of the Holy Spirit. In this connection the variant reading of D and others to Luke 11:2 (the Lord's Prayer) is interesting and in its order is evangelical and representative of New Testament teaching: "let thy Holy Spirit come upon us and cleanse us."

10 For a good development of the theme "conscious sin" see Helmut Thielicke,

e. The consequence of the New Testament doctrine of the condition for the gift of the Holy Spirit — the redeeming work of Christ (John 7:37-39; Gal. 3:10-14; 4:4-7; Rom. 8:1-4) — is the disqualification of the Pentecostal doctrine of sin and of the absolute conditions for sin's removal. Until it becomes clear to Pentecostalism that its absolute conditions, in the name of divine necessity and for the procuring of the divine gift, are poor modern translations of what the New Testament calls law, and that law of whatever kind does not remove but incites sin, gross or devout,[11] Pentecostalism must continue on what has been described as its "way." But if righteousness is through (any kind of) law, then Christ died for nothing (Gal. 2:21).

But the New Testament affirmation is clear. The solution for sin, the righteousness necessary for God's gift, comes not through conscious or unconscious sinlessness but by what we have seen is another Way:

> For our sake he made him to be sin who knew no sin, so that in him we might become the righteousness of God (II Cor. 5:21).

B. THE MEANS OF THE SPIRIT

1. THE MESSAGE OF FAITH

a. *The New Testament Doctrine (Gal. 3:1-5; Rom. 10:16-17).*[12] Once the essential pre-condition for the coming of the Spirit has been met — Christ's fulfillment of the law — how is the Holy Spirit actually communicated to men? The twin and magnetically attracted obstacles of holy law and unholy sin have been removed in the liberating work of Christ, but how does this work get to us? This is the question: How does God impart his fellowship (=his Holy Spirit) to men?

Paul, in an important and emotional passage, reminds the Galatian Christians of the means of their encounter. The passage begins in this manner:

> You stupid Galatians! You must have been bewitched — you before whose eyes Jesus Christ was openly displayed upon his cross! Answer me one question: did you receive the Spirit by keeping the law or by believing the gospel message (*ex akoës pisteōs;* margin and literally, "by the message of faith")? (Gal. 3:1-2 NEB).[13]

Theologische Ethik, 1. Prinzipienlehre: Dogmatische, philosophische, und kontroverstheologische Grundlegung (2d rev. ed.: Tübingen: Mohr, 1958), paragraphs 515-24.

[11] "Devout" is a particularly important signification in our context. See Schlier, *Gal.*[11], p. 182 to Gal. 5:18, and *idem,* art. *eleutheros, TWNT,* II, 493,8ff. Also Schweizer, art. *sarx, TWNT,* VII, 132,33ff. and 133 n. 274.

[12] Other texts which illumine this doctrine: I Thess. 1:4-5; 2:13; II Thess. 2:13-14; I Cor. 2:4-5; II Cor. 3:3, 6; Eph. 6:17; I Pet. 1:12; John 6:63; 16:8; 20:22-23; Acts *passim.*

[13] To *akoë pisteōs* as "message of faith" see Herman L. Strack and Paul Biller-

The *means* of the Spirit is nothing else than the *message* of the condition of the Spirit, namely the message of Jesus Christ upon his cross for us. This message, and the gift of the Spirit which comes through it, both calls for and creates what it calls for — faith — hence, "message of faith." We are in the presence of a happy and evangelical unity: the *means* of the Spirit is nothing else than the message of the *condition* of the Spirit: the work of Christ.

Paul considers the two competitive means of the Spirit in Galatia — the doing of the law and the message of faith — to be mutually exclusive (*ë*, "or," Gal. 3:2). The *ë* of the text allows no mixture of the law-works, on the one hand, and of the faith-message, on the other, as means for receiving God's free gift. The gift is received *either* freely *or* by devout effort. Not both-and.

In Galatians 3:2 Paul removes the Galatians to familiar and firm ground — to their becoming Christians in the beginning — because the Galatians are *now* in danger of being led to expect the Holy Spirit in greater measure through a means other or higher than the means which brought them the Spirit at first, i.e., through means other or higher than the message of simple faith in Christ. This is exactly the pathos of the Galatian problem. "Are you so foolish?" Paul asks. "Having begun with the Spirit, are you now ending with (*epiteleisthe*) the flesh?" (Gal. 3:3).

The Galatian letter is addressed to Christians who are being tempted to think that there is another, fuller gospel which will bring the Spirit to them in fulness, completion, or perfection (*epiteleisthai*) where the simple gospel message of Christ by faith brought only salvation's beginning.[14] Paul's message of faith is not totally repudiated by the bearers of the new gospel: they recognize faith as the way to initial salvation. But they believe that faith should be supplemented by fuller obedience to God's will and that this fuller obedience will be honored by God through a fuller gift of his Spirit or salvation. The new message

---

beck, *Kommentar zum Neuen Testament aus Talmud und Midrasch* (6 vols.; 2d ed.; München: C. H. Beck'sche Verlagsbuchhandlung, 1956), III, 283. Cf. Kittel, art. *akoë, TWNT,* I, 222; Schlier, *Gal.*[11], p. 81; Glöel, *Heilige Geist,* p. 130 n. 1. Hans Lietzmann translates the phrase "faith-message." *An die Galater* ("HNT," 10; 3d ed.; Tübingen: Mohr, 1932), p. 18. Friedrich Sieffert translates it "the preaching which counts on faith." *Der Brief an die Galater* ("MeyerK"; 9th ed.; Göttingen: Vandenhoeck & Ruprecht, 1899), p. 166. However, the faith-message not only counts on faith, it creates it. Cf. n. 28 below.

[14] "In the first of these contrasts ('begin' and 'end') Paul is probably facing a contention of the Judaizers that to attain to full salvation the Galatians must not rest satisfied with merely believing the gospel." George S. Duncan, *The Epistle of Paul to the Galatians* ("Moffatt NTC"; London: Hodder & Stoughton, 1948), p. 80. So also Schlier, *Gal.*[11], p. 83; Albrecht Oepke, *Der Brief des Paulus an die Galater* ("ThHK," 9; 2d rev. ed.; Berlin: Evangelische Verlagsanstalt, 1957), pp. 23, 68; Sieffert, *Gal.*[9], p. 167; Friedrich, art. *euaggelion, TWNT,* II, 731,42ff.; Schweizer, art. *sarx, TWNT,* VII, 132,30ff.

was thus earnest, plausible, appealing, and based on the Bible (cf. the entire argumentation of Gal. 3 and 4) — and therefore it was "bewitching," that is, attractive. Could God despise fuller obedience? The Galatians were simply being brought a fuller gospel with fuller conditions of obedience for a fuller salvation. The fact that Paul's Galatian opponents could appeal to such apparently high, spiritual, and biblical motives constituted the Galatian crisis.[15]

Paul must remind the Galatians all over again of how they received the Spirit in the very beginning, and in asking them, "having begun with the Spirit are you now ending with the flesh?" he is saying, "the greatest miracle in your life occurred without your assistance or effort through the power of the gospel alone; do you think now that you can go on to fulness through some higher means, if there is a higher means?" For Paul the message of faith was not simply a mathematical point at the beginning of the Christian life, or simply the fulcrum into the Christian life, to be superseded later by other means or messages bringing other and professedly greater blessings. For Paul the message of faith in Christ was the alpha and the omega, the beginning and the continuing means for the living of the Christian life. The message of faith yesterday, today, and tomorrow is God's one means of giving his Holy Spirit to men. That is the meaning of the extremely important Galatians 3:1-5 passage.

"When God gives you the Spirit and works miracles among you," Paul asks in his next question, "why is this? Is it because you keep the law, or is it because you have faith in the gospel message [again: *ex akoës pisteös*]?" (Gal. 3:5 NEB). Whereas Paul had placed his earlier and similar question (3:2) in the aorist, signifying the initial full reception of the Holy Spirit, the present question is placed in the present participle (*epichorëgön*), signifying both the constant (*-ön*) and, as the word itself represents (*epi-*), the rich, full giving of the Holy Spirit. In this second question Paul assumes that the Holy Spirit is continually and richly supplied just as he was initially: through the message of faith apart from works.

And once again it is Paul's contention — indeed, it is the distinctive feature of his gospel — that this faith message is God's *exclusive* means for the gift of the Spirit. The Spirit is either continually received, as he was initially received, through the attempt to do all that is com-

---

[15] "The recognition of the law [urged by the new teachers] is not intended to suppress faith in Christ; rather, obedience to the law, the 'law-work,' is a necessary supplementation and perfecting of faith in Christ (Gal. 3:2-5).... Only this call to recognition of the law in conjunction with faith in Christ is the full gospel (Gal. 1:7).... This doctrine seemed to be but a harmless rounding-off of the Pauline message." Goppelt, *Christentum und Judentum*, pp. 93-94. Cf. Bultmann: "The whole Galatian epistle fights the still possible misunderstanding that *pistis* [faith] has to be supplemented through fulfilling certain law-works." Art. *pistis*, *TWNT*, VI, 221,1-3.

manded, or he is received continually and always through faith in the gospel message.[16] Again the situation is either-or, and the immense subtlety of the Galatian heresy was its appeal to the both-and. It was being insisted in Galatia that the gospel of faith is, to be sure, absolutely indispensable for becoming a Christian, but for becoming a better Christian, for total filling by God (*epiteleisthai*), there must be obedience beyond mere faith. Paul does not contest obedience or the keeping of the commandments of God as such — indeed, he urges these most seriously — but he vigorously contests the necessity of any obedience except faith for a full relation with God. There is no other means for the full gift of the Holy Spirit than the message of faith in Christ's finished work, either initially (Gal. 3:2) or continually (Gal. 3:5).

The obedience of faith is the polar opposite of the obedience of conditions; the latter is apt to be an obedience not so much nourished as forced into activity and which in activity is often conceived as an immaculate preoccupation with oneself rather than the self-forgetting love of one's neighbor. Paul makes clear that God's constant and full supply of the Spirit, and of the miracles which are the Christian life, are *gifts* given as in the very beginning through the unconditioned message of faith in Christ (Gal. 3:2 and 5).

b. *The Consequences for the Pentecostal Doctrine of Fulness.* i. The Means of Fulness (The Galatian Consequences). As in Galatia the Pentecostal peril consists in seeking spiritual fulness through the fulfilling of special conditions rather than, as in the beginning, through the message of faith alone apart from all conditions.[17] Pentecostalism does not contest the conviction that a man begins the Christian life by the gospel alone — Pentecostalism can be rather orthodox in describing how a man becomes a Christian initially and, by their understanding, receives the Spirit, as we have seen, "in a sense."

It is possible to begin the Christian life through the gospel message of faith alone, it is said, but to go on to perfection and fulfillment this message must be supplemented, specifically, with conditions of absolute separation from all known sin, absolute surrender, and complete yielding, for while "as sinners we accept Christ; as saints we accept the Holy Spirit." It is this postulated difference in means — the gospel of faith for beginning in the Spirit, "deeper" conditions for fulfillment in the Spirit — which creates the Pentecostal difference in levels: Christians and Spirit-filled Christians.

Pentecostal conditions are not meant to be substitutes for the gospel; they are understood as implicates, as a "filling out" of the gospel, and

---

16 He is either a privilege or a "responsibility"— in Pauline language, either promise or law. See Gal. 3:16-18.

17 These conditions will often be interpreted by Pentecostals not as "additional" but as "inner" acts. Nevertheless.

therefore as steps into the "full gospel."[18] It will sometimes be conceded that other Christians preach, at least at times, a form of the gospel, but it is usually felt that as a rule it is only Pentecostals, or those who accept the Pentecostal message, who preach the full gospel, offering among other neglected blessings but especially the full gift of the Spirit.

The apostolic means of fulness, however, was no different than the apostolic means of initiation: the single message of faith (Gal. 3:2, 5). A principal error of Pentecostalism, shared by some of Pentecostalism's parents and relatives in conservative evangelicalism, is the conviction that the gospel is sufficient for the beginning but not for the continuing of the Christian life, for bringing the Holy Spirit initially but not fully. Faith suffices for a start but keys, secrets, steps, and conditions must bring the Christian into a higher, deeper, fuller or more victorious life.

It is one of the ironies of nomenclature among those going by the name "full gospel" (and even, at times, "evangelical") that the evangel or gospel itself is not considered full enough to cover and enable the whole of the Christian's life but must be joined with other means, conditions, steps, or laws of the spiritual life in order to be full. The remarkable feature in Paul on the other hand is the dogged insistence of the all-sufficiency of the *one* gospel for the beginning, for the continuing, and for the fulfilling of the Christian's life.

Christians not only once-and-for-all receive the Spirit through the message of faith apart from the fulfilling of conditions (Gal. 3:2) but they *continue* to be supplied *fully* with the Spirit and ministered miracles through the very same message without additional techniques or deeper messages or secret means (3:5).

Paul knew, and somehow it is true, that the faithful preaching of the grace of Jesus Christ is God's constant means of giving his Spirit. The apostolic means of initiation (the one gospel) is the apostolic means of fulfillment (the full gospel): the message of faith apart from the fulfilling of conditions.

The consequence for the Pentecostal doctrine of fulness must be the abandonment of any condition for the fulness of the Holy Spirit other than the one, initiating, sustaining, and powerful message of faith in Jesus Christ. There is for Christians no fuller, no more fulfilling gospel than the gospel that makes a man a Christian; to assert that there is, is to fall under Paul's severest censure (Gal. 1:6-9; 5:2-12).

---

[18] See the Pentecostal designations: full gospel people, or full gospel church, served by a full gospel minister, etc. The title of the major lay Pentecostal publication is "Full Gospel Business Men's Voice" published by "The Full Gospel Business Men's Association." One of the roots of this expression is the conviction that it is with the Pentecostal baptism in the Holy Spirit that the Spirit comes fully. Beyond salvation in Christ and the baptism in the Holy Spirit, as we have noted, the emphases on healing and the second coming round out the Pentecostal conviction of the full gospel.

ii. The Place of Fulness (The Special Colossian Implications). Pentecostalism advocates the seeking of the filling of the Holy Spirit by seeking the Holy Spirit himself. The New Testament locates the filling of the Holy Spirit in the proclamation of the Word of Christ (cf. Gal. 3:5 and 3:1) and in seeking to proclaim this Word (cf. Acts 4:29-30 with 4:31). The subsequent or later fillings of Christians with the Holy Spirit are due *not* to the fact — and this must be stressed — that Christians by their incorporation into Christ did not receive spiritual fulness (cf. Gal. 3:5 with 3:2 and Acts 4:29-31 with Acts 2); Christians can be filled with the Holy Spirit now precisely because when they were incorporated into Christ they were given every spiritual blessing, including the privilege of the continual filling of the Spirit as at the beginning (cf. e.g. Eph. 1:3 with 5:18).

It is the sustained doctrine of the Epistle to the Colossians that, according to the good pleasure of the Father, spiritual fulness is located for men in no other place — in no other be it ever so spiritual place — than in Jesus Christ.

(a) The theme of Colossians is the theme of Pentecostalism, "fulness" (*plëröma*). As Galatians poses the problem of the *means* to God's gift in the classic contradistinction of the "works of the law" and the "message of faith," so Colossians poses the problem of the *location* of God's gift in its pleroma-fulness. Over and again Paul reminds the Colossian church of the "all" that it has in Christ. Paul's opening prayer for the Colossians issues in a hymn of praise to the Son in one of the high christological passages of the New Testament terminating with the thematic, for the Colossians important, and for us relevant declaration:

> For in him [the Son] all the fulness was pleased to dwell (*pan to plëröma katoikësai*) and through him to reconcile to himself all things, whether on earth or in heaven, making peace by the blood of his cross (1:19-20).

The Colossians were being tempted by some to look for fulness in celestial powers *beyond* Christ.[19] Paul is eager for his church to know from the outset that not just "a" fulness, nor a transitional, passing, or initial fulness resided in the Son needing after him to be supplemented by another divine or semi-divine means. Rather, *the* fulness (*to plëröma*), *all* the fulness (*pan to plëröma*), was pleased to *dwell* (*katoikësai =*) permanently (and not visit passingly or preliminarily) in the Son.[20] There is no part of the divinity which is not placed — and fully,

---

[19] As in Galatia, the Colossian teachers apparently did not deny Christ — in fact, they probably felt that they especially honored him through a fuller means of devotion than faith. Cf. Wilfred L. Knox, *St. Paul and the Church of the Gentiles* (Cambridge: At the University Press, 1939), pp. 151-52. Our use of the name Paul in connection with Colossians is traditional.

[20] Cf. J. B. Lightfoot, *Saint Paul's Epistles to the Colossians and to Philemon: A Revised Text with Introductions, Notes and Dissertations* (Grand Rapids, Mich.: Zondervan Publishing House, 1879), p. 159.

permanently placed — in Jesus Christ. Therefore the man who believes
in Christ Jesus has every conceivable spiritual blessing and need not —
must not — look for other means than believing, other objects than
Christ in order to have "more," "filling," or "blessing" from the Divine.
The believer may declare with the author to the Ephesians, "blessed be
the God and Father of our Lord Jesus Christ who has blessed us *in
Christ* with *every* spiritual blessing in the heavenly places" (Eph. 1:3).[21]

Then in one of his most important remarks, paralleling but even
going beyond his encomium in Colossians 1:19, Paul explains why
Christ must be everything — absolutely everything — to the Colossian
believers: "For in him the whole fulness of deity dwells bodily, and
you have come to fulness of life in him" (2:9-10).[22] Every word is
important. "In him" is placed again at the head of the sentence for
emphasis repeating the theme of the Colossian letter that the "fulness"
be located by believers where it is located by God, in the incarnate Son.
Again the "fulness" *dwells* permanently (*katoikei,* present tense) in
the Son; again, the whole, full, and only "fulness" (*pan to*) there is.
And as if Paul were seeking to stretch this truth to its outermost limits
he adds: the whole "fulness *of deity.*" In the unified person ("bodily")
of the crucified and risen Christ God has been sovereignly pleased to
place his whole fulness. Therefore the Colossians must not be tempted
for a moment to seek rootage in any other heavenly being than Christ.

And the fulness which Christians have in Christ is *full,* not because
the Christian is capable of "appropriating" this fulness but because
Christ is capable of appropriating the Christian (see the *perfect* and
the *passive* form of the verb "to fill" in Col. 2:10).

Nowhere in Colossians is it suggested that pre-conditions of the
believer's self-emptying must precede God's filling; indeed, on the
contrary, it was precisely conditions of the rigorist and self-emptying sort which were most severely combatted by Paul in Colossians.
The Colossian teachers were advocating, variously, conditions of self-
abasement, visions, regulations, and severity to the body in order for
the Colossians finally to have fulfillment (2:18-23). Paul, however,
focuses the attention of the tempted Colossians not upon their subjective commitment but upon their objective condition: the Colossians,
Paul thunders, are *in Christ.* Therefore the Colossians *are fulfilled*
(*este . . . peplërömenoi*), Paul hammers home, because to be in Christ
is to be in him in whom all fulness dwells. Fulness is Christ's; the believer is in Christ; therefore the believer has fulness. To suggest that

---

[21] Cf. the anti *sola fide* polemic, above, pp. 109-10.
[22] The RSV translation here is inadequate. There is no "coming" of the Colossians in the text, there is only their *"Sein"* — here their passive being — in Christ:
kai este en autö peplërömenoi.

the believer, though in Christ, still needed some additional kind of spiritual fulfillment or appropriation, was the Colossian heresy.[23]

(b) The consequences of both the central Galatian and Colossian arguments for Pentecostalism's doctrine of fulness are far-reaching. Galatians forbids any other *means* to the Spirit than the Spirit's way to the believer, namely, through the message of faith in Christ apart from the fulfilling of the law's conditions, and this not only initially but continually. Colossians, in a remarkably parallel argument, forbids believers to contemplate fulfillment in any other *place* than where they *have* received it and where they *are* fulfilled — in Christ. The Pentecostal error in locating permanent spiritual fulness outside of or after initiation into Christ has been noted in Part I and may be reviewed succinctly in the following sampling, studied there.

> As the Spirit of Christ, He had come at conversion, imparting the Christ-life, revealing Christ, and making Him real. At the Baptism in the Spirit, He Himself in His own person comes upon and fills the waiting believer. This experience is as distinct from conversion as the Holy Spirit is distinct from Christ. His coming to the believer at the [spiritual] Baptism is the coming of the Third Person of the Trinity, in addition to the coming of Christ, which takes place at conversion.

> The central fact of the Pentecostal Experience consists in being *filled* with the Holy Spirit. This is distinct from His previous work in regeneration as the Giver of Life in Christ.

> This is not to say that children of God in whom dwells the Spirit of Christ and who have not received the Baptism in the Spirit will not have varying measures of wisdom, knowledge, faith, etc., which come from the Lord. Being partakers of His nature and dwelling in Christ as the branch in the vine, naturally brings one a measure of the qualities which Christ has.

> In the New Testament men always received a "measure" of the Spirit and were more or less filled with the Spirit at conversion. Every child of God received the "Spirit of adoption" and is filled with the Spirit in a "measure" when converted.

Is the "Christ-life" which the Spirit of Christ imparts so meager that it needs supplementation to be full? Is the believer still in a spiritually unfilled state in Christ or, in the curious expression, filled in a measure and first filled fully when he has an *added* initiation into the Spirit? Is to be indwelt by Christ distinct from being indwelt by the Spirit (Rom. 8:9-10; I Cor. 6:17; 15:45; II Cor. 3:17-18)? Does he whom the author above calls the Third Person of the Trinity come all by himself after and independently of the Second Person or does he come

---

23 "The Colossian [false] doctrine was distinguished by the special deeds and acts through which one was to make his way to fulness; conditions and rules are made to accompany the individual. But here [in Col. 2:10ff.] there are no human deeds, only a divine event; therefore all the verbs in this passage are passive." Lohmeyer, *Kol.*[11], pp. 107-08.

"in Christ Jesus" (Gal. 3:14; Rom. 8:2; John 14:26)? Is to be in
Christ to be in only a "measure" of God's provision (Col. 2:10)?

In fact, the fire of the apostle is directed at exactly those who allow
the believer in Christ only a measure of all God's fulness (which includes, of course, his Spirit) and who thereby have an opportunity to
introduce their armory of conditions into the believer's life in order to
provide him for the first time with the fulness lacking in "the Christ-
life." Paul's retort is that in Christ the believer has everything — and
perfectly (peplērōmenoi). When the believer is in Christ he does not
have but a measure of a power which he receives in Pentecostal fulness
only later: "measure" and "fulness" are mutually contradictory.

Of most importance, when the believer is in Christ he does not need
other conditions than faith or, in fact, other stipulated acts of faith
itself, if he wishes to have anything "more" than he already has in
Christ. For there is no such "more." For faith receives everything which
God gives — permanently, personally, fully — since faith receives
Christ, and in Paul's words, "in him the whole fulness of deity dwells
bodily and you have [perfect tense] . . . fulness [i.e., not a measure] of
life in him [repeated, and not in another spiritual entity]." "When men
have Christ they not only have everything one needs, they have everything one can possibly have" (Haupt).[24]

iii. Summary. The location of absolutes of obedience, surrender, and
faith upon the believer (the Galatian heresy) and the location of part-
fulness, part-life, and part-power in Christ (the Colossian heresy) in
order in both cases to offer a special spiritual fulness beyond what faith
receives in Christ is, in the judgment of Paul's letters to Galatia and
Colossae, nothing less than resorting to "another gospel which is not
another" (Gal. 1:6-7; cf. Col. 2:8, 18-19, 23) even if it is called
full. The absolutes and the parts are in each case in the wrong
place. The consequences for Pentecostalism of the omnisufficient message of faith concerning all the fulness in Christ are very considerable
indeed.

A text from John's Gospel summarizes the New Testament conviction:

> For he whom God has sent utters the words of God, for it is not by
> measure that he gives the Spirit; the Father loves the Son, and has given
> all things into his hand (John 3:34-35).[25]

> So it is final, says St. Paul, the whole, total Godhead dwells bodily, that
> is personally, in Jesus Christ. Therefore the fellow who does not find or
> get God in Christ shall never again and nowhere else have or find God

[24] Die Gefangenschaftsbriefe ("MeyerK"; 7th ed.; Göttingen: Vandenhoeck &
Ruprecht, 1897), pp. 86-87.
[25] "This means that the revelation which Jesus brings is complete, sufficient,
and needs no supplementation." Bultmann, Das Evangelium des Johannes
("MeyerK"; 14th ed.; Göttingen: Vandenhoeck & Ruprecht, 1956), p. 119.

outside of Christ, even if he goes, as it were, over heaven, under hell, or into space (Luther).[26]

2. THE HEARING OF FAITH

a. *The New Testament Doctrine (Gal. 3:1-14; Rom. 1:5, 16-17; cf. John 7:37-39; 4:13-14; 5:24; 6:35)*. i. "Did you receive the Spirit by works of the law, or by hearing [*akoë*] with faith?" (Gal. 3:2). The important Greek word *akoë* can be rendered not only by the term "message," "report," or "what is heard" (Isa. 53:1 LXX=John 12: 38=Rom. 10:16; cf. Rom. 10:17; I Thess. 2:13; Heb. 4:2) but also by simply "hearing" (see Mark 7:35; I Cor. 12:17; Acts 17:20; Heb. 5:11; I Pet. 2:8).[27] Paul may have chosen therefore to use *akoë* in Galatians 3:2, 5 because of its comprehensiveness, stressing at the same time, in the single word, the objective *message* and the subjective *hearing* of the message.

Of great importance in the phrase "heard-message of faith" is the controlling genitive: *"of faith."* "Of faith" in what sense? In the sense that the gospel message comes requiring faith and, because it is more than a law, it comes *giving* what it requires. The heard-message of faith gives not only the message of Christ, it gives the hearing of faith to receive the message. The "message of faith" is "the message which brings faith."[28]

ii. But the gospel is "of faith" in a still fuller sense. In his thematic introduction to Romans Paul calls the gospel a message which is "through faith for faith" (*ek pisteös eis pistin*, Rom. 1:17). "Through faith for faith" means that the gift of God is received not only initially by faith but that it is always and only received by faith alone, from beginning (*ek*) to end (*eis*). God gives us his righteousness and acceptance, Spirit and presence — and he gives them constantly — not to our

---

[26] Cited in Kurt Dietrich Schmidt, "Luthers Lehre vom Heiligen Geist," *Schrift und Bekenntnis: Zeugnisse Lutherischer Theologie* (Hamburg: Im Furche-Verlag, 1950), p. 157. Note Beasley-Murray's sharp conclusion: "However indignantly [Pentecostals] would repudiate the charge, their separation between the Church's experience of Christ and the work of the Holy Spirit entails them in the gravest heresy, and it should not for a moment be countenanced by the churches." "The Holy Spirit, Baptism, and the Body of Christ," *Review and Expositor, 63* (Spring 1966), 182.

[27] Schlatter prefers the meaning "hearing" exclusively and translates *akoë pisteös* with "believing hearing." *Gottes Gerechtigkeit: Ein Kommentar zum Römerbrief* (3d ed.; Stuttgart: Calwer Verlag, 1959), pp. 316-17. We are unable to be convinced that either the exclusive or the primary sense of *akoë* is "hearing." When Lightfoot (*Gal.*⁵, p. 135) argues that the context "requires some word expressing the part taken by the Galatians themselves," it seems to us that he misses the reason why *akoë* best lends itself to the objective interpretation as "message," namely as the opposite of *all* Galatian doing. Nevertheless, we can accept the nuance "hearing" which is present in *akoë*.

[28] Cf. Friedrich, art. *euaggelion, TWNT*, II, 730,5-6: "The message demands and *creates pistis* [faith]."

worthiness but to our faith. For "to one who works, his wages are not reckoned as a gift but as his due" and "if it is the adherents of the law who are to be the heirs, faith is null and the promise is void" (Rom. 4:4 and 14). Therefore the promise is of "faith, in order that the promise may rest on grace and be guaranteed" because "if it is by grace, it is no longer on the basis of works; otherwise grace would no longer be grace" (Rom. 4:16 and 11:6).[29]

iii. The important question, "What then is faith?" is probably best answered by observing that with which faith is constantly contrasted by Paul: again, the "works of the law." If God's gift is by faith apart from works then this means that there is at least one thing that faith cannot be: a work. Faith must be the opposite of a work or of something one does; it must be something which God does and enables and which one unworthily and unworked-for simply receives. This is exactly what the New Testament makes faith (see especially the important term, "the faith *of* Jesus Christ," Rom. 3:22; Gal. 2:16; Phil. 3:9).[30]

Wherever faith is defined as something emanating principally from the recipient, there faith is secretly a work and hence not Christian faith; but wherever faith is defined as that which emanates from God's gospel *to* the recipient, then this faith is *God's* work and gift and therefore Christian. Since faith must first of all be something that comes to us and only therefore from us if it is to avoid being our work, it is noteworthy that Paul in Galatians, writing to a situation where Christian faith was being misunderstood as in some sense human work, describes faith as *coming*— to men (Gal. 3:23, 25).

The mutual exclusiveness (Godward, not manward) of the two means of right standing with God — "works of the law" and "faith" — must be emphasized. The Galatian new teachers would not deny faith's primacy but they would deny its exclusiveness. Their formula for fulness before God was something like "faith *and* obedience," whereby the "and" could throw into question the sufficiency of faith for righteousness before God, and of the sufficiency of faith as the only legitimate and *effective* source

---

[29] The passages cited from Romans in this paragraph have their chief reference to the eschatological "righteousness," "promise," "inheritance," etc., and in Romans, except at 5:5 and ch. 8, are not brought into express relation to the Spirit. However, Pauline eschatological terms are not separable either from the promise of the Spirit or, what is the same thing, from the Christian dimension of the present.

[30] To this formative phrase cf. Schlatter, *Gottes Gerechtigkeit*[3], pp. 139-40 to Rom. 3:22; Schlier, *Gal.*[11], p. 56 to Gal. 2:16, who understands the phrase as an objective genitive but who nevertheless sees its fuller significance; Lohmeyer, *Phil.*[12], p. 137 n. 2 to Phil. 3:9. I am especially impressed by Greer M. Taylor's recent argument for *fidei commissum* in "The Function of PISTIS CHRISTOU in Galatians," *JBL, 85* (March 1966), summarized well theologically at p. 75.

of good works to men. (Observe the exclusive terms *ë* in Gal. 3:2, 5 and *ean më* in Gal. 2:16.)[31]

Paul knew how to refute the inevitable moral question (Gal. 2:17; Rom. 3:8; 6:1) which will arise in the presence of the evangelical *sola* and its exclusion of the works of the law toward God: "Is not a too radical message of *sola fide* antinomian and therefore ultimately immoral?" No. Faith is sufficient because it really identifies the believer with Christ (Gal. 2:20-21; Rom. 6:2ff.) and Christ is sufficient for the believer's moral direction. Paul is not antinomian, he is antinomistic.

The dangerous "and" on the other hand, in contrast to the evangelical *sola, causes* sin (Gal. 2:18-19; 3:19; Rom. 7:7-25) and places those who employ it under the curse accruing to those who wish to live before God and men on the basis of their obediences (Gal. 3:10).

iv. Finally, it is significant that in coming to the "hearing of faith" the Holy Spirit comes to the most passive of all the major organs of the personality. The ear does not create or emote, fulfill absolutes or "do"; its office is to receive what is given to it. From the human side the hearing of faith is the only condition for receiving God's gift and it is a condition, significantly, which is not "done" in the proper sense of the word. It is a condition, most accurately, which is enabled. The hearing of faith is made possible by the presence of the message of faith.

As all the *conditions* for the Spirit were fulfilled by Christ's work outside ourselves, and as the *means* of the Spirit is the message of Christ's work coming to us through the words of others, so even the hearing which receives the gift of Christ's work need not summon a power to believe which has not already been placed in the gospel "message of faith."[32] It is the glory of the gospel that it is not only a word *about* salvation, it is God's power *unto* salvation (Rom. 1:16).

God supplies his Spirit not to deeds but to the hearing of faith — alone — and even this hearing he supplies.

b. *The Consequences for the Pentecostal Doctrine of Faith.* i. Faith as Work. The crucial error in the Pentecostal doctrine of faith is the attempt to make faith a required accomplishment obtaining the reward of the Spirit. However, there is only one way for a *gift* — especially a *divine* gift — to be received — namely, received. The Pentecostal danger may be observed again in a review of Pentecostal remarks.

He gave Him to His Church ... and He waits to give each *individual*

---

[31] It is unfortunate that the NEB translated Paul's thematic and united *hupakoë pisteös* ("obedience of faith"), Rom. 1:5; 16:26, "faith *and* obedience." There is no "and" in Paul's expression. Cf. p. 326, n. 15 below.

[32] "Mit dem Evangelium ist auch der Glaube da." Friedrich, art. *euaggelion*, *TWNT*, II, 730,5. (The E. T. is a little less effective: "Faith is present with the Gospel," p. 732.) The entire Friedrich article is a revelation.

member of that Church his or her share in Pentecost on the one *condition* of applying for it by faith.

There was of course on the part of those present a perfect resignation ... and God honoured their child-like faith.[33]

He will give freely, as we meet His conditions and ask Him for His gifts.

All these scriptures [in Acts] emphasize the fact that this glorious experience is a gift from Heaven and is to be had by simply receiving on our part. Paul said in Galatians 3:14 "that we might *receive* the promise of the Spirit through faith"— *not* by works of righteousness which we have done; *not* by our own holiness or merit; *not* as a reward for any fasting and prayer; *not* as a payment to us in any way whatsoever; but as a sheer gift of His infinite grace and love. He is offered to us freely without money and without price. We simply extend our hand of faith, lay hold on Him, appropriate Him, and receive Him as our own.[34]

The rub is in the final sentence with its four qualifications: "We simply extend our hand" (the wrong hand is extended; and Pentecostal extension can be other than "simply" as speaking in tongues illustrates), "lay hold on Him" (still another way of making faith a work), "appropriate Him" (the classic way of making faith a work, see below), "and receive Him as our own" (the receiving, significantly, last). The sum result of the Pentecostal definition of faith not only in theory but in practice is that the Holy Spirit is not, as affirmed above, a "sheer gift" given to us (the Pentecostal sentence reads instead, noteworthily, "*offered* to us") "freely without money and without price," but faith itself is made the price for the gift of God.

The price of Pentecostal extension, laying-hold, appropriation, and reception, as the Pentecostal conditions and evidence detail, is high, for, as we have seen:

God has many lessons of humility and patience to teach us by withholding gifts and blessings that we seem to think should be always forthcoming. The more earnestly we covet a gift from God and the more we sacrifice to obtain it, the more we will prize it when it is obtained.

Yet the fact remains that things which are obtained cheaply are held cheaply; while that for which a great price is paid becomes a precious treasure for ever.

For the reception of God's gift, (inner) works are understood in Pentecostalism not as hindrances to faith or, with Paul, as the very opposite of faith, but as the cultivators of faith. We remember that:

If, upon searching your heart, you find that you are truly submissive to

---

[33] Rewarded faith was the doctrine of Rabbinic Judaism as well. Cf. Strack-Billerbeck, *Kommentar*[2], III, 191; Otto Michel, *Der Brief an die Römer* ("MeyerK"; 12th ed.; Göttingen: Vandenhoeck & Ruprecht, 1963), p. 57; and p. 173 above.

[34] It is interesting that Riggs speaks here of faith alone though in his list of conditions faith is fourth. See also the pre-Pentecostal F. B. Meyer placing faith fifth on a list of conditions and his argument, then, for *sola fide*. *A Castaway*, pp. 90-94; cf. Documents, below, p. 341. For a comparable "*ultima fide*" in Philo see Bultmann, *Theology of the New Testament*, I, 316.

> the revealed will of God and in harmony with your fellow man . . . *then* it
> will be easy for you to exercise that simple and childlike faith in the Lord
> that will bring a quick response from Him.

God is the responder to *man* the giver and faith, here, is a human
exercise. However in the New Testament when God gives it is God
who calls and man who responds and faith is a receiving.[35]

The Pentecostal equation for receiving God's gift is not the apostolic
faith *apart from* works but faith *after* works. We learned:

> We first make sure that we are right with God. Then [!] we cease from
> our own works [*n.b.*] or efforts, and apply to Him for the gift which we
> seek. He is waiting for us to come to this point.

Again, God is the waiter, men are the doers. Here it is not the absolutes which are in the wrong place but the action. According to
the New Testament it is God himself who makes men right with
himself in Christ — *apart* from "our own works or efforts" not *after*
them. It is God who comes to men in his gospel with his gift, not men
who come applying: it is God who gives the gift which men may
or may not have been seeking (cf. Rom. 9:30—10:4) and which they
are enabled through the power of that gift to answer with faith. "Who
has ever made a gift to him," Paul asks, "to receive a gift in return?"
(Rom. 11:35 NEB). No one.

A familiar citation should seal our consideration of faith as work as
it appears in Pentecostal teaching.

> Some have had the superficial conception that the Lord gives His Spirit as
> a reward for this work of making matters right. But this is not so. The
> heart must be made clean. When all conscious sin has been taken away,
> then [!] we really are in a place where it becomes easy to trust Him.

Here again we have the normal Pentecostal confusion of grace and
works, promise and command, gift and reward. It is protested by
Pentecostals that the Holy Spirit is not given as a reward for men's
making things right; nevertheless, the believer is responsible for the
work of cleansing his heart, for the removal of all conscious sin, and
only "then" does it become easy to have faith and thus only then will
the Holy Spirit be given. But when the Holy Spirit comes as a gift
at the end of this superhuman chain of deeds, then we do not see how

---

35 "Is it true that the man must always make the first move when cooperating
with God, to bring about a miracle?" asks the Pentecostal J. E. Stiles. "Answer:
Yes. If we go through the miracles of the Bible we will find that the man always
did something which constituted a step of faith." *Gift of the Holy Spirit*, p. 138;
cf. *ibid.*, pp. 104-06. Compare Luther's struggle with the Protestant "heavenly
prophets" in *LW* 40. Hutten sees as one of the most characteristic features of
sects in general the tendency to reverse in divine-human relationship the one who
calls and the one who responds. *Die Glaubenswelt des Sektierers: Das Sektentum
als Antireformatorische Konfession — Sein Anspruch und seine Tragödie* (Hamburg: Im Furche Verlag, 1957), pp. 37-38.

he may any longer be considered a gift.[36] And when faith is coupled with all the prior inner works enabling it or making it easier to receive God's great gift, then faith ceases to be the faith apart from works which the New Testament presents. For the receiving of God's great *gift,* faith is not easier where works are present, it is eliminated. Faith cannot be fifth on a list of conditions and still be alone. It cannot even be second. To receive God's gift faith must be left alone or it ceases to be faith in the sense in which Paul and John discuss it. True faith will produce works and good works as Paul himself, James, the other apostles, and the Reformers always insisted it must; but faith in Christ will not tolerate a single helper, as though it needed one, in bringing good works into being.[37]

It is the failure of Pentecostalism to see the utter antagonism of faith and works as the *means* by which God's gift is received that has contributed to the creation of the Pentecostal conditions.[38]

ii. Faith as Appropriation. A second attempt to circumnavigate the New Testament doctrine of faith will be found in the doctrine of a second faith or what is called appropriation. It is argued: Yes, faith alone receives God's gift of salvation and, in a sense, his Spirit, but there must be a second act of faith toward the Holy Spirit for appropriating the whole Spirit himself, for obtaining power, sanctification, victory, and the fulness of the Spirit, whereas the first faith obtained only grace, justification, and the forgiveness of sins. The watchwords in this argument are, as we noticed, "as there is a faith toward Christ for salvation, so there is a faith toward the Holy Spirit for power and consecration" and this second faith is necessary because "God's gift requires an appropriation."

It does not need to be stressed that where two faiths are required for God's giving, faith is again no longer *sola,* and where grace needs to be supplemented by power it is conceived as powerless grace and the proper sense of *sola gratia* no longer obtains. We have what has been called a system of "salvation by faiths" rather than the biblical salvation by faith.[39] The requirement of the second appropriating faith

---

[36] Cf. Augustine against Pelagius, *On the Grace of Christ,* ch. 34.

[37] Cf. the oft-cited words from Luther's preface to Romans: "Oh, faith is a living, busy, active, mighty thing, so that it is impossible for it not to be constantly doing what is good. Likewise, faith does not ask if good works are to be done, but before one can ask, faith has already done them and is constantly active." In *The Book of Concord: The Confessions of the Evangelical Lutheran Church,* tr. and ed. Theodore G. Tappert (Philadelphia: Fortress Press, 1959), pp. 552-53.

[38] We believe that we may say at the conclusion of this particular consideration of Pentecostal faith what Strack-Billerbeck, *Kommentar*[2], concludes at the end of the review of Rabbinic faith, III, 199.

[39] The phrase "salvation by faiths," used pejoratively, is B. B. Warfield's. See his *Perfectionism,* II, especially pp. 567-610. The book is an extensive critique of victorious-life evangelicalism. If it has been the frequent error of a theological

for the Holy Spirit — both as a requirement (prejudicing grace) and as a second (prejudicing Christ's sufficiency) makes the formula suspect. Two is the fatal number in Christian theology.

The second faith will usually be forwarded under specially constructed synonyms with which we have already become familiar: appropriate, claim, apply — all deeds or emotions to be effected by the believer to obtain what has not yet been given him or what has already been given but not yet fully appropriated by him in Christ. Indeed, the major reason offered by Pentecostalism for the insufficiency of the gift received by Christians is not Christ's insufficiency, since they do not wish to denigrate Christ, it is the believer's insufficient appropriation — a most important word and idea.

The notion of appropriation is central to Pentecostal and Anglo-Saxon evangelical usage and contains a serious danger. "Appropriate" lexically means "to make one's own . . . to take for one's own." It is what New Testament faith Godward is not: a "making," i.e., a doing, rather than a receiving. In Pentecostal appropriation the weight of the gift's transmission is shifted from the Giver's making it men's to men's making it theirs. Hence the gift ceases to be simply received, it is "made one's own" and so at least *in part* becomes our work.

Finally, when appropriation is made the condition of fulness then men are only and at every moment as sure of the fulness of God's presence as they themselves are at that moment capable of appropriating this fulness. However, it is doubtful that anyone this side of the general resurrection will ever be able to respond "appropriately" to all that there is in Christ. But if a man's *having* this fulness is thereby set in doubt or if to obtain it he is set to (even inward) work, then he is of all creatures most miserable.

It is our impression that "appropriation" has been the mother of more conditions, if not more misery, than any other word we have encountered in Pentecostalism except, perhaps, the word "full." The notion of appropriation tends to make the believer's faith even more central than God's gift, or to put it in another way, to make faith a work. But if faith is a work then salvation is not apart from works. If faith is an appropriation, that is, "a making one's own," then it is not apart from all our makings. If having what God in the fulness of Christ gives depends upon one's ability to make that fulness his, or even upon a believer's ability to "let go" which is the inverse (and as frequent side) of this emphasis, then the whole breadth and depth of salvation is transferred at the last possible moment, no matter how orthodox every prior moment may have been, from God to men. This is all to say that if faith is a human appropriation and not a

liberalism to claim God the Father apart from the exclusive mediation of Jesus Christ the Son, it is the as frequent error of a theological conservatism to place God the Spirit beyond simple faith in Christ the Savior.

human reception enabled completely and graciously by God then it is a devout work but it is not what the New Testament calls faith.[40]

iii. Faith as Absolute. Finally, faith will be defined as absolute surrender with its synonyms. This may be illustrated through two prior citations from Scandinavian Pentecostalism.

> As you were justified and regenerated by faith, and sanctified by faith, so also you must receive the Baptism of the Holy Ghost and Fire — the Comforter, by faith. I am supposing that you have yielded to God *at every point.* . . . Are you willing to go *all the way* with Christ?
>
> They have had wonderful experiences, and surrender after surrender has been made, but because they have not come all the way and made the yieldedness complete, they have not seen the fulness of the blessing.

Any number of features in these remarks could be commented upon — the separation of justification from sanctification as two separate events; the possibility of total obedience *prior* to the full reception of the Spirit — but we shall concentrate only on the definition of faith as yielding at "every point," going "all the way."

The believer is thrown upon himself to accomplish a dedication in order to receive God when, instead, he should be able simply to throw himself upon a God who has already given *himself* to us completely. Only the latter is New Testament faith, and the former, while adorned with all the adjectives of piety, is nevertheless nothing else than the call into the wilderness.

Works are not any less works for having to be done internally; they are, in fact, all the more excruciating and enslaving, for who can know his heart? Pentecostalism feels that it is speaking the language of Christian devotion when it invokes its internal absolutes of surrender. But because Pentecostalism almost completely misunderstands the character of New Testament faith in its noble simplicity, Pentecostalism's devotional absolutes call believers not to grace in Christ but to groveling within their own hearts to find what is not there: the absolute.

Interior works are more binding than exterior works because of their center in the self and they are more subtle because they appear more devotional. But what the New Testament calls faith stands sovereign and alone — and sufficient.

The Pentecostal pathfinder Andrew Murray provides an excellent illustration not only of abundant absolutes but also of interior works and of what we may call "the unevangelical reversal," namely, the making of *human* absolute surrender the condition of the *divine* fulness. As we have had occasion to see, Pentecostalism inherited not only the absolutes but the reversal:

---

[40] In connection with "appropriation" it can fairly be asked: Is a person "appropriated"? It is the frequently "thingish" understanding of the Holy Spirit in Pentecostalism which contributes to the offensiveness of the doctrine.

When once we strive to take in the full meaning of this preparation, the entire emptying of self, and of everything that this world can offer, we begin to understand how it is that there is often much prayer for the power of the Holy Spirit without any apparent answer. It is because the Holy Spirit claims nothing less than an absolute and entire surrender, for the life of heaven to take complete possession and exercise full mastery (*Back to Pentecost*, p. 13).

However, Luther's affirmation is evangelical, "Believe and you have it" (*Glaubst du, so hast du*). This is the New Testament doctrine in its purity. Yet the moment one adds, "*Absolutely* believe (or surrender, empty, yield) and you have it," though appearing more devout through its intensification, the sentence bears in fact the crushing weight of both the law and the impossible. When does one know he has believed *absolutely*? What must one do (or *not* do) to believe absolutely? What mortal can do the absolute?

To our knowledge, faith is never prefixed in Paul by an adjective, nor heightened by an absolute. This cannot be accidental.[41]

c. *Additional Note: John's Sola Fides.* A series of related Johannine texts with their aorists will conclude our consideration of the sufficiency of the New Testament's one faith. i. We begin with the programmatic announcement in John 7.

On the last day of the feast, the great day, Jesus stood up and proclaimed, "If any one thirst, let him come to me and drink. He who *believes* in *me*, as the scripture has said, 'Out of his heart shall flow rivers of living water.' " Now this he said about the Spirit, which those who *believed* in *him* were to receive; for as yet the Spirit had not been given, because Jesus was not yet glorified (John 7:37-39).

Faith in Jesus results in the gift of the Spirit: this has been and is here again the simple teaching of the New Testament. Faith in Jesus

---

[41] Note the absolutes in a representative Pentecostal assertion: "No person can receive or retain the Pentecostal experience without complete and unconditional obedience to all the revealed will of God. *The Bible gives no shortcuts or easy routes.* It is only when the person is entirely consecrated and fully obedient that the Spirit will come in. When every condition is met, no person or power can stop Him from taking up His abode." Wade Horton, *Pentecost Yesterday and Today* (Cleveland, Tenn.: Pathway, 1964), p. 28, emphasis his. The Bible has these notes also, of course. Yet it is the remarkable characteristic of the Pauline message in particular that where superlatives and absolutes are used it is usually in connection with God's work and provision in Christ toward us (Colossians is the classic example in the Pauline school); where Pentecostalism uses superlatives and absolutes, according to our observation, it is principally in connection with Christians and their requirements toward God.

The believer may be and rightly is called to complete devotion *because* he has been fully forgiven and accepted. However, if the devotion is ordered *in order* to get God in his fulness (e.g., in the fulness of his Spirit) then we are not in the presence of the gospel. The giving of the great commandment in the Gospels (Mark 12:28-34 par.), the contexts indicate, was a ministry of the law intended to show particular persons their prior need of the gospel — faith in Christ. Similarly, Romans 2 in relation to Romans 3.

and the reception of the Spirit are correlative. The faith need not be, indeed is never said to be, in the Spirit; the faith spoken of here (twice) is faith in Jesus. For the reception of the Spirit, Jesus Christ is the sole necessary object of faith: *solus Christus*. And the sole recipient of Christ in this text, as elsewhere, is faith: *sola fides*.

The John 7 passage teaches also that the Spirit given to *sola fides* is not anemic. The Spirit shall *"flow* with *rivers* of *living* water." It is not flattering to faith in Christ when it is identified only with a semi-initiation and is allowed only a trickle of nearly powerless life. For the Pentecostal formulation reads: faith in Christ brings spiritual *life;* but subsequent faith in the Spirit himself as evidenced by tongues brings spiritual *power.* However, according to John 7 faith in Christ brings not just enough water to wet the tongue of the believer, it receives from Christ in the Spirit not only spiritual existence and re-vivification, but spiritual power as well.

Pentecostalism seems to leave the simple believer in a condition some-what like that of the Jericho traveler in the story of the Good Samari-tan — "half-dead." For the believer, though made *alive* through faith in Christ, does not yet have what is called "power for service." The Pentecostal interpretation of simple faith in Christ thus detracts from Christ's sufficiency by teaching that faith gives only life enough to exist as a Christian, but that to have power to live, serve, witness, and work as a Christian requires a second transformation — the Pentecostal baptism in the Holy Spirit.

Pentecostalism's rebuttal is usually: the fault lies not with Christ but with the believer who, had he believed enough, would have re-ceived enough. But this answer is insufficient as we have already seen, since the *locus operandi* of the gift is transferred from the hands of the giver to the hands of the receiver which must be extended eagerly enough before the giver will fill them. But to demand of the spiritually lifeless initiate (John 5:24) that he make every necessary sacrifice, absolutely surrender, believe enough, and so forth, before God will give his full gift is to mock the dead, invoke the law, and to make a travesty of the gospel of grace. Faith is not a heroic work. Faith is letting God alone be heroic; it is letting God be God. Simple faith in Christ receives everything God has to give. This must be maintained or the gospel sinks.

ii. In his conversation with the Samaritan woman (John 4:7-15) Jesus declares: "Everyone who drinks of this water will thirst again, but whoever drinks [aorist: *once* drinks] of the water I shall give him will never thirst; . . . [it] will become in him a spring of water welling up to eternal life" (4:14). A single drink of Christ's gift of water suffices unto eternity. On receiving Christ there should be no thirsting after "deeper" spiritual experiences as though the water faith receives from Christ were not entirely satisfying or empowering. The sighing and thirsting of Pentecostal candidates for "more" is placed in question.

It is to be feared, furthermore, that *requiring* believers to thirst for more, in a second experience which alone brings spiritual fulness, is prejudicial to the honor of faith. The teaching that only the absolutely surrendered, tongues-speaking believers have attained to spiritual fulness while the great mass of Christians who have "only" faith must be satisfied with less than this, stands in direct contradiction to the meaning of the gospel, to the words of this text, and to experience.

iii. John 10:1, 9-10.

> Truly, truly I say to you, he who does not enter the sheepfold by the [*tës*=one] door, but climbs in by another way [*allachothen*=by another means], that man is a thief and a robber;... I am the [*hë*=single] door; if any one enters by me [emphasized] he will be saved,... the thief comes only... to destroy. I came that they may have life and have it abundantly.

There is only one door, there are not two. He who enters by this single door receives *abundant* life. Whoever suggests entering an abundant life by "another way" (*allachothen*) falls under unattractive light in this passage. Christ himself is "the way, the truth, and the life" (John 14:6). And we may say, in legitimate adaptation of John's teaching concerning Christ and the Father, that no one comes to the Holy Spirit except by Christ — indeed, Christ is not only the way to, he is the way of the Holy Spirit.

The Pentecostal quest for "more" through a second "way" should be transformed into evangelical thanksgiving for the "all" of the one way — the way who is Christ. Evangelical thanks and not Pentecostal aspiration is the only way to legitimate "more," for it alone honors the "all" given sufficiently to faith in Christ.

> He who believes is filled with God's work ... and no striving adds a "more" to this fulfillment (Lohmeyer).[42]

> God does not want to see us put our trust in anything else or commit our hearts to anything other than Christ in his Word, be it ever so holy and full of the Spirit (Luther).[43]

3. THE WATER OF BAPTISM

a. *The New Testament Doctrine (I Cor. 6:11; [12:13][44]; John 3:5-8; Tit. 3:4-8; cf. Rom. 6:1-11; Col. 2:11-23).* i. The preached and believed Word "becomes flesh" in the water of baptism. We observed in Acts that faith was incarnational, that is, that it never remained a soul-affair but

---

42 *Kol.*[11], p. 132.

43 Cited in "Der heilige Geist und das christliche Leben," in Karl Barth and Heinrich Barth, *Zur Lehre vom heiligen Geist* ("Zwischen den Zeiten," Beiheft Nr. 1; München: Kaiser, 1930), p. 68.

44 The important passage, I Cor. 12:13, is treated in the special Corinthian context, below, pp. 291-94.

became historical in the action of baptism in water. The fundamental pledge of allegiance according to the New Testament — God's pledge and the believer's — is laid down in baptism. Baptism is even more than the seal of the believer's faith — though it is that — it is the seal of the Spirit's coming.

The connection of water with the gift of the Holy Spirit is widely attested in the New Testament. The connection was sanctified and, in a significant sense, initiated by Jesus' own baptism (Mark 1:10 par.). After the church's first sermon at Pentecost the Holy Spirit was offered with the water of baptism (Acts 2:38). As we have observed, it was the careful plan of the Book of Acts to teach the divine will for the most intimate connection of baptism with the gift of the Spirit. This divine connection is taught the church most lucidly in the Acts' passage where a temporary suspension of the connection was allowed and recorded, a suspension which was then immediately and dramatically closed — at Acts 8. In each of the subsequent major Spirit texts in Acts — Acts 10-11 and 19:1-7 — the church is impressively taught that the gift of the Holy Spirit and the water of Christian baptism are co-ordinate.

ii. Consonant with the experience of Jesus and the earliest church as recorded in Acts, baptism and the Holy Spirit were understood in close relationship by the apostle Paul.

> But you were washed, you were sanctified, you were justified in the name of the Lord Jesus Christ and in the Spirit of our God (I Cor. 6:11).

The believer, according to the important I Corinthians 6:11 text, is washed clean of his past, sanctified into God's possession, and placed righteous before God — at once — "in the name of the Lord Jesus Christ and in the Spirit of our God." The name of Christ is pronounced and the Spirit of God is given not in imperfect or doubtful succession but, as the trebling of aorists in the text declares, in the one initiation act of baptism.

In baptism the believer is washed, sanctified, and justified by entering the new life of fellowship in the body of Christ in which, by definition, the Holy Spirit dwells (I Cor. 3:16; 6:19; cf. Rom. 8:9; Eph. 2:22).

> The gift of the Spirit in baptism stands in no contradiction to the gift of the Spirit in preaching. What is proclaimed to all in the Word is individually applied and received in baptism. Here the universality of the gospel becomes particular. Baptism is the place where the Spirit gives himself to the *individual* believer.

> Preaching and baptism stand together in a relationship somewhat analogous to engagement and marriage: the believer is truly engaged by the Holy Spirit through the message of faith and this engagement is then immediately and individually, sacramentally and publicly, ratified by baptism.

The whole chain of events from Christ's historical work to his baptismal work in our history — from the condition of the Spirit (Christ) through the means of the Spirit (faith) — may be described as "the coming of Christ," or "the coming of the Spirit," or as Paul in one interesting passage may be understood to be describing the whole, "the coming of faith" (Gal. 3:23-27):

> Now before faith came [n.b., faith comes], we were confined under the law, kept under restraint until faith should be revealed. So that the law was our custodian until Christ came [= the condition of the Spirit] that we might be justified by faith. But now that faith has come [= the means of the Spirit as the message of faith], we are no longer under a custodian; for in Christ Jesus you are all sons of God, through faith [= the means of the Spirit as the hearing of faith]. For as many of you as were baptized into Christ [= the means of the Spirit as baptism] have put on Christ.

Paul here is not describing a series of three or four experiences undergone by the Galatians in irregular order. God is not given in parcels — for example, first in Christ and justification, later in his Spirit and sanctification — but justification, sanctification, the Spirit are given at once and together in their single divine place — Jesus Christ (cf. I Cor. 1:30; 6:11). The whole is sealed and solemnly effected by baptism evidencing the Spirit and ushering the believer into the fellowship of the Spirit in Christ's body, the church.[45]

iii. The fourth evangelist presents the one New Testament initiation doctrine in all desirable clarity in his record of Jesus' conversation with Nicodemus.

> Jesus answered, "Truly, truly, I say to you, unless one is born of water and the Spirit [ean më tis gennëthë ex hudatos kai pneumatos], he cannot enter the kingdom of God" (John 3:5).

This may be the classic description of initiation in the New Testament — it is certainly John's major description.

Water and the gift of the Spirit cannot be more closely connected than they are in John 3:5: "of water and the Spirit." John does not place a second "of" (ex) before "Spirit" as he would if he were describing two different events. The single ex describes the single occasion.[46] This singularity is then completely established by the aorist

---

45 To sphragis as the seal of the Spirit in baptism cf. especially Lampe, Seal, passim; Schnackenburg, Heilsgeschehen, p. 81; Heitmüller, Im Namen Jesu, pp. 312-13, 333 n. 2a; and the Ephesians commentaries of Schlier and J. A. Robinson.

46 Lampe, Seal, p. 60; K. F. Nösgen, Der Heilige Geist: Sein Wesen und die Art seines Wirkens (2 vols.; Berlin: Trowitzsch und Sohn, 1905), I, 247, n. 32; the Baptist Beasley-Murray, Baptism in the New Testament, p. 30 — and the "water" is baptism, ibid., p. 228. Bultmann admits that the words "of water" "connect new birth with the sacrament of baptism," but he denies the words' authenticity and ascribes them to a church editor. John14, p. 98 n. 2. However, Bultmann's suspicion is without support in the text. See the helpful discussion in Raymond E. Brown, The Gospel according to John ("Anchor Bible"; Garden

subjunctive passive *gennëthë* which means literally *"once born"* of water and Spirit.

These facts taken together should caution against any tendency to find a reference in John 3:5 to two baptisms or births (after natural birth), namely, "water-baptism" and a later "Spirit-baptism," or a prior "regeneration" of justification and a later "Spirit-baptism" of sanctification. According to John's Gospel there *are* two births: the natural and the spiritual (3:6); there is not, however, a natural birth followed by a semi-spiritual birth, followed finally by a fully spiritual birth. A man must be "born again" (3:3) but not "again and again."

Spiritually a man is born only once and that "of water and the Spirit." That is why baptism is the baptism of the Holy Spirit. Christian baptism is *one* (the single "of"), really a baptism ("of water"), and at the same time really spiritual ("and the Spirit").

The accent in the Johannine passage lies clearly on the Spirit. A man's rebirth is not a perfunctory, unspiritual affair according to John 3. It is a real rebirth by the Holy Spirit. As always, however, any attempt to condition the Spirit's coming or going is forbidden (3:8). The descent of the Spirit in baptism remains a sovereign mystery and a wonder of grace. The only connection made for the Holy Spirit in this passage is with water. But *how* he relates himself to this water (coming immediately before, during, after?), or how or why he comes at all, is forbidden a too curious enquiry. Just as "the wind (*to pneuma*) blows where it wills, and you hear the sound of it, but you do not know whence (*pothen*) it comes or where (*pou*) it goes; so is everyone (*pas!*) who is born of the Spirit" (3:8). This is as clear a warning as the New Testament affords against prescribing conditions (*pothen*) or evidences (*pou*) for the Spirit apart from his sovereign coming in Christ Jesus in baptism. Neither in the water *per se* as a sacralized component (Tertullian), nor in the hands or privileges of the baptizing church (some Roman Catholicism), nor in the individual's remarkable experience (Pentecostalism), or obedience (some Protestant Christianity), should the decisive source or evidence of the Spirit's coming in baptism be sought. It is only important for us to know that the Spirit comes from *above* and in some connection with the water of baptism, but *how, whence, where, why,* apart from *faith* (John 3:9-21 interprets John 3:3-8) is placed beyond our ken.

John 3:5-8 teaches the unity, sovereignty, and grace of the baptism in the Holy Spirit as impressively as any passage in the New Testament.

iv. Finally, a kind of summary of New Testament doctrine of "the baptism with the Holy Spirit" can be discovered in Titus 3:4-8:

City, N.Y.: Doubleday, 1966), pp. 141-44; also C. K. Barrett, *The Gospel according to St. John: An Introduction with Commentary and Notes on the Greek Text* (London: S.P.C.K., 1958), *ad loc.*

> But when the goodness and loving kindness of God our Savior appeared, he saved us, not because of deeds done by us in righteousness, but in virtue of his own mercy [= the Spirit's condition, cf. Gal. 3:10-14], by the washing of regeneration and renewal in the Holy Spirit [dia loutrou paliggenesias kai anakainöseös pneumatos hagiou = the Holy Spirit as the means of initiation, cf. I Cor. 12:13a], which he poured out upon us richly [hou execheen eph hëmas plousiös = the Holy Spirit as the gift of initiation, cf. I Cor. 12:13b] through Jesus Christ our Savior, so that we might be justified by his grace and become heirs in hope of eternal life.

The whole saving event — from advent to end — is seen as one great deed. Salvation occurs because of the appearance of God the Savior's kindness and is applied terminally by the baptismal washing-of-regeneration-and-renewal in the Holy Spirit.

Significantly, the ruling preposition *dia* ("by") is placed only before "the washing of regeneration," which is immediately connected with "renewal in the Holy Spirit" indicating, as had John 3:5 so remarkably, that baptism should not be severed from the Spirit, nor regeneration from renewal: the single preposition in the single phrase again seals the single occasion.[47]

And once again (cf. I Cor. 12:13) the Holy Spirit is contemplated not only as the acting agent or means of spiritual initiation, but as the received gift of the same — and this not "partially" or poorly, but *ex expressis verbi,* "richly" (3:6).

v. We may make three definite declarations on the basis of the Spirit-baptismal texts of the New Testament as they find their summary in the Titus passage.

1. When the Holy Spirit works as the "agent" of salvation he does not leave to reappear in fulness and in person at a worthier or cleaner moment later in the believer's life — as though the believer could ever be worthier or cleaner than when "washed" by God; but the Spirit is also given as the gift of salvation (Tit. 3:6; cf. Acts 2 *passim;* I Cor. 12:13).

2. When the Spirit works rebirth and gives himself he does not do so partially, in a measure, or stingily — i.e., "in a sense" — as though he were given out of God's reluctance instead of God's grace; but he is, as it were, "drunk in" (I Cor. 12:13b), "poured out," "richly" (Tit. 3:6; cf. Rom. 5:5).

3. Then as both the agent *and* the gift, the rich gift, of spiritual ini-

---

47 The single *verb* — "washing" — used with the twin terms "regeneration" and "renewal" also indicates the single event. "*Loutron* is ... the comprehensive term including *both* of the following genitives." Oepke, art. *louö, TWNT,* IV, 306,37-38. Schnackenburg stresses the oneness of this saving deed by referring to the major verb of the entire sentence: "saved." *Heilsgeschehen,* p. 9. For the similarity between Tit. 3:5 and John 3:5 see Barrett, *John,* p. 53. See also the relevant comment on Tit. 3:5 in Dibelius-Conzelmann, *Die Pastoralbriefe* ("HNT," 13; 3d ed.; Tübingen: Mohr, 1955), p. 113.

tiation, the Holy Spirit is not understood in the New Testament as (a) an independent agent, (b) a separate gift, or (c) as privately wealthy. Rather: (a) as agent the Spirit baptizes into *Christ,* and it is by virtue of being baptized into Christ that the believer may derivatively be said to be baptized into the Spirit, for Christ and the Spirit are not divided; (b) as gift, in corollary, the Spirit in the New Testament comes in and through the name Christ Jesus and never in or through a discrete experience with himself as a separate gift which initiation into Christ was unable to convey, as though the Spirit were not fully given to Christ and in and through Christ to us; (c) for as the rich gift of salvation in Christ, the Spirit's wealth consists in his pointing not to a better, higher, or richer experience in himself, but to an accomplished justification in Christ (Tit. 3:6-7).

Therefore, God's one saving work accomplished in Christ at the cross and in the resurrection: *enabled* the gift of the Spirit in righteousness, which is then *communicated* in the message of faith, *received* by the hearing of faith, and *sealed* in baptism where the believer is planted with Christ in his saving work. According to the familiar words of Ephesians 4:4-5 there is only "one Lord" and "one faith" and consequently there is also only "one baptism" by which the one Lord is received, the one faith in him sealed, his "one body" entered, and his "one Spirit" given.

The "once" and "oneness" of God's saving application is removed from vagary, subjectivity, and doubt by God's gracious gift of visible, tangible, earthy baptism. Rather than making the visible occasion of the Spirit's reception an ecstatic or esoteric event to which only an emotionally equipped elite could attain, or an act requiring utmost effort and which for different persons would occur at different times and in different ways with more or less difficulty and for some persons perhaps not at all — all of which apply to the highly strenuous and unnatural Pentecostal doctrine of tongues — it was the grace of God that his gift should be connected so mundanely in an act administered so simply in the common, ordinary medium of water. Here too, in the final step in God's coming to men, his gift is given to us "outside ourselves" in order that it might reach inside ourselves, but especially "in order that the promise may rest on grace and be guaranteed to all" (Rom. 4:16). Baptism is something everyone can do — or better — receive.

   b. *The Consequences for the Pentecostal Doctrine of Two Baptisms.* It is, as we have seen, the momentum of Pentecostal doctrine inevitably to transform New Testament terms of grace into Pentecostal terms of work. This is most apparent in the Pentecostal understanding of faith examined above. But it can also be illustrated in the Pentecostal understanding of baptism.

Baptism, according to majority Pentecostal teaching, is primarily a place where *believers* act. Donald Gee, we recall, defines baptism as a principle which "applies to all-round obedience in everything. It means *actions* that witness before all that you have accepted the position of discipleship" (emphasis his). The "believer's-actions" understanding of baptism is not simply a part, it is, as far as we have been able to determine, the main meaning of baptism in Pentecostalism. What God wishes to give to believers freely, Pentecostalism wishes instead to give to God sacrificially — even in baptism.

i. The Consequences of the New Testament Pneumobaptistic Texts.[48] The first consequence of the New Testament's one baptism for Pentecostalism's two must be the dismantling of the isolated second spiritual baptism and its return to its original body — water. New Testament spiritual baptism was not a ghost. A Spirit-less baptism in water or a water-less baptism in the Spirit are ordinary impossibilities (cf. Acts 8:15-16 and 19:1-7 for exactly these convictions, respectively). The one baptism into Christ must be reinvested with all the power rightly accruing to Christ. The name of Christ must no longer be identified with power-less life, with Spirit-less faith, with regeneration which is not also renewal, with new birth which is not also new energy. That all of these latter predicates are denied to the baptism into Christ and are reserved in Pentecostalism for what is understood as a second baptism in the Spirit should no longer be able to be asserted in the presence of the New Testament doctrine.

When duPlessis, for example, writing in the *Religion in Geschichte und Gegenwart,* affirms, as we have seen, that in Pentecostalism "every new convert is encouraged 'to receive the Holy Spirit' and so to become a witness of Jesus Christ," he does not seem to see that a "new convert" is, by definition, a person who *has* received the Holy Spirit. When the Assemblies of God formulated their doctrine of baptism in the Holy Spirit to read, "All believers are entitled to and should ardently expect and earnestly seek the promise of the Father," they not only indicate their misunderstanding of what the New Testament calls a "promise" by making it conditioned on human ardor and earnest, but they are able to contemplate "believers" ("all"!) who have not yet received the Spirit. When the Pentecostal definition above therefore concludes, "this wonderful experience [of the baptism in the Holy Spirit] is distinct from and subsequent to the experience of the new birth," we must attribute this conviction to an insufficient acquaintance with the content with which the New Testament invests its one baptism.

Therefore, what Pentecostals take away from baptism they put back into conditions: cleansing, removal of sin, sanctification, and so forth.

---

[48] In a further section, below, we treat the texts where the Spirit is not expressly mentioned but which are so important to the New Testament's doctrine of baptism that in any systematic survey they could not be omitted — Rom. 6 and Col. 2.

What God gives *once-and-for-all* in Christian baptism, freely, by joining believers to Christ in his death to sin and resurrection to life, Pentecostalism subdivides into at least two separable events and makes them the candidate's costly responsibilities.

Pentecostalism relocates what in the New Testament happens in one act in baptism — death to sin and power for life — within a series of acts: first, identification with Christ (conversion), then (water) baptism, followed by the fulfilling of the conditions for the baptism in the Spirit, and thus finally the full identification with the Spirit through the Spirit-baptism with tongues. All along the line, and increasingly, the task of fulfillment lies with the believer.

New Testament initiation is at once simpler and more gracious. The whole is applied to the believer in baptism "in the name of the Lord Jesus Christ and in the Spirit of our God" (I Cor. 6:11). The burden of sin is carried away and the condition of righteousness is fulfilled by Christ's historical work; the gift of this fulfillment is conveyed to the believer in the gospel message of faith in Christ; the hearing of faith is enabled by this message; baptism is given; the believer is home.[49]

ii. The Consequences of the Romans Six Doctrine of Baptism. According to Romans 6 the Christian life has its foundation in the one baptism into Christ's death, burial, and resurrection. This baptism occurs once-and-for-all (*ephapax*, 6:10) and is not repeated. Therefore, the Christian need not undergo two deaths through two baptisms before he can have spiritual life. His baptism in water into Christ *is* his baptism in the Holy Spirit and is as fully spiritual as the Christ with whom he has been baptized.

All Christian exhortation for spiritual living is meant to flow out of this one full baptism and to be supported by it and be built upon it (Rom. 6-8). Christian ethical exhortation is not intended to lead the believer *to* this full baptism. Christian ethic and spirituality is based *upon* the already given Christian baptism. In the New Testament spiritual baptism is the base, it is not the goal of Christian effort.[50]

iii. The Consequences of Colossians' Doctrine of Baptism. The result of the believer's sufficient identification with Christ in baptism is deliverance not only from sin (Rom. 6:1-11) and law (Rom. 7:1-6) but also from the petty scrupulosity which attempts to remove its own sin, or to make sin what God does not. This "deliverance from scrupulosity" is taught most clearly in Colossians' doctrine of baptism.

---

[49] It is only a little embarrassing to Pentecostalism, as we have seen, that its two baptisms are not found in the Epistles or Gospels. Cf. pp. 61, 68-69, above.

[50] For an understanding of the important Rom. 6 passage see, in addition to the commentaries, the studies by Günther Bornkamm in *Das Ende des Gesetzes: Paulusstudien* ("BEvTh," 16: München, Kaiser, 1952), pp. 34-50; Schnackenburg, *Heilsgeschehen, passim;* and Johannes Schneider, art. *homoiōma, TWNT,* V, 191-95.

(a) To Pentecostalism's Doctrine of Symbolic Baptism. Having in baptism been "made alive together with [Christ]" (Col. 2:13), believers need no second or supplementary "making alive" or baptism. The Colossian desire for more was due at least in part to a failure to appreciate what had already been given to them when they became Christians at baptism.[51]

Paul's policy in discussing the Christians' source of life and power was not to look back to an *uncommon* experience appropriated only by some, nor to point ahead to a better, second experience which only the truly dedicated could obtain; rather, Paul looked back to the *common* experience of baptism received by all in the Colossian church, and thus he reminded the Colossians (and other Christians similarly in other letters) of all that this one baptism means and gives to all Christians. For Paul understood baptism not as a mere preliminary or symbol, but as the reception of the great *plērōma* of the Christian's career.

That Pentecostalism understands the "first" or "water" baptism to be only a symbol and not God's means for ministering the Holy Spirit, and hence that this symbolic baptism is seen primarily under the rubric of the believer's action rather than God's, may be observed again in the following remarks.

> Thus in water baptism, which is an action from our side, *we* seal God's trustworthiness, and in the Spirit-baptism, which is an action from God's side, *he* places the seal upon our sincerity, the sincerity which we have brought to him.

> Water baptism is the rite of entrance into the Christian church, and symbolizes spiritual life begun; ... Water baptism in itself has no saving power; people are baptized not in order to be saved but because they are saved. Therefore we cannot say that the rite is absolutely essential to salvation. But we may insist that it is essential to full obedience.

The difference between the Pentecostal understanding of baptism and the New Testament understanding is, in a word, that the former is seen as essentially the consecrated action of men while in the New Testament baptism is seen as essentially God's action for men. Baptism, according to the New Testament, is the place where God sacramentally, i.e., physically-individually, spiritually-really gives and applies what the spoken Word has creatively promised, the forgiveness of sins and the gift of the Holy Spirit (to speak with Luke), washing, justification, sanctification (to speak with Paul), new birth, regeneration, renewal (to speak with John and the Epistle to Titus).

Baptism is also the place of the believer's confession. But this "also"

---

51 However, it was just the appeal of another and higher blessing after baptism which characterized the doctrine of the Colossian teachers. With remarkably few adjustments one can take the reconstruction of the Colossian heresy and see Pentecostalism. Cf., e.g., Knox, *St. Paul and the Church of the Gentiles*, p. 154.

too easily becomes an "only" in Pentecostal development, and what is as serious, an "only" which is understood less as a grateful response to grace than as a work of obedience or sincerity with which God is impressed.

It is easy therefore to see why *this* baptism needs to be supplemented or filled — and really filled — for it receives nothing from God except an opportunity for the believer to show his dedication. A second baptism must finally give something divine, and this baptism is the Pentecostal baptism in the Holy Spirit with tongues. It is *this* physical-individual event which is the Pentecostal sacrament.

Where baptism is conceived as a symbol of the greater reality which occurs in the human heart, there the human heart assumes the place and center of interest and not the divine work. Baptism *is* a symbol of a work in the heart, but this is only one of its significations: it is first of all the *place* where God identifies the believer with Christ and his work, and this not merely symbolically but really. Even Baptist scholarship is coming to affirm that the interpretation of the New Testament baptismal texts requires what is called the "realistic" understanding of baptism rather than the merely symbolic.[52]

Furthermore, while the New Testament also knows how to take seriously the confession of the believer's faith at baptism (cf., e.g., Acts 22:16), we can find no place where the believer's action is emphasized, least of all celebrated as the theatre of the believer's admirable dedication which God then honors. It is precisely this tendency to glorify the believer's dedication which seems to us to vitiate any legitimacy which the Pentecostal "water baptism" might in itself seem to have. For grace is once again emptied of its content by the upstaging of devout human obedience.

A baptism evacuated of all spiritual content cries for a "greater," "higher," finally "spiritual" baptism. And thus, ironically, even in Pentecostalism the spiritual has to be evidenced by the physical and visible — speaking in tongues, the Pentecostal sacrament — as the locus of the Spirit's coming and of the believer's assurance of his coming.

However, the New Testament's much simpler baptism gives (and not simply offers) everything which God in Christ has done for men. This "everything" must be inviolably maintained. The critical point at which God's salvation enters the individual's life, according to the New

---

[52] For the newer Baptist understanding see especially Beasley-Murray, *Baptism in the New Testament*, pp. 126-46, 263, 276-77; R. E. O. White, *The Biblical Doctrine of Initiation*, pp. 217, 273, 280; Johannes Schneider, *Die Taufe im Neuen Testament* (Stuttgart: W. Kohlhammer, 1951), pp. 71-72. The realistic-sacramental interpretation of Paul's baptismal texts is the interpretation most widely represented in contemporary New Testament scholarship. See particularly the studies of Romans 6.

Testament at least, is where faith in the gospel becomes public in baptism into Christ. "There is no gift or power which the apostolic documents do not ascribe to baptism" (Schlatter).[53]

The rediscovery of the meaning of New Testament baptism is of the highest importance if aberrations offering "more" are to be resisted and if the church is to be itself. For Pentecostalism is an illustration of the fact that where the biblical one-baptism is emptied of its content other substitutes and supplements — other baptisms — rush in to fill the vacuum. Where the one-baptism is not the sufficient seal of certainty, then other certainties, other evidences *must* be found, for the certainty of salvation is a major human concern. And the substitute certainties cannot avoid jeopardizing the sufficiency of the *solus Christus* with whom the believer is identified in baptism, and of the *sola fides* which baptism concretizes.

(b) To Pentecostalism's Baptismal Substitutes. With the significance of baptism impressed upon the memories of the Colossian believers, Paul proceeded to ward from the believers' lives the sundry substitutes being circulated in Colossae in the form of scrupulous spiritual regulations (2:16-23). These included conditions of abstinence, observance in diet and days (2:16), and particularly and more internally, the condition of self-abasement (*tapeinophrosunë;* "self-mortification," NEB). The goal of self-abasement was, interestingly, called "seeing" and "fulness." Specifically, the condition of self-abasement in Colossae "required of the individual," Lohmeyer comments pointedly, "that he 'empty himself' in order, by this attitude, to possess the 'filling' content."[54]

Self-abasement, or as the RSV sometimes favorably renders *tapeinophrosunë,* "lowliness," was not a trait to be despised *per se,* for Paul can later list it among other characteristics to be "put on" by the believer (3:12). It was apparently not its *nature* which Paul disliked but its *place* and *significance* as a prior condition of Christian fulness. The self-emptying of self-abasement could be urged as a disposition flowing from all that one had in Christ (3:12), but it could not be employed as a special condition for believers to fulfill if they wished to *have* Christian fulness (2:18-23).

53 *Die Theologie der Apostel* (2d ed.; Stuttgart: Calwer Vereinsbuchhandlung, 1922), p. 515.

54 *Kol.*[11], p. 124. Cf. Pentecostal "emptying-yielding," above, pp. 99-101. *Tapeinophrosunë,* writes Dibelius, was "not only a term for a feeling, but for a (somehow cultic) attitude." *An die Kolosser, Epheser, an Philemon erklärt,* ed. Heinrich Greeven ("HNT," 12; 3d rev. ed.; Tübingen: Mohr, 1953), p. 35. Cf. the semi-cultic Pentecostal tarrying meeting where emptying is brought to its final expressions, above, p. 101. For historical parallels see the Schwärmer in Holl, *Gesammelte Aufsätze,* I, 428, n. 5. For a psychological discussion see William James, *The Varieties of Religious Experience: A Study in Human Nature* ("The Gifford Lectures," Edinburgh, 1901-02; 2d ed.; London: Longmans, Green & Co., 1907), pp. 206-10.

Some Pentecostal conditions are not in themselves reprehensible. However, by making Christian graces into Christian conditions, virtues are transformed into laws. When a grace becomes a condition then it ceases in the Christian sense to be virtuous. Self-emptying is a condition for the filling of the Spirit in Pentecostalism; it is a responsible consequence in Paul.

It must also be granted that, like the Colossians, the Pentecostal promotion of rigor of devotion, self-abnegation, and denials of the body, self, and mind not infrequently appear to be very spiritual. Pentecostal expression is filled with remarks such as the following (note particularly the derogatory references to the *natural* and *human,* and the normative Pentecostal stipulations prior to the full reception of the Spirit):

> Oh, the thrill of being fully yielded to Him! My mind had always been very active. Its natural workings had caused me most of my trouble in my Christian experience.... Nothing hinders faith and the operation of the Spirit so much as the self-assertiveness of the human spirit, the wisdom, strength and self-sufficiency of the human mind. This must be crucified, and here is where the fight comes in. We must become utterly undone, insufficient and helpless in our own consciousness, thoroughly humbled, before [n.b.] we can receive this possession of the Holy Spirit.... I never sought 'tongues'. My natural mind resisted the idea. This phenomena [sic] necessarily violates human reason. It means abandonment of this faculty for the time. And this is generally the last point to yield. The human mind is held in abeyance fully in this exercise. And this is 'foolishness', and a stone of stumbling, to the natural mind or reason.... We need not expect anyone who has not reached this depth of abandonment in their human spirit, this death to their own reason, to either accept or understand it. The natural reason must be yielded in this matter.... It is the underlying principle of the 'baptism'.... We must come 'naked' into this experience. All of self is gone (Bartleman, *How Pentecost Came to Los Angeles,* 2d ed., pp. 72-75).

From this lengthy but typical example we may observe again the antipathy to the human and the natural which is a hallmark of Pentecostal (and mystic) teaching — and of the Colossian teachers — in the promotion of "rigor of devotion and self-abasement and severity to the body." The goal of both the ancient and modern movements is the same: the unmixed participation in the spiritual; and the way is the same: the submersion of all that is natural and human — from will to body (*ethelothrëskia, apheidia sömatos,* 2:23). It is felt as axiomatic that wherever the human is sublimated the spiritual is elevated.[55]

---

[55] This "anti-human" strain has many sources besides mysticism of all varieties (cf. Holl, *Gesammelte Aufsätze,* I, 434-35). But in the United States what is called Dispensationalism, as inherited from Darby, has been a major contributor. See Clarence B. Bass, *Backgrounds to Dispensationalism: Its Historical Genesis and Ecclesiastical Implications* (Grand Rapids, Mich.: Eerdmans, 1960), *passim.* Anthony A. Hoekema believes that the major contribution of Pentecostalism to the contemporary church has been not speaking in tongues as such "but the state

However, though the spiritual disciplines and devotions in Colossae were of the most marvelous sort, their end was simply the glorification of those who made them — they satisfied not God but the flesh (2:18; 2:23?). Though "lowliness" was the required means to the end of the divine "fulness," the real end, and cause of this "way," according to Paul, was not the spirit which is divine but that which is "puffed up" (*phusioun,* 2:18).

There is a place for Christian discipline, devotion, and lowliness (3:1-12) but it is not before and for, it is after and because of the fulness which is once-for-all received in Christ by faith at baptism. Christian discipline never consists in the fulfilling of conditions for a "more" or for a fulness not received in Christ; rather it consists, in Paul's simpler language, in living by faith in Christ, abounding in thanksgiving (2:6-7), walking in the Spirit (Gal. 5; Rom. 8), and keeping the commandments of God (I Cor. 7:19) — all in gratitude for the past redemption, loyalty to the present Redeemer-Lord, and anticipation of the coming judgment.

Least of all does Christian devotion consist in the painfully petty minutiae of self-regulation and self-observation, the scrupulosity of the microscopic; it consists in the larger graces of Christian compassion and kindness toward others flowing gratefully out of the fulness in Christ toward us (3:12-17).

There is definitely a place for serious, attentive, and even rigorous spiritual warfare in believers' lives (3:5-11; cf. the present tense verbs in I Cor. 9:26-27; Rom. 8:13), but it is not the oppressive warfare *for* God or his power and fulness, it is the empowering warfare *in* and *from* his grace, power, and fulness (3:5 "therefore"!), all of which are given in Christian baptism (2:11-15; 3:9-11).

C. THE EVIDENCE OF THE SPIRIT: CHRISTIAN FAITH

1. THE NEW TESTAMENT DOCTRINE (GAL. 4:6-7; 5:5-6, 22-23; ROM. 5:5; 8:11-25; I COR. 2:12; II COR. 1:22; 5:5; I JOHN 3: 24; 4:1-3, 13-16; EPH. 1:13-14; 4:30; JOHN 14:16-17, 26; 15:26; 16:7-15)

a. *Introductory: Faith, Hope, and Love.* In drafting the New Testament evidence of the Holy Spirit one is obliged to outline nothing less than the New Testament's nearly entire doctrine of the Holy Spirit. For the evidence of the Holy Spirit is as wide· as his work. The center of his work is found, as we have already seen and shall see now again,

---

of mind of which it is said to be the evidence, or the spiritual disciplines which have preceded it." *What about Tongue-Speaking?* (Grand Rapids, Mich.: Eerdmans, 1966), p. 135. We would rather say that the major *problem* of Pentecostalism is not its speaking in tongues as such but the state of mind sought or the spiritual disciplines urged in order to achieve it.

in faith, which is another way of saying that it is found in Christ. From this center the Holy Spirit illumines the one grand saving work of God as this work sweeps in its wholeness from God's pre-creation counsel to God's post-historical or end-historical consummation.

The Holy Spirit, we may say then in preliminary summary, evidences a comprehensive ministry of faith, hope, and love. And hope and love are understood not as alternatives to, supplements of, or improvements on faith, but as the spiritual fruit of faith itself. This basic introductory fact is indicated in Paul's thematic reminder in Galatians (5:5-6):

> For through the Spirit, *by faith*, we wait for *the hope* of righteousness. For in Christ Jesus neither circumcision nor uncircumcision is of any avail, but *faith* working through *love*.

The Spirit "by faith" (*sola!*) works the entire Christian life of hope and love and so evidences himself. The Spirit gives first and fundamentally the assurance of faith. Then, by this assurance the Spirit works the purpose of hope and the patience of love. These are the major evidences of the Spirit in the life of believers. Therefore we shall take up each one — faith, hope, and love — in turn (b-d, below). The evidence of the Spirit is most comprehensively summarized as the work of Christocentricity, the work, that is, of bringing to effective remembrance — to oneself and to others — the person and the meaning of Christ (e, below). Christ is himself the classic evidence of the Spirit.

b. *Faith to Believe (The Assurance of Faith).* i. Galatians 4:6-7; Romans 8:15-17a. When Paul in his two fundamental theological arguments in Galatians and Romans has developed the redemptive work of Christ he reaches a certain conclusion in his description in remarkably similar formulations at remarkably similar junctures in the argument: the Spirit's essential — perhaps even his primary role — is to give men faith in the Father.

> And because you are sons, God has sent *the Spirit of his Son* into our hearts, crying, "*Abba! Father!*" So through God you are no longer a slave but a son, and if a son then an heir (Gal. 4:6-7).
>
> For you did not receive the spirit of slavery to fall back into fear, but you have received *the spirit of sonship*. When we cry, "*Abba! Father!*" it is the Spirit himself bearing witness with our spirit that we are children of God, and if children, then heirs (Rom. 8:15-17a).

For Paul, the ability to cry "Father!" was the work and therefore the evidence of the Spirit of the Son. The evidence of the Spirit is first of all Christian faith in God the Father or — Christian prayer.

The Spirit in these parallel texts is deliberately called "the Spirit of (the) Son(ship)," not only because the Spirit belongs to the Son and is given in him, but because it is the Spirit's work to assure believers that they are, through the Son, truly sons of God. The gift of the Spirit is first of all the subjective assurance of the gift of adoption or justification. The "objective" justification and the "subjective" gift of the Spirit cannot be separated for one is acceptance with God and the other is knowledge of this acceptance. And what God has joined together no man should put asunder. The "objective" justification never remains *merely* objective but is always accompanied mediately in the Word by its "subjective" revelation, and this is the first work of the Spirit — this *is* the Spirit. His evidence is Christian assurance.

It is the fulness of grace and the beauty and wholeness of the gospel that the Father not only sends his Son for men's salvation but as an integral part of this mission he sends *the Spirit* of his Son "downward" in the Christian gospel (*akoë*) and then "upward" in Christian prayer *(abba)* that men might both *have* and *know* of having this salvation. Here, in the prayer "dear Father," God's work of salvation reaches full circle. As God fulfills in Christ the *conditions* for the reception of his gift, and as he *communicates* this gift through the preaching of Christ and baptism in his name, so finally, and through the same gospel, he enables even the *response* of prayer Godward. From heaven through history into the heart and back to heaven again the entire circuit is God's (cf. Rom. 11:36: "from . . . , through . . . and *to* him are all things"). And the Spirit who comes enabling Christian prayer is not an influence or principle alien to the Father and the Son but in Paul's understanding he is God's own Spirit, or in Paul's exact, even trinitarian expression he is "the Spirit of his Son." The work of salvation is the work of the triune God, Father, Son, and Holy Spirit. So that even in the *closing* of the circle of salvation — in the prayer "dear Father"— the Spirit of God's Son is the giver and men are not burdened with themselves or their works.[56]

ii. Romans 5:5. What this gracious circle means finds a commentary in a parallel passage (Rom. 5:5): "God's love has been poured into our hearts through the Holy Spirit which has been given to us."

First, the fact that the Spirit is a divine bestowment and not a human procurement is underscored by the description of "the Holy Spirit which has been *given* to us." And the "given" is in the aorist indicating that God gives his Spirit decisively once — with a man's becoming a Christian. The Spirit is the gift of assurance.

Next, the work of the once-received Spirit is the *continual* distribution, pouring into, or shedding abroad of God's love in Christians'

---

56 Hendrikus Berkhof has written recently and well of the inner relations of Father, Son, and Holy Spirit in *The Doctrine of the Holy Spirit*, "The Annie Kinkead Warfield Lectures," 1963-64; Richmond, Va.: John Knox Press, 1964. Berkhof suggests that the biblical expressions "God is Spirit," and "the Lord is the Spirit" mean that "God is a moving God. . . . He seeks us in the Son; he reaches us in the Spirit; he brings us by the Spirit to the Son and in him to the Father." *Ibid.*, pp. 120-21. Rightly understood, the doctrine of the trinity is the doctrine of grace.

hearts. Paul describes *this* work, grammatically, as a *perfect* one *(ekkechutai en)* meaning that the Spirit's presence once decisively introduced in the past now remains and that the work he once-for-all introduced he now constantly continues.[57]

The *gift* of the Spirit as the subjective communicator of God's love is, according to Romans 5:5, once for all (aorist); the *work* of the Spirit as the disseminator of God's love is permanent (perfect) because he continues to distribute in believers' hearts the love which he once-and-for-all introduced (for gift and work of the Spirit, respectively, cf. Gal. 3:2, 5). Any doctrine which would suggest that the Spirit only *brings* God's love and then leaves until believers are obedient and empty enough to deserve the Spirit himself and his indwelling would cut believers from the source by which they are assured that they are loved by God at all and are even Christians.

iii. I Corinthians 2:12. In the three Galatians-Romans texts discussed above the essence as well as the evidence of the ministry of the received Spirit may be said to have been the unlocking of believers' hearts to the knowledge of the love of God. In the following Corinthian text the same truth is apparent:

> Now we have received not the spirit of the world, but the Spirit which is from God, that we might *understand the gifts bestowed* on us by God (I Cor. 2:12).

Paul addresses every Christian in Corinth (and beyond) inclusively as having received the Spirit of God ("we"). The guarantee of the sufficiency of this divine endowment to all Christians inclusively is the doubly stressed source: "from God, . . . by God."

Of most importance for our considerations, men are given the Spirit by God in order that they might *understand (eidömen)* the things graciously given them by God *(ta charisthenta)*. With *charisthenta* Paul employs his favorite root, *charis*, grace-free.[58] The purpose of the Spirit is to give understanding of grace. What God gives he gives *charis, gratis,* freely. And with his free gifts, as a most important part of them, he gives his Spirit so that men might understand and be assured of what they have been given. God's gift of his Spirit in and with the gifts of grace is to enable believers to understand what these gifts are and mean.

Interestingly, the Spirit's ministry is described here not as an un-

---

[57] Ingo Hermann correctly comments to Rom. 5:5: "It reads [poured] *en* [in], not *eis* [into]; this means that the love of God is seen as already indwelling our hearts; a lasting abiding, a perfect filling is meant." *Kyrios und Pneuma: Studien zur Christologie der paulinischen Hauptbriefe* ("Studien zum alten und neuen Testament," 2; München: Kösel Verlag, 1961), p. 112 n. 51.

[58] To this root's significance as it finds expression particularly in Paul's word *charisma*, see Ernst Käsemann, *Essays on New Testament Themes* ("Studies in Biblical Theology"; London: SCM Press, 1964), p. 64 n. 1.

veiling of future or exotic things, but of things which have already *been* graciously bestowed. Nor is the Spirit's ministry understood as an introduction to himself. Rather, we discover again that the Spirit's ministry is directed, as it were, away from himself and the numinous and toward grace and history. Grace, not the Spirit, is the focus of the Spirit's evidence.[59]

Through the gift of the Spirit the Christian not only *has* the gifts of grace, he is enabled to have some discernment of what these gifts are and mean. The Holy Spirit, in summary, is God's way for the Christian to understand God's work. "Pneuma ist also die christologische Kategorie der Realisation" (Ingo Hermann, *Kyrios und Pneuma,* p. 139).

iv. II Corinthians 1:22; 5:5; I John 3:24; 4:13. Paul also called the Holy Spirit the "guarantee": "He has put his seal upon us and given us his Spirit in our hearts as a guarantee" (II Cor. 1:22; cf. 5:5: "... God, who has given us the Spirit as a guarantee"). When God gives his great salvation, according to Paul's understanding, he not only *gives* it, he gives with it his *guarantee* that he has given it, and this is the Holy Spirit. John understood the Spirit in a similar way: "And by this we *know* that he abides in us, by the Spirit which he has given us" (I John 3:24; cf. 4:13: "By this we *know* that we abide in him and he in us, because he has given us of his own Spirit"). The knowledge or assurance that God is with us is indissolubly intertwined with his gift of the Spirit to us.

> Interestingly, in all four of the Pauline-Johannine texts cited above (cf. also Rom. 5:5) the Spirit is described as "given"— three times in the aorist, once in the perfect tense. The fact that he is always "given" heightens the "gift" character of the Spirit, who is never earned (Acts 8:20). The fact that his given-ness is aorist and perfect underlines again the decisive and unimprovable character of God's gift.

v. I John 4:1-3. Finally, there is a test or evidence by which the church may be assured that the witness of the Spirit it perceives is the witness of the Spirit of *God*:

> Beloved, do not believe every spirit, but test the spirits to see whether they are of God; for many false prophets have gone out into the world. By this you know the Spirit of *God*: every spirit which confesses that Jesus Christ has come in the *flesh* is of God, and every spirit which does not confess [variant reading: "looses"] Jesus is not of God. This is the spirit of antichrist, of which you heard that it was coming, and now it is in the world already (I John 4:1-3).

The evidence of the Spirit is not mystic or ecstatic, it is clear testimony to *the fleshly Jesus,* the incarnate Christ. This confession is

---

[59] Cf. Volz to the Holy Spirit in the Old Testament: "The *Ruah* [Spirit] ... is the *principle of interpretation* [*Erklärungsprinzip*], it is the *causality* of these phenomena, not the purpose." *Geist Gottes,* p. 56.

the first unambiguous public evidence of the Spirit's deity and presence (cf. I Cor. 12:1-3 and its exposition below, pp. 286-88).[60]

In all the Pauline-Johannine texts concerning the evidence of the Holy Spirit reviewed to this point it is interesting to observe that the Spirit's testimony is never to himself, nor to any unusual work which he does in order to point to himself specifically; rather, the Spirit is evidenced *indirectly,* through the ability to pray "dear Father," or through the confession of Jesus — as divine (I Cor. 12:3) and human (I John 4:3).[61]

It was the gnostic threat that Jesus Christ would be understood docetically, as not really human, as a transcendent miracle-worker, and no longer as the crucified, suffering Son of man who had come in the flesh, in the earthly, human Jesus. Significantly, gnosticism's danger lay in the direction not of stressing Jesus' humanity too greatly, but of stressing his deity at the expense of his real humanity.[62]

The Holy Spirit is not dependably evidenced in the outwardly extraordinary or superhuman — precisely these features were characteristic of the gnostic testimony. The Spirit is dependably evidenced in faithful confession of the Lord Jesus Christ's coming into the ordinary, the natural, and the human, i.e., in the flesh. Other spirits are characterized, particularly, by their "spiritual Christ"; but it is in the confession of the presence of the Christ in the earthly Jesus that John recognizes the Spirit of God.

vi. Summary. The gift of the Spirit of God enables believers to know, to be assured of, to pray to, to understand, to confess, and to discern the true love of God the Father in the grace of Jesus Christ his Son. We would not be mistaken in assuming, on the basis of the so far accumulated testimony of the New Testament to the evidence of the Holy Spirit, that wherever "the grace of the Lord Jesus Christ

---

[60] Ecstasy was a common phenomenon in the first-century mystery religions and could not therefore be made the indubitable Christian evidence. Cf. Büchsel, *Geist Gottes,* p. 103. Common to the mystery religions and our subject is the making of ecstasy into the high point of the spiritual experience. Of interest also is the similarity between Pentecostalism and the mysteries in the sequence: active obedience (preparation), passive obedience (emptying-yielding), followed by the audio-visual evidence (glossolalic ecstasy). Cf. Bultmann, *Das Urchristentum im Rahmen der antiken Religionen* (2d ed.; Zürich: Artemis-Verlag, 1954), p. 171; Schweizer, art. *pneuma, TWNT,* VI, 343 for the mantic parallel; finally, R. Reitzenstein, *Die Hellenistischen Mysterienreligionen nach ihren Grundgedanken und Wirkungen* (3d rev. ed.; Leipzig: Verlag von B. G. Teubner, 1927), p. 32.

[61] This is a slight corrective to Hermann's otherwise discerning remark that "God not only gives the Spirit *in fact,* but he bestows also the consciousness of this fact." *Kyrios und Pneuma,* p. 49 n. 49. It is nowhere said, to our knowledge, that God gives a consciousness of the gift of the Spirit — not even in Gal. 4:6; rather, God gives a consciousness of sonship in Jesus Christ, and one may know from this that he has the Spirit. Consciousness of Christ *is* the gift of the Spirit.

[62] See Schweizer to this situation in art. *sarx, TWNT,* VII, 141.

and the love of God" are central, *there* is "the fellowship of the Holy Spirit" (II Cor. 13:14).

c. *Faith to Hope (The Expectation of Faith).* The Spirit ministers faith not only in a present Father through the Son and to an aorist-perfect salvation given assuredly in him, but the Spirit exercises also a ministry (again *fide*) of hope. "For through the Spirit, by faith, we wait for the hope of righteousness" (Gal. 5:5). The Spirit, in other words, directs believers not only to the redeeming past and the living present, but also to the exciting future.

There is a peril in the occupation with the subject of spiritual fulness, as in the Colossian context for example, that sight will be lost of the true "not yet" of the Christian hope and of the authentic *un-fulness* of the Christian life in pilgrimage. Those who are in Christ not only *have* righteousness, fulness, life, and redemption, but they also wait, groan, press toward, and seek righteousness, fulness, life, and redemption in him (cf. especially Phil. 3:9-14; see also Rom. 8:18-25; Col. 3:1-4; Eph. 1:14; 4:30). If spiritual fulness were radically and un-evangelically understood, hope would be dispensable and faith therefore would no longer be faith. But by the Spirit the Christian not only believes, he hopes.

Yet the Christian hope is not an unsure wishing. That it is not — that it is able to be strong and sure expectation — is the work of the Holy Spirit. For the Holy Spirit is, as we have seen, "the guarantee," or as we might now say, "the down payment," "the first fruits" of our "adoption," "redemption," and "inheritance" (Gal. 4:5-7; Rom. 8:15-17, 23; Eph. 1:5, 14; 4:30). The Christian hope is not an unsure wishing and "does not disappoint us" *because* "God's love has been poured into our hearts *through the Holy Spirit* which has been given to us" (Rom. 5:5). Therefore the Christian does not passively, stoically, or, at the other extreme, anxiously wait for the catastrophic end, but by the Spirit he eagerly expects and inwardly groans for the trans-forming end, the glorious revealing of the sons of God (Rom. 8:18-25).

The waiting of hope in the New Testament is not a waiting for the fulness of the Holy Spirit. The goal of New Testament waiting and hope is not the Spirit — the Spirit is the *means* (*dia*, Rom. 8:11; *en*, Eph. 4:30) and the guarantee, but not the end and goal (never *eis*) of the Christian's expectation and aspiration. According to the New Testament no Christian waits, beyond Christ, for a second experience of the Spirit imperfectly received in the beginning. The verb "wait" is never used in expectation of the Holy Spirit after Pentecost. Rather, the Christian waits *through, by,* or *in* the Spirit (*pneumati*, Gal. 5:5), by faith, for the one hope of the church in the inheritance of Christ. For it is only *because* (*hoti*) of God's already having given the aorist-perfect (= full) gift of his Spirit that the Christian hope has any substance or possibility (Rom. 5:5).

Finally, according to Paul, "anyone who does not have the Spirit of Christ does not belong to him" (Rom. 8:9b). There is no such thing as a Christian without the Spirit, or the Spirit "without" (i.e., not *in*dwelling) a Christian. Romans 8:9a: "the Spirit of God . . . dwells in you." = Romans 8:10a: "Christ in you."

A passage in Ephesians provides a fitting conclusion to the consideration of the Spirit's ministry of hope and offers, at the same time, a panorama of the whole spectrum of the Spirit's "way" from his christological *condition* through his kerygmatic *means* to his eschatological *end*:

> In him [Christ the condition] you also, who have heard the word of truth, the gospel of your salvation [= the message], and have believed in him [= faith], were sealed [= baptism] with the promised Holy Spirit, which is the guarantee [= evidence] of our inheritance until we acquire possession of it, to the praise of his glory [= end] (Eph. 1:13-14).

d. *Faith to Love (The Energy of Faith).*[63] Faith, which is the work of the Spirit, evidences itself, in Paul's unforgettable expression it "energizes" itself in love (*pistis di agapës energoumenë*, Gal. 5:6b). Christian love requires the energy of the Spirit. This energy is received by faith (Gal. 3:5).

The Spirit's work of love is understood in the New Testament in two special relations: negatively, toward the flesh, and positively, toward the neighbor.

i. The Flesh. First of all, "faith working in love" is an energy in constant tension with a power which Paul calls "the flesh." Life in the Spirit, if it is real, is life at war with the flesh. And this war, according to Romans 8:13, is not a matter of the Christian's past — ending when the Spirit has been received. The Christian's war is the *continual* responsibility of "put[ting] to death" (*thanatoute*, present tense) his evil inclinations precisely *because* the Spirit has been received and is Holy. The man who suffers with Christ in his struggle with the flesh has *in that very struggle* a strong assurance that he is led by the Spirit and hence is a son of God. This is probably the significance of the juxtaposition of two important sentences in Romans 8:13-14: "if by the Spirit you [are constantly putting to death] the deeds of the body you will live. *For* all who are led by the Spirit of God are sons of God."[64]

---

[63] To the Spirit and love see Schweizer's treatment, art. *pneuma, TWNT,* VI, 428-30, entitled appropriately "Pneuma as Openness for God and the Other." The following development is much indebted to Schweizer's study.

[64] See Schweizer's section "Pneuma as Denial of the Sarx [Flesh]," art. *pneuma, TWNT,* VI, 425-28. Note also Berkhof's reflection: "Although in this fight the Spirit often seems to get the worst of it, this very fight is the sign of the Spirit's presence in our lives. The Spirit is absent when we stop fighting, not when we lose." *Doctrine of the Holy Spirit,* p. 78.

Thus to walk in love means essentially to walk according to the Spirit and *against* the flesh (Gal. 5; Rom. 8). This walk is itself an evidence of the Spirit; it is faith's daily way of energizing itself, faith's outer dimension. Once again, therefore, the evidence of the Spirit is not essentially ecstatic, it is ethical. It is not the Christian who can have the most or highest spiritual experiences or become least intelligible to his neighbor or to himself who has the evidence of the Spirit. For love is not the extinguishing of the ego in ecstasy, it is the bridling of the ego in restraint and then, as we shall see momentarily, the giving of the ego in love to the neighbor (and in this latter sense it is literally ec-static, "outside oneself"). Love however, first of all, is not so much the explosiveness of great emotion as it is the controlling of emotions; it is not so much great emotions at all as it is great patience (cf. I Cor. 13:4-7 in relation to 13:1-3); and at crucial moments it is not even so much a matter of the speaking of the tongue as it is a matter of the service of the hand (cf. I John 3:18).

ii. The Neighbor. In all types of gnosticism the highest goal of the spiritual life is the obtaining of divine substance for oneself. The Christian faith distinguishes itself from this seemingly devout but actually selfish piety by locating the focus of Christian life not in the accumulating of spirituality or spirit for oneself, but more mundanely, in giving oneself to the neighbor. In gnosticism the goal of spiritual life is the emptying of oneself in order to be filled with divine substance — it is vertical; in the Christian faith the goal is the emptying of oneself for the human neighbor — it is horizontal. This difference of directions in energy determines the difference in types of evidence. Special "spiritual experience" *(gnōsis)* "puffs up," but Christian love "builds up" (I Cor. 8:1b).

The very visible neighbor is the concern of authentic Christian spirituality; the invisible, the "spiritual" is the focus of all varieties of mystic-gnostic spirituality. Yet the gnostic is separated from his neighbor not only by his spiritual goals. He is separated also by the very spiritual experiences themselves. For with each experience the gnostic rises to a higher level of spiritual life. Above the mere pistic (believer) he becomes a gnostic (experiencer).[65] The neighbor is not only marginal to the gnostic, the neighbor, including the Christian brother, will usually be found *below* the gnostic. Thus gnosticism (experientialism) leads inevitably to schism. For the gnostic via his goals and experiences, i.e., by his whole understanding of the Spirit, comes increasingly to understand himself as spiritually superior to what he calls nominal Christians and, of course then, to all other people.

---

65 We may translate, in our context, "above the nominal Christian he becomes a Spirit-filled Christian." The expression "nominal Christian" is itself a perfect gnostic creation. See the histories of doctrine by Harnack and Seeberg under gnosticism. Cf. Bultmann, *Theology of the New Testament,* II, 74.

iii. The Special Relevance of the First Epistle of John. It was to the whole complex of gnostic ideas described above that I John in particular addressed itself. The gnostics claimed to be in possession of a special knowledge of God (I John 2:4).

> This knowledge of God, which is asserted to be superior to and beyond the reach of the average Christian, is the center of [the gnostics'] religion. Here they believe they have attained to a fellowship with God which lifts them high above the usual Church Christian.[66]

In contrast to this higher-life piety, John sets the only legitimate criterion of Christian faith as he understands it — the keeping of the commandments, i.e., *agapë*.

The gnostic ethical flaw derived from a deeper theological dislocation. As we saw, the gnostics were not able to center their version of Christianity in the *human* Jesus Christ since the human and the natural were to them by definition the opposite of the spiritual and supernatural (I John 4:2-3). They misunderstood *faith* by anchoring it in the "spiritual" rather than in the historical, namely, in a mainly spiritual being rather than in the Jesus Christ who became flesh. Consequently, they also misunderstood the *living* of the Christian life, the Christian ethic, by giving priority to "spiritual things" and higher experiences rather than to "historical things" like the brother and others (I John 4:12).

Thus the gnostic's assurance of high accomplishment in his spiritual experiences — experiences which were understood as the special evidences of union with God — was to John the decisive evidence of the gnostic "lie," for the gnostic's spirituality lifted him *over* rather than *to* his brother. Lovelessness, not lack of spiritual experiences, was for John the evidence that a man was not in the truth. The *test*, the *evidence* of authentic spirituality according to John was, in a word, love and not special experience.

Therefore John was obliged to deny the gnostics the name Christian (I John 2:4 *et al.*). Indeed, the gnostics' actual, though not always professed centering of their lives in the spiritual rather than in the incarnate Christ, and thus in experience rather than in the brother, i.e., ultimately the centering of their piety in themselves, was for John "the spirit of antichrist" (I John 4:3).

Consequently, for John as for Paul, gnostic piety could not be treated any longer as a legitimate form of the Christian faith though it professed to be so in a special degree. For, in summary, gnostic

---

[66] Friedrich Hauck, *Die Briefe des Jakobus, Petrus, Judas und Johannes. Kirchenbriefe* ("NTD," "Neues Göttinger Bibelwerk," 10; 5th ed.: Göttingen: Vandenhoeck & Ruprecht, 1949), p. 114. So also C. H. Dodd, *The Johannine Epistles* ("Moffatt NTC"; London: Hodder & Stoughton Ltd., 1946, 1953), p. 53. "John," here as elsewhere, indicates simply the author(s) of the literature by that name in the New Testament.

Christianity failed to make central to Christians' lives the *earthly* Jesus Christ and his service in the earthly brother. Gnostic Christianity centered its religion not in the concrete: the *fleischgewordene* Jesus Christ and the very tangible brother, but in the numinous. That is to say, gnostic Christianity saw spiritual evidences not so much in Christian faith, hope, and love as in — paradoxically — spiritual evidences.

e. *Faith to Remember (The Christocentricity of Faith)*. The Paraclete sayings of the Gospel of John contain the most concentrated New Testament witness to the doctrine of the evidence of the Holy Spirit and serve, therefore, as a useful summary. When one arranges the several sayings the most pervasive mark is Christocentricity. The Holy Spirit appears to have as not only the center but as the circumference of his mission the witness to Jesus.

For purposes of comprehension we shall depart in this section from the separate treatment of New Testament and Pentecostal doctrines in order to draw some immediate correspondences.

We may catalogue the Paraclete doctrine and its Pentecostal correspondences in the following manner.

i. "If you love me, you will keep my commandments. And I will pray the Father, and he will give you another Counselor, to be with you for ever" (John 14:15-16).

In this passage we have the New Testament's nearest approach to a human pre-condition for the decisive giving of the Holy Spirit. The keeping of Jesus' commandments (v. 15) appears in connection with the Father's gift of the other Counselor. (To be sure, the connection is not a strictly conditional one, for the "if" of the passage belongs, significantly, to v. 15 and not v. 16; nevertheless, there *is* a connection.) Does this passage prejudice the *sola fide* found elsewhere in the New Testament in relation to the Holy Spirit (not least in John itself; cf. especially 7:37-39)?

The Johannine juxtaposition here could be dangerous for the person eager to find conditions beyond faith for God's Spirit; it could be wholesome for the Christian apt to empty faith of its content as loyalty to a Person. However, the apparent pre-condition can be explained as a call not to obedience understood as works beyond or in addition to faith but, on John's own usage, as nothing else than the call to faith itself.[67]

If, however, v. 15 is understood discretely as the call to love, which the context in John can suggest (see 13:34; 15:12, 17), then the unity of the New Testament's doctrine will appear to be effected. But what is not effected, interestingly, is the relation of even this text to the

[67] So, e.g., Bultmann, *John*[14], pp. 474-75. The literature to the meaning of the Paraclete is vast. See recently the helpful interpretation by Raymond E. Brown, "The Paraclete in the Fourth Gospel," *NTSt, 13* (Jan. 1967), 113-32.

Pentecostal conditions. For to date — and this is to us significant — we have not discovered the command of love on a list of Pentecostal conditions for the Spirit. For as we have observed, the Pentecostal conditions revolve around the religious devotion or spiritual emptying of the Christian and very little around the Christian's relation to others. Most Pentecostal conditions can be fulfilled in one's own room, in isolation. The key and central concepts in the Pentecostal conditions are absolute surrender, emptying, prayer, and thus even in this apparently religious sense are fundamentally egocentric.

Whether the obedience spoken of in verse 15 is, with the rest of the New Testament, the obedience of *faith,* or whether it is the obedience of *love* (both of which are, in sequence, the inside and outside of the same reality), both fall outside the province of the conditions of Pentecostalism.[68]

ii. The Paraclete is not imperfectly or incompletely given, but in such a way as to be able "to be with you for ever" (14:16). Pentecostalism's doctrine ordinarily denies that when the Spirit is given "at first" he remains with the believer permanently; the Spirit has, as it is said, only imparted salvation and his permanence awaits the believer's fuller obedience. However, according to this text, when the Spirit is given it is forever. (Moreover, his coming is the result of Jesus' prayer, not men's: "And *I* will pray the Father," 14:16.)

iii. The Paraclete cannot be received by the world because it does not *see* him (14:17). In Pentecostal doctrine it is taught that the Spirit is not permanently received until, by the specific manifestation of tongues-speaking, he *is* seen. Until Pentecostals *see* what they understand to be the Spirit's only initial evidence, they do not believe the Spirit has been finally received.

Generally speaking, in the New Testament the demand to see a special evidence of the divine presence is not praised (cf. John 7:3-5; Matt. 12:38-42 par.; 16:4). The proverb "seeing is believing" is not true of the deepest kinds of biblical faith. The words to Thomas have a wider reference than the first century, "Blessed are those who have not seen and yet believe" (John 20:28).

iv. There can be no denial that Jesus identifies himself very closely with the other Counselor (14:16), the Holy Spirit, for Jesus says to his disciples, "you know him, for he dwells with you and will be in you. I will not leave you desolate, *I* will come to you" (14:17b-18).

---

[68] "The *agapē,* accordingly, is actually nothing else than the life in the Spirit which has become free of its trust in the [flesh] — insofar as this freedom expresses itself in the outward direction." Schweizer, art. *pneuma, TWNT,* VI, 429,14-16. True faith evidences itself, energizes, even justifies itself *before men* in love. For a sound treatment of the faith, love, and justification relations I should like to refer to the fundamental Protestant textbook, *The Book of Concord,* pp. 117-32.

The "coming" of the Spirit of Jesus, not as Substitute but as Continuator, is confirmed in the next Paraclete saying.

v. The Paraclete will be sent by the Father, Jesus promises, "in my name" (14:26). The functional identification of Jesus and the Spirit is so close that with the name of Jesus the Spirit is given. This correlation tallies interestingly with the doctrine of initiation discovered in Acts and Paul (Acts 2:38; 19:5-6; I Cor. 6:11).

In Pentecostalism the Spirit's full presence is not ordinarily given to faith in the name of Jesus Christ but to special conditions beyond mere faith in him (or to deeper faith in him). The Pentecostal doctrine thus misses the "co-incidence" of the name of the Son and the coming of the Spirit.

vi. Having come, the Paraclete's mission is essentially a remembering ministry: he will "bring to remembrance all that I have said to you" (14:26). The "I" is accentuated by its location in the Greek text. The sentence makes a real effort to stress that the Spirit's work is not an independent or even supplementary work, it is christocentric. If this is true, then it would be salutary for Pentecostalism to know that the Spirit's real evidence is his power to connect men with and to remind them of Jesus Christ, not carry men beyond him (cf. Acts 1:8; I Cor. 12:3).

In the verses which follow, particularly John 15:1-11, it is made clear that the one true source of Christian life is Jesus (15:1). Only apart from abiding in him is the believer unpowerful (15:5). It may be feared that seeking a second source of power beyond Jesus will tend to estrange the believer from the single source whom the Spirit lives not to supplant but to represent. The Spirit "will bear witness to *me*" (15:26b; see again Acts 1:8).

vii. The convicting mission of the Spirit (16:7-11) is a part of his christocentric mission. Through the church's preaching, the Spirit moves men to believe and he convicts them of unbelief in Jesus Christ ("of sin, because they do not believe in me," 16:9). The Spirit's convicting work is not related to any failure to believe in or seek the Spirit. Nor is the Spirit's reminding work the recalling of the disciples from mere recollection of Jesus to power for service. This is no doubt due to the apostolic conviction that power for service was the fruit of the Spirit's making Jesus real.

viii. The Paraclete not only reminds and convicts, he also guides into the future: "he will declare to you the things that are to come" (16:13). The church needs to be "reminded" of this future dimension of the Spirit's work.[69] Yet here too the passage is careful to declare

---

69 It could appear that in its strong future orientation Pentecostalism is least subject to criticism since eschatological expectation is a major characteristic of Pentecostalism. But if the representative remarks cited in "The Latter Rain" section (above, p. 28) are studied, and if one observes the manner of their

that this work is no independent or supra-christological mission of the Spirit, "for he will not speak on his own authority, but whatever he hears he will speak" (16:13). The Spirit will reflect to the churches the Word of Christ for the particular historical needs of the churches' existence.

ix. The Paraclete's entire mission may be gathered together in Jesus' own summary, "he will glorify me, for he will take what is mine and declare it to you" (16:14). The evidence of the Spirit *par excellence* is the glorification of Jesus Christ.

The Paraclete sayings end with the affirmation familiar elsewhere, but particularly in Colossians, "all that the Father has is mine" (John 16:15a), and it is of this all in Christ, of this *solus Christus,* that the Spirit reminds, the negligence of which he convicts, and the whole of which he glorifies. *All (panta)* has been given to Christ; therefore to all to whom Christ has given himself, all has been given. This is the now unanimous testimony of the New Testament concerning the way of the Holy Spirit in Christ Jesus.

2. THE CONSEQUENCES FOR THE PENTECOSTAL DOCTRINE OF INITIAL EVIDENCE

The importance to Pentecostalism of the doctrine of tongues as the initial evidence of the baptism in the Holy Spirit is, as we have seen, that speaking in tongues makes definite, manifest, audible, and visible the fact that the Christian has fully received the power of the Holy Spirit in what is considered to be the biblical way. Thus all "vague faith" is left behind. A passion for the certainty of the Holy Spirit's presence determines the Pentecostal doctrine of initial evidence.

However, all of the Pentecostal insistencies for the manifest and recognizable, even for the "tongue," are met adequately in the New Testament evidences of faith expressed in the prayer "dear Father" (Gal. 4:6; Rom. 8:16-17) or in the confession "Lord Jesus" (I Cor. 12:3; cf. I John 4:1-3). Both of these evidences are spoken, both

---

expression in meetings and literature it is difficult to avoid the conclusion that at least one source of Pentecostal eschatology is a profound misunderstanding of the gospel. Bonwetsch's conclusion concerning an earlier "Pentecostal" is worth comparing: The message of "the imminent world catastrophe was intended to serve only as a motivation of [Tertullian's] aescetic demand to give up the world." *Die Geschichte des Montanismus,* p. 126. It has become our impression, strengthened by personal experience in Pentecostal meetings, that the frequent motive of the near end of the world and of apocalyptic catastrophe, flows at least as often as not from the preacher's will to impress his message home to the hearers, i.e., in our opinion, to impress his law. We also believe that the Pentecostal eschatological exhortation falls on fertile soil because of the crisis character of our time, emotional and sometimes material poverty, and the strain of living — a strain not only occasionally relieved by Pentecostal meetings but frequently heightened by Pentecostal teachings on sin, righteousness, and the Spirit.

can be heard, and both touch the heart of the divine revelation as unintelligible tongues cannot.

In other words, everything Pentecostalism says it wants and needs in the initial evidence of the Spirit's coming can be simply provided in Christian prayer and confession of faith, comprehended initially in the evidence of baptism.

The basic New Testament word for the evidence of the Spirit is faith. Faith in Christ is not only the *means,* but it is also the *evidence* of the Holy Spirit's presence in Christian life. It is in this sense also that the Christian gospel is "through faith for faith" (Rom. 1:17).

The evidence of the *reality* of this faith, then, is first the confession of the Lordship, we may say, of the deity of the earthly *Jesus,* or what is another way of saying this, taking the humanity of Jesus with ultimate seriousness. The reality of Christian faith is tested first by the willingness to confess with the apostles and with the whole church that *kurios Iësous,* "Lord (is) Jesus" (I Cor. 12:3; Rom. 10:9; Phil. 2:11; Matt. 22:43 *et al.*), that is, that Jesus is *God;* that *Jesus* is God.[70]

Then and consequently, true as distinguished from counterfeit Christian faith will evidence itself not in being "carried away," but in being "carried to" the neighbor. This trans-portation is what the New Testament calls love.

Granted, these simple faith-evidences — baptism, the prayer "dear Father," the confession "Lord Jesus," the patience of Christian love — are not spectacular, but to the New Testament they are spiritual. There is a normalcy and simplicity in the New Testament evidences which one misses in the Pentecostal.

But something graver must be said about the Pentecostal evidence. The Pentecostal evidence is not simply a harmless idiosyncrasy which can be smiled upon in its naiveté and passed by. For since this evidence is *required* of Christians *in addition to faith* before they can have God

---

[70] See the excellent summary of New Testament and early Christian teaching concerning Christ in G. Sevenster, "Christologie des Urchristentums," *RGG*[3], I, 1745-62. That Jesus is, at the same time and without any confusion of natures, "true God and true man" is a fundamental theological doctrine and much more than a mere theologoumenon. But if, as is proper, the word *Jesus* is taken in its full and normal human sense, and if the word *God* is taken to mean God, then there seems to us no difference between the confession "Jesus is God" and the confession that he "is true God and true man." See, for a recent debate, Robert McAfee Brown's review of Thomas J. J. Altizer's *The Gospel of Christian Atheism* in *Theology Today,* 23 (July 1966), 286-87.

In looking retrospectively at the Bishop Pike affair in the church it is at least curious to see that the Bishop at one time officially combatted Pentecostal manifestation in his diocese because, in his words, it "tends to the neglect of the full Christology of the Catholic Faith: the assertion in objective terms of Jesus Christ as God and man" and thus, and for other reasons, "presents the Church with heresy in embryo." In "Pastoral Letter regarding 'Speaking in Tongues,'" *Pastoral Psychology,* 15 (May 1968), 58.

in his fulness, it threatens to remove Pentecostalism outside the sphere of Christian faith. The Pentecostal evidence bears the marks of the demand in the early church for circumcision (cf. Gal. *passim;* Acts 15). And Paul did not look upon this or any addition to faith as harmless.

When the circumcision party came requiring circumcision of believers in order for them to be (fully) pleasing to God Paul did not look on this requirement as an innocent novelty or as an ecumenical variation which in no way affected or endangered his gospel. When superlative apostles came bringing the Corinthian believers another, better, and fuller Jesus, Spirit, and gospel (II Cor. 11:4; see below, p. 308), Paul did not consider this to be merely interesting. The sternest words in the New Testament are directed at precisely the attempted supplementation of the gospel of faith alone.

When Pentecostalism comes requiring tongues of believers in order for them to have the fulness of the Holy Spirit and power for God — indeed, when Pentecostalism makes this experience the *sine qua non* of the Holy Spirit's full, personal, permanent, powerful, and indwelling presence, enabled by the fulfillment of conditions beyond faith in Christ — then we do not do the gospel honor when we fail to point out what this teaching means. Tongues-speaking in itself may be perfectly harmless; Paul, for instance, was willing to recognize circumcision itself as an at times harmless rite (cf. Gal. 5:6; 6:15; I Cor. 7:19) and could apparently even administer it where it was not made a requirement for spiritual completion (cf. Acts 16: 1-3). But the moment any rite, any obedience, any experience, no matter how buttressed with Scripture or with "angels from heaven," becomes a supplement to faith or a condition for fulness before God, then the anathema must be announced and the warning to avoid the false teaching urged with all possible seriousness.

This warning occurred in its classic form in Paul's Epistle to the Galatians (5:2-12; cf. 1:6-9). To give an indication of the gravity of supplements to faith we may conclude our systematic New Testament survey, then, by suggesting the simple comparison of the Pentecostal evidence of tongues with the Judaistic evidence of circumcision. The comparison is suggested by the remarkable similarities shared by both rites. Both base themselves upon Scripture, as supplements to (or, as extensions or consequences of) faith, and both are understood as requisite for God's favor or power in fulness. Interestingly, moreover, both are momentary physical phenomena, occurring at specific bodily organs, and both seem to have guaranteed, as it were, *ex opere operato,* the reality of what each purports to evidence. The physical event is in both cases invested with spiritual significance.

Finally, both share the tendency of all supplements to faith: to crowd center. The *supplement* to faith seems historically destined to become the *center* of a new faith. It is therefore not surprising that the earliest known "supplementary movement" was generally called the "circumcision party" (Gal. 2:12; Acts 10:45; 11:2). Nor is it accidental, rather it is quite understandable, that the most recent movement with a specific supplement is popularly known as "the tongues movement."

It appears to be historically true that every supplement to faith has within itself the almost irresistible tendency of becoming eventually a specific advancement beyond faith and thus to become inevitably the goal of a new spirituality of a purportedly higher Christian type. Faith itself then becomes but a step in the right direction. In a word, the supplement "and" is pregnant with the ineluctable tendency to become the central "more."

By careful attention to Paul's treatment of the major supplement of his time we may learn for our time something of the seriousness of any supplement.[71]

> Now I, Paul, say to you that if you receive circumcision, Christ will be of no advantage to you. I testify again to every man who receives circumcision that he is bound to keep the whole law. You are severed from Christ, you who would be justified by the law; you have fallen away from grace. For through the Spirit, by faith, we wait for the hope of righteousness. For in Christ Jesus neither circumcision nor uncircumcision is of any avail, but faith working through love. You were running well; who hindered you from obeying the truth? This persuasion is not from him who called you. A little yeast leavens the whole lump. I have confidence in the Lord that you will take no other view than mine; and he who is troubling you will bear his judgment, whoever he is. But if I, brethren, still preach circumcision, why am I still persecuted? In that case the stumbling block of the cross has been removed. I wish those who unsettle you would mutilate themselves! (Gal. 5:2-12).

---

[71] Oepke cautions that Paul's warning in Gal. 5:2-12 applies not to every *circumcised* man (for Paul himself was circumcised) but to all those who decide, on principle, to be circumcised in order to be complete before God. *Gal.*[2], p. 118. Neither circumcision *as such*, nor tongues-speaking *as such* is objectionable — both are biblically taught. The problem begins when any practice, obedience, or experience — even (and especially) any *biblical* practice, obedience, or experience — is made necessary for fulness before God beyond faith sealed in baptism. This means that no matter how innocent, harmless, even biblical the condition of tongues may be, by canceling the sole necessity of faith it cancels the sole sufficiency of Christ. "The *scandal of faith*," writes Stählin, "belongs to the essence of the gospel. It may not be put to one side for any reason whatsoever nor may it be moderated through a both-and.... Such an 'and' dilutes the uncompromising faith-challenge and makes the offending character of the gospel innocuous and so at the same time renders the saving power of the cross and the gospel empty." Art. *skandalon, TWNT*, VII, 354,12-21. The issue then is the elemental one: between faith and works. In the first century in Galatia the principle of works took the form of circumcision; in twentieth-century Pentecostalism the principle of works takes the form of tongues — only the form is different, the issue is the same.

As long as speaking in tongues remains the initial evidence and thus the ultimate condition of God's full gift, all of Paul's severe warnings in Galatians 5:2-12 must apply to Pentecostalism: severance from Christ, the falling away from grace, and the obligation to keep the whole law. No other judgment is fair to the gospel of the New Testament (though this judgment must seem unfair to the conditioners). Those who "trouble" and "unsettle" (Gal. 1:7; 5:10, 12; Acts 15:24) believers with "more," Paul insists, will have to bear their judgment, and those allowing themselves to be "fascinated" (Gal. 3:1) by the troublers must bear theirs (5:2-12). For the call to "more" for God's full gift is subversive of God's call to sufficiency in faith. "A little yeast leavens the whole lump" (Gal. 5:9), and a little "more" ruins the whole gospel. The issue is clear: either the believer receives everything God has to give in Christ, through faith, or he receives it by more (even by "more faith"). The New Testament flatly repudiates the second way (allachothen, John 10:1). Pentecostalism must draw its own consequences.

VII

HUPER: THE RELEVANT SPIRITUAL PROBLEMS IN CORINTH[1]

A serious study of the doctrine of the Holy Spirit in the New Testament in its relation to the doctrine of Pentecostalism is not complete without a penetration of the Corinthian letters. It is common knowledge that the issues treated in Corinthians are uniquely related to some of the inner issues in Pentecostalism. This relationship is most apparent in Paul's discussion of the spiritual gifts — I Corinthians 12 to 14 — but it may be most striking in Paul's development of the self-consciousness which apparently lay behind and under the entire Corinthian problem, at least in its more developed forms, in II Corinthians 10 to 13. To the person even introductorily acquainted with Pentecostal doctrine Paul's engagement with the Corinthian problems comes like light.

In the preface to I Corinthians Paul stresses all that the Corinthians already have "in Christ Jesus": sanctification (1:2), grace (1:4), enrichment in speech and knowledge (1:5), hence every spiritual gift (1:7). What they *have* in Christ is to be completed by, if we will, a second experience: "the day of our Lord Jesus Christ" (1:8), the return of Christ. The Corinthians have, in a word, one great call — whether past or future, experienced or expected — the call "into the fellowship of [God's] Son, Jesus Christ our Lord" (1:9). For everything the Corinthians already have, they have in Christ, and everything they are yet to have,

---

[1] Schlatter finds the key to the errant Corinthian theology in the word *huper,* specifically in the inclination to go "beyond" or "over" *(huper)* the Scriptures, as suggested by Paul in I Cor. 4:6, where *huper* occurs twice. *Die korinthische Theologie* ("BFChTh"; Gütersloh: C. Bertelsmann, 1914), pp. 7-8. Schlatter's development of this particular thesis, however, was not, for us, entirely convincing. Nevertheless, with him we find in the remarkably frequent incidence of *huper* in the Corinthian correspondence the clue to the Corinthian consciousness: if it was not a tendency to go "beyond" the Scriptures, it was a tendency to go beyond the apostle and other Christians, in ways that we hope to make clear in the course of the exposition.

they have in him as well. Did Paul load the preface to his first epistle with "baptismal" aorists and perfects (1:2, 4, 5, 6, 9) and "parousial" futures and participles (1:7, 8), and locate them all in Christ, because the Corinthians had zeals deflecting them from — or "beyond" *(huper)* — Christocentricity? The Corinthian correspondence, two major passages of which we shall investigate, is an extended answer to this question.

A. I CORINTHIANS 12-14: THE SPHERE OF THE SPIRIT AS THE BODY OF CHRIST

1. I CORINTHIANS 12: THE WORK OF THE SPIRIT *(Charismata)*

a. *12:1*. In the next three chapters we are face to face with the spiritual problem *par excellence* in Corinth. The Corinthians had probably asked Paul for his opinion (or defense) in a matter which was beginning to concern them: What, or who, is truly spiritual? How is it possible, or is it possible at all, to test spiritual things and persons? And in particular, how is Christian spirituality to be expressed in the congregational meeting?

b. *12:2*. Paul begins thematically by reminding the Corinthians negatively of what "spiritual things" (*ta pneumatika*) are not. The very characteristic of the Corinthians' heathen past, he argues, was the sense of being overpowered and carried away by spiritual forces.

> You know how, in the days when you were still pagan, you were swept off to those dumb heathen gods, however you happened to be led [I Cor. 12:2 NEB; margin: "you would be seized by some power which drove you to those dumb heathen gods"].

"There is no doubt at all," Schrenk comments, "that Paul intends to say here, 'The truly spiritual is not marked by a being swept away *(Hingerissenwerden)*; that was precisely the characteristic of your previous fanatical religion.' "[2] It is important to notice that Paul places this valuation of the spiritually "sweeping" at the very outset of his treatment of "spiritual things" in Corinth. As the superscripture to his

---

[2] "Geist und Enthusiasmus," *Studien zur Paulus* (Zürich: Zwingli Verlag, 1954), p. 116. "In *Enthusiasmus*," Schrenk observes, "ecstasy is always considered the most highly valued and sought condition, the peak and truly ultimate means for obtaining connection with the divine.... The states of *Enthusiasmus* and ecstasy are carefully observed and as such are cherished. One seeks to further and to implement them through carefully planned steps." *Ibid.*, p. 113. Cf. Oepke, art. *ekstasis, TWNT*, II, 449-60; Reitzenstein, *Hellenistische Mysterienreligionen*[3], p. 32. For a rich assortment of examples see Erwin Rohde, *Psyche: Seelencult und Unsterblichkeitsglaube der Griechen,* 2 vols. (5th and 6th ed.; Tübingen: Mohr, 1910), particularly II, 14-22, 60-61 and note his summary of Greek religious experience: "The Divine does not come down; man must struggle up to the divine height ... in order to unite himself with the One." *Ibid.*, II, 402. Kelsey's remark ignores history: "Actually there is nothing to be found in either Hebrew or Greek antecedents comparable to the experience described by Paul's letters and the Book of Acts as speaking in tongues." *Tongue Speaking*, p. 141.

essay in chapters twelve to fourteen Paul has written: Seizure is not necessarily Christian or paramountly spiritual. The relevance to Pentecostalism does not need to be stressed.

c. *12:3*

Therefore I want you to understand that no one speaking by the Spirit of God ever says 'Jesus be cursed!' and no one can say 'Jesus is Lord' except by the Holy Spirit.

Positively, Paul sees the characteristic, perhaps the classic work of the Holy Spirit in the intelligible and simple confession that Jesus is Lord. The man who confesses "Lord Jesus" has experienced the deep work of the Spirit. The Spirit does not exhibit himself supremely in sublimating the ego, in emptying it, removing it, overpowering it, or in ecstasy extinguishing or thrilling it, but in intelligently, intelligibly, christocentrically using it. It was the spectacular ego-enthralling understanding of the Spirit which had infiltrated the Corinthian church, and it is the thoughtful ego-employing understanding of the Spirit which Paul in these chapters seeks to reestablish.

Furthermore, in ascribing deity to *Jesus* — i.e., to the flesh-bearing, earthly, human Jesus — the genuine Spirit, the Holy Spirit, is distinguished from witnesses or spirits which minimize or deny the human, natural, or even weak Jesus. "Anathema *Iēsous!*"[3] The genuinely spiritual bears witness to the human; the counterfeit spiritual bears witness to the spiritual (cf. I John 4:1-3).

Thus in his opening paragraph Paul has set the guidelines for his entire discussion of spiritual things which follows. Paul is saying, "When you were non-Christians, the essence of your higher religious experiences was the feeling of being 'carried away' by spiritual forces; now, however, you experience the *Holy* Spirit, and you experience him supremely in your desire to honor Jesus in the intelligible and simple ascription of deity to him." With the essential nature or office of the Spirit defined now both positively and negatively the foundation

---

[3] We shall not enter extensively into the meaning of "anathema *Iēsous*": whether it is ecstatic, docetic, Jewish, hypothetical, or none of these seems difficult to say with certainty. The most general remark that can be made about the phrase is that it probably indicates not a disowning of Jesus *Christ* but the repugnance of the merely human Jesus, hence "anathema *Iēsous*." Cf. the additional note to I Cor. 15, below, p. 302 and Julius Schniewind, *Nachgelassene Reden und Ausätze* (Berlin: Alfred Töpelmann, 1952), p. 123; Schlatter, *Theologie der Apostel*[2], pp. 486-87.

Bultmann believes that I Cor. 12:3b (the phrase "no one can say 'Jesus is Lord' except by the Holy Spirit") "does not at all mean just speaking that is Christian, but rather a speaking in momentary seizure by the Spirit." *Theology of the New Testament*, I, 159-60. We doubt this since Paul uses *eipein* for the Christian confession here, probably in conscious opposition to the preceding *lalōn*. To *lalein* as an occasional *terminus technicus* for charismatic speech cf. Wilckens, art. *sophia*, *TWNT*, VII, 520 n. 380.

is laid for Paul's more detailed discussion of the gifts of the Spirit in the next paragraph.

d. *12:4-7.*

> Now there are varieties of gifts, but the same Spirit; and there are varieties of service, but the same Lord; and there are varieties of working, but it is the same God who inspires them all in every one. To each is given the manifestation of the Spirit for the common good.

If the central work of the Spirit is the honoring of Jesus in speech, this work is not in any sense monotonous or uni-form.[4] The Spirit is rich in the variety of his manifestations — hence the three-fold use of the word "varieties" and its emphasis by being placed at the beginning of each phrase in the sentence. The spiritualism in Corinth evidently needed to be impressed not only with the essential characteristic of the Spirit's work (vv. 1-3), but also with the wide variety of his characteristic work (vv. 4-30). There was apparently the tendency in Corinth to see the Spirit not only at work in a particular *way* (being swept away, v. 2), but in a *particular* way (speaking in tongues, vv. 10, 28, 30; 13:1, 8; 14 *passim*). The Corinthians needed to learn that the Spirit not only could and classically did reveal himself in talking rationally and reverently of Jesus, but that he had more ways of honoring Jesus than had occurred to them.[5]

It should be observed that Paul at this point shifts strategically in his vocabulary. He began by employing the word probably preferred by the Corinthians themselves in describing their experience: "spiritualities," or "spiritual things" (*pneumatika*, v. 1). In place of this term Paul now substitutes what is essentially his own word, *charismata*, i.e., "graces," or "grace-things" (v. 4).[6] Paul, throughout the Corinthian correspondence, may be observed in the attempt, so necessary apparently in Corinth, to subsume spiritual things under grace (see, e.g., I Cor. 2:12) and to see the Spirit's ministry not in the glorification of

---

[4] Berkhof believes that the biblical connection between the Spirit and speaking "is far more dominant than we are inclined to believe.... In general the Bible is less pious than we are. With striking frequency we are told that the main fruit of the Spirit is that he opens our mouths and encourages us to speak." *Doctrine of the Holy Spirit*, p. 36.

[5] John Coolidge Hurd summarizes, in an able recent study, the situation in Corinth: The Corinthians "maintained that glossolalia is the main (or only) evidence of possession by the Spirit.... only those Christians who have this gift are to be classed as spiritual." *The Origin of I Corinthians* (New York: Seabury Press, 1965), p. 193. Similarly, J. P. M. Sweet, "A Sign for Unbelievers: Paul's Attitude to Glossolalia," *NTSt*, 13 (April 1967), 240-41.

[6] For the word see Friedrich Grau, "Der neutestamentliche Begriff *Charisma*, seine Geschichte und seine Theologie" ("Inaugural-Dissertation zur Erlangung des Doktorgrades in der Hohen Evangelisch-Theologischen Fakultät der Ebehard-Karls-Universität"; Tübingen: Typewritten manuscript, 1946), pp. 79, 169; Käsemann, *Essays*, pp. 64-65; Küng, "The Charismatic Structure of the Church," *The Church and Ecumenism*, pp. 41, 49, 59.

the numinous, exotic, "spiritual," or useless, but in the illumination of the historical, concrete, crucified and risen Lord, and here, now, in the continual and varied distribution of free gifts of service in the visible church. As in the ascription "Lord" (v. 3), so in the distribution of charismata (vv. 4-11), the Spirit's mission is described as the earthly, intelligible, and now versatile honoring of the grace of the Lord Jesus Christ.

A charisma or "grace" is first of all defined as a "service" (*diakonia,* v. 5). It is not, therefore, first of all or primarily a spiritual privilege for the individual, for his own edification, enjoyment, or distinction. As a service, a grace is given for others; it is there for the church.

As service is another way of saying charisma (vv. 4a and 5a), so Lord is another way, to Paul, of saying the Spirit (vv. 4b and 5b; 6:17; 15:45; cf. II Cor. 3:17-18).[7] It was Paul's concern throughout his Corinthian letters (as we have seen with Luke in Acts) to see the Spirit in the most intimate connection with the Lord and thus with God (cf. e.g. II Cor. 13:14). Paul will not have deity severed as though the Spirit of the Lord went beyond the Lord himself! For as the Spirit's basic manifestation is the utterance "Lord Jesus," so now we are told that what the Spirit does is exactly what the Lord does; the Spirit's work is not an additional or special work *beyond* the Lord's; the Spirit *is* the Lord at work.

In fact, the Pentecostal progression — beyond the Lord to the Spirit — is prevented not only in verse 3 by the definition of the Spirit's essential work as the confession of Jesus, but here in verses 4 and 5 by proceeding not from the Lord's service to the Spirit's gifts, as though to a higher plane, but by proceeding from the Spirit to the Lord, which is the evangelical progression.

Paul uses every means possible — whether *kurios, charisma,* or syntax — to preserve the living inner-relationship of the Spirit to and for Christ, of the spiritual to and for grace, and of individual endowment to and for the church.[8]

Paul's trinity of source and distribution in I Corinthians 12:4-7 concludes then with a clear statement of purpose: the varied services of the grace-gifts are all "for the common good." It is for the commonality, the *communio,* and not first for the individuality, the integer, for which spiritual gifts principally exist. A charisma is given first of

---

7 The *functional* identification of the Lord and the Spirit is ably defended by Hermann, *Kyrios und Pneuma,* pp. 64-65, 140-44.

8 Schlatter points out that in I Cor. 12:4-7, as well as I Cor. 2:16 and II Cor. 3:17, Paul is seeking to guard the unity of the Spirit and Christ from the danger in Corinth of being "dissolved by the pneumatic experience taking an independent place next to incorporation into Jesus. For this reason the Corinthian letters express the Christian ideas of God in trinitarian formulas." *Die korinthische Theologie,* pp. 85-86.

all not for the sake of the saint, but for the sake of the *communion* of saints and that communion's good.

e. *12:8-11*. Paul now provides a list of some of the various gifts he has in mind. Prominent at the head are gifts of intelligent and thoughtful utterance. Prominent at the end are gifts of ecstatic utterance and their interpretation.

Important is the fact that Paul sees the significance of the head gifts in their "word" or "utterance" character — "the utterance of wisdom" and "the utterance of knowledge" (v. 8). It is not wisdom or intelligence *per se* which Paul treasures, but the wisdom and intelligence which are communicated, spoken, to the "common good" of the congregation. This is no less the case with the gifts listed last. Paul understands tongues as valueless to the congregation unless they are intelligibly *interpreted* (14:5c).

Paul looks at gifts from the paramount perspective of the *congregation* and from this view he does not value any gift simply in its existence but only in its understandable communication to others for their upbuilding. Indeed, it is questionable if, in Paul's thought, a gift can be said to "exist" for the individual if it is not employed for the church.[9] The gift of the "utterance of wisdom," according to Paul, becomes the *gift* of wisdom when it is in the *act* of utterance. The gift of tongues, similarly, becomes a gift in fact only when it is interpreted for the help of the congregation. In Paul's understanding, it appears, you cannot take a gift home with you.

And "all these [gifts] are inspired by one and the same Spirit, who apportions to each one individually as he wills" (v. 11). Spiritual gifts (or to use Paul's expression, graces) are not confined to a select few who, perhaps, can exhibit extraordinary manifestations as a result of their deeper dedication or greater nearness to the Spirit. The whole variety of gifts — from the more sober to the more ecstatic — *"all"* are being continually apportioned (present tense verb) by the one Spirit to *each* person as the *Spirit* wills. The Spirit's "gifting" work in the church is both completely universal and completely individual: he gives of all to each.

f. *Summary: 12:1-11*. Paul's treatment in these opening verses has sufficed to cancel (i) any view which sees the most spiritual in the most overpowering (v. 2); (ii) any narrow view of what is truly spiritual ("varieties," vv. 4-7); (iii) any view of gifts which sees "spiritual things" as primarily rewards for effort rather than presents of grace (*charismata*, "gifts," vv. 4 *et al.*); (iv) any view which sees in a variety of gifts only a variety of dedication rather than, mainly, the sovereign will of God (vv. 4-7; "as *he* wills," v. 11); (v) any view

---

[9] Moritz Lauterburg, *Der Begriff des Charisma und seine Bedeutung für die praktische Theologie* ("BFChTh"; Gütersloh: C. Bertelsmann, 1898), p. 9.

which treasures gifts for what they do for the recipient rather than or more than for what they do for the congregation ("service," "the common good," "utterance"); (vi) and perhaps primarily, any view which separates Jesus from the Spirit: be it in making the confession of Jesus only "nominal Christianity" and the demonstration of the Spirit, in some remarkable way, "deeper spirituality," or in seeing simple Christian testimony as less deeply spiritual than being swept away in enthusiasm, or in understanding the historical Jesus ("Lord Jesus") as preliminary and interesting but so definitely superseded as to be now superfluous ("anathema Jesus"), or in seeing the Spirit as leading one beyond what one has "merely" in Jesus Christ, instead of leading precisely to him (v. 3), or in leading the Christian above and beyond "most Christians" and other people instead of to them in service and ministry.

Paul understands the work of the Spirit to be the honoring of Jesus Christ. Therefore, it is not surprising that he understands the work of the spiritually gifted to be the service of the body of Christ.

It is the unity and variety of Christ's body and — of most relevance to us presently — the spiritual baptism into this body which next engage Paul's attention.

g. *12:12-13.*

> For just as the body is *one* and has many members, and all the members of the body, though many, are *one* body, so it is with Christ. For by *one* Spirit we were *all* baptized into *one* body — Jews or Greeks, slaves or free — and *all* were made to drink of *one* Spirit.

Just as a wide variety of organs and limbs in a single body does not endanger the body's unity so it is, Paul argues, with the variety of spiritual gifts in the single Christ. There is no necessary contradiction between many gifts and a single Christ, but in fact a fine congruence as the natural analogy of the body serves to illustrate (vv. 14-26).

Then we come to the important thirteenth verse. Here Paul comes closer to saying "baptism in the Holy Spirit" than anywhere else in his letters (he, like the other New Testament writers, nowhere uses the phrase itself).

> Paul's ruling object in the entire Corinthian context is to magnify the *one*ness of the body of Christ. For example, in opening his epistle Paul stressed all that all the Corinthians have *in Christ Jesus* (I Cor. 1:2-11). When Paul addresses the Corinthians as "those sanctified in Christ Jesus, called ... saints," he immediately adds "together with *all* those who in *every* place call on the name of our Lord Jesus Christ, both their Lord and ours" (I Cor. 1:2), as if to say, "You are sanctified and God's holy ones, but not you alone or any special group among you; you are his *together* with all those everywhere who call on Christ."

Paul wishes to stress again the oneness of Christians in the present context. How may Paul now demonstrate the real unity of Christians to a church threatening to splinter apart into "the Spiritual" and "the Christian" as though the two were distinct? In the opening verses of the twelfth chapter Paul had bound the Spirit, Christ, and believer as indissolubly as he knew how. Now Paul strikes upon the event — "the happening"— of baptism as the most adequate for conveying to the Corinthians their oneness in the one body of Christ.[10]

> For by one Spirit we were *all* baptized into *one* body — Jews or Greeks, slaves or free — and *all* were made to drink of *one* Spirit (I Cor. 12:13).

If this verse is interpreted as speaking of a second, subsequent, and separate baptism in the Holy Spirit, beyond baptism in Christ, for only *some* Christians, then violence is done not only to the words of the text — "all . . . all" — but to the purpose of the text in its Corinthian context. The burden of Paul's Corinthian message is the oneness of *all* the baptized in Christ Jesus. Twice in this single verse Paul employs the adjective "all," and by it he means all, the entire Corinthian church, and beyond the Corinthians (*n.b.: "we* were all baptized into one body") "all those who in every place call on the name of our Lord Jesus Christ" (1:2). In I Corinthians 12:13 Paul is not teaching an unusual spiritual baptism won by only a few, he is teaching the gracious Christian baptism through the Spirit given to *all*.

> Since it is precisely the apostle's concern [writes the elder Althaus] to show the inner consolidation of Christians in one unified organism by means of a public-fact-of-experience, he could not, for that reason, use an inner, purely "spiritual" event as his evidence [of unity]; he could call upon only an historical event (cf. the aorist) which had occurred in the same way to all members, by which their entrance into the spiritual "body" came also outwardly into view.[11]

This historical event is baptism. The unity of Christians is secured, assured, and displayed through the simple and yet profound initiation event through which every Christian passes and by which every Christian is given the same spiritual gift. Spiritual baptism is not a rite which only the ecstatically able can attain. Baptism, like the salvation it applies, has absolutely nothing to do with merit or evidence of ability. No reality can bring home to the Corinthians the grace of God and their unity as a church like the baptism through which all of them, old and young, emotional and reserved, wise and simple, Jew and Greek have passed.

Paul underscores the Corinthians' unity even further by employing

---

[10] Von Baer notes the significance of the fact that in this important verse it is baptism and not the laying on of hands which is connected with the gift of the Spirit. *Heilige Geist*, p. 175.

[11] *Die Heilsbedeutung der Taufe* (Gütersloh: G. Bertelsmann, 1897), p. 48. Cf. Schnackenburg, *Heilsgeschehen*, p. 24.

in this single verse no less than three times the great word of this chapter, "one" ("by one . . . into one . . . of one").

First, "by *one Spirit* we were all baptized." The Spirit is not "two" nor his office two-fold: for example, baptizing Christians into Christ at conversion in a partly spiritual way as the "initiating Spirit," and then coming subsequently and fully to only consecrated Christians as the indwelling Spirit.

Furthermore, all Christians are baptized by the one Spirit, Paul insists, "into *one body.*" There are not two Christian bodies: one (nominal Christianity) into which all name-Christians are baptized "in water," another (Spirit-filled Christianity) into which all deeper believers are baptized "in the Spirit."

Nor does it need to be thought, thirdly, that instead of the church's *one* baptism this text might possibly refer to *two* baptisms: for example, first, to the Spirit's baptism of all converts into the body of Christ (conversion, v. 13a), an experience then superseded subsequently by what Pentecostals call Christ's baptism of the consecrated believer into the Holy Spirit (Spirit-baptism, v. 13b). The imagery is somewhat grotesque and we mention it only because it is seriously taught (cf. p. 60 above). But such a second "Spirit-baptism" is destined to divide not only the divine trinity but the earthly body of Christ into lower and higher types. It was to avoid, not to introduce, such divisions that Paul wrote I Corinthians 12:13.[12]

Appropriate to the christological character and mission of the Holy Spirit, the baptism of the Holy Spirit is the baptism of the believer into Christ. Yet baptism into Christ can no more be separated from baptism into the Holy Spirit than Christ can be separated from the Holy Spirit. For in the depths the name by which we are baptized is one (I Cor. 6:17; 15:45; II Cor. 3:17-18; cf. the singular "name" in Matt. 28:19). For Christ and the Spirit are not so divided that each must separately and at appropriate times baptize into each other. Baptism into the body of Christ is not a Spirit-less matter upgraded later by a *spiritual* baptism into the Holy Spirit. For it is the *one Spirit,* according to our text, who baptizes into the body of Christ (v. 13a), and in so doing, as we shall exposit momentarily, he gives *himself* (v. 13b)! In baptism into Christ the baptism in the Holy Spirit occurs.[13]

---

12 Schism is, in fact, the historical result of the Pentecostal division of baptism into Christ for all Christians, baptism into the Spirit for specially dedicated Christians. A movement which begins by dividing the reception of deity culminates in dividing the fellowship of Christians.

13 The Pentecostal Hughes wrote recently of I Cor. 12:13: "This Scripture is definitely not talking about the baptism in the Holy Ghost, but the agency of the Holy Ghost in the unification of the body of Christ." *What Is Pentecost?*, p. 23. This analysis, familiar in Pentecostal justification for the special "baptism *in* the Spirit," fails both to take account of the *latter* part of v. 13 where the Spirit is the gift of Christian spiritual baptism, and to notice in the opening words of

The one baptism "of water and the Spirit" (see John 3:5) is the cumulative doctrine of Corinthians (cf. I Cor. 6:11) no less than of Acts (cf. especially Acts 2:38-39; 11:17). Therefore, because of the one baptism into the one body by the one Spirit the Corinthians, and beyond them all other Christians, should know their oneness.

Finally, Paul says that all Christians, baptized by one Spirit into one body, "were made to drink of one Spirit." The latter half of verse 13, again in the aorist, supplements the former half by stressing that the Spirit not only acts as agent by baptizing all Christians into the one body of Christ, but that as the Spirit baptizes he gives *himself,* fully, as the gift of Christian initiation. By the graphic picture of "drinking in" Paul wishes to emphasize that Christians are not only baptized *by* the Spirit (v. 13a), but they are at the same time filled *with* him. He fills their innermost being.[14]

I Corinthians 12:13 as a whole wishes simply to remind the Corinthians and not to prove to them that they are all one as they may most easily recollect from their initiation baptism into the body of Christ by which they were all filled with the Spirit. The heaping of "all's" upon "one's" in this important text should instruct even the most obdurate in Corinth that *all* Christians have been baptized in and by the one Spirit into the one body of Christ, giving them all the one indrinking of the Spirit, making them, all of them, one.

h. *12:14-31.* With the church's unity as signified by baptism classically sealed in the preceding sentences, Paul can now give his attention to the other side of the truth of organic unity — variety. In any living body there are "higher" and "lower" parts, or better, more or less prominent organs; but these differences in a single body, particularly in Christ's single body, are purely functional, they are not

---

the verse that the baptism of which Paul here speaks *is,* pointedly, the baptism in-by-with the Spirit: "For by [*en*] one Spirit we were all baptized." The Pentecostal distinction, studied earlier (above, p. 60), between a prior baptism *of* the Spirit (in which the Spirit is the agent) and a subsequent baptism *in* the Spirit (in which Christ is the agent) — the former as mere Christian initiation or conversion, the latter as the full Pentecostal Spirit-baptism — has no support in New Testament grammar or texts. In Matt. 3:11; Mark 1:8; Luke 3:16; Acts 1:4; 11:16, and here in I Cor. 12:13 the Greek text speaks of men being bap·tized *en* the Spirit. Thus in I Cor. 12:13 the Holy Spirit is both agent *and* gift of the *one* baptism. Note the strong remarks of Lampe, *Seal,* p. 57; Beasley-Murray, "The Holy Spirit, Baptism, and the Body of Christ," *Review and Expositor, 63* (Spring 1966), 181.

[14] "The Spirit is the fruit as well as the means of this process." Schnackenburg, *Heilsgeschehen,* p. 162. Cf. Hermann, *Kyrios und Pneuma,* pp. 30-31. The aorist in v. 13b (and the use of words) probably forbids the phrase to be understood as the sacrament of the Lord's Supper. In the light of the aorist and of I Cor. 6:11 we are probably best advised to see in the expression "drinking the Spirit" a reference to the vitalizing experience of becoming a Christian, i.e., baptism. See a discussion in Schweizer, art. *pneuma, TWNT,* VI, 415 n. 563.

qualitative or "spiritual." Paul in this passage aptly contrasts the sense of spiritual inferiority which lower and seemingly less important parts of the body could feel toward higher, and the superiority which higher and seemingly more impressive or spectacular parts could feel toward lower parts (vv. 14-17). But no part should feel either inferior or superior, for "*God* arranged the organs in the body, *each one* of them, as *he* chose" (v. 18)! Every part of the body needs every other part. The various parts are not in fierce competition with each other but are in rich supplementation of each other for the sake of the whole and hence for the sake of the God who has, himself, placed each in its appropriate place.

Paul concludes this particular part of his argument by offering a second list, this time of persons rather than of gifts (v. 28; cf. Eph. 4:11). As if to stress the fact that in his prior list no rigid, invariable inventory of "nine" gifts was proffered, Paul now lists several types not readily recognizable in the earlier grouping, notably apostles, helpers, and administrators. Unique to this list also is the stressed numerical order: "first . . . , second . . . , third," followed simply by "then . . . , then." Similar, however, in both lists in Corinthians are the entries at the very bottom — speaking (and interpreting) "various kinds of tongues" (vv. 10b, 28b, and so also in what may be considered a third list, a duplication in interrogative form of the second, v. 30b). Paul then discreetly places a period to this particular discussion by suggesting that the Corinthians "earnestly desire the *higher* gifts" (v. 31). Even he who runs may read.

2. I CORINTHIANS 13: THE MANNER OF THE SPIRIT (*Agapë*)

In the twelfth chapter Paul bound the church's thought of spiritual things to grace; in the thirteenth chapter Paul connects spiritual things with love *(agapë)*. In the present chapter Paul will teach the way in which the divine graces discussed in the twelfth chapter should be humanly expressed. Neither transported speech (13:1), nor profundity (v. 2), nor sacrifice (v. 3) are, by themselves, either substitutes for or even necessarily components of Christian love. Love is a more basic and a less spectacular grace than all the others. Without it the Christian graces are dis-graced.

To understand and rightly to interpret I Corinthians 13 we must keep in mind the context in which Paul's description of love is given: the context of the problem of spiritual things in the Corinthian church. The moment this is realized, Paul's "poem" is half-deciphered. For example, Paul's first positive definition of Christian love is *makrothumei* (v. 4), i.e., Christian love is not so much emotional, passionate, or fiery *(thumos)* as it is the "making broad," the stretching out, the extension of "fire" *(makro-*thumos). This "long-suffering" should be compared with the superscripture of the twelfth chapter where the emotionalism of heathendom is contrasted with the sober confession of the church (12:2-3). Paul would not wish for it to appear that superior Christian devotion were necessarily identical with ardent Christian expression — either vertically, toward God (12:2-3), or horizontally, toward men (13:4). Paul sees the essence of the Holy Spirit in the simple word for Christ (12:3), he sees the higher gifts of the Spirit in the cooler words of wisdom and knowledge (12:8, 28), and he sees the major characteristic of Christian love not so much in the expression as in the extension of emotion, the drawing out, taming, literally the "lengthening" *(makro-)* of emotion. In English this attribute is called patience. Each description of love in I Corinthians 13, when placed against the background of "Corinthianism," can be comparably highlighted.

It is interesting to observe, for example, that the spiritual pride or inflated sense of one's own spiritual experience ("puffed up," *phusioun*) which Paul saw as the peculiar affliction of the Corinthian higher-life Christians (cf. 4:6, 18, 19; 8:1) appears in its negative in this passage: "love is . . . not *phusioutai*" (v. 4).[15] Paul's description of love in chapter thirteen, then, is not simply poetry; it is a concrete apostolic application of truth to elements of a church in need of learning what being Christian really and not spectacularly meant.

The final description in chapter thirteen to which we shall refer is in verse 5, which reads, literally, that love "does not seek its own" (*ou zētei ta heautēs*). This definition becomes important for the understanding of the fourteenth chapter, especially the fourth verse. It is sufficient now to observe that Christian love has as the goal of its seeking something other than its own advancement. This again brings the thirteenth chapter into harmony with the twelfth where we observed the *diakonia* and "common good" character and direction of the graces in Paul's definition. Graces too, like their *modus vivendi* love, "do not seek their own." They exist for the service of the body into which they have been baptized. Love, in Lauterburg's figure, "is the burning-glass which unremittingly re-concentrates the diverse charismatic manifestations toward their unified goal," the common good.[16]

The "higher" way of spiritual experiences for individuals urged by the Corinthians should become the "lower" way of patient love for the church and her service in the world as taught by Paul.

3. I CORINTHIANS 14: THE GOAL OF THE SPIRIT (*Oikodomē*)

a. *14:1-3.* Paul wishes the ardor, which apparently the Corinthians did not lack, to be spent in the pursuit of the kind of life he has

---

[15] Does this self-consciousness appear in v. 3 in the other major word for the Corinthian problem — *kauchēsōmai* — as some of our best witnesses attest (P46, A, B, C, etc.)? "If I deliver my body that I may *glory*." RSV margin.

[16] *Charisma*, p. 38.

just described. At the same time, the Corinthians should eagerly seek gifts, "especially that you may prophesy" (v. 1). It appears in this chapter that Paul sees the highest expression of spiritual gifts in the free, helpful discussion of Christians together and their contribution in thoughtful speech to each other. (It is, in fact, our impression that expressions such as "thoughtful speech," "testimony," or even "counsel" better translate the word rendered now somewhat archaically "prophesy.")[17]

Paul says that, for himself, he prefers prophecy — we shall call it often testimony — to tongues-speaking because, among other reasons, "one who speaks in a tongue speaks not to men but to God; for no one understands him, but he utters mysteries in the Spirit" (v. 2). At first glance one might think that, on Paul's reasoning, tongues would be the preferable gift, for is not speaking to God a greater matter than speaking to men? Not to Paul, apparently, who values gifts for their ability to help men (feeling, no doubt, that God is not as needy).

However, the Corinthians evidently tended to see in the very extraordinary and supernatural character of tongues-speech directed, as it was, primarily to God and only secondarily to men, the final proof of the superiority and spirituality of this particular gift. "Surely there could be no more convincing proof of the indwelling Spirit than this abandonment of consciousness to supernatural power" (Moffatt).[18]

Paul, however, favorably contrasts intelligible testimony to unintelligible tongues: "he who prophesies speaks to men for their *upbuilding* and encouragement and consolation" (v. 3). This important sentence defines prophecy. "Upbuilding" *(oikodomë)* then becomes the theme of this chapter (vv. 3, 4, 5, 12, 17, 26). As the undivided Godhead is the source of the graces (ch. 12), and as love is their manner (ch. 13), so upbuilding is their goal (ch. 14). In Paul's thought the ultimate criterion for a gift of the Spirit is this: Does it upbuild the church?

b. *14:4 and 12.* "He who speaks in a tongue edifies himself, but he who prophesies edifies the church" (v. 4). Paul has not denied that the gift of tongues was a gift, nor has he said that it is undesir-

---

17 Berkhof believes that "we badly need a study of the content and the theological relevance of New Testament prophecy. In this context I cannot say more than that in my opinion prophecy is the gift of understanding and expressing what the will of God is for a given present situation." *Doctrine of the Holy Spirit,* p. 91. Committees often manifest this gift. The sometimes pastoral disparagement of committee meetings could be modified, perhaps, by appreciating that it is often only in committee meetings that the *charismata* given the church members have the opportunity of expression.

18 *The First Epistle of Paul to the Corinthians* ("Moffatt NTC"; London: Hodder & Stoughton, 1938), p. 211. Lütgert notes that to the Corinthian congregation "a gift seems more likely to be spiritual the more able it is to be contrasted with the natural, the ordinary, and the everyday." *Freiheitspredigt und Schwarmgeist in Korinth: Ein Beitrag zur Charakteristik der Christuspartei* (Gütersloh: C. Bertelsmann, 1908), p. 133.

able if one is given this gift for, in fact, in the following verse he says that he could wish that all the Corinthians enjoyed this gift, a comfort, certainly, for all who did. But, significantly, Paul never directed the Corinthians (or any other churches in his preserved letters) to *seek* the gift of tongues — even though, interestingly, Paul could say that the tongues-speaker edifies himself. In fact, as we observed in an earlier use of the verb "to seek," Paul specifically writes that Christian love does *not* seek its *own (ta heautës,* 13:5). Here, on the other hand, it is the special characteristic of the speaker in tongues that he "edifies *himself" (heauton).* Prophecy, by contrast, edifies the church. Paul, therefore, could urge the seeking of the gift of prophecy because the goal of this gift was beyond the seeker; the same fact was apparently not as often true of speaking in tongues. Self-edification is not a Christian goal.[19]

Two facts must be kept in mind, however, in order to be fair to Paul's representation of the tongues problem. There apparently was a gift of tongues and Paul did not despise it. While significant curbs and, as we shall see in a moment, regulations for the use of the gift will be observed, Paul did not deny that speaking in tongues was a gift. The second fact, in justice to Paul's development, is that he not only neglected expressly to urge that tongues be sought, he diplomatically substituted alternative goals of seeking. He urged seeking "the higher gifts" in chapter twelve, love in chapter thirteen, and testimony in chapter fourteen. Both of these dialectical facts — of tactful retention and of tactical substitution — deserve attention if Paul's own "testimony" in these three chapters is to be understood in its underlying intention.

Paul then thematically and definitively declared: "Since you are eager for manifestations of the Spirit, strive [literally, "seek"] to excel in *building up* the church" (v. 12). Paul wishes to see spiritual gifts become service (ch. 12), love become selfless (ch. 13), and the church be upbuilt (ch. 14). It is in the light of these criteria that Paul wishes the Corinthians to direct their zeals.

c. *14:5-20a.* Tongues-speaking *could* be useful — when supplemented with the gift of interpretation — "so that the church may be edified" (v. 5). The over-riding consideration in each case, for every

---

[19] *Contra* all advocacy of tongues for what tongues do for the individual Christian Michel concludes from the Corinthian context that it is "therefore false when, according to I Cor. 14:4, the tongues-speaker 'edifies himself': this spiritually-effected act is not directed to the congregation or the brother (I Cor. 14:17), it is not seen as a service, and it is not dictated by love, rather it remains directed toward itself." Art. *oikodomëö, TWNT,* V, 144. Cf. Berkhof's similar conclusions relative to Pentecostalism, *Doctrine of the Holy Spirit,* pp. 92-93. See also Helmut Thielicke's perceptive remarks in the chapter "Speaking in Tongues," in his *Between Heaven and Earth: Conversations with American Christians,* tr. and ed. John W. Doberstein (New York: Harper and Row, 1965), p. 89.

gift, is its service in equipping the church. The consequence to be drawn by a speaker in tongues is to "pray for the power to interpret" (v. 13). Paul can thank God that he speaks in tongues "more than you all" (v. 18), "nevertheless, in church I would rather speak five words with my mind, in order to instruct others, than ten thousand words in a tongue" (v. 19).[20] Paul's sense of the comparative usefulness of the gifts of "mind-words" and of "tongue-words" could not be more forcefully expressed. In fact, we have no record of Paul's ever speaking to his churches except with mind-words, that is, with considerable sense. "Brethren," Paul counsels, "do not be children in your thinking" (v. 20).[21]

d. *14:20b-25.* In the following paragraph comes perhaps the strongest consideration of all: the evangelistic. At an assembly of the whole church the effect of speaking in tongues on "outsiders" or "unbelievers" is adverse: they will think Christians are crazy (v. 23). The sense of the Old Testament quotation which is inserted in this context (v. 21) is more serious than may appear on the surface: the effect of tongues is to harden, not soften the hearts of unbelievers. Tongues are a divine "hardening-instrument."[22]

On the other hand, the missionary power of testimony is great: "But if all prophesy and an unbeliever or outsider enters, he is convicted [for the word used here cf. John 16:8-12] by all, he is called to account by all, the secrets of his heart are disclosed, and so, falling on his face, he will worship God and declare that God is really among

---

[20] Cf. Hurd, *Origins of I Cor.,* p. 188: "Since 'ten thousand' is the largest number for which the Greek system of numeration had a symbol, we may better translate: '... rather five words with my mind ... than an infinite number in a tongue.'"

[21] "That means, indeed, indirectly: 'Your striving for glossolalia is childish' (I Cor. 13:11)." Lietzmann-Kümmel, *Kor.*[4], p. 73. So also Hurd, *Origins of I Cor.,* pp. 112-13. Cf. Robert H. Gundry, whose defense of tongues as non-ecstatic does not convince. "'Ecstatic Utterance' (NEB)," *JTS,* New Series *17* (Oct. 1966), 299-307.

[22] Johannes Weiss, *Der erste Korintherbrief* ("MeyerK"; 10th ed.; Göttingen: Vandenhoeck & Ruprecht, 1925), p. 332. See the careful qualifications in J. P. M. Sweet, *art. cit., NTSt, 13* (April 1957), 241-44. Paul's meaning is, unbelievers will find the suspicions of their unbelief confirmed when they encounter this *absurdum.* I once attended a large breakfast sponsored by the Pentecostal group, the Full Gospel Business Men's Fellowship International. A local high school choir had been invited to participate in the program. After the choir's number the festivities became increasingly Pentecostal. Soon, to our embarrassment, the high school students, who were seated conspicuously near the head table, began gradually to leave the large hall until almost all of them had gone. Discourteous as this departure unquestionably was, I felt that it provided, nevertheless, a symbol of a disturbing fact. Many are turned away from the Christian faith by the irrational Pentecostal manifestation of it. I affirm this in the face of Pentecostalism's advertisement of its missionary successes. Unfortunately, those who are driven out cannot always, like those who come in, be counted.

you" (vv. 24-25).[23] On the one hand (tongues), the impression made on the non-Christian could not be more unfavorable, he is hardened; on the other hand (testimony), the impression could not be more favorable, he is converted. The evangelistic-missionary concern of the apostle should be taken into consideration in any final decision by a church on the public use of spiritual gifts.

e. *14:26-33*. Paul sums up his prior considerations by discussing now in comprehensive fashion a church meeting. Impressive again is the "each" (v. 26) in this context. It appears that "each" believer was to feel himself a vital and responsible participant in the congregation's life.

Again, Paul does not disdain to include speaking in tongues — with three qualifications (and later a fourth, cf. vv. 34-35): (1) not more than three; (2) in turn; and (3) with an interpreter. Without an interpreter, "let each of them keep silence in the church and speak to himself and to God." Prophets, too, should speak in turn (two or three) "while the rest exercise their judgment upon what is said" (v. 29 NEB). This sentence indicates that the critical faculty of the assembly was not to be held in abeyance when any gift, even the highest, was in use. Evidently discussion followed presentation.

At a time when there is a rising protest against monologous and therefore sometimes monotonous "one man ministries" in the churches, and when it is complained increasingly that the preacher is one of the few remaining public figures whose formal remarks allow no public interrogation or discussion (even Presidents are subjected now to the discipline of public interview), it is perhaps in order for the churches to look here in Corinthians to their earliest structures. Perhaps the worship service should include or append a period of thoughtful discussion following the sermon — or sermons (v. 29) — in place of the often dull and unprofitable responsive readings before it and of some of the singing which seems to be often, at the conscious or mental level at least, low-level glossolalia with instrumental accompaniment. However, it would be bad history and unevangelical theology to attempt to implement the precise Corinthian program outlined in I Cor. 14. But the underlying intention here, as elsewhere in Paul's thought, is sound: the ministry, not least in the congregational meeting, should be shared; or put in another way, there should be ample opportunity for discussion. Central to the nature of the church in I Cor. 12-14 is the prominent place of the knowl-

---

[23] Goppelt shows that the primary missionary locus of the early church was the *practicing congregation. Apostolische und nachapostolische Zeit*, p. 60. In this connection Fr. Johannes Hofinger, S. J., of Manila, writes that "today we are, perhaps, too preoccupied and anxious to discover the most effective way of reaching those outside. The Christians of the first centuries showed little of this concern. . . . And yet the worship of these centuries was a missionary force of the first order; regular participation in that worship made of the faithful fully formed Christians and 'missionaries.'" *Worship: The Life of the Missions* ("Liturgical Studies"; Notre Dame, Ind.: University of Notre Dame Press, 1958), p. 12.

edgeable, shared, spontaneous utterance in some kind of thoughtful conversational format. The churches should note this.

The goal of the total participation of the church ("for you can *all* prophesy one by one") was "that all may learn and all be encouraged" (v. 31). The three-fold use of "all" in this verse, underlining at least something of the nature of the ministry of the church, is impressive and should be convicting.[24]

f. *14:33b-38.* Paul then places a prohibition on the verbal, or perhaps more specifically, on the glosso-*lalic* participation of women in the congregational meetings: "For it is shameful for a woman to speak *(lalein)* in church" (v. 35b). The apparent contradiction observed between this verse and I Corinthians 11:5 ("any woman who prays or prophesies with her head unveiled dishonors her head") has been variously explained: that in chapter eleven Paul is speaking more hypothetically, here more concretely; or there of a somewhat private situation, here of a more public one; more plausibly, perhaps, there of intelligible contributions, here of glossolalia; or, finally, a not impossible solution, that even Paul himself is not above contradiction. The prohibition is, however, interesting in this context (ch. 14): Did most of the trouble with tongues-speaking in Corinth come from women?

g. *14:39-40.* Paul's final word on "spiritual things" is an exhortation, "earnestly desire to prophesy," with the again tactful concession "and do not forbid speaking in tongues." There should simply be strict attention that whatever is done "be done decently and in order" (cf. I Thess. 5:19-22). For, as Paul had stressed earlier, "God is not a God of confusion but of peace."

Paul's concern, then, in chapter fourteen is clear: the upbuilding of the church. Paul understands free discussion as especially fitted to this upbuilding. The problem in Corinth — tongues-speaking — Paul neither expressly forbids nor ever commands; but he places before the Corinthians in chapter fourteen these considerations: (1) the larger churchly helpfulness (vv. 1-19) and (2) the missionary preferability (vv. 20-25) of the thoughtfully and understandably shared word — prophecy. Paul trusts that Christian *agapē* with its concern for others will move the congregation to rethink the charismatic ministries in the meetings along the lines he has suggested so that all who come will receive maximum "upbuilding and encouragement and consolation" (v. 4).

SUMMARY

Paul's accomplishment in these three chapters is to have impressed upon the faith of the Corinthians that as the Spirit is united to Christ

---

[24] The congregation's active sharing of ministry is the most impressive lesson for the historic churches from I Cor. 14 — and from Pentecostalism.

so the varied *gifts* of the Spirit are committed to the upbuilding of the *body* of Christ. The triune God is the source, love is the way, and the upbuilding of the church is the goal of the spiritual graces.[25]

The impact of this three-chapter tract must be such as to make it difficult for any church to find the essence of the spiritual in the merely enthusiastic or the only visibly miraculous. One must have the impression instead that, according to Paul, the Christian spiritual is that which confesses the deity of Jesus by faith and which thus works through intelligent love for the upbuilding of Christ's body the church.

ADDITIONAL NOTE: I CORINTHIANS 15:1-11

The denial of the resurrection in Corinth countered by Paul was probably not a denial of Christ's resurrection but of the general resurrection of the *flesh* — i.e., a type of contention for the immortality of the soul.[26] The "transeschatological" mentality in Corinth (see I Cor. 4:8) probably led to a minimizing of the *bodily* resurrection in the interest of the greater and already fully accomplished resurrection or exaltation of the soul through the new experience of the Spirit. Such an emphasis would harmonize with the Corinthians' minimizing of the body, the natural, and the human in the interest of what was considered the spiritual, the supernatural, and the divine.

> The contempt for nature and the body which expressed itself in the unbelief in the resurrection had, in turn, its positive ground in an [exaggerated] estimation of the Spirit, as we have observed heretofore in the Corinthian church. Spirit and nature have become opposites. This is a fundamental trait of all spiritually unbalanced piety (Lütgert).[27]

In 15:1-11 Paul reviews for the Corinthians the apostolic gospel which he had preached to them. Conspicuous by its absence in this review is any reference to the Holy Spirit. The apostolic gospel, according to Paul's definitive account here, circles around Jesus Christ, his death for our sins according to the Scriptures, his burial, his resurrection from the dead, and his appearances to the brethren and apostles. There is apparently no "fuller" gospel with a doctrine of the Holy Spirit.

We may say, then, in theological summary of our studies to this point, that the Holy Spirit in biblical teaching is the almost wholly "functional" and intentionally non-objective member of the divine trinity, purposely hidden behind and operative in the illumination of the gospel of the Son. The gospel of Christ is the full gospel. There is no gospel of the Holy Spirit. To say this is not to deprecate the Spirit,

---

[25] Cf. Hurd's conclusion, *The Origin of I Cor.*, p. 192.

[26] Schniewind, "Die Leugner der Auferstehung in Korinth," *Nachgelassene Reden*, p. 111. Also Jack H. Wilson, "The Corinthians Who Say There Is No Resurrection of the Dead," *ZNW*, 59 (1968), 97. See Hurd's reconstruction of the Corinthians' contention, *The Origin of I Cor.*, pp. 199-200.

[27] *Freiheitspredigt*, p. 128. Cf. Bultmann, *Theology of the New Testament*, I, 169.

it is to co-operate with his office which is to point — even if necessary away from himself — to the Son.

B. II CORINTHIANS 10-13: THE SPHERE OF THE SPIRIT AS THE BELIEVER'S WEAKNESS

The second Corinthian letter in its near entirety is relevant to our subject. Nevertheless, it is in the four concluding chapters — which were perhaps originally (fragments of) a separate letter — that Paul comes with special point to those who are behind the problems in Corinth. In these four chapters all that Paul says in both epistles finds its summation, its sharpest expression and, for our subject, the most pointed correspondences.[28]

1. II CORINTHIANS 10: INTRODUCTORY

a. *10:1-5*

> I, Paul, myself entreat you, by the meekness and gentleness of Christ — I who am humble when face to face with you, but bold to you when I am away! — I beg of you that when I am present I may not have to show boldness with such confidence as I count on showing against some who suspect us of acting in worldly fashion. For though we live in the world we are not carrying on a worldly war, for the weapons of our warfare are not worldly but have divine power to destroy strongholds. We destroy arguments and every proud obstacle to the knowledge of God, and take every thought captive to obey Christ.

Paul begins by entreating the Corinthians through "the meekness and gentleness of Christ," for it is just this lowliness which the Corinthian Christians are in danger of losing through their high spiritual self-consciousness. "I, so feeble (you say) when I am face to face with you, so brave when I am away" (v. 1b NEB). What the entire second letter had heretofore been adumbrating begins now to become clear: Paul lacked the evidences of power which the Corinthians, under the influence of their new teachers, were beginning to associate with the spiritual life.

---

[28] For the identification of the new teachers in Corinth, the time of their arrival, the character and particularly the religious background of their message, see now Dieter Georgi, *Die Gegner des Paulus im 2. Korintherbrief: Studien zur religiösen Propaganda in der Spätantike* ("WMANT," 11; Assen, Niederlande: Neukirchener Verlag, 1964). Georgi's related findings: The opponents understood themselves as Christian world-missionaries (*ibid.*, p. 38) and felt uniquely successful in missionary work, apparently for good reasons (*ibid.*, p. 49). Indeed, "they claimed — for many credibly — to be better Christian missionaries than Paul" (*ibid.*, pp. 205-06). Georgi concludes, relevantly, that "*the opponents of Paul in Second Corinthians were not simply isolated individuals, they were representatives of a large group of missionaries — perhaps, indeed, the majority of missionaries — in the early Christian period*" (*ibid.*, p. 218, emphasis his). For discussion of the literary units — or perhaps letters — contained, sometimes fragmentarily, in the present Second Corinthian letter see the studies by Plummer, Strachan, Schmithals, and Georgi.

When one picks up this Corinthian letter he is struck by the pervasive sense of oppression, trouble, and difficulty to which Paul repeatedly alludes as the experience of his life (cf. especially II Cor. 1:3-11; 4:7-12; 6:4-10; 7:5-6; 11:23 — 12:10; in I Cor. cf. 2:3; 4:8-13). Paul begins the second letter by referring to his afflictions and sufferings (*thlipsis* and *pathēma*) eight times in less than six verses (1:3-8) ending this awesome introduction with the opinion, "we felt that we had received the sentence of death," and with the evaluation, "but that was to make us rely not on ourselves but on God who raises the dead" (1:9). The theology of Paul in II Corinthians is a "theology of death"; but it is a death (a sense of radical weakness) which one knows in oneself in order that God may give the life and receive the honor. As Paul formulates it in introducing another catalogue of suffering in this letter: "We have [present tense = we constantly have] this treasure in earthen vessels, to show that the transcendent power belongs to God and not to us" (4:7).

The absence of the power to avoid his difficulties, or the absence of impressiveness in his difficulties, was enough to make the Corinthians suspicious of Paul's full possession of the Spirit and now, therefore increasingly, to be suspicious of his apostleship. The Corinthians felt that Paul seemed able to be impressive and strong only at a distance — when he wrote, but not when he appeared or spoke. A saying concerning Paul began to circulate in Corinth: " 'His letters are weighty and strong, but his bodily presence is weak, and his speech of no account' " (NEB: " 'When he appears he has no presence, and as a speaker he is beneath contempt' ") (II Cor. 10:10).[29]

The personal unimpressiveness of a man supposed to be full of the Spirit was incomprehensible to those who understood the possession of the Spirit to grant power. According to the new Corinthian equation, to be spiritual = to be powerful; and to be weak = to be fleshly (or, RSV, "worldly," lit. *sarkika*, II Cor. 10:4; *kata sarka*, II Cor. 10:2). Therefore, Paul, who had acknowledged an evident weakness, was suspected of worldliness or of a lack of authentic spirituality. The source of this suspicion becomes clearer as the letter proceeds.

Paul affirms that the Christian (and he means here himself specifically) does live "*in* the world" (*en sarki*, emphasized). However, the Christian's warfare is not therefore "worldly" (*kata sarka*). The Christian's weapons, like his war, are not *sarkika* but are *dunata tö theö*, literally, "powerful to God" (10:4). That is, the Christian's weapons

---

[29] "The character of a carrier of *pneuma* [Spirit] was rendered suspicious, in the religious sense, if he evidenced *dunamis* [power] only in his labored letters but not in direct communication." Reitzenstein, *Hellenistische Mysterienreligionen*³, pp. 363-64. Cf. Lütgert, *Freiheitspredigt*, p. 69; Georgi, *Gegner*, pp. 46 n. 5, 192-93; Tertullian and the Montanists in Harnack's *History of Dogma*, II, 99-100.

are powerful — not necessarily *to men.* It is precisely the character of worldly weapons that they are seen, that they are impressive, that they are visible — to men.

Paul seems to be saying: "If I were personally impressive or overwhelming, if you did see me bristling with power, what would make me any different from any other powerful, impressive personality in the world? As it is, you see me in all my weaknesses, in this 'earthen vessel,' but this is exactly where God can be God. You can know the power in my ministry is God's because you can trace so little of it in me. The way I am you can be sure 'that the transcendent power belongs to God and not to me' " (II Cor. 4:7).

In another important passage in this epistle Paul contrasts what is visible and seen by men and therefore prized, with what is invisible, seen by God alone and therefore (since not seen) by men despised: II Corinthians 5:11-13. Paul speaks in these lines of "those whose pride (*kauchōmenous*) is all in outward show and not in inward worth" (v. 12b, NEB), introducing then an important example from his own life: "For if we are beside ourselves (*exestēmen*), it is for God (*theō*); if we are in our right mind, it is for you" (v. 13). Paul's ecstatic experiences, that is to say, are a matter between him *and God.* Before his churches Paul's desire is to be thoughtful. Paul thus contrasts his private spiritual experiences with those who in Corinth preen themselves publicly on theirs.[30]

Paul sees the "fleshly" not in that which *appears* weak — for it is just the property of the fleshly to be *apparent* — but in pride in that which appears to men to be powerful. This criterion was probably formed in Paul's mind by his consideration of the cross: there one sees total and even repugnant weakness. It was Jesus' "spiritual" contemporaries who called for Jesus to "come down now from the cross," i.e., from weakness, "that we may see [!] and believe" (Mark 15:32 par.). But this triumphalist view of life was not spiritual, it was "fleshly." It was reappearing now in Paul's spiritualist opponents in Corinth who could not *see* certain signs of power in Paul and therefore doubted the authenticity of his work and the fulness of the Spirit in his life. The call to see in order to believe is not the call of

---

[30] "Among the superiorities of which Paul's competitors boasted," notes Bultmann, "were the demonstrations of their possession of the Spirit, especially, as I Cor. 12:1ff. shows, ecstatic experiences." *Exegetische Probleme des zweiten Korintherbriefes: Zu 2. Kor. 5:1-5; 5:11 — 6:10; 10-13; 12:21* ("SBU," 9; Uppsala: Wretmans Boktryckeri A.-B., 1947), p. 14. In another place Bultmann observes perceptively that "if ... the real essence of Christian existence is held to lie in subjective emotional experiences and the activity of the Spirit accordingly to be the producing of emotional experiences, then an individualistic sort of spirit-endowment will arise which may, of course, express itself in deeds of power, but culminates in ecstasy." *Theology of the New Testament,* I, 163. This sentence contains a short history of a type of heart-religion from Methodism to Pentecostalism.

the Spirit. For even in the understanding of ourselves in the Christian life "we walk by faith, not by sight" (II Cor. 5:8).

In Paul's vivid description of the activity of his spiritual warfare in II Corinthians 10:3-5 the preposition *huper* and its "high" synonyms play an important role, as they do indeed throughout the Corinthian correspondence (cf. the thematic I Cor. 4:6 and in II Cor., besides the important 10:5, 14-16; 11:5, 23; 12:6, 7, 11). Paul in the present passage likens his enemies to high fortresses (*hups*ōma) whose thoughts, like ramparts, exalt them *above* the one true experience of God (*tēs gnōseōs tou theou*).[31] Their every "high" notion must be torn down and brought *under* obedience to *Christ* (eis tēn *hup*akoën tou Christou). All *huper* ("over") must become *hupo* ("under"), everything high must become low, and all exalted sense of spiritual power and fulness must become a deep sense of spiritual need. Christian spirituality is placing oneself under Christ, it is not going beyond him.

b. *10:7-18.* Paul continues by comparing himself with the new attitude in Corinth. "If any one is confident that he is Christ's, let him remind himself that as he is Christ's, so are we" (v. 7). There were apparently some in Corinth who felt themselves to be very especially "Christ's." The reader is reminded of Paul's reference in his first epistle to those whose boast sounded especially spiritual in claiming " 'I belong to Christ' " in contrast to those who said " 'I belong to Apollos,' 'I belong to Cephas,' or 'I belong to Paul' " (I Cor. 1:12). Some recent students of Corinthians feel that it is this "Christ-party" in special particular which is the spiritualist or problem group in Corinth.[32] Be-

---

[31] It has become our tentative conviction that *gnōsis* can be as legitimately rendered by "experience" as it can by "knowledge" since the Gnostic *gnōsis* was not primarily speculative but religious knowledge. In support of this hypothesis cf. Weiss, *I Kor.*[10], p. xviii; Reitzenstein, *Hellenistische Mysterienreligionen*[3], pp. 66, 68-69; Heinrich Weinel, *Die Wirkungen des Geistes und der Geister im nachapostolischen Zeitalter bis auf Irenäus* (Freiburg i. B.: Mohr, 1899), p. 195; Schlatter, *Paulus der Bote Jesu: Eine Deutung seiner Briefe an die Korinther* (2d ed.; Stuttgart: Calwer, 1956), p. 40; Büchsel, *Geist Gottes,* p. 371; Walter Schmithals, *Die Gnosis in Korinth: Eine Untersuchung zu den Korintherbriefen* (Göttingen: Vandenhoeck & Ruprecht, 1956), who remarks that " 'gnosis' is the substance of [the gnostic] Corinthian preaching — the central gift of the Spirit," p. 59. Note also the more gnostic-pneumatic than philosophical-intellectual meaning of the related term — *sophia,* "wisdom"— as demonstrated recently by Wilckens' art. *sophia, TWNT,* VII, 520,4-11, 523,17-49. There is a great deal of inner-exegetical debate about the legitimacy of the use of the terms "gnostic" and "gnosticism" as applied to New Testament problems. For our purposes these terms are convenient and dispensable — mystic(ism) or docetic(ism) would serve as well.

[32] So, e.g., Schmithals, *Gnosis in Korinth,* p. 165 n. 1. Not too differently, Georgi's conclusion, *Gegner,* p. 228 n. 1. Further Lietzmann-Kümmel, *Kor.*[4], pp. 6-7, 141. See, however, Hurd's scepticism concerning the Christ-party, *The Origin of I Cor.,* pp. 96-107 and *contra* Schmithals, *ibid.,* pp. 105-07.

cause of its special experience of the Spirit this group felt itself to be in *direct* contact with Christ rather than in indirect, human contact with him through men, even apostles, like the others in Corinth. Corinthian spiritualism demeaned what came indirectly through men in the interest of the direct, the spiritual, and the supernatural as these were then understood.[33] Speaking perhaps to these very persons in particular, Paul tells them to remind themselves that he too belongs to Christ no less than they (cf. I Cor. 7:40 *kagö*).

Paul then proceeds (vv. 12-18) to contrast his own lack of self-advertisement with the spiritual approach of his opponents in Corinth by ironically and thematically employing the verb that best characterizes for him their life-style: *kauchasthai* (the "boasting" of spiritual attainment: II Cor. 10:8, 13, 15, 17, 18; note also *huper* in vv. 14 and 16). Paul's boast is only in the work which God has given him to do and in God's blessing on that work; his vocation is his *kanön* of boasting. Paul *is* proud of the fact that he was enabled to be the first to reach the Corinthians with the gospel and he does not feel that he is *over*-extending himself (*huper*ekteinomen, v. 14) when he says this.

After a left-handed reference to the proselyting work of his opponents Paul ends this introductory section with the same command by which he ended the introductory argument of his first epistle, "Let him who boasts, boast of the Lord" (v. 17; cf. I Cor. 1:31) because, to paraphrase what Paul then writes, it is not those who talk about their spiritual experiences and thus commend themselves who are spiritual, but those whom by their work the Lord commends (v. 18).

2. II CORINTHIANS 11: THE QUEST FOR MORE AND PAUL'S SOLUS CHRISTUS

a. *11:1-4*. Paul now introduces a subject which he is to carry for some time now, his foolishness-theme (11:1 — 12:10). However, he momentarily checks this praise of folly for an important prefatory word. Paul expresses a divine jealousy for the Corinthians, "for I betrothed you to Christ to present you as a pure bride to her one (*heni*) husband" (v. 2). The fact that Paul expressly points to the church's *one* husband (ordinarily it would be sufficient to say simply "husband") points up the Corinthian problem well: the Corinthians were not satisfied with "one" — they were fascinated with the perilous "two" or "more."

Engaged to one husband they were threatening through their new teachers to become attached to someone or something beyond or beside Christ, beyond or beside the exclusive preoccupation with the one husband expected of a faithful bride. This one husband Paul ex-

---

[33] For this very reason — preference of the direct-spiritual to the indirect-human — Kelsey, in our time, suggests that tongues-speaking is a surer evidence of the spiritual presence than prophecy. *Tongue Speaking*, p. 17. The key words of the entire book, written in the mystic vein, are "immediate" and "direct."

pressly names: *tö Christö* (emphasized in the text). The church's
chaste devotion to Christ alone was endangered. Deceived by satanic
cunning, the Corinthians, like Eve, are in deadly peril of having their
thoughts led from "*single*-hearted" devotion to *Christ* (v. 3 NEB).[34]
Paul expresses his disappointment in the Corinthian submission to
the visiting missionaries (II Cor. 11:4):

> For if some one comes and preaches another Jesus than the one we
> preached, or if you receive a different spirit from the one you received,
> or if you accept a different gospel from the one you accepted, you submit
> to it well enough.

II Corinthians 11:4 is one of the most important texts in the
Corinthian correspondence. It places a wide-angled lens over the
Corinthian theology of the higher life taught by Paul's influential
opponents in Corinth. It was a theology of "another Jesus," "a different
Spirit," and "a different gospel" — and the Corinthians were very willing
"to submit to it."

First of all, the Jesus the new missionaries preached was "another,"
somewhat different (*allon*) Jesus than the Jesus Paul preached. The
difference probably existed in seeing the earthly Jesus primarily as a
divine miracle-worker and only peripherally (if at all) as a suffering
servant.[35]

In two respects particularly — the Spirit and the gospel — the
Corinthian teachers understood themselves as differing from Paul
(*pneuma heteron . . . , euaggelion heteron*). While it could not be denied
that Paul brought the Corinthians a knowledge of the gospel and the
Spirit in an at least introductory or intellectual way, nevertheless, the
more recent missionaries to Corinth can now claim, and evidently prove,
that they have been able to bring the Corinthians "exactly these things in
a greater measure than Paul."[36]

We may reconstruct the Corinthian situation, from the preceding
text, then, in approximately the following manner. A number of
Corinthians believed that only *post-Paulum,* only since the new teaching had come were they in fact living in the new life of the Spirit and
the gospel which seemed their appropriate birthright in the heavenly
Christ (I Cor. 4:8; cf. II Cor. 4:12). As they contrasted the wonder-

---

[34] Cf. duPlessis' commendation of Pentecostalism's *two* distinct experiences in
RGG[3], V, 311, above, p. 74.

[35] On the Christology of Paul's opponents in Corinth see especially Georgi,
Gegner, pp. 15, 290.

[36] Lütgert, *Freiheitspredigt,* p. 67. Cf. Skibstedt, *Geistestaufe,* p. 77, above p.
72. Karl Prümm, S.J., carries on a polemic against Lütgert's (and following
Lütgert, Schlatter's, Bultmann's, and Käsemann's) pneumatic interpretation of
Corinthianism and asks for one single piece of evidence for this theory. *Diakonia
Pneumatos: Der zweite Korintherbrief als Zugang zur apostolischen Botschaft,*
3 vols. (Rome: Herder, 1960-1967), I, 738. One might point to the use of *huper*
as evidence, or to this text, or even to Prümm's own remarks, *ibid.,* p. 748.

ful new experiences in their lives with Paul's now admitted weaknesses — his constant public difficulties and personal problems — the Corinthians were inevitably tempted to ask: Have we not in fact received the Spirit and the gospel in a fuller measure than Paul himself? II Corinthians 11:4 indicates that the higher teachers came talking about the same general subjects as Paul — Jesus, Spirit, gospel — but with a consciousness that whereas Paul had only partly known and presented these, as confirmed in his own confessed experience of omnipresent troubles and embarrassing lack of personal magnetism, they had experienced Jesus, the Spirit, and the gospel in a fuller way.[37]

b. *11:5-15*. For the first time in this letter Paul ventures a name for the new evangelists in Corinth: they are "superlative apostles" (*huper*lian apostoloi, v. 5). They were spiritual "hupermen." They were superlative because they claimed to go beyond Paul (and others) in both message and life. Paul made Christians in name, they made Christians in Spirit; Paul accented a crucified Messiah who gave grace, they brought a glorified Messiah who gave power; Paul brought the Spirit, but they brought him fully; Paul, in other words, brought something of the gospel, but they brought the full gospel. Yet Paul now declares — and the fact that he must even say it strikes us as somehow pathetic — "I think that I am not the least inferior to these" (II Cor. 11:5)![38] However, his commendable self-control will not last much longer.

After discussing financial matters briefly (vv. 7-12), Paul finally explodes: those who found him worldly because weak, less Christ's because less their "more," and who knew how to make full what he only knew how to begin, i.e., to over-(*huper*)-do him, he must now call by name: they are not only superapostles, they are "sham apostles" (*pseudapostoloi*) and "crooked in all their practices, masquerading as apostles of Christ" (11:13 NEB).

Paul felt that he must now say, of those to whom earlier he had seemed to attribute Christianity, the very opposite: they are not real. For Paul saw in their spiritual pride, in their superlatives, in their self-advertisement and large claims, perhaps even in their celebrated spiritual experiences, and certainly in their bringing schism, not apostles of a higher type of Christianity (though they saw miraculous evidences

---

[37] Cf. Lütgert, *Freiheitspredigt,* p. 75. Note the recorded beginnings of the Assembléias de Deus, the largest Pentecostal group in Brazil, in *Hollenweger* II, 886-87.

[38] See Lütgert's important observation to this text: "Out of the insistence of the apostle — that he does not think himself to be behind these men in anything — we may gather that these men did not purport to give something completely different than Paul had given — e.g., the law — rather, they intend to outdo him, give more than he gave, the Spirit, but *more* of the Spirit, a fuller Spirit, Jesus, but a more deeply understood Jesus." *Freiheitspredigt,* pp. 67-68. Héring calls these superapostles *"les apôtres transcendants." II Cor.,* p. 83.

of this all around them), but of a lower, indeed, of an anti-type.[39]
And so, though they glowed with a luminous message, warmth of devotion, and zeal of life, Paul was not impressed or surprised for he spied
the source of their illumination:

> Satan himself masquerades as an angel of light. It is therefore a simple
> thing for his agents to masquerade as agents of good. But they will meet
> the end their deeds deserve (vv. 14-15 NEB).

c. *11:16-21*. After touching the "fool theme" again (vv. 16-19),
into which he shall launch full force momentarily, Paul pauses to offer
one more picture of his higher-life opponents. In it he indicates with a
few vivid strokes something of the manner of their ministry as earlier
(11:4) he had outlined in a comparable passage the content of their
message.

> For you bear it [the same word is used at 11:4] if a man makes slaves
> of you, or preys upon you, or takes advantage of you, or puts on airs
> [*epairetai*, cf. II Cor. 10:5!], or strikes you in the face (v. 20).

Corresponding to their higher-life or *huper* theology, the way of
life of the new teachers with their pupils was supercilious (*kata-*, v.
20a). Being higher, they could not help seeing others as lower. Thus
the inevitable corollary of their granting the Corinthians a higher
experience was a certain creditor or master sense.[40] If one feels himself spiritually higher than others, then from this altitude it must be
difficult in looking around to look anywhere but down. Nor was it
psychologically incomprehensible that the Corinthians found a certain
fascination in their strong, masterful leaders; they "bore" this superior
manner as readily as they bore the superior message. Paul must confess,
"to my shame, I must say, we were too weak for that!" (11:21).

d. *11:21b-33*. Now in a sustained passage Paul commences at last
his "foolishness" — *his* boasting. He had been postponing this painful
assignment for as long as possible (since at least 11:1, but cf. 10:8).
He evidently did not compliment himself readily.

In beginning, as if talking to himself, he protests the absurdity of
what he is going to do as though the very idea of a Christian's dis-
coursing on his exploits was repugnant to him ("I am speaking as a
fool," 11:21; "I am talking like a madman," 11:23). And when his
boasting is over he almost audibly sighs, "I have been a fool!" (12:11).

The opponents had boasted of their spiritual (and Jewish) back-

---

[39] They probably had actual miracles to which they could point — the visibly
miraculous was not unfamiliar in even the post-apostolic period. See Weinel,
Wirkungen, pp. 13-14. Cf. also Braun, art. *poieö*, *TWNT*, VI, 482; Friedrich, art.
euaggelion, *TWNT*, II, 732,35 and the same author's "Die Gegner des Paulus im
2. Korintherbrief," in *Abraham Unser Vater: Juden und Christen im Gespräch
über die Bibel*. "Festschrift für Otto Michel zum 60. Geburtstag," ed. Otto Betz
et al. (Leiden: Brill, 1963), p. 183.

[40] Cf. Georgi, *Gegner*, p. 227 n. 3.

ground — so can Paul (11:22). They boasted of being special missionaries of Christ and Paul exerts himself and says, "I am a better one (*huper egö!*) — I am talking like a madman" (11:23).[41] Then Paul proceeds to show exactly how he was better, using his opponents' superlatives, but with a twist: "with far greater labors, far more imprisonments, with countless beatings, and often near death" (11:23b). The superlatives were employed by Paul in a way the Corinthians had not been accustomed to hearing: Paul praised his problems. Strange boasting.

Paul continues to count his painful trophies (vv. 24-29) in a way that reveals Paul's greatness as surely as it must have lashed his readers' consciences. Then Paul explains what he has already implied — his philosophy of sharing spiritual experiences: "If I must boast, I will boast of the things that show my weakness" (v. 30). And as if to carry this now to its fullest consequences he relates an experience in which he appears as anything but a *theios-anër,* a conquering hero with divine accoutrements: Paul being furtively lowered — by men not angels — from a city wall in a basket (vv. 32-33). Paul prefers appearing comical to appearing super.[42]

3. II CORINTHIANS 12: THE QUEST FOR POWER AND PAUL'S SOLA GRATIA

a. *12:1-6.* Finally, Paul is forced to a theme which his opponents had pressed him to discuss from the very first, if he were able: Had Paul ever had a special spiritual experience since becoming a Christian? Though Paul can see no use at all in sharing this ("it does no good," v. 1 NEB), he would lie if he should deny it. Specifically, had he ever had any visions or revelations as they had had? Paul says he will now come to that.

And immediately, as if attempting to distance himself as far as possible from what is as unnatural to him as his just completed boasting, Paul grammatically shifts persons. Rather than speaking in the first person, he writes, "I know a man" (v. 2). By using the anonymous third person — "a man" — Paul adroitly removes his own person from what he is for truth's sake forced to relate.

The Corinthian higher-life teachers, in their demotion of the body

---

[41] For an extended discussion of the opponents' self-designations see Georgi, *Gegner,* pp. 31-82 and for the meaning of the term *diakonos* ("missionary"!) see, in particular, *ibid.,* pp. 31-38.

[42] In itself, this escape "was nothing but absolutely humiliating." Héring, *II Cor.,* p. 92. However, Pentecostalism sees this passage in a different light. "Since Paul introduces this report of his rescue with the solemn assurance that he tells the pure truth, one must assume that the little wall-window was so narrow that it appeared to be impossible for a man to pass through it. . . . Thus the rescue of Paul was miraculous." Note to II Cor. 11:32-33 in the *Mülheimer New Testament, ad loc.*

in the interest of the Spirit, had made much of being completely transported out of their bodies by their spiritual experiences. Paul purposely confesses ignorance:

> I know a man in Christ who fourteen years ago was caught up to the third heaven — whether in the body or out of the body I do not know, God knows. And I know that this man was caught up into Paradise — whether in the body or out of the body I do not know, God knows — and he heard things that cannot be told, which man may not utter (vv. 2-4).

This was the extent of Paul's spiritual experience! He goes no further. In it he tells more of what he does not know than of what he does. What his opponents claim so certainly to know — that they were taken out of their bodies — he leaves to God. What his opponents in their spiritual experiences saw, heard, and described with exotic detail, Paul relates with hardly an adjective or traceable emotion. He describes not a single thing seen. And what he heard were things that "cannot be told" and which "man may not utter." This is all that Paul will tell the curious and miracle-hungry Corinthians.

Paul's vision, in which he neither describes what he saw, relates what he heard, nor details what he felt or thought, constitutes a rebuke of the first order to those in Corinth who cultivated marvelous spiritual experiences for public consumption. The fact, moreover, that Paul must go back fourteen years to relate an experience in the life of "a man in Christ" (whether in or out of the body he does not know), indicates eloquently that Paul was no ordinary or everyday visionary.

Paul then adds this footnote: "On behalf of this man [still in the third person!] I will boast, but on my own behalf [now first person!] I will not boast, except of my weaknesses" (v. 5). When Paul boasts of experiences he prefers to boast of his deflated experiences — such as imprisonments, beatings, anxieties, or embarrassments (11:23-33). But now Paul prepares to relate, at the conclusion of his long list of "boasts," his perhaps most painful experience. It is significant that Paul places this lowest of his Christian experiences at the end for emphasis — and not his "vision." For this lowest of experiences was in fact Paul's highest, for reasons he himself will explain.

b. *12:7-10.*

> And to keep me from being too elated [*huper*airömai] by the abundance [*huper*bolë] of revelations, a thorn was given me in the flesh, a messenger of Satan, to harass me, to keep me from being too elated (v. 7).

One may only cautiously guess what this thorn, this messenger of Satan, was. It was not in itself pleasant or good: it beat Paul. However, its end was good: to keep Paul from becoming *huper*. Thus the very trait granted the superapostles through their spiritual experiences was denied Paul: the sense of superiority.

Paul did not want to be esteemed because of anything unusual in him or in his experience; therefore he deliberately refrained from boasting "so that no one may think more of me than he sees in me or hears from me" (v. 6), that is, than one sees and hears in the usual, daily round of Paul's life and ministry.[43] Paul interpreted the nagging satanic messenger as "given" him to keep his feet on the ground, to keep him earthy and normal. We may even say that it was given to him to keep him from becoming (as his opponents understood it) "spiritual." Paul's Christian experiences could have carried him away, elevated him over others, but the thorn nailed him to earth, as he twice expresses it, "to keep me from being too elated."

Three times Paul besought the Lord to take the problem from him. But the Lord said (perfect tense verb: Paul still hears it!): " 'My grace is sufficient for you, for my power is made perfect in weakness' " (v. 9). May we gather from this answer that Paul had specifically asked for more power than he felt he had? That Paul felt inhibited by his thorn and sought the power to overcome this weakness? If so, his experience would correspond to that which we recognized earlier in those seeking a baptism in the Holy Spirit: the sense of self-frustration and of the lack of sufficient power for service.

In any case, Paul's answer was different. Power, he learned, was not something acquired beyond "mere grace," but "grace," he was told, "is all you need" (v. 9 NEB). Paul learned that grace was not simply a first blessing, succeeded by a second. Paul was not told how to go beyond mere grace. He was not told how to overcome his weakness through five steps. He was told that when a man had grace his weakness was precisely where God could be strong.

Power, the divine answer told Paul, comes not through overcoming weakness but through bearing it. Some weaknesses are apparently never to be overcome, they are to be used. They can in fact become the source of divine power in its perfection. For God's power perfects itself in human weakness. The cross is the paradigm of this formula. Worldly, i.e., "spiritualist" power is powerful when it is no longer weak.[44]

From the divine answer came the apostolic conclusion, determinative for Paul's whole life: "I shall therefore prefer to find my joy and pride ["my boast," kauchēsomai] in the very things that are my weakness: and then the power of Christ will come and rest upon me" (v. 9 NEB; the Greek word order is more impressive, literally, "in order that it might rest upon me the power of Christ"). The power of Christ is power in weakness; all other power — i.e., power in power — Paul must have found puny in comparison. In this life only power in

---

[43] "The transcending of the daily round, however, was precisely the intention of the opponents in their boasts." Georgi, Gegner, p. 228.
[44] See Lütgert's illuminating comment, Freiheitspredigt, p. 110.

weakness is divine and sure to keep divinity where it belongs — with God and not the vessel (II Cor. 4:7). Power in power is in danger of self-deification, for through its assumed contact with divine power it is tempted to believe *itself* powerful. Only power in real (not overcome) weakness is divine power and rescued from boasting in spiritual accomplishment. Radical, present weakness is the sphere of Christ's royal power.

Paul ends (v. 10 NEB): "Hence I am well content, for *Christ's* sake, with weakness, contempt [*hub*resin: Paul's Corinthian opponents?], persecution, hardship, and frustration; for when I am weak [present tense =continually], then I am strong [also present tense]." *Simul potens et debilis.*

Remarkable in this classic discussion of power in the New Testament is the absence of any reference to the Spirit. The reason may lie not only in the actual experience itself, but in Paul's studied effort, visible throughout the Corinthian letters, to turn the eyes of the Corinthian spiritualists from what they thought was the Spirit to the Spirit's true work, which is the magnification of the grace of Christ; and "grace is sufficient."

c. *12:11-21.* Paul has played the fool by talking liberally of his spiritual experiences (in a quite unanticipated way), but only because he was forced by the Corinthians' insistence. Paul ought not to have had to commend himself in defense; he should have had the Corinthians' commendation without this foolishness (v. 11).

Then Paul, in that curious irony which marks the whole epistle, claims to be behind the superapostles in nothing, even if he is nothing himself (v. 11b). Through the interesting contrast in this verse (cf. also II Cor. 11:5) between *husterēsa* (behind) and *huperlian* (beyond) we get an even more accurate description of Paul's opponents: they are "further" apostles. But however far their "further life" extends, Paul claims to be behind them in nothing at all. Whatever they may offer further or fuller, be it Jesus, the Spirit, or the gospel, power, victory, or holiness, Paul will not concede that he is behind them in anything, even if he does understand himself as nothing at all and as radically weak.

Paul then takes up what appears to be another phrase of the superlative teachers, "the signs of the apostle," and he uses it — again with that distance which characterizes Paul in this portion of the epistle — in the third person and the passive: "the signs of a true apostle were performed among you in all patience, with signs and wonders and mighty works" (v. 12). The opponents made much of miracles and claimed them; indeed, they claimed the very signs of an apostle. Again, Paul cannot honestly claim to have been without these signs himself. But he does not suggest what these signs were or offer any description of them either here or in any of his writings (cf. I Cor. 2:4; Rom. 15:19).[45]

We will not be far wrong in assuming that Paul talks only reluctantly of signs at all, for he had himself earlier written that "Jews demand signs and Greeks seek wisdom, but we preach Christ crucified [which is] a stumbling-block" (I Cor. 1:22-23). For miraculous signs themselves were not unambiguous. When Paul does mention signs (such as his "vision"), he will not specify for the curious.

After touching the sensitive financial question again, Paul lists what he fears encountering when he comes and what may have been among the serious spiritual problems of the Corinthian spiritualists in spite of their higher life: "quarreling, jealousy, anger, selfishness, slander, gossip, conceit (*phusiōseis;* cf. this word in I Cor. 4:6; 8:1; 13:4), and disorder (see this word at I Cor. 14:33)" (v. 20b). Bultmann says of the sins in this list, rightly, that they are the "consequences of spiritualism," and that most of these same sins "can be easily illustrated by the noticeable church circumstances in I Corinthians."[46] Yet one need not reach back to I Corinthians; the II Corinthian context itself portrays to us a theology (11:4) and a mentality (11:20) which this catalogue explicates ethically. It is an ethic caught most concisely in the signature word of Corinthianism: *huper.* The catalogue is interesting for its being composed almost exclusively of the "spiritual" sins, which do not often strike those involved in them as sinful.

But that sins of the spiritual sort, finally, are not guarantees for the absence of their erotic companions is indicated by the fear Paul expresses that the "impurity, immorality, and licentiousness" which used to find a home in many in Corinth may not have been repented of (v. 21).

4. II CORINTHIANS 13: THE QUEST FOR EVIDENCE AND PAUL'S SOLA FIDES

Paul fears his severity when he comes to Corinth. This severity, Paul insists, will be the evidence that Christ is in him; the evidence will not be any special spiritual proof such as they are now seeking from him in Corinth —"since you desire proof that Christ is speaking in me" (13:3). This is one of the most interesting phrases in the letter for our subject. The Corinthians wanted "proof" (*dokimē;* cf. the

---

[45] First pointed out to me by Hermann Bertrams, *Das Wesen des Geistes nach der Anschauung des Apostels Paulus: Eine biblisch-theologische Untersuchung* ("Neutestamentliche Abhandlungen"; Münster i. W.: Aschendorffsche Verlagsbuchhandlung, 1913), p. 43. Volz notices that in the Old Testament while the prophets were expected to perform miracles and could, nevertheless, "the great prophets themselves tell of none of their own miraculous deeds." *Geist Gottes,* p. 35.

[46] *Probleme,* p. 24.

English "documentation"), evidence, that Christ could really speak through Paul.[47]

The quest for evidence was behind all the earlier Corinthian demands to know Paul's experiences, visions, and victories, and behind the Corinthians' doubt of Paul's spirituality, in the highest sense. Is not Christ the victor, the Lord of glory, the all-powerful? Could, then, a Christian — indeed an apostle — in whom this Lord fully dwelt have, at the same time, personal and physical problems and unconquered weaknesses? Paul lacked the evidences of the Spirit as the Corinthians were now being taught to understand these evidences. Could Christ, then, be truly or fully in Paul?

The nature of the "documentation" sought of Paul by the Corinthians can only be surmised. Reasoning from the entire Corinthian context we may suppose that the evidence was something striking, for the striking manifestation was to the Corinthians the spiritual *par excellence.* Schmithals in his study of gnosticism in Corinth came to the conclusion that the Corinthian demand for an evidence of Christ speaking in Paul "in its symbolic roots . . . expresses . . . the desire for ecstatic speaking, i.e., primarily, for speaking in tongues."[48] Whatever the evidence, Paul would not supply the Corinthians the satisfaction of compliance; instead, he would prove Christ's speaking through him by his apostolic severity against unrepented sin in Corinth (vv. 1-3).

Then in pungent sentences, difficult to unravel for their irony and yet poignant precisely for their confusion, Paul stutters again his difficult theme in this letter — power in weakness:

> [Christ] is not weak in dealing with you, but is powerful in you [how does Paul mean this?]. For he was crucified in weakness, but lives by the power of God. For we are weak in him [!], but in dealing with you we shall live with him by the power of God (v. 4).

This much is clear: for Paul as for the Psalmist "power belongs to God." Even "in Christ" Paul sees *himself* as weak. Yet we know from his earlier and classic formula that precisely *when* he is weak, *then* he is

---

[47] "When they demand of Paul a 'certification' (*dokimē* 13:3)," writes Bultmann, "they thereby betray their position that a tangible accomplishment capable of being presented for inspection is to them the proof of possessing the Spirit." *Theology of the New Testament,* I, 241. "For the Corinthians," Schmithals adds, "everything depended upon giving themselves and others an evidence of the Spirit who indwelt them." *Gnosis in Korinth,* p. 141; also G. Bornkamm, *Die Vorgeschichte des sogenannten Zweiten Korintherbriefes* (Heidelberg: Carl Winter Universitäts Verlag, 1961), pp. 12-13; Hurd, *The Origin of I Cor.,* p. 193.

[48] *Gnosis in Korinth,* p. 159. Paul's opponents in Corinth believed and taught that tongues-speaking was "*the* manifestation of ecstatic religiosity." *Ibid.,* p. 142. Similarly, Friedrich, *art. cit.,* in *Abraham Unser Vater,* pp. 182-84. Friedrich, however, traces the opponents to Jewish rather than gnostic sources. Cf., finally, Sweet, *art. cit., NTSt, 13* (April 1967), 245.

strong (II Cor. 12:9-10; cf. II Cor. 4:7, 10-12). Paul is confident of exhibiting this evangelical strength in his pending visit to Corinth (v. 4b).

Then Paul goes on the offensive. Rather than testing *him* for evidences, Paul suggests that the Corinthians test themselves (see the emphasized "yourselves," three times in v. 5). "Examine *yourselves,* to see whether *you* are holding to *your* faith. Test *yourselves.* Do you not realize [Greek adds: "yourselves"] that Christ is in *you?* — unless indeed *you* fail to meet the test!" Paul calls, in Héring's word, for *"autocritique."*

It is important to mark the specific test which Paul sets: "Are you in *the faith?"* (literal rendering of v. 5a). Paul does not believe that a man ever gets beyond faith as the evidence of Christian reality. Paul knows no other evidence. Instead of submitting the Corinthians to some new sensational proof, of which they already knew too many, Paul probes them for what is not only basic but ultimate, not only initial but medial and terminal, for faith — more specifically, for their standing in the objective Christian faith of the gospel.

The simplicity of Paul's evidence of faith fits the simplicity of Paul's gospel of Christ. Paul wants the eyes of the Corinthians to be on Christ, their one husband, to whom they owe a single-hearted devotion. If the Corinthians wish to look at themselves, Paul submits only one test: Are they in the faith, that unique Christian faith (*të pistei; fides quae creditur*) which looks away from itself, its evidence and power included — indeed, even from its own inner faith — to the one object of its faith and subject of its engagement, the Christ. Paul does not ask anything more of his Corinthians in the midst of their Christian life than he asked at the beginning: faith. For the Christian life to Paul is not only "through faith," it is "for faith" (Rom. 1:17).

Paul ends the II Corinthian letter with a prayer by which, as in his entire correspondence, he links in union that which in Corinth was being parceled and apportioned but which he can see only whole: "The grace of the Lord Jesus Christ and the love of God and the fellowship of the Holy Spirit be with you all" (v. 14).[49]

SUMMARY AND CONCLUSION

Everywhere one turns in the Corinthian correspondence, particularly

---

[49] See Schlatter's conclusion to "the Corinthian theology." "The self-centered conception of faith which understands faith as participation in God's power by which one is brought higher life, ... a desire to be bound to the exalted Christ without appreciating God's grace in the crucified one, a filling with the Spirit ... which blessed one with one's own greatness, ... all this was in the deepest sense un-Pauline as it was also un-Johannine and unapostolic." *Korinthische Theologie,* pp. 123-24.

the second letter, one finds not only a superseded gnosticism but, we are obliged to believe, an anticipated Pentecostalism. From the pride of power (II Cor. 10), through the fuller ministry of Jesus, Spirit, and gospel (II Cor. 11), and the unusual interest in visions nd higher experiences (II Cor. 12), to the quest for oral evidences (II Cor. 13), we are in similar spiritual topography. The features most prominent in first-century Corinthianism are found to correspond to a remarkable degree with the features most distinctively present in twentieth-century Pentecostalism. We do not believe that these correspondences are forced.

Paul's approach to his problem is thoroughly christocentric. His strategy is to bring the church's every thought into captivity to obedience to Christ (II Cor. 10:1-6), to have all subsequent boasting in only the Lord (10:17), to have his church engaged with a single-hearted devotion to one husband, even to Christ (11:2), and consequently not to bear with any teaching of "another" and more striking or miraculous Jesus, or of a quite "different," deeply filling Spirit, or of a "different," fuller gospel (11:4).

The Corinthians' preoccupation with what they understood as the spiritual, namely the remarkable and the powerful, lifted them above (huper) both the Spirit's corporate and individual spheres of action: specifically, above the common lot of believers in the church, the body of Christ (I Cor. 12-14), and above personal weakness, the body of the Christian (II Cor. 10-13).

First, the Corinthians must become, in the best sense of the word, more churchly, more committed to the church (I Cor. 12-14). It is impossible at the same time to love the Head and hate the body, proclaim Christ and despise his church. As long as the Corinthians felt themselves the possessors of the special manifestations of the Spirit and of a new message on how to attain such they must necessarily find themselves exalted above all "nominal Christians" and their weaknesses in the crucified church. The church in many respects will always seem to be, like Paul himself, outwardly unimpressive and full of weaknesses. But instead of despising these weaknesses in the church — as the crucified Messiah himself was despised by his more spiritual contemporaries — Christians are called upon, with their particular and unique gifts (I Cor. 12), patiently and compassionately (I Cor. 13) to seek one thing for this always somewhat offensive, and generally rather unimpressive institution — its upbuilding (I Cor. 14). For to faith this unimpressive entity is the body of Christ.

In a word, Paul wants to turn the eyes of the Corinthians from the spirit of huper which boasts, to the spirit of agapë which builds; from being impressed with one's own spiritual relevance and power, to being concerned with finding a lowly and patient relevance of a quite different kind to the weaknesses of the church. If the Corinthian problem is in any way typical of problems in the early church, then the vaunted power and purity of the primitive church is really not much to boast about. The church, from its start, has been full of problems because it has been full of people.

The Corinthian letters are a sustained attempt to formulate what Luther later called a *theologia crucis,* a theology of the cross. God's way of working in the world — to men an inefficient way, and thus a proof of its divinity — is the way of weakness. The crucified Christ himself is this way's classic content; the cross its classic form; the struggling church (and church member) its classic sphere. Men are saved by believing this content and serve by assuming this form in this sphere. But hidden in the cross and weakness (corporate and individual) and revealed in the church to faith is resurrection power. "When . . . weak, then . . . strong" (II Cor. 12:10).

The churches no less than Pentecostalism need to hear the message of the Corinthian letters. If both the churches and Pentecostalism could be persuaded to hear what the Spirit says to them through Corinth, to look at Christ singly and to serve him simply through the ministry of varied gifts in the given local congregation and wherever else there is need, the churches would find life in (but never beyond) their weaknesses, and Pentecostalism would find not only the fulness of the Spirit it wrongly seeks, it would minister to the church it needs and which — if Pentecostalism were made responsibly christocentric — very much needs it.

Part Three

DOCUMENTS
BIBLIOGRAPHY
INDEXES

DOCUMENTS

A REPOSITORY OF THE MODERN THEOLOGICAL SOURCES OF THE PENTECOSTAL DOCTRINE AND EXPERIENCE OF THE HOLY SPIRIT

I. JOHN WESLEY'S DOCTRINE OF ENTIRE SANCTIFICATION (CHRISTIAN PERFECTION)[1]

A. THE DOCTRINE OF THE SUBSEQUENCE OF ENTIRE SANCTIFICATION

1. Subsequent to Justification

a. " 'Neither dare we affirm, as some have done, that all this salvation is given at once. There is indeed an instantaneous, as well as a gradual, work of God in His children; and there wants not, we know, a cloud of witnesses who have received, in one moment, either a clear sense of the forgiveness of their sins, or the abiding witness of the Holy Spirit. But we do not know a single instance, in any place, of a person's receiving, in one

---

[1] "This doctrine is the grand depositum which God has lodged with the people called Methodists, and for the sake of propagating this chiefly he appears to have raised us up." *The Letters of the Rev. John Wesley, A. M.,* ed. John Telford (8 vols.; "Standard Edition"; London: The Epworth Press, 1931), VIII, 238 (letter of Sept. 1790). Sources: John Wesley, *A Plain Account of Christian Perfection* (London: The Epworth Press, 1952 [1741; rev. ed. 1767]); *The Journal of the Rev. John Wesley, A. M.,* ed. Nehemiah Curnock (8 vols.; "Standard Edition"; London: The Epworth Press, 1938); *Wesley's Standard Sermons . . . ,* ed. Edward H. Sugden (2 vols.; 4th ed.; London: The Epworth Press, 1955); John Wesley, *Sermons on Several Occasions* ("First Series"; London: The Epworth Press, 1952). And see, particularly, the sermon "Christian Perfection" (1741), and the essays "The Scripture Way of Salvation" (1765), "Thoughts on Christian Perfection" (1759; 1787), and "Cautions and Directions . . ." (1762), all printed with admirable introduction in Albert C. Outler's *John Wesley* ("A Library of Protestant Thought"; New York: Oxford University Press, 1964), pp. 251-305. Further literature: R. Newton Flew, *The Idea of Perfection in Christian Theology: An Historical Study of the Christian Ideal for the Present Life.* London: Oxford University Press, 1934; H. Lindström, *Wesley and Sanctification,* 1946; John Leland Peters, *Christian Perfection and American Methodism.* Nashville: Abingdon, 1956; Lycurgus M. Starkey, Jr., *The Work of the Holy Spirit: A Study in Wesleyan Theology.* Nashville: Abingdon, 1962; Robert C. Monk, *John Wesley: His Puritan Heritage* (1966); and F. Platt, art. "Perfection (Christian)," *ERE,* IX, 728-37.

323

and the same moment, remission of sins, the abiding witness of the Spirit, and a new, a clean heart.' "[2]

b. " 'It is not so early as justification; for justified persons are to "go on unto perfection" (Heb. 6:1).' "[3]

c. "I differ [from some of the other clergy in the Church of England] in the points following: — First. They speak of justification, either as the same thing with sanctification, or as something consequent upon it. I believe justification to be wholly distinct from sanctification, and necessarily antecedent to it."[4]

2. Higher than Justification

a. " 'Nor does anything under heaven more quicken the desires of those who are justified, than to converse with those whom they believe to have experienced a still higher salvation. This places that salvation full in their view, and increases their hunger and thirst after it.' "[5]

b. " 'If a man be deeply and fully convinced, after justification, of inbred sin; if he then experience a gradual mortification of sin, and afterwards an entire renewal in the image of God; if to this change, immensely greater than that wrought when he was justified, be added a clear direct witness of the renewal, I judge it as impossible this man should be deceived herein, as that God would lie. And if one whom I know to be a man of veracity testify these things to me, I ought not, without some sufficient reason, to reject his testimony.' "[6]

c. " 'And as the change undergone when the body dies is of a different kind, and infinitely greater than any we had known before, yea, such as till then it is impossible to conceive; so the change wrought when the soul dies to sin is of a different kind, and infinitely greater than any before, and than any can conceive till he experience it.' "[7]

B. THE DOCTRINE OF THE EVIDENCE OF ENTIRE SANCTIFICATION

1. An Instantaneous Experience

a. "I like your doctrine of Perfection, or pure love; love excluding sin; your insisting that it is merely by faith; that consequently it is instantaneous (though preceded and followed by a gradual work), and that it may be now, at this instant."[8]

b. "It is also a plain fact, that this power does commonly overshadow

---

[2] Wesley, *Plain Account*, p. 24.
[3] *Ibid.*, p. 106.
[4] Wesley, *Journal*, II (Sept. 13, 1739), 275.
[5] Wesley, *Plain Account*, p. 47.
[6] *Ibid.*, pp. 52-53.
[7] *Ibid.*, p. 53. For similar remarks elsewhere in Wesley see, e.g., the sermon "Satan's Devices" in Wesley's *Sermons on Several Occasions*, p. 492. Cf. Flew, *The Idea of Perfection*, p. 316. Starkey notes that for Wesley "justification implies a 'relative change' in man while the new birth and sanctification mark the 'real change.' " *Work of the Holy Spirit*, p. 51.
[8] Wesley, *Journal*, IV (Nov. 1, 1762: Letter to Thomas Maxfield), 536.

them in an instant; and that from that time they enjoy that inward and outward holiness, to which they were utter strangers before."[9]

2. A Deeper Experience

" 'Q. When may a person judge himself to have attained this?'

" 'A. When, after having been fully convinced of inbred sin, by a far deeper and clearer conviction than that he experienced before justification, and after having experienced a gradual mortification of it, he experiences a total death to sin, and an entire renewal in the love and image of God, so as to rejoice evermore, to pray without ceasing, and in everything to give thanks.' "[10]

C. THE DOCTRINE OF THE CONDITIONS FOR ENTIRE SANCTIFICATION

1. The Doctrine of Faith

a. Sola Fide

i. "Exactly as we are justified by faith, so are we sanctified by faith. Faith is the condition, and the only condition of sanctification, exactly as it is of justification. It is the condition: none is sanctified but he that believes; without faith no man is sanctified. And it is the only condition: this alone is sufficient for sanctification."[11]

ii. "As to the manner. I believe this perfection is always wrought in the soul by a simple act of faith; consequently in an instant."[12]

iii. " 'Can anything be more clear than . . . [t]hat this is spoken of as receivable by mere faith?' "[13]

---

[9] Ibid., V (Aug. 27, 1768: Letter to Lawrence Coughlan), 284. For similar remarks on instantaneousness in Wesley cf. his Plain Account, pp. 24, 41.

[10] Wesley, Plain Account, p. 52. Cf. this exchange in ibid., p. 57: " 'Q. Is there no danger, then, of being thus deceived?' 'A. Not at the time that he feels no sin. . . . So long as he feels nothing but love animating all his thoughts and words and actions, he is in no danger." Key word: "feels." Wesley's diary, Sunday, Jan. 8, 1738, is introduced with the revealing entry: "By the most infallible of proofs, inward feeling, I am convinced. . . ." See Outler, John Wesley, p. 41.

[11] From "The Scripture Way of Salvation" (1765) in Outler, John Wesley, p. 278, who says of this essay that "if the Wesleyan theology had to be judged by a single essay, this one would do as well as any." Ibid., p. 271.

[12] Wesley, Plain Account, p. 112. Wesley adds, then, that this moment "generally is the instant of death . . . But I believe it may be ten, twenty, or forty years before." And he concludes: "I believe it is usually many years after justification; but that it may be within five years or five months after it, I know no conclusive argument to the contrary." To death's being the instant see, however, Wesley's objection (under the name of 'a plain man'): "If so, is it not something else, not 'the blood of Christ, which cleanseth' it 'from all sin'?" Ibid., p. 61. Robert Monk concludes that in spite of Wesley's occasional references to death as the instant of sanctification, nevertheless, Wesley's "whole doctrine of perfection depended on perfectibility in life, not at death." John Wesley, p. 57. This observation might be confirmed by a number of Charles Wesley's hymns.

[13] Ibid., p. 27. For further affirmations of sola fide, cf. ibid., p. 41; Journal, IV (Nov. 1, 1762), 536.

b. *Ultima Fides (Anti Sola Fide)*

i. " 'Q. How are we to wait for this change?'

" 'A. Not in careless indifference, or indolent inactivity; but in vigorous, universal obedience, in a zealous keeping of all the commandments, in watchfulness and painfulness, in denying ourselves, and taking up our cross daily; as well as in earnest prayer and fasting, and a close attendance on all the ordinances of God. And if any man dream of attaining it any other way (yea, or of keeping it when it is attained, when he has received it even in the largest measure), he deceiveth his own soul. It is true, we receive it by simple faith; but God does not, will not, give that faith unless we seek it with all diligence, in the way which He hath ordained.' "[14]

ii. " 'Once more, beware of Solifidianism; crying nothing but, "Believe, Believe!" and condemning those as ignorant or legal who speak in a more scriptural way.... for as "by.works faith is made perfect," so the completing or destroying the work of faith, and enjoying the favour or suffering the displeasure of God, greatly depends on every single act of obedience or disobedience.' "[15]

c. Faith as Inner Work

i. "And accordingly the next day [Peter Böhler] came again with three others, all of whom testified, of their own personal experience, that a true living faith in Christ is inseparable from a sense of pardon for all past and freedom from all present sins. They added with one mouth that this faith was the gift, the free gift of God; and that He would surely bestow it upon every soul who earnestly sought it. I was now throughly *(sic)* convinced; and, by the grace of God, I resolved to seek it unto the end, (1) By absolutely renouncing all dependence, in whole or in part, upon *my own* works or righteousness; on which I had really grounded my hope of salvation, though I knew it not, from my youth up; (2) by adding to the constant use of all the other means of grace, continual prayer for this very thing, justifying, saving faith, a full reliance on the blood of Christ shed for *me;* a trust in Him, as *my* Christ, as *my* sole justification; sanctification, and redemption."[16]

---

[14] Wesley, *Plain Account*, pp. 53-54. The final sentence is very important. Wesley's faith requires work for its attainment. Cf. Wesley's remarks on the necessity of prayer, *ibid.*, p. 54.

[15] *Ibid.*, p. 92. For Wesley's criticism of "Lutheran and Calvinist authors, whose confused and indigested accounts magnified faith to such an amazing size that it quite hid all the rest of the commandments," see Wesley's *Journal*, I (Jan. 24, 1738), 419. See further Wesley's biting criticism of Luther's Commentary on Galatians, *Journal*, II (June 5, 1741), 467, and cf. the editor's note. Outler comments: "The great Protestant watchwords of *sola fide* and *sola Scriptura* were also fundamentals in Wesley's doctrine of authority. But early and late, he interpreted *solus* to mean 'primarily' rather than 'solely' and 'exclusively.' " *John Wesley*, p. 28. Therefore we should agree with Outler when he concludes that "it is highly misleading to interpret [Wesley] as [Luther's and Calvin's] conscious debtor. Indeed, the bulk of his references to them are largely negative." *Ibid.*, pp. 119-20; cf. *ibid.*, p. 45.

[16] *Journal*, I (May 24, 1738), 475-76. Note especially point one. Since Wesley,

ii. " 'This faith, indeed, as well as the salvation it brings, is the free gift of God. But seek, and thou shalt find. Strip thyself naked of thy own works, and thy own righteousness, and fly to Him. For whosoever cometh unto Him He will in no wise cast out.' "[17]

d. Faith as Absolute

i. "In August following [1738], I had a long conversation with Arvid Gradin, in Germany. After he had given me an account of his experience, I desired him to give me, in writing, a definition of 'the full assurance of faith,' which he did in the following words: — 'Requies in sanguine Christi; firma fiducia in Deum, et persuasio de gratia divina; tranquillitas mentis summa, atque serenitas et pax; cum absentia omnis desiderii carnalis, et cessatione peccatorum etiam internorum.' ... — This was the first account I ever heard from any living man of what I had before learned myself from the oracles of God, and had been praying for (with the little company of my friends), and expecting for several years."[18]

ii. "So that when Peter Böhler, whom God prepared for me as soon as I came to London [in January 1738], affirmed of true faith in Christ (which is but one) that it had these two fruits inseparably attending it, 'dominion over sin and constant peace from a sense of forgiveness,' I was quite amazed, and looked upon it as a new gospel. If this was so, it was clear that I had not faith."[19]

e. Faith (or, Perfection) as Reward

i. " 'It is true, we receive it by simple faith; but God does not, will not, give that faith unless we seek it with all diligence, in the way which He hath ordained. — This consideration may satisfy those who inquire, why so few have received the blessing. Inquire how many are seeking it in this way; and you have a sufficient answer.' "[20]

ii. " 'God hardly gives His Spirit even to those whom He has established in grace, if they do not pray for it on all occasions, not only

---

there is an evangelicalism in which works are as often strenuous (inner) *un*-doings, in the mystic tradition, as they are strenuous (outer) doings in the moralist tradition.

[17] *Journal*, VIII, Appendix XXVI ("The Wesley-Law Correspondence of 1738," May 14, 1738), 319. The letter to Law is bitter and might seem inconsistent with Wesley's doctrine of perfect love and his (probably unfortunate) indebtedness to Law. See the editor's note to this letter in *Standard Sermons*, I, 269 note.

[18] *Plain Account*, pp. 9-10. Key words: "summa," "omnis." Two further points of interest: In this review of how he arrived at the doctrine of Christian perfection it is noteworthy that Wesley makes no reference to his May 1738 conversion. Second, the influence on Wesley of the Moravian Pietists, illustrated in Peter Böhler and Arvid Gradin, was strong. Behind Methodism stands Moravianism. An historical study would have to trace this indebtedness. See the useful material in Outler, *Wesley*, pp. 53-69 and especially pp. 353-76, "The Rift with the Moravians."

[19] *Journal*, I (May 24, 1738), 475. Key words: "a new gospel," and "if this was so, it was clear that I had not faith." Until faith became absolute it could not, under this new conception, be considered true faith.

[20] *Plain Account*, pp. 53-54.

once, but many times. — God does nothing but in answer to prayer.' "[21]

2. *The Condition of Sinlessness*

    a. *Absolute* Sinlessness

        i. " 'Q. What is implied in being a *perfect Christian?*'

        " 'A. The loving God with all our heart, and mind and soul (Deut. 6:5).'

        " 'Q. Does this imply that *all inward sin* is taken away?'

        " 'A. Undoubtedly: or how can we be said to be *"saved from all our uncleanness?"* (Ezek. 36:29).' "[22]

        ii. "I have been the more large in these extracts, because hence it appears, beyond all possibility of exception, that to this day both my brother and I maintained — (1) That Christian perfection is that love of God and our neighbour which implies deliverance from *all sin.*"[23]

        iii. " 'Q. What is Christian Perfection?'

        " 'A. The loving God with all our heart, mind, soul and strength. This implies that no wrong temper, none contrary to love, remains in the soul; and that all the thoughts, words, and actions are governed by pure love.' "[24]

        iv. "Entire sanctification, or Christian perfection, is neither more nor less than pure love — love expelling sin and governing both the heart and life of a child of God. The Refiner's fire purges out all that is contrary to love, and that many times by a pleasing smart. Leave all this to Him that does all things well and that loves you better than you do yourself."[25]

    b. *Relative* Sinlessness

        i. "What, then, does their arguing prove who object against *perfection?* 'Absolute and infallible perfection?' I never contended for it. *Sinless perfection?* Neither do I contend for this, seeing the term is not scriptural. A perfection that perfectly fulfills the whole law, and so needs not the merits of Christ? I acknowledge none such — I do now, and always did, protest against it.— 'But is there not *sin* in those that are *perfect?*' I believe not; but, be that as it may, they feel none, no temper but pure love, while they rejoice, pray, and give thanks continually. And whether sin is *suspended* or *extinguished,* I will not dispute; it is enough that they feel nothing but love. This you allow 'we should daily press after'; and this is all I contend for. O may God give you to taste of it today!"[26]

        ii. " 'We, secondly, believe that there is no such perfection in

---

[21] *Ibid.,* p. 100. Cf. Ockenga's similar remarks on prayer, above, p. 116.

[22] *Plain Account,* p. 33.

[23] *Ibid.,* p. 41. It is in the light of such remarks that it is difficult to understand the frequent parallel objection that Wesley does not teach *"sinless* perfection," e.g. Outler, *Wesley,* p. 299 and Wesley himself, below, b. i; c. ii.

[24] *Ibid.,* p. 42. Cf. *ibid.,* pp. 53, 57, 109; *Sermons on Several Occasions,* pp. 108, 404.

[25] *Letters,* V (To Walter Church, Feb. 21, 1771), 223.

[26] *Letters,* IV (To Mrs. Maitland, May 12, 1763), 213; cf. *Journal,* IV (Nov. 1, 1762), 536. Note especially the crucial use of the word "feel" (twice) above.

this life as implies an entire deliverance, either from ignorance or mistake, in things not essential to salvation, or from manifold temptations, or from numberless infirmities, wherewith the corruptible body more or less presses down the soul. We cannot find any ground in Scripture to suppose that any inhabitant of a house of clay is wholly exempt either from bodily infirmities, or from ignorance of many things; or to imagine any is incapable of mistake, or falling into divers temptations.' "[27]

iii. "Certainly sanctification (in the proper sense) is 'an instantaneous deliverance from all sin,' and includes 'an instantaneous power then given always to cleave to God.' Yet this sanctification (at least, in the lower degrees) does not include a power never to think an useless thought nor ever speak an useless word. I myself believe that such a perfection is inconsistent with living in a corruptible body; for this makes it impossible 'always to think right.' While we breathe we shall more or less mistake. If, therefore, Christian perfection implies this, we must not expect it till after death. — I want you to be all love. This is the perfection I believe and teach. And this perfection is consistent with a thousand nervous disorders, which that high-strained perfection is not. Indeed, my judgment is that (in this case particularly) to overdo is to undo, and that to set perfection too high (so high as no man that we ever heard or read of attained) is the most effectual (because unsuspected) way of driving it out of the world."[28]

iv. " 'But we may carry this thought farther yet. A mistake in judgment may possibly occasion a mistake in practice. For instance: Mr. De Renty's mistake touching the nature of mortification, arising from prejudice of education, occasioned that practical mistake, his wearing an iron girdle. And a thousand such instances there may be, even in those who are in the highest state of grace. Yet, where every word and action springs from love, such a mistake is not properly a sin. However, it cannot bear the rigour of God's justice, but needs the atoning blood.' "[29]

c. Summary: Absolute Relativity

i. "By Christian Perfection, I mean (1) loving God with all our heart. Do you object to this? I mean (2) a heart and life all devoted to God. Do you desire less? I mean (3) regaining the whole image of God. What objection to this? I mean (4) having all the mind that was in Christ. Is this going too far? I mean (5) walking uniformly as Christ walked. And this surely no Christian will object

ii. "In the year 1764, ... I wrote down the sum ... : '(1) There is such a thing as perfection; for it is again and again mentioned in Scripture. (2) It is not so early as justification; for justified persons are to 'go on unto perfection' (Heb. 6:1). (3) It is not so late as death; for St. Paul speaks of living men that were perfect (Phil. 3:15). (4) It is not absolute. Absolute perfection belongs not to

---

[27] *Plain Account*, p. 28.

[28] *Letters*, IV (To Dorothy Furly, Sept. 15, 1762), 188.

[29] *Plain Account*, p. 43. Cf. *ibid.*, p. 42; *Letters*, IV (To Elizabeth Hardy, April 4, 1758), 13.

to. If any one means anything more, or anything else by perfection, I have no concern with it."[30] man, ... but to God alone. (5) It does not make a man infallible; none is infallible while he remains in the body. (6) Is it sinless? It is not worth while to contend for a term. It is "salvation from sin." (7) It is "perfect love" (I John 4:18). This is the essence of it. ... (8) It is improveable.... (9) It is amissible, capable of being lost; ... (10) It is constantly both preceded and followed by a gradual work.' "[31]

iii.[32] " 'They [the entirely sanctified] are freed from evil thoughts, so that they cannot enter into them; no, not for a moment. Aforetime, when an evil thought came in, they looked up, and it vanished away. But now it does not come in, there being no room for this in a soul which is full of God. They are free from wanderings in prayer. Whensoever they pour out their hearts in a more immediate manner before God, they have no thought [note 1. This is far too strong. See the Sermon on *Wandering Thoughts*. J.W.] of anything past, or absent, or to come, but of God alone. In times past they had wandering thoughts darted in, which yet fled away like smoke; but now that smoke does not rise at all. They have no fear or doubt, either as to their state in general or as to any particular action [note 2. Frequently this is the case, but only *for a time*. J.W.]. The "unction from the Holy One" teacheth them every hour what they shall do, and what they shall speak [note 3. For a time it may be so; but not always. J.W.]. Nor, therefore, have they any need to reason concerning it [note 4. Sometimes they have no need; at other times they have. J.W.]. They are, in one sense, freed from temptation: for though numberless temptations fly about them, yet they trouble them not [note 5. Sometimes they do not; at other times they do, and that grievously. J.W.]. At all times their souls are even and calm, their hearts are steadfast and unmovable. Their peace, flowing as a river, "passeth all understanding," and they "rejoice with joy unspeakable and full of glory." For "They are sealed by the Spirit unto the day of redemption"; having the witness in themselves, that "there is laid up for them a crown of righteousness, which the Lord will give" them "in that day" [note 6. Not all who are saved from sin; many of them have not attained it yet. J.W.].' "[33]

---

[30] *Journal*, V (June 27, 1769), 324-25. Note the "all's."

[31] *Plain Account*, p. 106. Robert Monk, in his study sympathetic to Wesley, concludes, however, that "the inconsistencies present in Wesley's doctrine [of perfection]... tend to discount any real meaning in the term 'perfection.'" *John Wesley*, p. 249.

[32] The notes inserted within brackets and affixed with J.W. in this text are Wesley's later additions and illustrate the relativities of Wesley's absolutes.

[33] *Plain Account*, p. 23. The most interesting feature in this remarkable passage is the immoderate language.

D. SUMMA SUMMARUM: SAVIOR OF THE SINLESS AND JUSTIFICATION OF THE GODLY

1. *Christology-Soteriology*

a. " 'Q. Do we not then need Christ, even on this account [i.e., even when entirely sanctified]?'

" 'A. The holiest of men still need Christ as their Prophet, as "the light of the world." For He does not give them light but from moment to moment: the instant He withdraws, all is darkness. They still need Christ as their King; for God does not give them a stock of holiness. But unless they receive a supply every moment, nothing but unholiness would remain. They still need Christ as their Priest, to make atonement for their holy things. Even perfect holiness is acceptable to God only through Jesus Christ.' "[34]

b. " 'The best of men still need Christ, in His priestly office, to atone for their omissions, their shortcomings (as some not improperly speak), their mistakes in judgment and practice, and their defects of various kinds, for these are all deviations from the perfect law, and consequently need an atonement. Yet that they are not properly sins, we apprehend, may appear from the words of St. Paul: "He that loveth hath fulfilled the law; for love is the fulfilling of the law" (Rom. 13:10). Now, mistakes and whatever infirmities necessarily flow from the corruptible state of the body are no way contrary to love; nor therefore, in the Scripture sense, sin.' "[35]

c. " 'Beware of Antinomianism.... Even that great truth, that "Christ is the end of the law," may betray us into it, if we do not consider that He has adopted every point of the moral law, and grafted it into the law of love.' "[36]

2. *Justification*

"It is also far easier to take for granted, than to prove from any clear scripture testimony, that justification is the clearing us from the accusation brought against us by the law: at least, if this forced, unnatural way of speaking mean either more or less than this, that whereas we have transgressed the law of God, and thereby deserved the damnation of hell, God does not inflict on those who are justified the punishment which they had deserved.

"Least of all does justification imply, that God is deceived in those whom He justifies; that He thinks them to be what, in fact, they are not; that He accounts them to be otherwise than they are. It does by no means imply, that God judges concerning us contrary to the real nature of things;

---

[34] *Ibid.*, pp. 72-73. Key words: "to make atonement for their holy things." The most significant feature in this series of remarks is Wesley's unwillingness to assert that Christ is the mediator for the *sins* of the sanctified.

[35] *Ibid.*, p. 44. Contrast Luther's discussion of the same question in the *Heidelberg Disputation, LW, 31,* 60-64.

[36] *Ibid.*, p. 91. Wesley's polemic against *sola fide* immediately follows. To the theme of Christ and law cf. further *Sermons on Several Occasions,* p. 406; Platt, art. "Perfection (Christian)," *ERE,* IX, 731; Flew, *The Idea of Perfection,* pp. 247, 256.

that He esteems us better than we really are, or believes us righteous when we are unrighteous. Surely no. The judgment of the all-wise God is always according to truth. Neither can it ever consist with His unerring wisdom, to think that I am innocent, to judge that I am righteous or holy, because another is so. He can no more, in this manner, confound me with Christ, than with David or Abraham. Let any man, to whom God hath given understanding weigh this without prejudice; and he cannot but perceive that such a notion of justification is neither reconcileable to reason nor Scripture."[37]

II. CHARLES FINNEY'S DOCTRINE OF JUSTIFICATION[38]

A. The Condition beyond Faith: The Christian's Full Obedience

1. "We have seen that repentance, as well as faith, is a condition of justification. We shall see that perseverance in obedience to the end of life is also a condition of justification. Faith is often spoken of in scripture as if it were the sole condition of salvation, because, as we have seen, from its very nature it implies repentance and every virtue."[39]

2. "It has been shown that nothing is acceptable to God, as a condition of justification, and of consequent salvation, but a repentance that implies a return to full obedience to the moral law. . . . The relations of the old school view of justification to their view of depravity is obvious. They hold, as we have seen, that the constitution in every faculty and part is

---

[37] From the sermon "Justification by Faith," *Sermons on Several Occasions*, p. 53. Cf. further, *ibid.*, pp. 54, 498-502; *Letters*, IV (To Elizabeth Hardy, Apr. 4, 1758), 10-11; and Flew's remarks on George Fox in *The Idea of Perfection*, p. 282. Wesley's denial of the substitutionary work of Christ, of the imputation of Christ's righteousness, and of the non-imputation of the law was of fateful consequence theologically and historically.

[38] Primary sources: Charles G. Finney, *Lectures on Revivals of Religion* (New York: Fleming H. Revell Co., 1868); *idem, Lectures on Systematic Theology*, ed. J. H. Fairchild (South Gate, Calif.: Colporter Kemp, 1944 [1878]); *idem, Memoirs* (New York: Fleming H. Revell Co., 1903 [1876]). Further literature: V. Raymond Edman, *Finney Lives On: The Man, His Revival Methods and His Message* (New York: Fleming H. Revell Co., 1951); W. G. McLoughlin, Jr., *Modern Revivalism: Charles Grandison Finney to Billy Graham* (1959); James E. Johnson, "Charles G. Finney and Oberlin Perfectionism," *Journal of Presbyterian History, 46/1* (March 1968), 42-57 and *46/2* (June 1968), 128-38.

[39] *Systematic Theology*, p. 390. Cf. further: "A governmental consequence of faith is peace with God: — (1) In the sense that God is satisfied with the present obedience of the soul. . . . Of course God is at peace with the soul, so far as its present obedience is concerned." *Ibid.*, p. 380. See Finney's not entirely clear distinction: "Our own works, or obedience to the law or to the gospel, are not the ground or foundation of our justification. That is, neither our faith, nor repentance, nor love, nor life, nor anything done by us or wrought in us, is the ground of our justification. These are the conditions of our justification, in the sense of a 'not without which,' but not the ground of it. We are justified upon condition of our faith, but not for our faith; upon condition of our repentance, love, obedience, perseverance to the end, but not for these things. These are the conditions, but not the reason, ground, or procuring cause of our justification. We cannot be justified without them, neither are we or can we be justified by them." *Ibid.*, p. 400.

sinful. Of course, a return to personal, present holiness, in the sense of entire conformity to the law, cannot with them be a condition of justification. They must have a justification while yet at least in some degree of sin. This must be brought about by imputed righteousness. The intellect revolts at a justification in sin. So a scheme is devised to divert the eye of the law and of the law-giver from the sinner to his substitute, who has perfectly obeyed the law. But in order to make out the possibility of his obedience being imputed to them, it must be assumed, that he owed no obedience for himself; than which a greater absurdity cannot be conceived."[40]

B. The Corollaries and Consequences

1. *The Christian's Required Sinlessness*

"But again, to the question, can man be justified while sin remains in him? Surely he cannot, either upon legal or gospel principles, unless the law be repealed. That he cannot be justified by the law, while there is a particle of sin in him, is too plain to need proof. But can he be pardoned and accepted, and then justified, in the gospel sense, while sin, any degree of sin, remains in him? Certainly not. For the law, unless it be repealed, continues to condemn him while there is any degree of sin in him. It is a contradiction to say, that he can both be pardoned, and at the same time condemned. But if he is all the time coming short of full obedience, there never is a moment in which the law is not uttering its curses against him. 'Cursed is every one that continueth not in all things that are written in the book of the law to do them.' The fact is, there never has been, and there never can be any such thing as sin without condemnation. 'Beloved, if our heart condemn us, God is greater than our heart;' that is, he much more condemns us. 'But if our heart condemn us not, then have we confidence towards God.' "[41]

2. *Sola Fide as Total Obedience*

"Present evangelical faith implies a state of present sinlessness. Observe, faith is the yielding and committal of the whole will, and of the whole being to Christ. This, and nothing short of this, is evangelical faith. But this comprehends and implies the whole of present, true obedience to Christ. This is the reason why faith is spoken of as the condition, and as it were, the only condition, of salvation. It really implies all virtue. . . . its existence in the heart must be inconsistent with present sin there. Faith is an

---

[40] *Ibid.*, p. 402. See Edman's attempt to defend Finney's doctrines of atonement and justification in *Finney Lives On*, pp. 189-90. Cf. also the interesting recommendation of Finney's theology by a Dr. Redford in the Preface to Finney's *Systematic Theology*, p. vii.

[41] *Systematic Theology*, pp. 121-22. To Finney's understanding of justification see further *ibid.*, pp. 312-13, 395, 400; to sin, *ibid.*, pp. 122 24; to law and gospel see Finney's *Memoirs*, p. 339; to the "higher life," *ibid.*, pp. 340-41. In his autobiography Finney writes of the academic reception of his *Lectures on Systematic Theology*: "To these different reviews as they appeared, I published replies; and for many years past, so far as I am aware, no disposition has been shown to impugn our orthodoxy." *Memoirs*, p. 348. Incredible.

attitude of the will, and is wholly incompatible with present rebellion of will against Christ. This must be true, or what is faith?"[42]

3. Faith as Inner or Additional Work

a. "Nor is it that any are chosen to salvation for, or on account of their own foreseen merits, or good works. II Tim. 1:9 . . . God did not elect them to salvation, for or on account of their foreseen good works, but upon condition of their foreseen repentance, faith and perseverance."[43]

b. "I have no fear of the doctrine of holiness — perfect, instantaneous, perpetual holiness; and know full well that like justification, sanctification is to be received by faith."[44]

4. The Limited God

a. "God cannot repeal the law. It is not founded in his arbitrary will. It is as unalterable and unrepealable as his own nature. God can never repeal nor alter it. He can, for Christ's sake, dispense with the execution of the penalty, when the subject has returned to full present obedience to the precept, but in no other case, and upon no other possible conditions. To affirm that he can, is to affirm that God can alter the immutable and eternal principles of moral law and moral government."[45]

b. "We have seen in former lectures, that God is a moral agent, the self-existent and supreme; and is therefore himself, as ruler of all, subject to, and observant of, moral law in all his conduct. That is, his own infinite intelligence must affirm that a certain course of willing is suitable, fit, and right in him. This idea, or affirmation, is law to him; and to this his will must be conformed, or he is not good. This is moral law, a law founded in the eternal and self-existent nature of God. This law does, and must, demand benevolence in God. Benevolence is good-willing. God's intelligence must affirm that he ought to will good for its own intrinsic value. It must affirm his obligation to choose the highest possible good as the great end of his being. If God is good, the highest good of himself, and of the universe, must have been the end which he had in view in the work of creation. This is of infinite value, and ought to be willed by God. If God is good, this must have been his end."[46]

c. "But again, it is impossible that this view of justification [viz., reckoned or imputed righteousness] should be true; for the moral law did not originate in the arbitrary will of God, and he cannot abrogate it either as to its precept or its penalty . . . But set it aside in such a sense, that sin would not incur it, or that the soul that sins shall not be condemned by it, he cannot — it is naturally impossible! The law is as unalterable and unrepealable, both as to its precept and its penalty, as the nature of God. It

---

[42] Systematic Theology, p. 377.

[43] Ibid., p. 482. "In other words, they are chosen to salvation by means of sanctification. Their salvation is the end — their sanctification is a means." Ibid., p. 483.

[44] Letter of Finney to John Humphrey Noyes in James E. Johnson, art. cit., Journal of Presbyterian History, 46 (March 1968), 49.

[45] Systematic Theology, p. 122.

[46] Systematic Theology, p. 214. Note the use of the word "must."

cannot but be, in the very nature of things, that sin in any being, in any world, and at any time, will and must incur the penalty of the moral law. God may pardon as often as the soul sins, repents and believes, but to prevent real condemnation where there is sin, is not at the option of any being."[47]

III. R. A. TORREY'S DOCTRINE OF THE BAPTISM WITH THE HOLY SPIRIT

A. THE BASIC PROPOSITIONS

"First Proposition: A number of suggestive phrases ... are used in the New Testament to describe one and the same experience [: baptized or filled with the Holy Spirit; the gift, fell, poured out, received, etc. ...

"Second Proposition: The baptism with the Holy Spirit is a definite experience of which one may and ought to know whether he has received it or not [Acts 19:2]. ...

"Third Proposition: The Baptism with the Holy Spirit is an operation of the Holy Spirit distinct from and subsequent and additional to His regenerating work [Acts 8:12, 15-16; 19:1, 2, 6]. ... A man may be regenerated by the Holy Spirit and still not be baptized with the Holy Spirit. In regeneration there is an impartation of life, and the one who receives it is saved; in the Baptism with the Holy Spirit there is an impartation of power and the one who receives it is fitted for service.

"Every true believer has the Holy Spirit. But not every believer has the Baptism with the Holy Spirit, though every believer ... may have. The Baptism with the Holy Spirit may be received immediately after the new birth — as e.g., in the household of Cornelius. In a normal state of the church every believer would have the Baptism with the Holy Spirit, as in the Church at Corinth (I Cor. 12:13 ...).

"In such a normal state of the church the Baptism with the Holy Spirit would be received immediately upon repentance and baptism into the name of Jesus Christ for the remission of sins (Acts 2:38). But the doctrine of the Baptism with the Holy Spirit has been so allowed to drop out of sight, and the church has had so little expectancy along this line for its young children, that a large portion of the church is in the position of the churches in Samaria and Ephesus, where someone has to come and call the attention of the mass of believers to their privilege in the Risen Christ and claim it for them.

"Fourth Proposition: The Baptism with the Holy Spirit is an experience connected with and primarily for the purpose of service [Acts 1:5, 8; Luke 24:49; Acts 2:4; 9:17; I Cor. 12:4-14]. ... The Baptism with the Holy Spirit has no direct reference to cleansing from sin. It has to do with gifts for service rather than with graces of character. ... It is the impartation of

---

47 *Ibid.,* p. 393. See Finney's remarks in a sermon with the interesting title "Where Sin Occurs God Cannot Wisely Prevent It": "But if God cannot prevent sin will He not be unhappy? No. He is entirely satisfied to do the best He can, and accept the results." In Edman, *Finney Lives On,* pp. 196-97.

supernatural power or gifts in service, and sometimes one may have rare gifts by the Spirit's power and few graces.

"Fifth Proposition: . . . Jesus promised a two-fold baptism, 'with the Holy Ghost and with fire' . . . It is one twofold baptism. Many seem to get only part of it, 'the Holy Wind,' but the 'fire' is for us too, if we claim it. And fire searches, refines, consumes, illuminates, makes to glow, energizes, spreads. 'Fire' is what many need today, and it is for us.

"Sixth Proposition: The Baptism with the Holy Spirit causes one to be occupied with God and Christ and spiritual things. The man who is filled with the Holy Ghost will not be singing sentimental ballads, nor comic ditties, nor operatic airs while the power of the Holy Ghost is upon him. If the Holy Ghost should come upon one while listening to the most innocent of the world's songs he would not enjoy it. He would long to hear something about Christ."[48]

B. THE NECESSARY CONDITIONS

1. "The Conditions upon which the Baptism with the Holy Spirit is given: First Proposition: The fundamental conditions upon which the gift (or Baptism with the Holy Spirit) is bestowed are: Repentance, faith in Jesus Christ as an all-sufficient Saviour (apart from works of the law), and baptism in the name of Jesus Christ unto the remission of sins [Acts 2:38; 10:44; Gal. 3:2]. . . .

"Second Proposition: For those who believe on Jesus Christ the experimental reception of the Baptism with the Holy Spirit is sometimes conditioned on the believer's knowing that there is such a blessing and that it is for him now [Acts 19:2, 6]. . . .

"Third Proposition: God gives the Holy Ghost to them that obey Him. Obedience means *absolute surrender*. This is really involved in true repentance and faith in Jesus Christ. It is the point at which thousands fail of it to-day [Acts 5:32b]. . . .

"Fourth Proposition: The Baptism with the Holy Spirit is given to those who have already believed on Christ and been baptized with water . . . in answer to definite prayer (cf. Luke 11:13). But there may be much earnest praying and still the Holy Spirit not come because the prayer is not in faith (James 1:6, 7). The faith that receives this, as every other blessing at once, is the faith that counts it as its own (Mark 11:24 RV; I John 5:14, 15)."[49]

2. "The first step is that we *accept Jesus Christ as our Saviour and Lord*. . . . The second step in the path that leads into the blessing of being baptized with the Holy Spirit is *renunciation of sin*. . . . A controversy with God about the smallest thing is sufficient to shut one out of the blessing. Mr. Finney tells of a woman who was greatly exercised about the baptism with the Holy Spirit. Every night after the meetings, she would go to her

---

[48] *What the Bible Teaches*, pp. 270-76.

[49] *Ibid.*, pp. 279-80. See Torrey's orthodox depreciation of works, however, *ibid.*, pp. 318-22. How Torrey was able to combine this orthodoxy with his doctrine of the several conditions of the baptism with the Holy Spirit remains a mystery.

rooms and pray way into the night. . . . One night as she prayed, some little matter of head adornment, a matter that would probably not trouble many Christians to-day, but a matter of controversy between her and God, came up (as it had often come up before) as she knelt in prayer. She put her hand to her head and took the pins out of her hair and threw them across the room and said, 'There go!' and instantly the Holy Ghost fell upon her. It was not so much the matter of head adornment as the matter of controversy with God that had kept her out of the blessing. . . . The third step is an *open confession of our sin and our acceptance of Jesus Christ*. . . . The fourth step is *absolute surrender to God*. . . . What does obedience mean? Some one will say, doing as we are told. Right, but doing how much that we are told? Not merely one thing or two things or three . . . but all things. . . . The fifth step is *an intense desire for the Baptism with the Holy Spirit*. . . . The sixth step is *definite prayer for the Baptism with the Holy Spirit*. . . . The seventh and last step is *faith*. . . . Any one who will accept Jesus as their Saviour, and their Lord, put away all sin out of their life, publicly confess their renunciation of sin and acceptance of Jesus Christ, surrender absolutely to God, and ask God for the baptism . . . , and take it by simple faith in the naked word of God, can receive the Baptism with the Holy Spirit right now. . . . The seven steps given above lead with absolute certainty into the blessing."[50]

C. THE SPECIAL APPROPRIATIONS

1. To I Cor. 1:30. "Separation from sin and separation to God was provided for us in Christ. By the appropriation of Christ we obtain this sanctification thus provided. The more completely we appropriate Christ, the more completely we are sanctified. But perfect sanctification is provided in Him, just as perfect wisdom is provided in Him (Col. 2:3). We appropriate each in ever-increasing measure. Through the indwelling Christ, presented to us by the Spirit in the Word, we are made Christlike and bear fruit."[51]

2. To Acts 2:38. "Repentance is one of the primary conditions for receiving the gift of the Holy Ghost. The gift of the Holy Ghost is for all those who repent and are baptized in the name of Jesus Christ unto the remission of sins. It is for them to 'take' (the exact force of the word rendered 'receive')."[52]

3. "We enter into rest by faith. From beginning to end, at every step, salvation is by faith. God freely offers to us in Jesus Christ a manifold salvation; forgiveness, justification, eternal life, the right to be His sons, participation in His own nature, sanctification, heart-cleansing, an indwelling Christ, keeping unto a salvation ready to be revealed in the last time, power to stand, victory over the world and the evil one, rest. We appropriate to ourselves every item in this salvation by faith. By grace we are saved through faith from first to last."[53]

---

50 *The Person and Work of the Holy Spirit*, pp. 213-37.
51 *What the Bible Teaches*, pp. 344-45.
52 *Ibid.*, p. 358.
53 *Ibid.*, p. 375. For further examples cf. *ibid.*, pp. 376-77.

IV. ANDREW MURRAY'S DOCTRINE OF THE INDWELLING SPIRIT

A. THE DOCTRINE OF THE SECOND BLESSING ("TWO")

1. "The importance of recognizing this distinction [between our spirit and the Holy Spirit] can easily be perceived. We shall then be able to understand the true relation between regeneration and the indwelling of the Spirit. The former is that work of the Holy Spirit, by which He convinces us of sin, leads to repentance and faith in Christ, and imparts a new nature. Through the Spirit God thus fulfills the promise, 'I will put a new spirit within you.' The believer is now a child of God, a temple ready for the Spirit to dwell in. Where faith claims it, the second half of the promise is fulfilled as surely as the first. As long now as the believer only looks at regeneration, and the renewal wrought in his spirit, he will not come to the life of joy and strength which is meant for him. But when he accepts God's promise that there is something better than even the new nature, than the inner temple, that there is the Spirit of the Father and the Son to dwell within him, there opens up a wonderful prospect of holiness and blessedness. It becomes his one great desire to know this Holy Spirit aright, how He works and what He asks, to know how he may come to the full experience of His indwelling, and that revelation of the Son of God within us which it is His work to bestow.

"The question will be asked, How these two parts of the Divine promise are fulfilled? simultaneously or successively? The answer is very simple: From God's side the twofold gift is simultaneous. The Spirit is not divided: in giving the Spirit, God gives Himself and all He is. So it was on the day of Pentecost. The three thousand received the new spirit, with repentance and faith, and then, when they had been baptized, the Indwelling Spirit, as God's seal to their faith, on one day.... And yet we have indications in Scripture that there may be circumstances, dependent either on the enduement of the preacher or the faith of the hearers, in which the two halves of the promise are not so closely linked.... So Samaria ... Ephesus.

"When the standard of spiritual life in a Church is sickly and low, when neither in the preaching of the word nor in the testimony of believers, the glorious truth of an Indwelling Spirit is distinctly proclaimed, we must not wonder that, even where God gives His Spirit, He will be known and experienced only as the Spirit of regeneration. His indwelling Presence will remain a mystery. In the gift of God, the Spirit of Christ in all His fulness is bestowed once for all as an Indwelling Spirit; but He is received and possessed only as far as the faith of the believer reaches."[54]

2. "It may be objected that, for the believer who has the Holy Spirit within him, waiting for the promise of the Father is hardly consistent with the faith and joy of the consciousness that the Spirit has been received and is dwelling within.... The Father has indeed given us the Spirit; but He is still, and only works as the Spirit of the Father. Our asking for His working, that the Father would grant unto us to be strengthened with

---

[54] *Spirit of Christ*, pp. 17-20; cf. *ibid.*, p. 23.

might by His Spirit, and our waiting for this, must be as real and definite as if we had to ask for Him for the first time."[55]

3. "Just as there was a twofold operation of the one Spirit in the Old and New Testament, of which the state of the disciples before and after Pentecost was the most striking illustration, so there may be, and in the great majority of Christians is, a corresponding difference of experience. This difference between the bare knowledge of His presence and His full revelation of the indwelling Christ in His glory, is owing either to ignorance or unfaithfulness."[56]

B. THE DOCTRINE OF THE CONDITIONS FOR THE INDWELLING SPIRIT ("ABSOLUTE")

1. *Absolute Surrender*

"In studying the conditions of Pentecost the question naturally arises what there was in the disciples that made them fit to be the chosen recipients of the wonderful gift from heaven. . . . To Him it meant that death to sin and the world was the one condition for His being made partaker of the glory of heaven and the fulness of the Spirit to impart to His disciples on earth.

"Christ had . . . undertaken to fit them for the gift. When they forsook all and followed Him, when they accepted His teaching to hate and to lose their own life, to deny themselves and take up their cross, to follow Him even to the shame and utter darkness of Calvary, they were in reality being prepared to sacrifice the whole world and their own life, as the one thing that would prepare them for being filled with the Spirit of their crucified and glorified Lord.

"When once we strive to take in the full meaning of this preparation, the entire emptying of self, and of everything that this world can offer, we begin to understand how it is that there is often much prayer for the power of the Holy Spirit without any apparent answer. It is because the Holy Spirit claims nothing less than an absolute and entire surrender, for the life of heaven to take complete possession and exercise full mastery."[57]

2. *Prayer*

a. "As essential as the promise of the Father was the prayer of His children; the one was as indispensable [at Pentecost] as the other. As inconceivably glorious as the promise, was the glory and the power of the prayer by which the gift was to be brought down to earth. And such will be our prayer too, as we set ourselves with all our hearts to wait for the gift."[58]

b. "The question arises whether we [in comparison to the first disciples at Pentecost], in our prayer for the Spirit, do indeed yield our-

---

[55] *Ibid.*, p. 128.
[56] *Ibid.*, p. 323.
[57] *Back to Pentecost*, pp. 11-13. "It was this complete surrender of the whole heart and life [by the disciples] that made them capable of receiving the fulness of the Spirit." *Ibid.*, p. 39.
[58] *Back to Pentecost*, p. 36. Cf. *Spirit of Christ*, p. 323.

selves with the same passionate love, whole-hearted devotion, and absolute obedience to the Lord and all His commandments, to be led by the Spirit and to be used wholly and only in His service and the fulfilment of His will."[59]

c. "God has limited Himself, and made Himself dependent in the dispensing of His gifts, on what man really wills and desires. This is one of the highest tokens of man's nobility, that he has the power to say to God what he desires, and then to expect the answer."[60]

V. A. J. GORDON'S DOCTRINE OF TWO FAITHS

"On the contrary, it seems clear from the Scriptures that it is still the duty and privilege of believers to receive the Holy Spirit by a conscious, definite act of appropriating faith, just as they received Jesus Christ.... There is the same reason for accepting [the Paraclete] for his special ministry as for accepting the Lord Jesus for his special ministry. To say that in receiving Christ we necessarily received in the same act the gift of the Spirit, seems to confound what the Scriptures make distinct. For it is as sinners that we accept Christ for our justification, but it is as sons that we accept the Spirit for our sanctification....

"[Acts 2:38]: This passage shows that logically and chronologically the gift of the Spirit is subsequent to repentance....

"[Gal. 3:2, 14]: These texts seem to imply that just as there is a 'faith toward our Lord Jesus Christ' for salvation, there is a faith toward the Holy Ghost for power and consecration."[61]

"[The enduement of the Spirit] is not conversion, but something done upon a converted soul, a kind of crown of consecration put upon his faith. Indeed the two events stand in marked contrast. In conversion the believer receives the testimony of God and 'sets his seal to it that God is true' (John 3:33). In consecration God sets his seal upon the believer that he is true. The last is God's 'Amen' to the Christian, verifying the Christian's 'Amen' to God."[62]

VI. F. B. MEYER'S DOCTRINE OF THE POWER OF THE HOLY SPIRIT

"You say to me: 'Sir tell me how I may get this power myself.' I will. I know a little of it, thank God.... Any mechanic knows this law to be true: obey the law of a force, and the force will obey you.... Take water-force.... So it is with the Holy Spirit... you have never yet learned the law of the Holy Ghost; for if you had, the Holy Ghost would have come flowing through your life as much as through the life of a Peter or a John. You seem to think that God is a God of favoritism."[63]

"Five conditions: (1) You cannot have the power of the Holy Ghost

---

[59] *Back to Pentecost*, p. 40.

[60] *Ibid.*, p. 44. "Let us also see and make no mistake about *the condition* of this Divine Power. He that would command nature must first, and must absolutely, obey her." *Spirit of Christ*, p. 141.

[61] *The Ministry of the Spirit*, pp. 68-71.

[62] *Ibid.*, p. 78.

[63] *A Castaway and Other Addresses*, pp. 90-91.

without having the Holy Ghost Himself; ... (2) You must be cleansed. ...
(3) You must live for the glory of Christ. ... (4) Your preaching and
teaching must be in harmony with the word of God. ... (5) Fifth, and
last. The Holy Spirit must be received by faith. ... All God's dealings with
men are on the same principle, by faith. By faith you are regenerate, by
faith you are justified, by faith you are sanctified, by faith you receive the
Holy Ghost, by faith you receive Christ as the power of God into your
life. It is all by faith."[64]

"He gave [the Holy Spirit] to His church, to be its permanent possession
during the present age; and He waits to give each individual member of
that church his or her share in Pentecost, on the one condition of applying
for it by faith. As you took forgiveness from the hand of the dying Christ,
take your share of the Pentecostal gift from the hand of the living Christ. ...

"There are just *five tests* by which you may know that you have received
this infilling. ... (1) Is the Lord Jesus Christ a living reality to you? ... (2)
Have you assurance that you are a child of God? ... (3) Have you victory
over known sin? ... (4) Have you power in witness-bearing? ... (5) Have
you the spirit of holy love? This I need not dwell on.

"Is Jesus real to you? ... If not, there are three steps necessary — confession, surrender and faith. *Confession.* Before God can come into your
soul there will have to be a setting right of things which are not as they
should be. I have gone through it all myself. There were things in my
heart years ago that choked out all of God's fullness. ... *Surrender.* ...
Then follows *Faith.* Gal. 3:14 tells us that we may receive the promise of
the Holy Spirit by faith, just as we receive forgiveness, or any other
spiritual gift."[65]

---

[64] *Ibid.*, pp. 92-94.
[65] *Back to Bethel: Separation from Sin and Fellowship with God*, pp. 97-103.
The sum of the significance of the documents for Pentecostalism is, in the words
of the proverb (Ezek. 18:2), "The fathers have eaten sour grapes, and the
children's teeth are set on edge."

BIBLIOGRAPHICAL REMARKS
AND BIBLIOGRAPHY

The bibliography is divided into three parts: (1) literature to the understanding of the Pentecostal (including the Neo-Pentecostal) movement, consisting of primary sources; (2) literature to the understanding of the background of the Pentecostal movement, consisting of secondary sources and literature illuminating the historical, social, and theological traditions behind Pentecostalism; (3) literature to the understanding of the New Testament doctrine of the Spirit. A policy of exclusion has been necessary in forming the bibliography, particularly in the voluminous periodical literature. Consequently, only the more interesting or representative sources are listed. A short bibliographical essay suggesting the authors most helpful in each category in the preparation of the study precedes the bibliography itself.

I.

The single most important Pentecostal writer has been the Englishman Donald Gee. The publication which Gee edited for twenty years, from the postwar period until his death in 1966, *Pentecost: A Quarterly Review of World-Wide Missionary Activity,* was, for that generation, the fullest account of the international Pentecostal movements. Gee's several books and articles, moreover, provide unusually lucid exposition of essential Pentecostal beliefs.

Until recently David J. duPlessis' lectures, travel experiences, public articles, privately printed writings, and mimeographed newsletters provided, for those who wished it, a Neo-Pentecostal grapevine.

After Gee and duPlessis Pentecostal writers are primarily regional in their range and influence. First, there are the informative histories: by the American Pentecostals Brumback, Conn, Frodsham (older and standard), and especially Kendrick; the Brazilian by Conde; and the works by the pioneers themselves in their respective countries: Hoover in Chile; Barratt in Norway and beyond; and Pethrus in Sweden. The major European and somewhat more comprehensive treatment is Steiner's. Gee wrote a history of the Pentecostal movement in the forties which, though not as broad as might be wished, ranks with the studies by Kendrick and Steiner.

Doctrinally, the comprehensive Pentecostal statements are those of Krust, Nelson, Pearlman, the *Reglamento local,* and Williams. There are many writings on the major Pentecostal doctrine, the baptism in the Holy Spirit, of which the more important, in addition to Gee's contributions, are the works especially of Riggs, then Conn, A. S. McPherson, and Pearlman in North America; the prolific O. S. Boyer in Brazil; and Skibstedt, but also Barratt, Pethrus, and Steiner in Europe. There is as yet, to my knowledge, no major book from an Asian Pentecostal. In the ancillary area of the gifts of the Spirit, the charismata, the main presentations are the somewhat older works by Carter and Horton, and the newer and more cautious ones by Gee and Hodges. The specific gift of tongues is the subject of one of Brumback's earlier important works.

If one wishes to keep abreast of the *testimonia* of Neo-Pentecostalism the *Full Gospel Business Men's Voice* is especially recommended. The address of the rather important Full Gospel Business Men's Fellowship International, for information both Pentecostal and charismatic, is Box 17904, 836 So. Figueroa, Los Angeles, California, 90017, U.S.A.

There have been to date four noteworthy Neo-Pentecostal publications: John Sherrill's for a sympathetic and well-written inner view by a Protestant layman; the Ranaghans' for Catholic involvement and appreciation; Michael Harper's for an historical encomium by an English Anglican; and the American Lutheran pastor Laurence Christenson's for doctrine.

II.

Before all other secondary sources Hollenweger's multivolume achievement, "Handbuch der Pfingstbewegung," must be mentioned. It is a mine of historical and statistical information on Pentecostalism, with doctrinal texts and translations, from every responding country in the world. Dr. Hollen-weger is himself a former Pentecostal and serves presently as the Executive Secretary of the Department on Studies in Evangelism of the World Council of Churches, 150 route de Ferney, 1211 Geneva, Switzerland. His Handbuch is available, outside of Europe, in the libraries of several American east coast seminaries and in the major Pentecostal training centers across the country. His recent book, *Enthusiastisches Christentum* (1969), is a valuable summation of the Handbuch.

A well-equipped Catholic scholar has recently entered the study of Pentecostalism, Fr. Kilian McDonnell, O.S.B. All of his contributions are well written, researched, and sympathetic. His newly established Center for Ecumenical Research in Collegeville, Minnesota will be an important American base for Pentecostal studies.

Fr. Prudencio Damboriena's *Tongues As of Fire* (1969) is a comprehensive historical and theological treatment of Pentecostalism in every area except the exegetical. I regret that it was not at hand before my text reached the printer. Except for one or two Protestant reservations I believe that I can recommend Damboriena's study as the most thorough English-language treatment of Pentecostalism.

The understanding of the central experience and theology of the Pentecostal movement was considerably helped by advancing from a study of Wesley, especially his succinct *Plain Account,* through the nineteenth-century Finney, the holiness movement, and the turn of the century evangelical figures A. J. Gordon, F. B. Meyer, Andrew Murray, A. B. Simpson, and especially R. A. Torrey. Lindström helped us to see Wesley's doctrine of sanctification in perspective, though Flew and Peters were also informative. Monk and Pettit introduced us late in our studies to Wesley's Puritan forbears — and to our own need to study the seventeenth-century spiritual movements now known as Puritan. Outler's recently edited Wesley is valuable for understanding the whole man.

McLoughlin most helpfully interpreted the revivalist tradition from Finney forward, while Lawson's collection illumines the revival-holiness second experience tradition of evangelicalism from within. Boardman's work represented for us the holiness doctrine most clearly, while Timothy Smith's two historical studies provided scholarly interpretation of revivalism and of an important expression of the holiness movement, the Nazarenes.

The most useful general studies of Pentecostalism, in addition to the Hollenweger, McDonnell, and Damboriena publications, were those by Bloch-Hoell (from a Scandinavian perspective), Fleisch (in extremely thorough German studies over a fifty-year period), and recently Nichol whose heritage is Pentecostal and who writes sympathetically and fairly. Lighter, more popular, but also helpful were the essays by Eggenberger, the discussion by Newbigin, and the articles and statements by Mackay and Van Dusen. Mosiman's early monograph on tongues-speaking remains the most suggestive. Of the several modern discussions of tongues-speaking the article by Lapsley and Simpson points to possibilities of psychological interpretation. The books by Hutten, Pope, and Wilson and the article by Gerlach and Hine, but also the studies by Calley, Lalive, Léonard, Mintz, Vergara, Willems, and Wood provide sociological materials for understanding Pentecostalism.

A number of books will be found in the second bibliographical collection which are not secondary sources in the strict sense but are books independently illustrative of the Pentecostal spirituality of experience. These include, particularly, several of the conservative-evangelical studies of the Holy Spirit. The reading of these books might convince the hesitant that Pentecostalism is in several important respects the logical and theological consequence of an influential Protestantism.

Finally it should be mentioned that the person who provided the largest general theological assistance to us was — somewhat unexpectedly — Martin Luther. We took up the reading of Luther in Germany mainly as a kind of avocation and as a means of acculturation. Soon Luther had become our theological tutor. Luther's understanding of the gospel and his important controversy with the Protestant spiritual-movement of his time were very impressive to us. After the New Testament we feel we owe the most to our acquaintance with Luther and with those materially influenced by him for the understanding of the meanings of Christian theology.

III.

The commentary tradition (particularly the venerable Meyer series), the word studies of Kittel's theological dictionary, and the serious biblical theology of Adolf Schlatter were, after Luther, the main helps toward understanding the New Testament message.

The Pauline commentaries in the Meyer, then also in the HNT, ThHK, NTD, and Moffatt collections were particularly helpful interpreters. The reading of Friedrich's article on the gospel, *euaggelion*, in Kittel's wordbook was a "higher experience." Also helpful in Kittel were Gutbrod's article on the law (*nomos*) and Heidland's on reckoned righteousness (*logizomai*). Other word studies in Kittel to which I should like to point with gratitude are Bultmann's articles on boasting (*kauchaomai*) and faith (*pistis*), Schrenk's on righteousness (*dikaios*), Schweizer's on the Spirit (*pneuma*) — though the reader will know where I depart from this thorough study — Stählin's *skandalon,* and Wilckens' study of wisdom (*sophia*).

Adolf Schlatter — to whom, incidentally, the Kittel collection is dedicated — was an unknown quantity to me in the beginning of my German studies, though I had heard him mentioned admiringly by my Princeton Seminary teachers Otto Piper and James Martin. On making Schlatter's acquaintance I was immediately taken by his serious engagement with the biblical realities. I have not yet theologically reconciled Schlatter's earnestness and Luther's freedom; but the dialectic seems present even in the New Testament itself (in the Matthean and the Pauline traditions, respectively, though the Synoptic Jesus and even Paul himself combine both attitudes in a sometimes astonishing way). The Protestant Reformation in two of its main streams exhibits the perhaps not unimportant and probably not mutually exclusive differences between the "earnest" and the "free" in Calvin and the Reformed tradition, on the one hand, and the Lutheran movement on the other.

For the understanding of the New Testament doctrine of the Holy Spirit Büchsel's book seems still to me above all others. I should also like to mention von Baer's monograph on the Holy Spirit in the Lukan writings. New Testament baptism was a particularly fruitful mother of good books. I feel particular respect for the studies by the Roman Catholic exegete Schnackenburg and (perhaps surprisingly, at the other pole and incidentally Schnackenburg's English translator) the English and continental Baptist scholar Beasley-Murray, though the final chapter in his New Testament study, a polemic for believer baptism, was disappointing. For the relation of baptism and the Holy Spirit, particularly with reference to a specifically Anglican problem, I feel myself indebted to the book by Lampe. Several studies on baptism, in addition to Schnackenburg's, moved me from a symbolic to a realistic understanding of this sacrament: principally, the studies by the elder Althaus, G. Bornkamm, Heitmüller, and Kümmel. On the gifts of the Spirit the old study by Lauterburg remains the most solid, though Käsemann's recent essay was provocative. The general matrix of the New Testament world was interpreted to me helpfully by Goppelt's books and by the Strack-Billerbeck commentary.

Luke, probably the most embattled figure in recent New Testament scholarship, was (in especially his Acts' form) thoroughly dissected for me by Conzelmann and Haenchen and helpfully put more or less together again by Wilckens and Stählin. The Mattills' bibliography is an invaluable reference for Acts' study. Paul's Corinthians, particularly his Second Corinthian letter, was made more intelligible to me through the rich commentary tradition and the special studies, first of all, by Lütgert and Schmithals, but then also by Bultmann, Georgi, Schlatter, Wilckens, and recently and quite helpfully, by Hurd.

The books most helpful in understanding the general doctrine of the

Holy Spirit were, first of all, Regin Prenter's remarkable historical study, then also the works by Berkhof and Hendry. On the whole the doctrine of the Holy Spirit has been a rather uninteresting topic in theological treatments — perhaps the doctrine resists fascination for reasons indicated by our study.

I. TO THE UNDERSTANDING OF THE PENTECOSTAL MOVEMENT
(Primary Sources)

Abundant Life. Tulsa, Okla.: Oral Roberts Evangelistic Assoc., 1947ff.

Acts: Today's News of the Holy Spirit's Renewal, 1967ff.

Atter, Gordon F. *The Third Force.* Peterborough, Ontario: The College Press, 1962.

"Baptism." Springfield, Mo.: Gospel Publishing House, n.d. Tract No. 4617.

Barratt, Thomas Ball. *In the Days of the Latter Rain.* London: Simpkin, Marshall, Hamilton, Kent, 1909. Cited as *Rain.*

———. *When the Fire Fell and An Outline of My Life.* Oslo: Alfons Hansen and Sønner, 1927. Cited as *Fire.*

Bartleman, Frank. *How Pentecost Came to Los Angeles: As It Was in the Beginning.* 2d ed.; Los Angeles: Privately Printed, 1925.

*Basham, Don W. "They Dared to Believe," *Christian Life, 28* (April 1967), 28, 52-56.

*Bennett, Dennis J. " 'They Spake with Tongues and Magnified God!' " in *Full Gospel Business Men's Voice, 8* (Oct. 1960), 6-8; and "When Episcopalians Start Speaking in Tongues," *Full Gospel Business Men's Voice, 8* (Jan. 1961), 10-12.

*Bradford, George C. "Are Presbyterians Post-Pentecostals?" *Presbyterian Life, 21* (June 1, 1968), 30.

Brandt, R. L. "The Case for Speaking with Other Tongues," *Pentecostal Evangel, 48* (June 5, 1960), 4, 29-30.

Branham, William. "Beyond the Curtain of Time!" *Full Gospel Business Men's Voice, 9* (Feb. 1961), 3-5.

*Bredesen, Harald. "Discovery at Hillside," *Christian Life, 20* (Jan. 1959), 16-18.

———. "The Lord Who Healeth All Thy Diseases," *Full Gospel Business Men's Voice, 9* (May 1961), 3-11.

Bresson, Bernard L. *Studies in Ecstasy.* New York: Vantage Press, 1966.

*Brown, James D. "The Whole Gospel for the Whole Man," *Charisma Digest,* No. 2 (1969), pp. 2-6, 21-22.

Brumback, Carl. *God in Three Persons.* Cleveland, Tenn.: Pathway Press, 1959.

———. *Suddenly from Heaven: A History of the Assemblies of God.* Springfield, Mo.: Gospel Publishing House, 1961.

———. *What Meaneth This? A Pentecostal Answer to a Pentecostal Question.* Springfield, Mo.: Gospel Publishing House, 1947.

Buntain, D. N. *The Holy Ghost and Fire.* Springfield, Mo.: Gospel Publishing House, 1956.

Caldwell, William. *Pentecostal Baptism.* Tulsa, Okla.: Miracle Moments Evangelistic Assoc., Inc., 1963.

Campbell, Joseph E. *The Pentecostal Holiness Church, 1898-1948: Its Background and History.* Franklin Springs, Ga.: The Publishing House of the Pentecostal Holiness Church, 1951.

Cantelon, Willard. *El Bautismo en el Espiritu Santo.* 3d ed. Springfield, Mo.: Editorial Vida, 1955.

---

* Neo-Pentecostal in source, content, or emphasis.

Carter, Howard. *The Gifts of the Spirit*. Minneapolis, Minn.: Northern Gospel Publishing House, 1946.

Champion, Richard (ed.). *Our Mission in Today's World: Council on Evangelism Official Papers and Reports*. Springfield, Mo.: Gospel Publishing House, 1968.

Charisma Digest. Los Angeles: Full Gospel Business Men's Fellowship International, 1968ff.

Chinn, J. J. "May We Pentecostals Speak?" *Christianity Today*, 5 (July 17, 1961), 5.

*Christenson, Laurence. *Speaking in Tongues and Its Significance for the Church*. Minneapolis, Minn.: Bethany Fellowship, Inc., 1968.

Conde, Emilio. "Brazilian Assemblies of God Celebrate Fiftieth Anniversary," *Pentecost*, No. 57 (Sept. 1961), p. 1.

————. *Historia das Assembleias de Deus do Brazil*. Rio de Janeiro: Casa Publicador A.d.D., 1960.

————. "Phenomenal Growth in Brazil: 'Largest Evangelical Body,'" *Pentecost*, No. 44 (June 1958), p. 1.

————. *O Testemunho dos seculos*. Rio de Janeiro: Casa Publicador A.d.D., 1961.

Conn, Charles W. *Like a Mighty Army: Moves the Church of God, 1866-1955*. Cleveland, Tenn.: Church of God Publishing House, 1955.

————. *Pillars of Pentecost*. Cleveland, Tenn.: Pathway Press, 1956. Cited as *Pillars*.

————. *Where the Saints Have Trod*. Cleveland, Tenn.: Pathway Press, 1959.

Cross, James A. (ed.). *Healing in the Church*. Cleveland, Tenn.: Pathway Press, 1962.

Dalton, Robert Chandler. *Tongues Like As of Fire: A Critical Study of Modern Tongues Movements in the Light of Apostolic and Patristic Times*. Springfield, Mo.: Gospel Publishing House, 1945.

Duffield, Guy P., Jr. *Pentecostal Preaching*. New York: Vantage Press, 1957.

DuPlessis, David J. "Are We Going Back to the Churches?" in *Pentecost*, No. 35 (Dec. 1955), pp. 17-18.

————. "A Brief History of American Pentecostal Movements." Unpublished Notebook, [1959].

————. "A Brief History of Pentecostal Movements." Unpublished Notebook, [1959].

————. "A Confidential Report to Pentecostal Leaders." Circular Letter, [1960].

————. "An Ever More Insistent Challenge." Circular Letter, [1960].

————. "Golden Jubilees of Twentieth Century Pentecostal Movements," *IRM*, 47 (April 1958), 193-201.

————. "Jesus Christ the Baptizer." *Acts*, 1 (Sept.-Oct. 1967), 12-15.

*————. *Pentecost Outside "Pentecost": The Astounding Move of God in the Denominational Churches*. Dallas: Privately Printed, 1960. Cited as duPlessis, *Pentecost*.

————. "Mission der Pfingstbewegung," *RGG³*, V, 310-11.

*————. *The Spirit Bade Me Go: The Astounding Move of God in the Denominational Churches*. Dallas: Privately Printed, 1961. (2d rev. ed., 1963; not used.)

*————. "World Pentecostal and Ecumenical Movements," *Full Gospel Business Men's Voice*, 8 (Dec. 1960), 9-12.

————."The World-Wide Pentecostal Movement." A Paper read . . . on August 5, 1960 at St. Andrews, Scotland before the Commission on Faith and Order of the World Council of Churches. Dallas: Privately Printed, 1960.

————. "The World Pentecostal Movement," in *WChH* (1968), pp. 15-18.

348   A THEOLOGY OF THE HOLY SPIRIT

Ecke, Karl. *Der Durchbruch des Urchristentums infolge Luthers Reformation.* 2d rev. ed. Nürnberg: Süddeutschen Missionsverlag, n.d.
——. "Die Pfingstbewegung: Ein Gutachten von kirchlicher Seite." Privately Printed, 1950.

Edel, Eugen. *Der Kampf um die "Pfingstbewegung."* Mülheim-Ruhr: Emil Humburg. Schulte und Büscher, 1949.
——. *Miss den Tempel Gottes und die darinnen anbeten: Erlebnisse und Erkenntnisse.* 2d rev. ed. Schriftenmission Dillenburg, 1950.

*Evans, Leonard H. "A Witness," *Charisma Digest,* No. 2 (1969), pp. 11-13, 27-33.

Ewart, Frank. *The Phenomenon of Pentecost.* St. Louis, Mo.: Pentecostal Publishing House, 1947.

Faith Digest: The Monthly Voice of T. L. Osborn's Evangelistic Ministry. Tulsa, Okla.: T. L. Osborn Evangelistic Association, Inc., 1956ff.

*Farah, Charles. "The Laying on of Hands and the Reception of the Holy Spirit," *View,* No. 1 (1966), pp. 1-9.

Fischer, Harold A. "Progress of the Various Modern Pentecostal Movements toward World Fellowship." Fort Worth: Texas Christian University, 1952. Unpublished Master's thesis.

Flower, J. Roswell. "Birth of the Pentecostal Movement," *Pentecostal Evangel,* 38 (Nov. 26, 1950), 3.
——. "Flashes Back to the Beginning," *Pentecost,* No. 36 (June 1956), p. ii.
——. "Holiness, the Spirit's Infilling, and Speaking with Tongues," *Paraclete,* 2 (Summer 1968), 7-9.

Frodsham, Stanley H. *Jesus Is Victor: A Story of Grace, Gladness and Glory in the Life of Alice M. Frodsham.* Springfield, Mo.: Gospel Publishing House, 1930.
——. *Rivers of Living Water: The Secret of a Perpetual Pentecost.* Springfield, Mo.: Gospel Publishing House, n.d.
——. *Spirit-Filled, Led, and Taught.* Springfield, Mo.: Gospel Publishing House, n.d.
——. *With Signs Following: The Story of the Latter Day Pentecostal Revival.* Springfield, Mo.: Gospel Publishing House, 1926.

*Frost, Robert C. *Aglow with the Spirit.* Northridge, Calif.: Voice Christian Publications, Inc., 1965.

Full Gospel Business Men's Voice, 1953ff.

Garvin, Edna L. "Nine Words that Changed My Life," *Pentecostal Evangel, 48* (June 5, 1960), 5-7, 21-23.

Gause, R. H. *Church of God Polity.* Cleveland, Tenn.: Pathway Press, 1958.

Gee, Donald. *Concerning Spiritual Gifts: A Series of Bible Studies.* 2d rev. ed. Springfield, Mo.: Gospel Publishing House, 1947. Cited as *Spiritual Gifts.*
——. *Fruitful or Barren? Studies in the Fruit of the Spirit.* Springfield, Mo.: Gospel Publishing House, 1961.
——. *God's Great Gift: Seven Talks Together about the Holy Spirit.* Springfield, Mo.: Gospel Publishing House, n.d. Cited as *Gift.*
——. "The Initial Evidence of the Baptism in the Holy Spirit." Kenley, Surrey, 1959.
——. *The Ministry-Gifts of Christ.* Springfield, Mo.: Gospel Publishing House, 1930.
——. *Pentecost.* Springfield, Mo.: Gospel Publishing House, 1932.
—— (ed.). *Pentecost.* (See under *Pentecost,* below.)
——. *The Pentecostal Movement: Including the Story of the War Years (1940-47).* Rev. ed. London: Elim Publishing Co., 1949.
—— (ed.). *Pentecostal World Conference Messages: Preached at the Fifth*

Triennial Pentecostal World Conference, Toronto, Canada, 1958. Toronto: Full Gospel Publishing House, 1958.

————. *Spiritual Gifts in the Work of the Ministry Today.* "The L.I.F.E. Bible College Alumni Assoc. Lectureship on Spiritual Gifts"; Los Angeles: n.p., 1963.

————. *Upon All Flesh: A Pentecostal World Tour.* Springfield, Mo.: Gospel Publishing House, 1935.

Gericke, P., M.D. *Christliche Vollkommenheit und Geisteserlebnisse.* Rietenau, Germany: Privately Printed, [1950].

*Ghezzi, Bert. "Just the Beginning," *Acts, 1* (Sept.-Oct. 1967), 34.

Greenway, H. W. *This Emotionalism.* London: Victory Press, 1954.

Hall, J. G. "The Baptism in the Holy Spirit." Pamphlet, n.p., n.d.

*Harper, Michael. *As at the Beginning: The Twentieth Century Pentecostal Revival.* London: Hodder and Stoughton, 1965.

————. "Editorial," *Acts, 1* (Sept.-Oct. 1967), 1-2, 47-48.

*"Have Ye Received the Holy Ghost Since Ye Believed?" Van Nuys, Calif.: The Blessed Trinity Society of Prayer, n.d.

Hodges, Melvin L. "Creating Climate for Church Growth," in *Church Growth and Christian Mission,* ed. Donald A. McGavran (New York: Harper and Row, 1965), pp. 27-39.

————. "A Pentecostal's View of Mission Strategy," *IRM, 57* (July 1968), 304-10.

————. *Spiritual Gifts.* Springfield, Mo.: Gospel Publishing House, 1964.

Holdcroft, L. Thomas. "Spirit Baptism: Its Nature and Chronology," *Paraclete, 1* (Fall 1967), 27-30.

Hoover, Willis C. *Historia del Avivamiento Pentecostal en Chile.* Valparaiso: Imprenta Excelsior, [1909], 1948.

Horton, Harold. *The Baptism in the Holy Spirit.* London: Victory Press, 1956.

————. *The Gifts of the Spirit.* 2d rev. ed.; Bedfordshire, Eng.: Redemption Tidings Bookroom, 1946.

Horton, Wade H. (ed.). *The Glossolalia Phenomenon.* Cleveland, Tenn.: Pathway Press, 1966.

————. *Pentecost Yesterday and Today.* Cleveland, Tenn.: Pathway Press, 1964.

Hoy, Albert L. "The Holy Spirit in Imposition," *Paraclete, 1* (Fall 1967), 18-22; "The Gift of Interpretation," *Paraclete, 3* (Summer 1969), 28-31; "Public and Private Uses of the Gift of Tongues," *Paraclete, 2* (Fall 1968), 10-14.

Hughes, Ray H. *Church of God Distinctives.* Cleveland, Tenn.: Pathway Press, 1968.

————. *Religion on Fire.* Cleveland, Tenn.: Pathway Press, 1956.

————. *What Is Pentecost?* Cleveland, Tenn.: Pathway Press, 1963.

Hurst, D. V., and T. J. Jones. *The Church Begins: A Study Manual on the First Twelve Chapters of the Acts.* Springfield, Mo.: Gospel Publishing House, 1959.

Hurst, D. V. "The Evidence Points to the Evidence," *Paraclete, 2* (Winter 1968), 22-30.

"Introducing the Assemblies of God." Springfield, Mo.: Gospel Publishing House, [1960].

Jarvis, Edward J. "'This Is That,'" *Pentecostal Evangel, 49* (Jan. 15, 1961), 6-7.

*Jensen, Jerry (compiler). *Baptists and the Baptism of the Holy Spirit* (1963); *Catholics and the Baptism in the Holy Spirit* (1968); *Episcopalians and the Baptism in the Holy Spirit* (1964); *Lutherans and the Baptism in the Holy Spirit* (1966); *Methodists and the Baptism of the Holy Spirit* (1963);

Presbyterians and the Baptism of the Holy Spirit (1963). Los Angeles: Full Gospel Business Men's Fellowship International, 1963-1968.

———— (compiler). *Charisma in the Twentieth Century Church.* Los Angeles: Full Gospel Business Men's Fellowship International, 1968.

Kendrick, Klaude. "The Pentecostal Movement: Hopes and Hazards," *Christian Century, 80* (May 8, 1963), 608-10.

————. *The Promise Fulfilled: A History of the Modern Pentecostal Movement.* Springfield, Mo.: Gospel Publishing House, 1961.

Kortkamp, A. W. "What the Bible Says about the Baptism of the Spirit." Springfield, Mo.: Gospel Publishing House, n.d. Tract No. 4285.

Krust, Christian Hugo. *Fünfzig Jahre Deutsche Pfingstbewegung-Mülheimer-Richtung nach ihrem geschichtlichen Ablauf dargestellt.* Altdorf bei Nürnberg: Missionsbuchhandlung und Verlag, 1958.

————. *Was Wir Glauben, Lehren, und Bekennen.* Altdorf bei Nürnberg: Missionsbuchhandlung und Verlag, 1963.

*Kuhlman, Kathryn. *I Believe in Miracles.* Englewood Cliffs, N.J.: Prentice-Hall, Inc., 1962.

Lindsay, Gordon. *The Gordon Lindsay Story.* Dallas: The Voice of Healing, n.d.

Luce, Alice Evelyn. *Pictures of Pentecost in the Old Testament.* Springfield, Mo.: Gospel Publishing House, n.d.

McAllister, Robert. "Brazil: Pentecostal Opportunity," *Acts, 1* (July-Aug. 1967), 14-16.

MacDonald, William G. *Glossolalia in the New Testament.* Springfield, Mo.: Gospel Publishing House, [1964].

McPherson, Aimee Semple. *The Baptism of the Holy Spirit.* Four-Square Gospel Evangelism, vol. 2, lesson 6: "Jesus Christ, the Baptizer with the Holy Spirit." Los Angeles: Four-Square Correspondence Courses of the Lighthouse of International Foursquare Evangelism, 1928.

————. *The Foursquare Gospel.* Los Angeles: Echo Park Evangelistic Association, Inc., 1946.

————. *The Holy Spirit.* Los Angeles: Challpin Publishing Co., 1931.

————. *In the Service of the King.* New York: Boni and Liveright, 1927.

————. *The Story of My Life.* Hollywood, Calif.: An International Correspondents' Publication, 1951.

————. *This Is That: Personal Experiences, Sermons, and Writings.* Los Angeles: Echo Park Evangelistic Association, Inc., 1923.

Melodies of Praise. Edwin P. Anderson (ed.). Springfield, Mo.: Gospel Publishing House, 1957.

Menzies, William W. "The Spirit of Holiness: A Comparative Study," *Paraclete,* 2 (Summer 1968), 10-16.

Miller, Elmer C. *Pentecost Examined by a Baptist Lawyer.* Springfield, Mo.: Gospel Publishing House, 1936.

Mülheimer Ausgabe, Neue. Das Neue Testament in der Sprache der Gegenwart. 6th ed. Altdorf bei Nürnberg: Missionsbuchhandlung und Verlag, 1958. Cited as *Mülheimer NT.*

Myland, D. Wesley. *The Latter Rain Covenant and Pentecostal Power: With Testimony of Healings and Baptism.* Chicago: The Evangel Publishing House, 1910.

Nelson, P. C. *Bible Doctrines: A Series of Studies Based on the Statement of Fundamental Truths as Adopted by the General Council of the Assemblies of God.* 2d rev. ed. Springfield, Mo.: Gospel Publishing House, 1948.

Nickel, Thomas R. *The Amazing Shakarian Story.* Los Angeles: Full Gospel Business Men's Fellowship International, n.d.

Olson, N. Lawrence. "A Half-Century of Pentecost in Brazil," *Pentecostal Evangel*, 49 (Sept. 24, 1961), 6-7.

Osborn, T. L. *Impact*. Tulsa, Okla.: T. L. Osborn Evangelistic Association, Inc., 1960.

————. *The Purpose of Pentecost*. Tulsa, Okla.: T. L. Osborn Evangelistic Association, Inc., n.d.

*Osteen, John H. "Pentecost Is Not a Denomination: It Is an Experience," *Full Gospel Business Men's Voice*, 8 (June 1960), 4-9.

*Pagard, Ken. "American Baptists and the Holy Spirit," *Acts*, 1 (1969), 21-25.

Paraclete: A Journal concerning the Person and Work of the Holy Spirit, 1967ff.

Paulk, Earl P., Jr. *Your Pentecostal Neighbor*. Cleveland, Tenn.: Pathway Press, 1958.

Pearlman, Myer. *The Heavenly Gift: Studies in the Work of the Holy Spirit*. Springfield, Mo.: Gospel Publishing House, 1935. Cited as *Gift*.

————. *Knowing the Doctrines of the Bible*. Springfield, Mo.: Gospel Publishing House, 1937. Cited as *Doctrines*.

Pentecost: A Quarterly Review of World-Wide Pentecostal Activity. Published for the Pentecostal World Conferences, 1947-1966.

Pentecostal Evangel, 1913ff.

The Pentecostal Message. Franklin Springs, Ga.: Pentecostal Holiness Church, 1950.

Pethrus, Lewi. *The Wind Bloweth Where It Listeth: Thoughts and Experiences concerning the Baptism of the Holy Spirit*. 2d ed. Tr. Harry Lindblom. Chicago: Philadelphia Book Concern, 1945. Cited as *Wind*.

Pfingstjubel. 5th ed. Altdorf bei Nürnberg: Missionsbuchhandlung und Verlag, n.d.

The Phenomena of Pentecost. Springfield, Mo.: Gospel Publishing House, 1931.

Rabe, Paul. "Scriptural Principles for Receiving the Baptism in the Holy Spirit." An Address given at the World Conference [of Pentecostal Churches] in Stockholm, 1955. *Pentecost*, No. 38 (Dec. 1956), pp. 8-9.

Ramabai, Pandita. "Showers of Blessing at Mukti, India, 39 Years Ago," *Pentecostal Evangel*, 34 (May 4, 1946), 12-13.

*Ranaghan, Kevin and Dorothy. *Catholic Pentecostals*. "Deus Books"; Paramus, N.J.: Paulist Press, 1969.

Reed, Glenn A. "Pentecostal Truths 322." Mimeographed Notes to a Course Taught at Central Bible Institute, Springfield, Mo., 1952-54.

*Reed, William Standish, M.D. "God's Holy Calling: A Minister of Healing," *Full Gospel Business Men's Voice*, 8 (Dec. 1960), 3-6 (6-8).

Reglamento local. Rafael D. Williams (ed.). 9th ed. Santa Ana, El Salvador, C. A.: Conferencia Evangelica de los Asambleas de Dios en Centro America. Libreria "Bethel," Apartado 99, 1959.

*Rice, Robert. "Charismatic Revival," *Christian Life*, 25 (Nov. 1963), 30-32.

Riggs, Ralph M. *The Spirit Himself*. Springfield, Mo.: Gospel Publishing House, 1949.

————. "Those 'Store-Front' Churches: A Phenomenal Development in the Religious Life of America," *United Evangelical Action*, 6 (Aug. 1, 1945), 4.

Roberts, Oral. *The Baptism with the Holy Spirit and the Value of Speaking in Tongues Today*. Tulsa, Okla.: Oral Roberts, 1964.

————. *The Fourth Man*. Tulsa, Okla.: Oral Roberts, 1961.

————. *My Own Story*. New York: Summit Book Co., 1961.

Rutheven, Jon. "The Cessation of the Charismata," *Paraclete*, 3 (Spring 1969), 23-30, (Summer 1969), 21-27.

*Sherrill, John L. *They Speak with Other Tongues*. Westwood, N.J.: Revell, 1964.

Skibstedt, Werner. *Die Geistestaufe im Licht der Bibel*. Tr. and ed. Otto Witt.

352 A THEOLOGY OF THE HOLY SPIRIT

Reisach, Württemberg: Karl Fix, Verlag Deutsche Volksmission entschiedener Christen, 1946.

Spence, Hubert T. *Pentecost Is Not a Tangent.* 3d ed. Franklin Springs, Ga.: Pentecostal Holiness Church, n.d.

Squire, Fred H. *Divine Healing Today.* London: Victory Press, 1954.

Steiner, Leonhard. *Mit folgenden Zeichen: Eine Darstellung der Pfingstbewegung.* Basel: Verlag Mission für das Volle Evangelium, 1954.

———. "The Pentecostal Movement and World Evangelism." An Address given at the World Conference [of Pentecostal Churches at Stockholm] on June 20 [1955], in *Pentecost,* No. 33 (Sept. 1955), pp. 2-3.

Stiles, J. E. *The Gift of the Holy Spirit.* Burbank, Calif.: Privately Printed, n.d.

*Stone, Jean. "A High Church Episcopalian Becomes Pentecostal," *Full Gospel Business Men's Voice, 8* (Oct. 1960), 9-10.

Sumrall, Lester F. *Through Blood and Fire in Latin America.* Grand Rapids, Mich.: Zondervan, 1944.

Trinity. 1962-1966.

United Pentecostal Church. *What We Believe and Teach.* St. Louis: Pentecostal Publishing House, n.d.

*View: A Quarterly Journal Interpreting the World-Wide Charismatic Renewal, 1966-1968.

Wigglesworth, Smith. *Ever-Increasing Faith.* Springfield, Mo.: Gospel Publishing House, 1924.

Wilkerson, David, with John and Elizabeth Sherrill. *The Cross and the Switchblade.* New York: Bernard Geis Associates, 1963.

Williams, Ernest Swing. *Systematic Theology.* 3 vols. Springfield, Mo.: Gospel Publishing House, 1953.

Wilson, Elizabeth A. Galley. *Making Many Rich.* Springfield, Mo.: Gospel Publishing House, 1955.

Winehouse, Irwin. *The Assemblies of God: A Popular Survey.* New York: Vantage Press, 1959.

Womack, David A. "Are We Becoming Too Formal?" in *Pentecostal Evangel, 48* (Dec. 4, 1960), 3, 31.

———. *The Wellsprings of the Pentecostal Movement.* Springfield, Mo.: Gospel Publishing House, 1968.

"The Word of God on the Baptism of the Holy Ghost." Springfield, Mo.: Gospel Publishing House. Tract No. 4286.

Zimmerman, Thomas F. "What Is the Assemblies of God?" in *Pentecostal Evangel* (Special Outreach Issue), *48* (Sept. 11, 1960), 6-9, 15.

II. TO THE UNDERSTANDING OF THE BACKGROUND OF THE PENTECOSTAL MOVEMENT

(Secondary and Interpretive Sources and the Historical Tradition)

Allan, Tom. "Our Historic Churches Need Pentecostal Fire," *Full Gospel Business Men's Voice, 8* (Oct. 1960), 30.

Alland, Alexander, Jr. " 'Possession' in a Revivalistic Negro Church," *JSSR, 1* (April 1962), 204-13.

Althaus, Paul. *Die Theologie Martin Luthers.* Gütersloh: Gütersloher Verlagshaus. Gerd Mohn, 1962. Available in E.T.

Arlt, Augusto E. Fernandez. "The Significance of the Chilean Pentecostals' Admission to the World Council of Churches," *IRM, 51* (Oct. 1962), 480-82.

Baëta, Christian G. "Conflict in Mission: Historical and Separatist Churches," in *The Theology of the Christian Mission,* ed. Gerald H. Anderson (London: SCM, 1961), pp. 290-99.

Barnhouse, Donald Grey. "Finding Fellowship with Pentecostals," *Eternity, 9* (April 1958), 8-10.

Barth, Karl, and Heinrich Barth. "Der heilige Geist und das christliche Leben," in *Zur Lehre vom heiligen Geist.* "Zwischen den Zeiten," Beiheft No. 1. München: Kaiser, 1930, pp. 39-105.

*Barth, Markus. *Die Taufe — ein Sakrament? Ein exegetischer Beitrag zum Gespräch über die Kirchliche Taufe.* Zollikon-Zürich: Evangelischer Verlag, 1951.

Bass, Clarence B. *Backgrounds to Dispensationalism: Its Historical Genesis and Ecclesiastical Implications.* Grand Rapids, Mich.: Eerdmans, 1960.

Bauer, Walter. *Rechtgläubigkeit und Ketzerei im ältesten Christentum.* "BHTh," 10. Tübingen: Mohr, 1934.

Bergsma, Stuart. *Speaking with Tongues.* Grand Rapids, Mich.: Baker, 1965.

Bittlinger, Arnold. *Gifts and Graces: A Commentary on I Cor. 12-14.* Tr. Herbert Klassen and Michael Harper. London: Hodder and Stoughton, 1967.

Bloch-Hoell, Nils. *The Pentecostal Movement: Its Origin, Development, and Distinctive Character.* Oslo: Universitetsforlaget, 1964.

Bloesch, Donald G. "The Charismatic Revival: A Theological Critique," *Religion in Life, 35* (Summer 1966), 364-80.

Boardman, W. E. *The Higher Christian Life.* Boston: Henry Hoyt, 1859.

Boisen, A. T. "Religion and Hard Times: A Study of the Holy Rollers," *Social Action, 5* (March 15, 1939), 8-35.

Bonwetsch, G. Nathanael. *Die Geschichte des Montanismus.* Erlangen: Deichert, 1881.

———. "Montanismus," *RE, XIII,* 417-26.

The Book of Concord: The Confessions of the Evangelical Lutheran Church. Tr. and ed. Theodore G. Tappert *et al.* Philadelphia: Fortress, 1959.

Bornkamm, Heinrich. *Mystik, Spiritualismus und die Anfänge des Pietismus im Luthertum.* "Vorträge der theologischen Konferenz zu Giessen," 44. Giessen: Töpelmann, 1926.

Braden, Charles S. "Centrifugal Christian Sects," *Religion in Life, 25* (Summer 1956), 336-48.

Braga, Erasmo, and Kenneth G. Grubb. *The Republic of Brazil: A Survey of the Religious Situation.* London: World Dominion Press, 1932.

Brandenburg, H. "Heiligungsbewegung," *RGG³, II,* 182.

Bright, William. "Have You Made the Wonderful Discovery of the Spirit-Filled Life?" Los Angeles: Campus Crusade for Christ, 1966.

———. "The Christian and the Holy Spirit" and "Ye Shall Receive Power" in *Ten Basic Steps toward Christian Maturity: Step Eight;* Los Angeles: Campus Crusade for Christ, n.d.

Bruckner, A. *Erweckungsbewegungen: Ihre Geschichte und ihre Frucht für die christliche Kirche.* Hamburg: Agentur des Rauhen Hauses, 1909.

Buchner, Eberhard. "Die Pfingstleute," *Christliche Welt, 25* (1911), 29-34.

Calley, Malcolm J. C. "Aboriginal Pentecostalism: A Study of Changes in Religion." 4 vols. Sydney: University of Sydney, 1955. Unpublished Ph.D. dissertation.

———. *God's People: West Indian Pentecostal Sects in England.* London: Oxford University Press, 1965.

Calvin, John. *Institutes of the Christian Religion.* John T. McNeill (ed.). Tr.

---

* A number of sources in this list will appear, logically, to belong in the biblical-doctrinal bibliography (III); but theologically they are more useful for our purposes in illustrating Pentecostal doctrinal and experiential forms which, with the exception of speaking in tongues, they sometimes so independently represent that one might call them para-Pentecostal.

Ford Lewis Battles. "Library of Christian Classics," 20-21. 2 vols. Philadelphia: Westminster, 1965.

Castro, Emilio. "Ecumenical Relationships in Latin America," *Lutheran World*, 15 (1968), 271-78.

Chacon, Arturo. "The Pentecostal Movement in Chile," *Student World*, 57 (1964), 85-88.

Chadwick, Samuel. *The Way to Pentecost*. New York: Revell, n.d.

Chafer, Lewis Sperry. "The Baptism of the Holy Spirit," *Bibliotheca Sacra*, 109 (1952), 199-216.

Chandler, Russell. "Fanning the Charismatic Fire," *Christianity Today*, 12 (Nov. 24, 1967), 39-40.

Chery, H.-Ch., O.P. *L'Offensive des sectes en France*. Paris: Les Editions du Cerf, 1960.

Clark, Elmer T. "Non-Theological Factors in Religious Diversity," *EcRev, 3* (July 1951), 347-56.

———. *The Small Sects in America*. Rev. ed. Nashville: Abingdon-Cokesbury, 1949.

Clasen, L. " 'Heiligung im Glauben': Mit Rücksicht auf die heutige Heiligungsbewegung," *ZThK, 10* (1900), 439-88.

Coats, R. H. "Holiness. II. Historical Development," *ERE*, VI, 745-50.

Coxill, H. Wakelin. See *World Christian Handbook*, below.

Cremer, E. *Das vollkommene gegenwärtige Heil in Christo: Eine Untersuchung zum Dogma der Gemeinschaftsbewegung*. "BFChTh." Gütersloh: Bertelsmann, 1915.

———. *Rechtfertigung und Wiedergeburt*. "BFChTh." Gütersloh: Bertelsmann, 1907.

Criswell, W. A. *The Holy Spirit in Today's World*. Grand Rapids, Mich: Zondervan, 1966.

Cully, Kendig Brubaker (ed.). *Confirmation: History, Doctrine, and Practice*. Greenwich, Conn.: Seabury, 1962.

Cutten, George Barton. *Speaking with Tongues: Historically and Psychologically Considered*. New Haven: Yale University Press, 1927.

Dallmeyer, Heinrich. *Die Zungenbewegung: Ein Beitrag zu ihrer Geschichte und eine Kennzeichnung ihres Geistes*. Lindhorst: Adastra Verlag, n.d.

Damboriena, Prudencio, S. J. "The Pentecostals in Chile," *Catholic Mind, 60* (March 1962), 27-32.

———. *El Protestantismo en América Latina*. "Estudios Socio-Religiosos Latino-Americanos." 2 vols. Bogotá (Colombia): Oficina Internacional de Investigaciones Sociales de FERES, 1962-63.

———. *Tongues As of Fire: Pentecostalism in Contemporary Christianity*. Wash., D.C.: Corpus Books, 1969.

Davenport, Frederick Morgan. *Primitive Traits in Religious Revivals: A Study in Mental and Social Evolution*. New York: Macmillan, 1905.

Davies, Horton. "Pentecostalism: Threat or Promise?" *ExT, 76* (March 1965), 197-99.

Davis, George T. B. *Torrey and Alexander: The Story of a World-Wide Revival*. New York: Revell, 1905.

Davis, J. Merle. *How the Church Grows in Brazil: A Study of the Economic and Social Basis of the Evangelical Church in Brazil*. New York: Department of Social and Economic Research and Counsel, I.M.C., 1943.

De Haan, M. R. *Holy Spirit Baptism*. Grand Rapids: Radio Bible Class, 1964.

The Diocese of California, Division of Pastoral Services, Study Commission on Glossolalia. *Preliminary Report*. San Francisco, Calif., May 13, 1963.

The Diocese of Chicago. "Report on Spiritual Speaking," *The Living Church, 144* (Jan. 1, 1961), 10-11.

Douglass, Harlan Paul. "Cultural Differences and Recent Religious Divisions," *Christendom, 10* (1945), 89-105.

Doyle, Peter. "The Theology of Episcopalian Pentecostalism," *Churchman, 80* (Winter 1966), 303-12.

Drews, Paul. "Aus der Gemeinschaftsbewegung," *Christliche Welt, 22* (1908), 244-47, 271-76, 290-93.

Drummond, Andrew L. *Edward Irving and His Circle: Including Some Consideration of the 'Tongues' Movement in the Light of Modern Psychology.* London: James Clarke, n.d.

Dusenberry, Verne. "Montana Indians and the Pentecostals," *Christian Century, 75* (July 23, 1958), 850-51.

Dyer, Helen S. *Pandita Ramabai.* New York: Revell, 1911.

Dynes, Russel R. "Church-Sect Typology and Socio-Economic Status," *The American Sociological Review, 20* (Oct. 1955), 555-60.

Edman, V. Raymond. *Finney Lives On: The Man, His Revival Methods and His Message.* New York: Revell, 1951.

Edwards, Jonathan. *Religious Affections.* John E. Smith (ed.). New Haven: Yale University Press, 1959.

————. *Thoughts on the Revival of Religion in New England, 1740 and A Narrative of the Surprising Work of God in Northampton, Mass., 1735.* New York: American Tract Society, n.d.

Eggenberger, Oswald. *Evangelischer Glaube und Pfingstbewegung: Mit besonderer Berüchsichtigung der Verhältnisse in der Schweiz.* "Schriftenreihe zur Sektenkunde." Schweizerischer Protestantischen Volksbund (ed.). St. Gallen, Switzerland: Evangelischer Verlag A.G. Zollikon, 1956.

————. "Die Geistestaufe in der gegenwärtigen Pfingstbewegung (Darstellung und Versuch einer Beurteilung)," *ThZ, 11* (1955), 272-95.

————. "Pfingstbewegung. I. Konfessionskundlich," *RGG³,* V, 308-10.

Eliade, Mircea. *Shamanism: Archaic Techniques of Ecstasy.* Tr. Willard R. Trask. "Bollinger Series," 86; New York: Pantheon Books, 1964.

England, Stephen Jackson. "Simon Magus and Simonianism in the First Four Centuries." New Haven: Yale University, 1940. Unpublished Ph.D. dissertation.

Epp, Theodore H. *The Other Comforter: Practical Studies on the Holy Spirit.* Lincoln, Neb.: Back to the Bible Broadcast, 1966.

Farrell, Frank. "Outburst of Tongues," *Christianity Today, 7* (Sept. 13, 1963), 3-6.

"Fastest-Growing Church in the Hemisphere," *Time* (Nov. 2, 1962), p. 38.

Finney, Charles G. *Lectures on Revivals of Religion.* New York: Revell, 1868.

————. *Finney's Lectures on Theology.* Minneapolis, Minn.: Bethany Fellowship, [1840], 1968.

————. *Lectures on Systematic Theology.* J. H. Fairchild (ed.). South Gate, Calif.: Colporter Kemp, [1878], 1944.

————. *Memoirs.* New York: Revell, [1876], 1903.

Fischer, Max. *Der Kampf um die Geistestaufe.* Stuttgart: Quell-Verlag der Evang. Gesellschaft, 1950.

Fleisch, Paul. Articles on "Blankenburger Allianz," "Boardman," "Erweckungsbewegung," "Finney," "Gnadauer Verband," "Gemeinschaftsbewegung," "Heiligungsbewegung," "Jellinghaus," "Keswickbewegung," "Mahan," "Methodismus," "Paul," "Pfingstbewegung," "Smith," "Torrey," in *RGG²*.

————. "Die Entstehung der deutschen Heiligungsbewegung vor 50 Jahren," *Neue Kirchliche Zeitschrift, 38* (1927), 663-702.

————. "Gemeinschaftsbewegung," *EKL,* I, 1484-92.

————. *Die moderne Gemeinschaftsbewegung in Deutschland: Ein Versuch dieselbe nach ihren Ursprungen darzustellen und zu würdigen.* Leipzig: Wallmann, 1903. Cited as *Fleisch*, I/1.

———. *Die moderne Gemeinschaftsbewegung in Deutschland.* I: *Die Geschichte der deutschen Gemeinschaftsbewegung bis zum Auftreten des Zungenredens (1875-1907).* 3d rev. ed. Leipzig: Wallmann, 1912. Cited as *Fleisch*, I/2.

———. *Die Pfingstbewegung in Deutschland: Ihr Wesen und ihre Geschichte in fünfzig Jahren dargestellt.* "Die moderne Gemeinschaftsbewegung in Deutschland," vol. 2, part 2. Hannover: Heinr. Feescher Verlag, 1957. Cited as *Fleisch*, II/2.

———. *Die Zungenbewegung in Deutschland.* II: *Die deutsche Gemeinschaftsbewegung seit Auftreten des Zungenredens.* 3d rev. ed. Leipzig: Wallmann, 1914. Cited as *Fleisch*, II/1.

Flew, R. Newton. *The Idea of Perfection in Christian Theology: An Historical Study of the Christian Ideal for the Present Life.* London: Humphrey Milford: Oxford University Press, 1934. (Now in a 2d ed.)

Flugfeuer fremden Geistes. Offenbach am Main: Gnadauer Verlag, 1957.

Förster, Herbert. "Die Pfingstbewegung und ihr Verhältnis zur Okumene," *Evangelische Missionszeitschrift, 20* (Aug. 1963), 115-21.

Gaddis, Merle E. "Christian Perfectionism in America." Chicago: University of Chicago, 1929. Unpublished Ph.D. dissertation.

Gerdes, Hayo. "Zu Luthers Lehre vom Wirken des Geistes," *Luther Jahrbuch, 25* (1958), 42-60.

Gerlach, Luther P., and Virginia H. Hine. "Five Factors Crucial to the Growth of a Modern Religious Movement," *JSSR, 7* (Spring 1968), 23-40.

Gilbert, Arthur. "Pentecost among the Pentecostals," *Christian Century, 78* (June 28, 1961), 794-96.

Gingrich, Gerald Ira. *Protestant Revival Yesterday and Today: A Historical Study of the Characteristics of Twelve Revival Movements and of Their Application in the Mid-Twentieth Century.* New York: Exposition Press, 1959.

Goldschmidt, Walter R. "Class Denominationalism in Rural California Churches," *The American Journal of Sociology, 49* (Jan. 1944), 348-55.

Gordon, A. J. *The Ministry of the Spirit.* Grand Rapids, Mich.: Zondervan, [1894], 1949.

Graham, Billy. "Be Baptized with the Holy Spirit," *Full Gospel Business Men's Voice, 9* (April 1961), 31.

Gromacki, Robert Glenn. *The Modern Tongues Movement.* Philadelphia, Pa.: Presbyterian and Reformed Publishing Co., 1967.

Grützmacher, Richard H. *Wort und Geist: Eine historische und dogmatische Untersuchung zum Gnadenmittel des Wortes.* Leipzig: A. Deichert'sche Verlagsbuchhandlung Nachf. (Georg Böhme), 1902.

Hall, Gordon L. *The Sawdust Trail.* Philadelphia: Macrae Smith Co., 1964.

Hall, Thor. "A New Syntax for Religious Language," *Theology Today, 24* (July 1967), 172-84.

Harnack, Adolf. *History of Dogma.* Tr. Neil Buchanan. 7 vols. in 4. 3d ed. New York: Dover, 1961 [1900].

Haselden, Kurt. "The World Council Grows," *Christian Century, 78* (Dec. 13, 1961), 1487.

Hayes, D. A. *The Gift of Tongues.* New York: Methodist Book Concern, 1913.

Hebert, Gabriel. *Fundamentalism and the Church of God.* London: SCM, 1957.

Henke, Frederick G. "The Gift of Tongues and Related Phenomena at the Present Day," *American Journal of Theology, 13* (April 1909), 193-206.

Henry, Carl F. H. "Pentecostal Meeting Makes Holy Land History," *Christianity Today, 5* (May 22, 1961), 25, 30.

Herberg, Will. *Protestant-Catholic-Jew: An Essay in American Religious Sociology.* New York: Doubleday, 1955.

Hills, James W. L. "The New Pentecostalism: Its Pioneers and Promoters," *Eternity, 14* (July 1963), 17-18.

Hitt, Russell T. "The New Pentecostalism." Philadelphia: Evangelical Foundation, 1963.

Hoekema, Anthony A. *What about Tongue-Speaking?* Grand Rapids, Mich.: Eerdmans, 1966.

Hofinger, Johannes, S. J. *Worship: The Life of the Missions.* "Liturgical Studies." Notre Dame, Ind.: University of Notre Dame Press, 1958.

Holl, Karl. *Gesammelte Aufsätze zur Kirchengeschichte: I. Luther.* 7th ed. Tübingen: Mohr, 1948.

Hollenweger, Walter J. "Enthusiastisches Christentum in Brasilien," *Reformatio, 13* (1964), 484-88, 623-31.

―――. *Enthusiastisches Christentum: Die Pfingstbewegung in Geschichte und Gegenwart.* Zürich: Zwingli, 1969.

―――. "Evangelism and Brazilian Pentecostalism," *EcRev, 20* (April 1968), 163-70.

―――. "Geist- und Bibelverständnis bei Spiritualisten der Gegenwart: Eine frömmigkeits- und dogmengeschichtliche Untersuchung unter besonderer Berüchsichtigung der Schweizerischen Pfingstmission und ihrer historischen Wurzeln." Zürich: University of Zürich, 1960. Unpublished Akzessarbeit.

―――. "Handbuch der Pfingstbewegung." 9 vols. Geneva: Privately Photocopied, 1965. Unpublished Ph.D. dissertation, University of Zürich. Cited as *Hollenweger.*

―――. "Handbuch der Pfingstbewegung (Handbook of Pentecostalism)." Promotional Flier, n.d.

―――. "Literatur von und über die Pfingstbewegung (Weltkonferenzen, Holland, Belgien)," *Nederlands Theologisch Tijdschrift, 18* (1963), 289-306.

―――. "The Pentecostal Movement and the World Council of Churches," *EcRev, 18* (July 1966), 310-20.

―――. "Pfingstbewegung," *Handbuch des lateinamerikanischen Protestantismus.* [Projected]

―――. "Die Pfingstbewegung in Indonesien." Geneva: Unpublished manuscript, 1966.

―――. "Unusual Methods of Evangelism in the Pentecostal Movement in China," *A Monthly Letter about Evangelism,* Nos. 8-9 (Nov.-Dec. 1965), pp. 1-5.

Holt, John B. "Holiness Religion: Cultural Shock and Social Reorganization," *American Sociological Review, 5* (Oct. 1940), 740-47.

Hopewell, James F. "Protestant Theological Education in Latin America," *Lutheran World, 15* (1968), 329-34.

Hopkins, Charles Howard. *The Rise of the Social Gospel in American Protestantism, 1865-1915.* "Yale Studies in Religious Education," 14. New Haven: Yale University Press, 1950.

Horn, William M. "Speaking in Tongues: A Retrospective Appraisal," *Lutheran Quarterly, 17* (Nov. 1965), 316-29.

Housley, John B. "Protestant Failure in Chile," *Christianity and Crisis, 26* (Oct. 31, 1966), 244-46.

Hutten, Kurt. "Die Einheit der Kirche und die Sekten," *Deutsches Pfarrerblatt, 56* (1956), 366-69, 394-95.

―――. "Geistestaufe," *RGG³,* II, 1303-04.

―――. *Die Glaubenswelt des Sektierers: Das Sektentum als Antireformatorische Konfession — Sein Anspruch und seine Tragödie.* Hamburg: Im Furche Verlag, 1957.

————. Articles in *MD (Materialdienst: Langschnitt durch die geistigen Strömungen und Fragen der Gegenwart)*, especially 1951ff.

————. *Seher, Grübler, Enthusiasten: Sekten und religiöse Sondergemeinschaften der Gegenwart.* 5th rev. ed. Stuttgart: Quell-Verlag der Evang. Gesellschaft, 1958.

Ihmels, L. "Zur Lehre von der Heiligung bei Theodor Jellinghaus," *Neue Kirchliche Zeitschrift, 27* (1916), 89-128.

————. "Rechtfertigung," *RE,* XVI, 482-515.

Jacobs, Hayes B. "Oral Roberts: High Priest of Faith Healing," *Harper's, 124* (Feb. 1962), 40.

James, Maynard. *I Believe in the Holy Ghost.* Minneapolis, Minn.: Bethany Fellowship Inc., 1965.

James, William. *The Varieties of Religious Experience: A Study in Human Nature.* "Gifford Lectures, 1901-02." 2d ed. London: Longmans, Green, 1907.

Jellinghaus, Theodor. *Das völlige, gegenwärtige Heil durch Christum.* 2d ed. Basel: C. F. Spittler, 1886.

Jennings, George J. "An Ethnological Study of Glossolalia," *Journal of the American Scientific Affiliation, 20* (March 1968), 5-16.

Joest, Wilfred. *Gesetz und Freiheit: Das Problem des tertius usus legis bei Luther und die neutestamentliche Parainese.* 3d ed. Göttingen: Vandenhoeck und Ruprecht, 1961.

Johnson, Charles A. *The Frontier Camp Meeting: Religion's Harvest Time.* Dallas: Southern Methodist University Press, 1955.

Johnson, James E. "Charles G. Finney and Oberlin Perfectionism," *Journal of Presbyterian History, 46/1* (March 1968), 42-57 and *46/2* (June 1968), 128-38.

Kelsey, Morton T. *Tongue Speaking: An Experiment in Spiritual Experience.* Garden City, New York: Doubleday, 1964.

Kline, Meredith G. *By Oath Consigned: A Reinterpretation of the Covenant Signs of Circumcision and Baptism.* Grand Rapids, Mich.: Eerdmans, 1968.

Knox, R. A. *Enthusiasm: A Chapter in the History of Religion — with Special Reference to the Seventeenth and Eighteenth Centuries.* Oxford: At the Clarendon Press, 1950.

Knudsen, Ralph E. "Speaking in Tongues," *Foundations, 9* (Jan.-Mar. 1966), 43-57.

Köberle, Adolf. "Heilsordnung," *RGG³,* III, 189-90.

————. *Rechtfertigung und Heiligung: Eine biblische, theologiegeschichtliche und systematische Untersuchung.* 2d rev. ed. Leipzig: Dörffling und Franke, 1929. Available in E.T. as *The Quest for Holiness.*

Kolarz, Walter. *Religion in the Soviet Union.* London: Macmillan, 1961.

Krüger, H. "Pfingstbewegung," *EKL,* III, 172-74.

Kühn, Bernhard. *Was ist's mit der Geistestaufe? Schriftstudie über Eph. 5:18.* Neumünster i. H.: Vereinsbuchhandlung G. Ihloff, n.d.

LaBarre, Westen. *They Shall Take Up Serpents: Psychology of the Southern Snake-Handling Cult.* Minneapolis: University of Minnesota Press, 1962.

Lalive d'Epinay, Christian. "The Pentecostal 'Conquista' in Chile," *EcRev, 20* (January 1968), 16-32.

————. "The Training of Pastors and Theological Education: The Case of Chile," *IRM, 56* (April 1967), 185-92.

Lang, G. H. *The Modern Gift of Tongues: Whence Is It? A Testimony and an Examination.* London: Marshall Bros., n.d.

Lanternari, Vittorio. *The Religions of the Oppressed: A Study of Modern Messianic Cults.* Tr. Lisa Sergio. New York: Knopf, 1963.

Lapsley, James N., and John H. Simpson. "Speaking in Tongues," *Princeton*

Seminary Bulletin, 58 (Feb. 1965), 3-18 = *Pastoral Psychology*, 15 (May 1964), 48-55 and (Sept. 1964), 16-24.

Lawson, J. Gilchrist. *Deeper Experiences of Famous Christians: Gleaned from Their Biographies, Autobiographies and Writings*. Springfield, Mo.: Gospel Publishing House, 1911.

Léonard, Emile G. "L'Evangile au Bresil," *Revue de l'Evangelisation*, 7/38 (July-Aug. 1952), 208-35.

————. *L'Illuminisme dans un protestantismo de constitution recente (Bresil)*. Paris: Presses Universitaires de France, 1953.

————. "O Protestantismo Brasileiro: Estudo de eclesiologie e de historia social," *Revista de Historia*, No. 12 (1952), pp. 403-43.

Lindström, Harald. *Wesley and Sanctification: A Study in the Doctrine of Salvation*. Stockholm: Nya Bokförlags Aktiebolaget, 1946.

Lombard, Emile. *De la Glossolalie chez les premiers chretiens et des phenomenes similaires: Etude d'exegese et de psychologie*. Paris: G. Bridel, 1910.

Loofs, Friedrich. "Methodismus," *RE*, XII, 747-801.

Lowell, C. Stanley. "New Protestantism in Latin America," *Christianity Today*, 4 (Jan. 18, 1960), 9-14.

Luther, Martin. "Against the Heavenly Prophets in the Matter of Images and Sacraments, 1525." Tr. Bernhard Erling and Conrad Bergendoff. *Luther's Works*. American Edition. Vol. 40, "Church and Ministry: II." Conrad Bergendoff (ed.). Philadelphia: Muhlenberg Press, 1958, pp. 73-223.

————. "Heidelberg Disputation, 1518." Tr. Harold J. Grimm. *Luther's Works*. American Edition. Vol. 31, "Career of the Reformer: I." Harold J. Grimm (ed.). Philadelphia: Muhlenberg Press, 1957, pp. 35-70.

————. *Ausgewählte Werke*. Ed. H. H. Borcherdt and Georg Merz. Band 4: Der Kampf gegen Schwarm- und Rottengeister. 3d ed.: München: Kaiser, 1957.

McCrossan, T. J. *Are All Christians Baptized with the Holy Ghost at Conversion?* Seattle, Wash.: Privately Printed, 1932.

————. *Speaking with Other Tongues: Sign or Gift. Which?* New York: Christian Alliance Publishing Co., 1927.

McDonnell, Kilian, O.S.B. "Catholic Pentecostalism: Problems in Evaluation," *Dialog*, 9 (Winter 1970), 35-54.

————. "The Ecumenical Significance of the Pentecostal Movement," *Worship*, 40 (Dec. 1966), 608-33.

————. "Holy Spirit and Pentecostalism," *Commonweal*, 89 (Nov. 8, 1968), 198-204.

————. "The Ideology of Pentecostal Conversion," *JEcSt*, 5 (Winter 1968), 105-26.

McGavran, Donald; John Huegel; Jack Taylor. *Church Growth in Mexico*. Grand Rapids, Mich.: Eerdmans, 1963.

Mackay, John A. "The Christian Mission at This Hour," in *The Ghana Assembly of the International Missionary Council*. Ronald K. Orchard (ed.). London: Edinburgh House Press, 1958, pp. 100-24.

————. "Latin America and Revolution: II, The New Mood in the Churches," *Christian Century*, 82 (Nov. 24, 1965), 1439-43.

————. "The Latin American Churches and the Ecumenical Movement." New York: The Committee on Cooperation in Latin America, Division of Foreign Missions, National Council of the Churches of Christ in the USA, [1963].

————. "The Spiritual Spectrum of Latin America." New York: Latin America Department, Division of Overseas Ministries, National Council of the Churches of Christ in the USA, [1965].

Mackie, Alexander. *The Gift of Tongues: A Study in Pathological Aspects of Christianity*. New York: Doran, 1921.

McLoughlin, William G., Jr. *Modern Revivalism: Charles Grandison Finney to Billy Graham.* New York: The Ronald Press, 1959.

Mason, Arthur James. *The Relation of Confirmation to Baptism: As Taught in Holy Scripture and the Fathers.* London: Longmans, Green, 1891.

Maurer, Wilhelm. "Luther und die Schwärmer," *Schriften des theologischen Konvents Augsburgischen Bekenntnisses.* Friedrich Hübner (ed.). No. 6. Berlin: Lutherisches Verlagshaus, 1952, pp. 7-37.

Maxson, Charles Hartshorn. *The Great Awakening in the Middle Colonies.* Glouster, Mass.: Peter Smith, [1920], 1958.

Mayer, F. E. *The Religious Bodies of America.* 2d ed. St. Louis: Concordia, 1956.

Mead, Frank S. *Handbook of Denominations in the United States.* 2d rev. ed. Nashville: Abingdon, 1961.

Mead, Sidney E. "Denominationalism: The Shape of Protestantism in America," *Church History, 23* (Dec. 1954), 291-320.

Meinhold, Peter. "Pfingstbewegung," *Weltkirchen Lexikon,* 1140-43.

Meyer, F. B. *Back to Bethel: Separation from Sin and Fellowship with God.* Chicago: Revell, 1901.

———. *A Castaway and Other Addresses.* Chicago: Revell, 1897.

Miller, Haskell M. "Religion in the South," *Christendom, 7* (Summer 1942), 305-18.

Miller, Irving R. "The Prophetic Meaning of Sectarian Ecstasy," *Religion in Life, 17* (Winter 1947-48), 104-11.

Mintz, Sidney W. *Worker in the Cane: A Puerto Rican Life History.* New Haven: Yale University Press, 1960.

Molland, Einar. *Christendom: The Christian Churches, Their Doctrines, Constitutional Forms, and Ways of Worship.* London: A. R. Mowbray, 1959.

Monk, Robert C. *John Wesley: His Puritan Heritage.* Nashville: Abingdon, 1966.

Moore, Everett LeRoy. "Handbook of Pentecostal Denominations in the United States." Pasadena, Calif.: Pasadena College, 1954. Unpublished Master's thesis.

Mosiman, Eddison. *Das Zungenreden geschichtlich und psychologisch untersucht.* Tübingen: Mohr, 1911.

Les Mouvements de Pentecôte: Lettre pastoral du Synode général de l'Eglise Réformée des Pays-Bas. Tr. Frank van het Hof. Neuchâtel, Switzerland: Delachaux and Niestlé, 1964.

Muelder, Walter G. "From Sect to Church," *Christendom, 10* (1945), 450-62.

Müller, Alexander. "Die internationale Pfingstbewegung," *Informationsblatt, 8* (May 22, 1959), 157-61.

Müller, Karl. "Rechtfertigung oder Heiligung?" *Im Kampf um die Kirche: Versuch einer Lösung der Spannungen zwischen Kirche, Theologie und Gemeinschaft.* L. Thimme (ed.). (Gotha: Verlagsbuchhandlung P. Ott, 1930), pp. 94-116.

Murray, Andrew. *Absolute Surrender and Other Addresses.* Chicago: The Moody Press, 1897.

———. *Back to Pentecost: The Fulfillment of "The Promise of the Father."* London: Oliphants Ltd., n.d.

———. *The Spirit of Christ: Thoughts on the Indwelling of the Holy Spirit in the Believer and the Church.* New York: A. D. F. Randolph and Co., 1888.

Murray, J. S. "What We Can Learn from the Pentecostal Churches," *Christianity Today, 11* (June 9, 1967), 10-12.

Nee, Watchman. *The Normal Christian Life.* Fort Washington, Pa.: Christian Literature Crusade, 1961.

Neighbour, R. E. *The Baptism in the Holy Ghost, or Before and After Pentecost.* Cleveland, Ohio: The Union Gospel Press, 1930.

————. *Talking in Tongues*. Elyria, Ohio: Gems of Gold Publishing Co., n.d.

Nelson, Wilton M. "Evangelical Surge in Latin America," *Christianity Today, 7* (July 19, 1963), 5-6.

Newbigin, Lesslie. *The Household of God: Lectures on the Nature of the Church.* New York: Friendship Press, 1954.

Nichol, John Thomas. *Pentecostalism.* New York: Harper and Row, 1966.

————. "The Role of the Pentecostal Movement in American Church History," *The Gordon Review, 2* (Dec. 1956), 127-35.

Nida, Eugene A. *The Indigenous Churches in Latin America.* New York: The Committee on Cooperation in Latin America, Division of Foreign Missions, National Council of the Churches of Christ in the USA [1960].

Niebuhr, H. Richard. *The Kingdom of God in America.* New York: Willett, Clark and Co., 1937.

————. *The Social Sources of Denominationalism.* Hamden, Conn.: The Shoe String Press, [1929], 1954.

Nuttall, Geoffrey F. *The Holy Spirit in Puritan Faith and Experience.* Oxford: Basil Blackwell, 1946.

Oates, Wayne E. *The Holy Spirit in Five Worlds: The Psychedelic, the Nonverbal, the Articulate, the New Morality, the Administrative.* New York: Association Press, 1968.

Ockenga, Harold John. *Power through Pentecost.* "Preaching for Today." Grand Rapids, Mich.: Eerdmans, 1959.

————. *The Spirit of the Living God.* New York: Revell, 1947.

O'Connor, Edward, C.S.C. "A Catholic Pentecostal Movement," *Acts, 1* (Sept.-Oct. 1967), 31-34.

Oepke, Albrecht. "Die Kindertaufe — Eine Wunde unserer Kirche?" in *Evangelisch-lutherische Kirchenzeitung, 1* (Dec. 15, 1947), 29-35.

Oesterreich, Traugott Konstantin. *Einführung in die Religionspsychologie als Grundlage für Religionsphilosophie und Religionsgeschichte.* Berlin: Ernst Siegfried Mittler und Sohn, 1917.

O'Hanlon, Daniel, S.J. "The Pentecostals and Pope John's 'New Pentecost,'" *View*, No. 2 (1964), pp. 20-23.

Oman, John B. "On 'Speaking in Tongues': A Psychological Analysis," *Pastoral Psychology, 14* (Dec. 1963), 48-51.

Otto, Walter F. *Dionysos: Mythos und Kultus.* "Frankfurter Studien zur Religion und Kultur der Antike," 4. 2d ed. Frankfurt am Main: Vittorio Klostermann, 1933.

Outler, Albert C. *John Wesley.* "A Library of Protestant Thought." *New York:* Oxford University Press, 1964.

Parkes, William. "Pentecostalism: Its Historical Background and Recent Trends," *London Quarterly and Holborn Review, 191* (April 1966), 147-53.

Parsons, Anne. "The Pentecostal Immigrants: A Study of an Ethnic Central City Church," *Practical Anthropology, 14* (Nov.-Dec. 1967), 249-66.

Pattison, E. Mansell. "Behavioral Science Research on the Nature of Glossolalia," *Journal of the American Scientific Affiliation, 20* (Sept. 1968), 73-86.

"The Pentecostal Movement in Europe," *EcRev, 19* (Jan. 1967), 37-47.

"Pentecostal Tongues and Converts," *Time, 90* (July 28, 1967), 64.

Peters, John Leland. *Christian Perfection and American Methodism.* Nashville: Abingdon, 1956.

Pettit, Norman. *The Heart Prepared: Grace and Conversion in Puritan Spiritual Life.* "Yale Publications in American Studies," 11; New Haven: Yale University Press, 1966.

Pfister, Oskar. *Die psychologische Enträtselung der religiösen Glossolalie und der automatischen Kryptographie.* Leipzig: Deuticke, 1912.

Phillips, McCandlish. " 'And There Appeared to Them Tongues of Fire,' " *Saturday Evening Post* (May 16, 1964), 30-40.

Phillipson, John S. "Two Pentecostal Experiences," *America, 120* (March 29, 1969), 360-63.

Pike, James. "Glossolalia," *The Living Church, 146* (May 19, 1963), 11.

———. "Pastoral Letter Regarding 'Speaking in Tongues,' " *Pastoral Psychology, 15* (May 1964), 56-61.

Platt, Frederic. "Perfection (Christian)," *ERE,* IX, 728-37.

Pope, Liston. *Millhands and Preachers: A Study of Gastonia.* "Yale Studies in Religious Education," 15; New Haven: Yale University Press, 1953.

Powers, James F. "Catholic Pentecostals," *America, 119* (July 20, 1968), 43-44.

Prenter, Regin. *Spiritus Creator.* Tr. John M. Jensen. Philadelphia: Muhlenberg Press, 1953.

Ranson, Charles W. "Centrifugal Christian Sects," *Religion in Life, 25* (Summer 1956), 349-58.

Read, William R.; Victor M. Monterroso; Harmon A. Johnson. *Latin American Church Growth.* Grand Rapids, Mich.: Eerdmans, 1969.

———. *New Patterns of Church Growth in Brazil.* Grand Rapids, Mich.: Eerdmans, 1965.

Reuber, Kurt. *Mystik in der Heiligungsfrömmigkeit der Gemeinschaftsbewegung.* Gütersloh: Bertelsmann, 1938.

Roberts, W. Dayton. "Pentecost South of the Border," *Christianity Today, 7* (July 19, 1963), 32.

Robertson, Edwin. *Tomorrow Is a Holiday.* London: SCM, 1959.

Robinson, H. Wheeler. *The Christian Experience of the Holy Spirit.* London: Nisbet, 1928.

Rohde, Erwin. *Psyche: Seelencult und Unsterblichkeitsglaube der Griechen.* 2 vols. 5th and 6th ed.; Tübingen: Mohr, 1910.

Rose, Delbert R. *A Theology of Christian Experience: Interpreting the Historic Wesleyan Message.* Minneapolis, Minn.: Bethany Fellowship, Inc., 1965.

Roth, Alfred. *Fünfzig Jahre Gnadauer Konferenz in ihrem Zusammenhang mit der Geschichte Gnadaus.* Giessen: Brunnen-Verlag, 1938.

Roth, E. "Neuerer englische Literatur zum Taufproblem," *ThLZ, 76* (1951), 709-16.

Rust, Hans. *Das Zungenreden: Eine Studie zur kritischen Religionspsychologie.* "Grenzfragen des Nerven- und Seelenlebens," 118. München: J. F. Bergmann, 1924.

———. "Zungenreden," *RGG²,* V, 2142-43.

Ryrie, Charles Caldwell. *The Holy Spirit.* Chicago: Moody Press, 1965.

Sadler, A. W. "Glossolalia and Possession: An Appeal to the Episcopal Study Commission," *JSSR, 4* (Oct. 1964), 84-90.

Samarin, William J. "Glossolalia as Learned Behaviour," *Canadian Journal of Theology, 15* (Jan. 1969), 60-64.

Schepelern, Wilhelm. *Der Môntanismus und die phrygischen Kulte: Eine religionsgeschichtliche Untersuchung.* Tübingen: Mohr, 1929.

Schmidt, Kurt Dietrich. "Luthers Lehre vom Heiligen Geist," *Schrift und Bekenntnis: Zeugnisse Lutherischer Theologie.* Hamburg: Im Furche Verlag, 1950.

Schmidt, Martin. "Finney, Charles Grandison," *RGG³,* II, 957-58.

———. *John Wesley: A Theological Biography.* Vol. 1. From 17th June 1703 until 24th May 1738. Tr. Norman P. Goldhawk. Nashville: Abingdon, 1962.

———. "Wesley, John," *EKL,* III, 1783-85.

Schmidt, Wolfgang. *Die Pfingstbewegung in Finnland.* "Finska Kyrkohistoriska Somfundets Handlingar," 27. Helsingfors: Centraltryckereit, 1935.

Schulte, Walter, M.D. "Sektierer und Schwarmgeister — psychiatrisch gesehen," *Deutsches Pfarrerblatt, 53* (1953), 295-97.

Scroggie, W. Graham. *The Baptism of the Spirit: What Is It? Speaking with Tongues: What Saith the Scriptures?* London: Pickering and Inglis, n.d.

Seeberg, Reinhold. *Lehrbuch der Dogmengeschichte.* Vol I: Die Anfänge des Dogmas im nachapostolischen und altkatholischen Zeitalter. 6th ed. = unaltered reprographic production of the 3d ed. Darmstadt: Wissenschaftliche Buchgesellschaft, 1965.

————. *Text-Book of the History of Doctrines.* 2 vols. Tr. Charles E. Hay. Grand Rapids, Mich.: Baker, 1956.

Shaw, P. E. *The Catholic Apostolic Church.* New York: King's Crown Press, 1946.

Shoemaker, Samuel M. *With the Holy Spirit and with Fire.* New York: Harper and Bros., 1960.

Simpson, A. B. *The Holy Spirit, or Power from on High: An Unfolding of the Doctrine of the Holy Spirit in the Old and New Testaments.* Part II.: The New Testament. Harrisburg, Pa.: Christian Publications, 1896.

Simpson, J. G. "Irving and the Catholic Apostolic Church," *ERE,* VII, 422-28.

Singh, Sadhu Sundar. *Gesichte aus der jenseitigen Welt.* Aarau: Verlag der christlichen Buchhandlung, n.d.

Smith, Hannah Whitall. *The Christian's Secret of a Happy Life.* "Spire Books"; Westwood, N.J.: Revell, [1870], 1968.

Smith, Timothy L. "Historic Waves of Religious Interest in America," *The Annals of the American Academy of Political and Social Science, 332* (Nov. 1960), 9-19.

————. *Called unto Holiness: The Story of the Nazarenes: The Formative Years.* Kansas City, Mo.: Nazarene Publishing House, 1962.

————. *Revivalism and Social Reform.* Nashville: Abingdon, 1957.

Smith, Wilbur. "Notes on the Literature of Pentecostalism," *Moody Monthly, 55* (Dec. 1955), 31-35.

Sprague, William B. *Lectures on Revivals of Religions.* London: The Banner of Truth Trust, [1832], 1959.

Stagg, Frank; E. Glenn Hinson; Wayne E. Oates. *Glossolalia: Tongue Speaking in Biblical, Historical, and Psychological Perspective.* Nashville: Abingdon, 1967.

Stalker, James. "Revivals of Religion," *ERE,* X, 753-57.

Starkey, Lycurgus M., Jr. *The Work of the Holy Spirit: A Study in Wesleyan Theology.* Nashville: Abingdon, 1962.

Stolee, Haakon J. *Pentecostalism: The Problem of the Modern Tongues Movement.* Minneapolis, Minn.: Augsburg, 1936.

————. *Speaking in Tongues.* Rev. ed. [of *Pentecostalism,* above]. Minneapolis, Minn.: Augsburg, 1963.

Stott, John R. W. *The Baptism and Fullness of the Holy Spirit.* Chicago: Inter-Varsity Press, 1964.

Strachan, Kenneth. *The Missionary Movement of the Non-Historical Groups in Latin America.* "Part III of the Study Conference on the Message of the Evangelical Church in Latin America; Buck Hill Falls, Pa., Nov. 10-12, 1957." New York: Committee on Cooperation in Latin America of the Division of Foreign Missions of the National Council of the Churches of Christ in the USA, [1957].

Sundkler, Bengt G. M. *Bantu Prophets in South Africa.* 2d ed. London: Oxford University Press, 1961.

Sweet, William Warren. *The American Churches: An Interpretation.* Nashville: Abingdon-Cokesbury, 1948.

———. *Revivalism in America: Its Origin, Growth, and Decline.* New York: Scribner's, 1945.

———. *The Story of Religion in America.* Rev. ed. New York: Harper, 1950.

Swete, Henry Barclay. *The Holy Spirit in the Ancient Church: A Study of Christian Teaching in the Age of the Fathers.* London: Macmillan, 1912.

"A Symposium on Speaking in Tongues," *Dialog, 2* (Spring 1963), 152-63.

Taylor, Clyde W., and Wade T. Coggins. *Protestant Missions in Latin America: A Statistical Survey.* Washington, D.C.: Evangelical Foreign Missions Association, 1961.

Thielicke, Helmut. *Between Heaven and Earth: Conversations with American Christians.* Tr. John W. Doberstein. New York: Harper and Row, 1965.

———. *Theologische Ethik.* Erster Band: Prinzipienlehre. Dogmatische, philosophische, und kontroverstheologische Grundlegung. 2d rev. ed. Tübingen: Mohr, 1958. E.T. in progress.

Thimme, Ludwig. *Kirche, Sekte und Gemeinschaftsbewegung vom Standpunkt einer christlichen Soziologie aus.* 2d ed. Schwerin i. Mecklb.: Verlag von Friedrich Bahn, 1925.

Thompson, Claude H. "The Witness of American Methodism to the Historical Doctrine of Christian Perfection." Madison, New Jersey: Drew University, 1949. Unpublished Ph.D. dissertation.

Thornton, L. S. *The Common Life in the Body of Christ.* 3d ed. London: Dacre Press, 1950.

———. *Confirmation: Its Place in the Baptismal Mystery.* Westminster: Dacre Press, 1954.

Torrey, R. A. *The Baptism with the Holy Spirit.* New York: Revell, 1897.

———. *The Person and Work of the Holy Spirit: As Revealed in the Scriptures and in Personal Experience.* London: James Nisbet, 1910.

———. *What the Bible Teaches: A Thorough and Comprehensive Study of What the Bible Has to Say concerning the Great Doctrines of Which It Treats.* London: James Nisbet, [1898].

Troeltsch, Ernst. *Die Soziallehren der christlichen Kirchen und Gruppen.* "Gesammelte Schriften," 1. Tübingen: Mohr, 1919.

Tschuy, Theo. "Lateinamerika im Umbruch," *Der Wanderer, 37* (1963), 1-16.

———. "Shock Troops in Chile," *Christian Century, 77* (Sept. 28, 1960), 1118.

Unger, Merrill F. *The Baptizing Work of the Holy Spirit.* Chicago: Scripture Press, 1953.

Van Dusen, Henry P. "Caribbean Holiday," *Christian Century, 72* (Aug. 17, 1955), 946-48.

———. *Spirit, Son and Father: Christian Faith in the Light of the Holy Spirit.* New York: Scribner's, 1958.

———. "The Third Force in Christendom," *Life, 44* (June 9, 1958), 113-24.

Vergara, Ignacio, S.J. *El Protestantismo en Chile.* Santiago de Chile: Editorial del Pacifico, S.A., 1962.

Visser 't Hooft, W. A. (ed.). *The New Delhi Report: The Third Assembly of the World Council of Churches, 1961.* New York: Association Press, 1962.

Vivier, Lincoln M. van Eetveldt. "Glossolalia." Johannesburg: University of Witwatersrand, 1960. Unpublished M.D. dissertation.

Wach, Joachim. *Sociology of Religion.* Chicago: University of Chicago Press, 1944.

———. *Types of Religious Experience: Christian and Non-Christian.* Chicago: University of Chicago Press, 1954.

Walker, Alan. "Where Pentecostalism Is Mushrooming," *Christianity Today, 12* (Jan. 17, 1968), 81-82.

Walvoord, John F. *The Holy Spirit.* Wheaton, Ill.: Van Kampen Press, 1954.

Warburton, T. Rennie. "Holiness Religion: An Analogy of Sectarian Typologies," *JSSR, 8* (Spring 1969), 130-39.

Warfield, Benjamin Breckinridge. "Edwards and the New England Theology," *ERE,* V, 221-27.

————. *Miracles: Yesterday and Today, True and False.* Grand Rapids, Mich.: Eerdmans, [1918], 1953.

————. *Perfectionism.* 2 vols. New York: Oxford University Press, 1931.

Warren, Max. *Revival: An Enquiry.* London: SCM, 1954.

Watkin-Jones, Howard. *The Holy Spirit from Arminius to Wesley: A Study of Christian Teaching concerning the Holy Spirit and His Place in the Trinity in the Seventeenth and Eighteenth Centuries.* London: Epworth, 1929.

Webster, Douglas. *Pentecostalism and Speaking in Tongues.* London: Highway Press, 1964.

Weinel, Heinrich. *Die Wirkungen des Geistes und der Geister im nachapostolischen Zeitalter bis auf Irenaeus.* Freiburg i.B.: Mohr, 1899.

Welliver, Kenneth Bruce. "Pentecost and the Early Church: Patristic Interpretation of Acts 2." New Haven: Yale University, 1961. Unpublished Ph.D. dissertation.

Wesley, John. *The Journal of the Rev. John Wesley, A.M., Sometime Fellow of Lincoln College, Oxford.* Standard Edition. Nehemiah Curnock (ed.). 8 vols. London: Epworth, 1909.

————. *The Letters of the Rev. John Wesley, A.M., Sometime Fellow of Lincoln College, Oxford.* Standard Edition. John Telford (ed.). 8 vols. London: Epworth, 1931.

————. *A Plain Account of Christian Perfection.* London: Epworth, [1767], 1952.

————. *Sermons on Several Occasions.* First Series. London: Epworth, 1952.

————. *Standard Sermons.* Edward H. Sugden (ed.). 2 vols. 4th ed. London: Epworth, 1955.

Whale, J. S. *The Protestant Tradition: An Essay in Interpretation.* Cambridge, Eng.: At the University Press, 1955.

Whitam, Frederick L. "New York's Spanish Protestants," *Christian Century, 79* (Feb. 7, 1962), 162-64.

Whitley, W. T. "Enthusiasts (Religious)," *ERE,* V, 317-21.

Willems, Emilio. *Followers of the New Faith: Culture Change and the Rise of Protestantism in Brazil and Chile.* Nashville: Vanderbilt University Press, 1967.

————. "Validation of Authority in Pentecostal Sects of Chile and Brazil," *JSSR, 6* (Fall 1967), 253-58.

Williams, Charles. *The Descent of the Dove: The History of the Holy Spirit in the Church.* New York: Meridian Books, [1939], 1956.

Williams, George Huntston. *The Radical Reformation.* Philadelphia: Westminster, 1962.

Wilson, Bryan R. "The Pentecostal Minister: Role Conflicts and Status Contradictions," *The American Journal of Sociology, 64* (1959), 494-504.

————. *Sects and Society: A Sociological Study of Elim Tabernacle, Christian Science, and Christadelphians.* Berkeley: University of California Press, 1961.

Wolfram, Walter Andrew. "The Sociolinguistics of Glossolalia." Hartford, Conn.: Hartford Seminary Foundation, 1966. Unpublished M.A. thesis.

Wood, William W. *Culture and Personality Aspects of the Pentecostal Holiness Religion.* The Hague: Mouton and Co., 1965.

Woodside, Edmund R. "Glossolalia: The Gift of Tongues: A Bibliography," *Fuller [Seminary] Library Bulletin,* No. 11 (July-Sept. 1951), pp. 3-5.

World Christian Handbook. 1957 Edition: E. J. Bingle and Sir Kenneth Grubb (eds.). *1962 Edition:* H. Wakelin Coxill and Sir Kenneth Grubb (eds.). London: World Dominion Press, 1957, 1962. *1968 Edition: idem,* London: Lutterworth Press for the Survey Application Trust, 1967.

World Council of Churches. "The Pentecostal Movement and the Swedish Baptist Union," *Bulletin,* 6 (Spring 1960), 9-12.

Yinger, J. M. (ed.). *Religion, Society, and the Individual.* New York: Macmillan, 1957.

III. TO THE UNDERSTANDING OF THE NEW TESTAMENT DOCTRINE OF THE HOLY SPIRIT
(Biblical and Theological Sources)

Adler, Nikolaus. *Das erste christliche Pfingstfest: Sinn und Bedeutung des Pfingstberichtes Apg. 2:1-13.* "NTA," 18/1. Münster i.W.: Aschendorffsche Verlagsbuchhandlung, 1938.

————. *Taufe und Handauflegung: Eine exegetisch-theologische Untersuchung von Apg. 8:14-17.* "NTA," 19/3. Münster i.W.: Aschendorffsche Verlagsbuchhandlung, 1951.

Aland, Kurt. *Did the Early Church Baptize Infants?* Tr. G. R. Beasley-Murray. "The Library of History and Doctrine." Philadelphia: Westminster, 1963.

Allen, Roland. *Pentecost and the World: The Revelation of the Holy Spirit in the "Acts of the Apostles."* London: Oxford University Press, 1917.

Althaus, Paul. *Die Heilsbedeutung der Taufe.* Gütersloh: Bertelsmann, 1897.

Andrews, Elias. "Spiritual Gifts," *IDB,* IV, 435-37; "Tongues, Gift of," *IDB,* IV, 671-72.

Asting, Ragnar. *Die Heiligkeit im Urchristentum.* "FRLANT," N.F., 29. Göttingen: Vandenhoeck und Ruprecht, 1930.

Bachmann, Philipp, and Ethelbert Stauffer. *Der erste Brief des Paulus an die Korinther.* "KNT." 4th ed. Leipzig: A. Deichertsche Verlagsbuchhandlung, 1936.

Bachmann, Philipp. *Der zweite Brief des Paulus an die Korinther.* "KNT." 4th ed. Leipzig: A. Deichertsche Verlagsbuchhandlung, 1922.

Von Baer, Heinrich. *Der Heilige Geist in den Lukasschriften.* "BWANT." Stuttgart: Kohlhammer, 1926.

Barrett, C. K. *The Gospel according to St. John: An Introduction with Commentary and Notes on the Greek Text.* London: S.P.C.K., 1958.

————. *The Holy Spirit and the Gospel Tradition.* New York: Macmillan, 1947.

————. *Luke the Historian in Recent Study.* London: Epworth, 1961.

Barth, Karl. "The Christian Life (Fragment): Baptism As the Foundation of the Christian Life." *Church Dogmatics,* IV/4. Tr. G. W. Bromiley. Edinburgh: T. and T. Clark, 1969.

Bauer, Walter. *Griechisch-Deutsches Wörterbuch zu den Schriften des Neuen Testaments und der übrigen urchristlichen Literatur.* 5th rev. ed. Berlin: Töpelmann, 1958. Available in E.T.

————. *Der Wortgottesdienst der ältesten Christen.* Tübingen: Mohr, 1930.

Bauernfeind, Otto. *Die Apostelgeschichte.* "ThHK." Leipzig: A. Deichertsche Verlagsbuchhandlung, 1939.

Beare, Frank W. "Speaking with Tongues: A Critical Survey of the New Testament Evidence," *JBL,* 83 (Sept. 1964), 229-46.

Beasley-Murray, G. R. *Baptism in the New Testament.* London: Macmillan, 1962.

————. *Baptism Today and Tomorrow.* New York: St. Martin's Press, 1966.

————. "The Holy Spirit, Baptism, and the Body of Christ," *Review and Expositor,* 63 (Spring 1966), 177-85.

The Beginnings of Christianity. Part I: The Acts of the Apostles. F. J. Foakes-Jackson and Kirsopp Lake (eds.). Vol. 4: English Translation and Commentary by Kirsopp Lake and Henry J. Cadbury. London: Macmillan, 1933. (See also under Foakes-Jackson; Lake; and New, below.)

Behm, Johannes. *Glössa, TWNT,* I, 719-26.

―――. *Die Handauflegung im Urchristentum nach Verwendung, Herkunft, und Bedeutung in religionsgeschichtlichem Zusammenhang untersucht.* Leipzig: A. Deichertsche Verlagsbuchhandlung, 1911.

Berkhof, Hendrikus. *The Doctrine of the Holy Spirit.* "The Annie Kinkead Warfield Lectures," 1963-64; Richmond, Va.: Knox, 1964.

Bertrams, Hermann. *Das Wesen des Geistes nach der Anschauung des Apostels Paulus: Eine biblisch-theologische Untersuchung.* "NTA." Münster i.W.: Aschendorffsche Verlagsbuchhandlung, 1913.

Betz, Otto. *Der Paraklet: Fürsprecher im häretischen Spätjudentum, im Joh.-Ev., und in den neugefundenen gnostischen Schriften.* "Arbeiten zur Geschichte des Spätjudentums und Urchristentums," 2; Leiden: Brill, 1963.

Blass, Friedrich. *Grammatik des neutestamentlichen Griechisch.* Albert Debrunner (ed.). 10th ed. Göttingen: Vandenhoeck und Ruprecht, 1959. Available in E.T.

Bornkamm, Günther. *Das Ende des Gesetzes: Paulusstudien.* "BEvTh," 16. München: Kaiser, 1952.

―――. "Paulus," *RGG³,* V, 166-90.

―――. *Die Vorgeschichte des sogenannten Zweiten Korintherbriefes.* Heidelberg: Carl Winter, Universitätsverlag, 1961.

Brown, Raymond E., S.S. *The Gospel according to John (Chapters 1-12).* "Anchor Bible"; Garden City, New York: Doubleday, 1966.

―――. "The Kerygma of the Gospel according to John," *Interpretation, 21* (Oct. 1967), 387-400.

―――. "The Paraclete in the Fourth Gospel," *NTSt, 13* (January 1967), 113-32.

Bruce, F. F. *The Acts of the Apostles. Greek Text with Introduction and Commentary.* 2d ed. London: Tyndale Press, 1952.

―――. *Commentary on the Book of the Acts. English Text with Introduction, Exposition and Notes.* "The New International Commentary on the New Testament." Grand Rapids, Mich.: Eerdmans, 1954.

Büchsel, Friedrich. *Der Geist Gottes im Neuen Testament.* Gütersloh: Bertelsmann, 1926.

―――. *Die Johannesbriefe.* "ThHK." Leipzig: A. Deichertsche Verlagsbuchhandlung, 1933.

Bultmann, Rudolf. *Das Evangelium des Johannes.* "MeyerK." 14th ed. Göttingen: Vandenhoeck und Ruprecht, 1956.

―――. *Die drei Johannesbriefe.* "MeyerK." 7th ed.; Göttingen: Vandenhoeck und Ruprecht, 1967.

―――. *The History of the Synoptic Tradition.* Tr. John Marsh. Oxford: Basil Blackwell, 1963.

―――. *Kauchaomai, TWNT,* III, 646-54; *pistis, TWNT,* VI, 174-230.

―――. *Exegetische Probleme des zweiten Korintherbriefes zu 2. Kor. 5:1-5; 5:11 — 6:10; 10-13; 12:21.* "SBU," 9. Uppsala: Wietmans Boktryckerei A.-B., 1947.

―――. *Theology of the New Testament.* Tr. Kendrick Grobel. 2 vols. New York: Scribner's, 1951.

―――. *Das Urchristentum im Rahmen der antiken Religionen.* 2d ed. Zürich: Artemis-Verlag, 1954. Available in E.T.

Burton, Ernest De Witt. *A Critical and Exegetical Commentary on the Epistle to the Galatians.* "ICC." Edinburgh: T. and T. Clark, 1921.

Cadbury, Henry J. *The Book of Acts in History.* London: Adam and Charles Black, 1955.

Caird, G. B. *The Apostolic Age.* London: Gerald Duckworth, 1955.

Calvin, Johannes. *Die Apostelgeschichte.* "Auslegung der Heiligen Schrift in deutscher Übersetzung," 2. Neukirchen, Kreis Moers: Verlag der Buchhandlung des Erziehungsvereins, n.d.

Von Campenhausen, Hans Freiherr. *Kirchliches Amt und geistliche Vollmacht in den ersten drei Jahrhunderten.* "BHTh." Tübingen: Mohr, 1953.

Cerfaux, L. and J. Dupont, O.S.B. *Les Actes des Apôtres.* "La Sainte Bible." 3d rev. ed. Paris: Les Éditions du Cerf, 1964.

Conzelmann, Hans. *Die Apostelgeschichte.* "HNT," 7. Tübingen: Mohr, 1963.

————. *The Theology of St. Luke.* Tr. Geoffrey Buswell. London: Faber and Faber, 1960.

Cullmann, Oscar. *Baptism in the New Testament.* Tr. J. K. S. Reid. "Studies in Biblical Theology." London: SCM, 1961.

————. *Peter: Disciple, Apostle, Martyr: A Historical and Theological Study.* Tr. Floyd V. Filson. London: SCM, 1953.

————. *Urchristentum und Gottesdienst.* 2d rev. ed. Zürich: Zwingli Verlag, 1950. Available in E.T.

Currie, Stuart D. " 'Speaking in Tongues': Early Evidence outside the New Testament Bearing on 'Glössais Lalein,' " *Interpretation, 19* (July 1965), 274-94.

Davies, John Gordon. *Der Heilige Geist, die Kirche, und die Sakramente.* Stuttgart: Evangelische Verlagswerk, 1958.

————. "Pentecost and Glossolalia," *JTS,* N.S., *3* (Oct. 1952), 228-31.

Davies, W. D. "Paul and the Dead Sea Scrolls: Flesh and Spirit," in *The Scrolls and the New Testament,* ed. Krister Stendahl. New York: Harper, 1957.

Delling, Gerhard. *Der Gottesdienst im Neuen Testament.* Göttingen: Vandenhoeck und Ruprecht, 1952.

————. *Die Taufe im Neuen Testament.* Berlin: Evangelische Verlagsanstalt, 1963.

De Wette, W. M. L. *Kurze Erklärung der Apostelgeschichte.* Leipzig: Weidmannsche Buchhandlung, 1838.

Dibelius, Martin. *Aufsätze zur Apostelgeschichte.* Heinrich Greeven (ed.). Göttingen: Vandenhoeck und Ruprecht, 1951. Available in E.T.

————. *An die Kolosser, Ephesus; An Philemon erklärt.* Heinrich Greeven (ed.). "HNT," 12. 3d rev. ed. Tübingen: Mohr, 1953.

————. Hans Conzelmann. *Die Pastoralbriefe.* "HNT," 13. 3d ed. Tübingen: Mohr, 1955.

Dibelius, Otto. *Die werdende Kirche: Eine Einführung in die Apostelgeschichte.* "Die urchristliche Botschaft," 5. 5th rev. ed. Hamburg: Im Furche Verlag, 1951.

Dodd, C. H. *The Apostolic Preaching and Its Developments: Three Lectures, with an Appendix on Eschatology and History.* London: Hodder and Stoughton, 1936.

————. *The Johannine Epistles.* "Moffatt NTC." London: Hodder and Stoughton, 1953.

Duncan, George S. *The Epistle of Paul to the Galatians.* "Moffatt NTC." London: Hodder and Stoughton, 1948.

Dupont, Jacques, O.S.B. *The Sources of the Acts.* Tr. Kathleen Pond. New York: Herder and Herder, 1964.

Eichholz, Georg. "Was heisst charismatische Gemeinde? (I. Kor. 12)," *Kirch-*

liche Hochschule Wuppertal: Freundesgabe. Wuppertal-Barmen: Buchdruckerei Albert Sighart, 1959, pp. 1-25.

Flemington, W. F. "Baptism," *IDB,* I, 348-53.

————. *The New Testament Doctrine of Baptism.* London: S.P.C.K., 1953.

Flender, Helmut. *St. Luke: Theologian of Redemptive History.* Tr. Reginald H. and Ilse Fuller. London: S.P.C.K., 1967.

Foakes-Jackson, F. J. *The Acts of the Apostles.* "Moffatt NTC." London: Hodder and Stoughton, 1931.

Foakes-Jackson, F. J., and Kirsopp Lake. "The Development of Thought on the Spirit, the Church, and Baptism," *BC, 1* (1920), 321-44.

Friedrich, Gerhard. *Epaggelia, TWNT,* II, 573-83; *euaggelizomai, TWNT,* II, 705-35; *prophētēs, TWNT,* VI, 781-863.

————. "Die Gegner des Paulus im 2. Korintherbrief," in *Abraham Unser Vater: Juden und Christen im Gespräch über die Bibel.* "Festschrift für Otto Michel zum 60. Geburtstag. Otto Betz (ed.). Leiden: Brill, 1963.

Fuchs, Ernst. *Christus und der Geist bei Paulus: Eine biblisch-theologische Untersuchung.* "Untersuchungen zum Neuen Testament," 23. Leipzig: J. C. Hinrichs'sche Buchhandlung, 1932.

Fuller, Reginald H. "Tongues in the New Testament," *American Church Quarterly, 3* (Fall 1963), 162-68.

Gäumann, Niklaus. *Taufe und Ethik: Studien zu Römer 6.* Münich: Kaiser, 1967.

Georgi, Dieter. *Die Gegner des Paulus im 2. Korinterbrief: Studien zur religiösen Propaganda in der Spätantike.* "WMANT," 11. Assen, Niederlande: Neukirchener Verlag, 1964.

Gerhardsson, Birger. *Memory and Manuscript: Oral Tradition and Written Transmission in Rabbinic Judaism and Early Christianity.* Tr. Eric J. Sharpe. Uppsala: Almqvist und Wiksells, 1961.

Glöel, Johannes. *Der Heilige Geist in der Heilsverkündigung des Paulus: Eine biblisch-theologische Untersuchung.* Halle a.S.: Niemeyer, 1888.

Goppelt, Leonhard. *Christentum und Judentum im ersten und zweiten Jahrhundert: Ein Aufriss der Urgeschichte der Kirche.* "BFChTh." Gütersloh: Bertelsmann, 1954. The first half available in E.T.

————. "Kirche und Häresie nach Paulus." *Gedenkschrift für D. Werner Elert: Beiträge zur historischen und systematischen Theologie.* Friedrich Hübner, Wilhelm Maurer, und Ernst Kinder (eds.). Berlin: Lutherisches Verlagshaus, 1955, pp. 9-23.

————. *Die apostolische und nachapostolische Zeit.* "Die Kirche in ihrer Geschichte. Ein Handbuch," 1; Göttingen: Vandenhoeck und Ruprecht, [1962].

Goulder, M. D. *Type and History in Acts.* London: S.P.C.K., 1964.

Grässer, Erich. "Die Apostelgeschichte in der Forschung der Gegenwart," *ThLZ,* 26 (1960), 93-167.

Grau, Friedrich. "Der neutestamentliche Begriff *Charisma:* Seine Geschichte und seine Theologie." Tübingen: Ebehard-Karls-Universität, 1946. Unpublished Dr. Theol. dissertation.

Grundmann, Walter. *Der Begriff der Kraft in der neutestamentlichen Gedankenwelt.* "BWANT," 4/8. Stuttgart: Kohlhammer, 1932.

————. *Dunamai, TWNT,* II, 286-318.

Gundry, Robert H. " 'Ecstatic Utterance' (NEB)," *JTS,* N.S., *17* (Oct. 1966), 299-307.

Gunkel, Herman. *Die Wirkungen des Heiligen Geistes nach der populären Anschauung der apostolischen Zeit und der Lehre des Apostels Paulus: Eine biblisch-theologische Studie.* 2d ed. Göttingen: Vandenhoeck und Ruprecht, 1899.

Gutbrod, Walter. *Die paulinische Anthropologie.* "BWANT," 4/15. Stuttgart: Kohlhammer, 1934.

———. *Nomos, TWNT,* IV, 1016-84.

Haenchen, Ernst. *Die Apostelgeschichte.* "MeyerK." 12th rev. ed.: Göttingen: Vandenhoeck und Ruprecht, 1959.

———. "Gab es eine vorchristliche Gnosis?" in *ZThK, 49* (1952), 316-49.

Hamilton, Neill Q. *The Holy Spirit and Eschatology in Paul.* "Scottish Journal of Theology Occasional Papers," 6. Edinburgh: Oliver and Boyd, 1957.

Hanson, R. P. C. "The Divinity of the Holy Spirit." *Church Quarterly, 1* (April 1969), 298-306.

Hauck, Friedrich. *Die Briefe des Jakobus, Petrus, Judas und Johannes. Kirchenbriefe.* "NTD," 10. 5th ed. Göttingen: Vandenhoeck und Ruprecht, 1949.

Haupt, Erich. *Die Gefangenschaftsbriefe.* "MeyerK." 6th and 7th ed. Göttingen: Vandenhoeck und Ruprecht, 1897.

Heidland, Hans Wolfgang. *Logizomai, TWNT,* IV, 287-95.

Heitmüller, Wilhelm. *Im Namen Jesu: Eine sprach- und religionsgeschichtliche Untersuchung zum Neuen Testament, speziell zur altchristlichen Taufe.* "FRLANT," 1/2. Göttingen: Vandenhoeck und Ruprecht, 1903.

———. "Sphragis," in *Neutestamentlichen Studien: Georg Heinrici zu seinem 70. Geburtstag dargebracht von Fachgenossen, Freunden und Schülern.* Leipzig: J. C. Hinrichs'sche Buchhandlung, 1914, pp. 40-59.

———. *Taufe und Abendmahl im Urchristentum.* Tübingen: Mohr, 1911.

Hendry, George S. *The Holy Spirit in Christian Theology.* London: SCM, 1957.

Héring, Jean. *La Première Épitre de Saint Paul aux Corinthiens.* "Commentaire du Nouveau Testament," 7. 2d rev. ed. Neuchâtel, Switz.: Editions Delachaux et Niestlé, 1959. Available in E.T.

———. *La Seconde Épitre de Saint Paul aux Corinthiens.* "Commentaire du Nouveau Testament," 8. Neuchâtel, Switz.: Delachaux et Niestlé, 1958. Available in E.T.

Hermann, Ingo. *Kyrios und Pneuma: Studien zur Christologie der paulinischen Hauptbriefe.* "Studien zum Alten und Neuen Testament," 2. München: Kösel Verlag, 1961.

Hilgenfeld, Adolf. *Die Glossolalie in der alten Kirche in dem Zusammenhang der Geistesgaben und des Geisteslebens des alten Christenthums.* Leipzig: Breitkopf und Härtel, 1850.

Holtzmann, H. J. *Die Apostelgeschichte* in *Hand-Commentar zum Neuen Testament,* vol. 1. 2d ed. Freiburg i. B.: Akademische Verlagsbuchhandlung von Mohr, 1892, pp. 307-428.

Hull, J. H. E. *The Holy Spirit in the Acts of the Apostles.* London: Lutterworth, 1967.

Hurd, John Coolidge. *The Origin of I Corinthians.* New York: Seabury, 1965.

Jeremias, Joachim. *Infant Baptism in the First Four Centuries.* Tr. David Cairns. "Library of History and Doctrine." Philadelphia: Westminster, 1960.

———. *Samareia, TWNT,* VII, 88-94.

Joest, Wilfred. "Paulus und das Lutherische Simul Iustus et Peccator," *KuD, 1* (Oct. 1955), 269-320.

Johansson, Nils. "I Corinthians 13 and I Corinthians 14." *NTSt, 10* (April 1964), 383-92.

Jonas, Hans. *The Gnostic Religion: The Message of the Alien God and the Beginnings of Christianity.* Boston: Beacon, 1957.

Käsemann, Ernst. *Essays on New Testament Themes.* "Studies in Biblical Theology." London: SCM, 1964.

———. Review of Markus Barth's *Der Augenzeuge,* in *ThLZ, 73* (1948), 665-70.

Keck, Leander E., and J. Louis Martyn (eds.). *Studies in Luke-Acts: Essays in Honor of Paul Schubert.* Nashville: Abingdon, 1966.

Knopf, Rudolf. *Die Apostelgeschichte.* Göttingen: Vandenhoeck und Ruprecht, 1907.

Knox, Wilfred L. *St. Paul and the Church of the Gentiles.* Cambridge: At the University Press, 1939.

Kraeling, Carl H. *John the Baptist.* New York: Scribner's, 1951.

Kretschmar, Georg. "Zur religionsgeschichtlichen Einordnung der Gnosis," *EvTh, 13* (1953), 354-61.

————. "Himmelfahrt und Pfingsten," *ZKG, 66* (1954-55), 209-53.

Kümmel, Werner Georg. *Kirchenbegriff und Geschichtsbewusstsein in der Urgemeinde und bei Jesus.* "SBU." Uppsala: Wietmans Boktryckerei A.-B., 1943.

————. "Das Urchristentum. I. Gesamtdarstellungen," *ThR, 22* (1954), 138-70; "Das Urchristentum. Nachträge zu Teil I-III," *ThR, 18* (1950), 1-53.

Küng, Hans, S.J. "The Charismatic Structure of the Church," *The Church and Ecumenism.* "Concilium: Theology in the Age of Renewal," 4: "Ecumenical Theology." New York: Paulist Press, 1965, pp. 41-61.

Lake, Kirsopp. "Note 9. The Holy Spirit," *BC, 5* (1933), 96-111.

————. "Note 10. The Gift of the Spirit on the Day of Pentecost," *BC, 5* (1933), 111-21.

Lampe, G. W. H. "Acts." *Peake's Commentary on the Bible.* Matthew Black and H. H. Rowley (eds.). London: Nelson, 1962, pp. 882-926.

————. "Holy Spirit," *IDB,* II, 626-39.

————. "The Holy Spirit in the Writings of St. Luke," *Studies in the Gospels: Essays in Memory of R. H. Lightfoot.* D. E. Nineham (ed.). Oxford: Basil Blackwell, 1955, pp. 159-200.

————. *The Seal of the Spirit: A Study in the Doctrine of Baptism and Confirmation in the New Testament and the Fathers.* London: Longmans, Green, 1951.

Lauterburg, Moritz. *Der Begriff des Charisma und seine Bedeutung für die praktische Theologie.* "BFChTh," 2/1. Gütersloh: Bertelsmann, 1898.

Lietzmann, Hans. *An die Galater.* "HNT," 10. 3d ed. Tübingen: Mohr, 1932.

————. *An die Korinther I, II.* "HNT," 9. 4th rev. ed. Tübingen: Mohr, 1949.

Lightfoot, J. B. *Saint Paul's Epistles to the Colossians and to Philemon: A Revised Text with Introductions, Notes and Dissertations.* Grand Rapids, Mich.: Zondervan, 1879.

————. *Saint Paul's Epistle to the Galatians: A Revised Text with Introduction, Notes, and Dissertations.* 9th ed. London: Macmillan, 1887.

Lock, Walter. *A Critical and Exegetical Commentary on the Pastoral Epistles (I and II Timothy and Titus).* "ICC." Edinburgh: T. and T. Clark, [1924], 1952.

Lofthouse, W. F. "The Holy Spirit in the Acts and the Fourth Gospel," *ExT, 52* (June 1941), 334-36.

Lohmeyer, Ernst. *Die Briefe an die Philipper, an die Kolosser, und an Philemon.* "MeyerK." 11th ed. Göttingen: Vandenhoeck und Ruprecht, 1956.

————. *Das Evangelium des Markus übersetzt und erklärt.* "MeyerK." 15th ed. Göttingen: Vandenhoeck und Ruprecht, 1959.

————. *Das Evangelium des Matthäus. Nachgelassene Ausarbeitung und Entwürfe zur Übersetzung und Erklärung.* Werner Schmauch (ed.). "MeyerK." 3d ed. Göttingen: Vandenhoeck und Ruprecht, 1962.

————. " 'Gesetzeswerke': Probleme paulinischer Theologie, II.," *ZNW, 28* (1929), 177-207.

————. *Das Urchristentum. I. Buch: Johannes der Täufer.* Göttingen: Vandenhoeck und Ruprecht, 1932.

————. *Urchristliche Mystik: Neutestamentliche Studien.* Darmstadt: Wissenschaftliche Buchgesellschaft, 1955.

Lohse, Eduard. "Die Bedeutung des Pfingstberichtes im Rahmen des lukanischen Geschichtswerkes," *EvTh, 13* (1953), 422-36.

————. *Pentëkostë, TWNT,* VI, 44-53.

Lütgert, Wilhelm. *Freiheitspredigt und Schwarmgeist in Korinth: Ein Beitrag zur Charakteristik des Christuspartei.* "BFChTh." Gütersloh: Bertelsmann, 1908.

————. *Gesetz und Geist: Eine Untersuchung zur Vorgeschichte des Galaterbriefes.* "BFChTh." Gütersloh: Bertelsmann, 1919.

Martin, Ira Jay, 3rd. "Glossolalia in the Apostolic Church," *JBL, 63* (1944), 123-30.

————. *Glossolalia in the Apostolic Church: A Survey Study of Tongue-Speech.* Berea, Ky.: Berea College Press, 1960.

Mattill, A. J., Jr., and Mary Bedford Mattill. *A Classified Bibliography of Literature on the Acts of the Apostles.* "New Testament Tools and Studies," 7. Bruce M. Metzger (ed.). Leiden: Brill, 1966.

Mentz, Hermann. *Taufe und Kirche in ihrem ursprünglichen Zusammenhang.* "BEvTh," 29. München: Kaiser, 1960.

Meyer, Heinrich August Wilhelm. *Kritisch Exegetisches Handbuch über die Apostelgeschichte.* "MeyerK." 3d rev. ed. Göttingen: Vandenhoeck und Ruprecht, 1861.

Michaelis, Wilhelm. *Täufer, Jesus, Urgemeinde: Die Predigt vom Reiche Gottes vor und nach Pfingsten.* "Neutestamentliche Forschungen," 2/3. Gütersloh: Bertelsmann, 1928.

Michel, Otto. *Der Brief an die Römer übersetzt und erklärt.* "MeyerK." 11th ed. Göttingen: Vandenhoeck und Ruprecht, 1957.

Moffatt, James. *The First Epistle of Paul to the Corinthians.* "Moffatt NTC." London: Hodder and Stoughton, [1938], 1954.

Moody, Dale. *Baptism: Foundation for Christian Unity.* Philadelphia: Westminster, 1967.

Morton, A. Q., and G. H. C. Macgregor. *The Structure of Luke and Acts.* New York: Harper and Row, 1964.

Nestle, Eberhard (ed.). *Novum Testamentum Graeca cum apparatu critico curavit.* 21st ed. Stuttgart: Privilegierte Württembergische Bibelanstalt, 1952.

New, Silva. "Note 11. The Name, Baptism, and the Laying on of Hands," *BC, 5* (1933), 121-40.

Nösgen, K. F. *Der Heilige Geist: Sein Wesen und die Art seines Wirkens.* 2 vols. Berlin: Trowitzsch und Sohn, 1905.

Oepke, Albrecht. *Baptö, TWNT,* I, 527-43; *ekstasis, TWNT,* II, 447-56.

————. *Der Brief des Paulus an die Galater.* "ThHK," 9. 2d rev. ed. Berlin: Evangelische Verlagsanstalt, 1957.

O'Neill, J. C. *The Theology of Acts in Its Historical Setting.* London: S.P.C.K., 1961.

Ott, Wilhelm. *Gebet und Heil: Die Bedeutung der Gebetsparänese in der lukanischen Theologie.* "Studien zum Alten und Neuen Testament," 12. München: Kösel-Verlag, 1965.

Oulton, J. E. L. "The Holy Spirit, Baptism, and Laying on of Hands in Acts," *ExT, 66* (May 1955), 236-40.

Parratt, J. K. "The Laying on of Hands in the New Testament," *ExT, 80* (April 1969), 210-14; and "The Rebaptism of the Ephesian Disciples," *ExT, 79* (March 1968), 182-83.

Pieper, Karl. *Die Simon-Magus Perikope (Apg. 8:5-24): Ein Beitrag zur Quellenfrage in der Apostelgeschichte.* "NTA," 3/5. Münster i.W.: Aschendorffsche Verlagsbuchhandlung, 1911.

Pocknee, Cyril E. *Water and the Spirit: A Study in the Relation of Baptism and Confirmation.* London: Darton, Longman and Todd, 1967.

Preisker, Herbert. "Apollos und die Johannesjünger in Act. 18:24 — 19:6," *ZNW, 30* (1931), 301-04.

Preuschen, Erwin. *Die Apostelgeschichte.* "HNT," 4. Tübingen: Mohr, 1912.

Prümm, Karl, S.J. *Diakonia Pneumatos: Der Zweite Korintherbrief als Zugang zur apostolischen Botschaft.* 3 vols. Rome: Herder, 1960-1967.

Rackham, Richard Belward. *The Acts of the Apostles.* "Westminster Commentaries." 14th ed. London: Methuen, [1901], 1951.

Reicke, Bo. *Glaube und Leben der Urgemeinde: Bemerkungen zu Apostelgeschichte 1-7.* Zürich: Zwingli, 1957.

Reitzenstein, Richard. *Die hellenistischen Mysterienreligionen nach ihren Grundgedanken und Wirkungen.* 3d rev. ed. Leipzig: Verlag von B. G. Teubner, 1927.

Rengstorf, Karl Heinrich. *Apostolos, TWNT,* I, 397-448.

Robertson, Archibald, and Alfred Plummer. *A Critical and Exegetical Commentary on the First Epistle of St. Paul to the Corinthians.* "ICC." 2d ed. Edinburgh: T. and T. Clark, 1955 [1901].

Robinson, J. Armitage. *St. Paul's Epistle to the Ephesians: A Revised Text, and Translation with Exposition and Notes.* 2d ed. London: Macmillan, 1904.

Robinson, John A. T. *The Body: A Study in Pauline Theology.* "Studies in Biblical Theology." London: SCM, 1957.

Schlatter, Adolf. *Die Apostelgeschichte.* "Erläuterungen zum Neuen Testament." Stuttgart: Calwer, 1928.

————. *Einleitung in die Bibel.* 4th ed. Stuttgart: Calwer, 1923.

————. *Der Evangelist Johannes: Wie er spricht, denkt, und glaubt: Ein Kommentar zum vierten Evangelium.* 3d ed. Stuttgart: Calwer, 1960.

————. *Der Evangelist Matthäus: Seine Sprache, sein Ziel, seine Selbstständigkeit: Ein Kommentar zum ersten Evangelium.* 5th ed. Stuttgart: Calwer, 1959.

————. *Die Geschichte der ersten Christenheit.* 2d ed. Gütersloh: Bertelsmann, 1926. Available in E.T.

————. *Die Geschichte des Christus.* 2d ed. Stuttgart: Calwer, 1923.

————. *Der Glaube im Neuen Testament.* 2d ed. Calw und Stuttgart: Verlag der Vereinsbuchhandlung, 1896.

————. *Gottes Gerechtigkeit: Ein Kommentar zum Römerbrief.* 3d ed. Stuttgart: Calwer, 1959.

————. *Paulus der Bote Jesu: Eine Deutung seiner Briefe an die Korinther.* 2d ed. Stuttgart: Calwer, 1956.

————. *Die Theologie der Apostel.* 2d ed. Stuttgart: Calwer, 1922.

————. *Die korinthische Theologie.* "BFChTh," 18/2. Gütersloh: Bertelsmann, 1914.

————. "Der Wandel nach dem Geist in der Unterweisung des Paulus," *Jahrbuch der Theologischen Schule Bethel,* 4 (1933), 9-26.

Schlier, Heinrich. *Eleutheros, TWNT,* II, 484-500.

————. *Der Brief an die Epheser: Ein Kommentar.* Düsseldorf: Patmos, 1957.

————. *Der Brief an die Galater.* "MeyerK." 11th ed. Göttingen: Vandenhoeck und Ruprecht, 1951.

————. "Zur kirchlichen Lehre von der Taufe," *ThLZ, 72* (1947), 321-36.

————. "Die Taufe nach dem 6. Kapitel des Römerbriefes," *EvTh, 5* (1938), 335-47.

————. *Die Zeit der Kirche: Exegetische Aufsätze und Vorträge.* Freiburg: Herder, 1956.

Schmauch, Werner. *Beiheft: Die Briefe an die Philipper, an die Kolosser und an*

Philemon [by] Ernst Lohmeyer. "MeyerK," 9; Göttingen: Vandenhoeck und Ruprecht, 1964.

Schmidt, Karl Ludwig. *Die Pfingsterzählung und das Pfingstereignis.* "Arbeiten zur Religionsgeschichte des Urchristentums," 1/2. Leipzig: J. C. Hinrichs'sche Buchhandlung, 1919.

Schmithals, Walter. *Die Gnosis in Korinth: Eine Untersuchung zu den Korintherbriefen.* Göttingen: Vandenhoeck und Ruprecht, 1956. (Now in 2d ed.)

———. "Die Häretiker in Galatien," *ZNW, 47* (1956), 25-67.

Schmoller, Alfred. *Handkonkordanz zum griechischen Neuen Testament.* 12th ed. Stuttgart: Privileg. Württ. Bibelanstalt, 1960.

Schnackenburg, Rudolf. *Das Heilsgeschehen bei der Taufe nach dem Apostel Paulus: Eine Studie zur paulinische Theologie.* "Münchener Theologische Studien." München: Karl Zink Verlag, 1950. Available in E.T.

———. *Das Johannesevangelium.* I: Einleitung und Kommentar zu Kap. 1-4. "Herders Theologischer Kommentar zum Neuen Testament," 4; Freiburg: Herder, 1965.

Schneider, Johannes. *Die Taufe im Neuen Testament.* Stuttgart: Kohlhammer, 1951.

Schniewind, Julius. *Das Evangelium nach Markus übersetzt und erklärt.* "NTD." 9th ed. Göttingen: Vandenhoeck und Ruprecht, 1960.

———. *Das Evangelium nach Matthäus übersetzt und erklärt.* "NTD." 10th ed. Göttingen: Vandenhoeck und Ruprecht, 1962.

———. *Die Freude der Busse: Zur Grundfrage der Bibel.* Göttingen: Vandenhoeck und Ruprecht, 1956.

———. *Nachgelassene Reden und Aufsätze.* Berlin: Töpelmann, 1952.

Schrenk, Gottlob. *Dikē, dikaios, TWNT,* II, 176-229.

———. "Geist und Enthusiasmus," *Studien zu Paulus.* Zürich: Zwingli, 1954, pp. 107-27.

Schweitzer, Albert. *Die Mystik des Apostels Paulus.* 2d ed. Tübingen: Mohr, 1954. Available in E.T.

Schweizer, Eduard. *Pneuma, TWNT,* VI, 330-453; *sarx,* VII, 98-151; *sōma,* VII, 1024-91.

———. "Die Bekehrung des Apollos, Apg. 18:24-26," *EvTh, 15* (1955), 247-54.

———. "Gegenwart des Geistes und eschatologische Hoffnung bei Zarathustra, Spätjudischen Gruppen, Gnostikern und den Zeugen des Neuen Testamentes," in *The Background of the New Testament and Its Eschatology: In Honour of Charles Harold Dodd.* W. D. Davies and D. Daube (eds.). Cambridge: At the University Press, 1956, pp. 482-508.

———. *Geist und Gemeinde im Neuen Testament und Heute.* "Theologische Existenz Heute," N.F. 32. München: Kaiser, 1952.

———. *Gemeinde und Gemeindeordnung im Neuen Testament.* Zürich: Zwingli, 1959.

———. "The Spirit of Power: The Uniformity and Diversity of the Concept of the Holy Spirit in the New Testament." Tr. John Bright and Eugene Debor. *Interpretation, 6* (1952), 259-78.

Scobie, Charles H. H. *John the Baptist.* Philadelphia: Fortress, 1964.

Scroggs, Robin. "The Exaltation of the Spirit by Some Early Christians," *JBL, 84* (1965), 359-73.

Seeberg, Alfred. *Der Katechismus der Urchristenheit.* Leipzig: A. Deichertsche Verlagsbuchhandlung, 1903.

Sevenster, G. "Christologie des Urchristentums," *RGG³,* I, 1745-62.

Sieffert, Friedrich. *Der Brief an die Galater.* "MeyerK." 9th ed. Göttingen: Vandenhoeck und Ruprecht, 1899.

Sleeper, C. Freeman. "Pentecost and Resurrection," *JBL, 86* (Dec. 1965), 389-99.

Smalley, Stephen S. "Spiritual Gifts and I Corinthians 12-16," *JBL, 87* (Dec. 1968), 427-33.

Sohm, Rudolph. *Kirchenrecht.* "Systematisches Handbuch der Deutschen Rechtswissenschaft." Leipzig: Duncker und Humblot, 1892.

Sokolowski, Emil. *Die Begriffe Geist und Leben bei Paulus in ihren Beziehungen zu einander: Eine exegetisch-religionsgeschichtliche Untersuchung.* Göttingen: Vandenhoeck und Ruprecht, 1903.

Stählin, Gustav. *Skandalon, TWNT,* VII, 338-58.

————. *Die Apostelgeschichte.* "NTD." 10th ed. Göttingen: Vandenhoeck und Ruprecht, 1962.

Steinmann, Alphons. *Die Apostelgeschichte übersetzt und erklärt.* 4th rev. ed. Bonn: Peter Hanstein, 1934.

Strack, Herman L., and Paul Billerbeck. *Kommentar zum Neuen Testament aus Talmud und Midrasch.* 2d ed. 6 vols. München: C. H. Beck, 1956.

Sweet, J. P. M. "A Sign for Unbelievers: Paul's Attitude to Glossolalia," *NTSt, 13* (April 1967), 240-57.

Swete, Henry Barclay. *The Holy Spirit in the New Testament: A Study of Primitive Christian Teaching.* London: Macmillan, 1910.

Talbert, Charles H. *Luke and the Gnostics: An Examination of the Lukan Purpose.* Nashville: Abingdon, 1966.

Taylor, Greer M. "The Function of PISTIS CHRISTOU in Galatians," *JBL, 85* (March 1966), 58-76.

Taylor, Vincent. *The Gospel according to St. Mark: The Greek Text with Introduction, Notes, and Indexes.* London: Macmillan, 1959. (Now in 2d ed.)

Theologisches Wörterbuch zum Neuen Testament. Begründet von Gerhard Kittel, ed. Gerhard Friedrich. 8 vols. Stuttgart: W. Kohlhammer, 1932-1970. E.T.: *Theological Dictionary of the New Testament,* tr. and ed. Geoffrey W. Bromiley. 6 vols. Grand Rapids, Mich.: Eerdmans, 1964-1969. Cited as TWNT.

Vielhauer, Philipp. "Zum 'Paulinismus' der Apostelgeschichte," *EvTh, 10* (July 1950-51), 1-15. Available in E. T. in Keck and Martyn, above.

Volz, Paul. *Der Geist Gottes und die verwandten Erscheinungen im Alten Testament und im anschliessenden Judentum.* Tübingen: Mohr, 1910.

Weiss, Johannes. *Der erste Korintherbrief.* "MeyerK." 10th ed. Göttingen: Vandenhoeck und Ruprecht, 1925.

Wendland, Heinz-Dietrich. "Gesetz und Geist: Zum Problem des Schwärmertums bei Paulus," *Schriften des Theologischen Konvents Augsburgischen Bekenntnisses, 6* (1952), 38-64.

————. "Das Wirken des Heiligen Geistes in den Gläubigen nach Paulus," *ThLZ, 77* (1952), 457-70.

Wendt, Hans Heinrich. *Kritisch Exegetisches Handbuch über die Apostelgeschichte.* "MeyerK." 6th and 7th eds.; Göttingen: Vandenhoeck und Ruprecht, 1888.

White, R. E. O. *The Biblical Doctrine of Initiation.* London: Hodder and Stoughton, 1960.

Wikenhauser, Alfred. *Die Apostelgeschichte übersetzt und erklärt.* "Regensburger Neues Testament," 5. 3d rev. ed. Regensburg: Verlag Friedrich Pustel, 1956.

Wilckens, Ulrich. *Die Missionsreden der Apostelgeschichte: Form- und traditionsgeschichtliche Untersuchungen.* "WMANT," 5. Neukirchen Kreis Moers: Neukirchener Verlag, 1961.

————. *Sophia, TWNT,* VII, 465-529.

————. *Weisheit und Torheit: Eine exegetisch-religionsgeschichtliche Untersuchung zu I. Korintherbrief 1 und 2.* "BHTh." Tübingen: Mohr, 1959.

Wilkens, Wilhelm. "Wassertaufe und Geistesempfang bei Lukas," *ThZ, 23* (Jan.-Feb. 1967), 26-47.

Wilson, Jack H. "The Corinthians Who Say There Is No Resurrection of the Dead," *ZNW, 59* (1968), 90-107.

Wilson, R. McL. *The Gnostic Problem: A Study of the Relation between Hellenistic Judaism and the Gnostic Heresy.* London: A. R. Mowbray, 1958.

Windisch, Hans. *Die katholischen Briefe erklärt.* "HNT," 15. 3d rev. ed. Herbert Preisker (ed.). Tübingen: Mohr, 1951.

————. *Der zweite Korintherbrief.* "MeyerK." 9th ed. Göttingen: Vandenhoeck und Ruprecht, 1924.

————. *The Spirit-Paraclete in the Fourth Gospel.* Tr. James W. Cox. "Facet Books," Biblical Series, 20; Philadelphia: Fortress, 1968.

————. *Taufe und Sünde im ältesten Christentum bis auf Origenes: Ein Beitrag zur altchristlichen Dogmengeschichte.* Tübingen: Mohr, 1908.

Wink, Walter. *John the Baptist in the Gospel Tradition.* London: Cambridge University Press, 1968.

Yates, J. E. *The Spirit and the Kingdom.* London: S.P.C.K., 1963.

INDEX OF SUBJECTS

380

INDEX OF PERSONS AND AUTHORS

384

INDEX OF NEW TESTAMENT REFERENCES